CW00375470

ACCOUNTS OF
THE FEOFFEES OF THE
TOWN LANDS OF BURY ST EDMUNDS

1569–1622

SUFFOLK RECORDS SOCIETY

President
Norman Scarfe

Vice-Presidents
James Campbell, FBA
Geoffrey Martin
The Hon. David Erskine

Chairman
Dr John Blatchly

General Editors
David Dymond (co-ordinating editor)
Christopher Harper-Bill (Suffolk Charters)

Secretary
Gwyn Thomas
Suffolk Record Office
77 Raingate Street
Bury St Edmunds,
IP33 2AR

The Guildhall's porch, shown in Carter's drawing on the book jacket, was enlarged soon after the death of Jankin Smith in 1481. The room over the porch became a strongroom, entered from the minstrels' gallery through a stout oak door with several locks. In the thickness of the strongroom's inside wall is this 'wall safe' usually called the 'coffer', sometimes the 'hutch' or 'treasury' when, in these accounts, money was put in or taken out. It is no longer possible to open it, but a hook still survives in the ceiling from which a chain could pass through a ring in the door of the safe to raise or lower it. Until the early twentieth century traces of some verses in praise of Jankin Smith and his bequest to the town were visible on the wall above the safe. These were probably defaced during the Reformation in the belief that some of the wording was superstitious. © Crown Copyright NMR.

ACCOUNTS OF
THE FEOFFEES OF THE
TOWN LANDS OF BURY ST EDMUNDS

1569–1622

Edited by

MARGARET STATHAM

General Editor

D.N.J. MacCULLOCH

The Boydell Press

Suffolk Records Society
VOLUME XLVI

Editorial matter © The Trustees of the Suffolk Records Society

All Rights Reserved. Except as permitted under current legislation
no part of this work may be photocopied, stored in a retrieval system,
published, performed in public, adapted, broadcast,
transmitted, recorded or reproduced in any form or by any means,
without the prior permission of the copyright owner

A Suffolk Records Society publication
First published 2003
The Boydell Press, Woodbridge

ISBN 0 85115 921 4

Issued to subscribing members for the year 2002–2003

The Boydell Press is an imprint of Boydell & Brewer Ltd
PO Box 9, Woodbridge, Suffolk IP12 3DF, UK
and of Boydell & Brewer Inc.
PO Box 41026, Rochester, NY 14604–4126, USA
website: www.boydell.co.uk

A catalogue record for this book is available
from the British Library

This publication is printed on acid-free paper

Printed in Great Britain by
St Edmundsbury Press Ltd, Bury St Edmunds, Suffolk

Contents

Illustrations

Preface

I shall never forget the Saturday afternoon in 1981 when a young couple and their small children arrived at the Bury Record Office bringing with them a pile of books. These had been found when they were turning out a grandparent's house. They did not know what they had found, and were unable to read some of them. Eventually they were advised that the Record Offices in Suffolk and adjacent counties would be interested in them. Unannounced, they brought them to the Bury office that day. As I listed them I could see that one of the large, flat volumes at the bottom of the pile had the characteristic 'feffes' written on it, a sure sign that it was one of the items handled by John Sotheby when he sorted the records of the Bury corporation from those of the feoffees in 1664. Needless to say, I was anxious to know what this was, as it was almost certainly something to interest me. Someone – I think it was David Dymond – said I went into the stratosphere when I saw what had been brought in! It is a measure of the quality of this collection that this is the second text from it to be published by the Suffolk Records Society, the other being *The Bailiffs' Minute Book of Dunwich*, which appeared as volume xxxiv in 1992. After a number of years on loan, the Record Office (with the help of a grant from its Friends) bought the Suffolk items. The Friends of the Suffolk Record Office, who help the archive service financially and in other ways, will always welcome enquiries, donations and new members. They can be contacted at any of the three branches of the Suffolk Record Office.

Until these account books turned up, Bury records for the early modern period were few and none covered any length of time. Fortunately these two volumes cover the final years during which the feoffees of the town lands were virtually running the town, and overlap with the early years of the incorporated borough. They were known to John Gage and Samuel Tymms, who worked in the early part of the nineteenth century, but then disappeared for almost a hundred and fifty years. They provide a valuable source for a period of great change in the history of Bury. It therefore seemed sensible to abandon an earlier attempt to compile an anthology of documents illustrating aspects of Bury history, mainly from the early years of the seventeenth century, and undertake the daunting task of editing these two volumes.

I have to thank Gwyn Thomas, Senior Archivist, Suffolk Record Office, for permission to publish these volumes. He, Jane Isaac and Ed Button of the Bury office have given me much help on various points. Other members of the staff there have produced obscure items from the feoffees' records – which cause special difficulties in production – and other little-used Bury sources with unfailing good humour and patience.

It has been my great good fortune to have as my general editor Professor Diarmaid MacCulloch. His detailed knowledge of this period generally and Suffolk in particular has enriched the volume, and saved me from many errors. I am most grateful to him for all his help over many years. I am also grateful to David Dymond, the co-ordinating editor, who has been unstinting in time and effort as my drafts were prepared for publication, and has made a major contribution to the Glossary. John Craig has commented on several points and very generously let me have a typescript copy of the Bury chapter from his book *Reformation, Politics and*

Polemics, while it was going through the press. A number of people have given their time and expertise to help me with various points. These include John Blatchly, Tony Copsey, Audrey McLaughlin, Peter Northeast, Tony Redman, Jayne Ringrose, Anne Sutton and Charles Taylor. I wish to thank all of them most sincerely for their help. David Dymond and Zillah Halls gave much help with proof correction. The errors that remain are my own.

It is a source of great pride to me that for many years now I have been one of the Guildhall Feoffees and I must record my gratitude to my fellow feoffees for their generous support and encouragement in the preparation of this volume.

My interest in Bury history was first fostered by my husband, Martin. I am sad that we were never able to discuss these two volumes, for they touch on topics we had often speculated about. My daughter, Helen, has always encouraged me in my work on the history of Bury. Lastly, but by no means least, the friendship of Amanda Arrowsmith, Hugh Edgar, Zillah Halls and Valerie Moore has been a great help to me when the going seemed to be hard.

MARGARET STATHAM
Bury St Edmunds,
Candlemas Day, 2002

Introduction

The account books

The accounts are written in two paper books, now in the Bury St Edmunds branch of the Suffolk Record Office, where they have the reference numbers HD1150/1 and 2. As described below, they became at some stage separated from the bulk of the archive of the Guildhall Feoffment Trust, and were only brought back to Bury St Edmunds in 1981. The Record Office, with the help of a grant from the Friends of Suffolk Record Office, has since bought them and they are now safe for future students of the history of Elizabethan and Jacobean Bury St Edmunds.

The earlier of the two volumes is 16 x 12in., or 41 x 30cm. On the parchment cover, which is now loose, is written

The Booke of Accomts from 1570 to 1602
Feffes[1]
A.13 (in pencil)
29 March 1720
?Coia necliguntur
Boni civis est publica curare[2]

On the inside of the front cover is a pencilled signature – W.T. Jackson.

The book itself is made up of six gatherings. The first had sixteen leaves originally, but a page has been cut out between f.7v. and f.8r. The other five gatherings consist of sixteen leaves each. The paper of which the book is formed has a watermark of a wheel, with six spokes, 2cm in diameter. Between each spoke there is a 'tooth' on the circumference. Above the wheel is a stem with three leaves, perhaps oak or holly. It is 5.5cm high.[3] It has some similarities with examples shown by Briquet, but none are close.[4] An inventory of the Guildhall in 1584 was written on a loose sheet pinned to f.23r., and has been numbered 23a. Similarly, a note of arrears of rent stitched to f.46r. has been numbered 46a. The volume cost 1s.8d., which is recorded in the account for 1570–1, f.4v.

The second volume measures 15 x 11¼in., or 38 x 28.5cm. Its cover is also of parchment and on the front is written

Bury St Eds Guildhall foefees Jackson [*in pencil*]
Feffees [*?This*] Boke of Accomts from [*1603*] to 1623.
[?] March 1720
[*Some illegible words at the bottom.*]

---

[1] This seems to be in the hand of John Sotheby, the Recorder, who on 24 March 1664 was paid £8 for seven or eight days work sorting records, Minutes, H2/6/2.1, p.95.
[2] The reading of the first line is difficult. From the version here, it seems to mean 'matters concerning the community are neglected; it is the mark of a good citizen to care for public affairs'.
[3] The watermark is illustrated in Plate 1(a).
[4] C.M. Briquet, *Les Filigranes* (ed. Allan Stevenson) Jubilee edition, 4 vols. (Amsterdam, 1968), vol. 4, 13470 and 13510 for example, which were both found on French paper dating from 1520 and 1525 respectively. However, they have acorns as well as oak leaves.

On the inside of the front cover this volume also has the signature W.T. Jackson, and also the address Angel Hill.[5] Originally the book had two cords to fasten it, but only the lower one now survives.

This book is an early example of recycling paper. It is not formed in gatherings in the usual way, presumably because holes from an earlier stitching would have made this difficult. It consists of a pile of folded sheets placed one on top of the other, stitched together about a quarter of an inch in from the fold. At the front are two leaves of thin paper, a leaf of thicker paper and then the sheets on which the accounts are written. The *recto* of each folio is marked with an Arabic numeral of the early sixteenth century. In the following table the early numeral is given in square brackets:

Old and new folio numbers	*Date on which the account was made up*
fos. 2r.[130], 2v., 3r.[128]	3 January 1604
fos. 3v., 4r.[116], 4v.	2 January 1605
fos. 4v., 5r.[126], 5v., 6r.[20], 7r.[25]	2 January 1606
fos. 7r.[25], 7v., 8r.[44], 8v., 9r.[50], 9v., 10r.[42]	30 December 1606
fos. 10r.[42], 10v., 11r.[46], 11v., 12r.[26], 12v.	29 December 1607
fos. 13r.[48], 13v., 14r.[30], 14v., 15r.[39], 15v., 16r.[31], 16v.	3 January 1609
fos. 16v., 17r.[38], 17v., 18r.[33]	3 January 1610
fos. 18v., 19r.[36], 19v., 20r.[58]	2 January 1611
fos. 20v., 21r.[56], 21v., 22r.[64], 22v.	31 December 1611
fos. 23r.[65], 23v., 24r.[54], 24v., 25r.[63], 25v.	5 January 1613
fos. 26r.[70], 26v., 27r.[71], 27v., 28r.[35]	4 January 1614
fos. 28v., 29r.[69], 29v., 30r.[72], 30v.	4 January 1615
fos. 31r.[68], 31v., 32r.[67], 32v., 33r.[74], 33v.	[*space*] January 1616
fos. 34r.[66], 34v., 35r.[94], 35v., 36r.[95], 36v.	2 January 1617
fos. 37r.[93], 37v., 38r.[96], 38v.	6 January [*1618*]
fos. 39r.[92], 39v., 40r.[97], 40v., 41r.[91]	[*space*] January 1619
fos. 41v., 42r.[98], 42v., 43r.[90]	16 January 1620
fos. 43v., 44r.[99], 44v., 45r.[88]	3 January 1621
fos. 45v., 46r.[89], 46v.	2 January 1622
fos. 47r.[80], 47v., 48r.[78], 48v., 49r.[76]	9 January 1623
f.49v. is blank.	

The written sheets have a fleur-de-lis watermark, 4.5cm high and 4cm across at the widest part.[6] It is very similar to, if not identical with, Briquet's no. 6884 from paper made at Livorno in Italy in 1502.[7] At the end there is one leaf of fairly good paper and a leaf of thin paper. Two similar leaves seem to have been cut out. The watermark on the thin paper used at each end shows a flagon, perhaps with grapes above its lid. There are some marks on the body of the vessel, which cannot readily be identified. It is about 6cm high and 2cm wide.[8] One wonders what early sixteenth-century document was pulled apart to provide the paper for this account

---

5   Mr Jackson had his book shop at 4 Angel Hill, on the north side of the Angel. The shop can be seen in some early photographs, notably in the well-known view of the hustings outside the Angel.
6   Illustrated in Plate 1(b).
7   Briquet, *ut supra*, vol. 3.
8   The two versions of this watermark are illustrated in Plate 1 (c) and (d). They have similarities with Briquet, *ut supra*, vol. 4, nos. 12528 and 12526, which were made in 1583 and 1567 respectively.

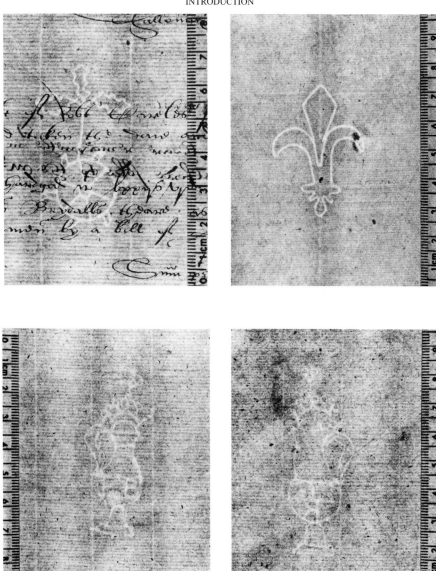

Plate 1. Watermarks
(a, top left) from the paper of HD1150/1; (b, top right) from the paper of
HD1150/2; (c, bottom left) from sheet at the beginning of HD1150/2;
(d, bottom right) from sheet at the end of HD1150/2. Reproduced by permission
of Suffolk Record Office.

book which cost 2s.0d., as is recorded in the account for 1604 on f.4r. There are a number of well known references to the re-use of paper for practical purposes.[9]

The last two accounts are not fully made up, probably because new account books, which no longer survive, had already been acquired, while the remaining pages in these volumes were used for a draft version. This is suggested by the account for 1622, when 2s.2d. was paid for 'two paper bookes to enter the receipts and payments of this accomptant'.

These accounts are written in English though Latin words are often used in dates and for technical accounting terms. The English, printed in its original spelling, may often seem strange to modern eyes, and would have been heavily edited had these accounts been printed by contemporaries. Obsolete and unusual words are defined in the Glossary. The first account book is written in three different hands. The second volume is written in several hands, one of which has been identified as that of Thomas Bright, who entered his own account into the book.

The history of the account books

These volumes were used by Gage in his *Thingoe Hundred*,[10] and also by Samuel Tymms both in the notes on his *Bury Wills* and in his history of *St Mary's church*.[11] After this use by Gage and Tymms in the nineteenth century, no evidence has been found of any scholar having access to them until they were deposited at the Bury Record Office in 1981. How they became divorced from the archive of the Guildhall Feoffment and came into the hands of W.T. Jackson, whose signature is in both books, is not clear. William Thomas Jackson was the son of Thomas and Frances Ann (*née* Martin) Jackson, born on 9 August 1807 and baptised at St Mary's on 15 August 1808.[12] He was a bookseller, printer and publisher in the town, active as a printer from 1836–48, and as a bookseller until his death in 1881.[13] Among other works published by Jackson and his partner Frost were Samuel Tymms *[A] notice of the Gate-Tower . . . known as the Norman Tower* (1846) and *An account of the church of St Mary* (1854) both of which were printed by Gedge and Barker of Bury St Edmunds. Jackson was an enthusiastic member of the Bury St Edmunds and West Suffolk Institute of Archaeology in its early days; whether he dealt in manuscripts is not clear, but that he had some interest in them is illustrated by the fact that he was

---

[9] See, for instance, Giles E. Dawson and Laetitia Kennedy-Skipton, *Elizabethan Handwriting* (Chichester, 1981) pp.6–7.

[10] John Gage, *The History and Antiquities of Suffolk: Thingoe Hundred* (1838) p.188 in describing Queen Elizabeth I's progress through Suffolk, 1578.

[11] Samuel Tymms, *Wills and Inventories from the Registers of the Commissary of Bury St Edmunds and the Archdeacon of Sudbury*, Camden Society, xlix (1850) used these accounts in a note about the alderman and dee or dye of Candlemas guild, p.243, and also in a note about the use of frieze for coats for the poor, p.254. In Samuel Tymms, *An Architectural and Historical Account of the Church of St Mary, Bury St Edmunds* (Bury St Edmunds, 1854) he again used them in discussing, for example, the alderman and dee of Candlemas guild, p.43; in connection with the annual payment made by the Crown to the town clergy, p.101; and when writing about the ministers' houses, p.104. They also provided him with the name of Mr Lewis, minister and later preacher of St Mary's, p.114, and gave an early reference to the Friday exercise, pp.133–4.

[12] Transcript (typescript) of St Mary's baptism register at the Bury Record Office.

[13] For Jackson's career see Tony Copsey, *Book Distribution and Printing in Suffolk, 1534–1850* (Ipswich, 1994) p.63.

once the owner of a letter from George Bloomfield which is now in the Bury St Edmunds Record Office.[14]

The names of Jackson's two eldest sons, James Burrough and Martin De Carle, suggest that he was not only of a local family but possibly allied to two distinguished Suffolk antiquaries.[15] On 20 March 1850 he exhibited a globe ring dated 1678 to the Suffolk Institute of Archaeology. His account of it stated that it had been once in the possession of the eighteenth-century antiquary and amateur architect, Sir James Burrough.[16] Sir James collected materials for the history of Bury St Edmunds, of which he left two volumes of notes to the library in St James's church; one volume of this still survives.[17] The globe ring which W.T. Jackson exhibited to the Suffolk Institute had fascinated Sir James when he was a child. From the Burrough family it had been left to a Mrs Martin, who had given it to Jackson. W.T. Jackson's mother was Frances Ann Martin, so it is quite possible that it was a family gift. Martin is quite a common name in Suffolk, but the mother of the antiquary, Thomas Martin, was Elizabeth Burrough, aunt of the antiquary, Sir James. The second child of W.T. Jackson was called Martin De Carle, his grandmother's maiden name linked with the name of the well-known Bury stone masons.[18] It seems more than likely that in some way William Thomas Jackson was connected with both Sir James Burrough and Thomas Martin, probably through his mother. That he possessed papers relating to the Burrough family is illustrated by the presence of a copy of the receipt given by the preachers of the two churches to Miss Elizabeth Burrough when they received Sir James Burrough's *Collectanea Buriensia*. It is written inside the front cover of the surviving volume with a note that the original receipt was in the possession of Mr W.T. Jackson.[19] The names of Dr Burrough, father of Sir James, and Thomas Martin are linked in the last known examination of the Black Book of Bury St Edmunds, which contained orders of the feoffees at one end and of the governors of the Grammar School at the other. Tom Martin made a note that it was at Dr Burrough's house when he saw it on 17 March 1722.[20] Several members of the Burrough family were feoffees and would have been well placed to borrow items from the archive of the town charities.[21]

---

[14] Acc. 406/1. This letter, which is incomplete, gives biographical information about Robert and Nathaniel Bloomfield.

[15] For Jackson's sons, see S.H.A. Hervey, *Biographical List of Boys educated at King Edward VI Free Grammar School from 1550 to 1900*, Suffolk Green Books, xiii (Bury St Edmunds, 1908).

[16] *PSIA*, i, p.155. On 14 December 1848 he drew attention to a misericord which had been presented to the Bury museum which depicted a fox preaching to geese and a fox running off with a goose, *PSIA*, i, p.57. On 15 March a Mr Jackson exhibited a rental of lands in Coney Weston, held of the abbot of Bury, 1435, *ibid.*, p.60. On Burrough, see *DNB*.

[17] This volume now forms part of the Cathedral Library and has been deposited at the Bury Record Office with the St James's parish records, where its reference is FL541/13/4.

[18] For the De Carle stone masons see Rupert Gunnis, *Dictionary of British Sculptors, 1660–1851* (new revised edition, n.d.) p.125.

[19] FL541/13/4, inside front cover.

[20] BL MS Egerton 2372, p.363 of which there is a photostat at SROB, P755/28. The first entry in the earliest surviving Minute Book, H2/6/2.1, is dated January 1590 while the earliest Minute Book of the Grammar School governors, E5/9/202.1 begins in December 1589. No doubt this volume contained minutes of the governors from the foundation of the school in 1550, and probably of the feoffees from 1481.

[21] Thomas Burrough was receiver in 1686, Dr James Burrough in 1697 and Matthew Burrough in 1726, BL MS Egerton 2374, p.155, photostat copy at SROB, P755/42.

The conflict between abbey and town

The organisation whose accounts are edited here arose out of the conflict between the Abbey of St Edmund and the town which grew up at its gates. A monastery was founded at *Bedericesworth* by Sigeberht, King of the East Angles, in the seventh century to which the body of Edmund, King of the East Angles, was brought for burial after he had been put to death by the invading Vikings in 869.[22] Cnut, who introduced Benedictine monks into the monastery in 1020 was, according the tradition of the abbey, also founder of the town, which soon after came to be known by place-names of which St Edmund was an element.[23] The town's grid-shaped plan took shape on the ground in the first half of the twelfth century.[24] Successive abbots secured valuable privileges for those who lived in Bury.[25] A guild merchant was set up at an early date, but the might of the abbey ensured that here it did not develop into an incorporated governing body for the town, as happened in most places.[26] However, it was the abbey, not the townsmen, to whom these privileges had been granted, and it was not long before the men of Bury began to hanker after some say in the administration of their town. The abbey, however, began to threaten those privileges which the townsmen already enjoyed, and they resisted all attempts to increase the townsmen's liberties. Trouble brewed on all sorts of fronts. By the time of Abbot Samson there were serious encroachments on the market place, and the abbey began to complain about loss of income.[27] The first of the local disturbances, which usually happened when the country as a whole was in turmoil, took place at the time of the Barons' War in the mid-thirteenth century.[28] As is well known, rebellion and revolt were rife in fourteenth-century Bury St Edmunds.

The earliest reference to Candlemas guild, as it was commonly known, is in the guild certificates of 1389. It states that the guild of St Mary in St James's church had been founded about sixty years before, soon after the rising of 1327, after which the townsmen lost their right to hold a guild merchant.[29] It is probable that this guild was founded, under a religious guise, to provide the townsmen with a forum in which affairs of interest to the town as a whole could be discussed.[30] Members of the guild met on the feast of the Purification of the Blessed Virgin Mary, 2 February, and attended mass at the altar before the image of St Mary.[31] On the following day,

---

[22] See E.O. Blake (ed.) *Liber Eliensis*, Camden Society, 3rd series, xcii (1962), p.11 for Sigeberht's foundation. For St Edmund, see Abbo of Fleury, *Passio Sancti Eadmundi* in Michael Winterbottom (ed.) *Three Lives of English Saints* (Toronto, 1972) p.82.

[23] Vatican MS Reg. Lat. 12, f.17v.

[24] See Bernard Gauthiez, 'The Planning of the Town of Bury St Edmunds' and Margaret Statham, 'The Medieval Town' in Antonia Gransden (ed.) *Bury St Edmunds, Medieval Art, Architecture and Economy*, BAA Conference Proceedings, xx (1998).

[25] For confirmation of market rights, see D.C. Douglas (ed.) *Feudal Documents from the Abbey of Bury St Edmunds*, British Academy Records of Social and Economic History, viii (Oxford, 1932), p.62. King John's charter suppressing markets which threatened the trade in Bury Market is printed in M.D. Lobel, *The Borough of Bury St Edmund's: a study in the government and development of a monastic town* (Oxford, 1935).

[26] The earliest reference is in H.E. Butler (ed.) *The Chronicle of Jocelin of Brakelond* (Nelson's Medieval Classics, 1949) p.74. The passage refers to 1198, at which date the guild merchant was very well established.

[27] *Ibid.*, pp.77, 78.

[28] For discussion of outbreaks of violence in medieval Bury see Lobel, *Borough*, pp.118–70.

[29] V.B. Redstone, 'Chapels, chantries and gilds in Suffolk', *PSIA* xii (1904) p.25.

[30] Lobel, *Borough*, p.147.

[31] This was in the north aisle of the church. See will of John Gardiner, cloth maker, d.1506, who was the father of Stephen Gardiner, Bishop of Winchester, IC500/2/4, f.196. In 1637 the Corporation pew was in

the brothers held a meeting called 'morwespeche' and elected their officers. The head of this guild, in the fifteenth century, was called the alderman, and it had an officer called the dee or dye. The guild merchant had also had officers who used these terms,[32] as did the company or fellowship whose activities are recorded in the earlier accounts in these books. Candlemas guild became very influential in the fifteenth century and the town élite were included in its membership, which was much sought after.[33] It provided the focus for yet another attempt to obtain a voice for the townsmen in the affairs of the town.

The charities which produced these accounts were founded by John, commonly called Jankin, Smith. He was many times alderman of Bury St Edmunds, so he was very well aware of the problems faced by the townsmen.[34] During his lifetime he paid for the building of the chancel aisles and sanctuary of St Mary's church, and he helped to endow the College of Jesus which provided residences for the town clergy.[35] When he made his will his only son, John, was childless, while his daughter, Rose, had already been dead for some years.[36] The esteem in which Jankin Smith was held may be judged by these lines which were used to introduce a summary of his bequest to the town. They were written by, perhaps, a younger contemporary, or at least by someone who had heard about him from those who knew him.

It is to be called and reduced to the perpetuall memory and remembrance off th'enhabitauntes of the town of Bury Seynt Edmund the grett bountevouus [sic] and profitable gifte of that honorable persone, Jhon [sic] Smyth, late of Bury Seynt Edmund, esquier, especiall lover and preferrer off the politik and comen well of the same inhabitauntes, whom God assoile, which disceasid in the vigill of Seynt Peter the xxviij day of June, the yere of our lord God mcccclxxxj . . .[37]

---

the north aisle of St James's, Archdeacon of Sudbury's faculty book, E14/1/13, f.3r. Then the wives of the Corporation men had a pew in the south aisle, though other pews in St James's were granted to households with no segregation by sex. For many years, perhaps from 1550 until 1972, the north aisle was virtually the chapel for King Edward's school, who even had their own entrance from the north side of the church.

[32] Lobel, *Borough*, p.75. See Glossary for 'dee' or 'dye'.

[33] John Hedge, who died in 1504, left two gallons of wine a year for twelve years to ensure that his brother Robert should have the goodwill of the guild and become a member in years to come, IC500/2/4, f.146. Robert Hedge was of the Inner Temple in London, had property in Bury, and left his manor of Purley in Essex to Candlemas guild for payment of taxes when he died, though no trace of this property coming into their hands has been found, PRO PROB 11/22, opening 198, left hand and right hand.

[34] His name is in the list of aldermen for the regnal years 2 Henry VI, 1423/4; 22 and 23 Henry VI, 1442/3 and 1443/4; 34 Henry VI, 1455/6; 2 and 3 Edward IV, 1462/3 and 1463/4: M.D. Lobel, 'A list of the Aldermen and Bailiffs of Bury St Edmunds from the twelfth to the sixteenth century', *PSIA*, xxii (1934) pp.26, 27. While Smith's Christian name is always given as John in formal documents, he has long been known by the diminutive form, Jankin, in Bury St Edmunds. Residents of the town often do not realise that Jankin is a diminutive form of John. This is probably reinforced by the practice of calling the annual commemoration of benefactors 'the Jankin Smith commemoration'.

[35] For these see the registered copy of Jankin Smith's will, IC500/2/2, f.304, printed in Tymms, *Wills*, pp.55–81.

[36] It will be observed in the course of this narrative that the feoffees often benefited from those who had no direct heirs to whom they could leave their wealth. Jankin Smith, however, provided handsomely for his Yaxley grandchildren who established a separate branch of the family at Mellis, Joan Corder, *Visitation of Suffolk, 1561*, Harleian Society's Publications, 2 vols., new series, ii (1981) p.139.

[37] From a photocopy of a benefactors' book, GB500/3/1, f.26v. The manuscript is now in the collection of Professor Toshiyuki Takamiya of Keio University, Tokyo.

Many documents relating to the affairs of the feoffees have only survived in the form of copies made by John Woodward, who was their clerk in the 1650s, in a most comprehensive register of evidences, which is referred to as Woodward's Register. Perhaps the most of outstanding of these copies is that of the deed by which Jankin Smith set up his charity. The foundation deed was sealed on 10 September 1470.[38] On the very same day an agreement, called the 'charter' by its Elizabethan transcriber, was drawn up between the abbot of St Edmunds and the then alderman of Bury St Edmunds in which the privileges allowed to the townsmen were set out.[39] The customs set out in this document allowed the alderman more influence than he was ever known to have had. They are symptomatic of renewed interest in town administration at this period, and an attempt to wrest more power for the urban élite. The duties of the alderman included responsibility for assessing and collecting any taxes which were imposed upon the town. This point cannot be overemphasised in connection with Jankin Smith's bequest to the town. In addition to national taxes, the townsmen of Bury were also required to pay a sum of 100 marks, £66 13s.4d., sometimes called the abbot's cope,[40] to each new abbot on his election. Smith had been alderman for a number of years in a period during which new abbots had been appointed frequently. The charter also described a body of greater and lesser burgesses which foreshadows the arrangements made in 1606. At about this date a few of the townsmen even described themselves as burgesses. Andrew Skarbot, sometime alderman, and Clement Drury, who were two of the first feoffees nominated by Jankin Smith, described themselves as burgess when they made their wills.[41] Reignold Chirche, bell-founder, who became a feoffee when the feoffment was renewed on 22 September 1473, also described himself as burgess.[42] Against the name of Robert Rose, chandler, the word *burgus* is written in the margin of the Probate Register.[43] The last of the five men so far discovered who described themselves in this way was Adam Newhawe. He was an executor of Jankin Smith's will, a benefactor of the town, and probably an officer of the abbey.[44] Records from this period are scanty, but it seems that litigation between abbey and town in 1478 marked the end of this attempt to set up a governing body. One of the complaints made was that the abbot had refused, without any reason, to confirm Jankin Smith's election as alderman.[45] Another complaint was that the payment of the abbot's cope was an 'importable', that is, an unbearable, charge.[46]

---

[38] Woodward's Register, H1/6/1, pp.13–16.

[39] Copied (by Sir James Burrough?) and included in his *Collectanea Buriensia*, FL541/13/4. The 'charter' was copied in the course of the dispute between the feoffees and the townsmen which was settled in 1585.

[40] As, for instance, in the will of John Baret, Tymms, *Wills*, p.21.

[41] Skarbot made his will in 1474 during Jankin Smith's lifetime, IC500/2/2, f.189r. Clement Drury was the brother-in-law of Jankin Smith's executor, Ralph Duke; his will proved in 1475 is IC500/2/2, f.207r.

[42] The first renewal of the feoffment is given in GB500/3/1; Chirche's will is IC500/2/4, f.74v.

[43] Probate Register, IC500/2/2, f.140r.

[44] Probate Register, IC500/2/4, f.49v. See W. Dugdale's *Monasticon Anglicanum*, ed. J. Caley, H. Ellis and B. Bandinel, 8 vols. (1817–30), III, p.130, no. 86, for the appointment of an Adam Newhawe as *stabularius*, keeper of the stables or master of the horses.

[45] Lobel, *Borough*, pp.161–2. It should be noted that Abbot Robert of Ixworth, who had granted the 'charter', had been replaced by Richard Hingham in 1475, while Thomas Rattlesden became abbot in 1479, A. Goodwin, *The Abbey of St Edmundsbury* (Oxford, 1931) p.82.

[46] N.M. Trenholme, 'The English Monastic Boroughs', *The University of Missouri Studies*, vol. 2, no. 3 (1927) p.104. The last three lines of the bidding prayer suggest that Jankin Smith had paid this imposition himself on three occasions during his lifetime.

The foundation deed of 1470 conveyed land in and near Bury St Edmunds to the first feoffees.[47] Its most unusual feature is its witness list. Not only are many of the gentlemen of Suffolk, for instance Cloptons, Highams and Waldegraves, among their number, but also gentlemen from elsewhere in the eastern counties, with Sir John Howard, Lord de Howard, who eventually became the first Howard duke of Norfolk, at their head. Jankin Smith augmented his first gift in 1473 when he gave an estate at Rougham.[48] The foundation deeds of 1470 and 1473 were confirmed when Jankin Smith made his will in 1480, where he set out how his gift was to be administered.[49] As long as he lived he himself was to receive the revenues from these lands. Thereafter, the alderman, burgesses and feoffees were to receive the profits and use them to keep his anniversary every year in St Mary's church. The rest of the income was to be used for paying the abbot's cope on the election of every abbot; any surplus could be used to pay other taxes, national or local, levied on the town as a whole. Under these arrangements, on Jankin Smith's death, the townsmen would begin to receive an income from which a hated imposition could be paid. Even their monastic masters were impressed by this novel arrangement. 'Moved by the pious example of Jankin Smyth' on 28 October 1491, the abbot and convent granted a 99-year lease of these lands, which were copyholds of the cellarer's manor of Great Barton, to Thomas Jermyn and others for the use of the inhabitants of Bury by the advice of the brethren of the guild of the Purification of the Blessed Virgin Mary called Candlemas guild, paying twelve shillings *per annum* at the usual terms.[50] Candlemas guild is not mentioned in Jankin Smith's will. How had this influential guild come to administer the land he had left?

Margaret Odeham and Candlemas guild

No one knew better than Jankin Smith that what was given by one abbot could as easily be taken away by another, and he made provision for the administration of his bequest should the arrangement set up by the 'charter' prove to be short-lived. In this case, according to the will, his feoffees were to administer the lands and distribute the profits in the event of the alderman and burgesses failing.[51] Probably all the original feoffees were members of Candlemas guild, for it drew up new statutes in 1472 to enable it to administer the charities which Jankin Smith and Margaret Odeham had already set up, to come into effect when they died.[52]

Like the founder, Margaret Odeham had no direct heirs at the time of her death. When her husband, John, made his will in 1470, they had two unmarried daughters, both of whom subsequently married. One married John Ansty, to whom John Odeham had left a black robe. The other son-in-law, whose surname was Marlborough, had remarried before Margaret Odeham's death. Both daughters,

[47] Details of the property given by Jankin Smith and the benefactors who followed his example are given in Appendix 8.

[48] Woodward's Register, H1/6/1, pp.34, 35. John Woodward, the feoffees' clerk, compiled this register c.1657–9, copying many deeds and other documents which no longer survive.

[49] An English version of the part of Jankin Smith's will relating to his gift for the payment of town taxes is printed in Appendix 1.

[50] Woodward's Register, H1/6/1, p.35.

[51] See Appendix 1, p.285.

[52] BL MS Harl. 4626, f.21.

therefore, died before their mother and had there been any grandchildren, it is certain that they would have have been left something.

Lack of direct heirs often led testators to think of the feoffees when making their wills. Some testators left land for charitable purposes should they have no heirs, or if all the heirs died – rather as present-day testators are urged to provide against the whole family being wiped out in some disaster. The childless Thomas Andrews, a very active feoffee until his death in 1585, arranged for his estate to pass to the Grammar School should his brother die without an heir. Richard King who lived at Moyses Hall, left the alderman and brethren of Candlemas guild as 'remainder men' should his heirs fail.[53] He had extensive estates which, if they had ever come into the hands of the guild, would have been a munificent benefaction. Only one small part may have become part of the town lands. King left a piece of arable in Fornham All Saints to the friars of Babwell for forty years to pray for him and to keep an *obit*, but at the end of forty years, this land was to go to Candlemas guild. Thereafter the guild should have paid 6s.8d. a year to the friars to pray for him, using the rest for the town of Bury. The feoffees may well have eventually received this land, for it could easily have been intermixed with land given by others.[54] It should be noted that the feoffees bought Moyses Hall, which had been Richard King's home, but it did not come to them as part of his conditional bequest to Candlemas guild.[55]

Margaret Odeham, whose will is dated 12 January 1478, left property in Bury and nearby villages to Candlemas guild.[56] The guild was enjoined to provide a chantry priest for her in St James church; he was to be 'non comown debyte but an helper at nede to devyne service'. He was also to say mass in the chapel of the gaol every Sunday and on every principal feast, and to bring the prisoners holy water and holy bread. In addition every week from Hallowmas (1 November) until Easter, the prisoners in the long ward of the gaol were to be given seven faggots of wood every week. They were to be stored in a house in Skinner Rowe which formed part of her gift.[57] Mrs Odeham insisted that 'seke and heyle' her priest was to keep his office, provided that mass was said at the gaol every Sunday.[58] The guild was also required to provide various services for the souls of the Odeham family, and for the brothers and sisters of the guild, including a mass on Candlemas day followed by the distribution of bread at the Guildhall. If Candlemas guild should fail, her feoffees were to administer the estate she left and carry out her charitable intentions. Part of Margaret Odeham's gift – two houses in Churchgate Street – was successfully concealed at the dissolution of the chantries and guilds and remained in the possession of the feoffees until early in the twentieth century.[59]

---

[53] Probate Register IC500/2/6, f.1v. Professor Gottfried did not appreciate the conditional nature of this bequest and his assertion that the feoffees took all King's estates has been followed by other scholars.

[54] Diarmaid MacCulloch has kindly drawn my attention to a letter, probably to be dated to April 1543, from Peter Brinkley, ex-warden of Babwell Friary, to Nicholas Bacon. Richard King's son Thomas, about seven years before, believing that all land given to spiritual uses for ever would be taken by the king unless the heir should enter before May Day, had entered 14 acres of land in Fornham All Saints. The warden had managed to preserve the payment to Babwell until the house was discharged and he suggested that Bacon should advise on this matter when he was in Suffolk, Regenstein Library, University of Chicago, Bacon Letter 4059.

[55] Payne's petition, K1/3.

[56] Benefactors' book, H1/2/1, fos. 6r. to 9v.

[57] *Ibid.*, f.7r.

[58] *Ibid.*, f.8r.

[59] See Particulars of Sale to be held 22 August 1918, lot 9, GB500/8/7.

Margaret Odeham's will shows that Candlemas guild had sisters as well as brothers, though it is impossible to tell whether these were, like her, competent career women in their own right or wives and widows of male members. It is perfectly possible, indeed likely, that guild members could have discussed problems in the town and agreed to do whatever they could to improve conditions, as Margaret Odeham did with the prisoners in the gaol. The will also shows that by the time of her death in 1492 the Candlemas guild was already administering Jankin Smith's charity and that they would administer her bequest on her own death.[60] The deeds of the land she left, and a terrier which described them, were to be kept in a hutch in the Guildhall. Jankin Smith had required his executors to provide a safe place in which the deeds of the land he left to the town could be stored, and once revenue came in, there would be need of somewhere to store money. The porch of the Guildhall shows signs of having been enlarged at this period, and in the room above the porch (sometimes called the tower, but more often the evidence house) in the thickness of the wall above the inner entrance arch, is a wall safe (Frontispiece). Early in the twentieth century these verses in praise of Jankin Smith were still legible on the wall above it.

> And in this chest [*words illegible*]
> [*words illegible*] blyssynges they may not mysse
> This fulfylling his Wyll as his wrytyng is
> And they that wyll the contrary do
> Shall have the blyssyng that longeth thereto.[61]

One hopes this has merely been painted over, not removed.

This coffer, hutch or treasury in which the money belonging to the town was kept, is often mentioned in the accounts when surplus balances were lodged there or money withdrawn for major expenses.[62] In the early days, individuals, perhaps members of Candlemas guild, also used it to store valuables. An interesting instance is set out in a will proved in 1516.[63] John Hovyll asked the abbot and convent to take care of £60 in money, eighteen silver spoons and the deeds of his two houses in Bury until his children came of age. His property was to be kept in the vestry of the abbey church, and the arrangement set out in an indenture under the common seal of the abbey. One part of this indenture was to be kept in the 'hooche' in the Guildhall 'wherin the bredryn of Candelmesse gilde kepe the money that longeth to the towne of Bury'. He left the guild £1 in return for this.

Other pre-dissolution benefactors and the Candlemas guild accounts

Others soon followed the example set by Jankin Smith and Margaret Odeham. On 22 July 1500 Sir John Frenze, Master of the Hospital of St Peter without the Risby Gate, made his will which confirmed a deed dated 20 April 1494 by which he gave land in Bury for the relief of lepers in St Peter's, or lepers who came to Bury St

---

60 IC500/2/4, f.8, printed Samuel Tymms, *Wills*, pp.73–81.
61 From a newspaper cutting which had been given the date 14 July 1907, which was a Sunday. Not found in either of the local papers, which were full of accounts of the Bury Pageant. Another version of these lines is reprinted from the *Bury and Norwich Post* 1888–91 in *Memorials of the Past*, p.112, and gives a line before those given here which reads '[*space*] wyll hath mad'.
62 For example, HD1150/1, fos. 3r., 17v., 18v., 19v. and 24v.
63 Probate Register IC500/2/4, f.21r.

Edmunds.[64] Like many other donors, Frenze required his feoffees to be renewed when Smith's feoffees were renewed; this was the normal pre-Reformation practice. It is interesting to speculate whether the fact that Frenze left his bequest to Candlemas guild reflects a lack of confidence in the abbey's administration of this major hospital in the town. An almshouse was later built on part of Frenze's gift, on the corner of Chalk Road.[65]

William Fish, whose will is dated 11 August 1499, left lands to John Allen, Thomas Clerk, William Baret and other brothers of Candlemas guild, after the death of his wife Ellen, to pay for the abbot's cope on the election of a new abbot, and also towards the payment of the task. As usual, their anniversaries were to be observed. Each year the members of Candlemas guild were to have a gallon of wine at their feast, which is a frequent bequest in wills such as this, and his will was to be read out each year before the guild.[66] Next, in 1503, John Salter made his will leaving property in Bury to his daughter Isabell for life and after her death to 'wholy remayne in the Gylde of the Purificacion of the blessed Virgine Mary of Bury aforesaid forever more according to the gyfte of John Smyth esquire'.[67]

According to Adam Newhawe's will, made in 1496, he intended the guild of the Holy Name of Jesus in the college to be his beneficiary.[68] However, when new feoffees were appointed on 10 January 1521, the feoffees were to hold it to the use and profit of the inhabitants and to keep an *obit* for Adam Newhawe and his three wives, Rose, Elizabeth and Margaret, in St Mary's on St Blaze's day (3 February),[69] and there is good evidence that this land was by then administered by Candlemas guild. Some connection with the guild and College of Jesus was maintained, as in 1532 the feoffees of Newhawe's gift included Robert Syllyard, clerk, master of the guild 'of the sweetest Name of Jesus' and Thomas Neche, master of the college.[70] The accounts of Candlemas guild, 1520–35, confirm that it administered Adam Newhawe's gift before the dissolution of the guilds and chantries.[71] Because Adam Newhawe's land was to be used by his widow, Margaret, during her lifetime, she is occasionally named as the benefactor; this is also the case with William Fish, whose wife Ellen is sometimes named as the donor.

The Candlemas guild accounts cover lands left by John Smith, Margaret Newhawe, William Fish and John Salter during the years from Michaelmas 1520 – Michaelmas 1529, and three further accounts headed 23, 24 [1531–3] and 26 Henry VIII, [1534–5].[72] From them it appears that the land left by John Smith at Cattishall in Great Barton was let for £6 13s.4d., Leyers in Rougham produced £2 in the first account, but rose to £3 in 1521, and the land in the South Field, £2 6s.8d. At first the rent of William Fish's land was received in malt, which was sometimes not

64 Woodward's Register, pp.55–7. Woodward's copy of the deed lacks the date, which is given in a deed of refeoffment dated 15 April 1519, H1/5/19.
65 When cholera was feared in the town in 1832, the feoffees agreed that the Court of Guardians and Board of Health could use this building as an isolation hospital providing they made other arrangement for the occupants, Minutes, H2/6/2.3, p.147.
66 Woodward's Register, H1/6/1, p.60.
67 Probate Register, IC500/2/4, f.141r.
68 Probate Register, IC500/2/4, f.49v.
69 Woodward's Register, H1/6/1, p.64.
70 Deed of re-enfeoffment forming part of H1/1/10 dated 1 October 1532.
71 Accounts of Candlemas guild, Bodl. MS Suffolk b.1., fos. 8r.–28v., where Newhawe's lands are administered with those of Smyth, Odeham and Fish. There is a photostat copy at SROB, Acc. 515.
72 Candlemas guild accounts, *ut supra*.

forthcoming and, of course, produced an amount which varied from year to year as grain prices fluctuated. In the account headed Michaelmas 1526–7, but more likely for 1525–6,[73] the feoffees sold the crops growing on Fish's land and in the following account, the first of those headed 1527–8, a rent of £3 15s.0d. was received for this land. When Margaret Newhawe's grange and land are listed separately, the rent received was 12s. In the first account, John Salter's land was let for 2s. In cases where several small pieces of land were let at small rents to the same tenant, it must have been very tempting to merge land given by different benefactors.

Out of the receipts of this land, the obits of John Smith and Margaret Newhawe were paid; in the early accounts Smith's and Fish's obits were put together, but Fish's soon disappears. These properties had to be repaired, and further money, usually only a few pence, was spent on the repair of the Guildhall. However, in 1523–4, the supervisors of the lands spent 2s.9d. on a table of the feoffees' names hanging in the hall, while in 1524–5 the large sum of £5 6s.0½d. was spent on repairing the Guildhall. The extra legal expenses incurred when the feoffments of Smith's and Fish's lands were renewed in 1531 are also accounted for here. Apart from one of the accounts headed 1527–8, which is incomplete, each account ends with the amount placed in the hutch at the end of the year. Among those who audited these accounts of Candlemas guild were Mr Stephen Gardiner, who was to become bishop of Winchester and, under Mary I, Lord Chancellor, and the abbot's brother, Roger Reve.[74]

Over the fourteen years for which we have information, an average of just over £10 14s.0d. a year was set aside for payment of taxes, when required. During the years covered by these early accounts, John Reve was abbot, so there was no expenditure on the election of a new abbot. However, there was heavy national taxation, and that it was still a cause of tension between abbey and town was demonstrated when a dispute between the townsmen and Abbot Reve about jurisdictions and taxation was referred to Cardinal Wolsey during his progress through East Anglia in 1515. Abbot Reve required the townsmen to pay £8 19s.6d. towards the fifteenths and tenths for property held by the abbey, which had formerly paid this sum towards the task.[75]

There are some documents copied into John Woodward's register which show that some early benefactions, not originally left to the feoffees, had nevertheless come into their hands. Margaret, widow of Clement Drury, for instance, left almshouses in Little Brackland.[76] Woodward also thought that Reginald Church gave property in Raingate Street which also came into the feoffees' hands.[77] In the case of

---

[73] *Ibid.* There is no heading for an account for 1525–6, but there are two for the year from Michaelmas 1527 to Michaelmas 1528.

[74] Stephen Gardiner in 1528–9, f.22r.; Roger Reve in 1522–3, 1526–7 and 1527–8, fos. 11r. 17r. and 19v.

[75] Diarmaid MacCulloch, *Suffolk and the Tudors: Politics and Religion in an English County, 1500–1600* (Oxford, 1986) p.137. The townsmen's complaints were published by Trenholme, 'The English Monastic Boroughs', p.102. If, by this date, the sum of £24 which the town later paid for fifteenths and tenths had been fixed, it was a considerable addition to the townsmen's financial burden.

[76] Probate Register IC500/2/4, f.36r. and Woodward's Register, H1/6/1, p.54.

[77] Woodward's Register, H1/6/1, p.59. Chirche's will, which was made 16 February 1499, is in Probate Register IC500/2/4, f.74v. From the 1587 rental it can be seen that the feoffees had three tenements in Raingate Street, from which they received rent of 10s., but some or all of these could be part of Tassell's gift.

Thomas Bereve, the houses he left on the corner of Burmans Lane and Garland Street – now the site of the Baptist Chapel – were conveyed to the feoffees by his heirs on 2 September 1527.[78] He intended that his heirs would administer these and other charitable gifts, but it must soon have become obvious that his immediate heirs were dying out and Candlemas guild was the body most suitable to take on the task of administration.

The dissolution and the purchase of the chantry lands

It might be thought that the dissolution of the abbey of St Edmund in November 1539 would have solved many of the problems which had beset the townsmen for so long. In fact this was far from the case, as the Crown took over the possessions of the abbey and controlled the town in much the same way as the abbey had done before. The townsmen found their new masters no more amenable than the old. It can be assumed that Candlemas guild continued to administer the charitable gifts until the dissolution of guilds and chantries in 1548. Even before then, there were the first signs of what was to come. In August 1547, aware that the church plate was likely to be confiscated by the Crown, the parishioners of both parishes agreed that their plate should be sold to provide a fund for repairing the churches and relieving the poor. Woodward preserved the texts of these agreements. That for St Mary's parish gives a fascinating list of the items to be sold, weighing an amazing forty stones and four ounces.[79] The document for St James's parish is very similar, but gives no description of the items of plate involved.

Next came a move towards the dissolution of the guilds and chantries. On 12 November 1548, a commission, which included, among others, the influential government official, Nicholas Bacon, made a certificate of the property belonging to the Bury guilds and chantries.[80] This covered the possessions of the guilds of St Botolph and St Nicholas which had formerly belonged to the College of Jesus, Newhawe's gift, Margaret Odeham's chantry, Beckett's chantry, the possessions of the Morrow Mass priest in St James's church, Jankin Smith's chantry in St Mary's church, Smith's *obit*, St Peter's hospital, the Charnel and St Nicholas's and St Petronilla's hospitals.[81] As far as this certificate is concerned, Candlemas guild might never have existed. Of Jankin Smith's gift for the payment of town taxes, only the rent charge of 10s.8d. which provided for his anniversary each year was deemed superstitious.[82] Inevitably, on its dissolution, Candlemas guild concealed some of its properties, including the Guildhall itself. The feoffees soon bought back land they had forfeited, and also took the opportunity to acquire additional land which had formerly belonged to other guilds and chantries. It was a rather involved process. On 12 January 1549 Roger Barber, Edmund Hawkins, William Parker and William Hammond agreed that Robert Bedys and Giles Levett should endeavour to obtain Odeham's and Beckett's chantries, the possessions of the Morrow Mass priest in St James's church,[83] and the guilds of St Nicholas and St Botolph, formerly held in the

78 Woodward's Register, H1/6/1, p.63.
79 Woodward's Register, H1/6/1, p.66. This document is dated 26 August 1547; the agreement for St James's Parish, *ibid.*, p.70 is dated only August 1547.
80 See Woodward's Register, H1/6/1, p.73. Another, slightly different version is printed by V.B. Redstone, 'Chapels, chantries and gilds in Suffolk', *PSIA*, xii (1904) pp.39–40.
81 Woodward's Register, H1/6/1, p.79.
82 Woodward's Register, H1/6/1, pp.79, 88.
83 The Morrow Mass priest said mass at dawn for labourers and others whose work began then, Eamon

College, for the relief of the poor in the town. The agreement ended with a list of those who had contributed sums ranging between £6 13s.4d. and £40 towards the purchase of these lands.[84] The acquittance for the purchase of these lands, which cost £348 5s.4d., is dated 18 January 1549, and the purchase was confirmed by Letters Patent issued on 12 February following. In his notes on the Commissioners' certificate, Woodward stated that the land endowing Newhawe's gift for Jesus Mass was bought by the feoffees, but this was not covered by the conveyance which he copied. As we have already seen the feoffees had this land long before the dissolution of the guilds.[85] It was probably never surrendered to the Crown.

A few days later, 16 February 1549, the churchwardens of both parishes entered into an agreement with certain inhabitants and parishioners about the use of the sum of £480 which had been raised by selling the church plate,[86] Quite near the beginning of this document we read that 'for that there is noe generall corporacion within the said towne of Bury' the yearly profit of the money given to the churchwardens by the parishioners was obtained by letting[87] it for gain 'wherein doe rest not only many parcells [?recte perils] and uncertenteys whereby the releife of the poore is unlike to have eny long continuance but also the same seemeth not soe Godly unto the said parishioners as if it were converted to some purchase of lands and tenements whereof the profitts should have continuance for ever'. The parishioners agreed that as the former chantry lands had been bought by individuals out of their own money, the money obtained from the sale of the church plate should be used to repay these sums, and that the former chantry lands should in future be in feoffment to parishioners for the relief of the poor and other godly purposes. The lands purchased were used as security for the money laid out by those who had financed the purchase from the Crown until, on 4 September 1555, the former chantry lands were conveyed to feoffees and became known as the 'new purchased lands'.[88]

Bury St Edmunds was by no means the only town to buy former chantry lands. In many towns the Corporation bought former chantry lands to use for a variety of civic purposes, and there are several instances where the church plate was sold to finance such ventures.[89]

More gifts and the purchase of the concealed lands

William Tassell, a nephew of Sir Thomas Jermyn, was for a long time one of the feoffees and made an outstanding gift in his own lifetime.[90] As we shall see, several members of the Jermyn family were benefactors of Bury St Edmunds and, from time

---

Duffy, *The Stripping of the Altars: Traditional Religion in England c.1400–c.1580* (Newhaven and London, 1992) p.140.

[84] Of those listed all were feoffees of what came to be called the town lands apart from John Swanton but he, like some of the others, was a feoffee of the manor of Bretts in Hepworth with which Jankin Smith had endowed his chantry in St Mary's.

[85] See above, p.xxiv.

[86] Woodward's Register, H1/6/1, p.94.

[87] That is, letting it out on bonds as a means of investment.

[88] Woodward's Register, H1/6/1, pp.103–7; the schedule of uses annexed to this document is printed as Appendix 4. Appendix 8, *sub* 1555 indicates the guilds or chantries which were endowed with the property bought as the new purchased lands.

[89] See for instance Colin Platt, *The English Medieval Town* (1986) pp.180–1 and Robert Tittler, *Townspeople and Nation: English urban experiences, 1540–1640* (Stanford, California, 2001) pp.12–13.

[90] A Richard Tassell, presumably his father, was a feoffee, *fl.* 1518–21, Woodward's Register, H1/6/1, p.64; H1/1/50 (15) (16) and (17). The Candlemas guild accounts Bodl. MS Suff. b.1, f.8r. show him as

to time, some of them were feoffees.[91] Although William Tassell was twice married, he died childless.[92] By far the most outstanding property he conveyed to the feoffees on 18 December 1557 was the Angel Inn, and more will be said later about its sale, during his own lifetime, and subsequent recovery.[93] All these properties had formerly belonged to the abbey of St Edmund, so here we see Tassell and the feoffees profiting from the brisk market in land in the years following the dissolution.

Tassell's gift was a very large and valuable one, but a number of smaller ones were also received at about this time.[94] Some, such as the houses in Northgate Street with which Edmund King, grocer, who died in 1483, had endowed a chantry, show how some of the land which had been surrendered at the dissolution returned to charitable ownership.[95] However, some almshouses in Crown Street were acquired on 22 November 1564 which had been concealed, presumably on the dissolution of the abbey of St Edmund. These almshouses were of medieval origin and are mentioned in the Sacrist's rentals of 1433 and 1526.[96] The deeds show that they had been conveyed by William Grice and Anthony Foster to Bartholomew Brockesby of London and John Walker. They were described as 'the almshouses or le poore mens rents, next the stone walls of the Great Churchyard, on the west side of the walls'. They were conveyed to the feoffees for the consolation and relief of the honest poor people of Bury St Edmunds on 22 November 1564.[97] These concealed almshouses were among many similar properties discovered and claimed by William Grice who was one of the patentees charged with seeking out concealed lands on behalf of the Crown. Edward Grimston was another.[98] As mentioned above, it seems likely that the feoffees themselves successfully concealed land given by Margaret Odeham and Adam Newhawe from the Commissioners. Other, more significant properties, which they had concealed were identified by the patentees and now had to be bought in. For the sum of £188 11s.0d., Grimston and le Grys on 6 July 1569 had been granted a former guildhall in Eastgate Street which had belonged to the guilds of St Thomas the martyr, the Assumption of the Blessed Virgin Mary and of St Peter the Apostle; this had been used as the Grammar School since it was founded by King Edward VI in 1550. Also included in their grant was the valuable manor of Bretts in Hepworth, Barningham and Weston with which Jankin Smith had endowed his chantry in St Mary's church,[99] and, no doubt most important of all to the feoffees, the Guildhall in Guildhall Street. This was the headquarters of the company or fellowship. It had

---

supervisor of Smith's and Fish's, 1520–1. William Tassell was a feoffee of Odeham's and Fish's from 1545, deed of refeoffment, H1/1/50 (6) and (9).

[91] See Woodward's Register, H1/6/1, pp.35, 55, 61 and 77; deeds of refeoffment, H1/1/48, 48(b); H1/1/49(c) (d) and (g); H1/1/50 (1) (3) (4) (6) (8) (9) (10) and (11) for the period before these accounts began.

[92] See Notes on People.

[93] Deeds of the Angel Inn, H1/5/23/1–18, transcribed, Woodward's Register, H1/6/1, pp.125–60. For brief details of his gift, see Appendix 8, *sub* 1557.

[94] For brief details of these gifts, see Appendix 8, *sub* 1557, 1558 and 1563.

[95] Edmund King's will has not been traced. The conveyance to the feoffees was made by Francis Boldero of Redgrave, gentleman, and Robert Parker of London, Woodward's Register, H1/6/1, p.53.

[96] Sacrist's rental 1433, BL MS Harl. 58, f.20v.; there is a photographic copy at SROB, Acc.1055. Sacrist's rental, 1526, A6/2/1, p.31.

[97] Woodward's Register, H1/6/1, p.169.

[98] For an account of those granted patents to search for concealed lands see Christopher J. Kitching, 'The quest for concealed lands in the reign of Elizabeth 1', *Transactions of the Royal Historical Society*, 5th series, xxiv (1974) pp.63–78.

[99] When the feoffment of Hepworth was renewed in 1542 the name of Stephen Gardiner, bishop of Winchester, stood at the head of the list of feoffees.

been built as the hall of the guild merchant and then became the hall of Candlemas guild. It was described in the grant from the Crown as a hall for considering or discussing [*ad tractandum*] matters concerning the common profit and benefit of Bury St Edmunds. On the following day, 7 July 1569, Grimston and Le Grice conveyed these properties to Lord Keeper Bacon and the other feoffees of the town lands of Bury.[100]

The vestigial Candlemas guild

Bury St Edmunds was a large town, which would have been incorporated long before but for the repressive power of the abbey of St Edmund. The townsmen did well to obtain so much property for the benefit of Bury as it came on to the market after the dissolution of the monastic houses and chantries. They were no doubt helped by powerful friends at court. Sir Nicholas Bacon, himself a feoffee, was Lord Keeper of the Great Seal from the accession of Elizabeth I in 1558 until his death in 1579; another Burian who was involved in politics at national level was Bishop Stephen Gardiner.[101] Powerful allies such as these helped the town through a difficult period and John Sotheby, recorder of Bury in the late seventeenth century, was right to point out to the new feoffees in 1682 that the town owed a great deal to them.[102]

As the account books open, we have a vestigial Candlemas guild, not quite sure what to call itself. The accounts at first are those of the feoffees of the lands left by the various benefactors, later those of the town lands. The word 'guild' is never used in them; that would have been politically incorrect. However, there are references which show that the organisation was still thought of informally as a guild until the end of the sixteenth century and beyond.[103] Moreover, some members of the company or fellowship were never feoffees; others were active in affairs long before they became enfeoffed in the sense of having a legal interest in the land. The names of those who were enfeoffed in the years immediately before and during the years covered by these volumes are set out in Appendix 6. A list of those enfeoffed and not enfeoffed in January 1585 was pinned into the earlier of these books.[104] Of the four who were not enfeoffed in 1585, two, John Gipps and Walter Brook, had been elected into the fellowship on 20 December 1582 by eighteen men. These eighteen, apart from the younger Thomas Cocksedge, were all feoffees at that date.[105] Men

---

[100] Woodward's Register, H1/6/1, p.109 for the Letters Patent, and p.114 for the conveyance to the feoffees.

[101] See above, n. 74. He was a feoffee of Odeham's and Fish's from 1531, H1/1/9 and 11. The deeds relating to the refeoffment of Smith's have not survived, but it was the intention that Odeham's feoffees at least should always be the same as the feoffees of Smith's, so it is likely that he was feoffee of all the charities administered by Candlemas guild. His name was at the head of those who in 1542 became feoffees of the manor of Bretts in Hepworth, with which Jankin Smith endowed his chantry in St Mary's church, H1/1/50/1 and Woodward's Register, H1/6/1, p.33.

[102] Two versions of parts of Sotheby's speech have survived; one is in the Borough records, Town Clerk's papers miscellaneous, D11/2/3 and the other is to be found in the feoffees' miscellaneous papers, H2/4/1.

[103] For instance the Candlemas guild was referred to, meaning the feoffees of the town land and, no doubt, other members of the company, in the will of Edward Reeve, 1597, IC500/1/56 (91). In correspondence about the Barton copyholds a letter dated in the 1630s is addressed to the alderman and brethren of Holy Trinity Guild, which perhaps does not count.

[104] HD1150/1, 23a.

[105] *Memorandum* of election, H2/1/1(b).

who were not enfeoffed seem to have been most likely to act as distributors to the poor and orphans. Their accounts were entered in the years 1586–92. Of the fifteen men involved only one, Thomas Goodrich the elder, was a feoffee when he undertook this task. Robert Spark, William Faircliff and John Gilly undertook the office of distributor immediately before or at the time they became feoffees in 1588. The names of Richard Moore and John Parker are in the list of those to whom William Baker released his title to the town lands in 1590. John Man became a feoffee in 1606, but the others, although some of them were very active, were never feoffees in the strict sense of having a legal interest in the town lands.[106] Those who were entrusted with such offices may well have been the up and coming men who were likely to be considered when the feoffment was next renewed.

The account for 1590[107] refers to the payment of the charges of a chancery suit brought against William Baker, and it is conjectured that the release that he made of all his interest in the town lands on 31 October 1590 may indicate either that he had been required to stand down from being a feoffee or that he resigned, either voluntarily or at the behest of his fellows. William Baker's release of his interest in the town lands was not made to the then surviving feoffees of the refeoffment of 1588. While most of the surviving feoffees were party to his release, the gentlemen, Sir Robert Jermyn and Sir John Heigham, were not involved. This suggests that those named in that deed were some of the members of the company or fellowship; it is perhaps significant that they were collectively described as inhabitants of Bury St Edmunds. Those who were parties to this deed but were never feoffees were William Alman, Gregory Bridon, Richard More and John Parker.

In 1606 Thomas Baker, named as a chief burgess in the charter of that year, also became a feoffee. However, when the feoffment was being renewed in 1616 Baker refused to sign the deed and the whole process of refeoffment was held up.[108] It is rather difficult to disentangle the legal cases which followed. It seems likely that the first step he took was directed against the Corporation for it appears from the draft decree, from which the information given here comes, that his first attempt to seek redress for alleged wrongs was brought against men appointed on behalf of the Corporation.[109] A later action was brought by Thomas Bright and Robert Martin who were appointed on behalf of the town of Bury St Edmunds, which almost certainly means the feoffees of the town lands. (Thomas Bright was also one of those appointed by the Corporation.) Thomas Baker considered that either the feoffees or the Corporation ought to reimburse him for a large sum of money which he had laid out in connection with a tithe suit, about obtaining a charter of incorporation for the borough and for provision money for the late Queen Elizabeth's household, that is, purveyance.

All these were matters of concern a long while before he refused to sign the renewal of the feoffment in 1616. So far it has not been possible to identify the tithe cause with which he was concerned; his name does not appear in the papers relating to the complaint about the tithes of the town made in 1593.[110] Thomas Baker was undoubtedly involved in a dispute about purveyance. In 1600 he was lent a confirmation of the abbey's privileges made in 1516 to take to London to show to the

---

[106] Similarly, although Thomas Bright was not among those who were re-enfeoffed in 1617, he nevertheless acted as receiver in 1619.
[107] HD1150/1, f.32v.
[108] Minutes, H2/6/2.1, p.45.
[109] Borough archives, legal papers, D10/5/1.
[110] Complaint of Anthony Payne and others to Sir William Cecil and others, C7/2/9.

Clerk of the Green Cloth.[111] As for the cost of incorporating the town, most of the more influential townsmen paid dearly for it in both time and money. Thomas Baker's name, on the evidence available, does not stand out in this respect. By the time the case was eventually settled, on 11 June 1624, Thomas Baker had fallen on hard times. Perhaps he wasted money on ill-advised litigation, for the document shows that he persisted in his allegations. As part of the agreement, Baker was required to relinquish his place as a [capital] burgess of the Corporation and to release the Corporation and feoffees from the claims he had made. The feoffees were also, in view of his poverty, required to pay him an annuity of twenty marks [£13 6s.8d.] throughout his life and after his death to pay twenty nobles [£6 13s.4d.] a year to his widow if she should survive him. While it is tempting to suppose that Thomas Baker was the son of William, it has not been possible for find a will for either of them, and it could be coincidence that two men called Baker fell out with their fellow feoffees.

Although Candlemas guild had long been dissolved, in the early years covered by these account books the company, as we must now call it, elected an alderman. One of the claims made in the agreement between abbey and town in 1470 was that the alderman, presumably meaning the alderman who was nominated by the townsmen and had his appointment confirmed by the abbot, held the Guildhall for his term of office.[112] It will be noted in the early accounts that whoever was alderman for the year was also keeper of the Guildhall and accounted for it as such. In the first three accounts, until, no doubt, they were absorbed into a new rental, £1 4s.0d. a year in rent was received by the keeper of the Guildhall, who was also always the alderman.[113] In the dispute between abbey and town in 1478 it was said that the alderman had the Guildhall and other property throughout his term of office and that he ought to have certain rents towards repairing the Guildhall and maintaining his office.[114] The rents noted in the first few accounts look as though they are those mentioned in this dispute. Could it possibly have been the case that before the dissolution the man chosen as alderman of Candlemas guild was also the person recommended to the abbot for confirmation as alderman of the town?[115]

By 1570 a company or fellowship, headed by an officer called the alderman, and with another officer known as the dee[116] had its headquarters in the Guildhall which was initially built as the hall of the guild merchant and, after the suppression of that body, had been used by Candlemas guild; the office of dee had previously existed in both the guild merchant and Candlemas guild. In addition to the alderman and dee, annual fees were paid by the company to a clerk, porter, chaplain and sexton. One of the clerk's tasks was to enter the orders (minutes) of the company. He or his deputy also copied the accounts into the account book from the loose paper accounts which were first drawn up. The first clerk whose name we know is William Cook, who was awarded a pension in 1615.[117] The porter or beadle of the hall was another officer

---

111 Minutes, H2/6/2.1, p.20. The *Inspeximus* Baker took to London is A1/1.

112 Sir James Burrough's *Collectanea Buriensia*, FL541/13/4, p.549.

113 A memorandum made in 1550 of rents to be received by the keeper of the Guildhall amounted in all to £2 7s.5d., but 14s.0d. of this was the rent for Frenze's gift for the lepers and other property may also have been added in. *Memorandum* of rents to be received by the Keeper of the Guildhall, H1/1/15.

114 *Ibid.*

115 This appears to have been the case with the guild merchant in the mid-thirteenth century. See Lobel, *Borough*, p.78, but the will of John Baret, proved 1467, suggests otherwise, Tymms, *Wills*, p.30.

116 See Glossary.

117 William Cook is mentioned by name as the clerk in the account for 1589, HD1150/1, f.31r. For his pension see Minutes, H2/6/2.1, p.43.

whose wages are regularly recorded in these accounts. Richard Yates copied into his notes for a history of the town the porter's promise or oath dated 1582, when John Annable took up the office. In addition to acting as caretaker and cleaner of the Guildhall he was required to inform members of the company when fellow members or their wives died so that the company could follow the coffin to burial and, more surprisingly, to keep two blood-hounds to apprehend felons and other malefactors when required to do so by the magistrates.[118] A chaplain was paid for the annual service, and in many years, a preacher's fee is also recorded.[119] This service might be held in either of the two churches.[120] Perhaps each church was used alternately, or the service may have been held in whichever church the alderman for that year attended. The sexton received a small payment (for putting out the cushions for the company) as did the cook who prepared the feast. In the earlier accounts, payments were made (or, at least, demanded) when men joined the company or fellowship[121] and bread given in alms on the death of members.[122] The newly agreed rules and articles of the house, which would no doubt have illuminated many obscure points, were engrossed by Robert Adams at a cost of 10s.0d. in the year ending Michaelmas 1573, but they have not survived.[123]

It seems certain that an alderman was appointed in the years between the two periods for which alderman's accounts survive, and also after the alderman's account ceased to be given separately. One who held the office in a year for which no special alderman's account was kept was Thomas Bright the younger, who was described as alderman when his son Walter was admitted to Caius College, Cambridge, in 1599.[124]

Common conference and other innovations

No doubt the purchase of the Guildhall, not to mention the school building, must have created confidence by removing the fear of losing essential buildings. The opening of the account book in 1570 and, in the following year, the Book of Orders of the body sometimes called 'common conference', seem to indicate a new era in the government of the town. Incorporation was still in the future. However, the feoffees had recovered much of the land which had been surrendered in 1549 together with some of the possessions of other dissolved guilds and chantries. Some of the former possessions of the abbey had come into their hands with Tassell's gift.

---

118   Yates Notes, BL MS Egerton 2374, pp.358–60, photostat copy at SROB, P755/42.
119   For example preachers' fees are recorded in the years ending Michaelmas 1573, 1574 and 1575 when many of the feoffees were still quite conservative in religious matters.
120   St Mary's in the year ending Michaelmas 1573, HD1150/1, f.9r.; St Mary's again in the year ending Michaelmas 1578, HD1150/1, f.17r.; St James in the year ending Michaelmas 1580, HD1150/1, f.18r.
121   Payments were received from Robert Careles and Thomas Goodrich on their admission to the company in the year ending Michaelmas 1570, HD1150/1/1, f.2v., and demanded from John Higham and Thomas Peyton in the year ending Michaelmas 1571, but not, apparently, received, HD1150/1 fos. 4v. and 6v. In the year ending Michaelmas 1574 a silver spoon weighing 2 ounces was received from Henry Collin on his admission, HD1150/1, f.11r.
122   In the first account 5s. was spent on bread distributed on the deaths of both William Smythis and John Holt, HD1150/1, f.3r., and the same amount was given in 1574 on the death of Thomas Cage, HD1150/1, f.10r.
123   HD1150/1, f.9r.
124   Hervey, *Grammar School List*, p.42.

Their title to some of the lands they had originally contrived to conceal was now secure, while legacies and gifts of land and money were still coming in.[125]

Outstanding among these was the bequest of Edmund Jermyn. He left an annuity of £40 a year out of the manor of Torksey in Lincolnshire, although this was subject to the payment of £20 a year to his brother, John Jermyn, until he died in 1607.[126] This was an exceedingly valuable gift, and members of the Jermyn family from time to time were involved in its application for the relief of the poor. Initially, in January 1573, the rent charge was conveyed to some of the feoffees, described as inhabitants of Bury St Edmunds, but in 1576 they conveyed it to the governors of the Grammar School.[127] The governors were to hold the annuity just as the inhabitants had done for the provision of a stock of wool, hemp, flax, iron or other materials to provide work for poor and needy people in Bury St Edmunds.[128] Of the sixteen governors named in the charter in 1550, by 21 January 1583 only Thomas Andrews, William Baker, Thomas Cocksedge and William Tassell survived, all of whom were also feoffees.[129] Gifts of money to buy a stock of materials, especially wool, to provide employment for the poor were made frequently at this time. Others who left money for a stock to set the poor to work were Thomas Browne, Francis Boldero, and, a little later, John Gipps.[130]

A Book of Orders made by the body sometimes called 'common conference' sheds light on administrative affairs in the town. This body met on forty-two occasions between 14 January 1571 and 11 December 1575. Seven of these meetings were held in January and February 1571 when 77 out of a total of 225 cases were heard in little over a month. Even if no formal census of the poor had been taken before these meetings were held, it is obvious that the constables had been very busy discovering whether or not the poor were employed. This body is found ordering incomers to return to their place of birth or to some place where they had lived for at least three years. Three years' residence in Bury St Edmunds entitled a person to be treated as a townsman or woman.[131] It was quite possible for someone to come and settle in the town, provided he or she had work which would support them, or someone would satisfy the authorities that they would not become chargeable upon the community.

The Book of Orders also shows that in the early 1570s wool was regularly handed out to poor women at church on Sunday morning for spinning and that they had to return the wool, converted into yarn for weaving, on the following Saturday.[132] It also contains lists of poor people, eighteen in all, to whom cards and/or spinning wheels were given one October.[133] In addition to a wheel, Mother Bateman was also given a pair of rakes. Two wheels were also supplied to the gaol.

---

125 Set out in Appendix 8.

126 For Edmund Jermyn's will see S.H.A. Hervey (ed.) *Rushbrooke Parish Registers, 1567–1850, with Jermyn and Davers Annals*, Suffolk Green Books, vi (Woodbridge, 1903), p.145; the last payment to John Jermyn is recorded HD1150/2, f.12r.

127 Woodward's Register, H1/6/1, pp.185–8.

128 *Ibid.*, 188–9. This annuity was probably entrusted to the governors because the money could be invested more safely by a body which was incorporated and could sue and be sued in a court of law.

129 The other governors named in the charter were William Maye, Dean of St Paul's, Richard Bacon, esquire, John Eyer, Christopher Peyton, Henry Payne, Stephen Heyward, Roger Barber, John Battie, Robert Sharpe, William Cheston, Thomas Horseman and Thomas Stacye.

130 Such stocks were used to buy raw materials which were then made into goods and sold, enabling the proceeds to be used to buy further raw materials.

131 Book of Orders, C2/1, f.25r.

132 *Ibid.*, f.1r.

133 *Ibid.*, fos. 39v., and 40r. The year is not given in the text.

A number of those given equipment with which they could earn a living were also given liveries or gowns in 1572 or 1574. Twenty-five poor people were named who were given 'gowns' in November 1572, fifteen from St Mary's parish and ten from St James's. Another list in the book actually gives the yardage of fabric allowed for providing the winter 'liveries' for the poor on 30 October 1574.[134] Whether the feoffees or the parish officers provided this clothing is not known. Looking overall at the names found in this book, it is possible to identify the hard core of really poor families in the town during these years. Those who were idle and frequented ale houses or spent their days in unlawful games were punished. Throughout, the fear of hungry mouths to be fed at the expense of the town foreshadows the thinking behind the by-laws drawn up by the Corporation in 1607.

The continuing post-dissolution existence of Candlemas guild has already been argued for, but common conference cannot be wholly equated with either the post-dissolution company or the feoffees. There are references in the Book of Orders to the 'company of this house'; for instance, on 17 August 1572, it was agreed that the company of this house should meet for common conference on the first Thursday in every month.[135] Many members of the company or fellowship which produced the account books also attended common conference. The list of those who attended common conference in 1571 shows that it consisted of twenty-two men from each parish, and included all the then feoffees who were resident in the town, besides many who were to become feoffees later in the century.[136] In all twenty-one of the forty-four men involved were or were to be feoffees. Two more seem to have been members of the vestigial Candlemas guild; one was one of those to whom William Baker released his interest in the town lands, while another signed the account for 1578–9.[137]

The activities of those who met for common conference were to a considerable degree connected with the administration of poor relief and in maintaining good order in the town. It seems possible that this body might have been a combined select vestry for the two parishes of the town, and they seem to have elected the collectors for the poor.[138] Although it is tempting to identify this body with the inhabitants who supervised the election of feoffees and attended the audit of their accounts, there is at present too little evidence to assert this with any confidence. It is quite obvious that those who became involved in town administration were a tightly knit group, and while the bodies which produced the Book of Orders and the account books were not the same, many men were involved with both groups. Activities recorded in the Book of Orders such as the admission of Alice Hill into an almshouse under the churchyard wall on 19 January 1571 suggest that those who met for common conference were in fact the feoffees plus others.[139]

One or two further points must be noted about the meetings of the township or common conference. Several of the orders demonstrate the activities of the justices of the peace, some of whom seem to have been present often at these meetings. The justices' authority seems to have been required when people were sent back to their

---

[134] *Ibid.*, f.37v.
[135] Book of Orders, C2/1, f.21r.
[136] *Ibid.*, f.42v. In Appendix 6 those feoffees who attended common conference are indicated in the column headed 1571 with either an 'M' or a 'J' to indicate which parish they represented.
[137] One was the Thomas Cocksedge who was not a feoffee but signed the account for the year ending 1578, HD1150/1, f.16v. The other was John Gilly.
[138] On 8 March 1573 it was noted that the justices and the rest of the company were to meet to elect the new collectors, Book of Orders, C2/1, f.23v.
[139] *Ibid.*, f.6r.

place of birth or other place of settlement.[140] Probably it was a question of whether John Brewer, a Dutchman, could remain in the town which was to be settled by Sir Ambrose Jermyn and Mr Badby.[141] Again, Mr Badby was involved in allowing Philip Jones to remain in Bury provided that his father-in-law, Mr John Clark of London, gave his word that Jones should not become a charge to the town.[142] Justices of the peace could, of course, take action alone, as Thomas Andrews had done about Robert Cowper, a sixteen-year-old who had lived in Norwich. The company did not know what Andrews had ordered, so he was put in the care of Robert Walls until Mr Andrews returned home.[143] On one occasion, however, although most of the company attended, business was deferred because no justice of the peace was present.[144] The magistrates were required to use their authority to compel the authorities in Newmarket to receive John Rolfe, a butcher, who had been ordered to return there but found that Newmarket would not accept him.[145] Rather different was the case of Anne Johnson who had a licence from Higham and Badby to earn her living within the franchise of Bury. She was suspected of prostitution and referred back to them by common conference to see whether she should have her passport revoked and be ordered to leave the town.[146] On 11 December 1575 Elizabeth Gardiner was ordered to bring a testimonial of credit under the alderman's hand for her good behaviour before Christmas.[147] Here is evidence that the alderman was still involved in judicial or quasi-judicial matters in the town. Finally, on 5 August 1571 James Maydnell, physician, was bound in £10, and Jeffrey Talbot, yeoman, in £5, and James Maydnell was to appear at the next sitting of the portmanmoot, and to be of good behaviour in the meantime.[148]

One case recorded in the Book of Orders is quite unlike any other. William Pole, shoemaker, promised to provide his mother-in-law, Margaret Corton, with sufficient meat, drink, washing, wringing and 3s.4d. a quarter throughout her natural life. If he failed to do so, he promised that she should have her house in Southgate Street again in fee simple, as she had had it before they first bargained. The first payment of 6s.8d. was to be made on the feast of St John the Baptist, 1574.[149] William Pole made his mark in the book, and the entry was witnessed by ten men, Thomas Badby's name at the head.[150]

Another reflection of an increased interest in local government following the acquisition of the concealed lands and the activity of common conference, is to be found in the renewal of the feoffment on 1 February 1572.[151] Unlike later general feoffments, it does not give the date of the previous general feoffment; the last

---

[140] On 28 January 1572 Harry Potter and his wife were ordered to leave the town before Easter on pain of a fine of £10. There is a note that this order was ratified in the presence of Mr Badby, one of the justices, on 28 March following, *ibid.*, f.11v. On 12 August John Day, who had been ordered to leave the town by Easter was required to attend at the hall when Mr Andrews came home, *ibid.*, f.15v.

[141] *Ibid.*, f.16r.

[142] *Ibid.*, f.25v.

[143] *Ibid.*, f.18v.

[144] *Ibid.*, f.13r.

[145] *Ibid.*, f.25r.

[146] *Ibid.*, f.19r.

[147] *Ibid.*, f.31r.

[148] *Ibid.*, f.15v. The Portmanmoot was the ancient court to which the men of Bury owed suit and which become the court of record after 1606.

[149] The nativity of St John the Baptist is 24 June; the decollation or nativity 29 August, C.R. Cheney (ed.) *Handbook of Dates for Students of English History* (1948).

[150] Book of Orders, C2/1, f.28r.

[151] See Appendix 6.

surviving documents, when each donor's lands were separately enfeoffed, had been drawn up as long ago as 1545. It seems that in the confusion of the reformation period no general refeoffment had been made, and that men were co-opted as required in transactions concerning the town lands.

There is evidence that problems which had arisen as a result of the way in which the abbey had treated the town were now being tackled. A long standing problem arose because the Sacrist had provided chaplains to carry out his duties as titular parson of both parishes, but no vicarages had ever been endowed, and no official parsonage houses existed in the town.[152] The first reference to the feoffees' involvement is in the account for the year ending Michaelmas 1574, in the alderman's account, where payment was made for repairing glass windows.[153] The ministers' houses were near the Norman Tower. There are references to buying a house next to St James's steeple for this purpose, for which the last instalment was paid in the year ending Michaelmas 1577.[154] The house on the north side of St James's church, now the cathedral shop, was bought for £40 in 1584–6.[155]

Before the dissolution, the abbot and convent refused to allow royal courts to meet within the borough boundary. The assizes and quarter sessions had been held in temporary accommodation just north of the town at Henhowe. When Thomas Badby conveyed the monastic school to the feoffees on 12 July 1578[156] the people of the town would already have known that the queen was likely to visit Bury that summer.[157] Badby, a prominent puritan justice as well as an active feoffee, knew by then that if the queen did visit Bury that year, he was to entertain her in his house which his father-in-law, John Eyer, had made out of some of the abbey buildings.[158] Temporary, even ramshackle, accommodation on the outskirts of Bury, highlighting the abbey's control of the town, had made a point before the dissolution, but was no longer an acceptable place for the magistrates to meet.[159] Needless to say, Elizabeth I's visit to the town produced a special effort to improve its appearance. These accounts show that three of the town gates were repaired in the years 1579–80.[160]

1578 was also the year in which Thomas Bright the elder, one of the major benefactors, died. The application of his gift of £300 and the litigation about his grant of tithes are discussed below.[161] Much of Bright's bequest was to relieve the poor, who must have been very numerous at this period. A Bridewell or house of correction for

---

[152] The College of Jesus, to which Jankin Smith left his manor of Swifts in Preston, had provided residences for both the parochial clergy and chantry priests in the fifteenth and early sixteenth centuries, but it had been dissolved with the other guilds and chantries, Woodward's Register, H1/6/1, p.73.

[153] HD1150/1, f.12v.

[154] HD1150/1, f.15r.

[155] HD1150/1, fos. 23r., 23v. and 25v.

[156] Woodward's Register, H1/6/1, p.198. Badby is usually said to have given the Shire House, but the conveyance states that it was granted out of good will and by fine; there is a payment of £10 for it in the account for 1580, HD1150/1, f.18v. No doubt a medieval school would require considerable modification to fit it for use as a shire house; such work may account for some of the very large, vaguely described payment in 1579, HD1150/1, f.16r.

[157] News of the proposed progress had been sent to Thetford and Norwich in June, Zillah Dovey, *An Elizabethan Progress: the Queen's Journey into East Anglia 1578* (Stroud, 1996) p.17.

[158] Suitable houses had been inspected earlier in the year, Dovey, *ut supra*, pp.17, 18.

[159] In this year Thomas Seckford levied a rate for building the Shire House at Woodbridge, MacCulloch, *Suffolk*, p.122.

[160] HD1150/1 fos.17r. and 18v. It would not have been surprising to find a present for the Queen recorded in the accounts.

[161] See pp.xlviii and li below.

the whole town was provided in 1580, although there had been houses of correction for each parish before this.[162] This must have been prompted by Sir Ambrose Jermyn's bequest of £40 to provide work for the poor when a workhouse had been established.[163]

Improvements at a price

In 1580 and 1581 the feoffees received two rather unusual cash gifts, amounting to £44 18s.0d., from 'a frinde E.R., gentleman'.[164] John Craig is no doubt correct to identify 'E.R.' with the wealthy Catholic recusant, Edward Rookwood.[165] In the following year, the feoffment was renewed, and the almshouse regulations made on 8 December 1582 may reflect new brooms sweeping clean.[166] The requirement that residents should nurse those who were suffering from the plague or other epidemics were as much to be expected as those requiring them to live at peace with their neighbours.[167]

In 1582 the governors of the school, on behalf of and with a large financial contribution from the feoffees, bought St Peter's Hospital. Why they bought the property at this juncture is not clear. From the earliest account, the feoffees had been making regular payments to the poor people in St Peter's Hospital. It is usually called the 'spittle', sometimes the 'poor hospital', sometimes the 'hospital almshouse' in these accounts, and it was certainly used as an isolation hospital in times of plague or other epidemics.[168] St Peter's had been one of the possessions of the abbey of St Edmund, and a note of its suppression is included in the Chantry Certificate of 1548 along with the guilds, chantries and the other hospitals in the town.[169] However, a well known clause at the end of the Bury chantry certificate indicated the feeling that much had been lost by the townsmen at the dissolution 'and soe [*they*] petition for some foundation of an hospitall for the poore and schoole for the education of youth'. Modern writers have rightly dismissed the view that the hospital was not dissolved.[170] However, the hospital building could well have been rented by the feoffees for much, if not all, the period between its dissolution and its purchase, so that they could continue to use it as a hospital. Surviving deeds show that it was conveyed by the Crown to Sir George Somerset on 6 July 1545 who, on

---

[162] HD1150/1, f.18r. Henry Horningold bought reed and thatch from one of the houses of correction.

[163] S.H.A. Hervey, *Rushbrooke*, pp.145, 146. There is no evidence that the feoffees received Sir Ambrose's legacy.

[164] HD1150/1 fos. 18r. and 19r.

[165] John S. Craig, *Reformation Politics and Polemics: the Growth of Protestantism in East Anglian market towns, 1500–1610* (Aldershot, 2001) p.98.

[166] Almshouse regulations, 1582 H2/1/1/(a).

[167] It was difficult to persuade people to care for those with plague, so in some towns residence in an almshouse was conditional on help during times of plague. Paul Slack, *The Impact of Plague in Tudor and Stuart England* (Oxford, 1990) p.274.

[168] This happened in the great plague of 1637. The governors were compensated by those who handled the money collected for relief of the infected who burnt down some of the buildings at St Peter's, school accounts, 1623–1657, E/5/9/18–45.

[169] Woodward's Register, H1/6/1, p.79; for its history see C. Harper-Bill (ed.) *Charters of the Medieval Hospitals of Bury St Edmunds*, SRS, Suffolk Charters, xi (Woodbridge, 1994) pp.7–9.

[170] M. Joy Rowe, 'The Medieval Hospitals of Bury St Edmunds', *Medical History*, ii (1959) p.259 dismissed the idea and C. Harper-Bill, *ut supra*, ignored it. *VCH: Suffolk*, II, p.135 cited a licence to beg, granted to George Hodgson, 'guide' of the house, noted by Strype, *Ecclesiastical Memorials of the Reign of Edward VI*, ii, p.249 in support of its survival. Knowles and Hadcock, *Medieval Religious Houses*, p.316 say St Peter's was not suppressed.

25 September that year, leased St Peter's and the land which went with it to Edward Reve.[171] From the account for the year ending Michaelmas 1576, it is clear that the purchase was already under consideration; Mr Andrews had £30 in his hands for that purpose.[172] The purchase in 1582 was from Charles Somerset of Wickhambrook.[173] The feoffees spent £45 5s.2d. to obtain the licence in mortmain, although it was granted to the governors, and Mr Andrews was reimbursed for £66 3s.4d. which he had laid out about the purchasing of St Peter's lands.[174] Before this, however, two payments had been made to Edward Reve, the then lessee, which were probably in connection with St Peter's.[175] All these sums together come to £185 10s.4d.; some seventeenth-century notes analysing the accounts from 1581–1602 give the sum of £106 8s.6d. for the purchase of St Peter's in 1582, which does not agree with the figures given here.[176]

Expenditure on the ministers' houses, and the purchase of St Peter's must have strained the feoffees' resources, and may account for the fact that part of Tassell's gift, including the Angel, was alienated in 1582, while Mr Tassell was still alive, although these properties were later recovered under a decree of the Commissioners for Charitable Uses. The Angel was bought by Roger Potter, one of the feoffees, for a total of £120 over a period of six years.[177] In the same year, 1582, the feoffees extinguished a rent charge on a piece of ground adjoining Sir John Heigham's house in Crown Street. He paid £12 for this, £7 10s.0d. plus £4 10s.0d. for arrears of rent.[178] Some land in Great Barton was also exchanged with John Bright, described as being of Great Barton, in 1584, when he paid £1 6s.8d. to make up the value of the land he had received.[179]

The Market Cross which was built in 1583 to replace the simple medieval stone cross certainly proved expensive and may have been another factor influencing the sale of some of Tassell's lands.[180] Sir Thomas Jermyn, who died in 1552, had left £40 to the town of Bury to spend upon 'such things as shalbe most pleasure unto Almightie God and profytt of the towne'.[181] The greater part of his legacy, £30, was spent on building the Market Cross during the year ending at Michaelmas 1583.[182] On 11 December 1583 John Heigham and Thomas Andrews wrote to constables in Cockfield, Shimpling and Lawshall informing them that 'a very fayer large house for cornesellers' had recently been built in the market place in Bury St Edmunds 'wherein they may stande to their great ease very comodiouslye in the heate of somer and also in the tyme of reynye and cold wet winter'. The cost was greater than the inhabitants could bear so the writers asked that everyone 'within your hundred' should be asked to contribute to the cost. Any contributions were to be brought to the sign of the Angel on 'Saturday next before the feast of the Epiphanie comonly

---

171 Lease, E5/9/305.7. For Edward Reve, see Notes on People.
172 HD1150/1, f.14r.
173 Conveyance dated 20 March 24 Eliz. I [1582], E5/9/305.8. The licence in mortmain sanctioning this is among the feoffees' records, H1/5/33.
174 HD1150/1, f.20v.
175 HD1150/1, fos. 15r. and 18v.
176 H2/3/1. These notes were probably compiled by John Sotheby when preparing his address on the history of the feoffees for the new feoffees appointed in 1682.
177 HD1150/1, fos. 20r., 21v., 22v., 24r., 25v. and 27v.
178 Ibid., f.20r.
179 Ibid., f.22v. Bright was probably the tenant of Catishall; see f.15r.
180 There was also a cross to mark the horse market, now St Mary's Square. See the will of Thomas Clerk, proved 1506, IC500/2/4, f.190r.
181 Hervey, Rushbrook, p.134.
182 HD1150/1, fos. 21v., 22r.

called twelf day next' with a list of contributors so that 'we may yelde them thanks accordingly'. On the back is a list of those in Lawshall who subscribed a total of 3s.1d.[183] The account ending at Michaelmas 1584 shows the very large sum of £121 18s.8d had been spent on finishing the Market Cross, while the stones of the old cross were sold for £2.[184]

At about this time, a disagreement occurred between the feoffees and the townsmen, in the course of which questions were asked about the status of the alderman and burgesses. The copy of the 'charter' of 1470 which Sir James Burrough saw and copied was made in connection with this enquiry. It concluded with an agreement dated 27 January 1585.[185] This document is in very poor condition, and holes in the paper mean that some words or phrases have been lost. The first clause of this agreement could well mean that twenty townsmen who were not feoffees should elect those who were to be enfeoffed and it is clear that each year they were to meet with the feoffees for the account, and that four gentlemen who lived in and about the town 'at their will and pleasure' should be present at elections and audits. From the second clause it appears that the inhabitants who had been elected were to approve the feoffees who were to keep the keys of 'the howse, chamber and chests wherein the evidence, treasure and suche other things belonginge to the towne dothe [space] soe that the said feoffes be inhabitinge within the town of Burye'. The inhabitants who were to supervise the feoffees might have been those who attended common conference, assuming that it still met at this date. It also seems possible that the feoffees' accounts, which had been consolidated for several years, reverted to the ancient division according to the donors of the land for the years from 1585 to 1594 as a result of this enquiry. A new general feoffment was made on 5 March 1588, which introduced the feoffees who were to manage the town lands until just after the incorporation of the borough.

When the feoffees began to pay the stipends of the town preachers, they assumed a heavy annual charge. The payments which the two parochial chaplains received from the sacrist, a shilling a week each, were inadequate long before the dissolution; after 1539 the Crown paid (sometimes irregularly) a pension or exhibition of about £8 10s.0d. a year out of the possessions of the abbey for the priests' wages.[186] The controversy surrounding the ministers of St James's in 1570s has been the subject of extensive analysis in recent years, and it is clear from the accounts of these troubles that the townspeople were already contributing towards the cost of providing the town clergy.[187] The feoffees, however, did not become involved with the distribution of money collected for the clergy, or for augmenting their livings, until after the 'Bury stirs' had subsided; they made their first payment in 1586.[188] Until the special accounts for the lands given by different groups of donors were abandoned, some of the money was recorded in the account for Smith's lands and the rest in the account for the new purchased lands and Tassell's lands. As may be seen from the table giving these payments year by year, the name of neither clergyman is given in the

---

[183] Town Clerk's papers miscellaneous, D11/2/3. It is often the case that strays from the feoffees' archive are to be found among the records of the Corporation, and *vice versa*.

[184] HD1150/1, fos. 22v., 23r.

[185] Agreement between townsmen and feoffees, 1585, C2/2.

[186] In 1589 it was £8 11s.6d., in 1590 it was £8 12s.4d. and in 1591 £8 12s.4d: HD1150/1, fos. 30r., 34v. and 35r. The reference in 1571 to a decree in the exchequer for the priests' wages suggests litigation had been required to secure payment of this sum. Note the use of the word 'priests' at this date rather than 'minister' or 'clergyman', HD1150/1, f.5r.

[187] MacCulloch, *Suffolk*, pp.199, 200; Craig, *Reformation, Politics and Polemics*, p.90.

[188] HD1150/1, f.25v.

first two years. Then both Mr Hill and Mr Moss seem to have been attached to St James's. For some reason Mr Mosse was not paid for the whole year; perhaps he was taking the sixteenth-century equivalent of a sabbatical, in trouble with the authorities or even travelling abroad, as William Bedell did in the seventeenth century.

Sometimes in the early years the feoffees received contributions from the parishioners towards clerical stipends. Such income was noted from 1589 until 1591, some of it, in the latter year, being specified as the exhibition granted by the Crown.[189] These offerings may not have been given entirely of the freewill of the townspeople, for on one occasion Mr Mountford is recorded to have paid 6d. for Dr Wood's arrears under this heading.[190] It is therefore likely that these contributions were in fact a rate assessed at so much per house. In the absence of evidence to the contrary, it must be assumed that in future the payments to the town clergy were met from the feoffees' own funds. However, it will be noted that the amount paid tended to fluctuate, so anything given by the feoffees, in the earlier years at least, might have been in addition to contributions managed by the parish officers.

Although one would never guess from the account books, at sessions held at Bury St Edmunds on 22 April 1589, the feoffees entered into an agreement with the county justices of the peace 'for punnishinge and suppressinge of roages, vaccabonds, idle loyteringe and lewde persons which doe or shall hereafter wander and goe aboute' within those hundreds which made up the Liberty of St Edmund.[191] The conditions set out for those who were taken to the working house or house of correction were very hard indeed. The agreement and the regime prescribed for the poor in the document of 1589, were set up in accordance with an Act of Parliament passed in 14 Elizabeth I [1571–2], at the very period when the authorities in Bury were making strenuous efforts to provide the poor of the town with work.[192] After this agreement between the feoffees and the county magistrates, the existing house of correction, which had been set up by the feoffees, was used. This was in Master Andrew Street, which has become the present Bridewell Lane. So far the site has not been ascertained. The house was to be administered by wardens chosen annually at Easter, two of them by the justices from among the chief constables of the Liberty of St Edmund, and another two who were to be inhabitants of Bury St Edmunds.

Hard times and financial problems

The 1590s were notoriously difficult for the poor. Harvests failed and money must have been short. It seems certain that the winter of 1593–4 must have been a very hard one. The account for the new purchased lands and Tassell's lands included the receipt of £12 which had been collected for providing wood to those in the south and west wards, that is the whole of St Mary's parish.[193] Whether no similar collection was made for St James's parish, or whether it was accounted for elsewhere, cannot

---

189 HD1150/1, fos. 30r., 31r., 32r., 33r., 34v., 35r.
190 HD1150/1, f.33r.
191 Orders made by Justices of the Peace at Sessions held at Bury St Edmunds, 22 April 31 Eliz. I [1589], BL MS Harl. 364, fos. 144–52; photostat copy at SROB, Acc. 829. Lack of space has made it impossible to describe in detail the harsh regime set up by this document. Some idea may be had from Margaret Statham, *The Book of Bury St Edmunds* (revised edition, Whittlebury, 1996) p.66. It deserves a properly documented paper.
192 Book of Orders, C2/1.
193 HD1150/1, f.38r.

now be discerned. However, meeting on 23 May 1594 the feoffees decided that the sum of £28 which had been received the previous year from the sale of wood[194] and another £32, to make up £60 in all, was to be used to buy eighty cauldrons 'of the great measure' of sea coal for the poor. It was to be laid up in the yard between St James's church and the Norman Tower, with John Cadge, or Cage, in charge. The idea must have been to sell it to the poor at affordable prices for he was to make a monthly account of his receipts.[195] A little later, on 26 July 1594 it was agreed that Mr Pead and William Browne should receive some of the money which had been left to the town by Thomas Bright the elder, and that it should be used to buy sea coal for the poor.[196] It was also in 1594 that the town gates were manned to prevent grain being taken out of the town when food was scarce following a failed harvest.[197]

These difficult conditions no doubt led to the appointment of overseers of the poor, first mentioned on 23 May 1594.[198] Six men were appointed for each of the five wards; in many cases their names are familiar from the account books. At a meeting on 9 August 1598 it was agreed that 3s.4d. weekly should be paid to the collectors and overseers lately appointed for the collection of a weekly contribution to the poor of each parish.[199] No special entry can be found for this and it was presumably included in the sum of £33 8s.4d. expended on the poor and orphans that year.[200] Ever increasing demands on the revenues may explain why eleven acres of land in Bury St Edmunds were sold to Thomas Overend in 1594 for £110. Some of this money was used to provide stock to set the poor to work, more to pay the salary of Mr Lewis, preacher of St Mary's, but £20 was used to repay a debt to one Page and to Thomas Overend himself.[201]

In the meantime, Dr Miles Moss, whose name occurs regularly for many years as preacher of St James, established a library in his church which must surely have been the resource centre for the combination lecture or prophesying for which the town was noted. Although some feoffees as individuals gave books to the library, at this stage they were not as a body concerned with it.[202] The title page of a volume of the *Works of Calvin* given by Sir Robert Jermyn in 1595, with its contemporary bookplate noting the gift, is reproduced as Plate 2; as can be seen from the marks at the bottom of the volume, it was originally chained, but some of these books are known to have been lent to readers. John Ward, who was briefly preacher of St James's in 1598 came to Bury St Edmunds after a distinguished ministry at Haverhill. He was the father of Samuel Ward who is now recognised as the founding father of the Ipswich town library. It is possible that Samuel Ward was inspired by the library founded in Bury during Dr Moss's long ministry.

A meeting held on 30 December 1595 agreed that from the annuity of £20 out of Torksey left by Edmund Jermyn, his kinsman, Sir Robert Jermyn, would bear the

---

[194] £16 was said to have been received for wood, HD1150/1, f.37v., and further sums, amounting to £2 10s.0d., can be found on f.38v. in the account for 1595. The entry confirms that the provision of fuel for the poor was undertaken in May 1595.

[195] Minutes, H2/6/2.1, p.12. See Glossary for 'cauldron of the great measure'.

[196] *Ibid.*, p.13.

[197] HD1150/1, f.39v. The original account reads 'malt', the account book 'corn'.

[198] Minutes, H2/6/2.1, p.12.

[199] *Ibid.*, p.19.

[200] HD1150/1, f.42.

[201] *Ibid.*, f.38v.

[202] Where it is known that a feoffee (or other person) gave a book, or books, to the library, this has been mentioned in that person's entry in Notes on People.

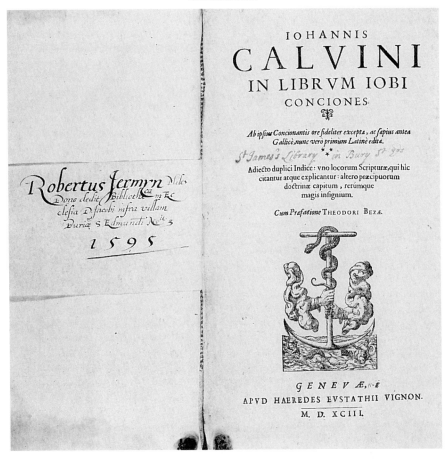

Plate 2. Title page of Calvin's *In Librum Jobi Conciones* (Geneva, 1593). Given to the library in St James's church by Sir Robert Jermyn in 1595. Reproduced by kind permission of the Dean and Chapter of St Edmundsbury Cathedral.

charges of the working house or house of correction. He would pay the rent, and repair it, so that the arrears which were then due could be discharged and the house maintained. The poor who were committed to the working house were to be clothed on entering it, and John Man and William Faircliff were to pay for the clothing at the next receipt.[203] A year later, on 30 December 1596, the sums of money owed to Sir Robert were reported to the feoffees. They were £4 0s.4d. to be paid at the next receipt, £12 for thirty-six loads of wood which he had brought to the house of correction, 12s. for spinning wheels and cards, and £2 3s.4d. which he had lent to the keeper of the house.[204] These sums were duly paid to him, partly at that account and partly in the following year. The account for 1596 included the sum of £40 which had been given to William Faircliff in 1594 to provide work for the poor. Among other things, it was noted that he had paid £10 13s.4d. in rent arrears due to

---

203 Minutes, H2/6/2.1, p.17b.
204 *Ibid.*, p.18.

Thomas Short, from whom the working house or house of correction was now leased.[205] References to the payment of rent for either the working house or for the Bridewell to Thomas Short show that the same establishment is meant whichever term was used.[206]

Incorporation at last

It is well known that Sir Nicholas Bacon was asked to help obtain a corporation for Bury St Edmunds in 1562, and that he refused on the grounds that too many corporations had been created in recent years.[207] After that, no further attempt was made to obtain incorporation until the townsmen petitioned for it in 1601.[208] The surviving copy of the petition is undated, but must have been made before 19 August 1601 when Sir Robert Jermyn wrote the first of a series of letters in which the county gentlemen complained to Cecil that an incorporation would take control of the town out of their hands.[209] One of those who opposed incorporation was Sir Nicholas Bacon the younger, concerned, no doubt, for his income from grants of rights in the town made to his father. The charter petition shows that the townsmen wanted to control the fairs and markets, which they said were leased to strangers who thought nothing of the town. Between 1604 and 1608 the feoffees gave William Scott £10 towards his costs in litigation with Sir Nicholas Bacon about the liberties of the townsmen in the markets and fairs. As we shall see, Sir Nicholas was later to be involved in litigation relating to other matters of great concern to the town.

This petition was drawn up at the request of a number of men, most of whose names are familiar to us from the feoffees' account books. Thomas Bright, in both his memoranda and in the first chamberlain's account of the new Corporation, explained that he was asked to do his best to obtain a corporation by John Gipps, John Revell, Stephen Ashwell, Francis Pinner, John Man, Thomas Baker, George Boldero, Henry Gipps, John Goodrich, Anthony Smith, James Baxter, John Gilly, Christopher Cox and Roger Lowdale. Of these men only John Gipps, enfeoffed in 1582, and John Gilly, enfeoffed in 1588, were feoffees. These two and John Revell are among those to whom William Baker released his interest in the town lands in 1590. Stephen Ashwell, Francis Pinner, John Man, Thomas Baker, George Boldero and Henry Gipps became feoffees in 1606 while John Goodrich, Anthony Smith and Roger Lowdale were only enfeoffed in 1617. Although James Baxter became a benefactor neither he nor Christopher Cox were ever feoffees. Neither James Baxter nor John Gilly ever became members of the Corporation either. At this stage there was no mention of John Mallowes, whose legal work probably did much to shape the Corporation. He was eventually to become the feoffees' clerk after the retirement of William Cook. The only significant reference to Mallowes in the feoffees' minutes (before he too became a feoffee in September 1606) occurs on 11 March of that year when he was lent the foundation deed of Jankin Smith's charity 'to the

---

205 HD1150/1 fos. 40r., 40v. and 41v.
206 The feoffees continued to pay the rent to Thomas Short or his widow, and then to Mr Howman, from 1605 until 1609.
207 Letter from Nicholas Bacon to Sir Clement Higham and others about incorporation, C4/1.
208 The petition was copied by Dr Richard Yates, who did not give his source, in his manuscript notes on the History of Bury St Edmunds, BL MS Egerton 2373, pp.350–5, photostat copy at SROB, P755/38.
209 *Calendar of the Manuscripts of the Marquis of Salisbury* XI (Historic Manuscripts Commission, 1883–date), p 351. In addition to Sir Robert Jermyn those who were concerned about their loss of authority were named as North, Bacon, Mawe and Smith (these two being counsellors at law), Barber, Dandy and Sir John Higham.

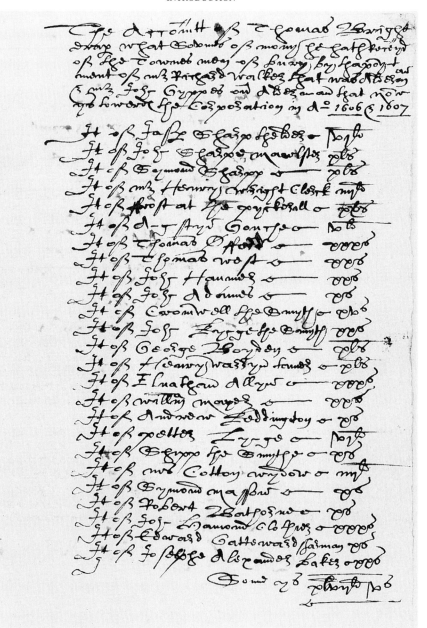

Plate 3. An account kept by Thomas Bright of sums of money given by the townsmen and women of Bury towards the cost of the incorporation, 1606 (D6/4/1). Reproduced by permission of St Edmundsbury Borough Council.

intent that he should use some travell abowte the passage of the said londs from the King's Majestie to certain of the feoffees of the town londs of Bury aforesaid accordinge to a beginninge thereof made the last terme by Mr Walker and the said John Mallowes by the consent of the feoffees of the said towne londs', which is followed by a note that he returned the document on 30 December 1607.[210] Richard Walker who is mentioned here in connection with John Mallowes was to be the first alderman of the newly incorporated Borough, while John Mallowes became the first Town Clerk.

From 1603 the feoffees made an annual payment of £1 to the minister of each parish in addition to paying the town preachers. From 1604 to 1610 Mr Bedell, the preacher of St Mary's, left his post to act as chaplain to Sir Henry Wotton's embassy to Venice. His place was taken by Mr Sotheby from 1608 to 1610. On his return, William Bedell brought with him a Venetian protestant, Jasper Despotine, who established a flourishing medical practice in the town.[211] Thomas Bright provides information about the appointment of town preachers; surprising as it may seem, the townsmen claimed the right to appoint the town clergy. He noted in his memoranda book the cost incurred in obtaining a new preacher for St James's after Mr Newton's departure – perhaps he was churchwarden of St James's at this time.[212] Although it is not dated it is to be found with other *memoranda* dating from 1606, among which there is reference to making a 'stoelle' (stool was the word normally used in Bury for any seat in church) for Mr Walker then alderman, in St James's church. This places it more precisely between April and September 1606. The first sum was 9s.4d. paid to an innkeeper, Edward Cropley at the Bell, for horse-meat for three journeys by Mr Daynes and his man.[213] A pound was paid to 'Mr Howgrave'[214] of King's College for horse hire and his travelling expenses. In addition, it had cost 4s. to hire horses for Benett Barker and John Bye to ride to Cambridge to persuade him to come to Bury St Edmunds. He was, however, an unsuccessful candidate for the post. Another pound was given to Mr Healey,[215] who was appointed, again towards his horse hire and travel. Christopher Buller, the minister of St James's at the time, was given 5s. for providing for a meeting of ministers at his house. It appears likely that we should envisage a board composed of clergy of the combination lecture called together to select the new preacher, who no doubt played a full part in all the theological activities for which Bury St Edmunds was then noted.[216] Finally 6s.8d. was paid for horse-meat and 'mansmeatt' at Newmarket when Mr Healey and his family came from Wallyn [*?Welwyn*] with his family.[217] He is almost certainly the unnamed preacher who was paid in 1607.

Documents survive which show that questions about the administration of the feoffees' land had been raised before the incorporation was granted. In this instance

---

[210] Minutes, H2/6/2.1, p.27. The assurance of the town lands was granted in the 1614 charter.

[211] As demonstrated by his will, printed in Tymms, *Wills*, pp.200–8.

[212] The account for 1607, HD1150/2, f.11r., records payment of a gratuity to Mr Newton for finding preachers after his departure while there was no preacher in the parish.

[213] For John Daynes, see Notes on People.

[214] Probably Henry Howgrave; see Notes on People.

[215] For John Healey, see Notes on People. Apart from his education at Cambridge, nothing is known of him before he came to Bury, so the identification of 'Wallyn' has not been settled.

[216] Dr John Craig thinks it probable that it was the clergy of the combination lecture who made this appointment. Professor Collinson noted that the townsmen delegated an earlier appointment at Bury to John Knewstubb of Cockfield and Dr John Still, Archdeacon of Sudbury, P. Collinson, *The Elizabethan Puritan Movement* (Oxford, 1990), p.338.

[217] Thomas Bright's memoranda book, H1/4/16, f.4r.

it was John Mallowes who made the complaint against the feoffees. Long ago, the land left by John Salter, augmented by some left by Jankin Smith and Margaret Odeham, had been leased for a long term of years to John Holt, himself a feoffee. Holt had left his leases to his daughter Anne and his son-in-law, Henry Collin, also a feoffee. As early as 1585 the feoffees had attempted to strengthen their title to these lands, fearing that some of the land was being appropriated by the lessee.[218] However, some of the feoffees were induced to make a further lease of part of the land to Henry, the young son of Henry Collin the elder, in 1586. Another lease was made in 1598, this one, it seems, by all the then feoffees. This litigation identifies Mallowes as a man who was prepared to take on the establishment. That this began before the chartering of the borough is shown in the draft decree in Chancery which makes it clear that the second hearing was held on 28–30 March 1606.[219] As well as the obvious complaints that leases had been made for long terms at minimal rents, and that the lands had not been properly defined so that it had been possible for the lessee to 'swallow up the greatest part of them', Collin, in Mallowes' view, only wanted the leases at a low rent so that he could sub-let for his own profit. Moreover, by 1606 Henry Collin the elder was dead and his son no longer lived in Bury St Edmunds so that he made no contribution to town charges. It is obvious that some of the more conservative feoffees, including William Cook and Richard Walker, were reluctant to press Collin. Matters dragged on until 1612 when the lands were restored to the feoffees and they were able to let them to John King, a local husbandman who, they knew, would cultivate them well. Mallows may have been the prime instigator against Collin, but those who had agreed to contribute to the cost of the incorporation may also have been motivated in part by concerns about the feoffees' stewardship.

When the charter petition was made in c.1600 at least ten of the feoffees appointed in 1588 were already dead. Perhaps the feoffees' reluctance to renew the feoffment was another factor which further encouraged those who sought incorporation. Of the feoffees who survived to 1606 there were three of the county gentlemen, who all opposed the incorporation, William Cook, the long serving and very conservative clerk of the feoffees, and Anthony Payne, who, to judge from the response to William Payne's complaint, was regarded by the new men as the most unscrupulous steward of the town lands. According to Jankin Smith's will the feoffment was always to be renewed as soon as the number of feoffees fell to fourteen. Over the centuries this was not always done, and difficulties arose on occasions when the number became very low and the administration of the trust became difficult if not impossible.[220]

The new Corporation created by Letters Patent dated 3 April 1606 consisted of thirty-seven members: the alderman himself, twelve chief or capital burgesses and twenty-four burgesses of the common council.[221] From the twelve chief burgesses four assistants, or justices of the peace were to be elected every year. The usual borough officers, Recorder, Town Clerk, and two Sergeants-at-Mace were granted

---

[218] See HD1150/1, f.24r.

[219] Draft Decree in Chancery, H3/1/1.

[220] Francis Pinner made his bequests to the feoffees on condition that the feoffment be renewed within three months after his death. His will is printed in Tymms, *Wills*, pp.170–85. He had long been urging a renewal which was eventually made shortly before his death, H1/1/53.

[221] Charter or, technically, Letters Patent of Incorporation dated 3 April 1606, D1/1/1. It was printed by Richard Yates in his *An Illustration of the Monastic History and Antiquities of the Town and Abbey of St Edmund's Bury* (illustrated edition, 1843), appendix, pp.14–37.

to the new Corporation, along with the fundamental rights of incorporation: the right to sue and be sued, to have a common seal, to make by-laws and to hold land to the value of £100. On that day in 1606 Bury St Edmunds had at last become an incorporated borough, but those things the town leadership most desired, the churches, the tithes, the fairs and markets and parliamentary representation, were still denied them. The incorporation cannot have been cheap. A list of sums owing to Edward Mallowes, dating from 1604, shows that those who promised Thomas Bright to underwrite the incorporation had, on the whole, subscribed £10 each towards the cost, and that Edward Mallowes, who must have been a relation of John Mallowes, was acting as banker in the City for these sums and handing money out to those who travelled to London about the business as it was required. Part of the list of subscriptions given by the townspeople towards the cost is reproduced in Plate 3 (p.xliv).

While the negotiations for the chartering were going on, steps were also being taken to recover the large part of Tassell's gift which had been sold in 1582. No papers about the enquiry have survived, but it would be interesting to know who brought this sale to the notice of the Commissioners for Charitable Uses. The first moves to recover this property must have been taken before the incorporation in 1606, and may even be reflected in the payment, from 1603, of £1 to the minister for each parish. From 1609 it was expressly stated that this was the gift of William Tassell. This could be the first step in the recovery of Tassell's gift. It is probable that the ministers or curates at this period, as was the case much later in the seventeenth century, took all the fees for occasional services such as marriages and burials. Small as it was, they also received the exhibition from the Crown as part of their remuneration.[222]

The first piece of Tassell's land to be recovered was in Southgate Street. It was reconveyed to them on 12 June 1606 and is now the site of the Long Row almshouses.[223] This was also the very day when the Commissioners ordered that the Angel was to be bought back from Katherine, daughter of Roger Potter, formerly a feoffee, to whom it had been sold in 1582.[224] Woodward copied a deed to levy the uses of a fine which was drawn up on 20 March 1607; it related to the Angel, a messuage in Abbeygate Street near the Fishmarket, two messuages with a stable and woodhouse in the Marketstead and Skinners Lane, another messuage in Northgate Street (which had been alienated by Roger Barber and other feoffees in 1561)[225] and a close and a piece of land near Stamford Bridge which had been sold to Thomas Overend.[226] A garden or piece of ground in Brentgovel Street was reconveyed to them on 8 May 1612; in this case the deed expressly stated that it was under a decree of the Commissioners on the Statute for Charitable Uses, and that the property was to be held to the uses of Tassell's gift.[227] Careful reading of the accounts will show that when properties were recovered the feoffees usually recompensed the former occupiers. Where land had been let on too favourable terms and the leases were

---

[222] A receipt for payment of an exhibition of £8 18s.10d. by Richard Millar, His Majesty's Receiver General, dated 12 October 1630, has survived. It was signed by John Jewell and Jeremy Burroughes, who were then the curates, and witnessed by John Sudbury and Thomas Smith, churchwardens of St James's, and Thomas Barker and Jeremy Stafford, churchwardens of St Mary's, Town Clerk's papers miscellaneous, D11/3/2.

[223] Woodward's Register, H1/6/1, p.141. The almshouses were built on the site in 1811 by William Steggles.

[224] *Ibid.*, p.136.

[225] *Ibid.*, p.148.

[226] *Ibid.*, pp.154–60.

[227] *Ibid.*, p.152.

terminated by the Commissioners, annuities had to be paid to the former lessees; the first of these to appear was paid to John Bedwall who had been tenant of some land in Hepworth. A little later annuities to Henry Collin[228] and Francis Pinner, who had leased St Peter's, also became regular annual payments. The years immediately before and after the incorporation and the refeoffment of 1606 were a period of intense activity, as property which had been mismanaged in the past was restored to the feoffees or let at a reasonable rent. As far as is known Edmund Jermyn's annuity was always used to provide materials to employ those who were in the house of correction, but, when the governors reconveyed the annuity to the feoffees in 1609, it may also have been part of the programme of reform which was obviously in hand.[229]

The fire of 1608 and another charter

Any town would have reeled under the impact of the fire which broke out on 11 April 1608 in a thatched house in Eastgate Street beyond the East Gate. The flames eventually spread into the market place, sparks blowing from one thatched roof to another, destroying in all one hundred and sixty dwelling houses and four hundred out-houses and 'houses of necessary use'. The loss was estimated by the Corporation at £60,000, and a new by-law was hastily passed prohibiting the use of thatch for roofing new houses.[230]

Soon after the fire, the second charter was sealed on 1 July 1608; it granted five hundred loads of timber from the royal woods at Hitcham to help with the rebuilding. It also granted many things which the Corporation were anxious to acquire, but in reversion, that is, on the termination of a lease which had almost forty years still to run. They were also granted a number of public buildings which had been badly damaged, if not entirely destroyed, in the fire and made responsible for rebuilding them; these included the Market Cross, the gaol, the gaol-keeper's house and the tollhouse.[231] It is impossible to tell how the problems created by the fire were handled. Several hundred people must have been made homeless and some temporary arrangements made for them until they were able to move back to repaired or rebuilt property, while businessmen like Francis Pinner who lost all the goods in their shops and warehouses had to set up their businesses again.[232]

According to an order in their book, the feoffees met the cost of obtaining the grant of 1608. There is an undated entry which probably belongs to the year beginning Michaelmas 1612. It appears that Bright's legacy of £300 had been put out at interest because it had not yet been used to buy land. This was considered 'unlawful and not fitte to be contynued' and on several occasions it had almost been lost. Both the inhabitants and the Commissioners for Charitable Uses in Suffolk had many times ordered that this money should have been invested in land 'or some other thinge whereof some certein yearely revenue may aryse otherwise than by waye of

---

228 See above, pp.xlvi, xlvii.
229 Woodward's Register, H1/6/1, pp.194–5.
230 By-laws of 1608 and later, D14/2/1, fos. 23r. and v. Other accounts give a higher figure, but the Corporation would have no reason to minimise the loss.
231 Charter of 1608, D1/2/1. Although the Market Cross had been built at public expense it was obviously regarded as part of the market which belonged to the Crown.
232 A photograph of the brief appealing for relief for the people of Bury who had suffered losses in the fire is reproduced in Plate 4 on p.xlix.

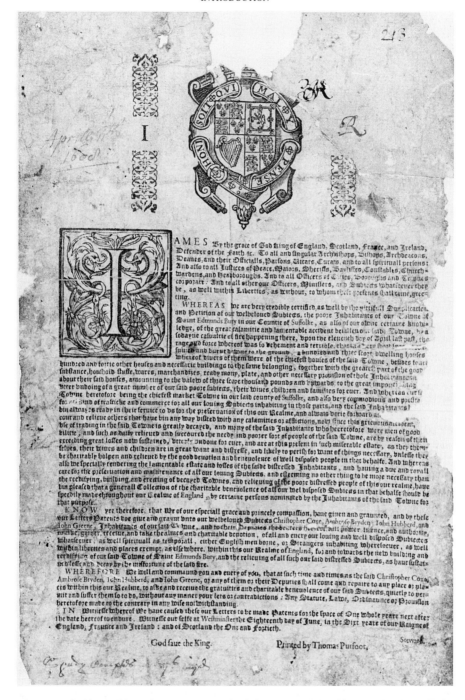

Plate 4. Brief issued by King James I authorising a general collection for the relief of Bury St Edmunds after the fire of 1608. At the bottom a note shows that 3s.4d. was collected in Shudy Camps, Cambs (SROI, HD695/3). Reproduced by permission of Suffolk Record Office.

interest'. The 1608 charter by which the reversion of the leases of the tithes, fairs, markets and glebe lands had been granted to the alderman and burgesses had cost over £300. The things granted by that charter 'in tyme to come wilbe of great benefitt and avayle to the saide towne for the convenient maintenance of the preachers and ministers of the parishe churches there and for the bearing and defraying of divers towne charges'. It was therefore considered right that the cost of obtaining these things should be paid for with money belonging to the town as a whole.

About two years before, the alderman and burgesses, the feoffees and other chief inhabitants had agreed that 'nothing was thought or could be found mor fitt and proper for that use and purpose than to be holpen by the saide three hundred pounds'. The money had therefore been given to John Mallowes, the Town Clerk, who had laid out the charges in obtaining the grant of these reversions. It was agreed that for the time being £24 a year should be allowed out of the feoffees' revenues for clothing the poor, but that as soon as possible – within ten years it was hoped – the feoffees' revenues would have been built up sufficiently to make £300 available with which to buy a suitable estate.[233] Moreover, although much of the town centre was ruined by fire and some of the Corporation men are known to have suffered severely, they were not prepared to wait until the 1640s before they held the tithes, markets and fairs. As private men, some of them bought in the unexpired part of Sir Robert Drury's lease for £2,500. These men were occasionally called the 'feoffees of the Almoners Barns', but more often the 'purchasers of the Almoners Barns'; to avoid any confusion they will henceforth be referred to as the 'purchasers'. The feoffees were not the only body who had to help to finance the purchase of Sir Robert Drury's lease. The governors of the Grammar School used a fine of £100 which they received in 1615 on granting a lease of their farm in Waldingfield to enable them to lend money to help the purchasers.[234] At some later date the purchasers used the property they had bought from Sir Robert Drury as security for a loan which they had negotiated from the governors.[235] By 1622 the purchasers were paying interest on £1800 which the governors had lent them for seven years.[236]

On 31 December 1611 the feoffees agreed that the £40 given by Edmund Jermyn, which had hitherto been used to finance the house of correction, should in future be used for clothing poor children and orphans, putting them to service or apprenticing them so that they could earn their own living, and providing them with meat, drink, fire and lodging until they could earn their own living. This was taken to be agreeable with the will until 'better matter shall be provided and allowed'.[237] Children were excluded from the house of correction in the 1589 regulations, while those in the workhouse in 1619 were all children.[238] It appears that the workhouse was seen

---

[233] Minutes, H2/6/2.1, pp.36–42. John Boldero signed first, which almost certainly indicates that he was alderman when this agreement was made. For his being alderman for the year beginning Michaelmas 1612, see D7/7/2, E5/9/202.1, when he was described as alderman, and H1/2/9(a) where he was described as late alderman.

[234] Governors' Minutes, E5/9/202.1, p.73.

[235] The Corporation records contain a number of counterpart conveyances of parts of the Almoner's Barns estate which were sold off c.1621–3, to which the governors were a party, D7/10/1.

[236] Governors' accounts, E5/9/203.18. One has to wonder to what extent the governors could have educated more boys and given the staff more generous salaries, had they not loaned this money. A scholarly account of the early years of the school is long overdue.

[237] H2/6/2.1, p.34.

[238] A note on the back of a memorandum about the Great Barton copyholds, H1/2/7, has a list of the children in the workhouse, 1619, and an inventory of goods at the workhouse, 1618.

as a place where children could be brought up and given training which would in time enable them to earn their own livings. On 2 May 1612 the governors agreed that St Peter's hospital should be used as the workhouse.[239] By 1622 the two houses in Churchgate Street which Richard Walker had given had been fitted up as a workhouse; a rate was levied towards the cost of it, to which the feoffees had paid 13s. for one quarter, in addition to £25 for the keeper's salary. In the same account, it is stated that St Peter's was then used as the house of correction.[240]

In addition to £300 in money, Thomas Bright the elder had also given some tithes coming out of the manor of Brook Hall in Foxearth, Essex, for repairing the churches and for relieving the poor and the prisoners in the gaol. Through no fault of the feoffees, the tithes were alienated and litigation was required to recover them. Before the dissolution, these tithes had belonged to the abbess of Barking in Essex. Later they were sold by the Crown, eventually coming into the possession of Thomas Bright. From the surviving papers,[241] it seems that Richard Carter, who was Sir Nicholas Bacon's farmer of the demesne of Brook Hall, contrived to get a lease of these tithes (which Thomas Bright had made) assigned to George Atherton. Carter then paid John Firmin, the parson of Foxearth, to claim that he had a right to these tithes and to say that Carter had the necessary evidences. Although Sir Nicholas Bacon agreed to accept the decision of the court, it seems obvious that, if he did not instigate this scam, he encouraged it. On 12 July 1613 Lord Chancellor Ellesmere ordered that from then on the feoffees were to enjoy these tithes according to the will of Thomas Bright the elder. The payment made to the curates or ministers out of this gift was then resumed and was doubled from 1613 onwards, when they began to receive the money allotted to them in lieu of their interest in the so-called ministers' houses which were occupied by the preachers.[242]

The 1614 charter and after

It was only in 1614 that the third charter gave Bury St Edmunds its own court of quarter sessions, the right to hold the court leet, and to have its own coroner, an office which until the reforms of 1836 was always held by the immediate past alderman.[243] No longer were cases from the town referred to quarter sessions for the Liberty of St Edmund, nor had the county coroner to be brought in when required. The right to have four maces carried before the alderman instead of two must have increased civic pride. This charter also gave the Corporation the churches and their advowsons. The lands held by the feoffees were confirmed as being given for the use of the alderman, burgesses and commonalty of Bury St Edmunds and, at last, the borough was given the right to return two members of Parliament who in theory at least would act as their advocates when necessary at Westminster. The thirty-seven members of the Corporation were the sole electors of these two members.

Meanwhile, rebuilding after the fire continued as funds became available. The

---

[239] Governors' Minutes, E5/9/202.1, p.66.
[240] HD1150/2, f.48r.
[241] Papers about Foxearth tithes, H3/1/6.
[242] Minutes, H2/6/2.1, p.33. This was agreed on 31 December 1611.
[243] A bundle of mainly seventeenth-century coroners' papers has survived. They illustrate the danger of open wells, from which most of the population would have obtained their water supply at this period, D11/11/1.

Market Cross was rebuilt on a different site. Rotten Row had formerly extended south from the north side of Cornhill. Even in the seventeenth century it must have impeded traffic in the market place and, apart from the Market Cross, which stands in part on its extreme south end, the rest of this medieval row was never rebuilt.[244] The rebuilding of the cross after the fire was a joint venture by the feoffees and Corporation, as these accounts, augmented by such Corporation accounts as survive, demonstrate. It was only finished in 1620 when £50 18s.2d. was paid for its completion, and must have greatly enhanced the market place.[245]

Another sign of the civic pride which arose at this time can be seen in the improvements carried out at the Guildhall. A new oven was made in 1613, which is probably that still to be seen in the former kitchen. Although the fifteenth-century detached kitchen was used for providing food for the poor on the account day, it was also used for the feoffees' feasts and also for the corporate feasts which became part of the town's social calendar.[246] In 1616 and later a new or inner chamber was constructed; it may have been a fore-runner of the mayor's parlour of the present day. The chamber in which the feoffees and Corporation met was a first-floor room in a wing at right angles to the northern part of the hall.[247] This chamber was decorated with portraits of King James I and the two major benefactors, Jankin Smith and Thomas Bright the elder.[248] There is also a handsome portrait of Edmund Jermyn at the Guildhall, but it is not known how it came to be there. Silver badges for the beadles and the town waits were bought by the feoffees, who long continued to provide the liveries for various civic officers.

The feoffees continued to receive additions to their endowment. In 1619 they made their first payment to the parish clerk of St James's church for looking after the library. This came from the revenue of land left by James Baxter who made his will on 6 August 1612.[249] Francis Pinner the younger made a bequest to help to fund the Monday Exercise, the combination lecture for which Bury was so famous; the first payment was received in 1620, when his own father was receiver.

In the last few years covered by the accounts, the feoffees assisted the Corporation by contributing towards the cost of litigation brought by Sir Nicholas Bacon the younger regarding the profits of the town courts. Sir Nicholas claimed these by virtue of a grant which he said had been made to his father. On the other hand, the Corporation claimed that these had been granted to them by the 1614 charter and that they paid a fee-farm for them to the Crown. No decree has survived among the borough's or feoffees' records, but as the Corporation continued to receive income from the courts it is concluded that they won their case.[250]

---

244 Deeds of Rotten Row, H1/2/9/1–6. The old cross must have been nearer Moyses Hall than the present one.
245 HD1150/2, f.44v. The main timbers of the seventeenth-century building were found under Adam's façade when the Market Cross was refurbished in the 1970s.
246 HD1150/2, f.27v.
247 The chamber wing was rebuilt in 1806, Margaret Statham, 'The Guildhall, Bury St Edmunds', *PSIA* xxxi, part 2 (1968) p.152.
248 HD1150/2, fos. 34v. and 35r. See Plates I–III.
249 For Baxter's gift, see Woodward's Register, H1/6/1, p.200; payments for the library are noted in HD1150/2, fos. 42r., 44r., 46v. and 48v. The library was housed in the eastern bay of the north aisle of the church.
250 Copy of Bacon's bill of complaint (endorsed as having been examined by Edward Mallowes, clerk in Chancery) is D10/1. An incomplete copy of the Corporation's reply is D10/6.

William Payne's complaint

Near-contemporary comment on the stewardship of the feoffees and the alderman and burgesses is to be found in the surviving papers of the Commissioners appointed under the Statute for Charitable Uses.[251] These relate to many places in Suffolk and probably survived among the records kept in the Guildhall because John Mallowes was their clerk. William Payne, whose father and great uncle had been feoffees in their time – and who, on the evidence of these papers emerge as wicked feoffees – complained to the Privy Council that the lands belonging to the town were not competently administered.[252] The Council referred Payne's petition to the Commissioners on 28 February 1632, and his complaint was considered by them at a hearing held in the Shire House on 1 May 1633.[253] It is strange to modern notions that two of the Commissioners were to be the then alderman, Robert Davy, who was also a feoffee, and the recorder, John Godbold. John Mallowes, who acted as clerk to the Commissioners for Charitable Uses was both town clerk, feoffee, and the feoffees' clerk. One hopes that Chinese Walls were scrupulously observed in seventeenth-century Bury St Edmunds.

The answers and depositions make it clear that Payne lived outside the town, but owned a considerable amount of land within it. He had been sued because he had refused to pay poor and church rates and tithes payable for land he held in the town. However, he won a following among the numerous poor people in the town, as he claimed that they were not receiving the full benefit of land and money which had been given to them. Payne was also aware that Jankin Smith and other town benefactors had given land or money specifically to provide for the payment of town taxes, which assisted those who were sufficiently well-off to be assessed for them. He argued that if the town charities were better administered, not only would the poor be more fully relieved, but the better-off, such as himself, would not be so heavily burdened with both national and local taxes. The Corporation and feoffees were exonerated by the Commissioners.

As Payne's petition has not survived among the papers, his allegations have to be determined from the answers given by the Corporation and feoffees. He seems, for instance, to have considered that the town revenues amounted to £2,000 a year. The alderman and burgesses retorted that their income was in fact far less than this, that they had borrowed £800 on which interest was payable, and that they had been much more indebted in earlier years. They gave the fire of 1608 and the misgovernment by Payne's ancestors as reasons for their difficult financial state. While they admitted that a great many poor people lived in the town, many of these had entered by stealth and settled there so that they could not be removed. It was accepted that they were 'combersome' at gleaning time, and that they broke hedges and begged at other seasons, but as these offences were committed outside the borough boundaries, the county magistrates and the parish constables must punish them.

In the feoffees' answer to a question about their Great Barton estate at Catishall it becomes clear that Richard Walker, a long-standing feoffee, was not considered to have acted as he ought, although he is now accepted as one of the town's benefactors. Mr Payne's father, if we are to believe the feoffees of 1633, had made a lease of Cattishall to William Webbe, who had been named in trust because Richard Walker,

---

251 Class K at the Bury Record Office has papers relating to the Commissioners for Charitable Uses.

252 For William and Anthony Payne, see Notes on People.

253 Payne's complaint, K1/3. These papers will form the basis of a paper, and so comments given here relate only to matters covered by the accounts.

as one of the feoffees, could not take a lease in his own name.[254] Although Catishall was worth £50 *per annum*, it had been let for only £20 *per annum*. When Walker was questioned by the 'now feoffees' before the Commissioners for Charitable Uses, he realised that the lease would be overthrown and asked to be allowed to retain it for its full term, promising to make some recompense to the trust. The 'now feoffees' must mean those who were appointed in 1606.[255] Although Richard Walker gave a house and £40, the feoffees in 1633 considered those a poor return for the lease of Cattishall, although they had done all that Walker had required in return for his gift of houses in Churchgate Street.

Payne thought that the feoffees ought to have spent all their income on the poor and he condemned their purchase of additional property. It was conceded that the feoffees had bought houses for the preachers. In 1633 Mr White, preacher of St James's, lived in one of them, but the other, next to St James's steeple, was 'soe annoyed with the often ringing of bells as it was unfitt for the preacher of St Maries to dwell in it'. This they had sold and with the proceeds bought another house in which Mr Calamy lived at the time of the hearing. They had also bought two or three acres of wood from Sir Henry Bokenham as it was intermixed with the feoffees' woods in Hepworth. It was explained that in 1626 they had bought Moyses Hall, which in 1633 was used for the gaol, common workhouse and house of correction.[256] Although the gaoler should have paid them £10 for its use, they in fact received nothing for it. As the accounts show, although St Peter's had been granted to the Grammar School, the purchase money had been found jointly by the feoffees and the governors.[257] The Brooms in Bradfield, it was explained, had not been bought by the feoffees but by the governors who had given it to them in lieu of their part of St Peter's.[258]

Payne was also of the opinion that too little of the feoffees' income was devoted to church repairs. He had been prosecuted for not paying his church rate, and made great play of the fact the money raised from the sale of the church plate was no longer used to fund the repair of the churches. It is quite obvious that he was familiar with the indenture for St Mary's parish drawn up on 26 August 1547.[259] Unlike other documents which John Woodward copied in the 1650s, this one did not form part of the feoffees' archive, but was copied from 'Mr Jewell's book'. Woodward noted that Mr Jewell, the long serving curate of St Mary's, had copied it from the original in St Mary's parish chest. Reference is made in the register[260] to a suit between William Payne and the parishioners of St Mary's in 1637, in connection with which John Mallowes had made a deposition about this document. It seems that William Payne was not content with the Commissioners' report in 1633, and had continued to harass the authorities on such matters.

This querulous man had criticism to make of poor rates as well as church rates.

---

254 William Webb is named as tenant in the accounts for 1607, 1612 and 1613. He was also named as Walker's executor, Probate Register IC550/2/47, p.206.

255 Deed of refeoffment, H1/1/52.

256 K1/3. Moyses Hall was leased by the Corporation in 1606, see chamberlain's account, D6/4/1, when money was spent on adapting it for use as the borough gaol. This use may well have continued until the purchase.

257 William Payne's complaint, K1/3.

258 In 1631 an agreement was made between governors and feoffees by which the feoffees accepted the Brooms estate in Bradfield Combust in lieu of their interest in St Peter's. The terms suggested by John Godbold are set out in G1/4.

259 Woodward's Register, H1/6/1, pp.66–7.

260 *Ibid.*, p.67.

Payne alleged that the feoffees only paid £14 in weekly contributions. In fact, they replied, they paid £18 13s.4d. and the purchasers £6. He had said that the amount collected for the poor was £320 *per annum* and that this sum was sufficient to provide weekly contributions for the poor without charging the town lands. If this were true, replied the feoffees, the overseers abused both the feoffees and the poor, and Mr Payne must prove that this was so. A note in the margin states that the collection in St James's parish in 1632 amounted to £139 3s.9d.[261] As some guide to the number of people who received financial relief, it was said in 1633 that about 1,000 poor people were given a dole of 2d. in money each Christmas.[262]

From the information given about the sale of property and leasing of land for less than its true value, Payne's father and uncle who had been feoffees begin to emerge as the wicked feoffees.[263] In answer to his complaint, the feoffees of the 1630s observed that 'Mr Payne his father and the rest of his cofeoffees had soe litle regard of the good of the towne, as that they solde away theis things even whilest Mr Tassell lyved, to his great discontent, and to the great discouragement of all benefactors.' The recovery of these properties has already been discussed.

William Payne felt that the feoffees ought to devote more of their income to paying various impositions levied on the town, although he conceded that they paid the tax, meaning fifteenths and tenths, which were often referred to in the accounts as the 'task'. It was admitted that cope silver was no longer an issue in 1633. However, the responses made in 1633 show that after 1622 the feoffees had begun to pay composition money for purveyance on behalf of the town, so that individuals were not taxed. It was also pointed out that the sum of £40 a year from Edmund Jermyn's annuity was used to maintain the workhouse and house of correction 'as otherwise they would have been charged by rates according to the Statute'.[264]

The long account of the £300 given by Thomas Bright the elder setting out an agreement for its use in 1612 has already been noted.[265] In the course of this enquiry the feoffees said that Mr Bright's £300 had been received by William Payne's father and others who had put it out at interest and been in danger of losing it. The feoffees appointed in 1606 found that lands had been given away or sold and the rest let for small rents, while the buildings were in need of repair. The company had been in debt and they had often needed great sums of money to satisfy those whose conveyances and leases had been overthrown by the Commissioners. When they got the £300 into their hands it was used they said, 'towards the relief of th'aforesaide decayed and incumbred estate, and yet nevertheles they have yearly ever since allowed £24 *per annum* for the profict thereof which hathe ben yearly bestowed in clothing the poore according to Mr Bright's intencion'. As soon as the feoffees were out of debt, they intended to buy land with the capital.[266] John Woodward, writing in the 1650s, believed that this £300 had been lent to the purchasers (whom he called the trustees of the Corporation) for seven years, and that this was made clear by the books of orders of both feoffees and Corporation. He concluded his account by saying 'but never any penny was yet repayd' nor £100 of Mr Ashwell's £200, which had also been lent to the purchasers.[267] For once William Payne seems to have been

---

261 William Payne's complaint, K1/3.
262 *Ibid.*
263 His uncle was also a wicked governor of the grammar school.
264 William Payne's complaint, K1/3.
265 See above, p.xlviii.
266 William Payne's complaint, K1/3.
267 Woodward's Register, H1/6/1, p.174.

correct in saying that clothing provided for the poor was the result of two specific gifts, £24 given by Thomas Bright the elder, even after the capital had been used in connection with the 1608 charter, and the gift of Stephen Ashwell, which produced an additional £20 a year after these account books closed.[268]

The feoffees today

By the time these accounts end, Bury St Edmunds, like many other towns, could boast of numerous displays of civic pride. The Guildhall, concealed on the dissolution of the abbey, had been bought back as the home of the feoffees and, after 1606, of the Corporation. The Guildhall chamber, or meeting room, had been enhanced and an inner chamber provided, perhaps used when the capital burgesses or magistrates alone met. A series of portraits of benefactors embellished the chamber. The market place had been improved by the building of the Market Cross which probably had a clock, another favourite embellishment for a forward-looking town of the early seventeenth century.[269]

The charity founded by Jankin Smith is still active today. It is now known as the Guildhall Feoffment Trust (though the trustees still call themselves feoffees). Nowadays it is chiefly an almshouse charity, providing homes for over thirty elderly people. The Guildhall, which had been the headquarters in turn of the guild merchant, Candlemas guild and the post-dissolution company or fellowship from which the feoffees were drawn, also served as the home of the Corporation from 1606. Council meetings only ceased to be held there in 1966. There is little wonder that at about the time this series of accounts ends, the feoffees were coming to be called the Feoffees of the Guildhall, or the Guildhall Feoffees.[270]

In the account for 1622, the last in the series, the Commemoration Day is first mentioned.[271] Jankin Smith's request to be remembered by his feoffees each year has always been scrupulously observed. The other benefactors of the town were soon included in this act of remembrance. It would have been unthinkable to keep the founder's anniversary in the form he suggested in his will after the reformation, but, as with so many traditional ceremonies, it has been constantly adapted to suit changing circumstances. The early accounts here edited show that a service and the audit were still held on Candlemas Day. Later, when the accounting year ended at Christmas or 31 December, the accounts were audited early in January, and the feast and a service was held then. In the seventeenth century the Thursday in Plough Monday week (Plough Monday was the Monday after Twelfth Night) became the day on which the commemoration was held, sometimes in dreadful weather. In the 1960s the feoffees decided that it should again be held in June, at about the time of

---

268 William Payne's complaint, K1/3.
269 A man called Docking was paid for looking after the market clock in 1622, HD1150/2, f.48v. A clock is shown on the Market Cross in two paintings of the market place which are exhibited at the Manor House Museum and date from c.1700. When Celia Fiennes visited Bury St Edmunds in 1698 she mentioned the lanthorn and dial on the Market Cross, C. Morris (ed.), *The Journeys of Celia Fiennes* (1949) p.151.
270 The wills of the benefactors James Baxter (1612), IC500/2/000 and Edward Bourne (1637), IC500/2/48, f.151 are early examples of the use of 'feoffees of the Guildhall'. A list of documents deposited in, or returned to, the Evidence House by John Mallowes on 16 April 1619 described the deed of refeoffment made in 1617 as the 'Guildhall Feoffment renewed from Mr Boldero and Mr Bright to Sir John Heigham and others', Minutes, H2/6/2.1, p.46.
271 HD1150/2, f.49r.

the anniversary of Jankin Smith's death. Although it is sometimes not practicable to do so, if the service can be held on the Thursday before St Peter's day, 29 June, from time to time it is held on the anniversary itself, 28 June, as it was in the year 2001.

For over seventy years, after the service in St Mary's church, a reception has been held in the Guildhall known as the cake and ale ceremony. Thomas Bright the younger, who took the lead in obtaining the charter of incorporation for Bury St Edmunds gave, by deed dated 13 February 1625, two houses in the Buttermarket to provide, among other things, 3s.4d. to be laid out in wine and cakes at the annual meeting of the feoffees.[272] This is, undoubtedly, the origin of the so-called cake and ale ceremony – refreshment for the feoffees as they strove to balance the accounts. This pleasant custom ceased along with the feoffees' feast (which seems to have reached gargantuan proportions) in the scheme of 1842. When the Revd J.H. Sandford, vicar of St Mary's, was chairman in 1929, he invited his fellow feoffees to join him after the Commemoration Service in the Guildhall to partake of cakes and ale 'according to the ancient custom'. Perhaps cakes and ale sounded more medieval than cake and wine.[273]

If there is one building in Bury which enshrines the town's hopes and aspirations for municipal freedom, it is, of course, the Guildhall, which ought to be regarded as the focus of civic pride. Thomas Bright and those who supported him strove to gain freedom for the town – freedom, as far as possible, from royal interference and intervention by the county authorities. If it served their purposes, the corporation would even plead that the 1614 charter, which granted them the churches and confirmed their right to appoint the town clergy, granted them episcopal exemption such as the abbot of Bury had enjoyed. The present arrangement of the service in St Mary's followed by the cakes and ale ceremony in the Guildhall brings together two men who deserve to be better known, and remembered more generally, than they are at present. The service carries out in modern manner the will of Jankin Smith, the founder of the town's most prominent charity. The cake and ale ceremony is derived from a gift made by Thomas Bright the younger who took the lead in obtaining the charter which gave the town the self-government which it had sought for centuries.

The method of accounting

These accounts will seem strange to the modern reader. In some of the early examples, accountants for individual charities (or groups of the charities) handed over any surplus balance they had to the alderman; sometimes, and always in the later years, one account covers all the feoffees' income and expenditure. At this period the person(s) responsible for keeping the accounts were entrusted with the task, charge or burden, represented by the Latin word *onus*, of collecting all the sums set out in the rental. A rental is not an account of rent actually received, but a list of the rents due, which often included customary rents which were paid by the land owner (or, more accurately, holder) to the chief lords of the fee, or to the lord of the manor, or for some special purpose. The rental for all the feoffees' property for 1587 and a

---

[272] J.B. Bright, *The Brights of Suffolk* (Boston, Mass., 1858). Although this is a late, printed source, there seems no good reason to doubt its accuracy, and it confirms statements elsewhere that Thomas Bright the younger originated the 'cakes and ale' ceremony, as it is now called.

[273] Although the feoffees' records contain constant references to cake and wine at the account, they nowhere mention cakes and ale. The latter phrase was used by Shakespeare in *Twelfth Night*.

new rental made in 1621 are printed as Appendices 1 and 2, and the rents payable are listed individually in the accounts for 1607 and for 1612–15. The amount of rent given under the heading *onus* is, therefore, the theoretical amount which would have been received if every tenant had paid rent in full. After recording his receipts, the accountant noted down the sums paid out, represented by the Latin word *allocacio*, meaning 'allowance' or 'expenditure' in English.

Once the final balance had been worked out further expenditure might be considered at the audit or account. The arithmetic is not always correct, but this is probably due to careless copying from the original account, and no attempt has been made to add the figures given in these books.[274] Many of the accounts contain lists of 'supers',[275] that is rents that had not been paid, sometimes divided into 'supers *de antiquo*', arrears carried forward from previous years, and the arrears on that year's account, 'supers *de novo*'. Money in hand at the end of the year is said to have been put into the coffer, or, if the accountants had overspent, money might have to be taken out of it.[276] Accountants who ended their year with money in hand indicated this with the phrase *et debet* or *et sic debent*, literally meaning that the accountant or accountants still owed some of the money, with the collection of which they had been entrusted, to the company. If they ended the year having spent more than was received, then the account was *in surplusagio*, indicating that the payments were in excess of receipts. These and many other words are explained in the Glossary, where Latin words are printed in ***bold italic***.

The method of accounting displayed in these volumes shows some progress towards modern practice. In the early years long narrative passages are used with no attempt to put amounts in a column at the right-hand side as in modern accounts. In the early years, all amounts are given in Roman numerals, but in the second volume Arabic numerals begin to be used increasingly, though never to the extent that the predominance of Roman numerals is threatened.

Income

Rent was by far the largest source of income for the feoffees. In the earliest accounts, the rents are arranged in groups, varying slightly over the years, according to the donors of the lands from which they arose. When the feoffees acquired a new property, its rent sometimes appeared on its own for a year or two until it was absorbed when the rental was renewed. Similarly, increased rents were now and then entered individually until reflected in a new rental. The two rentals printed as Appendices 2 and 3 serve to indicate the general increase of rental income over the period covered by the accounts.

There are frequent references to arrears of rent, and their payment. From time to time a strenuous effort was made either to gather in small rents which had been in arrears for years, or, in the case of very small rents, to compound them for a cash sum. Some rents were always paid in kind. The first one to appear in the account books was a gallon of wine, provided by the occupier of land which had once belonged to John Baret, and which Baret had left to the alderman to see his will

---

[274] The original accounts for 1592–95, 1603, 1606, 1609 and 1611 have survived, and discrepancies in amounts have been noted in footnotes.

[275] See Glossary.

[276] For the coffer, see above, p.xxiii.

executed.[277] Later on, from 1608,[278] a boar was taken as part of the rent of Bretts in Hepworth, which was given to the alderman each year as his Christmas present. Towards the end of the run of accounts, quantities of rye were taken as rent and baked into bread for distribution to the poor on the account day.[279] At least two surviving leases stipulate that rent was to be paid in the south aisle of St James's church.[280]

Edmund Jermyn's annuity was first received in 1573,[281] where it is given its own heading. As it was used to provide materials to enable the poor to work, it is usually mentioned only in connection with the annuity of £20 which the feoffees had to pay to Mr John Jermyn for life.

In the sixteenth and seventeenth centuries, the Guildhall was much used for wedding parties, as it was until it was closed in 2001. Payments for bride ales or marriage dinners are to be found in the account of the keeper of the Guildhall, in those years when the accounts are divided into such sections. Receipts for marriages were off-set against casual expenditure by the keeper and his fixed annual wage. The evidence suggests that the charge made for use of the Guildhall was variable, although it often seems to have been 5s.[282] In the account for the year ending Michaelmas 1573 money was owing for marriages from three people, five shillings each. Two of those who owed money were servants of prominent feoffees, Sir Ambrose Jermyn and Mr John Higham, while the other, called Hammond, was very likely related to members of the company.[283] Perhaps use of the Guildhall for marriages was restricted to members of the company or their servants. In one instance a refund was made. Whether this was because the wedding had not taken place, or for some other reason, is not clear.

From time to time, especially in the earlier accounts, a payment called a 'fine' was received when tenants entered, renewed or assigned their leases to another person. In a few of the earlier accounts, money was also received from members of the company on their admission, but it appears that by this date there was difficulty in collecting these sums.[284] These payments derive from the medieval practice of guild members making a payment, called a gage, which provided money to pay for their funerals and for doles of bread to the poor on the day of their burial.[285] Legacies were often received and can be traced through the Index, Notes on People, and in Appendix 8. In many years additional income was received from the sale of wood or timber grown on the feoffees' estates. There is evidence that wood used in repairing properties often, perhaps usually, came from the estates whenever suitable timber was available.[286] 'Timber', as Dr Rackham has made clear, meant large,

---

277 Printed in Tymms, *Wills*, p.27. This will was made in 1463 and proved in 1467. In the benefactors' book, H1/2/1, which contains the English version of Smith's will and the bidding prayer, there is a much defaced passage about John Baret as a benefactor in which the reference to the gallon of wine can still be read.

278 HD1150/2, f.13r. is the first reference to this. The custom only ended when the first Scheme of the Charity Commissioners was implemented in 1842.

279 These rents are set out in the rental made in 1621, printed in Appendix 3.

280 Hepworth leases, H1/3/4/9.

281 HD1150/1, f.8v.

282 HD1150/1, fos. 19r., 20r.

283 HD1150/1, f.8r.

284 See above, p.xxxii.

285 Bread was distributed on the deaths of John Holt and William Smythis in the year ending 1570, HD1150/1, f.3r., and on the death of Thomas Cage in the year ending at Michaelmas 1574, HD1150/1, f.10r.

286 At a later period the feoffees were able to make a gift of timber to the governors when they built the

heavy beams, to be used in building or for gate-posts, while 'wood' was much lighter, suitable for poles, light construction or fire-wood.[287] In the account for 1612 the cost of preparing wood and faggots is set out, including 311 faggots paid as tithe.[288]

At this period, the purchase of land was deemed the safest investment, but at times money was in hand which had to be put to work, either before a suitable estate came on to the market or before it was spent upon some purpose laid down by the donor. This was done by one or more people making a bond with financial penalties to ensure that the money was repaid at specified times. Usury, if legal, was still not considered quite respectable.[289] On a few occasions the feoffees themselves borrowed money.[290]

A certain amount of income arose from property sales although, in many instances, the Commissioners for Charitable Uses later insisted that these properties should be re-purchased. From 1570–2, £2 was received each year from Christopher Johnson who had bought a house in Well Street under a deed of re-entry. The total recorded for this property was £6, although the payments might have begun before this account book was opened.[291] At the end of the alderman's account for the year ending Michaelmas 1576, a memorandum states that £60 paid by Sir William Cordell, Master of the Rolls, for land in Melford was in the hands of Mr Andrews.[292] In that and the following year, in the account of the new purchased lands, John Bright paid a total of £5 for a piece of ground in Mr Andrews Street.[293] Soon after the feoffees received a cottage and garden in Church Street, Lavenham, from Walter and Robert Brunwyn; they sold the property for a total of £19 10s.0d. to Henry Garrard of Lavenham, from whom money was received over four years from 1580 to 1584, but none in 1583.[294] In the early years of the seventeenth century, the feoffees were required, by decree of the Commissioners for Charitable Uses, to buy back land which they had sold earlier.[295]

In the early years, credit balances at the end of each accounting year, if any, were often recorded as having been put into the coffer or treasury.[296] In these early accounts the outgoing receivers do not hand over their balances to their successors. In 1582 £59 7s.1½d. was taken from the coffer 'at two severall tymes as appereth by the register of the sayde coffer'. Sadly this register has not survived, but the need to pay the task for the town, the purchase of St Peter's Hospital and a heavy bill for repairs (probably largely related to the purchase of St Peter's Hospital) made

---

new school hall in Northgate Street in 1662, Minutes H2/6/2.1, p.92. The timber in this instance came from the Broomes in Bradfield which the feoffees only acquired after these accounts ended.

[287] Oliver Rackham, *Trees and Woodland in the British Landscape* (1976), p.23.

[288] HD1150/2, f.24v.

[289] It was first sanctioned by law in 1545, repealed in 1552 and re-enacted in 1571.

[290] For example, HD1150/1, fos. 28v. and 29r.; HD1150/2, fos. 10v. and 13r.

[291] HD1150/1, fos. 2v., 4v. and 6v. There are deeds dating from 1457 to 1485 which relate to cottages in Well Street bequeathed by Geoffrey of Glemsford and later sold by the feoffees which may relate to this property, H1/5/6/1–7. At this date Well Street could mean the present Well Street, High Baxter Street or Angel Lane.

[292] *Ibid.*, f.14r. The feoffees may have acquired land in Long Melford when they bought the guild of St Nicholas which had been held in the College. Land in Melford was mentioned among its possessions in the chantry certificate, Woodward's Register, H1/6/1, p.73, but is not mentioned among the lands granted with the guild, *ibid.* p.88.

[293] HD1150/1 fos. 14r. and 15r. This formed part of Tassell's gift.

[294] *Ibid.*, fos. 18r., 19r., 20r. and 22v. The deeds are H1/7/1–2.

[295] See above, pp.xlvi–xlviii.

[296] See above, p.xxiii.

recourse to the coffer, or treasury as it was sometimes called, inevitable. The habit of handing on a credit balance only came in gradually during the 1580s and 1590s, to become a regular feature of the accounts from 1593.

Expenditure

Repairs

On the whole, repairs to the feoffees' property were carried out by tenants in accordance with covenants in their leases. They themselves repaired public buildings, such as the Guildhall, Market Cross, St Peter's Hospital and other buildings needed to provide for the poor and offenders. In many years the amount spent on repairs appears as one item; it seems likely that the building which comes first in the year's list may well have had a large sum spent upon it that year. Work carried out on individual buildings can be traced through the Index. It is not clear whether the Shire House was already let to the county justices, as was the case later; however, the thatch was repaired in 1609.[297] From time to time the pillory and cage, which the magistrates used to punish offenders, were also repaired. By the charter of 1608, the Crown had placed responsibility for repairing bridges on the Corporation although the rental of 1621 makes it clear that the feoffees accepted this duty.[298] Drainage and road repairs seem to be involved in the 8s.7d. spent in 1612 on mending the channel near the Abbeygate and setting four stones against the church door,[299] while in 1620 2s.6d. was spent on setting the way from the Abbey Gate to the Church Gate; a highway rate would have been levied by the highway surveyors to raise the bulk of the money required.[300]

Taxation

The bequests of Jankin Smith and others for the payment of national taxes levied on the town continued after the dissolution.[301] During the years covered by the accounts, the feoffees paid the medieval national tax called the fifteenths and tenths, commonly known as the task, as shown in Table I. Though usually collected in May,[302] the task was sometimes not paid on time[303] and sometimes the name of the collector is given.[304] Even as late as 1610 it looks as though the alderman retained his long-established responsibility for tax collection.[305]

---

[297] HD1150/2, f.17r.
[298] Charter of 1608, D1/2/1; the rental of 1621 is H2/3/4/11.
[299] HD1150/2, f.24v.
[300] *Ibid.*, f.44v.
[301] For donors who gave bequests for payment of town taxes, see Appendix 8, *passim*. For taxation at this period generally, see J.D. Alsop, 'The Theory and Practice of Tudor Taxation', *EHR*, xcvii (1982) and 'Innovation in Tudor Taxation', *EHR*, xcix (1984).
[302] For example in 1610, HD1150/2, f.19r.
[303] HD1150/1, fos. 24v., 35v., 36r. and v. and HD1150/2, fos. 13v. and 14r.
[304] HD1150/2, fos.13v. and 14r.
[305] Original account, 1610, H2/3/4/9.

Table I. Fifteenths and tenths (called the task) paid on behalf of the whole town

1570		1584		1598	£24
1571	£24	1585	£24	1599	£24
1572	£24	1586	£24	1600	£24
1573		1587		1601	
1574		1588	£24	1602	£72
1575		1589		1603	£48
1576	£24	1590	£24	1604	£48
1577	£24	1591	£24	1605	£24
1578		1592	£24	1606	£24
1579		1593	£48	1607	
1580		1594	£48	1608	£48
1581	£24	1595	£24	1609	£24
1582	£24	1596	£24	1610	£24
1583		1597			

As property owners the feoffees themselves paid taxes. From time to time, no doubt depending on the covenants of current leases, they paid the task for various parts of the St Peter's lands[306] as well as for Leyers in Rougham.[307] The annual tenth out of St Peter's lands, which is noted in account after account, must not be confused with fifteenths and tenths. It was a virtual rent, which had been reserved to the Crown when the grant was made to the governors of the Grammar School. As a body the feoffees were assessed for and paid other taxes. Their contributions to the subsidy were noted in the published lists for 1524 and 1568.[308] Payment of subsidy is set out in Table II. The names of those who collected the subsidy are sometimes given in the accounts, and include a Mrs Boldero, probably a widow acting as her husband's executrix.[309] The final reference to subsidies is in 1622 when two pursuivants who brought books for the subsidy were rewarded with ten shillings.[310] In 1609 the feoffees reimbursed some tenants the sums they had paid for the Prince's Aid.[311]

Robert Ryece, who wrote in the early years of the seventeenth century, is a good starting point for the problems of purveyance, the hated procedure whereby food and other commodities were taken by purveyors to provide for the needs of the royal household.[312] He discussed it in the section of his work headed 'The discommodities of the scite'. Proximity to London meant Suffolk was 'ever groaning under the remedylesse burden of the oppressing purveyors and takers'[313] while the county's fertility produced abundant foods and other things and the ports made transport to

---

[306] HD1150/1, fos. 24v., 27v., 29r., 32v., 34v., 36r. and 37v. and HD1150/2 fos. 2v., 8r., 11v., 13v., 17v. and 19r.

[307] HD1150/1, fos. 28v., 32v., 34r., 35v., 37r and 38r.

[308] S.H.A. Hervey (ed.) *Suffolk in 1524: being a return for a subsidy granted in 1523* (Woodbridge, 1910) p.355 (at the end of entries for the Risbygate ward) and *Suffolk in 1568: being the return for a subsidy granted in 1566* (Bury St Edmunds, 1909) p.87, where it comes at the end of the west ward list. The Guildhall was in the west ward.

[309] HD1150/2, f.11v.

[310] *Ibid.*, f.49r.

[311] *Ibid.*, fos. 17r., 17v. and 18v.

[312] Lord Francis Hervey (ed.) *Suffolk in the XVIIth Century: the Brieviary of Suffolk by Robert Reyce, 1618* (1902) pp.15–20 is all very relevant. For purveyance generally see Allegra Woodworth, 'Purveyance for the Royal Household of Queen Elizabeth', *Transctions of the American Philosophical Society*, new series, xxxv, part 1 (1945).

[313] Lord Francis Hervey, *ut supra*, p.15.

Table II. Subsidy paid by the feoffees on their property

1570		1584		1598	£2 13s.4d.
1571		1585	£1 13s.4d.	1599	£2 13s.4d.
1572		1586	£1 0s.0d.	1600	£2 13s.4d.
1573		1587	£1 13s.4d.	1601	
1574		1588		1602	£5 6s.8d.
1575		1589	£2 13s.4d.	1603	£2 13s.4d.
1576		1590		1604	£2 13s.4d.
1577	£1 10s.0d.	1591	£1 0s.0d.	1605	
1578		1592	£1 13s.4d.	1606	£1 13s.4d.
1579		1593	£3 13s.4d.	1607	£2 13s.4d.
1580		1594	£2 13s.4d.	1608	£1 0s.0d.
1581	£1 13s.4d.	1595		1609	£1 13s.4d.
1582	£1 0s.0d.	1596			
1583		1597			

London convenient and easy. Suffolk only began to compound, that is, negotiate a fixed sum in lieu of produce, from 1593 onwards.[314] As in many towns, where men lived by wages and had no produce to contribute towards purveyance, Bury St Edmunds seems to have had special difficulties.[315] The amounts paid for purveyance were not, at first, large, though a much higher sum, £3 15s.0d. in all, was paid in 1618.[316]

There are also a few references to county and other local taxation. The small sum of 3s.4d. paid in 1605 for the king's wood-yard and Sudbury bridge may have been the feoffees' assessment for a county rate.[317] Ballingdon Bridge, then a wooden bridge which provided a crossing of the Stour near Sudbury, was notoriously in need of constant repair at this period.[318] Among the yearly revenues listed at Michaelmas 1588 the sum of 5s. had been received from Robert Davison on the orders of Sir Robert Jermyn and Sir John Heigham. This money was said to be part of a sum collected in the south ward towards the charges of putting forth soldiers; it may have been the residue of money collected on a county rate.[319]

In 1607 a church rate was levied for repairing St Mary's church. The feoffees paid £1 on the Guildhall, which was taxed or rated at £20, at 1s. in the pound.[320] Road repairs loomed large in 1620 when the feoffees paid £4 7s.8d. for setting the street before the Guildhall. It seems likely that this work was an initiative on their own part. However, the next entry related to 2s.6d. for setting the way from the Abbey Gate to the Norman Tower 'over and besides what was collected'.[321] It seems likely that a highway rate had been made for this work and that the feoffees made up a shortfall.

---

[314] *Ibid.*, pp.17–19.
[315] Two versions of a petition protesting at the amount of composition money demanded from the town have survived among the Borough Records, D11/3/2 and D11/11/3. They are undated but addressed to Sir Thomas Edmonds, who was appointed Treasurer of the Household in 1618.
[316] HD1150/2, f.40v. See above, p.lv.
[317] *Ibid.*, f.5v.
[318] See F.C.D.Sperling, *Hodson's History of the Borough of Sudbury* (Sudbury, 1896) p.216.
[319] HD1150/1, f.29r.
[320] HD1150/2, f.11v.
[321] *Ibid.*, f.44v.

The poor

The 1587 rental shows that the feoffees then had a total of twenty-eight almshouses, which provided homes for thirty-nine people; the sites of almshouses are marked on the Map (p.300). Various entries in the minute books show that from time to time the almshouses were cleared of those thought unworthy to live in them; on one occasion young people were specially targeted.[322] In addition to rent-free almshouses there were some for which rent was, or should have been, received each year. The rent was intended to provide an income for repairing other almshouses in the block.

The terms 'Bridewell' and 'house of correction' were used interchangeably by those who wrote these accounts.[323] Repairs at St Peter's in 1622 reveal that it was then used as the house of correction.[324] A workhouse is first mentioned in the account for 1620,[325] but evidence elsewhere shows that it was set up in 1611.[326]

In most years some money is spent on clothing for the poor. Sometimes this was for an individual and the item purchased was identified, but at other times an entry merely gave a total sum spent on clothing the poor that year; these instances may be found in the index under 'Clothing'. The first of these payments is for the year ending Michaelmas 1573 when £6 13s.4d. was paid for frieze to clothe the poor in both parishes.[327] This, it should be remembered, was the first year in which Edmund Jermyn's annuity was received, and it is quite probable that with the extra revenue at their disposal the feoffees felt able to spend money for this purpose. When clothing was given, it was often expressly described as being of frieze, an exceptionally warm and hardwearing fabric usually worn by poor people.[328]

Every effort was made to ensure that the poor always had work to do. Sometimes the feoffees spent money on implements with which the poor could work to provide for themselves: invariably spinning wheels and cards, of various types, with which wool was prepared for spinning.[329] Yet another aspect of encouraging the poor to work was apprenticing, which is mentioned from time to time in both the Book of Orders and these account books. It seems likely that the few references to apprenticeship all relate to orphans who had been brought up at the expense of the feoffees. This was certainly the case with, for example, Thomas Claydon and Barbara Langley.[330]

These accounts contain very many notes of money paid to or for the poor in general. The annual allowance of £1 to each parish from Tassell's gift was paid throughout the period covered by these books. An identical payment was left by Thomas Bright the elder out of Foxearth's tithes; the first payment of this was received in 1604.[331] The feoffees also, like other property owners, paid their local

---

[322] Minutes, H2/6/2.1, pp.4 and 23.
[323] For its establishment see Introduction, pp.xxxvi, xxxvii.
[324] HD1150/2, f 48r.
[325] HD1150/2, f.44r.
[326] See above, pp.l–li.
[327] HD1150/1, f.9r.
[328] See Glossary for 'frieze'.
[329] For example, for cards for the house of correction, see HD1150/1, fos. 41r., 43v. and 44v.; for cards provided for individuals, HD1150/2, fos. 46r. and 47v. and for spinning wheels, HD1150/1, fos. 7v., 41r., and HD1150/2, f.17v.
[330] HD1150/1, fos. 30v. and 39r.
[331] HD1150/2, f.4r.

rates and taxes for the support of the poor. At a meeting on 30 December 1595 it was agreed that the 'quarters' for the poor were to be paid at once 'as it is newly sett downe'.[332] These may be included in the payment of £10 in 1596, which the accountant had paid 'for this house', and an additional £6 13s.4d. which the accountant had paid 'likewise' for a debt of the house.[333] The accounts for a number of years give a sum which was distributed to the poor at Christmas.[334]

On a very few occasions, loans were made to poor men. In 1597 three poor men were lent a total of £1 17s.0d.,[335] most of which remained unpaid for a long time. On 4 January 1604, Clarke the card-maker was lent £2 which had not been repaid by the end of that year, but the account for 1605 shows that 10s. was repaid in that year.[336]

Although it may sometimes have been used as an almshouse, it is quite certain that St Peter's was being used as a hospital for much of the period covered by the accounts, and it was certainly used as an isolation hospital in time of plague. These account books show how the feoffees provided a health service for those who lived in late sixteenth- and early seventeenth-century Bury St Edmunds; the relevant entries are brought together under the heading of 'medical care' in the Index, where the names of practioners employed are listed. Some medical men other than those who regularly attended the poor are mentioned, such as the surgeon Jessop, who healed Pounsabie's eye,[337] and a German doctor who in 1621 was paid 10s. for curing a rupture.[338] There are two references to women surgeons. One of these was the redoubtable Margaret Stone *alias* Oliver, who lived on the north side of Abbeygate Street and mentions in her will both her instruments of surgery and her tools for goldsmith's work.[339] A total of £1 5s.0d. was paid for healing Bekon's daughter in 1574, of which 10s. was paid to Mrs Stone, as she appears in this source.[340] In 1582 a woman surgeon of Colchester was paid for curing the wife of John Willys of Bury, sherman, and many others.[341] As both patients who are named and who were attended by these women were female, it is tempting to suppose that the complaints they were required to deal with were gynaecological, although there is no real evidence for this. Porter notes instances of female surgeons working on the continent at an early date, but not in this country.[342]

Plague hit the poor much harder than the better-off.[343] Epidemics of one kind or another were frequent at this period, although the material relating to them in the

[332] Minutes, H2/6/2.1, p.17b.
[333] HD1150/1, f.40r.
[334] For example, HD1150/1, f.46v. (1602).
[335] HD1150/1, f.42r.
[336] The loan is noted in the Minutes, H2/6/2.1, pp.23 and 26, and also in HD1150/2 fos. 3r.and 4v.
[337] HD1150/2, f.39v.
[338] *Ibid.*, f.46r.
[339] See Notes on People. Her will is Probate Register IC500/2/37, f.242v.
[340] HD1150/1, f.11r.
[341] *Ibid.*, f.20v.
[342] Roy Porter, *The Greatest Benefit to Mankind: a medical history of humanity from antiquity to the present* (1997) p.113. There is an illumination of a woman performing a Caesarean section in a French manuscript of *c*.1375 reproduced in Sally Fox (ed.) *The Medieval Woman: an illuminated book of days* (1985). Rosemary O'Day, *The Professions in Early Modern England, 1450–1800: servants of the Commonweal* (Harlow 2000), in the section devoted to the medical profession, has useful references to women practitioners.
[343] Paul Slack, *The Impact of Plague*, esp. chapter 5, 'The Urban Impact', pp.111–43. Francis Pinner had plague in 1637 and survived to describe his experiences in his will (printed in Tymms, *Wills*, p.172). John Mallowes and Edward Bourne, a benefactor, both died in the summer of 1637. The St Mary's parish register makes it clear that Bourne did not die of plague, but Mallowes may well have been a victim.

accounts is less than might have been expected. In all probability the bulk of the relief needed would have been provided by the parish overseers and financed by a rate. There is always some doubt about the accuracy of diagnosis at this period. The term 'sickness' was constantly used, and sometimes does mean plague, but not always. In the original account for 1609, which has survived, when 'sickness' was used in the account book, the original account reads 'small pox'.[344] The parish registers show sharp increases in the number of deaths in 1578–9, 1587, 1592, 1609, when small pox was said to be in the town, and 1615. The accounts for 1578–9, 1592–3 and 1615 have no entries to suggest that the feoffees were involved in relief. In 1587, however, £10 3s.0d. was paid for keepers and bearers.[345] A couple of years later, but again probably in connection with some outbreak of plague, there is a payment of 5s. for a load of poles, presumably for rough shelters, during the last 'plagge'.[346] Since plague was essentially a disease of the summer months, those who were isolated to try to prevent the spread of infection were sometimes housed in tents in the open air, as seems to have been done here.[347] Although in neither 1603 nor 1606 are the number of deaths especially high, there is evidence both in these accounts and elsewhere that the town had some epidemic at this time. In 1603 there are payments relating to the burial of the dead from the hospital and also for the provision of coal, apparently stored at the Guildhall, for the sick.[348] Both the new Corporation and the feoffees provided for the sick in 1606. The feoffees paid £1 5s.0d. for people who were shut up in their houses and in other places,[349] while the Corporation paid 15s.6d.to Inglethorpe, whose name is familiar as the beadle or keeper of the Guildhall, for 4 yards of sky colour fabric and 6 yards of white cotton[350] for the keepers of the 'pest house'.[351]

The clergy and churches

The payments to the town clergy have already been considered. The amounts paid to the preachers and ministers are set out in Appendix 7.

Regular payments were made from Tassell's gift of £1 a year to each church towards the cost of repairs,[352] and from 1600 onwards the same amount was paid to the churchwardens out of income from the tithes at Foxearth which had been given by Thomas Bright the elder.[353] Otherwise, very little is to be found in these accounts about repairing the parish churches. Normally references to church repairs show that the feoffees were paying their rates (sometimes called a taxation) like all other property owners in the town.[354]

---

344 The variant readings have been indicated in the footnotes.
345 HD1150/1, f.27r. The keepers were those who took food and other necessities to those who were confined to their houses or in some other place.
346 HD1150/1, f.30v.
347 Slack, *The Impact of Plague*, p.203, cites instances of those with plague being housed in sheds outside the walls in provincial towns.
348 HD1150/2, f.2v.
349 HD1150/2, f.8r.
350 See Glossary for this woollen fabric.
351 Both in Bright's memoranda book, H1/4/16, f.6r. and in the Corporation chamberlain's account for 1606, D6/4/1, p.6.
352 Woodward's Register, H1/6/1, p.127.
353 HD1150/1, f.44v. has the first payment.
354 HD1150/2, fos. 5v., 11v. and 48v.

Military matters

In a period which included the year of the Armada, it is only to be expected that an organisation such as this, which was virtually running the town before 1606, would have to make some expenditure connected with the defence of the realm. Among the objects of his charity, William Tassell had included the equipping of soldiers. To take but two examples, the sum of £14 15s.0d. was spent on this in 1570, over and above an additional £22 which was taken out of the coffer.[355] However, in 1593 the accountant was paid only £1 which he was owed for providing equipment for soldiers.[356] As the years pass by, much more emphasis is placed on the musters. Mustering is virtually unknown before 1573, and in Bury St Edmunds, to judge from these accounts, may have become usual even later.[357] The muster master was sometimes treated to a dinner, once at the Angel.[358] This was in 1614, when the coroner, the immediate past alderman, was his host.[359] There were payments, for example 16s. in 1594, to those who wore the town armour at the muster.[360] The town armour was cleaned or scoured in most years; like so many other things it was stored in the Guildhall.[361] From time to time new armour had to be bought for the town, as in 1613 and 1617.[362] Living in Bury St Edmunds it is quite easy to forget that Suffolk is a maritime county, and in 1601 and 1602 payments of 8s.4d. and 10s.0d. were made for provisioning the navy.[363]

Legal expenses

Anyone owning land as the feoffees did, inevitably incurred legal expenses as a matter of routine for drafting and engrossing leases and such like.[364] Now and then they had to sue the executors of those who had left legacies to encourage their payment.[365] From time to time the feoffees had also to undertake the task of renewing the feoffment.[366]

The 1621 rental concludes with a very full list of all the payments for which the feoffees accepted responsibility as the account books come to an end.[367]

---

[355] HD1150/1, fos. 2r., 3r.

[356] HD1150/1, f.37r.

[357] Lindsay Boynton, *The Elizabethan Militia, 1558–1638* (1967) p.13. Boynton points out that the towns were 'pugnaciously independent' and difficult to incorporate in county schemes, *ibid*, p.37.

[358] HD1150/2, f.30r.

[359] The muster began at 8 or 9 in the morning with prayer or even a sermon, followed by the inspection of the men and their weapons. In the seventeenth century there might have been a mock battle. When all the males between sixteen and sixty years of age attended, they had to be sorted into three groups according to the ability ('choyce men', 'second sort' and 'unable but to keep [guard] the county'). After 1573 the men were paid, there was usually a large quantity of beer available and the official party rounded off the day with a dinner, Boynton, *ut supra*, pp.26, 27.

[360] HD1150/1, f.39v.

[361] HD1150/1, f.25v.

[362] HDHD1150/2, fos. 27v. and 38r.

[363] HD1150/1, fos. 45v. and 46v.

[364] For example, HD1150/2, f.24r.

[365] For example, HD1150/1, f.38r.

[366] For example, HD1150/2, f.30r.

[367] Printed in Appendix 3.

Editorial Conventions

This volume presents a full and exact transcription of the original documents, which are mainly in English but with some Latin words and phrases. The latter are printed in italics, and appear in the Glossary (pp.327–44) with English translation. As a further aid to readers, modern punctuation has been added, but never where it might impose a questionable reading. Similarly, the use of capital letters has been modernised.

The layout of the originals has been followed closely, except in the signatures found at the end of some accounts, which have been placed in columns instead of haphazardly on the page. The main heading for each account is printed in bold, as are those in the early years when several officers had their own headed accounts. The year, and sometimes the name of the accountant, which in the original are either above the heading or in the left-hand margin, have been placed in bold in the centre before each main heading. Marginal sub-headings, and comments have also been printed in bold. Those in the left margin are placed before the passage to which they relate, while those on the right are placed after the relevant passage.

Where items in the accounts take up more than one line, the second and subsequent lines have been indented. All numbers are given in Arabic numerals, apart from deletions which can still be read. In these cases the Roman numerals have been struck through.

The following editorial conventions have been used:

\ /	for insertions
~~alderman~~	for deletions which are legible (strike-through)
<deletion>	for whole words or groups of words, which are deleted and illegible
<..>	for a few illegible letters
[*space*]	for omitted words

All editorial insertions are given in italics within square brackets, e.g. [*f. 25v.*] or [*sic*].

Note that all obvious abbreviations have been extended without comment. The abbreviation 'lre' has been extended to 'lettre'.

Various forms of 'Mistress' have been printed as 'Mrs'.

The occasional use of Middle English or earlier characters has been modernised. The 'thorn' (þ) is rendered as 'th' as in 'the' and 'that'. Similarly, in the English version of Jankin Smith's will the 'yogh' (ȝ) is replaced by the modern English 'g' or 'y' as appropriate, and 'x' is printed as 'sh'.

All places mentioned are in Suffolk unless otherwise indicated.

Unless otherwise indicated, all manuscripts cited are at Suffolk Record Office, Bury Branch.

Money and Measurements

Money
1 pound (£) contained 20 shillings (s.) or 240 pennies (d.), the same as £1 today
1 shilling (s.) contained 12 pennies (d.), equivalent to 5p today
1 mark was a sum of money (not a coin), 13s.4d., approximately equivalent to 67p today

Weight
1 pound (lb) contained 16 ounces, approximately equivalent to 0.45 kg
1 stone contained 14 pounds (lb)
1 hundredweight contained 112 pounds (lb), approximately equivalent to 50.8 kg

Length
1 foot contained 12 inches, equivalent to 30 cm
1 yard contained 3 feet, approximately equivalent to 0.9 m
1 perch contained 5½ yards

Liquid measure
1 gallon contained 8 pints, equivalent to 4.55 litres
1 quart contained 2 pints, equivalent to 1.14 litres

Corn measure
1 quarter contained 8 bushels, approximately equivalent to 217 kg
1 bushel contained 4 pecks, approximately equivalent to 27 kg
1 coomb contained 4 bushels

Land area
1 acre (ac) contained 4 roods, approximately equivalent to 0.4 hectares

Abbreviations

BAA	British Archaeological Association
Bodl.	Bodleian Library, Oxford
BL	British Library
CSPD	*Calendars of State Papers Domestic*
DNB	*Dictionary of National Biography*
EHR	*English Historical Review*
n.d.	no date
OED	*Oxford English Dictionary*
PCC	Prerogative Court of Canterbury
PRO	Public Record Office
PSIA(H)	*Proceedings of the Suffolk Institute of Archaeology (and History)*
SROB	Suffolk Record Office, Bury St Edmunds
SROI	Suffolk Record Office, Ipswich
SRS	Suffolk Records Society
VCH	*Victoria County History*

ACCOUNTS OF
THE FEOFFEES OF THE
TOWN LANDS OF BURY ST EDMUNDS

1569–1622

SUFFOLK RECORD OFFICE (BURY ST EDMUNDS)

HD1150/1, 2

[*f.2r.*]

At Candylmas[1] *anno* 1570 [*1*]

The londes and tenementes sometyme John Smythes, esquier, Hepworthe,[2] Mrs Odams and William Tassell, gentleman[3]

Th'accompte of Thomas Cage, Stephyn Heyward, gentleman, Thomas Andrewes, esquire, and Sir Ambrose Jermyn, knight,[4] surveyors and collectors of the saide londes and tenementes made and taken the morowe after Candilmas daye *Anno* 1570 [*3 February 1571*] for one holle yere ended at Michelmas laste paste[5]

Arreragia nulla

Inprimis the saide accomptauntes do yelde ther accompte of £8 1s.4d. by them received within the said tyme of ther accompte of th'issues and proffittes of the manor, londes and tenementes in Hepworthe as by the rentall therof yt dothe appere. And of £7 18s.8d. of th'issues and proffittes of the londes and tenementes late William Tassell, gentleman, as by the rental therof it dothe appere. And allso of £18 15s.0d. of th'issues and proffittes of the londes and tenementes sometyme John Smyth, esquier, Mrs Odams and others in Bury St Edmond and other townes adjoynynge

    Summa totalis £34 15s.0d.

Item the saide accomptantes do allso yelde ther accompte of £16 14s.6d. by them received within the said tyme of ther accompte for certeyne fynes for the renewinge of certeyne leases of the londes in Hepworthe, *videlicet*, of William Muryell £10 0s.0d., of Valentyne Roose £4 16s.8d., and of Gyles Rust £1 10s.0d.[6] And of 7s.10d. for too hundrid and a half of woode, besides the makeing[7] and carriage

    Summa £16 13s.6d.

    Summa totalis oneris predicti £51 9s.6d., whereof

The saide accomptauntes do praye 8s.5½d. for certeyne owte rentes goinge owte of the londes in Hepworthe. And of 6s.1d. for certeyne tenthes and owte rentes goinge owte of the londes and tenementes sometyme William Tassell, gentleman. And of £1 3s.6½d. for certeyne rentes goinge owte of the londes and tenementes sometyme John Smyth, esquier, and others in Bury and other townes adjoynyng. And of 6d. a yere for a certeyne pece of ground nowe in th'occupacion of Anthony Payne, gentleman, nowe in suspens for certeyne yeres. And of 15s.0d.for the said collectors fees. And they praye allso to be allowed of £4 10s.0d. by them laide owte towardes the setteinge forthe of certeyne shouldiers as apperith by ther bill.

---

1   For the significance of Candlemas see Introduction, p.xxi.

2   For the purchase of the concealed lands at Hepworth in Suffolk see Introduction, p.xxviii.

3   Details of the land, and the purposes for which it was given, by these and other benefactors, are given in Appendix 8.

4   Where biographical information about the feoffees and others mentioned in these accounts is available, it is to be found in the Notes on People. The names of those who were feoffees during the period covered by the accounts are given in Appendix 6.

5   That is 29 September 1569 to the same date in 1570.

6   For William Muriell see H1/3/4/8; for Valentine Roose see H1/3/4/9; Rust's lease granted this year has not survived, but there is a lease to him dated 1561 of ten pieces of land in Hepworth, H1/3/5. The rental of 1587 (Appendix 2) shows that his son rented land at Osmond Crouch and in Russhe Leys then, as well as in the town meadow.

7   For this and other unusual words or usages, see Glossary.

Summa totalis allocationis predicte £7 3s.9¾d.
Et sic debent £44 5s.8¼d. *solutum aldermanno super*
determinacionem huius compoti

The newe purchased londes

Th'accompte of Robert Bronwyn and John Cutteras, surveyors and collectors of the same londes made and taken the daye and year abovesaid

Arreragia nulla

The saide accomptauntes do yelde ther accompte of £16 5s.8d. of th'issues and proffittes of the same londes by them receyved within the tyme of ther accompte. And of £1 0s.0d. by them received of William Jellowe for a fine for a newe lease of a tanners stall in the Marketsted[8]

> *Summa totalis oneris* £17 5s.8d., whereof

[*f.2v.*]   1570

The said accomptauntes do praye allowauns of 5s.0d. for ther fee. And of £1 18s.7d. for certeyne reparacions done by them of certeyne howses in Garlonde Strete[9] and for the makeinge of the conveyauns for the Almois Howses in the Colledge Strete[10] as apperith by too billes of the parcelles

> *Summa totalis allocationis predicte* £2 3s.7d.
> And so they do owe £15 2s.1d. which is paid unto the alderman
> uppon the determynacion of this accompt, and so evyn

The Guyldehall

Th'accompte of Henry Hornyngold, keper of the said hall, made and taken the daye and yere aforesaid

Arreragia nulla

The said accompteaunte dothe yelde his accompte of 14s.0d. by hym received of Thomas Buttery. And of 1s.0d. received of Robert Cheston. And of 1s.0d. received of John Whight for the gardeyne.[11] And allso the same accomptaunte dothe yelde accompte of £4 2s.0d. by hym received of dyverse persons for suche marriages as have ben kepte within the said hall within the tyme of his accompt

> *Summa totalis oneris predicti* £4 18s.0d., whereof

The said accomptaunte prayeth allowauns of £2 15s.2d. for certeyne reparacions and other thinges by hym laide owte as apperith by a bill of parcelles

> *Summa allocationis* £2 15s.2d., and so with £2 2s.10d. which is
> paid to the alderman uppon the determynacion of this accompt,
> and so evyn

---

[8]   This had been part of the endowment of the Morrow Mass priest in St James's church, Woodward's register, H1/6/1, p.77.

[9]   The feoffees had property in Garland Street from both Thomas Bereve and Thomas Browse. See Appendix 8, *sub* 1527 and 1558.

[10]   These almshouses were acquired on 22 August 1570, Woodward's Register, H1/6/1, p.181. See also Appendix 8, *sub* 1570.

[11]   These seem to be the rents for upkeep of Guildhall which had long been paid to the alderman during his year of office. See Introduction, p.xxxi.

The aldermans accompte

Th'accompte of Henry Hornyngold, alderman, made and taken the daye and yere aforesaid

Arreragia nulla

Firste the said alderman dothe yelde his accompte of £44 5s.8d. by hym received of Thomas Cage, Stephyn Heyward, gentleman, Thomas Andrewes, esquier, and Sir Ambrose Jermyn, knight, collectors of the londes and tenementes late John Smyth, esquier, Hepworthe, Mrs Odams, William Tassell, gentleman, and others. And of £15 2s.1d. received of Robert Bronwyn and John Cutteras, collectors of the newe purchased landes. And of £2 2s.10d. wherewith he hathe charged hym silf byfore in his accompte for the Guyldehall. And the said accomptaunte dothe further charge hym silf with the recepte of £5 0s.0d. of Richard Coppynge due by obligacion. And of £2 0s.0d. of Cristofer Johnson due for the purchase of a certeyne tenemente by dede of re-entrie.[12] And of £1 0s.0d. received of Robert Careles and Thomas Goodriche uppon ther admyssion into our company and felloweshipp, accordeinge to the old order of the howse[13]

    Summa totalis oneris predicte £69 10s.8¼d., whereof

[f.3r.]   1570

He prayeth allowauns of theis sommes underwritten by hym disburste and paide for dyverse charges and allowaunces, *videlicet*, of £4 0s.0d. paid to the dee for bringinge forthe of the dynner. 3s.4d. for his owne fee. 3s.4d. for the dees fee. 3s.4d. for the clerkes fee. 8d. for the porters fee. 2s.0d. for the chapleyns fee. 1s.4d. for the sextons fee.[14] £1 0s.0d. for the provision of woode for the gaiole.[15] £1 0s.0d. for the releif of the poore in the spittle.[16] £3 6s.8d. for the relief of the poore in St Jamys parisshe. £3 6s.8d. for the releif of the poore in St Maryes parisshe.[17] £2 0s.0d. towardes the reparacions of bothe churches.[18] 5s.0d. for breade delte at the deathe of William Smythis. 5s.0d. in like sorte for John Holt gentleman.[19] 5s.0d. more allowed to the dee for wyne and suger. And of £1 0s.0d. allso allowed more unto the dee for the provision of meat for the poore

    Summa totalis allocationis predicte £17 2s.4d.

    And so remeyneth £52 8s.4¼d. adde to this 16s.0d. received for a tenemente late Browse[20] in Garlond Strete, and so resteth £53 4s.4¼d. owte of which some paid to Bronwyn uppon his billes of reconynge for setteinge forthe of certeyne shouldiers this laste sommer, over and above £22 0s.0d. deliverid owte of the coffer to hym the 22th daye of Marche laste, £10 5s.0d., and £1 10s.0d. allowed to Walter Payne[21] for certeyne reparacions done by hym

---

[12] A deed of re-entry was used where property which had been alienated was re-entered, often because there had been a breach of covenant.

[13] See Introduction, p.xxxii (and n.121).

[14] The sexton prepared the church for the service; one of his duties was to put out cushions, see p.32 below.

[15] This is a payment from Margaret Odeham's gift.

[16] This annual commitment to provide for the relief of the poor comes from the uses of the new purchased lands.

[17] This is also an object of the new purchased lands.

[18] This is a regular payment out of Tassell's gift.

[19] See Introduction, p.xxxii (and n.122).

[20] This may well be a rent for this property, not yet included in the rental.

[21] See Notes on People.

uppon the almas houses in the Colledge Strete byfore they came to our handes. And so remeyneth £41 9s.3¼d. which was putt into the coffer[22] uppon the determynacion of this accompte, and so evyn.

[f.3v.]   At Candylmas *anno* 1571 [2]

The londes and tenementes sometyme John Smyth, esquier, Mrs Odams, Hepworth, and William Tassell, gentleman

Th'accompte of Thomas Andrewes, esquier, Sir Ambrose Jermyn, knight, William Tassell, gentleman, and Henry Horningold, surveyors and collectors of the saide londes and tenementes made and taken the Monday next after Candylmas daye[23] *anno* 1571 [*1572*] for one holle yere endid at Michelmas laste paste

Arreragia nulla

Firste the saide accomptauntes do yelde ther accompte of £8 1s.4d. by them received within the said tyme of ther accompte of th'issues and proffittes of the manor, of landes and tenementes in Hepworthe as by the rentall therof it dothe appere. And of £7 18s.8d. of th'issues and proffittes of the landes and tenementes late William Tassell, gentleman, as by the rentall therof it dothe appere. And allso of £18 15s.0d. of th'issues and proffittes of the londes and tenementes sometyme John Smyth, esquier, Mrs Odams and others in Bury St Edmond and other townes adjoynynge

    Summa totalis oneris predicte £34 15s. 0d., whereof

The said accomptauntes do aske to be allowed of 8s.5½d. for certeyne owte rentes goinge of owte of the landes and tenementes in Hepworthe as by the rentall of the same londes and tenementes it dothe appere. And allso of 1s.1¾d. for castellward rent[24] goinge owte of the same londes \to/ the Manor of Bardwell Hall, after the rate of 2¾d. for every 20 weekes, paid for five termes ~~weekes~~ ended the 29th daye of September nowe laste paste. And allso of 6s.1d. for certeyne rentes and tenthes paid owte of the londes and tenementes late William Tassell, gentleman, as by the rentall of the same londes it dothe likewise appere. And of £1 3s.6½d. for certeyne owte rentes going owte of the londes and tenementes sometyme John Smyth, esquier, and others in Bury and other townes adjoynynge as by the rental of the same londes dothe allso appere. And of 6d. a yere for the rent of a pece of ground nowe in th'occupacion of Anthony Payne, gentleman, nowe in suspens for a certeyne tyme by reason of an extente made of the same [?]\amogest/ of other londes and tenementes uppon the Statute for Recoverey of debtes by one Thomas Bacon,[25] citizen and salter of London, after the deathe of Nicholas Platte. And allso of 15s.0d. for the fee of the said accomptauntes for the collecion of the said rentes.

    Summa £2 14s.8d.

And allso the said accomptauntes do praye allso to be allowed of £31 9s.11d. by them laid [*out*] within the tyme of ther accompte, as well towardes the paymente

---

22 See Introduction, p.xxiii.
23 That is, Monday 5 February 1572.
24 See Glossary.
25 Thomas Bacon was the elder brother of the Lord Keeper, Sir Nicholas Bacon. See Notes on People.

of the taxe graunted to the Quenes Majestie at the laste Parliamente, and certeyne reparacions done uppon the Angell, as for dyverse other thinges, as by a bill of parcelles therof it dothe appere

> *Summa* £31 9s.11d.
> *Summa totalis allocationis predicte* £34 4s.7d.
> *Et sic debent* 10s.4½d. *solutum aldermanno super determinacionem huius compoti. Et sic eque.*

[*f.4r.*]   1571

The newe purchased londes

Th'accompte of John Cutteras and Thomas Kytson esquier, collectors of the londes aforesaid, made and taken the daye and yere aforesaid

Arreragia nulla

The said accomptauntes do yelde ther accompte of £16 5s.8d. of th'issues and proffittes of the said londes by them received within the tyme of ther accompte

> *Summa totalis oneris predicte* £16 5s.8d., whereof

The said accomptauntes do ~~yelde ther accompte~~ praye to be allowed of £10 0s.0d. by them laide owte towardes the payment of the taxe, over and besides £14 0s.0d. paid by Henry Hornyngold for the same. And of £5 0s.0d. paid for the fyne for certeyne copiehold londe holden of the Manor of Barton.[26] And of 5s.0d. for the collectors fee.

> *Summa totalis allocacionis predicte* £15 5s.0d.
> *et sic debet* £1 0s.8d. *solutum aldermanno super determinacionem huius compoti. Et sic eque.*

The Guylde hall

Th'accompte of William Axton, keper of the Guylde Hall, made and taken the daye and yere aforesaid

Arreragia nulla

The said accomptaunte dothe yelde his accompte of 14s.0d. by hym received of Thomas Buttery for the rent of too ~~peces~~ parcelles of londe and pasture in Risbiegate Strete and at Stanyware Bridge. And of 1s.0d. received of John White for the ferme of a gardeyne plott lyinge at the northe side of the said hall. And allso of 1s.0d. received of Robert Cheston for a gardeyne in the Estgate Strete. And of 8s.0d. for the rent of a tenemente lying at the south end of the said hall

> *Summa* £1 4s.0d.

And futher the said accomptaunte doth charge hym silf with the recepte of £2 0s.0d. by hym received of sondry persones for dyverse brydalles kepte within the said hall, within the tyme of his accompte

> *Summa* £2 0s.0d.
> *Summa totalis oneris predicte* £3 4s.0d., whereof

He praieth allowauns of £1 6s.10d. by hym laide owte for dyverse thinges as apperith by a bill of parcelles therof. And of 8s.0d. for the rent of the said howse at the south end of the said hall, for that <deletion>~~£1 6s.10d., Et sic debet~~ \the tenante craves respite for the same/ in respect of hir povertie

> *Summa totalis allocacionis* £1 14s.10d.
> *Et sic debet* £1 9s.2d.

---

[26] Some of the land in Barton left by Jankin Smith was copyhold. See Introduction, p.xxi.

[f.4v.]   1571
The aldermans accompte

The accompte of ~~Thomas Coksage~~ the said William Axton, alderman, made and taken the daye and yere aforesaid

Arreragia nulla

Firste the said alderman dothe yelde his accompte of £5 0s.0d. by hym received of Thomas Carre[27] for the discharge of an obligacion made by Coppinge. And of £2 0s.0d. received of Johnson in parte of paymente for the purchase of his howse in Wel Strete.[28] And of £1 0s.8d. received of John Cutteras and Thomas Kitson, esquier, surveiors and collectors of the newe purchased [*land*]. And of 10s.4¼d. received of Thomas Andrewes, esquier, Sir Ambrose Jermyn, knight, William Tassell, gentleman, and Henry Hornyngold, surveiors and collectors of the londes and tenementes late John Smyth and others. And of £1 9s.2d. wherewith he hathe charged hym silf byfore in his accompte for the Guylde hall. And allso of £1 0s.0d. by hym received of John Heigham and Thomas Peyton, esquier, uppon ther admission into this felowshipp[29]

    Summa totalis oneris predicte £11 0s.2¼d., whereof

Super[30]

He prayeth to be allowed of £1 0s.0d still remeynynge in th'andes of the said John Heigham and Thomas Peyton, unpaid uppon ther admyssion, until the next accompte

    Summa £1 0s.0d.

And of £4 0s.0d. paid to the dee for the bringinge forthe of the dynner   £4 0s. 0d.

To Axton

And of 3s.4d. for the aldermans fee. 3s.4d for the dees fee. 3s.4d. for the clerkes fee. 8d. for the porters fee. 2s.0d. for the chapleyns fee. 1s.4d for the sexteyns fee. *In toto*   14s. 0d.

Delivered to Careles.

Item for the provision of woode for the gaiole   £1 0s. 0d.

Cage and Hornyngold

Item for the releif of the poore in bothe parishes   £6 13s. 4d.

Careles, Bronwyn

Item for the reparacions of bothe the churches, *videlicet,* to either churche £1 0s.0d.   £2 0s. 0d.

Item allowed more to the clerke for a new paper booke to enter the accomptes in[31]   1s. 8d.

Item allowed more unto the dee above the ordynaire some of £4 0s.0d. for diverse respectes \<deletion\> \thought good unto the company/   £2 13s. 4d.

---

[27] For investment by bond, see Introduction, p.lx. Thomas Carre may have been the wealthy yeoman of Bury St Edmunds who died in 1590. Although this identification is only tentative, the witnesses of his will included Edmund Inglethorpe, who was for some years the beadle or the porter of the hall, Thomas Spittlehouse, bailiff of Thingoe Hundred, and his wife, Margaret, who worked as a scrivener and wrote this will. For Carre's will see IC500/2/4, f.349v.

[28] This property has not yet been identified.

[29] See Introduction, p.xxxii.

[30] See Glossary for the use of 'super' in these accounts.

[31] This records the purchase of the book in which these accounts are entered.

Delivered to ~~Careles~~ Coksedge

Item for the relief of the poore in the spittell £1 0s. 0d.

    Summa totalis allocacionis predice £19 2s.3d.

    Et sic in surplusagio £8 2s.0¾d. And paid more to Baylif Skott,
    Bayliff of the Hundred of Thingo, for the rent of a tenement next
    unto the Guyldehall due for 2 yeres at Michelmas laste, 7s.0d.

    Et sic in surplusagio £8 9s.0¾d.

[*f.5r.*] 1571

Which surplusag'[32] is paid unto hym owte of the coffer uppon the determynacion of
this accompte, excepte the £1 0s.0d. which resteth upon Mr Heighams hed and
Mr Peytons untill the next accompte.

Ambrose Jermyn	Tho: Badby	Thomas Andrews
Francis Boldero	Wyllm. Tassell	Anthony Payne
Thomas Peyton	Jamys Wright	Willm. Hill
Robarte Brunwyn	Wyllm Axton	John Cutteris
Robert Mlyes [*sic*]	H[*enry*] H[*orningold*]	Thomas Gooderyche

Memorandum that at this accompte the Decre of the Exchequer concernynge the
preistes wages was deliverd unto Mr Andrewes.[33]

                 By me Thomas Andrews

[*f.5v.*] At Candlemas *anno* 1572 [*3*]

**The londes and tenementes sometyme John Smithe, esquier, Mrs Odhams,
Hepworthe, and William Tassell, gentleman**

**Th'accompte of William Tassell, gentleman, Henry Horningeolde, William
Axten and Thomas Cockesage, surveyors or collectors of the saide londes taken
the seconde daie of Februar[*y*] beinge Candelmas daie *anno* 1572[*/3*] for one
hole yere ended at Michelmes last past**

Arreragia nulla

Onus

First the saide accomptantes do yelde th'accompte of £8 1s.4d. by them receyved
    within the saide tyme of their accompte of th'issues and profittes of the mannor
    londes and tenementes in Hepworthe as by the rentall theareof yt doethe appeare.
    And of £7 18s.8d. of th'issues and proffites of the londes and tenementes late
    William Tassel, gentleman, as by the rental theareof yt doethe appeare. And also
    of £18 15s.0d of th'issues and proffites of the londes and tenementes late or
    sometyme John Smithe, esquier, Mrs Od[*eha*]ms and others in Bury St Edmunde
    and other townes adjoy[n]inge

    Summa £34 15s.0d.

The saide accomptantes do yelde accompte of £8 13s.4d. for serten woode and
    tymbere by them solde oute of the landes and tenementes aforesaide. And also of
    £2 0s.0d. receyved by them of Futter

    Summa £10 13s.4d.

    Summa totalis oneris predicte £45 8s.4d., *unde*

---

[32] For this usage see Glossary and Introduction, p.lviii.
[33] See Introduction, p.xxxix.

Allocacio

The saide accomptauntes do aske to be allowed of 8s.5½d. for serten owte rentes goeinge owte of the londes and tenementes in Hepworthe as by the rental doethe appeare. And also of 6s.1d. likewise paied oute of the londes and tenementes of William Tassell, gentleman, as by the rental doethe appeare. And of £1 3s.6½d. paied oute of the londes and tenementes of John Smythe, esquier, and others in Bury and other townes adjoyninge to the same as likewise maye appeare. And of 6d. *per annum* for the rent of a pece of grounde nowe in th'occupacion of Anthony Payne, gentleman, now in suspens for a serten tyme by reason of an extenthe made of the same emonges other londes and tenementes uppon the Statute of Recovery of Debtes by one Thomas Bacon, cytizen and salter of London, after the deathe of Nicholas Platte.[34] And of 15s.0d. for the fee of the saide accomptantes for collectinge the saide rentes

> *Summa huius allocacionis* £2 13s.7d. Note
> that the castel warde rent is not allowed in this accompte
> because it is not payed

And also the saide accomptantes do praie allowance of serten rentes and other chardges paied oute, *videlicet*, in rentes £1 16s.1½d., and in reparacions and for the taske[35] and other chardges, as doethe appeare in a bill of parcells, £24 1s.7d.. And of £2 4s.0d. for reparacions of th'Aungell. And of 4s.0d. for a copie holde at Catsall by them paied as in the saide bill

> *Summa huius allocacionis* £28 5s.8½d.
> *Summa totalis allocacionis* £30 19s.3½d.
> *Et debent* £14 9s.0½d. *solutum aldermanno super determinacionem huius compoti, et quietus.*

[*f.6r.*]

The newe purchased londes

Th'accompte of Thomas Kytson and Frauncis Boldero, esquiers, collectors of the londes aforesaide made and taken the daye and yere aforesaide

Arreragia nulla

Onus

The saide accomptantes do yelde their accompte of £16 5s.8d. of th'issues and proffites of the saide londes by them receyved within the tyme of their accompte

> *Summa totalis oneris predicte* £16 5s.8d., *unde*

Allocacio

The same accomptantes do praie allowaunce of £10 0s.0d. paied for the taske, over and besides £14 0s.0d. paied by Henry Hornigeolde for the same. And of £1 5s.8d. paied to Edmonde Boldero, Mr Andrewes man, for wrightinge of serten evidences belonginge to the Gildehalle or fellowship.[36] And of £2 5s.11d. for reparacions laied uppon the pillory by Robert Brownyne, one of this company.[37]

---

[34] Tassell had bought the land which he gave to the town from Nicholas Platt, Woodward's Register, H1/6/1, p.125. See also n.25 above.

[35] This word is invariably used for the tax known as tenths and fifteenths.

[36] There are numerous instances of a clerk or servant of one of the company being employed to prepare legal documents.

[37] In an incorporated town, this would have been the responsibility of the corporation. After Bury St Edmunds was incorporated in 1606, the feoffees still accepted many civic responsibilities.

And of 2s.8d. paied to Mr Freeman, Clarke of the Peace, for a wrightinge made for the saide felloweship.[38] And of 5s.0d. for the fee of the saide collectors.

Summa totalis allocacionis predicte £13 19s.3d.

Et sic debent £2 6s.5d. *solutum aldermanno super determinacionem huius compoti, et quietus.*

The Gyldehalle

Th'accompte of Thomas Cockesage, keper of the Guyldehalle, made and taken the daie and yeare aforesaide

Arreragia

£2 0s.0d. forgotten in his last accompte by his owne confession and by the knowladge of the Company

Onus

The saide accomptante dothe yelde his accompte of 14s.0d. by him received of Thomas Buttery for the rent of 2 parcells of londe and pasture in Rysbegate Strete and at Stannewaye Bridge. And of 1s.0d. received of John White for the farme of a garden plotte at the northe end of the saide halle. And of 1s.0d. received of Robert Cheston for a garden in th'Eastegate Strete. And of 4s.0d. for the halfe yere rent of a tenement, lyinge at the southe end of the halle, deu at the feaste of St Michael th'Archangel last past

Summa huius oneris £1 0s.0d.

And further th'accomptaunte dothe chardge him selfe with receipte of £1 8s.4d. for brydealles kepte in the halle

Summa £1 18s.4d.

Summa totalis huius oneris cum arreragio £4 18s.4d., *unde*

Allocacio

The saide accomptante praiethe allowance for mendinge of the leades aboute the halle 2s.8d. And of 1s.0d. for one daies worke of a ploomer. And of 4d. for mendinge of the glasse wyndeowes. And of 6d. nowe paied (as parcell of the aforesaide chardge) unto the house

Super

And of 14s 0d. for Butteryes rent not received at this accompte.

Summa allocacionis £1 4s.0d. *Et sic debent super determinacionem huius compoti* £3 14s.0d.

[f.6v.]

The aldermans accompte

The accompte of Thomas Cockesage, alderman, made and taken the daye and yere aforesaide

Arreragia nulla

Onus

First the saide accomptante dothe yelde accompte of £5 0s.0d. by him received for the full dischardge of Thomas Carre his obligacion made by Coppyne.[39] And of

---

[38] John Freeman was Clerk of the Peace for the county of Suffolk 1559-1581: Sir Edgar Stephens, *The Clerks of the Counties, 1360–1960* (1961).

[39] See above, n.27.

£2 0s.0d. likewise received in full dischardge of Johnsons house in the Well
Streate, beinge bounde in a re-entre for the same, which is dischardged. And of
£2 6s.5d. likewise received of Thomas Kytson and Fraunces Boldero, esquiers,
for th'accompte of the newe purchased londes. And of £14 9s.0½d. likewise
received of William Tassel, gentleman, Henry Horningeolde, William Axten and
this accomptaunte, surveyors and collectors of the londes and tenementes late
John Smythes and others. And of £3 14s.4d. for the Guyldehalle. And of
£1 0s.0d. received of John Heigham and Thomas Peyton, esquiers, for their
admission into this felloweship. And of 6s.5d. for a tenement, late Broweses, in
Baxter Streate,[40] nowe in the tenure of Nicholas Marshall. And of 1s.6d. by him
receyved of Sir Ambrose Jermyne, knight, beinge paied by Sir Ambrose him
selfe at this accompte for a rent in Hepworthe *per annum* 9d. as appeare [*by*] the
rentall, behinde before this accompte for 2 yeres
> *Summa totalis huius oneris* £28 17s.8½d., *unde*

Allocacio
Super[41]
The saide accomptaunte praiethe allowance of £1 0s.0d. still in th'handes of John
Heigham and Thomas Peyton, esquiers, for their admission into the fellowship
> *Summa* £1 0s.0d.

Fees payed
And of £4 0s.0d. paied to the dee for providinge the dynner. And of 3s.4d. for the
aldermans fee. And of 3s.4d. for the dee his fee. And of 3s.4d. for the clarkes fee.
And of 5s.0d. for the preachers fee. And of 1s.4d.for the sextens fee. And of
1s.0d. for the porters fee. And of 1s.0d. in rewarde to Callowe the baker for his
attendaunce at the halle in service by the space of 2 daies
> *Summa* £4 18s.4d.

To Careles
And for the provision of woode for the gaole	£1	0s.	0d.

Cage and Horningeolde
Item for the reliefe of the poore in bothe the parishes	£6	13s.	4d.

Careles and Brownyne
Item for the reperacions of bothe the churches, *videlicet* for each parishe £1 0s.0d.	£2	0s.	0d.

Careles
Item for the relyefe of the poore in the almes house called the Spyttle House	£1	0s.	0d.
And of rentes and arrerages paied to Sir Ambrose Jermyne, knighte[42]		8s.	8d.
Item for paper at this accompte			1d.

> *Summa huius allocacionis cum super* £17 0s.5d.

[*f. 7r.*] *Adhuc allocacio*
The saide accomptaunte demaunedethe allowaunce of £8 6s.11d. laied up in the
house at this presente accompte
> *Summa huius allocacionis* £8 6s.11d.
> *Summa totalis allocacionis* £25 7s.4d.
> *Et debent super determinacionem huius compotis* £3 10s.4½d.

---

[40] At this period Garland Street and Baxter Street were used interchangeably for the streets now called
Garland Street and Lower Baxter Street.
[41] See Glossary.
[42] The out-rent for Leyers must have been paid directly to Sir Ambrose Jermyn, who was present at the
account this year.

Per me Ambrose Jermyn	Jo: Heigham	Thomas Badby
Thomas Peyton	Anthony Payne	Steven Hayward
John Boldero	Jamys Wryte	Wyllm. Axton
Willm. Hill	Thomas Cocksadge	

[*f. 7v.*] At Candelmas *anno Domini* 1573[*4*]
The londes and tenementes sometyme John Smythe, esquier, Mrs Odhams, Hepworthe and William Tassell, gentleman

Th'accompte of Henry Horningeolde, William Axten, Thomas Cocksage and James Wrighte taken the seconde daie of February, beinge Candelmas daye, *anno* 1573 [*4*] for one hole yere ended at Michelmes last past

Arreragia nulla

Onus
First the saide accomptantes do yelde accompte of £8 1s.4d. by them receyved within the saide tyme of their accompte of th'issues and proffites of the mannor, londes and tenementes in Hepworthe, as by the rentall therof yt dothe appeare. And of £10 8s.8d. for th'issues and profites of the londes and tenementes late William Tassell, gentleman, as by the rental theareof yt dothe appeare. And also of £18 15s.0d. for th'issues and profites of the londes and tenementes sometyme John Smythe, esquyer, Mrs Odhams and others in Bury St Edmonde and other townes adjoyninge
> *Summa totalis redditum predictorum* £37 15s.0d.

The saide accomptantes do yelde accompte of £4 0s.0d. by them receyved of John Cole for a pece of grounde solde to him by deade, from the hole fellowship[43]
> *Summa* £4 0s.0d.
> *Summa totalis oneris predicte* £41 15s.0d., *unde*

Allocacio
The saide accomptantes do aske to be allowed of 13s.8¼d. for rentes resolutes together with the fee of the collector, goeinge owte of the londes and tenementes in Hepworthe as by the rentall dothe appeare. And of 11s.1d. for rentes resolutes together with the fee of the collector goeinge owte of the londes and tenementes of William Tassell, gentleman, as by the rentall dothe appeare. And of £1 8s.6½d. for rentes resolutes together with the fee of the collector owte of the londes and tenementes of John Smythe, esquyer, and others in Bury and other townes adjoyninge to the same, as likewise may appeare. And of 6d. *per annum* for the rent of a pece of grounde, nowe in th'occupacion of Anthony Payne, gentleman, and in suspens for a serten tyme, by reason of an extenthe made of the same, emonges other londes and tenementes, uppon the Statute of Recovery of Debtes by one Thomas Bacon, citizen and salter of London, after the deathe of Nicolas Platt. And of 2s.2d. for the farme of a stalle with a garden in Punche Lane solde nowe to James Cole
> *Summa huius allocacionis* £2 15s.11¾d.
> Note that the castel warde rent is not allowed in this
> accompte because it is not payed

---

[43] A stable or tenement with a garden adjoining in Punch, now Athenaeum, Lane, was part of Tassell's gift, Woodward's Register, H1/6/1, p.124. Woodward implied that it had been exchanged rather than sold. It is described as a stall when the rent was accounted for under the heading *allocatio*.

And also the saide accomptantes do pray allowance of £23 18s.5¼d. for serten reparacions done aboute the halle, and other necessarie chardges by them laied oute, as appeared at this accompte by a severall byll of parcells. And also of £13 16s.5½d. likewise for reparacions aboute the allmes houses (as likewyse appeared). And of 7s.6d. for 6 spynninge wheles boughte for poore folkes that ware not hable to set them selves on worke

> *Summa huius allocacionis* £38 2s.5¾d.
> *Summa totalis allocacionis predicte* £40 18s.5½d.
> *Et debent* 16s.6½d. *solutum aldermanno super determinacionem huius compoti, et eque.*

[*f.8r.*] The newe purchased londes

Th'accompte of Frauncis Boldero, esquyer, and William Hyll, collectors of the landes aforesaide made and taken the daye and yere aforesaide

Arreragia nulla

Onus

The saide accomptantes do yelde accompte of £16 5s.8d. by them receyved of th'issues and proffites of the saide newe purchased londes within the saide tyme of their accompte

> *Summa totalis oneris predicte* £15 5s.8d., *unde*

Allocacio

The saide accomptantes do praye allowance of 5s.0d. for the fee of the collectors. And of £3 1s.4d. for serten money payed to William Carter, the carpenter, for worke done aboute the towne house.

> *Summa huius allocacionis* £3 6s.4d.

Super

Memorandum the £1 5s.8d. is answered in *anno* 1575.

The saide accomptants do praie allowance of serten rentes not gathered at this accompte, *videlicet*: of Anne Barbor £1 5s.8d. And of John Jellowe 2s.0d. And of Sir William Cordell, knighte, 13s.4d.

> *Summa huius allocacionis* £2 1s.0d.
> *Summa totalis allocacionis* £5 7s.4d.
> *Et debent super determinacionem huius compoti* £10 18s.4d.

The Gylde Hall

Th'accompte of James Wrighte, gentleman, made and taken the daye and yere aforesaide

Arreragium

For Butryes rent dependinge in super in the last yeres accompte for the Gylde Hall as yt maye appeare 14s.0d.

> *Arreragium patet*

Onus

The saide accomptante do chardge him selfe for mony receyved for serten bridalles kepte at the saide hall, sythens the last accompte, as appeared by a byll of particulers showed at this accompte to the some of £3 8s.4d.

> *Summa oneris cum arreragio* £4 2s.4d., *unde*

Allocacio

The saide accomptante dothe praie allowaunce of a byll of chardges done aboute mendinge of necessarie thinges belonginge to the saide halle as appeared by the bill to the somme of 8s.9d.

> *Summa huius allocacionis patet*

Super

The saide accomptaunte do praie allowance of serten mony deu for mariages in the saide house not yet receyved *videlicet*: of [*space*] Hamonde, 5s.0d., of [*space*] Sir Ambrose Jermyns man, 5s.0d. and of [*space*] Mr John Highams man, 5s.0d.[44]

> *Summa huius allocacionis* 15s.0d.
>
> *Summa totalis allocacionis predicte* £1 3s.9d.
>
> *Et debet* £2 18s.7d. *solutum aldermanno super determinacionen huius compoti, et eque.*

[f. 8v.] The annuytie geven by Edmonde Jermyne, esquyer, of Debden

Th'accompte of Thomas Andrews, esquyer, of the mony receyved for the saide annuytie made and taken the daye and yere afoaresaide[45]

Onus

The saide accomptaunte dothe chardge him selfe with the receipte of the saide annuytie the 10th daie of October last past, by the handes of Philip Barrowe, physicyan,[46] and due the 20th daie of July then last past, for the first payment due for one hole yere ended the saide 20th daye of July, £20 0s.0d.

> *Summa oneris predicte ut patet* £20 0s.0d., *unde*

Allocacio

The saide accomptaunte praiethe allowance for the halfe yeres annuytye due the saide 20th daie of July and paied to John Jermyne, esquyer,[47] as appearethe by his acquyttance dated the 21th of October last past, which is to the some of £10 0s.0d. And of £1 9s.2d. by him laide oute for the assueraunce of the saide annuytie, as appeared by a severall bill of accompte. And of £4 6s.8d. by him laied oute for serten chardges of necessarie thinges bestowed uppon the almes house or hospitall as apeared likewise[48]

> *Summa totalis allocacionis* £15 15s.10d.
>
> *Et debet super determinacionem huius compoti*
>
> £4 4s.2d. *solutum aldermanno, et eque.*

The alderman his accompte

Th'accompte of Sir Nicholas Bacon, knighte, Lord Keper of the Greate Seale of Inglonde, by th'handes of James Wrighte, gentleman, his deputie, made and taken the daie and yere aforesaide[49]

Arreragio £3 10s.4½d. uppon Thomas Coksage

The saide accomptante dothe chardge himselfe with £11 0s.0d. unto him paied by th'handes of Robert Browninge in full dischardge of the sale of a tenement and a

---

[44] The names noted here of those who paid for marriages at the Guildhall suggest that it may have been made available only to members of the company and their servants.

[45] For Jermyn's gift see Appendix 8, *sub* 1573 and Introduction, p.xxxiii.

[46] For Philip Barrow, see Notes on People.

[47] John Jermyn, Edmund Jermyn's half brother, received an annuity of £10 *per annum* throughout his life.

[48] For the Hospital see Introduction, p.xxxvii.

[49] Sir Nicholas Bacon's duties as Lord Keeper would have kept him in London; hence he served his office as alderman by deputy. See Notes on People for both Sir Nicholas Bacon and James Wright.

pece of grounde in Burntegovel Lane.[50] And also dothe yelde accompte of 16s.6½d. by him receyved for th'issues and proffittes of the londes and tenementes late John Smithes, esquier, and other of Henrie Horningeolde, William Axten, Thomas Cocksage and James Wrighte. And of £10 18s.4d. likewise received of Frauncis Boldero and William Hill for the new purchased londes. And of £2 18s.7d. likewise received of James Wrighte for the proffites of the Gyldehall. And of £4 4s.2d. likewise received of Thomas Andreus, esquier, remayninge uppon his accompte for th'annuytie of Edmonde Jermyne, esquier. And of £1 0s.0d. likewise received of John Higham and Thomas Peyton, esquyers, for their admission into the fellowship

> *Summa oneris cum arreragio recepto et soluto*
> £34 8s.0d., *unde*

Allocacio

The saide accomptante dothe praie allowaunce of £10 18s.4d. still in th'handes of Frauncis Boldero and William Hyll for the newe purchased londes. And of £1 0s.0d. still in th'handes of John Hygham and Thomas Peyton

> *Summa huius allocacionis* £11 18s.4d.

The saide accomptante dothe praie allowaunce of £5 0s.0d. layed owte for corne for the provision of the poore within the towne of Bury St Edmonde. And of £1 17s.4d. for serten chardges in th'interteyninge of the saide Lorde Keper uppon Henowe Heathe the last sommer as appeared by a severall bill of chardges.[51] And of 10s.6d. for the porter his lyvery. And of 6s.0d. geven to Roodinges wife for her reliefe and her children. And of 17s.4d. for certen cariages of stone and sande by Frogge as likewise appeared by a bill[52]

> *Summa huius allocacionis* £8 11s.2d.

[*f.9r.*] *Adhuc allocacio*
Fees paied

And of £4 0s.0d. to the dee for providinge the dynner. And of 3s.4d. for th'aldermans fee. And of 3s.4d. for the dees fee. And of 3s.4d. for the clarkes fee. And of 5s.0d. for the preachers fee. And of 2s.0d. to the curate of St Maries parishe. And of 1s.4d. to the sexten. And of 1s.0d. for the porters fee. And of 10s.0d. paied to Robert Adams for th'ingrossinge of the rules and articles of the house nowe agreed uppon[53]

> *Summa huius allocacionis* £5 9s.4d.

To Careles

And for provision of woode for gaole   £1 0s. 0d.

---

[50] This property was probably the messuage lately occupied by Kiseing which formed part of Tassell's gift, Woodward's Register, H1/6/1, p.125.

[51] The Lord Keeper visited Bury St Edmunds in the course of a journey or even a virtual progress in the summer of 1573, beginning on the day after midsummer. He intended travelling to Sir Robert Chester's that day, and on the following day to Lord North's. On the Saturday his journey was from Lord North's house at Kirtling, just over the county boundary in Cambridgeshire, to Redgrave and that is when he would have passed through Bury St Edmunds. The assizes were held at Henhowe, to the north of the town, near Thingoe Hill, until they moved into the town at about this time. James Wright, who acted as Bacon's deputy as alderman was asked to provide a hogshead of claret against his coming to Redgrave. I am indebted to Diarmaid MacCulloch for bringing to my attention Joseph Regenstein Library, Chicago University, Redgrave Bacon Letter 4127 which provides this information.

[52] An entry in the burial Register of St James's church states that Frog's son and his man, who were 'slayne at the clay pitts', were buried 9 August 1583.

[53] These ordinances have not survived among the records of the Guildhall feoffees.

Cage and Horningeolde
And for serten frizes to relyve the poore in bothe parishes   £6 13s. 4d.
Memorandum **this was layed oute in fryses and answered by the**
  saide parties *anno* **1572.**

James Wrighte and Browninge
And for reparacions in bothe the churches, *videlicet*, in eche parishes
£1 0s.0d.   £2   0s   0d.

To Carles
And for the reliefe of the poore in th'almes house called the spitellhouse   £1   0s.   0d.
   Summa huius allocacionis £10 13s.4d.
   Summa totalis tote allocacionis £36 12s.2d.
   Et sic in surplusagio £2 4s.2d., whereof

Super
Allowed for th'arrerages of £3 10s.4d. still in th'handes of Thomas Cocksage

Money owte of the treashr'
Memorandum theare was taken owte to dischardge paiements owte of the commen
  treash'[54] £1 6s.2d., *et sic eque.*

Ambros Jermyn	Thomas Badby	Thomas Peyton
John Chetham	Anthony Payne	William Hill
Hen: Collyng	Robert Brunwyn	John Boldero
John Cutteris	W. Axton	Thomas Gooderych

[*f.9v*]   At Candelmas *anno Domini* 1574[5]
**The mannor of Brettes and other londes and tenementes in Hepworthe, certen
londes and tenementes sometyme John Smythes, esquyer, Margaret Odham,
Elene Fishe, Adam Newhawe and John Salter, and serten mesuages londes and
tenementes late William Tassell, gentleman, and others in Bury and other
townes adioyninge**

**Th'accompte of Thomas Badby, esquyer, James Wrighte and Anthony Payne,
gentleman, surveyors and collectors of the saide mannors londes and
tenementes made and taken the daie and yere aforesaide for one hole yere than
ended**

Arreragia nulla

Onus
The said accomptantes do yelde their accompte of £8 1s.4d. by them received within
  the saide tyme of their accompte of th'issues and revenewes of the saide mannor
  of Bretes and other the londes and tenementes in Hepworthe as by the rentall
  therof yt dothe appere. And of £18 15s.0d. of th'issues and revenewes of the
  saide londes and tenementes sometyme John Smythes, esquyer, and others, as by
  the rentals of the same londes yt dothe likewise appeare. And also of £10 19s.8d.
  by them receyved of th'issues and revenewes of the saide mesuage, londes and

---

[54] This word obviously means the coffer in the room above the porch in which surplus money was kept,
but it is not clear whether the clerk who entered this account meant treasure or treasury; either could be
used for a place or container in which valuables were kept at this date.

tenementes late William Tassell, gentleman, and others as by the rental of the same yt dothe also appeare

Summa totalis of the hole chardge aforesaide £37 16s.0d., whereof

Allocacio

The saide accomptantes do pray allowance of 8s.0½d. by them disbursed for serten owte rentes goeinge owte of the saide mannor of Bretes and other the londes and tenementes in Hepworthe. And of 7d. for castell warde rent payed to the mannor of Bardewell after 2¾d. for every 20ᵗⁱᵉ wekes. And also of 5s.0d. for th'accomptantes fee for the same londes. And of £1 3s.6½d. for the owte rentes goeinge owte of the said londes and tenementes sometyme John Smythe, esquyer, Margeret Odham and others as by the rentals therof dothe appeare. And of 8s.0d. for rent decayed for a shoppe and a seller, parcell of the same londes solde to Robert Brownyne. And also of 5s.0d. for th'accomptantes fee of the same londes. And of 6s.1d. for tenthes and owte rentes goeinge owte of Mr Tassels londes as appearethe by the rental. And of 3d. payed owte of the tenementes late Browses to [space].⁵⁵ And of 5s.0d. for th'accomptantes fee for the collection of the same. And of £1 6s.8d. payed to George Atherton, servaunte to the house, for his yeres wages ended at Michelmas last past. And of £6 13s.4d. appoyncted to be layed owte towardes the repayringe of Yearmothe Haven, beinge chardged to be levyed uppon th'inha[b]ytantes of this towne of Bury.⁵⁶ And of 15s.10d. laied owte at thre severall tymes for the relyefe of serten poore children within the said towne of Bury. And of £8 6s.11d. delyvered at 7 severall tymes to Henry Hornigolde, Robert Carles and Thomas Goderiche for the reliefe and kepinge of dyvers poore children beinge borne within the towne. And of £1 6s.9d. [f.10r] Adhuc alloc[acio] allowed to Roger Potter for serten reparacions done this yere uppon the Aungell, as apperethe by his bill of parcells therof. And of 6d. not to be payed at this accompte for the Wydowe Cheston⁵⁷

Summa totalis of all the saide allowances £21 11s.11d.

And so in debet £16 4s.1d., which is payed to the alderman upon the determynacion of this accompte, and so even.

The newe purchased londes and anuyty of Mr Edmonde Jermyne, esquyer

Th'accompte of William Hill and Robert Carles, collectors of the saide londes and tenementes made and taken the daye and yere aforesaide

Arreragio

The saide accomptantes do chardge them with £10 18s.4d. by them receyved of Mr Frauncis Boldero for the super remayninge uppon his headde as maye appeare in the last yeres accompte

Onus

The saide accomptantes do yelde accompte of £16 5s.8d. by them receyved of th'issues and proffites of the saide newe purchased londes within the saide tyme of their accompte, as by the rental therof dothe appeare. And of £40 0s.0d. by

---

⁵⁵ For Browse's gift see Appendix 8, sub 1558.
⁵⁶ The completion of Yarmouth haven was a matter of great concern at this time. A letter from the Privy Council to the Sheriff and Justices of Suffolk dated 24 May 1573 required them 'to use some meanes to procure contribucion of the countrey to the towne of Yarmouth for the finishing of their haven', PRO (CSPD VIII, 1571–1575).
⁵⁷ The feoffees leased a garden at Sparrow Hill in Eastgate Street to Barbara Cheston in 1574, H1/3/6.

them receyved of Sir Ambrose Jermyne, knighte, for the anuytie geven by Mr Edmonde Jermyne, esquyer, for one hole yere ended the 20^tie daie of July last past And of £6 0s.0d. by them receyved of Mr Anthony Payne[58]

Summa totalis of the hole chardge with th'arrerage £73 4s.0d.

Allocacio

The saide accomptantes do pray allowance of £20 0s.0d. for the yerely anuytie payed to Mr John Jermyne of Debden, esquyer, and due to him for one hole yere ended the 20^tie daie of July last past as apperethe by his acquytance. And of 18s.6d. for one pounde of pepper and one suger loffe geven to my Lorde Chefe Justyce at th'assises in sommer last past. And of 5s.0d. for serten breade geven to the poore at the deceasse of Thomas Cage. And of 5s.0d. for the fee of the saide accomptantes. And of £13 14s.0½d. for serten reparacions done at the poore hospitall of Bury as appered by a bill of parcells. And of £10 17s.4½d. for serten mony bestowed and geven to the poore as appeared by a byll of parcells. And of £19 2s.5d. for serten reparacions done uppon the common halle as appeared by a bill of parcells. And of £7 19s.8d. for serten mony layed owte for nurssinge of serten poore children, wekely, as by a bill of parcells likewise ded appeare

torne over

[f.10v.] Summa totalis of the hole allowaunce £73 2s.0d.

And so the saide accomptantes owe uppon the determynacion of their accompte 2s.0d., which is payed to the alderman, and so even.

The Guylde or Common Hall

Th'accompte of Robert Carles made and taken the daye and yere aforesaide.

Arreragio

The arrerages of 14s.0d. in the last yeres accompte for Butreys rent was payed by th'andes of Henry Horningeolde, and so taken by the consent of all the company, and therfor nulla

Onus

The saide accomptante dothe chardge him selfe with £1 3s.4d. for mony receyved by him for the keppinge of serten brydals in the saide hall, as appered particularly to be receyved of dyvers men in a severall bill of parcells

Sum[m]e of this chardge £1 3s.4d. Payed to the alderman uppon the determynacion of this accompte, and so even.

The alderman his accompte

Th'accompte of James Wright, gentleman, made and taken the daie and yere aforesaide

Arreragio

Memorandum this mony was not geven but paied by this accompte

The arrerages of £3 10s.4½d. dependinge uppon Thomas Cocksage is by the consent of the hole company geven and pardoned therfor

Arreragio nulla

---

58 See Notes on People.

Onus

The saide accomptante do chardge him selfe with £16 4s.1d. received by him at the handes of Thomas Badby, esquyer, and Anthony Payne, gentleman, for th'issues and proffites clerly growinge of the londes and tenementes of the manor of Bretes, John Smithes, \esquyer/, and others, as in th'ende of the saide accompte dothe playnly appeare. And with 2s.0d. likewise receyved of William Hill and Robert Carles, accomptants for the newe purchased londes, and for the annuytie of Mr Edmonde Jermyne, esquyer. And with £1 3s.4d. likewise received of Robert Carles for th'use of brydalls in the commen hall. And with £20 0s.0d. likewise receyved for the [*f.11r.*] *Adhuc onus* bonde of Thomas Cocksage. And with £1 0s.0d. geven by William Hill in consideracion of £20 0s.0d. payed to him for Waltons house before his daie of the due therof

> Sum[*me*] of th'aldermans chardge £38 9s.5d., whereof

Allocacio

The saide alderman prayethe allowance of £19 0s.0d. payed to William Hill for Waltons house, for the which a release was made from Mr Groome for all paymentes due for the saide house, and Mr Collinge, Robert Carles and Robert Browneyne do stonde bownde for the payment of £10 0s.0d. to William Hill at Pentecost *anno Domini* 1577.[59] And of £4 0s.0d. for the dynner payed to the dee this yere. And of 3s.4d. for th'aldermans fee. And of 3s.4d. for the dees fee. And of 3s.4d. for the clarkes fee. And of 5s.0d. for the preachers fee. And of 2s.0d. for the curate or mynister. And of 1s.4d. for the sexten. And of 1s.0d. for the porter. And of 13s.4d. for the porters lyvery. And of 10s.0d. paied to Mrs Stone for healinge of Bekons daughter.[60] And of 15s.0d. for other chardges of the saide Becons daughter. And of £1 0s.0d. to Henry Horningolde for placinge of Martynes sonne, beinge bownde prentyse to one [*space*] Roades, a shoemaker in the Churchegate Strete. And of £2 7s.0d. payed to Jaffery Talbot for serten seelinge in the commen hall And of £1 0s.0d. for a hogeshedde of beere geven to the judges at the last assises[61]

In th'handes of Robert Carles

And for the nurse children unlikely to be paied	£3	4s.	2d.
The provision of the gaole	£1	0s.	0d.
The Spittlehouse	£1	0s.	0d.

James Wright and Brownyne

The reparacions of the churches	£2	0s.	0d.
And for paper			4d.

> Summe of th'allowance £37 8s.6d.
> And so th'alderman owethe £1 0s.11d.

Super

Memorandum theare is layed into the treshry one spone, 2 ounces, geven by Henry Collinge, gentleman, at his admission into the fellowship.[62]

---

[59] This property has not been identified.

[60] For Margaret Oliver *alias* Stone, see Notes on People and Introduction, p.lxv.

[61] Throughout these accounts there are many instances of gifts of food and drink to the judges who visited the town for the assizes.

[62] In this instance, instead of money a spoon must have been given as the fee on Collin's admission to the company.

Thomas Badby	Thomas Peyton	Steven Haward
Anthony Payne	W. Axton	Henry Collynges
Willm. Hill	Robert ~~Roberte~~ Brunwyn	H.H.[*in different hand*]
		Harry Hornyggold
Thomas Gooderyche	John Boldero	Thomas Coksedges marke.[63]

[f.11v] Candelmas *anno Domini* 1575[*6*]
The londes and tenementes in Hepworthe, certen londes and tenementes sometyme John Smithes, esquyer, and others, certen londes and tenementes sometyme William Tassell, gentleman, and the annuytie of Mr Edmonde Jermyne, esquyor

Th'accompte of Thomas Badby, esquyor, Anthony Payne and Frauncis Boldero, gentleman and Robert Brownewyne, surveyors and collectors of the saide londes and tenementes with the annuytie aforesaide, made and taken the daie and yere aforesaide for one hole yere at Michelmas last past

Arreragia nulla

Onus
The saide accomptantes do yelde their accompte of £8 1s.4d. by them received within the saide tyme of their accompte of th'issues and revenewes in Hepworthe as by the rentall dothe appeare. And of £18 7s.0d. of th'issues and revenewes of John Smithe, esquyor, and others as by the rentall of the same londes dothe likewise appeare. And of £10 15s.8d. of th'issues and proffites of the londes and tenementes Mr Tassells as by the rentall dothe also appeare. And of £40 0s.0d. beinge a yerelie rent of annuytie geven by the saide Edmonde Jermyne, esquyor, to the feoffes of this companye or felloweshippe. And of £1 0s.0d. of them receyved of one [*space*] Murrell for serten pollardes by him beinge felled of the towne grownde
Summa totalis of the hole chardge aforesaide £78 4s.0d., whereof

Allocacio
The saide accomptantes do praie allowance of 13s.8¼d. for certen owte rentes yerelie payable owte of the saide londes in Hepworthe duringe the saide yere. And of £1 8s.6½d. for certen owte rentes likewise owte of Mr Smithes londes duringe the saide yere. And of 11s.4d. for the like rentes paieable likewise oute of Mr Tassells londes. And of £20 0s.0d. for the yerelie annuytie payed to Mr John Jermyne, esquyor, of Debden and due to him for one hole yere ended the 20^{tie} daie of July last past as appearethe by his acquytaunce. And of £14 1s.6½d. for dyvers somes of mony payed and layed owte by the saide accomptantes in the repayringe of the allmoes houses in the Garlonde Strete[64] in Bury, as by a bill of particularities maie appeare. And of £7 10s.8d. for mony geven to the poore and other chardges as by a bill particularly likewise appeare

---

[63] There were two men of this name, one of whom signed and the other made his mark. See Notes on People.
[64] The feoffees had two blocks of almshouses in Garland Street, Bereve's which stood on the site of the Baptist Chapel and Browse's which, as rebuilt after the 1608 fire, still stand and are now private houses, the present nos. 7 and 8.

Summa totalis of all the saide allowaunces £44 5s.9¼d.
and so in debt £33 18s.2¾d. *solutum* to th'alderman uppon
the determynacion of this accompte and so even.

[*f.12r.*]
The newe purchased londe

Th'accompte of Robert Careles and Thomas Gooderiche, collectors of the saide londes and tenementes made and taken the ~~th~~ daie and yere aforesaide

Arreragia nulla

Onus

The saide accomptantes do yelde accompte of £16 5s.8d. by them receyved of the issues and proffites of the saide londes within the tyme of their accompte for one hole yere at Michelmas last past as by the rentall dothe appeare. And of £3 4s.2d. by them receyved (towardes the relieffe of the pore) of this company. And of £4 0s.0d. by them likewise receyved of Robert Brownyne likewise for the relyeffe of the poore[65]

Summa of the hole chardge £23 9s.10d., whereof

Allocacio

The saide accomptantes do praie allowaunce for certen mony by them layed owte wekely for the relieffe of dyvers pore orphanes within this towne of Bury, as appearethe by a boke of wekely distribucion, to the somme of £24 17s.10½d. And of 6s.8d. for a rent not receyved of Sir William Cordell, knight, parcell of th'above saide rentall.[66] And of 12s.2d. by them layed owte aboute certen necessarie causes, together with the collectors fee, as by a bill of parcells appeared uppon this accompte

Summa of all the allowances £25 16s.8½d. and so remain due to thes accomptantes £2 6s.10½d. which thaie are payed at the tyme of this accompte by th'alderman as appearethe in the fote of the next accompte.

The Guylde or Common Hall

Th'accompte of Robert Careles for the proffites of the saide hall made and taken the daie and yere aforesaide

Onus

The saide accomptante dothe chardge him selfe with £4 5s.4d. for mony by him receyved for the kepeinge of certen brydalls theare as appeared particularly to be receyved of divers men in a bill of parcells

Summa £4 5s.4d. paied to the alderman upon the determynacion of this accompte. *Et debet* over and besides £2 6s.10½d. allowed him in th'accompte of the newe purchased londes, as theare dothe appeare, £1 18s.5½d. *solutum aldermanno*[67]

---

[65] Despite these special gifts for the poor, nothing indicates that this was either a very dear year, or that the town was suffering an epidemic.

[66] As soon becomes apparent, Sir William Cordell was in the process of buying this land in Long Melford.

[67] It is not clear whether alderman was intended to be in English or Latin.

[*f. 12v.*]
The alderman his accompte

Th'accompte of Thomas Badby, esquyer, alderman this yere

Arreragia

£1 0s.11d. oweinge by James Wrighte, gentleman, as appearethe in the fote of the aldermans accompte the last yere

Onus

The saide accomptante is chardged with £33 18s.2¾d. by him receyved of Anthony Payne, Robert Brownyne and Frauncis Boldero for the issues and proffites clerely groweinge owte of the londes and tenementes of Hepworthe, John Smithes, esquyor and others as in the ende of their accompte dothe appeare. And with £1 18s.5½d. by him receyved of Robert Careles clerely cominge owte of the new purchased londes and the proffites of the common hall as in the saide accomptes dothe appeare. And with 8s.8d. of him receyved of William Hill in parte of a super dependinge uppon upon Anne Barber in the saide William his accompte in *anno* 1573, the residue of the saide super beinge accompted for as parcell of Robert Careles and Thomas Gooderiches accompte, within suche somes as thaie receyved to the use of the pore and other causes as by a severall bill dothe appeare

    Summa totalis of the chardge with th'arrerages £37 6s.3¼d., whereof

Supers £1 0s.11d.

The saide accomptante praiethe allowance of £1 0s.11d. dependinge still uppon James Wrighte, alderman for the last yere, as dothe appeare in the ende of his accompte. And of £4 0s.0d. for the dynner this yere beinge payed to the dee. And of 3s.4d. for th'aldermans fee. And of 3s.4d. for the dees fee. And of 3s.4d. for the clarkes fee. And of 6s.8d. for the preachers fee. And of 2s.0d. for the mynister or curates fee. And of 1s.4d. for the sexten. And of 1s.0d. for the porter. And of 3s.4d. for the cokes fee. And of £1 6s.8d. paied to John Bearcham for the healinge of a pore disseased wenche. And of 13s.4d. to Liechefilde for the healinge of Claydons legge. And of £3 6s.8d. nowe **William Axten** delyvered aforehande to William Axten for the wekely paiment of the nurse children. And of 12s.3½d. for certen chardges of reparacions of glaseinge done by John Powle uppon the houses appoincted for the mynisters of bothe parishes.[68] And of £1 0s.0d. for money geven by the company for the reliefe of Mr Browne, the phisitian.[69] And of £1 0s.0d. for mony geven by the consent of the company this yere to Thomas Cockesage

To Careles

The provision of the Gaolle	£1	0s.	0d.
The Spittell house	£1	0s.	0d.
To James Wright and Thomas Bright, churche wardens			
The reparacions of bothe the churches	£2	0s.	0d.
And for paper for this accompte			4d.

    Summa of all the allowaunces £18 4s.6½d
    Et remanet £19 1s.8¾d.

---

[68] For the ministers' houses see Introduction, p.xxxvi.
[69] See Notes on People for a possible identification of Mr Browne the physician.

[f.13r.]
Mony layed up at this accompte
Memorandum theare remaynethe in the treashry in mony layed up
    together with the aforesaide £19 1s.8¾d., in all to the some of   £26 3s. 8d.

Super
Memorandum this answered in the next accompte.

Memorandum that at the 20^tie daie of January last past theare was
    due by Robert Thorpe, gentleman, for th'annuytie graunted to
    Mr Edmonde Jermyne by the saide Robert Thorpe and geven
    by the saide Mr Edmond Jermyne to the township of Bury for
    one half yere than ended the some of   £20 0s. 0d.

Thomas Browne	Thomas Andrews	Anthony Payne
John Chetham	Thomas Peyton	Hary Collyng
James Wrighte	Robert Caryel	Thomas Gooderyche
John Boldero	Robert Brunwyn	William Hill

[f. 13v.]   At Candelmas *anno Domini* 1576[7]
The londes and tenementes in Hepworthe, John Smithes, esquyor, and others, the londes of William Tassell, gentleman, and the anuytie of Mr Edmonde Jermyn, esquior

Th'accompte of Robert Browneyn for all the saide proffites belonginge to the towneship of Bury St Edmonde for one hole yere at Michelmas last past as folowethe

Arreragia nulla

Onus
The saide accomptante dothe yelde accompte of £8 1s.4d. by him receyved for the
    rentes and proffites of the mannor of Brettes and other mesuages, londes and
    tenementes in Hepworthe as by the rentall of the saide londes may appeare. And
    of £10 15s.8d. by him receyved for the rentes and proffites of Mr Tassels
    tenementes as by the rentall also may appeare. And of £18 7s.0d. likewise
    receyved for the rentes and proffites of the mesuages, londes and tenementes
    sometyme Jankyne Smithes, Mrs Odeham and other, as by the rentall may
    appeare. And of £40 0s.0d. by him receyved beinge a yerely rent of annuytie
    geven by the saide Edmonde Jermyne, esquyor, to the feoffes of this company or
    felloweship. And of £26 3s.8d. by him receyved in redy mony owte of the towne
    house the 20^tie daie of July last past for certen necessarie paymentes in the
    behalfe of the towne of Bury aforesaide, as maie appere in th'allowances of this
    accompte, unto this accomptante[70]
        Summa totalis of the hole chardge aforesaide
        £103 7s.8d., whereof

Allocacio
The saide accomptante dothe praie allowance of 13s.8¼d. for certen owte rentes
    payable owte of the saide londes in Hepworthe, together with 5s.0d. for the fee of

---

[70] Money is here seen being taken from the accumulated balances of the feoffees in the coffer to pay the
fifteenths and tenths on behalf of the town.

the collector, as in the rentall maie appeare. And of 11s.4d. for the rentes and charges owte of Mr Tassels tenementes, with 5s.0d. likewise for the fee of the collector, as in the rentall maie also appeare. And of £1 8s.6½d. for the like rentes payable owte of the londes of the saide Jankyne Smithes, with 5s.0d. also allowed for the fee of the collector, as in the rentall for the same londes maie also appeare. And of 7s.0d. for an owte rent paied to Bayliffe Scotte, goeinge owte of a tenement by the hall in th'occupacion of Thomas Shorte for 2 yeres. And of £2 14s.0d. for dyvers sommes of mony by him layed owte for repayringe of th'Aungell, as by a particular bill ded appeare. And of £6 0s.0d. paied to the handes of William Axten for money geven to the poore, as appeared by the saide William Axtens acquyttance. And of £2 0s.0d. for the porters wages paied by this accomptante. And of £20 0s.0d. paied to Mr John Jermyne, esquior, for his annuytie due for one hole yere the 20^{tie} daie of July last past. And of £24 0s.0d. by this accomptante paied to [*the*] Quenes Majesties collectors for the taske of the towne of Bury, as by the acquyttances maie appeare. And of £1 13s.4d. paied to her Majesties collectors for the subsidie of the towne house of Bury. And of 8d. for 2 aquyttances

    Sum of th'allowances £59 8s.6 d. *et debet*
    £43 19s.1¼d. *solutum aldermanno*

[*f.14r.*]
The newe purchased londes

Th'accompte of Thomas Gooderiche, collector of the saide londes and tenementes made and taken the daie and yere aforesaide

Arreragia nulla

Onus
The saide accomptante dothe yelde accompte of £16 5s.8d. by him receyved of th'issues and proffites of the saide londes within the tyme of his accomte for one hole yere at Michelmas last past, as by the rentall maie appeare. And of £3 0s.0d. by him receyved of John Brighte of Bury, clothier, in part of paiement for one pece of grounde to him solde lyinge in Mr Andrews Strete

    Sum' of the chardge £19 5s.8d., whareof

Allocacio
The saide accomptante praiethe allowance of 13s.4d. to be deducted oute of the chardge of the saide rentall for 4^{or} acres of pasture and one acre and halfe of medowe in Melford beinge solde to Sir William Cordall, knight, Master of the Rolles, for £60 0s.0d. by the company of this fellowship.[71] And of £18 3s.6d. by him layed owte for sondrie causes as appeared by a bill of parcells, together with 5s.0d. for the collectors fee

    Summa of th'allowances £18 16s.10d.,
    et remanet 8s.10d. *solutum aldermanno*

The Guylde or Common Hall

Th'accompte of Robert Careles for the proffites of the saide hall made and taken the daie and yere aforesaide

---

[71] According to the chantry certificate, the guild of St Nicholas held land in Melford, Woodward's Register, H1/6/1, p.73. Edward VI's grant of the guilds and chantries mentions the purchase of this guild and property in Bury, but does not mention land in Melford, *ibid.*, p.88.

Onus

The saide accomptante is chardged with £3 12s.6d. for mony by him received for the kepinge of cearten brydalls theare, as appeared particularly to be receyved of dyvers men by a bill of parcells

Summa patet, whareof

Allocacio

He praiethe allowance for certen reparacions by him layed oute for the common halle 7s.6d., as appeared by a particular bill.

Et remanet £3 5s.0d. *solutum aldermanno*

The aldermans accompte

Th'accompte of Anthony Payne, gentleman, alderman this yere, as folowethe

Onus

The saide accomptante dothe chardge him selfe with £43 19s.1¼d. by him receyved of Robert Browneyn for th'issues and proffites cominge this yere owte of the londes, tenementes and hereditamentes of Jankyne Smithe, Mrs Odeham, the mannor of Bretes, Mr Tassels and th'annuytie of Mr Edmonde Jermyne, esquior, as appearethe in the fote of the same accompte. And with 8s.10d. by him receyved of Thomas Gooderiche for th'issues and proffites of the newe purchased londes. And with £3 5s.0d. by him receyved of Robert Careles for the proffites of the common hall, as in ther severall accomptes dothe appeare. And with £6 13s.4d. by him [*f.14v.*] receyved in parte of payment of £13 6s.8d. for Powles lease,[72] which is agreed by the hole company or felloweship

Summa of the hole chardge £54 6s.3¼d., whareof

Allocacio

Super £30 0s.0d.

The saide accomptante praiethe allowance of £30 0s.0d. paied into Mr Thomas Andrews, esquior, his handes for the purchasinge of Mr Reves londes.[73] And of £4 0s.0d. for the dynner this yere, beinge paied to the dee. And of 3s.4d. for th'aldermans fee. And of 3s.4d. for the dees fee. And of 3s.4d. for the clarkes fee. And of 6s.8d. for the preachers fee. And of 2s.0d. for the mynisters fee. And of 1s.4d. for the sexten. And of 1s.0d. for the porter. And of 3s.4d. for the cokes fee.

To Careles

The provision for the gaole	£1 0s.	0d.
The Spittlehouse	£1 0s.	0d.
To the churchewardens		
The reparacions of bothe churches	£2 0d.	0d.
And for paper at this accompte		4d.
And of £3 9s.0d. paied to William Axten for mony by him layed owt and allredy paied for the pore orphanes as appeared in a bil of particularities		[£3 9s. 0d.]

Summa of th'allowances £42 13s.10d.
And so is layed up into the Treashry of the
house at this accompte £11 12s.5¼d.

---

[72] Powle was a tenant at Hepworth, but the counterpart lease has not survived.

[73] The purchase of St Peters Hospital is discussed in the Introduction, p.xxxvii.

Super £60 0s.0d.
[*Also in the margin, but in a different hand, perhaps that of Robert Carlyes*] **Mr
Andrewes for londes sold to Sir William Cordell, knight, in Melford**
Memorandum theare remaynethe in Mr Andreus handes for the londe in Melforde
solde to the Master of the Rolles, £60 0s.0d.

Thomas Peyton	Anthony Payne	Harry Collyng
Robert Carlyes	*per me* Willm. Hill	Wyllm. Axen
Thomas Gooderyche	H[*enry*] H[*orningold*]	Thom[*as*] Coksag mark

[*f.15r.*]   Candlemas 1577[*8*][74]

**The landes and tenementes in Hepworth sometyme John Smythes, esquyer, the
landes of William Tassell, gentleman, the newe purchased landes, the annuytie
of Mr Edmunde Jermyn, esquyer, together with the fynes of leases and the
commodytie of the Guyldehall**

**Th'accompte of Frauncis Boldero, gentleman, and William Hill, merser,
surveyors and receyvors of the profittes belonging to the towneshipp of St
Edmundes Bury in the county of Suffolk for one wholle yere ended at
Michaelmas last past**

Arreragia[75]

The said accomptantes do yelde accompte of £18 7s.0d. by them
received of the rentes and profittes of the mesuages, landes and
tenements sometyme Jankyn Smythes, Mrs Odeham and others
as by the rental maye appere. And of £8 1s.4d. by them
receyved for the rentes and profittes of the mannor of Brettes
and other mesuages, landes and tenementes in Hepworth. And
also of £10 16s.2d. by them received for Mr Tasselles
tenementes. And of £40 0s.0d., a yerely annuytie geven by Mr
Edmunde Jarmyn esquyer. And of £13 12s.5d. received of the
company or felowshipp. And of £10 0s.0d. received of Thomas
Carre for a fyne of a closse by Stanforde Bredge. And of
£1 0s.0d. received of John Bright of Catshall for an ashe and
certeyne hollowe trees. And of £15 12s.4d. received for the
neewe purchased landes. And of £6 13s.4d. received for a fine
of John Powle for his lease. And of £2 0s.0d. received of John
Bright for a parcell in Mr Andrews Streate. And also of
£3 5s.0d. received of the profittes of the Guyldehall   £129 6s. 7d.
    Summa patet, wherof
The sayde accomptantes praye allowance of 13s.8¼d. for the out
rentes payeable out of the landes in Hepworth, together with
5s.0d. for the fee of the collectors, as by the rentall maye
appere. And of 11s.4d. the out rentes of Mr Tasselles
tenementes, with 5s.0d. fee lykewyse allowed to the collector.

---

[74] A new clerk entered this account. For the first time income from rents and other sources is brought
together, as are all kinds of expenditure. Whoever wrote this and the following accounts until 1585 wrote
an elegant engrossing hand. See Plate 5 for an example of his handwriting.
[75] Although the new clerk entered a heading '*arreragia*' he inserted neither an amount nor the word
'*nulla*' beside it. He also omitted the heading '*onus*' and begins to enter the receipts.

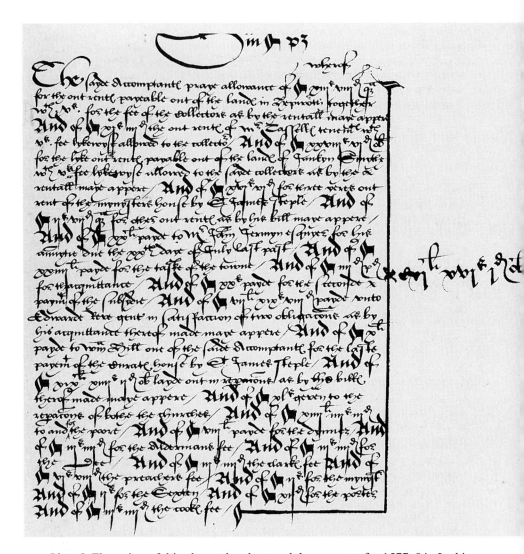

Plate 5. The writer of this elegant hand entered the accounts for 1577–84. In this, his first effort, no heading indicates that these are expenses. The accounts for all properties were brought together, and his entries were very brief (HD1150/1, f.15r.). Reproduced by permission of Suffolk Record Office.

And of £1 8s.6½d. for the lyke out rentes payable out of the landes of Jankyn Smythe, with 5s.0d. fee lykewyse allowed to the sayde collectors, as by the rentall maye appere. And of 16s.6d. for three yeres out rent of the mynysters house by St James steple. And of 2s.7¼d. for other out rentes as by his bill maye appere. And of £20 0s.0d. payde to Mr. John Jermyn, esquyer, for his annuytie due the 20th daye of July last past. And of £24 0s.0d. payde for the taske of the towne. And of 4d. paid for th'acquittance. And of £1 0s.0d. payde for the sceconde[*sic*] payment of the subsydie. And of £7 19s.8d. payde unto Edwarde Reve, gentleman, in satisfaccion of two obligacions, as by his acquittance thereof may appere. And of £10 0s.0d. payde to William Hill, one of the saide accomptantes, for the laste payment of the curates house by St James steple.[76] And of £19 14s.2½d. layde out in reparacions as by the billes therof made maye appere. And of £2 0s.0d. geven to the reparacions of bothe the churches. And of £14 4s.3d. to and \for/ the poore. And of £8 0s.0d. payde for the dynner. And of 3s.4d. for the aldermans fee. And of 3s.4d. for the dee. And of 3s.4d. the clarkes fee. And of 6s.8d. the preachers fee. And of 2s.0d. for the mynyster. And of 2s.0d. for the sexten. And of 1s.0d. for the porter. And of 3s.4d. the cookes fee   £106 16s. 1½d.

[*f.15v.*]

Super

And further the sayde accomptantes praye allowance of £20 0s.0d., behynde and unpayde unto them by Mr Thorpe. And of 16s.0d. behynde and unpayde by John Pyttman. And of 9d. due by Sir Ambrose Jermyn, knight. And of 6d. due by Mr. Anthony Payne   £20 17s. 3d.

Summa totalis of the payments and allowances is £132 13s.4½d. And so remayne due to the sayde accomptantes £3 6s.9½d paid unto the said accomptantes

Jo. Heigham	Anthony Payne	Hnry Collyng
Jamys Wyther[77]	John Cuttiris	Robert Carlyees
HH this Hary Hornyngoldes marke[78]		Thomas Cocksagys marke

[*f.16r.*]

Th'accompt of Thomas Payton, esquyer, and Henry Collyn, gentleman, William Hill and Robert Carelys, surveyors and recyvors of the profittes belonging to the towneshipp of St Edmundes Bury in Suffolk for one whole yere ended at Michaelmas last past 1578

---

[76] It seems possible that both ministers lived here until another house, on the north side of St James's church, was bought.

[77] So read by myself and Jane Isaac of Suffolk Record Office, but it appears from a lease, H1/3/4/8, that it is the signature of James Wright.

[78] Henry Horningold presumably could not sign his name in full, but his distinctive HH is to be found on a number of accounts. Obviously someone else wrote his name, but this has not been noted in other accounts.

Arreragia nulla

Onus

The saide accomptantes do yeilde theire accompt of £18 7s.0d. by
them receyved of the rentes and profittes of the mesuages,
landes and tenementes sometyme Janckyn Smythes, Mrs
Odeham and others, as by a rentall thereof made may appere.
And of £8 1s.4d. by them receyved for the rentes and profittes
of the mannor of Brettes and other mesuages, landes and
tenementes in Hepworth. And of £10 16s.2d. by them receyved
for Mr Tasselles tenementes. And of £40 0s.0d. being a yerely
annuytie geven by Mr Edmunde Jermyn, esquyer. And
of £15 12s.4d. receyved for the newe purchased landes. And
of £1 0s.0d. receyved for the shopp and seller by St James
steeple. And of £110 17d.4d. receyved of Thomas Badby,
esquyer, being due unto this house by the saide Thomas and
others their bonde.[79] And of £3 11s.8d. receyved for the
profittes of the Guyldehall. And also the saide accomptantes do
yelde accompt of £20 17s.3d. due by dyvers persons as by the
particulers therof in the title of supers in the last accompt maye
appere   £129 3s. 1d.

Summa patet

Redditus resoluti

The saide accomptantes praye allowaunce of 13s.8¼d. for the out
rentes payeable out of the landes in Hepworth, together with
5s.0d. the collectors fee. And of 11s.4d. paide out of Mr
Tasselles tenementes, with 5s.0d. the collectors fee. And of
£1 8s.6½d. for the oute rentes paide out of Janckyn Smythes
landes, with 5s.0d. the collectors fee, as by the severall
rentalles maye appere. And of 5s.6d. paide out of the
mynysters house by St James Steeple. And of 3s.6d. paide out
of a tenement in the occupacion of Thomas Shorte. And of
5s.0d. for the collectors fee of the new purchased landes.   £3 7s. 6¾d.

Feoda

Also the saide accomptantes praye allowance of 3s.4d. the
aldermans fee. And of 3s.4d. for the fee of the dee And of
£4 0s.0d. for the dynner. And of 3s.4d. for the clarkes fee for
the ingrossing th'accompte. And of 2s.0d. the curates fee. And
of 2s.0d. for the sextens fee for preparing the stoolles. And of
3s.4d. the cookes fee. And of £2 0s.0d. for the beadles wages
for ordering of the poore. And of 1s.0d. the porters fee.   £6 18s. 4d.

Denarii soluti pauperibus et pro reparacionibus

Also they praie allowance of £20 2s.8d. laide out for releife of the
poore. And of £1 0s.0d. geven for the releife of the poore in the
hospital. And of £1 0s.0d. geven to the releife of the prisoners.
And of £2 0s.0d. geven for reparacions of the churches.   £24 2s. 8d.

---

[79] Perhaps this loan was called in because money was needed for preparations for the queen's visit.

Also they praye allowance of £124 3s.0¼d. laide out for dyvers
    charges and reparacions, as by their bills thereof made maye
    appere £124 3s.0¼d.[80]   £124 3s. 0¼d.
        Summa totalis £158 11s.7d.
        And so remayne £70 11s.6d., whereof

[*f.16v.*]
Super
Also the saide accomptantes doe praye allowance of £20 0s.0d.,
    behynde and unpaide unto them by Mr Thorpe, due upon the
    last accompt. And of 16s.0d. due by John Pytman. And of 9d.
    due by Sir Ambrose Jermyn knight, deceased. And of 6d. due
    by Mr Anthony Payne, as by the last accompt in the title of
    supers dothe appere   £20 17s. 3d.
Also they praye allowaunce of £40 0s.0d., behynde and unpaide
    by Mr Thorpe due the 20th of January last past   £40 0s. 0d.

        Summa £60 17s. 3d.
        And so remayne due by the saide accomptantes
        £9 14s.3d. which is put into the cofer upon the
        determynacion of this accompt.

Jo. Heigham	Anthony Payne	Hary Collynge
Jamys Wyther[81]	John Cutteris	HH Harrye Hornyngoldes marke
Robert Carlyees	Thos. Coksag his mark	Thomas Gooderych the elder

[*f. 17r.*]
**Th'accompte of Robert Careles, Thomas Gooderiche, Stephen Haywarde,
gentleman, and Thomas Andrews, gentleman, surveyors and recyvors of the
messuages, landes and tenements belonging to the township of Bury for one
whole year ended at the feast of St Michaell th'archangell last past 1579.**

Arrerages
The said accomptantes yelde their accompt of £60 17s.3d. for
    th'arrerages as appeareth upon the fote of the last accompte   £60 17s. 3d.

Yerely rents
Item they yelde their accompte of £18 7s.0d. for the rentes and
    proffitts of the messuages, landes and tenements sometyme of

---

[80] This very large sum may represent expenditure on the queen's visit to the town this year. She was the guest of Thomas Badby at the abbey from 5 to 8 August. As Badby's house was not large enough for the whole entourage, Burghley and Leicester stayed with Thomas Andrews. She must have been given a present when she visited Bury; Norwich gave her a silver gilt cup containing £100 while Thetford gave a silver gilt covered cup weighing 16½ ounces. The Thetford civic insignia was in poor repair, and one mace had been lost, so the other was sent to Bury to be copied. The following account shows that the town gates were repaired for the visit, and there may well have been other expenditure to ensure that the town looked its best for the royal visitor. See Zillah Dovey, *An Elizabethan Progress* (Gloucester, 1999) for a detailed account of the progress. On the final day of the queen's visit, the first deaths from plague were noted in St James's parish register. Additional expense might have been in connection with those who suffered from this disease.

[81] See n.77 above.

Jenkyn Smythes, Maistres Odeham and other, as by a rental
thereof may appere. And of £8 1s.4d. for the rents and profits
of the maner of Bretts and other messuages, landes and tenements in Hepworthe. And of £10 16s.2d. for the messuages,
landes ~~landes~~ and tenements late Mr Tassells. And of
£40 0s.0d. for the yerely annuytie gyven by Mr Jermyn,
esquyer. And of £15 12s.4d. for the new purchased landes. And
of £1 0s.0d. for the shopp and cellar adjoyninge to St Jeames
steple   £93 16s. 10d.

Money out of the coffer and gyftes

And also of £3 0s.0d. delivered out of the coffers to the saide
accomptauntes. And of £30 0s.0d. given by Thomas Browne,
late citisen and marchant tailor of London,[82] for a contynuall
stocke for the relief of the pore people in Bury. And of
£1 4s.0d. for the rent of a howse in Lavenham, due for one yere
ended at Michaelmas last past. And of 6s.8d. for a legacie
given by Robert Brunnynge, deceased
  Summa totalis £189 4s.9d., whereof

Rents resol[*ute*]

The saide accomptauntes pray allowance of 13s.8d. payeable
yerely out the maner of Bretts and other landes in Hepworth,
together with five shillinges the collectors fee. And of 11s.4d.
payable yerely out of Mr Tassells tenements, together with five
shillinges the collectors fee. And of £1 8s.6½ d. payeable out
of Jenkyn Smythes landes and tenements, together with fyve
shillinges the collectors fee. And of 5s.6d. payable out of the
howse next adjoynynge to St Jeames steple. And of 3s.6d.
payable out of the messuage next adjoynynge to the sowth end
of the Gildehall. And of 5s.0d. for the collectors fee for the
newe purchased landes   £3 7s. 6½d.

Fees and rewards

And also of £4 0s.0d. for the dynner this yere. And of 3s.4d. for
the aldermans fee. And of 3s.4d. for the dees fee. And of 3s.4d.
for the clerkes. And of £2 0s.0d. for the lyvery and fee of the
chief porter. And of 1s.0d. for the under porters fee. And of
three shillinges 4d. for the cookes fee. And of 2s.0d. given this
yere of benevolence to the curate of St Maryes church. And of
2s.0d. gyven of like beneveolence to the sexten of the same
church for preparynge cushions and seates in the church for the
fellowship   £6 18s. 4d.

Reparacions and other charges extraordinary

And of 4s.4d. for leade bestowed on the gutters of the howse
adjoyninge to St Jeames steple. And of £6 5s.11d. bestowed in
repairinge the West Gate at the Quenes Majesties comynge to
this towne of Burye.   £8 10s. 3½d.

---

82 For Thomas Browne, see Notes on People.

32

And of £1 17s.4d. likewise bestowed on the Northe Gate.[83] And
  of 2s.8½d. for papir and other thinges layed out this yere by
  John Smythie   £8 10s. 3½d.

[f.17v.]
Reparacions ordinary
And also of £2 0s.0d. gyven yerely to the repayring of St Mary
  and St Jeames churches in this towne   £2 0s. 0d.

Almoyse
And also £1 0s.0d. given yerely in almoyse to the prisoners in the gaioll.
And of £1 0s.0d. gyven yerely in almoyse to the pore people in the
  hospitall. And of £33 9s.8d. bestowed this yere on the
  orphantes founde at the charge of the howse and in relief of
  other pore people as appereth by sondry bills   £35 9s. 8d.

        Sum total of the saide money whereof the
        saide accomptantes pray allowance £56 5s. 10d.

        And so there remayneth to be answeared
        by the saide accomptantes £132 18s.6½d., whereof

Super
There is in the handes of Mr Thorpe for Mr Edmund Jermyns
  annuytie   £100 0s. 0d.
Item in the handes of Thomas Badby, esquyer, for his fearme rent   £4 15s. 0d.
Item in the handes of Doctor Wode for a rent goynge out of a
  piece of ground lyenge by the streat ledinge from the Horse   6d.
  Market toward the late Gramer Schole Hall, nowe the Shire
  Howse.[84] **5s.0d. composicion by Mr Mountford '99**[85]
Item in the handes of Jellowe for the fearme of a stall in the Greate
  Markett   2s. 0d.
Item in the handes of the saide accomptaunts   £28 1s. 4½d.
        which summe of £28 1s.4½d. was payde by the saide
        accomptaunts and put into the coffer.

Jo. Heigham	Thomas Andrews	Anthony Payne
Wm. Cooke	Symond Cage	Roger Barber
Hary Collyng	Thomas Coksage	HH [*Henry Horningold*]
Willm. Hill	Roger Potter	Thom. Gooderych th'elder
Thomas Gyppes	Thomas Bryght	

---

[83] This probably relates to Queen Elizabeth I's visit to Bury St Edmunds in the course of her progress
through the eastern counties in 1578, but see n.93 below.
[84] See Introduction, p.xxxvi and n.159 for the benefits of having a building within the town in which the
royal courts of assizes and quarter sessions could be held. The former monastic school, which was used
as the Shire House, was conveyed to the feoffees on 12 July 1578, Woodward's Register, H1/6/1, p.196.
[85] This is the first of many notes in the right-hand margin which were made as the feoffees attempted to
collect arrears of rents which had grown up over the years. Sometimes, as here, a lump sum was agreed in
satisfaction of the sum which was owed.

[f. 18r.]

Th'accompte of Thomas Andrews, Stephen Haywarde, Henry Collyn, gentleman, and Thomas Gooderiche, surveyors and receyvors of the messuages, landes and tenementes belonginge to the towneship of Bury for one whole yere ended at the feast of St Michaell th'Archangell last past 1580

Arrearages

The said accomptantes yelde their accompt of £104 17s.6d. as appereth in the foote of the last accompte   £104 17s. 6d.

Yerely rents

Item they yelde their accompt of £18 7s.0d. for the rentes and profits of the messuages, landes and tenements sometyme Jenkyn Smythes, Mrs Odeham and other, as by a rentall thereof made maye appere. And of £8 1s.4d. for the rents and profits of the maner of Bretts and other messuages, landes and tenementes in Hepworth. And of £10 16s.2d. for the messuages landes and tenements late Mr Tassells. And of £20 0s.0d. for the yerely annuitie given by Mr Edmund Jermyn, esquyer, due for one half yere ended the 21th of July last past. And of £15 12s.4d. for the newe purchased landes. And of £1 0s.0d. for the shop and cellar adjoynynge to St Jeames steple   £73 16s. 10d.

Money owt of the coffer and giftes

And of £34 15s.7½d. delivered out of the coffer to the saide accomptaunts. And of £1 6s.8d. for the profitts of diverse dyners kept this yere within the hall. And of £5 0s.0d. received of Henry Colyn, gentleman, for a fyne for a lease.[86] And of £14 0s.0d. received \of the bequest/ of Sir Nicholas Bacon, knight, late Lord Keper of the Great Seale of Englande.[87] And of £15 0s.0d. given by a frinde, E.R., gentleman.[88] And of £5 16s.0d. received of John Boldroe to th'use of the howse[89]   £75 18s. 3½d.

Debts and Sales

And of £25 16s.8d. received of Thomas Badby, esquyer, in full discharge of an obligation of £60 0s.0d. And of £5 0s.0d. received of Henry Garrarde in parte of payment of the purchase of a howse in Lavenham solde to the saide Henry Garrarde.[90] And of 6s.3d. received of Henry Horningolde for the reede and thatch of one of the howses of correction   £31 2s. 11d.

    Summa totalis £285 15s.6½d., whereof

Rents resol[ute]

They praye allowance of 13s.8d. payable yerely out of the maner of Bretts and other landes in Hepworth, together with five shillinges for the collectors fee. And of 11s.4d. paiable yerely out of Mr Tassells tenementes, with five shillinges the

---

[86] See Introduction, p.xlvi.
[87] See Appendix 8, *sub* 1580.
[88] For the identity of E.R. gentleman, see Introduction, p.xxxvii.
[89] John Boldero's payment was a further instalment of his father's legacy.
[90] Robert Brunwyn, one of the feoffees, left them this property, Deed, H1/7/1.

collectors fee. And of £1 8s.6½d. paiable yerely out of Jenkyn
Smythes lands, together with five shillinges for the collectors
fee. And of 5s.6d. paiable yerely out of the howse next
adjoyninge to St Jeames steple. And of 3s.6d. payable yerely
out of the messuage next adjoyning to the southe ende of the
Guylde Hall. And of 5s.0d. for the collectors fee of the new
purchased landes. And of £60 0s.0d. payde to John Jermyn,
esquyer, for thre wholl yeres ended the 21th day of July last
past as by his acquittaunce appereth shewed at this accompte   £63 7s. 6½d.

Fearme Rent
And of £1 0s.0d. payed to Robert Wordewell for one half yere
ended at Michaelmas last past for the howse of correccion[91]   £1 0s. 0d.

Fees and rewardes
And of £4 0s.0d. for the dinner this yere. And of 3s.4d. for the
aldermans fee. And of 3s.4d. for the dees fee. And of 3s.4d. for
the clarkes fee. And of £2 0s.0d. for the livery and fee of the
chief porter. And of 1s.0d. for the under porters fee. And of
3s.4d. for the cookes fee. And of 2s.0d. gyven this yere of
benevolence to the curate of St Jeames church.[92] And of 2s.0d.
given of the like benevolence to the sextyn of the same church
for preparinge of cushions in the churche for the fellowship   £6 18s. 4d.

[f.18v.]
Giftes and rewardes
And of 13s.4d. payed to Andrewe Skynner for powder and match
at the tyme of the Quenes Majesties late beinge at Bury. And of
£1 18s.8d. payed to John Baker and Robert Smythe for the
repayringe of the South Gate at her Majesties saide beinge at
Bury. And of 5s.0d. given of benevolence to Jonas Rowte for
his paynes taken in redinge post at Her Majesties saide being at
Bury[93]   £2 17s. 0d.

Reparacions and other extraordinary charges
And of £30 3s.8d. bestowed this yere for reparacions of the
almoise howses and St. Peters and the gylde hall and diverse
other necessary charges as appered by diverse bills of
particulers shewed upon this accompte   £30 3s. 8d.

Money lent and paide for purchases
And of £10 0s.0d. lent to Robert Collyn, keper of the howse of
correccion, for the which he standeth bounde by two
obligacions to repay to the company of this howse. And of
£40 12s.2d. payed to Edwarde Reve, gentleman, as appereth by
his acquitance.[94] And of £10 0s.0d. payde \to/ Thomas Badby,

---

91 See Introduction, pp.xxxvi and xli–xliii.
92 The clerk does not always indicate in which church the fellowship met. See Introduction, p.xxxii.
93 These entries may refer to the queen's visit in 1578. Another progress through the eastern counties
was proposed for 1579, but so far there is no real evidence that it ever took place. See John Webb, *Town
Finances of Ipswich*, SRS, xxxviii (1996) p.46, n.4.
94 See Introduction, pp.xxxvii, xxxviii.

esquyer, for the full purchasing of the Shirehowse in the
Scholehall Strete within this towne of Bury[95]   £40 12s. 2d.

The howse of correction

And of 1s.0d. given to Robert Wordewell in parte of a bargayne
for the hyre of his howse, nowe the howse of correccion. And
of £1 0s.0d. given to the saide Robert for a fyne for a lease of
the saide howse. And of £45 5s.8d. bestowed in reparacions
and in other thinges bought and delivered into the saide howse
as appereth by bills of particulers shewed upon this accompte   £46 6s. 8d.

Reparacions ordinary

And of £2 0s.0d. given yerely to the repairinge of St Maryes and
St James churches within this towne   £2 0s. 0d.

Almoyse

And of £1 0s.0d. given yerely in almoise to the prisoners within
this towne. And of £1 0s.0d. given yerely in almoise to the pore
people in the hospitall. And of £29 8s.10d. bestowed this yere
upon the pore orphantes founde at the charge of this howse,
and in relief of other pore people within the said towne. And of
£4 0s.0d. given to the saide prisoners according to the legacie
of the saide Sir Nicholas Bacon, late Lorde Keper   £35 8s. 10d.

> *Summa totalis* of the saide money whereof the saide
> accomptantes pray allowance £248 14s.2½d.
> And so there remayneth to be answeared by the saide
> accomptantes, whereof £37 1s.4d.

Supers

There is in the handes of Mr Thorpe for Mr Edmund Jermyns
annuitie due the 21th day of July last past   £13 6s. 8d.

Item in th'andes of the administrators of Stephen Haiwarde,
gentleman, deceased, one of the collectors of the revenues of
this howse   £15 12s. 4d.

Item in th'andes of Dr Wode for a piece of grounde lyeng by the
streat leading from the Horsemarkett at sixe pence by the yere
for two whole yeres at Michaelmas last past. **5s.0d.**
composicion by Mr Montford '89   1s. 0d.

Item in th'andes of the saide administrators of the saide Stephen
Haywarde charged in the fote of the last accompt to be in the
handes of Jellowe for the ferme of a stall in the Great Markett   2s. 0d.

Item in th'andes of Sir Robert Jermyn, knight, for a parcell of
ground in Hepworth for one yere. **5s.0d. for this** *in fine*
compoti **'96**   9d.

Item in th'andes of Landesdall. **5s.0d. for this** *ibidem* **'96**   2s. 0d.
Item in th'andes of the saide accomptauntes   £7 16s. 7d.

> Which somme of £7 16s.7d. was paied by the saide
> accomptantes and put into the coffer and after delivered
> to the handes of the saide Thomas Gooderiche, one of the

---

[95] While Badby's name is in all the lists of benefactors, it appears from this entry that the feoffees at
least contributed to the purchase of the Shire Hall. See Introduction, p.xxxvi.

saide accomptantes, for the wekely payment of the
orphans founde at the charge of this howse and thereof to
yelde his accompt at our next audite.

[*In another hand*] Receyvd by me Thomas Gooderyche

Thomas Andrews	Hnrry Collyng	Willm. Hill
HH Harry Hornygold	Anthony Payne	Robert Carlyees
Wm. Cooke	Thomas Bryght	Roger Ptter.

[*f.19r.*]

The 8th of January 1581[*2*][96]

Th'accompt of Henry Collynge, William Coke, Anthony Payne, gentleman, Henry Horningolde and Thomas Gooderiche, surveyors and receivors of the landes, tenementes and hereditamentes belonginge to this ~~house~~ towne of Bury as also of the house of correction within the saide towne from the feast of St Michaell the Archangell 1580 unto the saide feast last past 1581

The arrears of the last accompt

The saide accomptantes do charge them selves with £29 4s.9d. as
appereth upon sondry persones in the fote of the last accompte   £29 4s. 9d.
Item with £7 16s.7d. put into the coffer and after that delivered to
the handes of the saide Thomas Gooderiche as appeareth also
in the fote of the sayde accompte   £7 16s. 7d.

Rentes certeyn

And they yelde their accompt of £18 7s.0d. for the rentes and
profyttes of the landes and tenementes sometyme Jenken
Smythes, Mrs Odeham and other, as by a rentall therof made
may appere. And of £8 1s.4d. for the rentes and profittes of the
maner of Brettes and other messuages, landes and tenementes
in Hepworth. And of £10 16s.2d. for the messuages, landes and
tenementes late Mr Tassells. And of £40 0s.0d. for the yerely
annuytie given by Mr Edmund Jermyn, esquier, for one whole
yere ended the 21th day of July last past. And of £15 12s.4d.
for the newe purchased landes. And of £1 0s.0d. for the shop
and cellar adjoynynge to St James steple. And of £4 10s.0d.
due by Sir John Heigham, knyght, for a parcell of ground
lyenge by his house in the Crowne Streat in Bury for nyne
whole yeres ended at the sayde feast of St Michaell
th'Archangell last past, at ten shillinges by the yere   £98 6s. 10d.

Fynes for leases

And of £1 5s.0d. receyved this yere for fyve dynners kept this yere
within the hall. And of £116 13s.4d. receyved for sondry fynes
for leases made this yere   £117 18s. 4d.

---

[96] In a different hand.

Gyftes

And of £13 0s.0d. received of the gyfte of Mr Edmund Markant, late of Colchester in Essex, gentleman, deceased.[97] And of £29 18s.0d. given by a frinde, E.R., gentleman. And of £4 0s.0d. given this yere by John Boldero of Forneham[98]   £46 18s. 0d.

Sales

And of £4 0s.0d. received of Henry Garrarde in parte of payement of the purchase of a howse in Lavenham. And of £1 0s.0d. received of Henrye Hornyngolde for certeyne olde tymber to him solde of a decayed house at the hospitall at the Risbygate   £5 0s. 0d.

     Summa totalis £305 4s.6d., [*In a different hand*] whereof

Rentes resolute

They pray allowance of 8s.8¼d. payable yerely out of the maner of Brettes and other landes in Hepworth. And of 6s.4d. payable yerely out of Mr Tassels tenementes. And of £1 3s.6½d. payeable yerely out of the landes and tenementes of Jenken Smythe, Mrs Odeham and other. And of 5s.6d. payable yerely out of the howse next adjoynynge to St Jeames steple. And of 3s.6d. payable yerely out of the messuage next adjoynynge to the southe ende of the Gylde Hall. And of £20 0s.0d. payde to John Jermyn, esquyer, for one whole yeres [*annuity*] ended the 21th day of July last past as by his acquittance appereth   £32 7s. 6¾d.

Ferme rent

And of £2 0s.0d. payde to Robert Wordewell for one whole yeres fearme rent, ended at Michaelmas last past, for the howse of correction   £2 0s. 0d.

[*f. 19v.*]

Fees and rewards

And of £4 0s.0d. for the dynner this yere. And of 3s.4d. for the aldermans fee. And of 3s.4d. for the dees fee. And of 3s.4d. for the clerkes fee. And of 5s.0d. for the collectors fee of the maner of Brettes. And of 5s.0d. for the collectors fee of the revenues, landes and tenementes of Jenken Smythe. And of 5s.0d. for the collectors fee of Mr Tassells tenementes. And of 5s.0d. for the collectors fee of the new purchased landes. And of £2 0s.0d. for the lyvery and fee of the chief porter. And of 1s.0d. for the under porters fee. And of three shillinges 4d. for the cookes fee. And of 2s.0d. gyven this yere of benevolence to the curate of St Maries church. And of 2s.0d. given of the like benevolence to the sexten of the same churche for preparinge of cushions in the saide church for the feloweship   £7 18s. 4d.

And of £2 0s.0d. given this yere and yerely to the reparacions of the parishe churches of St Mary and St James in this towne of Bury   £2 0s. 0d.

And of £1 0s.0d. given this yere in almoise to the hospitall without the Rysbygate. And of £1 0s.0d. gyven to the gaioll   £2 0s. 0d.

---

[97] See Appendix 8, 1581.
[98] See n.89 above.

Almes uncerteine

And of £18 1s.3d. given this yere for the dyet and apparailing of the orphantes. And of £17 2s.8d. bestowed this yere in garmentes for the pore within this saide towne. And of £44 12s.8d. bestowed this yere for the diet, apparaile and other necessaries for the house of correccion. And of £2 0s.0d. given to Lichfild, surgen, for curinge of a pore man grievously skalt with hote water[99]   £81 16s. 7d.

Reparacions

And of £75 4s.3d. bestowed this yere for reparacions of the hospitall, the almoyse houses, the mynisters houses, the house of correccion, and other houses belonginge to this feloweship as appereth by bills of pariculers shewd upon this accompt   £75 4s. 3d.

The taxe and subsidie paide to the Queens Majestie

And of £24 0s.0d. payde this yere for this towne of Bury to the Queenes Majestie for her highnes taxe of the 10[ths] and 15[ths] granted this yere to her highnes in the last Parliament. And of £1 13s.4d. for her highnes subsidie for the stocke of this house.[100] And of 4d. for the receivors acquittance   £25 13s. 8d.

> *Summa totalis* of the saide allowance £86 4s. 1¼d.
> And so remaineth to be answered by the saide
> accomptantes £86 4s. 1¼d., whereof

Supers

There is in the handes of Sir John Heigham £4 10s.0d. for a rente charge goinge out of certeyne groundes adjoyninge to his house in the Crowne Strete, beinge behinde for 9 yeres   £4 5s. 0d.

Item in the handes of Thomas Yonges, glasier, £1 0s.0d. for a rent of the shop next to St. James steple   £1 0s. 0d.

Item in the handes of John Landsdall 4s.0d. for two yeres rent of a piece of grounde in the Horsemarket   4s. 0d.

Item in the handes of Sir Robert Jermyn \knight/ 1s.6d. for two yeres rent of certeine landes in Hepworth, at 9d. the yere [*The last two items are bracketed*] **5s. pro hiis in compoto '96**   1s. 6d.

Item in the handes of Dr Wode 1s. 6d. for three yeres rent at 6d. the yere. **5s. composicion by Mr Mountford '89**   1s. 6d.

> *Summa* £5 17s.0d.
> And so resteth in the handes of the sayde accomptantes £4 7s.1¼d.
> [*In a different hand*] Which some is paid into the cofer upon the determynacion of this accompt.

Thomas Andrews	Anthony Payne	Thomas Gooderyche
Roger Potter	Robert Carlyes	H[enry] H[orningold]
Hary Collyng	Thomas Bryght	Thomas Gyppes
Willm. Hill	Thomas Coksage	

---

99 For medical care see Introduction, p.lxv. Details of practitioners are given in Notes on People.
100 See Introduction, pp.lxi–lxiii.

[*f.20r.*]

The 7th of January 1582[*3*]

Th'accompt of William Cooke, Roger Barber, Anthony Payne, gentleman, Henry Hornyngolde and Thomas Gooderiche, surveyors and receivors of the landes, tenementes and hereditamentes belonginge to the town of Bury, and also of the house of correccion within the said towne, from the feast of St Michaell th'archangell 1581 unto the sayde feast last past 1582

Arrerag[*es*]

The saide accomptantes do charge them selves with £5 17s.0d. as appereth upon diverse supers in the last accompte   £5 17s. 0d.

Mony out of the coffer

And with £59 7s.1¼d. taken owt of the coffer at two severall tymes as appereth by the register of the sayde coffer[101]   £59 7s. 1¼d.

The yerely revenues

And they yeld their accompt of £18 7s.0d. for the rentes and profites of the landes and tenementes sometyme Jenken Smythes, Mrs Odyham and other. And of £8 1s.4d. for the rentes and profytes of the manor of Brettes and other mesuages, landes and tenementes in Hepworth. And of £4 16s.2d. this yere for the mesuages, landes and tenementes late Mr Tassels, whereof the Angell nowe solde was parcell.[102] And of £40 0s.0d. for the yerely annuytie given by Mr Edmund Jermyn, esquyer, for one whole yere ended the 21th day of July last past. And of £15 12s.4d. for the newe purchased landes. And of £1 0s.0d. for the shop and cellar adjoyninge to St James steple. And of 5s.0d. for one yeres rent for a stable in the Westgate Streat in the tenure of Robert Scott. And of 8s.0d. for the half yeres rent of a closse by the hospitall due at Michaelmas last, lately dimised to Robert Careles. And of £29 18s.0d. for an annuytie graunted by the Governors of the Free Grammer Schole in Bury for one whole yere ended at Michaelmas last[103]   £118 7s. 10d.

Dynners

And of 15s.0d. received this yere of Roger Potter for three dynners kept in the Guylde Hall. And of 18s.4d. received of Mr Collinge for other three dynners kept in the same hall   £1 13s. 4d.

Fynes

And of £100 0s.0d. for the fyne of a lease of the manor of Brettes dymised to Stephen Murryell. And of £10 0s.0d. for the fyne of a lease of Great Atlye dimised also to the sayde Stephen Murryell. And of £4 0s.0d. for the fyne of a lease of 18ten acres of lande in Bury dimised to Robert Heathe[104]   £114 0s. 0d.

---

101   Unfortunately the register of the coffer has not survived.
102   The sale of the Angel and other properties, and their eventual repurchase, at the insistence of the Commissioners for Charitable Uses, is discussed in the Introduction, p.xxxviii and p.xlvii.
103   The last two items result from the purchase of St Peter's, discussed in the Introduction, p.xxxviii.
104   These leases have not survived.

Debtes

And of £20 0s.0d. received of Roger Potter for parte of the
purchase of the Angell due at the Annunciacion of our Ladie
last. And of £7 0s.0d. received of Henry Garrard in parte of
payment of a house at Lavenham. And of 13s.4d.for certeyne
wode solde to Edmund Clarke of Rougham. And of £12 0s.0d.
received of Sir John Heigham, knight, for the purchase of
10s.0d. rent and the arrerages of the s[ame][105] payable out of
this house in the Crowne Strete[106]   £39 13s. 4d.

Almoyse

And of £3 10s.0d. received of John Boldero to the relief of pore
orphans[107]   £3 10s. 0d.

    Summa totalis £342 8s.7¼d., whereof

Rents resolute

They pray allowance of 9s.1d. payable yerely out of the manor of
Bretes and other landes in Hepworth. And of 1s.4d. payable
yerely out of Mr Tassels tenementes. And of £1 3s.6½d.
payable yerely out of the landes and tenementes of Jenken
Smythe, Mrs Odyham and others. And of 5s.6d. payable yerely
out of the house next adjoyninge to St James steple. And of
3s.6d. paiable yerely out of the mesuage next adjoyninge to the
southe ende of the Guyld Hall. And of £20 0s.0d. payde to
John Jermyn, esquier, for one whol yere ended the 21th day of
July last past as by his acquittance appereth. And of £1 1s.0d.
payd to the Queenes Majestie for a yerely tenth at 10s.6d. by
the yere payable out of St Peters landes due for two whol yeres
ended at Michaelmas last as appereth by two severall acquittances shewde upon this accompte.[108] And of 8d. for the saide
acquittances   £23 4s. 7½d.

[f. 20v.]

Ferme rent[109]

And of £2 0s.0d. payde to Robert Wordwell for one whol yeres
ferme due at Michaelmas last past for the House of Correccion   £2 0s. 0d.

Ordynarye Fes and rewardes

And of £4 0s.0d. for the dynner this yere. And of 3s.4d for the
aldermans fee. And of 3s.4d. for the dees fee. And of 3s.4d. for
the clarkes fee. And of 5s.0d. for the collectors fee for the
manor of Brettes and other landes in Hepworth. And of 5s.0d.
for the collectors fee of the revenues of the landes and
tenementes of Jenken Smythe. And of 5s.0d. for the collectors
fee of Mr Tassels tenementes. And of 5s.0d. for the collectors

---

[105] Apart from the 's', this word is obscured by a blot.
[106] Sir John Heigham had extinguished the rent charge payable out of his house in Crown Street. It was
part of Catherine Cage's gift.
[107] This was part of his father's legacy.
[108] This annual tenth, payable to the Crown, was reserved in the grant of St Peter's. It must not be
confused with the tax known as tenths and fifteenths.
[109] See Glossary.

fee of the purchased landes. And of £2 0s.0d. for the lyvery and fee of the chief porter. And of 1s.0d. for the under porters fee. And of 3s.4d. for the cokes fee. And of 2s.0d. given of benevolence to the sexten of St James church for preparinge of cushians in the same churche for the felowship	£7 16s. 4d.

The Churches
And of £2 0s.0d. given this yere to the reparacion of the parishe church of St Mary and St James in this towne of Bury — £2 0s. 0d.

Hospitall and gaioll
And of £1 8s.0d. given this yere in almoyse to the hospitall without the Risbiegate. And of £1 0s.0d. given to the gayoll — £2 8s. 0d.

Almoyse
And of £18 12s.0½d. payde this yere for the dyet and apparailing of the orphans. And of £29 18s.1½d. bestowed this yere for the dyet, apparaile and other necessaries for the House of Correccion. And of £2 9s.0d.~~18s.1½d~~ bestowed this yere upon a woman surgen of Colchester and Lychfilde for curing of the wife of John Willys of Bury, sherman, and diverse other — £50 19s. 2d.

Reparacions
And of £32 14s.2d. bestowed this yere for reparacions of th'ospitall, th'almoyse houses, the mynisters houses, the House of Correccion and other houses belonginge to this feloweship — £32 14s. 2d.

The Taxe
And of £24 0s.0d. payde this yere for this towne of Bury for the Queenes Majestie for the seconde payment of Her Highnes taxe of the 10th and 15^{mi} graunted in the last parliament. And of £1 0s.0d. for the seconde payment of Her Highnes subsidie for the stocke of this house. And of 4d. for the receivors acquittance — £25 0s. 4d.

Debtes
And of £66 3s.4d. payde to Thomas Andrewes, gentleman, for diverse somes of money by him layde out for the purchasing of St Peters landes and diverse other thinges by him disbursed as appereth by two bylls of particulers shewed at this accompt — £66 3s. 4d.

Fynes
And of £1 0s.0d. for the fyne of certen copiehold lande in Barton — £1 0s. 0d.

Charges at Lawe
And of £40 5s.2d. for the charges of a lycence of alienacion[110] for St Peters and the graunge landes, and for diverse expences in attendinge about the same, as appereth by diverse bylls exhibited at this accompt — £40 5s. 2d.

Thinges bought
And of 11s.0d. for a loade of coale bought for the hall. And of 19s.2d. payde for a carpet of grene cloth for the hall — £1 10s. 2d.

---

110 See Glossary. The licence to alienate in mortmain survives, H1/5/33.

Giftes

And of £1 0s.0d. given to Mr Bourdman for the obteyninge of a
    sute for the mynisters lyvinge[111]   £1 0s. 0d.

Reparacions

And of £1 12s.7½d. for glasing and casementes for the hall   £1 12s. 7½d.

Thinges bought

And of 1s.5½d. payd to John Annable for candle, papir and wax
    spent in the hall   1s. 5½d.

And of £4 10s.0d. for arrerages of the arrerages [*sic*] of Sir John
    Heighams house in the super of the last accompt and nowe
    solde to the saide Sir John Heigham, knight   £4 10s. 0d.

        Summa totalis of the sayd allowances £262 5s.0½d.

        And so remayneth due by the saide accomptantes £80 3s.2½d.,
        whereof

[*f. 21r.*]

Supers

There is in the handes of Sir John Heigham, knight, £2 0s.0d. in
    full payement of the purchase of the yerely rent of 10s.0d. and
    of £4 10s.0d. for the arrerages of the saide rent goinge out of
    certeyne grounde adjoyninge to his house as appereth in the
    fote of the last accompt   £2 0s. 0d.

And in the handes of John Landesdale 6s.0d. for thre yeres ferme
    of a piece of grounde in the Horsemarket   6s. 0d.

And in the handes of Sir Robert Jermyn, knight, for three yeres
    ferme rent of certeyn landes in Hepworthe at 9d. by the yere.
    5s.0d. *pro hiis in fine compoti* '96   2s. 3d.

And in the handes of Doctor Wode[112] 2s.0d. for fower yeres rent
    at 6d. by the yere. **5s.0d. composicion by Mr Mountford '89**   2s. 0d.

And in the handes of William Futter for the half yeres ferme of
    Brettes Closse in Hepworth at Michaelmas last ended   £2 2s. 1d.

And in the handes of [*space*] Hoy for one yeres rent of a tenement
    in Longe Brackland ended at Michaelmas last   8d

        Summa £4 13s.0d.

        And so due by the sayde accomptantes £75 10s.2½d.

        [*In another hand*] Which mony was put into the coffer upon the
        determynacion of this accompt.

Thomas Badby	Thomas Andrewes	Anthony Payne
Hary Collyng	Wm. Cook	Roger Barber
Harry HH Hornyngold	Thomas Bryght	Thomas Gooderyche th'elder
Edward Ubanke	Walter Brooke	Roger Potter
Thomas Cokseg	Thomas Gyppes	

---

[111] The exhibition granted by the Crown to the ministers is discussed in the Introduction, p.xxxvi.
[112] See Notes on People.

[f.21v.]   **1583**

Th'accompte of Roger Barber, gentleman, Thomas Bright, Henry Horningolde, James Wright, gentleman and Thomas Gooderiche, surveyors and receivors of the landes, tenementes and hereditamentes belonging to the towne of Bury, and also of the House of Correccion within the saide towne, from the feast of St Michaell th'archangell 1582 untill the saide feast 1583

Arrerages

First the sayde accomptantes do charge them selves with
£4 13s.0d. as appereth upon the supers in the fote of the last
accompt   £4 13s. 0d.

The yerely revenues

And with £123 9s.1½d. for the yerely revenues of the landes,
tenementes and hereditamentes of this house for one whole
yere ended at the feast of St Michaell last past as appereth by
the rentalls   £123 9s. 1½d.

Money delivered out of the coffer

And with £30 0s.0d. delivered out of the coffer to the saide Roger
Barber towarde the buyldinge of the Market Howse, beinge
given by Sir Thomas Jermyn, knight, towarde the buyldinge of
the saide house.[113] And with £10 0s.0d. delivered to Thomas
Gooderich, one of the companye of this house, as appeareth by
the register of the saide coffer   £40 0s. 0d.

Dynners

And with £3 5s.0d. received by the saide accomptantes for diverse
dynners kept within the hall   £3 5s. 0d.

Wodesales

And with £6 13s.4d. received by the saide accomptantes for the
sale of certeyn elmes at Hepworth to Stephen Muryell   £6 13s. 4d.

Debtes

And with £20 0s.0d. received of Roger Potter for parte of the
purchase of the Angell in Bury due at the feast of the Annunciation of Our Ladie last past. And with £10 0s.0d. payde to the
handes of the saide Roger Barber by Thomas Peyton, gentleman, due by him and Thomas Badby, esquier, decessed, as
parcell of £20 0s.0d. payable to this house. And with £2 2s.1d.
due by William Futter, late fermer of Bretes Closse in
Hepworth, for the last half yeres ferme of the said closse   £32 2s. 1d.

Allmoyse

And with £4 0s.0d. given by William Hill, late one of the
company, decessed.[114] And with £5 0s.0d. given by the
parsone, William Page, late of Hesset, for the relief of the
pore[115]   £9 0s. 0d.

---

[113] See Introduction, p.xxxviii. No evidence has been found to explain why this legacy was not used before this.

[114] See Appendix 8, *sub* 1583, and Notes on People.

[115] William Page's induction as rector of Hesset is not recorded in the Archdeaconry of Sudbury Induction Book, E14/5/1.

And with one gallon of wyne payable yerely by John Revell for
certen lands lyenge in \Burye/ Horningserth feldes, late Jenken
Barrett, esquyer[116]

One gallon of
wine

Summa totalis £219 2s. 6½d., whereof

Rentes resolut'

They pray allowance of 9s.1d. payable yerely out of the Manor of
Brettes and other landes in Hepworthe. And of 1s.4d. payable
yerely out of Mr Tassels tenements. And of £1 3s.6½d. payable
yerely out of the landes and tenementes of Jenken Smythe, Mrs
Odeham and others. And of 5s.6d. payable yerely out of the
house next adjoyninge to St James steple. And of 3s.6d.
payable yerely out of the mesuage next adjoyninge to the
southe ende of the Guylde Hall. And of £20 0s.0d. payde to
John Jermyn, esquier, for one wholl yere ended the 21th day of
July last past as by his acquittance appereth. And of 10s.6d.
payeable as a yerely tenth due to the Quenes Majestie at the
feast of St Michaell th'archangell last past out \of/ of the St
Peters landes for one yere then ended as appereth by an
acquittance shewed at this accompt. And of 4d. for the saide
acquittance

£32 13s. 9½d.

[f.22r.]
Ferme rents

And of £2 0s.0d. payde to Robert Wordewell for one wholl yeres
ferme due at Michaelmas last past for the House of Correccion

£2 0s. 0d.

Ordynarye fees and rewardes

And of £7 16s.4d. for diverse fees and rewardes given this yere to
officers as appereth by the last accompt

£7 16s. 4d.

The churches

And of £2 0s.0d. given this yere to the reparacion of the two
parish churches

£2 0s. 0d.

The hospitall and gaioll

And of £2 8s.0d. given this yere to the hospitall and gayoll in
Bury

£2 8s. 0d.

Almoyse

And of £18 7s.1d. given this yere for the dyet and apparailing of
orphantes. And of £15 7s.7d. bestowed this yere in freeses for
the apparailinge of the pore. And of £13 6s.11d. bestowed this
yere for the dyet, apparaile and other necessaries for the house
of correccion

£47 1s. 7d.

Reparacions

And of £24 0s.3½d. bestowed on the mynisters houses and other
howses belonging to this felowship

£24 14s. 3½d.

---

[116] The passage in John Baret's will leaving wine to Candlemas guild is to be found in Tymms, *Wills*,
p.30.

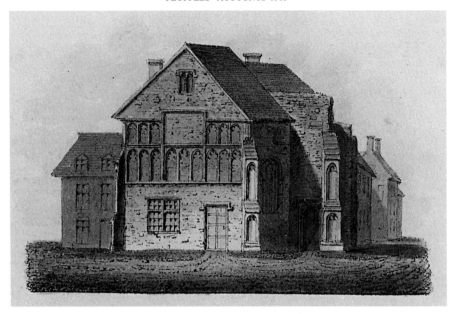

Plate 6. Drawing by Isaac Johnson, titled 'St Peter's Hospital, Risby Gate', but in fact depicts the stone chapel adjoining the Risbygate which was bought by the feoffees in 1583 and used as an almshouse (SROI, HD484/3). Reproduced by permission of Suffolk Record Office.

Purchase

And of £2 11s.0d. payde this yere for the purchase of \a/ litle house adjoyninge to the south side of the Risby Gate scituat without the saide gate, next to the wateringe there[117]   £2 11s. 0d.

The Market Crosse

And of £30 0s.0d. given by Sir Thomas Jermyn of Rushbroke in the Countie of Suffolk, knight, decessed, given by his last will and testament towarde the buyldinge of a Market Crosse in Bury market and this yere bestowed accordingly[118]   £30 0s. 0d.

Wyne

And of one gallon of wyne bestowed this yere at the common dynner for the feloweship   One gallon of wyne

> *Summa totalis* of the said allowances £141 5s.0d
> And so remayneth due by the said accomptantes £77 17s.6½d., wherof

---

[117] The deed by which Richard More conveyed this small house to the feoffees is Bodl. Suffolk Charter 170; when it was conveyed to Moore, Bodl. Suff. Ch.168, it was described as a stone chapel formerly belonging to the monastery of Bury St Edmunds, Copinger, *County of Suffolk*, I, p.393.
[118] See Introduction, p.xxxviii.

Supers

There is in the handes of John Landesdale 8s. 0d. for fower yeres
    ferme of a piece of grounde in the Horsemarket   8s. 0d.

And in the handes of Sir Robert Jermyn, knight, for fower yeres
    ferme rent of certeyn landes in Hepworth, at 9d. by the yere.
    [*These two items bracketed together, and in another hand*]
    5s.0d. *pro hiis in fine compoti* **'96**   3s. 0d.

And in the handes of Doctor Wode 2s.6d. for five yeres rent at 6d.
    by the yere. [*In a different hand*] **5s.0d. composicion by Mr.**
    Mountford '89   2s. 6d.

And in the handes of [*space*] Hoye for one yeres rent of a tene-
    ment in Brakelande ended Michaelmas last   8d.

        Summa   14s.2d.

        And so due by the said accomptantes £77 3s.4½d.

        [*In a different hand*] All which saide money is delivered
        to the handes of the saide accomptantes to be answered at
        the next accompt.

Thomas Andrews   Henry H H Hornyngold   Thomas Gooderyche th'elder
Thomas Bryght   Roger Potter

[*f.22v.*]   **1584**

**Th'accompte of James Wright, gentleman, Thomas Gooderiche the elder,
Thomas Bright and Roger Potter, surveiors and receivors of the landes
tenementes and hereditamentes belonging to the towne of Bury and of the
House of Correccion within the said towne from the feast of St Michaell
th'archangell 1583 untyll the saide feast 1584**

Arrerages

First the saide accomptantes charge them selves with 14s.2d. as
    appereth by the supers in the fote of the last accompte   14s.   2d.

And with £77 3s.4½d. due by the last accomptantes, as also
    appereth in the fote of the said accompt   £77 3s. 4½d.

Yerely revenues

And with £123 9s.1½d. for the yerely revenues of the landes
    tenementes and hereditamentes belonging to this house as
    appereth in the last accompt   £123 9s. 1½d

And with 14s.0d. in augmentacion of the ferme rent of the closse
    next to the hospitall lately dimised to Nicholas Raby, carpenter 14s. 0d.

Dynners

And with £3 5s.0d. received for the keepinge of diverse dynners
    within this house   £3 5s. 0d.

Debtes

And with £20 0s.0d. received of Roger Potter in parte of payement
    of a more some for the purchace of the Angell due at the
    Annunciacion of Our Ladie last past. And with £10 0s.0d.
    paide by Roger Barber, gentleman, for so much mony due to
    this house by Thomas Peyton, gentleman, and Thomas Badby,
    esquier, lately decessed *Memorandum* **for 10s.0d. here**

unpaid. And with £3 10s.0d., parcell of £4 0s.0d., due by
Henry Garrard for purchace of an house in Lanham   £33 10s. 0d.

Sales

And with £2 0s.0d. for certeyne elmes and 3 okes solde to Stephen
Muriell of Hepworthe   £2 0s. 0d.
And with 7s.0d. for certeine pieces of almaine rivetes solde   7s. 0d.
And with £2 0.0d. for the stones \of the olde Crosse/ in the Great
Markett solde   £2 0s. 0d.
And with 3s.0d. for certeyne drie fattes solde   3s. 0d.

Giftes

And with £2 0s.0d. received of John Heath, given by Christopher
Peyton, gentleman   £2 0s. 0d.

Legacies

And with £30 0s.0d. received of Thomas Andrews, esquier, for
mony by him received of Sir Thomas Lucas, knight, one of the
executors of William Markant, gentleman, decessed, parcell of
£60 0s.0d. bequeathed by the said William for the relief of the
pore people in Bury   £30 0s. 0d.

Exchange

And with £1 6s.8d. received of John Bright of Barton for
exchange of a parcell of lande there   £1 6s. 8d.
And with one gallon of wyne payable yerely by John Revell for
certeyn landes lieing in Burye fildes, late Jenken Barretes,
esquier   A gallon of
                                                                     wyne

Summa totalis £276 12s. 4d.
Wherof

Rentes resolute

They pray allowance of £22 13s.9½d. for diverse rentes payable
yerely out of the saide landes, tenementes and hereditamentes
as appereth by the last accompt   £22 13s. 9½d.

Rewardes and ferme rentes [*and, in another hand*] ferme rent

And of £2 0s.0d. for the yerely \ferme/ rent of the house of correction. And of £7 16s.4d. paiable yerely to th'officers as also
appereth by the last accompt   £9 16s. 4d.

Extraordinary rewardes

And of £1 0s.0d. given to Mr Bordeman and Mr Rodes in rewarde
of two sermons   £1 0s. 0d.

Churches

And of £2 0s.0d. given this yere for the repayringe of the two
parishe churches   £2 0s. 0d.

Gayoll and hospitall

And of £2 10s.0d. given to the prisoners in the gaioll and the pore
in the hospitall   £2 10s. 0d.

[f.23r.]

Almoise

And of £19 6s.10d. given this yere for the diett and apparailinge of orphantes. And of £23 11s.8d. bestowed this yere for the apparailinge of the pore people with frieses. And of £20 4s.5½d. bestowed this yere for th'apparaile and other necessaries for the house of correccion. And of £3 1s.8d. bestowed this yere in chirurgery for the curing of Gosse and his wife, of [*space*] Willis infected with the Frenche pockes. And of £1 0s.0d. given for the placinge of a pore childe to be prentise with Philip Streaker of Burye, tailor. And of 10s.0d. given to the Widowe Hawsted, being a pore woman, to paye her house rent   £67 9s. 7½d.

Buyldinges

And of £121 18s.8d. payde this yere for the finishinge of the Market Crosse   £121 18s. 8d.

Reparacions and purchaces

And of £12 3s.4d. bestowed this yere in reparacions on this house and on other belonging to this felowship   £12 3s. 4d.

And of £10 0s.0d. payde to Richard Collyn in parte of payement of his house next to St James churche   £10 0s. 0d.

And of £1 12s.0d. paied for the knoweledg and passinge of a fyne by Mr Collyn, gentleman, and others for certeyn landes in the fildes of Bury and Forneham All Saintes, late Salters landes   £1 12s. 0d.

And of £1 10s.0d. for 12 water bucketes of lether for fier   £1 10s. 0d.

Thinges bought

And of £49 19s.2d. for diverse parcels of lynnen bought of Mr Anthony Cage of London, lately decessed   £49 19s. 2d.

And of £1 15s.6d. for borde. And of 11s.6d. for coales bought for this house   £2 6s. 6d.

Expenses and chardges

And of £1 7s.0d. for deverse issues lost in th'exchequier   £1 7s. 0d.

And of £4 17s.7d. for skoring and trymmynge of the towne harneis, nowe in our hall   £4 17s. 7d.

Lynnen [*in another hand*]

And of £1 4s.0d. for washinge of sondrie pieces of lynnen   £2 4s. 0d.

Supers

And of 14s.2d. as appereth in the supers of the last accompt which the saide accomptantes have not yet received   14s. 2d.

And of 2s.0d. for the rent due by John Landesdale. And of 9d. due by Sir Robert Jermyn, knight. And of 6d. due this yere by Doctor Wode **5s.0d. composicion by Mr. Mountford '89. 5s.0d.** *pro hiis in fine compoti* **'96**   3s. 3d.

> *Summa totalis* of the sayde allowances £313 5s.3d.
> And so the sayde accompt[*ants*] be in surplusage upon this ~~this~~ their accompt £36 12s.11d.

All which mony was taken out of the coffer and paid to the saide accomptantes upon the determynacion of this accompt and so quite.

Thomas Andrews	Henry HH Hornyngold	Thomas Gooderiche the elder
Thomas Bryght	Roger Potter	Thomas Gooderich, junior

On a sheet of paper pinned to f.23r., now numbered 23a.]

Certeyne parcels belonging to the feoffes of the towne
landes in Bury the 11th day of January 1584[5]

The Kitchin
First a great brasse pot weighing 114 poundes
Item a lesser pot weighing 61 poundes
Item two cobyrons weighinge together 150 poundes
Item three spyttes weighinge 123 poundes

The Chamber
Item two andyrons, a paier of tonges and a fier sholve garnished with brasse together 54 poundes
Item a longe grene carpet of broad clothe fringed with grene the length of the same clothe beinge in length 7 yardes
Item fower wyned[119] formes, two tables, one liverye cupborde
Item twelve leather bucketes, market with a sheof of arrowes, agenest fier
Item fower great scovels ageinst fier given by Mr Thomas Andrews of Bury, gentleman
Item two great hookes or cromes ageinst fier given by the said Thomas Andrews

The names of the persones that stand seised the day and yere abovesaid of and in the said towne land.

Infeoffed
Sir Thomas Kitson, *miles*
Thomas Gipps
Sir John Heigham, knight
John Cutteras
Thomas Andrews, *armiger*
Roger Potter
William Tassell, *armiger*
Robert Goldinge, *armiger*
Thomas Peyton, gentleman
Anthony Payne, gentleman
William Cooke, gentleman
Roger Barber, gentleman
John Chetham, gentleman
Henry Collyn, gentleman
James Wright, gentleman
Edward Hubank, gentleman
Thomas Gooderich, senior
Thomas Bright

---

119 See Glossary.

Thomas Cocksage
~~Walter Broke~~
Henry Horningolde

Not infeoffed
John Gipps
William Heiward, gentleman
Thomas Gooderich, junior
Walter Brooke [*this added in a different hand.*]

[*f. 23v.*]

[120]4 January 1585[6]

Th'accompte of Roger Potter and Thomas Gippes, surveiors and collectors of the londes and tenementes late John Smythe, esquier, Margarett Odeham, Hellen Fissher, Adam Newhawe and John Salter and of certeine almes howses and other londes and tenementes in Burie St Edmunde and other townes adjoyninge made and taken the 4th daie of Januarie 1585[6] and in the 28 yere of the reign of Our Sovereign Ladie, Quene Elizabethe, for one hole yere endid at Michelmas last past

Arreragia nulla, quia in compoto aldermani

The yerelie revenues
First the said accomptauntes doo charge theym silves with £75 9s.11½d. by theym receyved of the issues, revenues and profittes of the londes and tenementes aforesaid for one yere endid at Michelmas last, as appearithe by the rentall of the same. And with £1 2s.0d. received of Father Bull and Bumpsted for one yeres rent endid at the said feast as an encreasid rent for two tenementes in the Churchegate Strete, late in lease to John Evans. And with 14s.0d. received of Nicholas Rabye as an encreasid rent for the hospitall closse, late in lease to Robert Careles, for one hole yere endid at Michelmas last. And also with certeine encreasid rentes by theym received for one hole yere endid at Michelmas last accordinge to th'order made by Sir Robert Jermyn, knight, and others the commissioners, as folowethe, *videlicet*: of Henry Collyn, gentleman, £1 0s.0d., of John Cutteris £5 6s.8d., of Edward Ubank, gentleman, £3 7s.6d.,[121] *in toto*   £87 0s. 1½d.

Mony delivered owte of the coffer
And with £4 14s.3d. delivered to the said Roger Potter owte of the coffer towardes the discharge of diverse charges   £4 14s. 3d.

---

[120] A new scribe takes over here and reverts to the original arrangement in which several sub-accounts with the balances are brought together in the alderman's account.

[121] There had been an enquiry into the conduct of the feoffees which no doubt led to three of their number having their rents increased, while the named commissioner who ordered the increases was yet another feoffee. Increased rents are often noted individually in a few accounts until a new rental was drawn up.

51

Dinners in the hall

And with £2 0s.0d. received by the said accomptauntes for diverse
  dynners kept within the hall

£2 0s. 0d.

Summa totalis oneris predict £93 14s.4½d., whereof

Rentes resolutes

They praie allowans of 9s.0½d. paiable yerelie owte of the
  mannor of Brettes and other londes in Hepworthe. And of
  £1 3s.6½d. paiable yerely owte of the londes and tenementes of
  Jenkyn Smythe, Mrs Odeham and others. And of 3s.6d. paiable
  yerelie owte of the mesuage adjoyning to the sowthe end of the
  Guildhall. And of 1s.0d. yerelie paiable to the Quenis Majestie
  for 4 tenementes in Garlond Strete And of £10 0s.0d. paid to
  John Jermyn, esquier, for his half yere anuytie due the 20th
  daie of Julie last. And of 10s.0d. for the collectors fee

£12 7s. 1d.

And of £20 0s.0d. received by Thomas Goderiche th'elder of Sir
  Robert Jermyn, knight, for the half yeres anuytie given by Mr
  Edmund Jermyn, due the 20th daie of Januarie last, of which
  they are bifore chargid, and which the said Thomas Goderiche
  hathe in charge as hereafter appearithe

£20 0s. 0d.

Purchase

And of £10 0s.0d. paid to Richard Collin in parte of the purchase
  of his howse

£10 0s. 0d.

And of £6 13s.3d. paid to John Smythe, gentleman, by the handes
  of Thomas Goderiche the yonger, by the assignement of
  diverse of the feoffees, for certeine arrerages due to the said
  John Smythe of a yerelie annuytie of £1 6s.8d., to hym heretofore graunted by indenture, for levyinge of Torckesey rent and
  for costes of suyte and charges abowte distresses by him taken
  for the same, and for his release of the same annuytie as
  appearithe by his acquittauns bearinge date the 16 daie of
  November last past, and for the surrender and yeldinge uppe of
  the said indenture of annuytie brought in at this accompt[122]

£6 13s. 4d.

[f. 24r.]

And of £2 8s.0d. laid owte the last terme of St Michaell by the
  said Thomas Goderiche the yonger and paid to him by the said
  accomptantes, for charges of plea in th'exchequer and makinge
  the right tenure to appeare to cease proces for certeine londes
  callid Salters londes upon the fine levied betwene Sir John
  Heigham and others, pleynants, and Henry Collyn, gentleman,
  and others, deforciants, as appearith by his bill of charges
  thereof shewed at this accompt[123]

£2 8s. 0d.

And of £27 18s.2d. laid owte for diverse charges paid by the said
  accomptantes, as appearithe by a bill of particulers shewed at
  this accompt, whereof £15 0s.0d. delivered to Thomas
  Goderiche th'elder towardes the payment of the taske, as hereafter appearithe in his charge

£27 18s. 2d.

---

[122] This suggests that there had been difficulty in enforcing payment of the rent charge out of the manor
of Torksey.
[123] See Introduction, p.xlvi.

Supers

And of 8s.6d. which John Evans received of Father Bull and
Bumpsted for one quarters rent endid at Christmas 1584. **This
8s.6d. paid, as appearithe in the next accompt.** And of
£1 0s.0d. which remainethe in Mr Paynes handes. And of
2s.0d. for half yeres rent for the Widowe Haggas which
William Baker received. *Pardon[atur] Haggas, quia
in manibus Willelmi Baker.* And of 8d. for a tenemente in
Hepworthe, which the said accomptauntes are charged with in
the said rentall, and there is no suche. And of 9d. in th'handes
of Sir Robert Jermyn, knight. [*In another hand*] **5s.0d. for this
in fine compoti '96**   £1 11s.11d.

> *Summa totalis allocationis* £80 18s.6d.
> *Et sic debent* £12 15s.10½d.
> *Solutum aldermano super determinacionem
> huius compoti et sic eque.*

**Th'accompt of Thomas Goderiche th'elder and Henry Collyn, gentleman,
surveiors and collectors of the newe purchasid londes and Mr Tasselles londes
bilonginge to the towne of Burie, made and taken the daie and yere abovesaid**

Arreragia nulla, quia in compoto aldermanni

The yerlie revenewes

First the said accomptauntes doo charge theymsilves with
£47 19s.2d. by theym received of th'issues, revenues and
profittes of the londes and tenementes aforesaid for one yere
endid at Michelmas last, as appearithe by the rentall of the
same. And also with certeine encreasid rentes by theym
received for one hole yere endid at the same feast accordinge to
th'order made by Sir Robert Jermyn, knight, and other the
commissioners as followethe, *videlicet*: Of Roger Barbour,
gentleman, £2 17s.8d., of Henry Collyn, gentleman, £1 10s.0d.,
of Thomas Goderiche th'elder £1 10s.0d., and of Walter
Brooke 8s.0d., *in toto*   £54 5s. 2d.

Dettes

And with £20 0s.0d. received of Roger Potter in parte of payment
of the purchace of the Angell in Burie, due at the feast of
th'annunciacion of Our Ladie last past   £20 0s. 0d.

And with £20 0s.0d. received of Sir Robert Jermyn, knight, for the
half yeres annuytie given by Mr Edmunde Jermyn and due the
20th daie of Januarie last past, beinge parcell of the charge of
the said Roger Potter, and whereof he hathe allowans as bifore
appearithe   £20 0s. 0d.

And of £15 0s.0d. received of the said Roger Potter toward the
payment of the taske of which he hathe likewise allowans in
th'above said somme of £27 17s.2d.   £15 0s. 0d.

> *Summa totalis oneris predicte* £109 5s.2d., whereof

Rentes resolutes

They praie allowans of 1s.1d. paiable yerelie owte of Mr Tasselles
londes. And of 5s.6d. paiable yerelie owte of the house next

adjoyning to St James steple. And of £10 0s.0d. paid to John Jermyn, esquier, for his half yere anuytie due the 20th of Januarie last past. And of 10s.6d. paiable as a yerelie tenthe due to the Quenis Majestie at Michelmas last owt of St Peters londes for one yere then endid as appearith by th'acquittans. And of 4d. for the same acquittans. And of 5s.0d. for the collectors fee

£11 2s. 5d.

[*f. 24v.*]
Fearme rent
And of £2 0s.0d. paid to Robert Wordewell for one hole yeres rent and fearme endid at Michelmas last past for the howse of correccion

£2 0s. 0d.

The Taske
And of £24 0s.0d. paid this yere for the towne of Burie to the Quenis Majestie for Hir Highenes taxe of the 10ths and 15ths graunted this yere to Hir Highenes in the last Parliament. And of 4d. for the acquittans. And of 6s.8d. paid to the collector for the forbearinge of task money for a tyme. And of £1 13s.4d. for Hir Highenes subsidie for the stocke of this howse. And of 2s.6d. for the taske of St Peters and the grange londes paid to the towne of Westley

£26 2s. 0d.

Reparacions and other charges
And of £20 18s.4d. paid and laid owte by the said accomptantes this yere as appearithe by a bill of particulers shewed at this accompt

£20 18s. 4d.

The Howse of Correccion
And of £11 15s.2d. paid for charges of the house of correccion for 3 quarters of a yere endid at Michelmas last past, as appearithe by particuler billes shewed at this accompt

£11 15s. 2d.

Orphantes
And of £30 5s.0d. paid and laid owte this yere for the orphanes and poore, as appearithe by bill of particulers shewed at this accompt

£30 5s. 0d.

Lynnen
And of £1 0s.0d. for washinge of sondrie peces of lynnen[124]

£1 0s. 0d.

Supers
And of £1 0s.0d. for rent not received for the shoppe and chamber next St James steple, late in th'occupacion of Thomas Yongs. **Dischargid q/ui/a in manibus ministri.** And of 5s.0d. for rent not received for the litle house in the Risbie Gate in the occupacion of [*space*] Pye **Now an almes howse.** And of 6d. rent not received of a parcell of ground, late Doctor Woods. **5s.0d. composicion by Mr. Mountford '89.** And of 2s.0d.

---

[124] Payments for washing linen for the judges who visited the town for the assizes are to be found in many of these accounts.

rent not received of a parcell of \ground/ in th'occupacion of
John Lansdale. **5s.0d. for this in fine compoti '96**   £1   7s.   6d.

    Summa totalis allocacionis £104 11s.3d.

    Et sic debent £4 13s.11d.

    Solutum aldermano super determinacionem huius
    compoti et sic eque.

The aldermans accompt
Th'accompte of Henry Collin, gentleman, alderman, made and taken the daie and yere aforesaid

Arreragia

First the said alderman dothe charge him silf with 17s.5d. as
appearethe in the supers of the last accompt   17s.   5d.

Onus

And the said alderman dothe yeld his accompt of £12 15s.10½d.
by him received of Roger Potter and Thomas Gippes, collectors of the londes and tenementes late John Smythe, esquier,
Margarett Odeham, Hellen Fissher, Adam Newhawe and John
Salter and others. And of £4 13s.11d. by him received of
Thomas Goderiche th'elder, collector of the newe purchased
londes and Mr Tasselles londes   £17 9s. 10½d.

    Summa totalis oneris predicte £18 7s.2½d.

                     Whereof

Allocacio

He praiethe allowans of these sommes underwritten, by him
disbursed for diverse charges and allowances as folowethe,
videlicet:

Delivered[125] to Thomas Bright and Robert Sparke.

Of £1 0s.0d. given to eche parishe churche towardes the
reparacions of the same, *in toto*   £2   0s. 0d.

Delivered to Thomas Bright

And of £1 0s.0d. for provision of wood in the goale   £1   0s. 0d.

Delivered to John Parker

And of £1 10s.0d. given to the hospitall withowte the Risbiegate   £1 10s. 0d.

And of £2 0s.0d. for the livery and fee of Annable, the porter   £2   0s. 0d.

And of 9s.8d. for diverse thinges bought by him and laid owte as
appearithe by a bill of particulers shewed at this accompt, and
parcell thereof for sweepinge the doore   9s. 8d.

[*f. 25r.*]

And of 6s.8d. given to Lichfield for curinge of certeine poore
folkes   6s. 8d.

And of 3s.4d. for the clerkes fee   3s. 4d.

---

[125] The abbreviation 'dd' is a regular contraction for *dederunt*, but 'delivered' could equally well be
represented.

Supers

And of 17s.5d. of arrerages of certeine rentes not yet received,
whereof he standethe chargid as bifore appearethe   17s.   5d.

> *Summa totalis allocationis*   £8   7s.   1d.
> *Et sic debet*   £10   0s.   1½d.
> Which is putt into the chist upon the determynacion of
> this accompt. [*In a different ink*] And after delivered to
> Thomas Godderiche to distribute to the poore [?]4s.2½d.
> more.

Paid as appearithe in the next accompt

Memorandum that it is agreed that £19 5s.1\½/d. shalbe paid to Thomas Bright,
draper, by the collectors of the revenues aforesaid which shalbe received the next
half yere for certeine fryses and clothe taken of him for garmentes for the poore this
yere past, bifore the takinge of this accompt conteyned in a bill of particulers delivered to the said collectors.

Jo. Heigham	Wm. Cooke	*Signum* Thome /V Coxsedg
Roger Barber	Thomas Bryght	*Signum* Henrici HH Horningold
Walter Brooke	Thomas Gooderyche th'elder	Richard Heigham
Edward Ubancke	Roger Potter	John Cutteris
John Gyppes		

[*f. 25v.*]

2 January 1586[7]

**Th'accompt of Thomas Gippes and Edward Ubank, gentleman, surveiors and
collectors of the londes and tenementes late John Smythe, esquier, Margarett
Odeham, Hellen Fissher, \Adam Newhawe/ and John Salter and of certeine
almes howses and other londes and tenementes in Burie St Edmunde and other
townes adjoyninge made and taken the second daie of Januarie 1586[7] and in
the 29ᵗⁱᵉ yere of the reign of Our Soveraigne Ladie Quene Elizabeth for one hole
yere endid at Michelmas last past**

Arreragia nulla quia in compoto aldermani

The yerelie revenues

First the said accomptauntes doo charge theym silves with £75
9s.11½d. by theym received of th'issues, revenues and
profittes of the londes and tenementes aforesaid for one yere
endid at Michelmas last as appearithe by the rentall of the
same. And with £11 0s.2d. of new increasid rents, *videlicet*: of
John Evans 12s.0d., of Nicholas Rabye 14s.0d., of Henry
Colling, gentleman, £1 0s.0d., of John Cutteris, £5 6s.8d., and
of Edward Ubank, gentleman, £3 7s.6d., and of John Evans 8s.
6d. for rent due the last yere, remayninge in his hand, as
appearithe in the super of the last accompt. And of £1 10s.0d.
for the half yeres rent of a tenemente late purchasid of Richard
Collyn and letten againe to him, *in toto*   £88 8s. 7½d.

Dettes

And with £20 0s.0d. received of Roger Potter in parte of payment

of the purchace of the Angell in Burie due at the feast of
th'annunciacion of Our Ladie last past   £20 0s. 0d.

Dyners in the hall
And with £3 5s.0d. received by the said accomptauntes for diverse
diners kept within the hall this yere   £3 5s. 0d.
　　　　Summa totalis oneris £111 13s.7½d., whereof

Rentes resolutes
They praie allowans of 9s. 0½d. paiable yerelie owte of the
mannor of Brettes and other londes in Hepworthe. And of
£1 3s.6½d. paiable yerelie owte of the londes and tenementes
of Jenkyn Smythe and others. And of 3s.6d. yerelie paiable owt
of the mesuage adjoyninge to the sowthe end of the Guildhall
And of 1s.0d. yerelie paiable to the Quenis Majestie for 4
tenementes in Garlond Strete. And of £20 0s.0d. paid to John
Jermyn, esquier, for one hoole yere annuytie as appearithe by
two severall acquittances shewed at this accompt. And of
10s.0d. for the collectors fee, *in toto*   £22 7s. 1d.

The Taske
And of £12 0s.0d. paid by the said accomptauntes for parte of the
seconde payment of the taske paiable this yere for the towne of
Burie to the Quenis Majestie. And of 2s.6d. paid for the taske
of St Peters londes and the grange londes paid to the towne of
Westley   £12 2s. 6d.

Purchase
And of £20 0s.0d. paid to Richard Collyn in full payment for the
purchase of his howse   £20 0s. 0d.

Orphanes
And of £13 0s.0d. delivered to Thomas Goderiche and Robert
Sparke to distribute to the poore and for the orphanes   £13 0s. 0d.

Paymentes
And of £10 0s.0d. paid to Thomas Bright in parte of payment of a
dett due to him for clothe for garmentes for the poore the laste
yere as appearithe in the foote of the last accompt   £10 0s. 0d.
And of £3 0s.0d. paid towardes the stipend of the mynister of St
James at Michelmas last. And of £6 0s.0d. for the same
purpose for a quarter endid at Christmas last[126]   £9 0s. 0d.
And of 15s 0d. paid to Roberte Collin, keper of the hospitall, for
half yeres rent of the hospitall closse leaton to Nicholas Rabye   15s. 0d.
And of £1 3s.3d. paid for wasshinge of the lynnen for the judges
this yere   £1 3s. 3d.
And of 7s.0d. paid this yere for skowringe of the harneys lying at
the hall   7s. 0d.

---

[126] This is the first year in which the feoffees contributed towards the ministers' stipends.

Reparacions

And of £14 3s.8½d. laid owt this yere for reparacions done at the hall, and at the mynisters howses, and the hospitall and other places as appearithe by bill of particulers shewed at this accompt

£14 3s. 8½d.

Supers

And of £2 0s.0d. remayninge unpaid in th'handes of Anthonye Payne, gentleman, for one hole yeres rent due at Michelmas last for a closse in the Westgate Strete. And of 9d. in th'andes of Sir Robert Jermyn, knight, for londes in Hepworthe. **5s.0d. for this 9d.** *in fine compoti* **'96.** And of 4s.0d. for one hole yeres rent for the widowe Haggas which William Baker received. *Pardonatur Haggas, in manibus Baker.* And of 8d. for a tenemente in Hepworthe which the said accomptauntes are chargid with in the said rentall and there is no suche

£2 5s. 0d.

> *Summa totalis allocacionum* £105 3s.11½d.
> *Et sic debent* £6 9s.8d.
> *Solutum aldermano super determinacionem huius compoti, et sic eque.*

[f. 26r.]

Th'accompt of Henry Collinge and William Cooke, gentlemen, surveiors and collectors of the newe purchased londes and Mr Tasselles londes bilonging to the towne of Burie, made and taken the daie and yere aforesaid

Arreragia nulla, quia in compoto aldermanni

The yerelie revenues

First the said accomptauntes doo charge theym silves with £47 19s.2d. by theym received of th'issues, revenues and profittes of the londes and tenementes aforesaid for one yere endid at Michelmas last as appearithe by the rentall of the same. And also with certeine newe encreasid rentes by theym received for one hole yere endid at the same feaste, *videlicet:* of Roger Barbor, gentleman, £2 7s.8d., of Henry Collinge, th'elder gentleman, £1 10s.4d., of Thomas Goderiche, th'elder, £1 10s.0d., and of Walter Brooke 8s.0d. *In toto*

£54 5s. 2d.

> *Summa oneris* £54 5s.2d., whereof

Rentes resolutes

They praye allowans of 1s.1d. paiable yerelie owte of Mr Tasselles londes. And of 5s.6d. paiable yerelie owt of the howse next adjoyning to St James steple. And of 5s.0d. for the collectors fee

11s. 7d.

The Taske

And of £12 0s.0d. paid by the said accomptantes for the residue of the seconde payment of the taske paiable this yere for the towne of Burie to the Quenis Majestie. And of 4d. for th'acquittans. And of £1 0s.0d. for the seconde payment of the subsidie for the stocke of this howse

£13 0s. 4d.

Orphanes

And of £9 0s.0d. delivered to Thomas Goderiche th'elder and

<deletion> of £3 0s.0d. delivered to Robert Sparke to distribute to the poore and for the orphanes	£12 0s.	0d.

Paymentes

And of 6s.8d. for a post fyne for Salters londes	6s.	8d.
And of £12 0s.0d. paid to the minister of St Maries for his stypend for half a yere, *videlicet*, for Michelmas and Christmas quarters	£12 0s.	0d.
And of £9 5s.1½d. paid to Thomas Bright, draper, in full discharge of the frises and clothe for garmentes for the poore the last yere as appearithe in the foote of the last accompt	£9 5s.	1½d.

Supers

This £1 0s.0d. not to be chargid *quia in manibus ministri*. And of £1 0s.0d. not received for the shoppe and chamber next St James steple late in th'occupacion of Thomas Yonges. And of 5s.0d. rent not received for the litle howse in the Risbie Gate in th'occupacion of Pye. **Now an almes howse.** And of 6d. rent not received of a litle parcell of ground late Doctor Woodes. **5s.0d. composicion by Mr Mountford '89.** And of 2s.0d. rent not received of a parcell of ground in th'occupacion of John Landisdale. **5s.0d. for this 2s.0d. *in fine compoti* '89**

£1 7s. 6d.

> *Summa totalis allocationis* £48 11s.2½d.
> *Et sic debent* £5 13s.11½d.
> *Solutum aldermano super determinacionem huius compoti et sic eque*

Compotus aldermani
Th'accompt of William Cooke, gentleman, alderman, made and taken the daie and yere aforesaid

Arrerages

First the said accomptaunt dothe charge him silf with £1 3s.5d., parcell of a super in the last accompt. And of £1 7s.6d. one other super as appeareth in the same accompt, *in toto*	£2 10s. 11d.

Onus

And dothe yeld his accompt of £6 9s.8d. by him received of Thomas Gippes and Edward Ubank, collectors of the londes and tenementes late John Smythe, esquier, and others. And of £5 13s.11½d. received of Henry Collinge, gentleman, collector of the new purchased londes and Mr Tasselles londes	£12 3s. 7½d.

> *Summa totalis oneris predicte* £14 14s.6½d., whereof

He praiethe allowans of theis somes under written by him disbursed for diverse charges and allowances as folowithe *videlicet:*

Delivered to Thomas Bright and Robert Spark

Of £1 0s.0d. given to eche parishe towards the reparacions of the same, *in toto*	£2 0s. 0d.

Delivered to Thomas Bright

And of £1 0s.0d. for provision of woode in the gaole	£1 0s. 0d.

Delivered to Thomas Bright

And of 15s.0d. given to the hospitall withowt the Risbiegate   15s. 0d.

Paid to Annable

And of £2 0s.0d. for the livery and fee of Annable the porter. And
of 14s. 0d. paid to him for thinges bought and done by him as
appearithe by a bill of particulers shewed at this accompt, and
parcell thereof for sweping the dore   £2 14s. 0d.

And of 3s.4d. for the clerkes fee   3s. 4d.

And of £2 10s.11d. of arrerages of certeine rentes not yet received
whereof he standithe charged as bifore appearithe   £2 10s.11d.

> *Summa totalis allocationis* £9 3s.3d.
>
> *Et sic debet* £5 11s.3½d.
>
> which some was delivered to William Faiercliff and John
> Parker, distributors to the poore and orphanes for the yere,
> *videlicet inde* £4 1s.3½d. to William Faiercliff and to John
> Parker £1 10s.0d.

[f. 26v.]

Th'accompt of the Distributors for the poore and orphanes[127]

Memorandum that the daie and yere aforesaid Thomas Goderiche
th'elder, Robert Sparke and Richard Moore did yeld their
accompt of £35 8s.7d. by theym received to distribute to the
relief of the poore and orphanes, *videlicet*: £10 0s.4d. delivered
owt of the chist as appearithe in the foot of the last accompt.
And £13 0s.0d. delivered to theym by Thomas Gippes as
appearith bifore in his accompt. And £12 0s.0d. likewise delivered to theym by Henry Collinge, gentleman, as appearithe
bifore in his accompt, and of 8s.3d. receyvid by theym for
certeine thinges sold by theym, *in toto*   £35 8s. 7d.

And it appearithe by particulers by theym particulerlie shewed at
this accompt that since the last accompt they have fullie given
and distributed the said somes received as afore by wekelie
contribucion untill the takinge of this accompt and over and
above the same have disbursed and laid owt for that purpose
the some of £8 19s.10d. and so remaynethe due to the same
accomptauntes the same some last recited, *videlicet*: to Thomas
Goderiche 10s.2d., to Robert Sparke £4 7s.5d., and to Richard
Moore £4 2s.3d., *in toto*   £8 19s. 10d.

Which said some of £8 19s.10d. it is agreid ~~it is agreid~~ shalbe paid
unto theym upon the resceite of £20 0s.0d. which is paiable by
Sir Robert Jermyn, knight, the 20tie daie of this present
monethe of Januarie, which some is paid to theym as it
appearithe in the next yeres accompt

Dettes all paid

And it is likewise agreid that Richard Lichefield shall have paid
unto him by the collectors and receyvors of the revenues of this
howse to be appointed for this yere to come, upon the next
resceit of the same revenues, the some of £8 0s.0d. for diverse

---

[127] This is the first year in which the account of the distributors appears.

cures done by him to diverse poore men and women within this towne daungerouslie hurte and maymed as appearithe by a bill of particulers exhibited by him at this accompt £8 0s. 0d.

Theise 2 somes paid as appearithe in the next yeres accompt
And likewise that the said receivors shall paie unto Roger Potter the some of 15s.0d., parcell of £2 0s.0d., for goodes left by Mr. Bourdman, late minister of St Maries parishe, in the howse next St James steple which shall remayne and contynue in that howse for the use of the mynisters which shall inhabit there, and th'other £1 5s.0d. he hathe alreadie received, *videlicet* £1 0s.0d. of Richard Collyn for rent of the howse, late purchased of him, which he received the last yere, and 5s. 0d. received of Mr Anthony Payne at Michelmas last, due by him for the stipend of the mynister of St Maries parishe, paid into this howse in consideracion of the allowans aforesaid made to the mynister of the same parishe for his stypend 15s. 0d.

    Summa debiti £17 14s.10d.

    Which some is agreed to be paid as aforesaid upon the determynacion of this accompt.

Jo. Heigham	Henrye Blagge	Robert Goldynge
William Cooke	Henry Collyng	Wyllm. Baker
Thomas Peade	John Gippes	Thomas Coxshag
Henry HH Hornyngold	Roger Potter	Thomas Gooderyche th'elder
Thomas Bright		

[*f. 27r.*]

9 *Januarii* 1587[*8*]

Th'accompt of John Gippes, surveior and collector of the londes and tenementes late John Smythe, esquier, Margarett Odeham, Hellen Fissher, Adam Newhawe and John Salter, and of certeine almes howses and other londes and tenementes in Burie and other townes adjoyninge, made and taken the ninethe daye of Januarie 1587[*8*] and in the thirtie yere of the reigne of Our Soveraigne Ladie Quene Elizabethe, for one hoole yere endid at Michelmas last past

Arreragia nulla hic quia in compoto aldermani

The yerelie revenues
First the said accomptaunt dothe charge him silf with £89 10s.1½d. of th'issues, revenewes and profittes of the londes and tenementes aforesaid for one yere endid at Michelmas last as appearithe by the rentall of the same[128] £89 10s. 1½d.

Dyners in the hall
And with £1 0s.0d. received for diverse diners kept in the hall this yere £1 0s. 0d.

---

[128] The rental for this year is one of only two to survive from the period covered by these account books. Although it has been damaged by damp, much of it can still be read and it is printed as Appendix 2.

Summa totalis oneris £90 10s.1½d., whereof

Rentes resolutes

He praiethe allowans of 18s.3d. for land moll rent. And of 1s.1½d.
for the rent of Leyers. And of 6d. for a barne withowt the
Sowthegate. And of 2s.6d. for a tenemente in the Churchegate
Strete. And of 3s.6d. for the rent of a mesuage adjoyninge to
the sowthe end of the Guildhall. And of £20 0s.0d. paid to John
Jermyn, esquier, for one hole yere annuytie as appearithe by
two severall acquittaunces shewed at this accompt. And of
10s.0d. for the collectors fee, *in toto*   £21 15s. 10½d.

Poore and Orphanes

And of £10 3s.0d. bestowed in the tyme of the sickenes towardes
the charges of the kepers and bearers and in the relief of the
poore beinge visited with sickenes[129]   £10 3s. 0d.

And of £6 0s.0d delivered to William Faiercliff and John Parker to
distribute to the poore and for orphanes   £6 0s. 0d.

Paymentes

And of £12 0s.0d. paid to the minister of St Maries for his stipend
for half a yere *videlicet*, for Michelmas and Christmas quarters.
And of £2 0s.0d. in parte of payment of the next quarter for the
same minister, *videlicet*, at Easter next. And of £12 0s.0d. paid
to the minister of St James for his stipend half a yere, *videlicet*,
for Easter and midsomer quarters. And of £1 0s.0d. in parte of
payment of his stipend for Michelmas quarter   £27 0s. 0d.

And of £8 19s.10d. paid to Thomas Goderiche, Robert Sparke and
Richard Moore for money by theym disbursed as appearithe in
the last accompt   £8 19s. 10d.

And of 8s.0d. paid this yere for skowringe the harneys at the hall   8s. 0d.

And of £1 10s.0d. paid to Robert Collin, keper of the hospitall   £1 10s. 0d.

And of 8s.0d. paid to John Heathe in recompence of 16s.0d. due to
him   8s. 0d.

And of £2 0s.0d. for the liverey and fee of Annable the porter.
And of £1 5s.4d. paid to him for thinges bought by him, and
makinge cleane the doore, and for his charges and horse hyer in
ridinge to Yarmowthe abowte the towne busynes   £3 5s. 4d.

Reparacions

And of £6 10s.9½d. laid owte this yere for reparacions done at the
hall, the mynisters howses and the hospitall as appearithe by
bill of particulers shewed at this accompt   £6 10s. 9½d.

Supers

And of 9s.0d. in the handes of Sir Robert Jermyn, knight, for
londes in Hepworthe. **5s.0d. for this *in fine compoti* '96.** And
of 8d. for a tenemente there not receyved. **No suche tenement
as shewithe bifore.** And of 3s.10½d. for the half yeres rent of

---

[129] The severity of the epidemic, probably plague, which was rife in the town in the summer of 1587,
can be seen from the higher than usual number of burials recorded in each parish. For St James's see
Hervey, *St James Parish Registers, Burials* and for St Mary's transcript of the parish register at SROB.

Valentyne Rose for londes in Hepworthe. And of 1s.2d. for the half yeres rent of John Deynes for londes there. **This 3s.10½d. and 1s.2d. answered** *in proximo compoto.* And of 4s.0d. for one hoole yeres rent of the Widowe Haggas in Burie. *Pardonatur Haggas in manibus Bakr.* And of £3 0s.0d. for the hole yeres rent of a tenement next St James churche late purchasid of Richard Collin. **This £3 0s.0d. answered** *in proximo compoto.* And of 6s.0d. for the hole yeres rent of Thomas Harryson in Garlond Strete. **This 6s.0d. then likewise answerid.** And of 2s.6d. for the half yeres rent of Roger Abelyt there. **This 2s.6d. then also answerid.** *In toto* £3 18s.11½d.

> *Summa totalis allocationis* £89 9s.9½d.
> *Et sic debet* 10s.4d.
> *Solutum aldermano super determinacionem huius compoti et sic eque*

[f. 27v.]

Th'accompt of William Cooke, gentleman, surveior and collector of the newe purchased londes and Mr Tasselles londes bilonginge to the towne of Burie, made and taken the daie and yere aforesaid

Arreragia nulla hic quia in compoto aldermani

The yerelie revenues

The said accomptaunt dothe charge him silf with £53 5s.2d. of the issues, revenues and profittes of the londes and tenementes aforesaid for one yere endid at Michelmas last as appearithe by the rentall of the same £53 5s. 2d.

Dettes

And with £20 0s.0d. received of Roger Potter for the purchase of the Angell in Burie due at the feast of th'Annunciacion of Our Ladie last past £20 0s. 0d.

> *Summa totalis oneris* £73 5s.2d., whereof

Rentes resolutes

He praiethe allowans of 1s.1d. paid yerelie owte of Mr Tasselles londes. And of 5s.6d. paiable yerelie owte of the howse next adjoininge to St James steple. And of 5s.0d. for the collectors fee 11s. 7d.

Orphanes

And of £16 0s.0d. delivered at sondrie tymes to William Faiercliff to distribute to the poore and orphanes £16 0s. 0d.

Paymentes

And of £8 0s.0d. paid to Richard Lichefield for diverse cures by him done to diverse poore folkes accordinge to order therein taken at the last accompt £8 0s. 0d.

And of 15s.0d. paid to Roger Potter for certeine thinges according to order likewise taken at the last accompt 15s. 0d.

And of £1 3s.0d. paid for wasshinge of the lynnen for the judges this yere £1 3s. 0d.

And of £12 0s.0d. paid to the minister of St Maries for his stipend for half a yere, *videlicet,* for Easter and midsomer quarters.

And of £1 0s.0d. in parte of payment of the next quarter for the same minister. And of £5 0s.0d. paid to the minister of St James in parte of payment of his stypend for Michelmas quarter £18 0s. 0d.

And of 2s.6d. for the taske of certeine londes bilonging to St Peters and the graunge, due for the towne of Westley 2s. 6d.

And of £1 13s.4d. for Hir Highenes subsidie for the stocke of this howse £1 13s. 4d.

Supers

Of this £14 19s.0d. is paid £3 8s.8d., as after appearithe in Mr Barbers accompt. And of £14 19s.0d. for the half yeres rent of St Peters, not received, due at Michelmas last. **This for St Peters discharged upon newe order.** And of 6d. rent for a litle parcell of ground late Doctor Woodes. **5s.0d. composicion by Mr Mountford '89.** And of 2s.0d. rent for a parcell of ground in th'occupacion of John Landisdale. **5s.0d. for this 2s.0d. in fine compoti '96.** And of 5s.0d. rent not received of a litle howse in the Risbie Gate in th'occupacion of Pye. **Now an almes howse.** And of 6s.8d. rent not received for a peece of ground in th'occupacion of Robert Sparke, baker. **5s.0d. composicion '89.** *In toto* £15 13s. 4d.

> *Summa totalis allocacionis* £61 18s.7d.
> *Et sic debet* £11 6s.7d.
> *Solutum aldermano super determinacionem huius compoti, et sic eque*

Compotus aldermani

Th'accompt of Roger Barber, gentleman, alderman, made and taken the daie and yere aforesaid

Arreragia

First the said accomptaunt dothe charge him silf with 7s.6d. parcell of a super in the last accompt. And of £2 5s.5d., one other super as appearithe in the same accompt, *in toto* £2 12s. 11d.

Onus

And dothe yeld his accompte of 10s.4d. by him receyved of John Gippes, collector of the londes and tenementes late John Smythe, esquier, and others. And of £11 6s.7d. received of William Cooke, collector of the newe purchased londes and Mr Tasselles londes, *in toto* £11 16s. 11d.

> *Summa totalis oneris* £14 9s.10d., whereof

He praiethe allowans of £2 12s.11d. of arrerages of certeine rentes, not yet received, whereof he standith chargid as bifore appearithe £2 12s. 11d.

And also of theis sommes folowinge by him disbursed for diverse charges and allowances *[f.28r.]* as folowithe, *videlicet*:

Of £1 0s.0d. given to eche parishe towardes the reparacions of the same, *in toto* £2 0s. 0d.

And of £1 0s.0d. for provision of woode in the gaole £1 0s. 0d.

And of 3s.4d. for the clerkes fee 3s. 4d.

And of £6 0s.0d. paid to Mr Mosse, mynister of St. James parishe,
for his stypend for Christmas quarter last past   £6 0s. 0d.

And of £3 0s.0d. delivered to the distributors for the poore and
orphanes for the yere to come, *videlicet*, to John Gillye,
£2 10s.0d. and to Ambrose Brydon,10s.0d.   £3 0s. 0d.

Th'accompt of the distributors for the poore and orphanes

Memorandum that the daie and yere aforesaid William Faiercliff
and John Parker did yeld their accompt of £27 11s.3½d. by
theym received to distribute to the relief of the poore and
orphanes, *videlicet*, £5 11s.3½d. delivered to theym upon the
determynacion of the last accompt, as appearithe in the foot of
the last accompt. And £6 0s.0d. delivered to theym by John
Gippes, as appearithe in his accompt. And £16 0s.0d. delivered
to theym by William Cooke, gentleman, as appearithe before in
his accompt, *in toto*   £27 11s. 3½d.

And it appearithe by particulers by theym particulerlie shewed at
this accompt that since the last accompt they have fullie given
and distributed the said sommes, received as afore, by wekelie
conribucion untill the taking of this accompt, and over and
above the same have disbursed and laid owte for that purpose
the somme of £5 18s.9½d. and so remaynethe to the same
accomptantes the same somme last recited, *videlicet*, to
William Faiercliff £3 0s.8½d. and to John Parker £2 18.1d.   £5 18s. 9½d.

Which somme it is agreed shalbe paid to theym by the collectors
appointed for this yere for receyvinge of the rentes this yere to
come, as the same shalbe received.

And it is likewise agreid that Richard Lichefield shall have likewise paid unto him by the said collectors and receyvors upon
the next resceipt of the said rent the somme of £4 0s.0d. for
diverse cures done by him to diverse poore folkes within this
towne sore hurt and greved as appearithe by a bill of particulers
by him exhibited at this accompt   £4 0s. 0d.

And likewise that the said collectors shall paie unto John Man for
money by him disbursed for reparacions done abowt the house
of Mr Mosse, mynister of St James parishe, the somme of   £2 9s. 0d.

And also that the said collectors shall paie to Robert Sparke for
money by him disbursed, as appearithe by a bill shewed at this
accompt   £4 0s. 0d.

And also that £1 0s.0d. shalbe paid by the said collectors to the
churchwardens of eche parishe towardes the reparacions of the
same, *in toto*   £2 0s. 0d.

And also that they shall paie for provision of woode in the gaole   £1 0s. 0d.

And likewise that they shall paye to Sir Thomas Kitson, knight,
for the fyne of Bell Meadowe,[130] the somme of   £5 0s. 0d.

The somes above paiable are paid as appeare in the next yeres accompt.

---

[130] It is not clear whether this is the land left by John Baret for the repair of the clock and chimes at St
Mary's church, or that given by John Parfay, whose will was proved in 1509, for the repair of the great
bell known as the curfew bell, in St Mary's church. The latter is still known as Bell Meadow. Both were
left to St Mary's church, not the feoffees. See Tymms, *Wills*, pp.28, 29 and 113.

[f. 28v.]

18 January 1588[9]

Th'accompt of Thomas Goderiche th'elder, surveior and collector of the londes and tenementes late John Smythe, esquier, Margarett Odeham, Hellen Fissher, Adam Newhawe and John Salter and certeine almes howses and other londes and tenementes in Burye St Edmunde and other townes adjoyning, made and taken the 18 daie of Januarye in the 31 yere of the reign of the reign [sic] of our Soveraigne Ladie, Quene Elizabeth, for one hole yere endid at \St/ Michaell th'Archaungell last past

Arreragia
Patet in le supers ultimi compoti

The yerelie revenues

First the said accomptaunt dothe charge himsilf with £89 10s.1½d. being the hoole yeres rent and profitt of the londes and tenementes aforesaid endid at Michelmas last as appearithe by the rentall of the same   £89 10s. 1½d.

Parcell of the supers in the last accompt

And with £3 13s.6½d. for certeine rentes \unpaid/ ~~upon~~ as appearithe in the supers of the last accompt, *videlicet*, of William Rowge for one hole yeres rent for a tenemente by St James churche, late purchased of Richard Collin, due at Michelmas 1587, £3 0s.0d. And of 3s.10½d. receyved of George Nunne, gentleman, for the half yeres rent of lond in Hepworthe, late Valentyne Rose. And of 1s.2d. receyved of the said George Nunne for the half yeres rent for londes there, late John Deynes. And of 6s.0s. receyved of Thomas Harryson for one hole yeres rent of a tenement in Garlond Strete. And of 2s.6d. receyved of Roger Abelye for the half yeres rent of a tenement there, *in toto*   £3 13s. 6d.

And with £20 0s.0d. receyved of Walter Brooke, which was borowed of Thomas Turner, for repayment whereof he stand bound.[131]   £20 0s. 0d.

    Summa oneris £113 3s.8d., whereof

Rentes resolutes

He prayethe allowans of 9s. 0½d. paiable yerelie owte of the mannor of Brettes and other londes in Hepworthe. And of £1 4s.6½d. payable yerelie owte of the londes and tenementes of Jenkyn Smythe and others. And of 2s.6d. yerelie paiable owte of the mesuage adjoyning to the sowthe end of the Guildhall. And of 1s.0d. yerlie paiable to the Quenis Majestie for 4 tenementes in Garlond strete. And of 10s.0d. for the Collectors fee, *in toto*   £2 17s. 1d.

And of £20 0s.0d. receyved by Roger Barber, gentleman, of Sir Roberte Jermyn, knight, for the half yeres annuytie given by

---

[131] This and another sum of £80 borrowed this year were no doubt required because of the double task which had to be paid, in addition to the usual expenditure. The purchase of St Peter's must have used up any reserves that had been built up, while the plague in the previous year involved additional expenditure.

Mr Edmunde Jermyn of which he is bifore chargid and which
the said Roger hathe in charge as hereafter appearithe   £20 0s. 0d.

And of £20 0s.0d. wherewith this accomptaunt is bifore charged
for th'other half yeres anuytie given by Mr Edmunde Jermyn
and paiable to John Jermyn of Debden, esquier, not yet
receyved by this accomptant nor acquitaunce made by the said
John Jermyn   £20 0s. 0d.

Poore and orphanes

And of £28 8s.0d. paid by this accomptaunt towardes the charges
of the poore and orphanes this yere   £28 8s. 0d.

Paymentes

And of £3 0s.0d. paid to Mr Morgan, mynister of St Maryes for
the residue of his stypend for Easter quarter. And of £12 0s.0d.
paid to him for his stypend for midsomer and Michelmas quarters. And of £8 0s.0d. paid to Mr Hill for his stipend for
Christmas quarter for serving the cure there   £23 0s. 0d.

And of £1 10s.0d. paid the keper of the hospitall   £1 10s. 0d.

And of £3 0s.0d. paid to William Faiercliff for money by him
disbursed as appeare in the last accompt   £3 0s. 0d.

And of £4 13s.6d. for certeine armour bought for the towne   £4 13s. 6d.

And of 1s.2d. for sealinge of 2 busshelles for the markett   1s. 2d.

And of £3 5s.10d. for certeine course lynnen bought in Burye by
this accomptaunt by appointement of diverse of this companye,
1583, for the use of the justices of assise, as appearithe by a bill
of particulers shewed at this accompt   £3 5s. 10d.

Taske

And of 6s.8d. paid for the taske of Leyers in Rowgham   6s. 8d.

Supers

And of 9d. in the handes of Sir Robert Jermyn, knight, for londes
in Hepworth. **5s.0d. for this *in fine compoti* '96. No suche
tenemente.** And of 8d. for a tenemente there, not receyved.
And of 4s.0d. for one hole yeres rent of the the Widowe
Haggas in Burye. ***Pardonatur Haggas, in manibus Baker***   5s. 0d.

    Summa allocationis £106 17s.8d.

    Et sic debet £6 7s.0d.

    Which is this 21 of Januarie *anno predicto* delivered by the
said accomptant to the distributors for the poore as hereunder appearithe.

Delivered by the said accomptant to John Gillie to distribute to the
poore and orphanes untill the fynishing of this accompt
£5 0s.0d. and unto Ambrose Brydon for the same purpose
£1 6s.0d.

    Summa £6 6s.0d.

    And so the said accomptant clere.

[f. 29r.]

**Th'accompt of Roger Barber, gentleman, surveior and collector of the newe
purchasid londes and Mr Tasselles londes bilonging to the towne of Burie,
made and taken the daie and yere aforesaid**

Arreragia
Patet in le supers ultimi compoti

The yerelie revenues

First the said accomptant dothe charge himsilf with £53 5s.2d. being the hole yeres rentes and profittes of the londes and tenementes aforesaid endid at Michelmas last, as appearithe by the rentall of the same — £53 5s. 2d.

And with £80 0s.0d. by him receyved of Thomas Turner of Burie to th'use of the feoffees of the londes bilonging to the same towne, as lent for repayment, whereof to the said Thomas Turnor at th'end of one yere, Sir Robert [*Jermyn*] knight, Robert Grome, gentleman, John Gippes and this accomptant stand severallie bound to the said Thomas Turnor, *videlicet*, every of them for payment of £20 0s.0d. — £80 0s. 0d.

And with £20 0s.0d. by him received of Sir Robert Jermyn, knight, for one half yeres annuytie given by Edmunde Jermyn, esquier, disceased, parcell of the charg of Thomas Goderiche, as bifore appearithe — £20 0s. 0d.

And with £3 8s.8d. by him receyved as part of th'arrerages of the rent of St Peters — £3 8s. 8d.

And with 5s.0d. by him receyved of Roberte Davison by th'appointement of Sir Roberte Jermyn and Sir John Heigham, knightes, as parte of the money by the said Davison receyved within the sowthe ward of Burye, 1585, towardes the charges of setting forthe of soldiers — 5s. 0d.

Summa oneris £156 8s.10d., whereof

Rentes resolutes

He praiethe allowans of 1s.1d. paid yerelie owt of Mr Tasselles lond. And of 5s.6d. paiable yerelie owt of the howse next adjoyning to St James steple. And of 10s.6d. paiable as a yerelie tenthe due to the Quenis Majestie at Michelmas last owt of St Peters lond, for one yere then ended. And of 5s.0d. for the collectors fee — £1 2s. 1d.

Poore and Orphanes

And of £8 2s.0d. paid by this accomptaunt towardes the charges of the poore and orphanes this yere — £8 2s. 0d.

Paymentes

And of £1 0s.0d. paid to Mr Mosse, mynister of St James parishe, for parte of the offeringes not receyved at Midsomer 1586. And of £6 0s.0d. paid to him for his stipend for a quarter endid at the feast of th'Annunciation of Our Ladie last past. And of £12 0s.0d. paid to him for his stipend for midsomer and Michelmas quarters. And of £10 0s.0d. paid to him for his stipend for a quarter endid at the feast of the Natyvitie of Christ last past. And of £1 0s.0d. paid biforehand to Mr Morgan for parte of his stypend to be due at Michelmas 1588 — £30 0s. 0d.

And of £5 1s.0d. paid for armour and setting forthe of soldiers — £5 1s. 0d.

And of £25 4s.7d. paid for certeine dettes due \to/ <deletion> diverse persons as in part appearithe in the last accompt and for

68

other thinges, as by a note shewed at this accompt dothe
appeare   £25 4s. 7d.

And of £1 11s.0d. given to Rogers, keper of the hospitall, at his
first entraunce in consideracion of diverse sicke persons which
were then there   £1 11s. 0d.

And of £1 4s.0d. for wasshinge the lynnen for the judges this yere   £1 4s. 0d.

Taske

And of £48 0s.0d. for the first and second paymentes of the taske
for the towne of Burie. And of 2s.6d. for the taske of certein
londes bilonging to St Peters and the graunge   £48 2s. 6d.

Reparacions

And of £15 3s.0d. laid owte this yere for reparacions as appeare
by billes of particulers shewed at this accompt   £15 3s. 0d.

Supers

And of £29 18s.0d. for the hole yeres rent of St Peters, not
received, endid at Michelmas last. **This for St Peters
discharged upon new order.** And of 10s.0d. for the hole yeres
rent of thre tenementes in Raynegate Strete ended at
Michelmas last, late Cutbert Smythes . And of 6d. rent for a
litle parcell of ground late Doctor Woodes. **This 6d.
discharged upon composicion '89.** And of 2s.0d. rent for a
parcell of ground in th'occupacion of John Landisdale. **5s.0d.
for this 2s.0d.** *in fine compoti* **'96.** And of 6s.8d. rent for a
peece of ground in the occupacion of Robert Sparke, baker.
This 6s.8d. paid. And of 5s.0d. rent of a litle howse in the
Risbyegate in th'occupacion of Pye. **This 5s.0d. discharged,
now an almes howse.** *In toto*   £31 2s. 2d.

> *Summa allocationis* £166 12s.3d.
> *Et sic in surplusagio* £9 13s.0d.
> This some is paid as appearith in th'accompt made
> by William Faiercliff, 1590.

[f. 29v.]

Th'accompt of the distributors for the poore and orphanes

Memorandum that the daye and yere aforesaid John Gillye and
Ambrose Brydon did yeld their accompt of certeine money by
theym receyved to distribute to the relief of the poore and
orphanes, *videlicet*, the said John Gillye did receyve
£18 10s.0d. and the said Ambrose Brydon £3 10s.0d., *in toto*   £22 0s. 0d.

And it appearithe by particulers by theym particulerlie shewed at
this accompt that since the last accompt they have fullie given
and distributed the said sommes receyved as afore by wekelie
contribuciones untill the fift daye of this moneth of Januarye,
and over and besides the same have disbursed and laid owte for
that purpose £3 12s.8d. and so remayneth to the same
accomptauntes the same somme last recited, *videlicet*, to John
Gillie £2 4s.8d. and to Ambrose Brydon £1 8s.0d, *in toto*   £3 12s. 8d.

More delivered the 21 daye of this present moneth of Januarie
before the fynishing of this accompt to the said John Gillye by
Thomas Goderich th'elder, as bifore appearithe in the foote of

his accompt as parcell of his debet upon his accompt, to distribute to the poore and orphanes untill the finishing of this accompt, £5 0s.0d. And to Ambrose Brydon, for the same purpose, £1 6s.0d., *in toto*   £6 6s. 0d.
    whereof

The said John Gillye since the said 21 daie of Januarie untill the 10th of Februarie next folowing and bifore the fynishing of this accompt hathe for the same purpose distributed as appearithe by his bill of particulers the somme of £2 18s.0d. And the said Ambrose Brydon for like purpose untill the second of Marche anno predicto as appeare by his bill the somme of 8s.0d., *in toto*   £3 6s. 0d.

    Sum of their recepts £28 6s.0d.
    And paid by theym £28 18s. 8d.

Debet 10s.0d. paid to Ambrose Briden *ut patet in comptoto* 95
And so rest due to the said John Gillye 2s.8d., and to the said Ambrose Brydon 10s.0d., *in toto*   12s. 8d.
    which some it is agreid shall be \paid/ to
    theym upon the next receipt

Paid as appearithe in the next accompt made by Thomas Goderiche the yonger. And shall likewise paye unto Richard Lichefield the some of £4 0s.0d. for diverse cures by him done to diverse poore folkes within this towne sore hurt and greved as appearithe by a bill of particulers shewed at this accompt   £4 0s. 0d.

Due to Annable clere for this yere £1 17s.10d., which is answerid him as appearithe in the accompt 1590. And shall likewise paye unto Annable, the porter, for his fee and livery, over and besides £1 0s.0d. remayning in his handes for dyners kept in the hall this yere which he hath receyved   £1 0s. 0d.
And likewise to him for sweping the doore and for thinges by him done as appearithe by a bill of particulers nowe shewed   17s. 10d.

£1 0s.0d. hereof \to be/ paid to John Man for St James churche by order taken at th'accompt 1590, entrid in the booke of orders, which somme is answered and paid as appears in th'accompt 1591[132] And shall also paye to the churche wardens of eche parishe towards the reparacions of the churches £1 0s.0d., *in toto*   £2 0s. 0d.

£1 0s.0d. hereof paid as appeare in th'accompt of th'executors of Erasmus Cooke to John Gillie, 1590
And shall also paye to [*space*] for provision of woode in the gaole   £1 0s. 0d.

Paid as appearthe on the next accompt made by Thomas Peade
And shall also paie to William Cooke £1 11s.0d. by him laid owte for the copie of the will and inventorie of Thomas Bright[133]   £1 11s. 0d.
And likewise to hym for the clerkes fee   3s. 4d.

---

[132] At a meeting on 21 January 1591 it was ordered that John Man and other parishioners of St James's, were to be paid £3 at the next receipt towards repairing the church, Minutes, H2/6/2.1, p.5.

[133] Thomas Bright the elder, a major benefactor, who died in 1587, left his moveable goods (after

[f. 30r.]

9 *Januarii* 1589[*90*]

Th'accompt of Thomas Goderiche the yonger and William Faiercliff, surveiors and receyvors of the londes and tenementes late of John Smyth, esquier, Margarett Odeham, Hellen Fissher, Adam Newhawe and John Salter and certeine almes howses and other londes and tenementes in Burie St Edmund, Hepworthe and other townes adjoyninge made and taken the ninethe daie of Januarie in the 32 yere of the reign of our Soveraign Ladie Quene Elizabeth for one hoole yere ended the last daie of December last past

Arrerages

First the said accomptantes doo charge theym silves with 5s.5d.
for certeine arrerages of rentes unpaid, as appearithe in the
supers of the last accompt of Thomas Goderiche th'elder. And
with 6s.0s. for the arrerages of a yerelie fearme rent of 9d.
deteyned by Sir Robert Jermyn, knight, for certeine londes in
Hepworthe by the space of 8 yeres, *videlicet*, for the yere 1580
and so forthe untill and for the yere 1587, as appearithe by the
supers of th'accomptes of the same yeres. And with 10s.0d. for
the arrerages of a yerlie fearme rent of 4s.0d., receyved and
deteyned by William Baker for a tenemente in the Northegate
Strete, in th'occupacion of the Widowe Haggas by the space of
two yeres and *dimidia, videlicet*, 1585, '86 and '87 as likewise
appearithe by the supers of th'accomptes of the same yeres.
And with 2s.0d. for th'arrerages of a yerelie fearme rent of 8d.
late deteyned by Margerye Canham, widowe, for the fearme of
a mesuage and an acre of lond in Hepworthe, late in the
occupacion of Wyllys, by the space of thre hole yeres, *videlicet*, 1585, '86, and '87, as likewise dothe appeare by the
supers of th'accomptes of the same yeres, *in toto*   £1   3s.   5d.

The yerelie revenues

And with £89 10s.1½d. beinge the hoole yeres fearme rentes and
profittes of all the londes and tenementes aforesaid for the yere
abovesaid, as appearithe by the rentall of the same   £89 10s. 1½d.

Fynes

And with £2 0s.0d. for a fyne paid by Ed[*ward*]e Clerke, late
fermor of the tenemente Leyers, in Rowgham, for licence to
alyen his lease thereof to Roger Hempston   £2   0s.   0d.

Churchegraces and offrings

And with 4s.2d. beinge th'arrerages of certeine churche graces[134]
happened in the parishe of St Maryes of the former yere next

---

paying all legacies) to be divided between his nine children and the feoffees; hence the feoffees' interest
in his inventory.
[134] See Glossary.

bifore the charge of theis accomptauntes. And with £8 7s.0d. beinge the clere some of the hoole yeres offringes and churche graces in the said parishe, endid at Michelmas last, over and besides the fees of the parishe clerke for his colleccion thereof, as appears by his notes. And also with £8 11s.6d. being the clere somme of this yeres exhibicion allowed yerelie by Hir Majestie towardes the findinge of the mynisters in bothe parishes in Burie aforesaid, over and besides the fees and charges paid at the audyte by the churche wardens abowte the [*f.30r.*] receipt thereof.   £17 2s. 8d.

And with £2 0s.0d. receyved by theis accomptauntes of Mr Peade, whereof he stand chargid in his accompt, parcell of his receipt.   £2 0s. 0d.

And with one galon of wyne ~~by~~ payable yerelie by John Revell and his heires for certeine lond in Burye field, sometyme of Jenkyn Barrett   one gallon of wyne

Summa oneris £111 16s.2½d. one galon of wyne, whereof

Rentes resolutes

They praie allowans of 9s.0½d. for owt rentes paid yerelie owte of the mannor of Brettes and other londes in Hepworthe. And of £1 8s.0½d. paiable yerelie owte of the londes and tenementes of Jenkyn Smythe and others. And of £20 0s.0d. paid to John Jermyn, esquier, for one hoole yeres rent and anuytie, as appearithe by his acquittaunce shewed at this accompt. And of 10s.0d. for the collectors fee, *in toto*   £22 7s. 1d.

[*f.30v.*]

Subsidies

And of £1 0s.0d. for the last payment of the subsidie, due the last yere and not paid. And of £1 13s.4d. for the first payment of the subsidie graunted at the last parliament   £2 13s. 4d.

Poore and orphantes

And of £1 0s.0d. paid to John Browne for receyvinge Thomas Sharpe, orphant, into his service as apprentize   £1 0s. 0d.

And of 7s.0d. paid to Margarett Earle for kepinge Bardwelles orphant 14 weekes from Misdomer forthe, and of 6s.0d. for 12 weekes from Michelmas to Christemas   13s. 0d.

And of £21 16s.8d. delivered at diverse tymes to Roberte Sparke and Thomas Michell, distributors, for the relief of the poore and orphantes   £21 16s. 8d.

Paymentes

And of £20 0s.0d. paid to Mr Lewis, mynister of St. Maryes churche, for his stipend for Our Ladie daye and midsomer last. And of £6 2s.0d. for parte of the stipend to Mr Mosse, mynister of St. James churche, at midsomer aforesaid   £26 16s. 0d.

And of £1 10s.0d. paid to Rogers for kepinge of the hospitall   £1 10s. 0d.

And of £2 0s.0d. paid to Mr Hill for the brasse and furnace in the mynisters howse. And of £3 10s.0d. to Mr Mosse for certeine curteynes and hanginges there. And of 5s.0d. to Josephe Nunne

for a loode of pooles[135] in the tyme of the last plagge, bought of him and ymploied abowte the making of tentes for th'infected. And of £3 10s.0d. to William Rowge in full repayment of his fyne, and for release of a promise to him for a lease to have been made of the tenemente late Richard Collins in Burie.[136] And of £4 0s.0d. to Richard Lichefield for a dett to him for surgerie of poore people, examined and allowed of at the last generall accompt	£13 5s. 0d.
And of £2 0s.0d. paid to John Annable, porter, for his wages for this year past	£2 0s. 0d.
And of 3s.0d. for a paper booke newlie provided for the remembraunces to remayne in this howse[137]	3s. 0d.

Reparacions

And of £12 8s.7d. laid owte abowte reparacions and building of the mynisters howses and others, and for a newe buckett to the well at the hospitall	£12 8s. 7d.

Supers

And of £3 0s.0d. rent, nowe withdrawen, for the tenement late purchased of Richard Collyn nere St James churche, by reason that the widowe of the same Collyn hathe thereof an estate for hir lief, by assuerauns, bifore the said purchase. **5s.0d. *in fine compoti* '96.** And of 7s.6d. in th'handes of Sir Roberte Jermyn, knight, for the fearme rent of lond in Hepworthe \at 9d. per annum/ deteyned by ten yeres nowe endid. **5s. for this *in fine compoti* '96.** And of 18s.0d. in th'handes of William Baker for the ferme rent of a tenemente in th'occupacion of Elizabeth Haggas, widowe, in the Northgate Strete, deteyned by foure yeres and *dimidia*, nowe ended. ***Pardonantur arreragia Haggas viduae in manibus William Baker***	£4 5s. 6d.
And of one gallon of wyne bestowed this yere at the common dynner of this felowshippe	One gallon of wyne

Summa allocacionis £108 4s 2d. one gallon of wyne
Et sic remanent £3 12s.0½d., whereof

Orphantes

The somme of £1 0s.0d. was presentlie paid and given to Richard Cowper, sherman, for enterteyninge Thomas Cleydon, an orphant, as an apprentize according to the statute

And 12s.0½d. paid to Robert Sparke and Thomas Michell in full discharg of the surplusage due to theym upon their accompt for the poore

And £2 0s.0d. residue delivered to Mr Barber towardes the payment of Mr Mosses stypend due at Christmas last
Summa £3 12s.0½d.
And so the said accomptantes clere

---

[135] Placing those infected with plague in temporary dwellings outside the town walls was an accepted means of isolation, Slack, *Impact of Plague*, p.203.
[136] It was discovered that Collin's wife was entitled to dower from this property, so the fine which the prospective tenant had paid was refunded.
[137] This is the earliest surviving Minute Book of the feoffees, H2/6/2.1.

[*f. 31r.*]

9 *Januarii* [15]89[90]

Th'accompt of Thomas Peede and Erasmus Cooke, surveiors and receyvors of the newe purchased londes bilonging to the towne of Burie, made and taken the daie and yere aforesaid

Arrerages

First the said accomptantes do charge theym silves with £31 2s.2d. for certeine arrerages of rentes unpaid, as appearithe in the supers of the last accompt made by Mr Barber. And with £15 13s.2d. for certeine arrerages of rentes unpaid as appearithe in the supers of the accompt of William Cooke, 1587. And of 4s.0d. for the arrerages of a yerelie rent of 6d. unpaid for a parcell of ground, late Doctor Woodes, by the space of 8 yeres, *videlicet*, for the yere 1579 and so forthe untill and for the yere 1586, as appearithe by the supers of th'accomptes of the same yeres. And with 14s.0d. for th'arrerages of a yerelie rent of 2s.0s. for a parcell of ground in th'occupacion of John Landisdale by the space of 7 yeres, *videlicet* for the yere 1580 and so forthe untill and for the yere 1586, as appearithe by the supers of th'accomptes of the same yeres. And with 10s.0d. for th'arrerages of a rent of 5s.0s. unpaid for a litle howse in the Risbie Gate, late in th'occupacion of Pye, by the space of 2 yeres, *videlicet*, for the yeres 1585 and '86, as appearithe by the supers of th'accomptes of the same yeres, *in toto*   £48 3s. 4d.

The yerlie revenues

And with £46 7s.2d. being the yerelie rentes and profittes of the londes and tenementes aforesaid for one hole yere endid at Michelmas last, as appearithe by the rentall of the same   £46 7s. 2d.

And with £11 10s.0d. paiable at Christmas for the half yeres rent of St Peters to end at th'annunciacion of Our Ladie next   £11 10s. 0d.

Churchgraces

And with £9 12s.3d. beinge the clere somme of the hole offeringes and churchegraces in St James parishe endid at Michelmas last, over and besides the parishe clerkes fee for collectinge the same, as appeare by his notes   £9 12s. 3d.

Dyners in the hall

And with £3 5s.0d. receyved for dyners kept in the hall this yere   £3 5s. 0d.

   Summa oneris £118 17s.9d., whereof

Rentes resolutes

They praye allowans of 1s.1d. paid yerelie owte of Mr Tasselles londes. And of 5s.6d. paiable yerelie owte of the mynisters howses by St James steple. And of 5s.0d. for the collectors fee   11s. 7d.

Poore and orphantes

And of £10 10s.6d. paid \towardes the charge of the poore and orphantes/ ~~to Mr Mosse, mynister of St James parishe in parte of~~ this yere   £10 10s. 6d.

74

Paymentes

And of £27 18s.11d. paid to Mr Mosse, mynister of St James
parishe in parte of his stipend for one yere endid at the feast of
the Nativitie of Christ last past. And of £20 0s.0d. paid to Mr
Lewys, mynister of St Maryes parishe for his half yeres
stypend due for the feastes of St Michaell th'Archangell and
the Nativitie of Christ last   £47 18s. 11d.

And of £1 4s.0d. for wasshinge the lynnen for the judges this yere   £1 4s. 0d.

And of 2s.6d. for the taske of certeine londes bilonging to St
Peters and the graunge, due for the towne of Westley   2s. 6d.

And of £2 0s.0d. paid to Thomas Goderiche the yonger towardes
the payment of th'annuytie due to John Jermyn, esquier, of
which the same Thomas stand chargid in his accompt   £2 0s. 0d.

And of £1 14s.4d. paid to William Cooke for a dett due to him as
appearithe in the last accompt   £1 14s. 4d.

And of £1 18s.0d. paid to him for money by him disbursed abowte
the suyte against Sir Thomas Lucas, knight, for a legacie given
to the poore of this towne of Burye by William Markaunt[138]   £1 18s. 0d.

And of 3s.4d. paid to the said William Cooke for the clerkes fee   3s. 4d.

And of £1 0s.0d. delivered to William Faiercliff, one of the
receyvors of the yere to come. And of 2s.3d. given to Yell. And
of 3s.4d. paid to Dodde for keping St Peters 8 daies[139]   £1 5s. 6d.

[*f. 31v.*]

Supers

And of £30 5s.6d., parcell of £31 2s.2d., of arrerages of rentes not
receyved, whereof they stand chargid as bifore appearith in this
accompt. **So much of thees arrerages as concerne St Peters
are discharged by newe order taken at th'accompt 1590,
which is for the payment of £20 0s.0d. by £3 6s.8d. yerlie
and after upon a newe lease this rent was reserved to be
paid in 20 yeres.** And of £15 6s.6d., parcell of £15 13s.2d.,
whereof they likewise stand chargid as bifore appearithe. **Mr.
Mountford compounded for th'arrerages hereof, being
now tenant of the ground late Doctor Woodes at
th'accompt 1590, and paid the rent for that yere.** And of
4s.6d. of arrerages \for a/ parcell of ground, late Doctor
Woodes, deteyned in all by 11 yeres, endid at Michelmas last.
And of 16s.0d, in th'handes of John Landisdale for the rent of a
parcell of ground deteyned in all by ten yeres endid at
Michelmas last. **5s.0d. for Landisdale *in fine compoti*. This
howse of Pye is now used for an almes howse and
th'arrerages pardoned.** And of 15s.0s. of arrerages for a litle
howse in the Risbie Gate, late in th'occupacion of Pye,
deteyned in all by fyve yeres at Michelmas last. **Sparke
compounded for all his arrerages *ideo vacat*.** And of 6s.8d.
in th'handes of ~~Sir~~ Robert ~~Jermyn~~ Sparke, baker, for the rent of
a parcell of ground in his occupacion due for one yere at

---

138   See Introduction, p.lxvii.

139   It is not certain what this means; it seems unlikely that St Peter's was only used for a short time this
year.

Michelmas last. And of 8d. in th'handes of William Johnson
for a yeres rent of a mesuage in Longe Brackelond, late
Ed[*ward*]e' Hoyes, endid at Michelmas last   £47 14s. 10d.
> *Summa allocationis* £115 3s.7d.
> *Et sic remanet* £3 14s.2d.,whereof

there remaynethe in th'handes of John Annable for dyners kept in the hall this yere,
and bifore chargid upon theis accomptaunts £3 5s.0d.
> So that to theym allowed there remayne 9s. 2d.,
> which somme was presentlie paid *et sic eque*

Annable 5s.0d. the next accompt.

John Annable is to be allowed for charges and money by him disbursed as by a bill
of particulers appearithe shewed at this accompt the somme of £1 7s.6d. And
demaundethe by the same bill allowans for his journey to Colchester for serving
the citacion upon Sir Thomas Lucas, knight, for the legacie given by William
Markaunt, and by assent of the companye he is allowed 3s.0d.
> *Summa* due by Annable upon this accompt £1 14s.6d.,
> which somme is answered as appearithe in the next accompt.

Th'accompt for the poore and orphantes

Th'accompt of Robert Sparke and Thomas Michell, distributors to the poore and
orphantes, made the daye and yere aforesaid, of certeine money by theym
received for that purpose as bifore appearithe, *videlicet*, of Thomas Godriche the
yonger and William Fayercliff £21 16s.5d. and of Thomas Peade and Erasmus
Cooke £10 10s.6d.
> *Summa* £32 7s.2d., which somme it

appearithe, by particulers by theym particulerlie shewed at this accompt, that they
have fullie given and distributed the said sommes receyved, as afore, by wekelie
paymentes to and for the poore and orphantes, and over and besides the same
have disbursed and laid owte for that purpose 12s.0½d., which is paid unto theym
as appearithe bifore in th'accompt of Thomas Goderiche the younger
> *Summa totalis* for the poore and orphantes this yere as
> here and bifore appearithe in this accompt £35 12s.2½d.

**Debentur £1 0s.0d. hereof for St Maries churche paid to John Gillie, as appeare
in the next accompt, and th'other £1 0s.0d.to be paid to John Man by order
taken at the accompt 1590, entered in the booke of orders, which somme is
answered and paid in the accompt 1591.**

To eche parishe churche towardes the reparacions of the same
£1 0s.0d., *in toto*   £2 0s. 0d.
For provision of woode in the goale   £1 0s. 0d.

[*f. 32r.*]

18 *Januarii* 1590[*1*]

**Th'accompt of William Faiercliff, surveior and receyvor of the londes and
tenementes sometyme of John Smythe, esquier, Magarett Odeham, Hellen
Fissher, Adam Newhawe, John Salter and certeine almes howses and other
londes and tenementes in Bury St Edmunde, Hepworthe and other townes
adjoyning, made and taken the 18 daie of Januarie in the 33° yere of the reign
of Our Soveraigne Ladie Quene Elizabeth, and *anno Domini* 1590, for one hole
yere endid the last of December last past, as folowithe**

Arreragia

First the said accomptaunt dothe charge him silf with £4 5s.6d. for
certeine arrerages of rentes unpaid, as appearith in the supers of
the last accompt made by Thomas Goderiche, junior £4 5s. 6d.

The yerelie revenues

And with £89 10s.1½d. beinge the hole yeres rentes, fearmes and
profittes of all the londes and tenementes aforesaid, for the yere
abovesaid, as appearithe by the rentall of the same £89 10s. 0½d.

And with £1 0s.0d. by him receyved at the last accompt, as
appearithe in the same accompt made by Thomas \Peede/
~~Goderiche~~ £1 0s. 0d.

Legacies

And with £40 0s.0d. receyved of th'executors of John Boldero,
disceasid, given by his last will and testament[140] £4 0s. 0d.

And with £30 0s.0d., residue of a legacie of £60 0s.0d. receyved
of Sir Thomas Lucas, knight, given to the poore of Burie by the
last [*will of*] William Markaunt[141] £30 0s. 0d.

Sales

And with £32 0s.0d. receyved for sale of certeine tymber at
Hepworthe. And with £13 0s.0d. likewise receyved for sale of
tymber there £45 0s. 0d.

Churchegraces and offeringes

And with £9 19s.8d. beinge the clere ħ somme of the hoole yeres
offringes and churchegraces in the parishe of St Maries, endid
at Michelmas last, over and besides the fees of the parishe
clerke for his colleccion thereof, as appearithe by his notes.
And also with £4 4s.0d., beinge the clere somme of the half
yeres exhibicion allowed yerelie by Hir Majestie towardes the
findinge of the ministers in the parishes of this towne, over and
besides the fees and charges paid at the awdyt abowt the resceit
of the same £14 3s. 8d.

And with one gallon of wyne paiable yerelie by John Revell and
his heires for certeine londes in Burie fieldes, sometyme of
Jenkyn Barrett a gallon of
wyne

Summa oneris £223 19s.3½d., one gallon of wyne, whereof

Rentes reolutes

The said accomptaunt praieth allowans of 9s.0d. for the owt rentes
paid yerelie owt of the mannor of Brettes and other londes in
Hepworth. And of £1 6s.0d. paid to Bailief Spittlehowse for
owt rentes paid yerelie owt of the londes and tenementes in
Burie St Edmunde, Barton and Rowgham And of 8d. for an
owt rent paid yerlie for Leyers. And of £20 0s.0d. paid to John
Jermyn, esquier, for one hoole yeres rent and annuytie, as
appearithe by his acquittaunces shewed at this accompt. And of
10s.0d. for the collectors fee £22 5s. 8d.

---

[140] See Notes on People and Appendix 8, *sub* 1584.
[141] See Notes on People and Appendix 8, *sub* 1590.

And of 10s.6d. paiable as a yerelie tenthe due to the Queins
Majestie for St Peters at the feast of St Michaell th'archaungell
31 Elizabeth *regine* as appearithe by th'acquittauns of Hir
Majesties receyvor shewed at this accompt   10s. 6d.

And for the acquittauns of the receipt of the same   4d.

[*f. 32 v.*]

Subsidies and taske

And of £1 0s.0d. paid for the second payment of the first subsidie
graunted at the last parlyament   £1 0s. 0d.

And of 3s.4d. paid to the towne of Rowgham for the taske of
Leyers

And of 2s.6d. for the taske of certeine londes bilonging to St
Peters and the graunge due for the towne of Westley   5s. 10d.

And of £24 0s.0d. for the payment of the first 15th and tenthe
graunted to Hir Highenes at the last parliament   £24 0s. 0d.

And for th'acquittauns for the same   4d.

Mynisters wages

And of £40 0s.0d. paid Mr Lewys, mynister of St Maries churche,
for his stipend for one hole yere endid at the feaste of the
Nativitie of Our Lord last past, bifore the taking of this
accompt   £40 0s. 0d.

And of £4 0s.0d. paid to Mr Mosse, mynister of St James churche,
for parte of his stipend due the last yere   £4 0s. 0d.

Paymentes

And of £5 0s.0d. paid to Mr Hill   £5 0s. 0d.

And of £60 0s.0d. paid to Thomas Tillott of Rowgham for a dett
due to him   £60 0s. 0d.

And of £1 4s.0d. for wasshinge of lynnen for the judges this yere £1 4s. 0d.

And of £2 0s.0d. laid owt by this accomptant abowt Stamford
Bridge and for certeine armour taken of him for setting forth of
soldiers. And of 2s.0d. paid to the bailief for his arrest abowt
matters concerning this towne   £2 2s. 0d.

And of £9 13s.6d. paid to Mr Barber, due to him as appearithe by
his accompt made 1588. And of £10 19s.0d. paid to John
Gillie. And of £6 4s.6d. paid to Mr Cooke for certeine charges
abowt the suyt in Chauncerie against William Baker, and the
matter of Sir Thomas Lucas, knight, for the legacie of William
Markaunt, disceased, as appearithe by a bill of particulers
shewed at this accompt   £26 17s. 0d.

Poore and orphanes

And of £25 0s.0d. paid at sondrie tymes to Robert Cotton, gentleman, one of the distributors for the poore and orphanes   £25 0s. 0d.

And of £2 4s.0d. given and distributed by this accomptaunt at
severall tymes to diverse poore and sicke persons   £2 4s. 0d.

Reparacions

And of 8s.8d. laid owt for reparacions this yere   8s. 8d.

Supers

And of £4 5s.6d. of arrerages not yet receyved, whereof this accomptaunt standethe chargid as bifore appearithe in this accompt   £4 5s. 6d.

And of £3 0s.0d. rent, parcell of the revenues in the charge of this accomptaunt and nowe withdrawen, for the tenement late purchased of Richard Collyn in Burie aforesaid. **5s.0d. in fine compoti '96.** And of 2s.0d. for the half yeres rent of a tene-ment in th'occupacion of the Widowe Haggas *Pardonatur quia in manibus* **Will[elm]i Baker.** And of 9d. for a yeres rent endid at Michelmas last for lond in Hepworthe deteyned by Sir Robert Jermyn, knight. **5s.0d. for this** *in fine compoti* **96**   £3 2s. 9d.

And of one gallon of wyne bestowed this yere at the common dyner of this felowshippe   one gallon of wyne

   Summa allocacionis £222 6s.8d., one gallon of wyne
   Et sic debet £1 12s.8½d. which somme is answered
   and paid as appeare in the next accompt.

[*f. 33r.*]

Th'accompt of th'executor of Erasmus Cooke, disceased,[142] surveior and receyvor of the newe purchasid londes and Mr Tasselles londes, bilonging to the towne of Burie, made and taken the daie and yere aforesaid

Arreragia

Patet in le supers ultimi compoti M[agist]ri Peade

The yerelie revenues

First the said accomptant dothe charge him silf with £46 12s.2d., beinge the rentes and profittes of the londes and tenementes aforesaid for one hoole yere, with the rent of St Peters, nowe paid, for the half yere to end at the Annunciacion of Our Ladie next and paiable at Christmas   £47 12s. 2d.

Churchegraces and offringes

And with £8 6s.9d. for part of the offringes and churchegraces in the parishe of St James, over and besides the fee of the parishe clerk for his colleccion thereof, as appearith by his notes. And with £1 19s.8d. more of the offringes and churche graces of the same parishe receyved by Mr Mosse, as dothe appeare under his hand. And also with £4 5s.0d. beinge the clere some of the half yeres exhibicion allowed yerelie by Hir Majestie for the finding of the ministers in the parishes of this towne, over and besides the fees and charges paid at the awdyte abowte the resceit of the same   £14 11s. 6d.

And with 6d. receyved of Mr Mountford in consideracion of the arrerages for his howse, late Doctor Woodes   6d.

   Summa oneris £61 4s.1d., whereof

---

[142] Erasmus Cooke died in 1590. He appointed his son-in-law, Robert Hyndes, like himself a goldsmith, as his executor. See Notes on People for more about both Cooke and Hyndes.

Rentes resolutes

The said accomptaunt dothe praie allowans of 5s.6d. paiable yerelie owt of the ministers howses by St James steple. And of 1s.1d. paid for Mr Tasselles londes. And of 5s.0d. for the collectors fee   11s. 7d.

Poore and Orphanes

And of £7 0s.0d. paid to Mr Cotton, one of the distributors of the poore and orphanes towardes their relief. And of £5 0s.0d. paid to William Kellam, one other of the distributors for the same purpose   £12 0s. 0d.

Paymentes and mynisters wages

And of £1 0s.0d. paid to John Man for the churche of St James paiable 1587   £1 0s. 0d.

And of £38 0s.4d. paid to Mr Mosse, minister of St James parishe, for part of his stipend for a yere endid at the feaste of the Nativitie of Christ last past. And of £1 19s.8d. received by Mr Mosse for the residue of his stipend for this yere past, as appearithe under his hand, and wherewith this accomptaunt is bifore chargid as bifore appearithe   £40 0s. 0d.

And of £2 0s.0d. paid to John Gillie, one of the churche wardens of the churche of St Maries, for the same churche for two yeres nowe past, *videlicet*, 1588 *et* 1589   £2 0s. 0d.

And of 3s.4d. to the clerke for his fee   3s. 4d.

Reparacions

And of 15s.1d. laid owt for certeine reparacions this yere   15s. 1d.

[*f. 33v.*]

Rentes deteyned by reason of paymentes for this howse

And of £2 1s.8d. for the half yeres rent of certeine londes in the fearme of Mr Barber, unpaid in consideracion of certeine money by him paid for this howse. And of £1 10s.0d. for the half yeres rent of certeine londes late in the fearme of Edward Goderiche and nowe of Mr Barber, also unpaid for the consideracion aforesaid. And of 6s.8d. for the half yeres rent of certein londes, late in the fearme of John Keale and nowe of Mr Barber, likewise unpaid for the cause aforesaid   £3 18s. 4d.

Supers

And of 2s.0d. of arrerages of rent for this yere past in th'handes of John Landisdale. **5s.0d. for this *in fine compoti* 96**   2s. 0d.

    Summa allocacionis £10 10s.4d.

    Et sic debet 13s.9d.

    Which somme was paid to John Gippes, one of the receivors appointed for the yere to come upon the taking of this accompt with 13s.4d. then receyved of William Jellowe for his fyne of a stall let to him for 21 yeres, so in all receyved £1 7s.1d. [*In another ink, perhaps also in another hand*] which somme is in charge in the next yeres accompt of John Gippes

Th'accompt for the poore and orphanes

Th'accompt of Robert Cotton, gentleman, and William Kellam, distributors to the poore and orphanes made the daie and yere aforesaid of certeine money by theym receyved for that purpose as bifore appearithe, *videlicet*, the said Robert Cotton receyved £32 0s.0d., and the said William Kellam £5 0s.0d.

> *Summa* £37 0s.0d.

Which somme as appearith by particulers by theym particulerlie showed at this accompt is by theym fullie given and distributed by wekelie paymentes to and for the poore and orphanes. **Debetur Will[el]mo Kellam 11s.0d.** [*In another ink, perhaps another hand*] **This paid to William Faiercliffe as appeare in the next accompt.** And, over and besides the same, the said William Kellam hathe paid and laid owte for that purpose 11s.0d.

> *Summa totalis* for the poore and orphanes as here
> bifore appearithe in this accompt £39 4s.0d.

Annable

It appearithe in th'accompt bifore, 1588, that Annable is to have for his wages and bill, besides £1 0s.0d. by him receyved for mariages that yere	£1 17s.	10d.
And in th'accompt 1589 he receyved for mariages that yere £3 5s.0d., and his wages for that yere is paid him, as appearithe by the same accompt. And he is to be allowed upon a bill £1 10s.6d., and so owethe clere for that yere	£1 14s.	6d.
And for this yere Annable do yeld accompt for dyners kept in this hall £2 0s.0d., and is to be allowed for his wages £2 0s.0d., and upon a bill 8s.0d., and so remaine due to him for this yere	8s.	0d.
So due to Annable clere upon theis 3 accompts	11s.	8d.

Which somme is answered in the next accompt

Dettes

£1 0s.0d. hereof for St James churche paid as appear in the next yeres accompt. Due for this yere to eche parishe churche toward the reparacions of the same £1 0s.0d., *in toto.* **£1 0s.0d. hereof due to St Maries churche paid as appear in the accompt of Mr Colling '93**	£2	0s.	0d.
For provision of wode in the gaol	£1	0s.	0d.
Agreid at this accompt that Richard Lichefield shall have for diverse cures by him done to diverse poore folkes within this \towne/ sore hurte and greved, as appearithe by a bill of particulers. **Paid as appearithe in th'accompte of Robert Spark '92**	£5	0s.	0d.

[*f. 34r.*]

3 *Januarii* [*15*]91[*2*]

Th'accompt of John Gippes and Robert Sparke, surveiors and receyvours of the londes and tenementes sometyme of John Smythe, esquier, Margarett Odeham, Hellen Fissher, Adam Newhawe and John Salter and certeine almes howses and other londes and tenementes in Burie St Edmunde, Hepworthe and other townes adjoyninge, made and taken the third daye of Januarie in the 34 yere of the reign of Our Soveraign Ladie Quene Elizabethe and *anno Domini*

81

1591[/2] for one hoole yere endid the last daye of December last past as followithe

Arreragia

Patet in le supers ultimi compoti Willelmi Faiercliff

The yerelie revenues

First the said accomptauntes do charge theymsilves with £89 10s.1½d. beinge the hoole yeres rentes, fearmes and profittes of all the londes and tenementes aforesaid for the yere abovesaid as appearithe by the rentall of the same £89 10s. 1½d.

Encreased rent

And with 15s.0d. of encreased rent for londes in th'occupacion of William Astye[143]   15s. 0d.

And with £1 7s.1d. by theym receyved at the last accompt, as appearithe in the foote of the same accompt £1 7s. 1d.

Woodesales

And with £12 0s.0d. receyved for sale of woode and tymber at Rowgham £12 0s. 0d.

And with £2 0s.0d. receyved of Mr Walker, as appearithe in his accompt £2 0s. 0d.

One gallon of wyne

And with one gallon of wyne paiable yerelie by John Revell and his heires for certeine londes in Burie fieldes, late of Jenkyn Barrett One gallon of wyne

        Summa oneris £105 12s.2½d., one gallon of wyne, whereof

Rentes resolutes

They praye allowans of 9s.0d. for the owte rentes paid yerelie owt of the mannor of Brettes and other londes in Hepworthe. And of £1 6s.0d. paid to bailief Spittlehowse for owte rentes paid yerelie owte of the londes and tenementes in Burie St Edmunde, Barton and Rowgham. And of 8d. for an owte rent paid yerelie for Leyers. And of 1s.0d. paid yerelie for 4 tenementes in Garlond Strete. And of £20 0s.0d. paid yerelie to John Jermyn, esquier, for one hole yeres rent and annuytie, as appearithe by his acquittans shewed at this accompt. And of 10s.0d. for the collectors fee £22 6s. 8d.

Mynisters wages

And of £30 0s.0d. paid to Mr Lewys, mynister of St Maries churche for parte of his stipend, *videlicet*, for 3 quarters of a yere £30 0s. 0d.

Taske

And of £16 0s.0d. for parte of the second payment of the firste 15th and 10th graunted to Hir Highenes at the last parliament, and of 4d. for the acquittauns £16 0s. 4d.

---

[143] At a meeting on 9 January 1590 it was agreed that, on the surrender of his old lease, William Aste was to have a new one for twenty-one years at a rent of 18s.0d., Minutes, H2/6/2.1, p.1.

And of 3s.4d. paid to the towne of Rowgham for the taske of
Leiers   3s. 4d.

Paymentes

And of £5 0s.0d. allowed to Mr Hill \claymed/ as due at the
Nativitie of Christ '90[144]   £5 0s. 0d.

And of £1 4s.0d. for wasshinge of lynnen for the judges this yere   £1 4s. 0d.

And of 13s.4d. for settinge forthe of soldiers   13s. 4d.

And of 15s.0d. paid to the keper of the Spittlehowse   15s. 0d.

And of 6s.0d. paid to Motte for surgerye   6s. 0d.

And of £2 0s.0d. paid to Page for interest, with 4d. for an
obligacion   £2 0s. 4d.

And of £1 4s.0d. paid to Henry Horningold for money by him
disbursed abowte Stamford Bridge   £1 4s. 0d.

Poore and orphanes

And of £5 10s.0d. paid to Colyes wief due to hir for kepinge of
thre poore children   £5 10s. 0d.

And of £2 0s.0d. delivered to ~~the~~ John Sterne, one of the distributors of the poore and orphanes   £2 0s. 0d.

And of £1 16s.8d. paid to Normans wief for kepinge of poore
orphanes   £1 16s. 8d.

And of 10s.0d. paid to Roodes wief for kepinge a poore child   10s. 0d.

Reparacions

And of £2 5s.9d. laid owte for reparacions of certeine howses   £2 5s. 9d.

Supers

And of £10 0s.0d. remayninge in th'handes of Sir Robert Jermyn,
knight, for parte of th'annuytie given by Mr Edmunde Jermyn,
due the 20[ti] daie of Julie last. **This £10 0s.0d. paid as
appearithe in the next accompt of Roberte Sparke.** And of
9d. rent unpaid by the said Sir Roberte Jermyn for londes in
Hepworthe. **5s.0d. for this 9d.** *in fine compoti* **'96.** And of
3s.9½d. for the half yeres rent of londes in Hepworthe due by
Rust. **5s.0d.** *per* **Collin** *in fine compoti* **'96.** And of £3 0s.0d.
withdrawen for a tenement, late Collins, in Burie. And of
6s.0d. for the rent of a tenemente in Garlond Strete in
th'occupacion of Harrison. **This 6s.0d. allowed for keping of
poor children.** And of 5s. for the rent of a bearne in Westgate
Street letton to Scott. **5s.0d. for this 5s.0d.** *in fine compoti* **'96.**
And of 15s.0d. for the half yeres rent of Rabye. **This 15s.0d.
allowed for a curble for a well and other thinges.** And of a
gallon of wyne bestowed at th'accompt   £19 10s. 6½d.

    Summa allocacionis £111 5s.11½d.

    Sic remanet computanto £5 13s.9d., whereof paid as
appearithe in th'accompt '92 and the residue by Mr.
Collinge as appearithe in his accompt '93.

---

[144] At a meeting on 15 January 1590 it was agreed that £5 which was due to Mr Hill, minister, should be
paid by Mr Faircliff at the next receipt if no further order was made, Minutes, H2/6/2.1, p.2.

[f. 34v.]

Th'accompt of Richard Walker, gentleman, and John Gillie, surveiors and receyvors of the newe purchased londes and Mr Tasselles londes bilonging to the towne of Burie St Edmunde, made and taken the daie and yere aforesaid.

Arreragia
Patet in le supers ultimi compoti executoris Erasmi Cooke

The yerelie revenues
First the said accomptauntes doo charge theymsilves with £46 12s.2d., beinge the rentes and profittes of the said londes and tenementes for one yere, as appeare by the rentall of the same £46 12s. 2d.

Wood sales
And with £4 0s.0d. receyved for woode and tymber sold at Rowgham £4 0s. 0d.

Churchegraces and offringes
And with £9 8s.2d. for offringes and churchegraces in the parishe of St James, over and besides the fee of the parishe clerke for colleccion thereof, as appearithe by his notes. And with £4 6s.0d. for the half yeres exhibicion allowed yerelie by Hir Majestie for the finding of the mynisters in the parisshes of this towne, being the clere somme, over and besides the fees and charges paid at the awdit abowt the resceit of the same £13 14s. 2d.
     Summa oneris £64 6s.4d., whereof

Rentes resolutes
They praye allowans of 5s.6d. paiable yerelie owte of the mynisters howses by St James steple. And of 1s.1d. paid for Mr Tasselles londes. And of 5s.0d. for the collectors fee 11s. 7d.

Mynisters wages
And of £30 0s.0d. paid to Mr Mosse, mynister of St James churche, for parte of his stipend, *videlicet*, for 3 quarters of a yere £30 0s. 0d.

Taske
And of £8 0s.0d. for parte of the second payment of the first 15th and 10th graunted to Hir Majestie at the last Parliament £8 0s. 0d.
And of 2s.6d. paid for taske to the towne of Westley 2s. 6d.

Paymentes
And of £2 0s.0d. paid to Page for interest £2 0s. 0d.
And of 2s.8d. for wearinge the towne armour at the trayninge 2s. 8d.
And of 7s.6d. paid to the keper of the Spittlehowse 7s. 6d.
And of £1 0s.0d. paid to Boyton the plommer for parte of a dett to him due for reparacions in St James churche £1 0s. 0d.
And of 10s.0d. paid to Yonges for half yeres wages for repayringe the glasse abowte the same churche[145] 10s. 0d.

---

[145] David Dymond, in his article 'God's disputed acre', cites references to windows broken by ball games played in churchyards, p.491. Although it is from the late eighteenth century, he also gives a reference, p.476, to cricket being played in the Great Churchyard in Bury.

And of £2 0s.0d. paid to John Gippes, one other accompant for
this yere, wherewith he standithe charged in his accompt   £2   0s. 0d.

And of £3 10s.0d. paid to John Gillie for dett to him due   £3 10s. 0d.

And of 3s.4d. to the clerke for his fee   3s. 4d.

And of 2s.0d. to John Sterne, one of the distributors for the poore,
by him laid owte   2s. 0d.

Poore and Orphanes

And of £1 6s.8d. paid to Roodes wief for keping a pore child   £1   6s. 8d.

And of 2s.0d. to Colyes wief for keping of orphanes   2s. 0d.

And of £2 0s.0d. to Thomas Davye, one of the distributors to the
poore   £2   0s. 0d.

Reparacions

And of 10s.0d. laid owte for reparacions of certeine howses   10s. 0d.

Supers

And of £11 0s.0d. for the half yeres rent of St Peters, unpaid. **10s.
paid to John Gippes as appeareithe on his accompt**   £11   0s. 0d.

And of 2s.0d. of arrerages in th'handes of John Landsdale. **5s.0d.
for this 2s.** *in fine compoti* **'9**   2s. 0d.

    Summa allocationis £64 0s.4d.

    Et sic debet 6s.1d.

    which was presentlie given to the poore

Th'accompt for the poore and orphanes

Th'accompt of Thomas Davye and John Sterne, distributors to the
poore and orphanes, made the daye and yere aforesaid of
certeine money by theym receyved for that purpose, as bifore
appearithe, *videlicet*, eche of theym the somme of £2 0s.0d., *in
toto*   £4   0s. 0d.

Debetur to Thomas Davye £4 18s.8d. Paid *ut patet in compoto* '95

Which somme as appearithe by particulers by theym shewed at this accompt is by
theym fullie given and distributed by wekelie paymentes to and for the poore and
ophanes [*sic*] and over and besides the same the said Thomas Davye hathe paid
and laid owte for that purpose £4 10s.4d., over and besides 8s.4d. by him laid
owte for matters concerning this towne, and so due to him £4 18s.8d., and the
said John Sterne hathe laid owte, over and besides the somme by him receyved,
2s.0d., which is to him allowed as appearithe bifore in Mr Walkers accompt

    Summa totalis for the poore and orphanes paid as appearithe here
and hereafter in this accompt £14 1s.8d. and 6s.7d. as above
appearithe,[146] over and above £9 5s.4d. as before appearithe, so in
all £23 13s.1d.

[*f. 35r.*]
Dett to William Faiercliffe paid to him as appeare hereunder

It appearithe in the last yeres accompt of William Faiercliffe that
he upon his accompt did owe £1 12s.8½d. and at this accompt,
as appearid by his bill, he hadd disbursed and laid owte for

---

146 In the original, the words from '*Summa totalis*' to 'accompt' are bracketed together and these
amounts written beside them.

matters concerning this towne £1 6s.0d., and for a dett of 11s.0d. due to William Kellam, as appearithe in the last accompt, the same William Faiercliffe demaundid allowans, which sommes being to him allowed there remaine due to him clere

4s. 3½d.

Dett to Annable £1 13s.9d.

At this accompt the wieff of John Annable, disceased, late porter of this howse, yelded accompt of £1 15s.0d. for 7 dynners kept in the Guildhall this yere, and demaunded allowans for his wages £2 0s.0d., and upon a bill by hir shewed at this accompt by him bestowed, 17s.1d. And for a dett to him due as in the last accompt 11s.8d., so rest clere due to hir. **Paid by Mr. Colling as appeare in his accompt '93**

£1 13s. 9d.

Debet Ricardo Lichefield £3 6.8d.[147]

Due to Richard Lichefield for surgerie of diverse poore people within this towne allowed him yerelie by order owte of the howse. **Paid by Mr Colling as appeare in his accompt '93**

£3 6s. 8d.

Debitur

Due for this yere to the parishe of St Maries towardes the reparacions thereof. **Paid as appeare in th'accompt of Mr Collinge '93**

£1 0s. 0d.

And for provision of woode in the gaole

£1 0s. 0d.

Churchegraces and offringes for the parishe of St Maries

Churchegraces and offringes this yere past gatherid by the parishe clerke in the parishe of St Maryes, over and besides the clerkes fee for collecting thereof, £6 6s.7d., whereof he paid to Mr Hill £5 12.0d., and so answerithe onelie the somme of

14s. 7d.

All sommes of money due to St James churche paid at this accompt.

The Quenis Majesties allowans for the half yeres exhibicion of the mynisters, over and besides the fees and charges paid at the awdit abowt the resceite of the same, £4 6s.4d., owt of which was nowe allowed for arrerages of money due for St James churche £1 0s.0d., and for this yere nowe past £1 10s.0d. and so answered and paid thereof clere

£1 16s. 4d.

Money lent by Thomas Overend. [*In another hand*] Paid to him upon a reckonning as appearithe in th'end of th'accompt '94.

Lent to this companye by Thomas Overend at this accompt, to be repaid to him upon the second daye of Februarie next insuyng, the somme of

£10 0s. 0d.

Summa of the last 3 sommes £12 10s.11d., whereof

Paymentes

Paid owte presentlie to Pond, the cutler, for dressinge 8 corseletts 3 yeres

£1 4s. 0d.

---

[147] At a meeting held on 21 January 1591, it was agreed that Richard Lichefield was to be paid £3 6s.8d. yearly for curing the sick.

Mynisters [*In another hand*] **This paid owte to John Gillie receyvor for the yere to come**

And to John Man for part of Mr Mosses stipend for the Nativitie of Christ last	£2 10s. 0d.
And to William Faiercliff for a dett to him due as above appearithe	4s. 3d.
And to the plommer for mending the Guildhall	£1 19s. 0d.

Poore and orphanes

And to Roodes wieff for keping a poore child	10s. 0d.
And to certeine poore women	2s. 0d.
And to Moores wief for keping a poore child	£1 0s. 0d.
And to Margarett Erle for a poore child which she must kepe untill Easter come 3 yeres	£1 6s. 8d.
And to Normans wief for orphanes for parte of the yere past	£1 0s. 0d.
And to Colies wieff for keping of orphanes	£1 10s. 0d.
And delivered to John Gillye, one of the receyvors for the yere to come	£1 5s. 0d.

Summa soluc[*ionis*] £12 10s.11d.

J. Heigham	Robt. Ashefeld	Henrye Blagge
Anthony Payne	Wm. Cooke	Thomas Gooderich
Richard Walker	Edmond Ubanke	John Gylly
Wylliam Fayerclif	Robrte Sparke	H[*enry*] H[*orningold*]

[*f. 35v.*]

3 Januarii [15]92[3]

Th'accompt of Robert Sparke, surveior and receyvor of the londes and tenementes sometyme of John Smythe, esquier, Margarett Odeham, Hellen Fissher, Adam Newhawe and John Salter and certeine almes howses and other londes and tenementes in Burie St Edmunde, Hepworth and other townes adjoyning made and taken the third daie of Januarie in the 35° yere of the reign of Our Soveraign Ladie Quene Elizabethe for one hoole yere endid ~~at Michelmas last~~ \the last daie of/ December last past as followethe

Arrerages

Inprimis the said accomptaunt dothe charge him silf with £10 0s.0d., parcell of th'annuytie of Mr Edmunde Jermyn due in Julie 33 *Elizabethae regine* as appearithe in the supers of the last accompt of John Gippes	£10 0s. 0d.

The yerelie revenues

And with £89 10s.1½d. the hoole yeres rent of the said londes for the yere abovesaid, as appearithe by the rentall of the same	£89 10s. 1½d.

Encreasid rentes

And with 18s.11d. of encreasid \rent/ for certeine woode in the tenure of Mr Nunne[148] in Hepworthe[149]	18s. 11d.

---

[148] The original account, gives his Christian name, George, Account, H2/3/4/1.

[149] On 3 January 1592 Mr Barber and John Gippes were asked to view the fourteen acres of wood which Mr Nunne was to lease and to report its value and what they considered a reasonable rent, Minutes, H2/6/2.1, pp.5, 6.

And with 2s.0d. of encreasid rent for lond there, in the tenure of
Lawrence Coldham[150]   2s.   0d.

And with £1 2s.5d. of encreasid rent for certeine lond and
meadowe late in the tenure of Rust,[151] and nowe of Sir Robert
Jermyn, knight[152]   £1 2s. 5d.

And with 15s.0d. of encreasid rent for londes there in the tenure of
William Astye   15s. 0d.

And with 6s.8d. of encreasid rent for a bearne and ortyard in Burie
in the tenure of John Cadge   6s. 8d.

A galon of wine

And with one gallon of wyne paiable yerelie by John Revell and
his heires for certeine londes in Burie fieldes, late Jenkyn   One gallon of
Barrettes   wine

    Summa oneris £102 15s.1½d., one gallon of wine, whereof

Rentes resolutes

He praiethe allowans of 9s.0d. for the owte rentes paid yerelie
owte of the mannor of Brettes and other londes in Hepworthe.
And of £1 6s.0d. paid to Bailief Spittlehowse, for owte rentes
paid yerelie owte of the londes and tenementes in Burie St
Edmunde, Barton and Rowgham. And of 8d. paid yerelie for an
owte rent for Leyers. And of 1s.0d. paid yerelie for ?two 4
tenementes in Garlond Strete. And of £20 0s.0d. paid yerelie to
John Jermyn, esquier, for one hole yeres anuytie, as appearithe
by his acquittauns shewed at this accompt, and of 10s.0d. for
the collectors fee   £22 6s. 8d.

Mynisters

And of £40 0s.0d. paid to Mr Lewys for his stipend for a yere
endid at the feast of St Michaell th'archaungell last past   £40 0s. 0d.

Taske

And of £12 0s.0d. paid for parte of the first payment of the second
taske graunted at the last Parliament   £12 0s. 0d.

And of 3s.4d. for the taske of Leyers   3s. 4d.

Subsidie

And of £1 13s.4d. paid for the first payment of the second subsidie
graunted at the last Parliament   £1 3s. 4d.

Poor and orphanes

And of £6 10s.0d. delivered to Thomas Overend, \one/ of the
distributors to the poore and orphanes to distribute for that
purpose   £6 10s. 0d.

---

[150] On 21 January 1591 it was agreed that Lawrence Colman, clerk to Mr George Kempe, should have a lease of a piece of ground in Barningham for twenty-one years at a rent to be agreed, Minutes, H2/6/2.1, p.5.

[151] The original account gives Rust's Christian name as Giles, Account, H2/3/4/1.

[152] The Minute Book is silent about Sir Robert Jermyn's lease of land which had formerly been held by Rust. On 9 January 1590, William Hodgkins was granted a lease of lands and meadows formerly Rust's for twenty-one years at £1 6s.8d. a year, Minutes, H2/6/2.1, p.1. It is not clear whether these lands were the same as those which, on 21 July 1592, were offered to Edward Tailor for twenty-one years at a rent of £1 10s.0d., Minutes, H2/6/2.1, p.7.

Paymentes

And of £1 4s.0d. for wasshing of the lynnen for the judges this
    yere   £1 4s. 0d.

And of £5 0s.0d. paid to Richard Lichefield for a dett due to him
    for curinge of diverse poore persons as s appearithe by
    th'accompt '90   £5 0s. 0d.

And of £1 10s.0d. paid to the keper of the spittlehowse   £1 10s. 0d.

And of £3 0s.0d. paid to John Gippes for parte of a dett to him as
    appearithe in his last accompt   £3 0s. 0d.

Reparacions

And of £5 0s.10d. for reparacions at the Guildhall and other places
    this yere   £5 0s. 10d.

Supers

And of 9d. remayning in th'handes of Sir Robert Jermyn, knight,
for a yeres rent unpaid for londes in Hepworthe. **5s.0d. for this
in fine compoti '96.** And of 5s.0d. for the yeres rent of a bearne
in Westgate Strete letton to Scott.[153] **5s.0d. for this ibidem.**
And of £3 0s.0d. for the yeres rent of a mesuage by St James
churche purchased of Richard Collyn. **5s.0d. in fine compoti
'96**   £3 5s. 9d.

And of a gallon of wine bestowed at th'accompt   A gallon of
        wine

        Summa allocationis £101 13s.11d., a gallon of wine.
        Et sic remanet £1 1s.2½d. *Et debet* 1s.0d. which he
        rec[*eived*] of Robert Jellowe and 7s.1d. receyved of
        Inglethorpe, *in toto*, 8s.1d., which is disbursed as
        hereafter followethe, *videlicet*

[f. 36r.]

Paid to the Widowe Potter by Robert Sparke which wanted of the
    nomber of 30 provided for at the common dyner   8s. 0d.

And more for hir for biere for the poore and the fier in the
    chamber   7s. 0d.

Given to Widowe Bentham at 2 severall tymes   3s. 6d.

And for a quarte of sacke and a pottell of clarett wyne   2s. 4d.
        Summa ~~8s.5½d.~~ £1 0s.10d.
        Sic debet 8s.5½d., which was presentlie
        delilvered to William Heyward, gentleman,
        one of the receyvors for the yere tocome.

3 Januarii [15]92[3]

**Th'accompt of John Gillie, receivor of the newe purchased londes and Mr
Tasselles londes bilonging to the towne of Burie St Edmunde made and taken
the daie and yere aforesaid**

Arrerages

First the said accomptaunt dothe charge himsilf with £11 10s.0d.
    arrerages for St Peters, as appearithe in the last accompt of Mr
    Walker   £11 10s. 0d.

---

[153] On 21 July 1592 a lease for twenty-one years was granted to Mr Peede of the barn in Westgate
Street, formerly let to Scott, for 10s. a year, Minutes, H2/6/2.1, p.7.

The yerelie revenue

And with £46 12s.2d. being the hoole yeres rent and profittes of
the londes and tenementes aforesaid, for one hole yere endid
the daye and yere aforesaid, as appearithe by the rentall of the
same   £46 12s. 2d.

Encreased rent

And £8 19s.4d. of encreasid rent for the londes nowe in the tenure
of Thomas Turnor, late of Carre[154]   £8 19s. 4d.

And with £2 10s.0d. by him received at the last accompt   £2 10s. 0d.

And with £1 5s.0d. by him then likewise receyved   £1 5s. 0d.

     Summa oneris £70 16s.6d., whereof

Rentes resolutes

He praiethe allowans of 1s.1d. paid yerelie owte of Mr Tasselles
londes And of 5s.6d. paiable yerelie owte of the ministers
howses by St James steple. And of 5s.0d. for the collectors fee   11s. 7d.

And of £2 14s.11¼d. paid to the Governors of the Free Grammer
Schole, parcell of the rent of St Peters   £2 14s. 11¼d.

And of £1 1s.0d. for a yerelie tenthe paid to the Quenis Majestie
owte of St Peters and the graunge londes, due for 2 yeres endid
at Michelmas '91   £1 1s. 0d.

And of £1 0s.0d. paid to the messenger which was sent for the
same, for his fee   £1 0s. 0d.

Poore and Orphanes

And of £2 10s.0d. paid to Thomas Overend, one of the distributors
to the poore and orphanes, for that purpose   £2 10s. 0d.

And of 8s.6d. given to the poore by this accomptaunt   8s. 6d.

Taske

And of £6 0s.0d. paid by this accomptaunt for parcell of the first
payment of the second taske graunted at the last Parliament   £6 0s. 0d.

And of 2s.6d. paid to the towne of Westley for the last payment of
the taske for St Peters and the graunge londes   2s. 6d.

Mynisters

And of £40 0s.0d. paid to Mr Mosse, mynister of St James
parishe, for his stipend endid at Michelmas, *videlicet* for 4
quarters   £40 0s. 0d.

Paymentes

And of £4 0s.0d. paid to Page for interest   £4 0s. 0d.

Supers

**This £11 10s.0d. paid upon a newe lease made to William Payne as
appeare in Mr Collinges accompt '93**

And of £11 10s.0d. for St Peters, the half yeres rent paiable at
Christmas \last/ or within 28 daies after yet not paid. And of
2s.0d. remayning in th'handes of John Landisdale for a yeres
rent of a peece of ground. And of 8d., for a yeres rent not paid

---

[154] On 9 January 1590, Thomas Turner was given a lease for twenty-one years of the lands late occupied by Carre, on the termination of the old lease, for 6s. an acre, Minutes, H2/6/2.1, p.1.

by William Johnson, for a tenemente in Longe Brackelond, *in
toto* **5s.0d.** *pro hiis in fine compoti '96*   £11 12s. 8d.

> *Summa allocacionis* £69 11s.2d.
> *Et sic remanet* £1 5s.3¾d., whereof

Paid by this accomptaunt for a quarter of beef for the poore   12s. 6d.
And for breade for theym   5s. 0d.
> *Summa* 17s.6d.
> *Et sic debet* 7s.9¾d., which was presentlie delivered to
> Mr Heyward, one of the receyvors for the yere to come.

[*f. 36v.*]
The Accompt for the poore and orphanes
                         3 Januarii [*15*]*92*[*3*]
**Th'accompt of Thomas Overend and John Man, distributors to the poore and
orphanes, made and taken the daye and yere aforesaid**

The said Thomas Overend hathe receyved of Robert Sparke and
   John Gillie as bifore appearithe in their severall acoomptes   £8 10s. 0d.
And he hathe paid and disbursed to and for the ϑ and orphanes as
   appearithe by a bill of particulers by him shewed at this
   accompt   £12 12s. 10d.
> So rest to him £4 2s.10d., whereof
> [*In another hand*] Allowed to hym as appere
> in th'end of th'accompt 1594

Dettes to Thomas Overend and John Man, [*in another hand*] **bothe paid**
And the said John Man hathe \laid out/ and disbursed to and for
   the poore and orphanes as appearithe by a bill of particulers by
   him showed at this accompt which is due and owing to him
   Paid him as appeare in th'accompt of Mr Peede '94   £7 7s. 4d.
                                                                    whereof

Dyners at the hall this yere
Receyved by Inglethorpe for dyners kept at the hall this yere   £2 18s. 4d.
Whereof allowed \him/ for his wages and other thinges, as
   appearithe by bill of particulers by him shewed at this accompt £2 11s. 3d.
> So he answerithe and paiethe 7s.1d., which was
> paid to Robert Sparke, as appearethe bifore in his accompt

Dett to William Faiercliff [*In another hand*] **This is repaid him
upon the buying of the same lynnen**
Lent by William Faiercliff at this accompt to the companye upon
   certeine lynnen remayning in his hand   £5 0s. 0d.
                                                                    whereof

Orphanes
Paid presentlie to Roodes wief for keping a poore child   £1 4s. 0d.
And to Colyes wief, in parte of payment of a greater \somme/, for
   keping 3 poore children   £2 0s. 0d.
And to John Moore for taking Barbara Langley as apprentize for 8
   yeres   £1 0s. 0d.
And to Moores wief, in part of payment of a greater somme, for
   keping of the said Barbara   10s. 0d.
And given to the bearers for helping in tyme of the sickenes   2s. 0d.

Fees

And to the clerke for his fee	3s. 4d.
And to the scryvener for one parte of the indenture of apprentizeshippe of John Hoors	8d.

Summa soluc[ionis] £5 0s.0d.

Debet **[*In another hand*] £1 0s.0d. to St James churche paid by Mr Heyward as appears in his accompt '93**

Due for this yere to eche of the parishe s churches towardes reparacions £1.0.0d., *in toto*	£2 0s. 0d.

£1 0s.0d. to St Maries churche paid by Mr Colling as appeare in his accompt '93

And for provision of woode in the gaole	£1 0s. 0d.

Dett to Richard Lichefield. Paid by Mr Colling as appeare in his accompt '93

Due to Richard Lichefield for surgerie of diverse poore people within this towne, allowed him yerelie by order of owte of this howse.	£3 6s. 8d.

Taske paid by Wyther, Man and Overend

Due to John Wyther, laid owte by him for parte of the first payment of the seconde taske. **Paid by Mr Heyward as appeare in his accompt '93**	£6 0s. 0d.
Due to John Man, laid owte by him for parte of the last payment of the seconde taske. **Paid to him by Sir Robert Jermyn, knight.** *<deletion>* **the accompt of Mr Peede**	£12 0s. 0d.
Due to Thomas Overend, laid owte by him for the residue of the same taske, and 10s.0d. given to the collector for his travell abowte \the/ resceit of the same. **Paid upon reckoning, as appeare in th'end of th'accompt '94**	£12 10s. 0d.

Jo. Heigham	Henrye Blagge	Anthony Payne
Wm. Cooke	Willia' Hayward	Thos. Hammond
Roger Barber	Henry Collyne	John Gippes
Edward Ubanke	Wyllm Ferclif	Thomas Goodryche the elder

[*f. 37r.*]

2 Januarii [15]93[4]

Th'accompt of William Heyward, gentleman, surveyor and receyvor of the londes and tenementes, sometime of John Smythe, esquire, Margarett Odeham, Hellen Fissher, Adam Newhawe and John Salter and certeine almeshowses and other londes and tenementes in Burie St Edmunde, Hepworthe and other townes adjoyning, made and taken the second daie of Januarie in the 36° yere of the reign of our Soveraigne Ladie Quene Elizabethe, for one yere endid the last daie of December last past

Arrerages

Patet in le supers ultimi compoti Roberti Sparke

The yerelie revenues

Inprimis the said accomptaunt dothe charge himsilf with £92

92

15s.1½d., being the whole yeres rentes and fearmes of the londes and tenementes aforesaid, for the yere abovesaid, conteyned in the rentall, and also \£3 5s.0d./, the old encrease rentes added to the same rentall

£92 15s. 1½d.

Encreasid rentes

And with £33 2s.4d. of newe improved rentes, for one hoole yere endid as bifore[155]

£33 2s. 4d.

And with 16s.3d. to him delivered at the last accompt

16s. 3d.

And with £1 0s.0d. receyved of Thomas Cutteris, fermor of Catshall for his neglect in not making a surveie according to his covenants

£1 0s. 0d.

And with one gallon of wine paiable yerelie by John Revell and his heires for certeine londes in Burie fieldes, sometime of Jenkyn Barrett

One gallon of wine

Summa oneris £127 13s.8½d., and one gallon of wine, whereof

Rentes resolutes

The said accomptant praiethe allowans of 9s.0d. for the owte rentes paid yerelie owte of the mannor of Brettes and other londes in Hepworthe. And of £1 6s.0d. paid to Bailieff Spittlehowse for owte rentes paid yerelie owte of the londes and tenementes in Burie St Edmunde, Barton and Rowgham. And of 8d. paid yerelie for an owte rent for Leyers. And of 1s.0d. paid yerelie for 4 tenementes in Garlond Strete. And of £20 0s.0d. paid to John Jermyn, esquier, for one whole yeres rent or annuytie, as appearithe by his acquittance shewed at this accompt. And of 10s.0d. for the collectors fee. *In toto*

£22 6s. 8d.

Subsidie and Taske

And of £1 0s.0d. paid for the last payment of the last subsidie. And of £2 13s.4d. paid for the first entier subsidie graunted at the Parliament 35 Elizabeth *regine nunc*

£3 13s. 4d.

And of 6s.8d. for the double taske of Leyers for the towne of Rowgham

6s. 8d.

And of £24 0s.0d. paid for the moytie of the same double taske, graunted at the last Parliament, for this towne. And of 5s.0d. given to the collector for sending for the same. And of 4d. for th'acquittauns

£24 5s. 4d.

Mynisters

And of £30 0s.0d. paid to Mr Mosse, mynister of St James churche for 3 quarters stipend endid at midsomer laste past

£30 0s. 0d.

Poore and orphans

And of £3 0s.6d. paid to Normans wief to hir due for keping of orphans at the last accompt. And of £1 6s.0d. due to hir for keping of theym for half of the yere past

£4 6s. 0d.

---

[155] On 19 January 1593, Anthony Payne, Thomas Hammond, William Heyward, Roger Barber, William Cooke and Richard Walker were asked to consider the leases with a view to increasing rents and to report to the rest of the feoffees before 25 March 1593, Minutes, H2/6/2.1, p.8.

And of 15s.4d. paid to Robert Sparke for providing a howse and fryse for the widowe Bentham	15s. 4d.
And of 10s.0d. paid to Colies wieff to apparell the children which she kepe[156]	10s. 0d.
And of 17s.0d. paid to Roodes wief for keping an orphan	17s. 0d.
And of £1 0s.0d. delivered to John Man for John Robertson	£1 0s. 0d.

Reparacions

And of £4 0s.5d. for reparacions done abowte the almes howses in the Northegate Strete and at the hospitall	£4 0s. 0d.

Paymentes
St James Churche

And of £1 0s.0d. due to St James churche '92, ~~and~~ nowe paid, and of £1 0s.0d. paid for this yere '93	£2 0s. 0d.

Lynnen

And of £1 4s.0d. paid for wasshing of the lynnen for the judges this yere	£1 4s. 0d.
And of £1 10s.0d. paid to the keper of the Spittlehowse	£1 10s. 0d.
And of £1 0s.0d. due to the said accomptant as a dett due to him \for setting forthe soldiors/	£1 0s. 0d.
And of £6 0s.0d. paid to John Wyther as a dett due to him, as appearthe in the last accompt	£6 0s. 0d.
And of £1 0s.0d. paid to John Revell as a dett due to him, laid owte for this howse \for old taske/	£1 0s. 0d.

Supers

And of £3 0s.0d. for the yeres rent of a mesuage by St James steple, late purchased of Richard Collin. *Vide in fine compoti '96.* And of 2s.0d. for the half yeres rent of a tenemente, in the occupacion of the Widowe Haggas, unpaid. And of £1 10s.0d. for the whole yeres rent of londes in Hepworthe, late in th'occupacion of Rust. **This 2s.0d. and £1 10.0d. answered in Mr Peedes accompt.** And of 9d. remayning in th'handes of Sir Robert Jermyn, knight, for a yeres rentes for londes in Hepworthe aforesaid. And of 5s.0d. for the yeres rent of a bearne in Westgate Strete, late letton to Scott. *Vide for this* **9d. and 5s.0d.** *in fine compoti '96.* And of £10 0s.0d. remayning in th'hands of Sir Robert Jermyn, knight, for parte of th'annuytie given by Edmond Jermyn, esquire, disceased, due the 20 daie of Julie last. **This £10 0s.0d. answered in Mr Peedes accompt.** And of 1½d., the half yeres rent of a tenemente in Garlond Strete, in th'occupacion of Buckenham. **This 1½d. answered in Mr Peedes accompt.** *In toto*

£14 17s. 10½d.

And of a gallon of wyne bestowed at this accompte

A gallon of wine

---

[156] This is probably the same person as Cowell's wife who was keeping Thomas, Elizabeth and Alice Fowler. She was to have 10s. for the girls' clothing, and 10s. for each quarter of the year that had ended. In the coming year she was to be paid £1 quarterly until £4 had been paid if the children lived so long in her keeping. The boy, Thomas, was to be removed from her care, Minutes, 2 January 1594, H2/6/2.1, p.9.

Summa allocationis £119 13s.1½d. and a gallon of wine ~~whereof~~
So rest due by this accomptaunt £8 0s.7d., whereof

Paid to Henry Hasell for meate, breade and drincke bestowed upon the poore at th'accompt, and other thinges	£1 10s. 0d.
More given then to prisoners in the gaole	2s. 0d.
More given then to 2 which brought the lynnen, and the keper thereof	10d.
More paid to Inglethorpe, the bedell, due to him besides his resceit for mariages, as appeare hereafter	7s. 8d.
More paid to Mr Colling, as appeare hereafter in his accompt	£6 0s. 1d.

Summa £8 0s.7d. paid as afore, and so this accomptaunt clere

Examinatur

[f.37v.]
Th'accompt of Henry Collinge, gentleman, receyvor of the newe purchased londes and Mr Tassells londes, bilonging to the towne of Burie St Edmunde, made and taken the daie and yere aforesaid

Arrerages

First the said accomptaunt dothe charge himsilff with £8 15s.0¾d., parcell of the arrerages mencioned in th'accompt of John Gillie, and the residue paid to the schole £8 15s. 0¾d.

Yerelie rentes

And with £53 16s.7½d. beinge the rentes and profittes of the londes and tenementes aforesaid for a yere, as appearithe by the rentall of the same £53 16s. 7½d.

Encreased rentes

And with £15 2s.8d. for newe encreased rentes for the yere past £15 2s. 8d.

Summa oneris £77 14s.4¼d., whereof

Owte rentes

He praiethe allowans of 1s.1d. paid yerelie owte of Mr Tasselles londes. And of 5s.6d. paiable yerelie for the mynisters howses by St James steple. And of 5s.0d. for the collectors fee. And of 10s.6d. for a tenthe owte of St Peters due at Michelmas '92. And of 4d. for th'acquittauns. And of 4d. to the receyvors, paide in all £1 2s. 9d.

Mynisters

And of £20 0s.0d. paid to Mr Lewys, preacher of St Maries parishe, for his stipend for the feastes of the birthe of Christ '92 and th'annunciacion of the Virgin Marie last past £20 0s. 0d.

Paymentes

And of £2 0s.0d. paid for interest for £20 0s.0d. for a yere endid abowte Michaelmas last. And of £2 13s.9d. paid to John Gippes for a dett due to him, as appearithe in th'accompt '91. And of £1 13s.9d. paid to Widowe Annable, for dett due to hir husband, as appearithe in the same accompt. And of £6 13s.4d. paid to Richard Lichefield, for dett due to him, as appeare in th'accomptes '91 and '92. And of £3 6s.8d. paid to the same Richard for this present yere past, graunted to him yerelie for curing of the poore, hurte and diseased. **St Maries churche**

And of £3 0s.0d. paid to the churche wardens of the parishe of St Marie for the yeres '90, '91, '92. And of £1 0s.0d. paid to the same churche wardens for this present yere paste. And of £3 0s.0d. for writing of diverse deedes of feofement, releases, rentalles and entering of orders into the booke, and matters concerning this companye and the londes bilonging to this towne for diverse yeres bifore this accompte. And of 3s.4d. for the clerks fee. *In toto*   £23 10s. 10d.

Poore and orphans

And of £3 0s.0d. paid to Colyes wief, due to hir for keping of 3 poore children as appeare in the last accompt. And of 2s.6d. given to Mother Erle of Felsham, which kepe a poore child. And of 5s.0d. given for carying a lettre to Colchester, for a child of Darnels left to the towne. And of £1 10s.0d. paid to Goodday, for taking Hoare, an orphan, as apprentize. And of 15s.0d. given to Mores wieff in discharge of £1 10s.0d., due to hir upon the last accompt for keping a poore child, and in discharge of the towne of the child. And of 7s.0d. paid to Roodes wief, in parte of money to hir due for keping a poore child.[157] And of £1 1s.0d. given at severall tymes in reliefe of diverse poore, sicke and ympotent persons, *in toto*   £7 0s. 6d.

Reparacions

And of £1 0s.2d. for reparacions done upon the almes howses in the Colledge Strete. And of 12s.6d. for reparacions done upon the mynisters howses   £1 12s. 8d.

Taske

And of £24 0s.0d. paid for the moitie of the taske graunted at the last Parliament. And of 5s.0d. for the taske of certeine of St Peters and the graunge londes paid to the towne of Westley   £24 5s. 0d.

Supers answered *proximo compote*

And of £1 4s.0d. for the yeres rent of certeine lond sold to Thomas Overend. And of 2s.0d. unpaid by John Landisdale, for a yeres rent of a parcell of ground in the Horsemarkett endid at Michelmas last. *Vide for this 2s.0d. in fine compoti.* And of £17 10s.1½d. remayning in th'andes of William Payne, for a whole yeres rent of St Peters due at the birthe of Christ last. And of £1 15s.0d. for half a yeres rent, due by Roger Reve, *et cetera.* And of £1 15s.8d., parcell of £2 0s.0d., for a yeres rent, due by Mr Richard Heigham for a tenement in Guildhall Strete. *Vide for this in fine compoti '96. In toto*   £22 6s. 9½d.

     Summa allocacionis £99 18s.6½d.

     Sic debet computantis £32 4s.2¼d.

     Whereof received of Mr Heyward as appeare in his accompte £6 0s. 1d.

     And so remaine due to this accomptaunt £16 4s.1¼d.

---

[157] The details of those who cared for orphans which are found in these accounts and in the Minute Books throw much light on the care provided in the town and could make a useful paper.

Which £16 0s.0d. is paid to ~~w~~ \him by returne/ of £16 0s.0d. which he receyvid for woode this yeare, and the 4s.1¼d. residue is paid to him by Mr Barber, one of the accomptauntes for the yere following, and so this accomptaunt clere discharged

Edmond Inglethorpe, the porter, did nowe accompt for money receyved for dyners kept at the Guildhall this yere, and answerid for the same £2 1s. 8d.

And demaundid allowans for his wages for the yere past, £2 0s. 0d., and for money by him laid owte for candle and fier and keping the doore cleane 9s.4d.

So due to him 7s.8d., which was paid him by Mr Heyward th'other accomptaunt

Examinatur

[*f. 38r.*]

1594

Th'accompte of Thomas Peede, gentleman, surveior and receyvor of the londes and tenementes sometyme of John Smythe, esquier, Margarett Odeham, Hellen Fissher, Adam Newhawe and John Salter, and certeine almes howses and other londes and tenementes in Burie St Edmunde, Hepworthe and other townes adjoyninge, made and taken the second daie of Januarie in the 37 yere of the reign of our Soveraigne Ladie Quene Elizabethe *anno Domini* 1594 [*1595*], for one whole yere endid the last daie of December last past

Arrerages

First the said accomptaunt dothe charge himsilf with £11 17s.10½d., part of the arrerages in super upon the last accompt of Mr Heyward. And with £4 19s.8d. of arrerages of part of the newe encreasid rentes of the londes in Hepworthe and Weston, letton to John Bedwall,[158] due for the last yere and not then receyved, *in toto* £16 17s. 6½d.

Yerelie revenues

And with £131 0s.7d. beinge the whole yeres rentes and fearmes of the londes and tenementes aforesaid, for the yere abovesaid, as appearithe by the rentall of the same £131 0s. 7d.

And with £11 0s.0d. receyved of Mr Barber, one of the receyvors for this yere, towardes the payment of the taske, as appearithe in his accompt £11 0s. 0d.

And with £1 0s.0d. received of Mr Henry Boldero for part of the charges of suyte for the legacie given by his father[159] £1 0s. 0d.

A gallon of wine

And with one gallon of wine paiable yerelie by John Revell and his heires for certeine londes in Burie fieldes, sometime of Jenken Barrett — One gallon of wine

---

[158] John Bedwell, of Wickham Skeith, leased a messuage, house and lands in Hepworth, this year, Lease, H1/3/4/18.

[159] It was agreed at a meeting on 8 March 1595 that Mrs Boldero was to be asked for the residue of her husband's legacy for setting the poor on work. Thomas Harwell was to pay £13 6s.8d. at Michaelmas 1595 and he and Henry Boldero were to be bound for payment of both the residue and the costs of the suit in the two years following, Minutes, H2/6/2.1, p.17.

Summa oneris £159 18s.1½d., and a gallon of wine, whereof

Owte rentes

The said accomptaunt praiethe allowans of 9s.0d. for the owte rentes paid yerelie owte of the mannor of Brettes and other londes in Hepworthe.

And of £1 6s.0d. paid to Bailieff Spittlehowse for owte rentes paid yerelie owte of the londes and tenementes in Burie St Edmunde, Barton and Rowgham. And of 8d. paid yerelie for an owte rent for Leiers. And of 1s.0d. paid yerelie for 4 tenementes in Garlond Strete. And of £20 0s.0d. paid to John Jermyn, esquier, for one whole yere rent or anuytie, whereof an acquittauns for £10 0s.0d. due in Julie last was shewed at this accompt. And of 10s.0d. for the collectors fee, *in toto*   £22 6s. 8d.

Taske

And of £48 0s.0d. for the second payment of the double taske for this towne of Burie, graunted at the last Parliament. And of 1s.0d. given to the collector man for his charges   £48 1s. 0d.

And of 6s.8d. paid for the same double taske for Leyers, to the towne of Rowgham   6s. 8d.

Mynisters

And of £30 0s.0d. paid to Mr Lewis, preacher of St Maries churche, for 3 quarters stipend endid at the feaste of St Michaell th'archaungell last past, as appearithe by his acquittaunce   £30 0s. 0d.

Poore and orphans

And of £2 5s.4d. paid to Roodes wief for kepinge of an orphant. And of £2 12s.0d. paid to Colies wief for keping of two orphans. And of 4s.0d. paid to the Widowe Abell for keping of two poore children. And of £3 8s.10d. paid to Normans wief for keping of orphans. And of 5s.0d. given to Mother Erle of Felsham, which kepethe a poore child. And of 6s.0d. paid for lynnen clothe, to make the poore children shirtes, which Normans wieff do kepe, *in toto*   £9 1s. 2d.

Reparacions

And of certeine money paid and laid owte for and abowt reparacions at the Guildhall, the mynisters howses, the hospital and the almes howses, as by billes of particlers appeare, shewed at this accompt   £12 1s. 9½d.

Paymentes

And of £1 10s.0d. paid to the keper of the Spittlehowse. And of £2 16s.2d. laid owte abowte the suyte against Mistress Boldero for the legacie given by Mr Fraunces Boldero, hir husbond. And of £20 0s.0d. paid to John Man for a dett due to him, for money by him disbursed for this towne. And of 3s.4d. paid to the clerke for his fee, *in toto*   £24 9s. 6d.

Supers

And of 9d. remayning in th'handes of Sir Robert Jermyn, knight, for londes in Hepworthe, for arrerages of the last yere chargid

upon this accomptaunt. **5s.0d. for this** *in fine compoti* **'96.**
And of 9d. for this yere, for the same lond, not paid. And of
£3 0s.0d. for the yeres rent of a mesuage by St James steple,
late purchased of Richard Collin, not paid. **5s.0d.** *in fine*
compoti **'96.** And of 5s.0d. for the rent of the last yere of a
bearne in Westgate Strete, late letton to Scott, nowe in possession of the salt peter man,[160] chargid upon this accompt.
5s.0d. for this *in fine compoti* **'96.** And of 5s.0d. for this yere
for the same bearne not paid. And of 3s.0d., parcell of the rent
of a tenemente in th'occupacion of the Widowe Aggas unpaid.

Answered *proximo compoto. In toto*	£3 14s. 6d.
And of a gallon of wine bestowed at this accompt	A gallon of wine

Summa allocacionis £150 1s.3½d. and a gallon of wine

Debet

Sic debet £9 16s.10d.
This soome[sic] full paid *in onere compoti* '96.

Th'accompt of Roger Barber, gentleman, surveior and receyvor of the newe purchasid londes and Mr Tassells londes bilonging to the towne of Burye St Edmunde, made and taken the daye and yere aforesaid

Arrerages
First the said accomptaunt dothe charge him silff with
£17 13s.5½d., beinge parte of th'arrerages in the supers of the
last accompt, for St Peters for rent due at the feast of St John
Baptiste and the birth of Christ 1593 and res'[161] *patet* in the
same supers   £17 13s. 5½d.

Yerelie rentes
And with £68 16s.11½d., beinge the rentes and profitts of the
londes and tenementes aforesaid, for one whole yere endid the
daie and yere abovesaid, as appearithe by the rentall of the
same   £68 16s.11½d.

Money receyved by waie of contribucion and for woode
And with £12 0s.0d. receyved of Frauncis Moundford, gentleman,
John Sterne, John Gillie and William Faiercliffe, as money
delivered to theym *anno* 1593, for provision of woode for the
poore within the sowthe and west wardes in Burie[162] £12 0s. 0d.
And with £44 18s.0d. receyved of sundrie th'inhabitaunts of the
towne of Burie by waie of contribucion for the payment of
some arrerages due to the preachers within the same towne, for
their yerelie stipendes, and for making uppe the somme of
£80 0s.0d., to be delivered into the handes of two clothiers
within the same towne, to sett the poore of the same towne to
worke, whereof £30 18s.0d. receyved by this accomptaunt
and £14 0s.0d. receyved by Thomas Hamond, gentleman £44 18s. 0d.

---

160 See Glossary.
161 This word might read 'resid' followed by something like the tail of an 'h'.
162 See Introduction, p.xl.

99

Summa oneris £143 8s.5d., whereof

Rentes resolutes

The said accomptaunt dothe praie allowans of 5s.6d., paiable
yerelie for the mynisters howses by St James steple. And of
1s.1d. paid yerelie owte of Mr Tassells londes. And of 5s.0d.
for the collectors fee. And of 10s.6d. for a tenthe owte of St
Peters, due at Michelmas 35 *Elizabethe regine, anno Domini*
1593, and 4d. for th'acquittauns, and 4d. for his porter. And of
11s.2d. for the like tenthe due at Michelmas 36 *reginae*, '94,
with like fees to the receyvor   £1 13s.11d.

examinatur

[*f.38v.*]
Poore and orphans

And of £1 0s.0d. paid to Robinsons wief for keping a poore child.
And of £1 0s.0d. more paid to hir at severall tymes for keping
the same child. And of 16s.0d. paid to Widowe Abell at
severall tymes for keping two poore children. And of 3s.4d.
laid owte for the burying of a child in Colyes keping, and
releving the same child in the tyme of sickenes, *in toto*   £2 19s. 4d.

Mynisters Mr Lewis and Mr Mosse

And of £10 0s.0d. paid to Mr Lewis, preacher of St Maries
parishe, for part of th'arrerages of his stipend due at midsomer
1593. And of £40 0s.0d. paid to Mr Mosse, preacher in St
Jeames parishe, for foure quarters stipend *videlicet*, the
nativitie of Christ, 1593, th'annunciacion of Our Ladie, 1594,
St John Baptist '94 and St Michaell th'archaungell '94 as by
his 4 several acquittaunces do appeare. And of £10 0s.0d. paid
to the same Mr Mosse by th'andes of Thomas Hamond, gentleman, parcell of the money aforemencioned receyved by waie
of contribucion for arrerages of his quarters stipend due at the
feaste of St Michaell th'archaungell 1593. **Paymentes.** And of
4s.2d. paid to Mr Colling in full payment of the money to him
due upon the fynissing of his accompt. And of £11 0s.0d. paid
to Mr Peede, one other of the receyvors for this yere towardes
the payment of the taske, and by him receyved as appeare by
his accompt. And of £28 5s.0d. paid to Henry Hamond of
Burie, clothier, in parte of payment of £40 0s.0d. appointed by
th'order of sundrie the feoffees, to be paid to him to sett the
poore people in St Jeames parish to worke[163] And of £4 0s.0d.
paid to him more for that purpose by the said Thomas Hamond,
residue of the contribucion money by him receyved. And of
£3 15s.0d. paid to the said Henry Hamond more towardes the
said somme of £40 0s.0d. by William Cooke, gentleman, of
money remayning in his handes. And of £4 0s.0d. remayning in
th'andes of the same William Cooke, which he require in
allowans of his paynes taken of long tyme abowte the busynes

---

[163] On 23 May 1594 a long list of sums to be disbursed and debts to be paid was entered in the Minute
Book. It includes this sum of £40, and a like sum for St Mary's parish, Minutes, H2/6/2.1, p.11.

of this howse. **Debet.** [*In a different hand?*] **Allocatur pro
servicis incipenso et impendend[o] secundo Maii 1595.** And
of 10s.0d., parcell of £4 0s.0d. for woode in th'andes of
William Faiercliff answered him to make uppe £40 0s.0d. to
sett the poore to worke in St Maries parisshe. And of £2 0s.0d.
paid for the woode making provided for this yere for the
poore. **Debet** [*In a different hand*] **Nota** And of 15s.0d. paid to
the said William Faiercliff for the losse in 500 woode, provided
for the poore the yere bifore

£114 9s. 2d.

Reparacions
And of £2 16s.2d. for reparacions done this yere upon the almes
howses in Garlond Strete. And of 12s.0d. paid to Alman the
cutler for skowringe the towne armour and mending two
corselettes

£3 8s. 2d.

Supers
And of 2s.0d. for one yeres rent due at the feaste of St Michaell
th'archaungell last past for a peece of ground in Horse Markett
in occupacion of John Landisdale. And of £2 0s.0d. for one
yeres rent \due/ at the same feaste for a mesuag and gardeine in
the Guildhall Strete late in th'occupacion of Robert Leder, not
paid. And of 5s.0d. for a tenemente and garden in
th'occupacion of William Heyward, gentleman, not paid. And
of 8d. for one yeres rent of a tenemente in Longe Brackelond,
due at Michelmas last, in th'occupacion of William Johnson.
And of £8 18s.4¾d. for the half yeres rent of St Peters, due and
paiable by William Payne at the feaste of the birthe of Christ
now past or within 28 \twentie/ daies after, yet not receyved.
This £8 18s.4¾d. answered *in proximo compoto, prohibitur
per concensum.* And of 5s.0d., parcell of the rent of Roger
Reve and Roberte Reve for St Peters, not receyved. And of
2s.0d. for the rent of a stall in the markett in th'occupacion of
William Jellowe, not receyved. **5s.0d. for this 2s.0d.** *in fine
compoti '96. In toto*

£11 13s. 0¾d.

And of £1 18s.8d. for the charges of parte of the dynner nowe
made for the feoffees, *videlicet*, for the absence of 13 of the
same feoffees, 13s.0d. And for 6 stone of beef for the poore,
and the boyling thereof, 15s.8d.. And for 6 dossen of breade for
the poore 6s.0d., *in toto*

£1 14s. 8d.

And of 5s.0d. for wyne

5s. 0d.

Summa allocacionis £136 3s.3¾d.
Sic debet £7 5s.1¼d., whereof

Poore and orphans
Paid presentlie upon the taking of this accompt to Robinsons
wieff, in full payment for keping a child untill the daie of this
accompt, 9s. 4d.. And to Widowe Abell 15s.0d. for kepinge
two children untill the same daye. And to Abraham Skarpe
10s.0d. to bringe uppe Abraham Cleydon, a bastard, and
10s.0d. more to be paid him in discharg of the keping of the
same child. And to Roodes wieff 1s.0d., in full payment for

kepinge Elizabethe Wilfree untill the daie of this accompt.
Subsidie And paid to Mr Walker for the second entier subsidie
graunted at the last Parliament, £2 13s.4d. **The churches of St
James and St Marie** And paid to the churche of St Maries for
the yere nowe past, £1 0s.0d.. And to the churche of St James
for the same yere, £1 0s.0d., *in toto*   £6 8s. 8d.

And <deletion> 12s.0d. paid to Edmunde Inglethorpe as hereunder appearithe in his accompt.   10s. 0d.
      Summa solucionis £7 0s.8d.
      Sic debet 4s.5¼d., which was given to the Widowe Abell
      bifore th'engrossment of this accompt, *et sic eque.*

Onus

Edmond Inglethorpe, the porter, did nowe accompt for money by
    him receyved for dyners kept at the Guildhall this yere, and did
    answere for the same.   £1 18s. 4d.

Allocacio

And demaunded allowans for his wages this yere past, £2 0s.0d..
    And laid owte for candle \and/ fier by him, and demaundithe
    for kepinge the doore cleane 10s.4d.*, in toto*   £2 10s. 4d.
      So due to him 12s. 0d., which is paid him
      by Mr Barber as above appearithe.

The accompt of the £110 received of Thomas Overend

An accompt of £110 receyved of Thomas Overend for 11 acres of lond to him sold
    by the feoffees of the londes and tenementes bilonging to this towne of Burie,
    whereof £42 10s.0d. was receyved by William Faiercliff, and £40 0s.0d. by John
    Gippes. **Mr Lewis, mynister, £20 0s.0d.** Of which £42 10s.0d. receyved by the
    said William Faiercliff he paid to Mr Lewis 20 0s.0d. for arrerages of his stipend
    due at the feaste of St Michaell th'archaungell '93 and the feast of the birthe of
    Christe then next ensuying. And of £22 10s.0d. residue, with 10s.0d., as
    appeare above in Mr Barbers accompt. **£40 0s.0d. in th'andes of William
    Faiercliff answered *in compoto* '96.** And £17 0s.0d., parcell of the £40 0s.0d. in
    th'handes of John Gippes, the said William Faiercliff hathe and reteynethe for a
    stocke to sett the poore on work for one yere in St Maries parishe and th'other
    £23 0s.0d., parcell of the £40 0s.0d., received by John Gippes as aforesaid, is
    paid by him for a dett of £20 0s.0d. for which he stoode bound to one Page, for
    this howse, and interest for the same. **Payment of dettes, Page and Overend.**
    And the residue of the said £110 0s.0d. was allowed to the said Thomas Overend
    for dett to him due on this howse.

                                                 examinatur

[f.39r.]

Memorandum that \the/ second daye of Maye 1595 it is agreed that, towchinge Mr
    Barbers accompt, we whose names been underwritten ~~we~~ do allowe and ratifie
    the same with our handes, and for Mr Peedes accompt, bifore mencioned, we
    staye th'allowans thereof untill further consideracion, by reason of allowans
    demaunded for the Shire Howse which is not convenient for this ~~tyme~~ present
    \tyme/ to be allowed by this howse, and for the howse of correccion.[164] [*In*

---

[164] Nothing in the Minute Book helps to explain this passage.

another hand] It is agreid that this accompt for Mr Peede shall be allowed, for that he hathe paid unto John Gippes the money due as appeare in his accompt.

Roberte Jermyn	Jo. Heigham	Wm. Cooke
Tho: Gooderich junior	Tho. Hammond	John Gippes
Thomas Gooderyche the elder	Wylliam Fayerclif	

After agreid upon payment of the debt of Mr Peede here bifore mencioned that his accompt shuld be allowed and ratified.

[*f.39r.*]

1595

Th'accompt of William Faiercliff, surveior and receyvor of all the mesuages, londes, tenementes and hereditamentes bilonginge to the common benefite of this towne of Burie St. Edmunde, sometime John Smythe, \esquier/, and others, made and taken the 30^tie daie of December in the 38° yere of the reign of our soveraign Ladie Quene Elizabethe *et cetera, anno Domini* 1595, for one whole yere nowe endid

Arrerages
First the said accomptaunt dothe charge himsilf with £15 7s.6¾d., beinge th'arrerages of the last accompt, as appearithe in the supers therof   £15   7s. 6¾d.

Yerelie revenues
And with £199 17s.6½d., beinge the whole yeres rent and fearme of the londes and tenementes abovesaid, as appearithe by the rentall of the same   £199 17s. 6½d.

Legacies
And with £10 0s.0d. receyved of th'executors of Mrs Heigham as a legacie given by hir to this towne.[165]   £10   0s.   0d.

And with £40 0s.0d. receyved of Mrs Boldero as a legacie, given likewise to this towne, by Fraunces Boldero, hir husband, disceased[166]   £40   0s.   0d.

A galon of wine
And with one gallon of wine, paiable yerelie by John Revell and his heires, for certeine londes in Burie fields, sometime Jenkin Barrettes

One gallon of wine

      Summa oneris £265 5s.1¼d. and a gallon of wine, whereof

Rentes resolutes
The said accomptaunt dothe praie allowans of £22 16s.0d., *videlicet*, £20 0s.0d. paid to John Jermyn, esquier, parcell of th'annuitie given by Edmunde Jermyn, esquier, for one whole yere, and of other rentes paid owte of the said londes and tenementes, and for the receyvors fees, as appeare by the rentall of the same shewed at this accompt   £22 16s. 0d.

---

165 See Appendix 8, *sub* 1595, and Notes on People.
166 See Appendix 8, *sub* 1595, and Notes on People.

And of 10s.6d. for a tenthe owte of St. Peters due at the feast of St
Michaell th'archaungell last past, and of 4d. for th'acquittauns   10s. 10d.

Mynisters
And of £40 0s.0d. paid to Mr Lewis, preacher in St Maries ~~parch~~
parishe for one yeres stipend endid at Michelmas. And of
£40 0s.0d. paid to Mr Mosse, preacher in St James parishe, for
his stipend for one yere then endid   £80 0s. 0d.

Taske
And of £24 0s.0d. paid for the taske of the towne of Burie this
yere   £24 0s. 0d.

Poore and orphans
And of £3 8s.0d. paid to Colies wief for kepinge of 2 orphans.
And of £1 12s.0d. paid to Robinsons wief for kepinge one
orphan. And of £2 12s.0d. paid to Widowe Abell for kepinge 2
orphanes. And of £1 6s.8d. paid to Roodes wief for kepinge an
orphan. And of 12s.0d. paid in [*f. 39r.*] charitie for the rent of
Marthas howse. And of 13s.4d. paid to Normans wief for
kepinge an orphan. And of 14s.4d. given to Thomas Inglishe
for taking as apprentize Barbara Langley, an orphan, and
makinge hir indentures. And of 10s.0d. paid to Abraham
Skarpe as a full recompence to take an orphan to kepe. And of
10s.0d. given to certeine poore women for busynes of this
towne. And of 10s.0d. given to Wiborowghes wief for kepinge
of Barbara Langley. And of 4s.0d. given hir for kepinge of one
of Darnells children. And of 6s.8d. given in relief of Mother
Muriell in hir sickenes, and for her burial. And of 6s.2d. given
to Darnels wief at severall times, and for a paire of stockardes.
And of 5s.0d. given in relief of Franke, a poore man, to redeme
his howshold stuff pledged. And of 5s.0d. given in reliefe of a
poore blind woman. And of 4s.0d. given to relieve Leves, a
poore man, at several tymes. And of 5s.0d. given in reliefe of
Gantes wief in tyme of hir sickenes, and for hir buriall. And of
3s.0d. given in relief to Mother Spere. And of 2s.0d. given to 4
poore widowes. And of 10s.0d. given to Wretham[167] the
surgion, for curing poore folkes. And of 3s.4d. given to Peerce
the bocher. And of 18s.0d. to diverse poore women at severall
times. And of 1s.4d. to lame Halles wief. And of 11s.0d. paid
in charitie for Darneles house rent, *in toto*   £16 12s. 10d.
[*f. 39v.*]

Paymentes
And of £4 0s.0d. paid for th'interest of £20 0s.0d. for 2 yeres. And
of £1 10s.0d. paid to the keper of the spittlehowse. And of
3s.4d. paid to the clerke for his fee. And of 16s.0d. paid to the
soldiers which did weare the towne armour at the muster   £6 9s. 4d.

---

[167] See Introduction, p.lxv.

Reparacions

And of £7 11s.0d. bestowed this yere in reparacions abowte the
Guildhall, the mynisters howses, and others, as appeare by
billes of particulers shewed at this accompt

£7 11s. 0d.

Supers

And of £3 0s.0d. for the yeres rent of a mesuage by St James
steple, late purchasid of Richard Collin, unpaid. *Vide in fine
proximi compoti.* And of £2 0s.0d. for one yeres rent endid at
the feaste of St Michaell th'archaungell last, for a mesuage and
garden in Guildhall Strete, unpaid, letten to Richard Heigham,
gentleman. And of 5s.0d. due at the same feast for the rent of a
bearne in Westgate Strete in th'occupacion of the saltpeter
man,[168] unpaid. And of 5s.0d. due at the same feaste for a
tenemente and gardene in th'occupacion of William Heyward,
gentleman, unpaid. And of 9d. remayning in th'andes of Sir
Robert Jermyn for rent of londes in Hepworthe, unpaid. *Vide
pro hiis in fine proximi compoti.* And of 2s.0d. for a yeres rent
due at Michelmas last for a peec of ground in Horse Markett, in
th'occupacion of John Landisdale. And of 8d. for a yeres rent
for a tenemente in the Longe Brackelond then due, in
th'occupacion of William Johnson. And of 1s.0d. parcell of
the rent of Widowe Aggas. And of 6d., parcell of the rent of
Anne Holte, unpaid. *Aggas and Holt pardonantur pro
paupertate. In toto*

£5 14s. 11d.

And of £8 18s.4¾d. for the half yeres rent of St Peters, paiable by
John Fletcher at the feast of the birthe of Christ last past or
within 28 daies after, not yet receyved. **This somme answered
in proximo compoto.**

£8 18s. 4¾d.

And of £5 18s.5d., parcell of £15 7s.6¾d. of arrerages wherewith
this accomptaunt is bifore chargid and not by him receyved.
This is in charge in proximo compoto.

£5 18s. 5d.

Bondes delivered for payment of money.

**£13 6s.8d. hereof answerid *in proximo compoto* and th'other
bond deliverid to Mr Walker *ut patet in eodem compoto* and
answerid by him in his accompte.**

And of £26 13s.4d., parcell of £40 0s.0d. for the legacie given by
Mr Fraunces Boldero, wherewith this accomptaunt standeth
bifore chargid, for which he hathe nowe delivered him two
obligacions of 40 markes a peece for payment thereof, *videlicet*, 20 markes at midsomer next, and 20 markes at Midsomer
next after, wherein Henry Boldero and Thomas Harwell doo
stand bound to Sir Robert Jermyn, knight, and others, and are
nowe delivered to John Gippes, receyvor for this yere to come,
to receive the money which shall be due bifore his accompt

£26 13s. 4d.

---

[168] See Glossary for this unwelcome official. His surname was given as Robinson when he took the
lease of the barn and garden in Westgate Street, late Scott, on 2 January 1595, Minutes, H2/6/2.1, p.15.

A galon of wine

And of a gallon \of wine/ spent at the dyner of this felowshippe	A gallon of wine

> *Summa allocationis* £205 5s.0¾d. and a gallon of wine
> *Sic debet* £60 0s.0½d., whereof

Dett paid

Nowe paid for a dett of this companye for which Mr Barber did stand bound	£20 10s. 0d.

Mynisters

And also paid to Mr Mosse for his quarters stipend due at the feast of the birthe of Christ £10 0s.0d., and to Mr Lewis for his quarters stipend then due, £10 0s.0d., *in toto*	£20 0s. 0d.

Money given

And given to Thomas Shippe for watching the gates for carying corne owt of this towne[169]	5s. 0d.

Dett paid

And paid to Thomas Davye for a dett due to him as appeare in th'accompt '91	£4 18s. 8d.

Money given

And to Ambrose Bridon for a dett due to him as appearith in th'accompt '88	10s. 0d.
And more given upon the taking of this accompt	8s. 0d.

The dyner and for the poore

And paid for the dyner of this felowshippe at that tyme	£2	6s. 8d.
And for wine then		7s. 0d.
More for 13 stone and 4 pound of beef for the poore then	£1	3s. 4d.
And for 20 dossen of breade for theym	£1	0s. 0d.
And for half a busshell of otemeale to make theym porrage		1s. 8d.
And for 18 gallons of beere for theym		3s. 0d.
Given to the cooke for dressinge the meate for theym, and his helpe		1s. 4d.

Poore and orphans

Paid to Thomas Overend for clothe delivered for the poore	6s. 0d.
Paid to Normans wief due to hir for keping an orphane	£1 15s. 4d.
Given to a poore woman for keping Darnels child	2s. 0d.

Corselettes keping

Paid for keping of 2 corselettes 2 yeres, at 1s.1d. the peece for a yere, and 1s.0d. for buckeling of theym	5s. 0d.

> *Summa totalis solucionis* £54 3s.0d.
> *Sic remanet* £5 17s.0½d. Adde thereunto 3s.6d. restinge due by Inglethorpe, the porter, upon his accompt. *Et sic in toto debet per computantem* £6 6s.0½d., which somme was presentlie deliverd to

---

[169] This payment illustrates how the poor harvests of these years had made corn an exceedingly valuable commodity which the unscrupulous might well attempt to take away from the town to sell elsewhere at a profit.

John Gippes, receyvor for the yere to come, to be answered to upon his accompt. *Et sic eque*

Onus

Edmond Inglethorpe, the porter, dothe yelde accompt for money
    by him receyved for dyners kept at the Guildhall this yere   £2 11s. 8d.
        Summa £2 11s.8d.

Allocacio

And demaund allowans for his wages for this yere past £2 0s 0d.
    And for making cleane the doore 4s. 0d.. And for fier and
    candle 2s.4d.. And for a loode of sand 10d.   £2 8s. 2d.
        Summa £2 8s.2d.
        Sic debet 3s.6d., which was presentlie paid to John Gippes,
        receyvor for the yere to come, as above appearithe. *Examinatur*

Roger Barber	Henry Collyne	Wm. Cooke
Hen. Walker	Thomas Peade	John Gylle, senior
John Gippes	Robrte Sparke	H[*enry*] H[*orningold*]

[*f. 40r.*]

1596

Th'accompt of John Gippes, surveior and receyvor of all the mesuages, londes, tenementes and hereditamentes bilonging to the common benefit of this towne of Burie St Edmunde, sometime John Smythes, esquier, and others, made and taken the 30⁰ daie of Decemeber in the 39⁰ yere of the reign of our Soveraign Ladie, Quene Elizabethe, and *anno Domini* 1596, for one whole yere nowe endid

Arrerages

First the said accomptaunt dothe charge himsilf with £6 15s.3d.
    old arrerages *ut patet in diversis compotis precedentis* and
    particulerlie sett downe amongest \others/ in th'end of this
    accompt   £6 15s. 3d.
And with £5 13s.5d., parcell of £5 14s.11d., *ut patet in ultimo*
    compoto   £5 13s. 5d.
And with £8 18s.4¾d. for St Peters, as appeare in the supers of the
    last accompt   £8 18s. 4¾d.
And with £5 18s.5d. of arrerages, as likewise appeare in the
    supers of the last accompte   £5 18s. 5d.

Yerelie revenues

And with £199 17s.6½d., beinge the whole yeres rent and fearme
    of the londes and tenementes abovesaid, as appearithe by the
    rentall of the same   £199 17s. 6½d.
And with 6s.0d. as an encrease, receyved at Michelmas last, for a
    tenemente late Anne Holte[170]   6s. 0d.

---

[170] On 21 July 1592 William Holt and his wife Agnes were granted a lease of the house next to the Guildhall, in which they lived, for twenty-one years from the end of the lease to Thomas Short, should either of them live so long, paying the queen's rent and 8s. to the feoffees, Minutes, H2/6/2.1, p.7.

Money received

And with £6 0s.6d., received at the last accompt by this
accompt[*ant*] as appeare by the same   £6 0s. 6d.

And with £6 2s.3d. received of Mr Peede, the residue of a debet
due by him upon his accompt '94   £6 2s. 3d.

Legacies

And with £13 6s.8d. received of Henry Boldero, gentleman, part
of £40 0s.0d., given for relief of the poore within this towne by
Fraunces Boldero, gentleman, his father   £13 6s. 8d.

A gallon of wine

And with a gallon of wine, paiable yerelie by John Revell and his
heires, for certeine londes in Burie fieldes, sometime Jenkyn   One gallon of
Barrettes   wine

     Summa oneris £252 18s.0¾d. and a gallon of wine whereof

Rentes resolutes

The said accomptaunt dothe praie allowans of £22 16s.6d., *videlicet*, £20 0s.0d. paid to John Jermyn, esquier, parcell of
th'annuytie given by Edmunde Jermyn, esquier, for one whole
yere, whereof two acquittaunces for this yere past were shewed
at this accompt, and for other rentes paid owte of the aforesaid
londes and tenementes, and for the receyvors fees, as by the
rentall dothe appeare, which was shewed at this accompt, the
some of   £22 16s. 6d.

Mynesters

And of £40 0s.0d. paid to Mr Doctor Mosse, preacher of St James
parishe, for one whole yere \stipend/ endid at the feast of the
birthe of Christ last past. And of £40 0s.0d. paid to Mr Lewes,
preacher of St Maries parish for his stipend for one yere then
ended, *in toto*   £80 0s. 0d.

Taske and Subsidie

And of £24 0s.0d. paid for the taske of the towne of Burie this
yere   £24 0s. 0d.

And of £1 13s.4d. for the subsidie paiable the last yere   £1 14s. 4d.

And of £1 0s.0d. paid for the subsidie for this yere   £1 0s. 0d.

Poore and orphans

And of £2 0s.0d. paid to Colyes wief for kepinge of two poore
children, and of 2s.0d. given her in tyme of hir sickenes. And
of £1 12s.0d. paid to Robinsons wief for kepinge a poore child.
And of £1 13s.0d. given to Widow Abell for keping 2 poore
children, and to relieve hir in hir sickenes. And of £1 15s.0d.
paid to Widowe Cornehill for kepinge Darnelles child. And of
£1 2s.0d. paid to Widowe Glover for keping a poore child. And
of 5s.0d. given to Turnor for kepinge Gauntes child. And of
10s.0d. delivered to Mr Blagge, to bind a poore boye
apprentize. And of 10s.0d. paid to Roodes wief for keping a
poore child. And of £1 0s.0d. given to Robert Wretham, for
diverse cures done upon the poore, hurte and sore. And of
10s.0d. given to Atkin for setting of Godfreis legge which was

broken. And of £2 8s.8d. given by this accomptaunt in relief to diverse poore folkes at severall tymes. And of £10 15s.0d., parcell of the yerelie rent and annuytie paiable by Sir Robert Jermyn, knight, disbursed abowte parte of the charge of the working howse, hereafter mencioned in th'end of this accompt in the demaund of the said Sir Robert Jermyn,[171] *in toto* £24 2s. 8d.

Paymentes

And of £1 10s.0d. paid to the keper of the sickehowse. And of £2 0s.0d. paid for setting forthe of soldiors. And of 3s.4d. for the clerkes fee. And of £10 0s.0d. which the said accomptaunt paid for this howse. And of £6 13s.4d. which the same accomptaunts likewise paid for a dett of this howse ~~in toto~~ **St Maries Churche**. And of £1 0s.0d. paid to Thomas Overend, one of the churche wardeins of St Maries parishe, for the yere bifore past, *in toto* £21 6s. 8d.

Reparacions

And of £24 4s.8d. bestowed this yere in reparacions abowte the Guildhall, the ministers howses and certeine almes howses bilonginge to the feoffees of the londes and tenementes aforesaid, as by billes of particulers shewed at this accompt appearithe £24 4s. 8d.

[*f. 40v.*]

Supers

And of £6 15s.3d. of arrerages wherewith this accomptant is bifore chargid, not receyved. And of £5 13s.5d., wherewith he is likewise bifore chargid, not receyved. And of £5 18s.5d. wherewith this accomptaunt is likewise bifore chargid, not receyved. **All theis be old arrerages and sett down** <*deletion*> **in th'ende of this accompt as parcell of the same.** And of 9d. remayning in the handes of Sir Robert Jermyn, knight, for a yeres rent endid at Michelmas last, for londes in Hepworthe. And of £3 0s.0d. for the yeres rent of a mesuage by St James churche, late Collins, which his wief clayme to hold frelie for her lief. **5s.0d. for this £3 0s.0d.** *in fine huius compoti.* And of £2 0s.0d. for a yeres rent of a mesuage and gardein in Guildhall Strete due by Mr Richard Heigham, not paid at Michelmas last. And of 5s.0d. for the rent of a bearne in the occupacion of the saltpeter man then due. And of 2s.0d. for a yeres rent then due for a peece of ground in the Horse Markett in th'occupacion of John Landisdale. And of 8d. for a yeres rent of a tenemente in Longe Brackelond, then due, in th'occupacion of William Johnson. And of 13s.4d. for a yeres rent of a tenemente in Colledge Strete then due by John Cobbe. **5s.0d for this** *in fine huius compoti.* And of 16s.0d. for a yeres rent, then due, for a tenemente there in th'occcupacion of Umfrey Crowder. And of 6s.8d. due for a yeres rent then due for a parcell of ground in th'occupacion of Robert Sparke,

171 See Introduction, p.xxxiii.

baker, in Mr Andrewe Strete. **Theis 2 somes answered in the next accompt,** *videlicet,* **the 6s.8d. by payment and the 16s.0d. by bond taken for payment thereof.** And of 2s.0d. for the half yeres rent of a tenemente in th'occupacion of Widowe Sutton

£7 6s. 5d.

And of £8 18s.4¾d for the half yeres rent of St Peters, paiable by Mr William Revell, at the feast of the birth of Christ last past or within 28 daies after, not yet receyved. **This answered** *in proximo compoto.*

£8 18s. 4¾d.

A gallon of wine
And of a gallon of wine spent at the dyner of this company at this accompt

A gallon of wine

Money lent to poore men
And of £5 11s.0d. lent to diverse poore men to sett theym on worke, hereafter speciallie named and sett downe

£5 11s. 0d.

> *Summa allocacionis* £239 6s.8¾d. and a gallon of wine.
> *Et sic debet* £13 11s.8½d., whereof

The Churches
Delivered to Robert Sparke
Paid to William Brewster, one of the churche wardens of St James churche, for two yeres past at this accompt

£2 0s. 0d.

Delivered to John Gippes
And to Thomas Overend, one of the churche wardens of St Maries, for this yere past

£1 0s. 0d.

The dyner and for the poore
And paid for the dyner of this felowshippe at this accompt — £2 10s. 0d.

And for wine then spent — 8s. 8d.

And paid for 20 stone and half of beeff then bestowed upon the poore — £1 17s. 7d.

And for 30 dossen of breade for theym — £1 0s. 0d.

And for otemeale woode for the poore — 5s. 6d.

And for 36 gallons of beere for theym — 6s. 8d.

And given to the cooke, and his helpe, to dresse the dyner — 3s. 4d.

The gaole and poore
And given to the wief of Lewis, being in the gaole, to relieve hir and hir childrene — 2s. 0d.

And given to the poore prisoners in the goale — £1 0s. 0d.

And given to Turnor for keping one of Gauntes children — 2s. 0d.

And to Widowe Bird for keping 5 children, left by hir son and his wief — 5s. 0d.

And to Robinsons wief for the helping of old Thriste — 3s. 0d.

And for fire upon the meeting the daie after this accompt, and fynissing the same — 1s. 6d.

> *Summa* £11 5s.3d.
> *Sic debet* £2 6s.5½d. Adde hereunto £1 0s.3d. due by Inglethorpe upon his accompt underwritten, and so in all is due by th'accomptaunt £3 6s.8½d., which somme of £3 6s.8½d. was

delivered to Richard Walker, gentleman, nowe chosen receyvor
for the yere to come, to be answered by him upon his accompt. *Et
sic predictus Johannes Gippes eque*

Onus

Edmond Inglethorpe, the porter, dothe yeld his accompt for
money by him receyved for dyners kept at this hall this yere.   \£3/ 6s. 8d.
> *Summa* £3 6s.8d.

Allocacio

And dothe demaund allowans for his wages for this yere past £2
0s.0d. And for makinge cleane the doore, 4s.0d. And for candle
5d. And for fier 2s.0d., *in toto*   £2   6s.   5d.
> *Summa* £2 6s.5d.
>
> *Sic debet* £1 0s.3d., which was presentlie paid to Richard Walker,
> gentleman, receyvor for the yere to come, as above appearithe.

Onus

Th'accompt \of William Faiercliff/ of £40 0s.0d. by him receyved
to sett the poore on worke, as appearithe in th'accompt of Mr
Barber, 1594, parcell of Overendes money
> *Summa* £40 0s.0d.

Allocacio

The same William Faiercliff dothe demaund allowans of
£10 13s.4d. for arrerages of rent paid to Thomas Shorte for the
working howse, and of diverse other sommes of money
bestowed there, in reparacions of the same, and for buyinge of
certeine necessarie thinges into the same house as well for
settinge theym on worke as otherwise, and for diverse other
sommes of money by him disbursed about the mainteynauns
and settinge such to worke as have been kept there since the
last accompt, as by a bill of particulers now shewed dothe
appeare, the somme of
> *Summa* £40 19s.3d.
>
> *Sic debet computanto* 19s.3d.

Debetur Willielmo Faiercliff 19s.3d.

This paid by Mr Walker, the new receyvor, with other money, to the
poore upon the fynisshing of this accompt.

[f.41r.]

Debetur Johanni Man, paid

John Man demaundethe as due to him for certeine wares by him
delivered since the last accompt for th'appareileinge of suche
as were committed to the workinge howse as appearith by a bill
of perticulers shewed at this accompt the somme of   £8 10s. 1½d.
> *Summa* £8 10s.1½d. **This paid as
> appeare in the next accompt.**

Debetur Roberto Jermyn, militi. **Paid *ut patet in proximo compoto***

Item Sir Robert Jermyn, knight, dothe demaund for 36 loades of
woode by him sent and laid into the workinge howse to be
spent there for two yeres   £12   0s.   0d.

And for wheles and cardes bought and delivered by him into the same howse	12s.	0d.
And for money lent by him to the keper of the same howse	£2 3s.	4d.

Summa £14 15s.4d.

And there remaine in th'andes of the same Sir Robert Jermyn for one half yeres annuytie goinge owte of the mannor of Torkesey paiable the 20 daie of Julie last past	£10 0s.	0d.
And for the rent for half a yere paiable at Michelmas last for londes in Hepworth, letton to Edward Tailor	15s.	0d.

Of which sommes the said John Gippes receyvor and accomptaunt is bifore charged and therefore bifore mencionid in the title of poore and orphans as allowed to him

> Summa £10 15s.0d., which somme is allowed to the said Sir Robert Jermyn owte of the said some of £14 15s.4d. and so remaine due to him £4 0s.4d., which is now agreid shalbe paid to the same Sir Robert Jermyn upon the resceipt of £10 0s.0d. for the half yeres annuytie paiable by the same Sir Robert Jermyn owte of the said manor of Torkesey, which shalbe due the 20 daye of Januarie next coming

Debetur Thome Peade. **Paid *ut patet in proximo compoto***

Thomas Peade demaundeth for money by him disbursed by appointement for kepinge two poore children for 23 weekes left to the towne and for other thinges by him disbursed for the poore by appointement, as appeare by a bill of particlers nowe shewed	£1 9s.	10d.

Summa £1 9s.10d.

Money lent to poore men bifore mencioned

Lent to Bullyvant for which Thomas Baker hathe promised payment.	10s.	0d.
And to William Johnson.	£1 0s.	0d.
And to William Streete for which he hathe putt in bond with suretie now in the next accomptauntes hands. **£1 0s.0d. *unde paid ut patet in compoto '99***	£2 0s.	0d.
And to \John/ Clement by bill	10s.	0d.
And to \Edmond/ Talbott by bill	10s.	0d.
And to Freeman, for which he hathe also putt in bond, now likewise in the next accomptauntes hand	£1 0s.	0d.

> Summa £5 10s.0d., which is to be answered by Mr Walker at his accompt, with also the some of £13 6s.8d. paiable at midsomer next by one obligacion now delivered to him made by Hary Boldero and Thomas Harwell to Sir Robert Jermyn, knight, and others.

Memorandum that theis rentes underwritten are bihind unpaid as appeare in former accomptes, over and besides the supers bifore mencionid in this accompt[172]

---

[172] This list marks a determined effort to collect arrears that had been outstanding for some years. A number of the marginal notes about arrears in former accounts were also connected with this endeavour.

Rentes arere and unpaid for diverse yeres.

Imprimis for a mesuage in Churchegate Strete letton to Mr
Richard Heigham, sometime Leders, for 2 yeres at £2 0s.0d.
per annum, videlicet '94, '95 and one yere, *videlicet* '93,
£1 15s.8d., the rest beinge answerid, *in toto*   £5 15s. 8d.

Item for a bearne in the Westgate Stret, in th'occupacion of the
saltpeter man, at 5s.0d. *per annum*, for 5 yeres, *videlicet* '91,
'92, '93, '94, '95, *in toto*   £1 5s. 0d.

Item for a howse and gardein in th'occupacion of William
Heyward, gentleman, at 5s.0d. *per annum* for 2 yeres, *videlicet*
'94, '95   10s. 0d.

Item for londes in Hepworthe in th'occupacion of Sir Robert
Jermyn, knight, at 9d. *per annum* for 16 yeres endid in *anno
Domini* '95, and beginnynge 1580 to be unpaid   12s. 0d.

Item for a peece of ground in th'occupacion of John Landisdale at
2s.0d. *per annum* for 16 yeres endid in *anno Domini* '95, and
beginning to be unpaid 1580   £1 12s. 0d.

Item for a tenemente in Longe Brackelond in th'occupacion of
William Johnson at 8d. per annum for 3 yeres, *videlicet* '93,
'94, '95   2s. 0d.

Item for a stall in the markett in th'occupacion of William Jellowe
for a yeres rent endid at Michelmas '94. **This paid.**   2s. 0d.

    Summa £9 18s. 8d., which some, or so muche thereof as can be
received is to \be/ answerid at the next accompt, with the supers
bifore mencionid in this accompt, *videlicet*, £4 5s.9d. parcell of
£7 6s.9d. and £8 8s.4¾d.

Rent suspendid for the lief of Collins wief

Memorandum that the rent of £3 0s.0d. reserved upon a lease made to Richard
Collin, disceasid, of a mesuage purchasid of him, \lyinge / by St James churche, is
not demandable duringe the lief of his wief for that she claymithe an estate for lief in
the same mesuage.

Roberte Jermyn	Roger Barber	William Cooke
Richard Walker	Thomas Hamond	Thomas Peade

[f. 41v.]

1597

**Th'accompt of Richard Walker, gentleman, survieor and receyvor of all the
mesuages, londes, tenementes and hereditamentes bilonginge to the common
benefit of this towne of Burie St Edmunde, sometime John Smythes, esquier,
and others, made and taken the thirde daye of Januarie in \the/ fouretie yere of
the reign of our soveraign Ladie Quene Elizabethe, and *anno Domini* 1597[/8]
for one whole yere nowe endid**

Arrerages

First the said accomptaunt dothe charge himsilf with £9 18s.8d.
old arrerages, gathered and collectid owte of former
accomptes, as appeare in th'end of the last accompt, not
received   £9 18s. 8d.

And with £4 6s.5d., likewise arrerages in super, as also appeare in th'end of the same accompt   £4   6s.   5d.

And with £8 18s.4¾d. receyved, beinge a super of the last accompt for St Peters   £8 18s. 4¾d.

Yerelie revenues

And with £200 8s.6½d., beinge the whole yeres rent and fearme of the londes and tenementes aforesaid, as appear by the rentall thereof shewed at this accompt   £200   8s. 6½d.

Money received

And with £1 0s.3d. receyved at the last accompt by this accomptaunt, as appeare by the same   £1   0s.   3d.

Legacie

And with £13 6s.8d. received of Henry Boldero, gentleman, parte of £40 0s.0d. given in relief to the poore within this towne, by Frauncis Boldero, gentleman, his father, by his will, now all paid   £13   6s.   8d.

And with £5 10s.0d. for money lent bifore the last accompt, as appeare by the same accompt   £5 10s.   0d.

A gallon of wine

And with a gallon of wine paiable by John Revell and his heires, for certeine londes in Burie fieldes, sometime Jenkyn Barrettes   A gallon of wine

Summa oneris £243 8s.11¾d.

and a gallon of wine, whereof

Allowans of money lent and not received

The said accomptaunt dothe praie allowans of £5 10s.0d. lent bifore the last accompt, wherewith he standethe bifore chargid, and hathe not receyved eny parte of the same, and hathe brought in and delivered the billes bifore taken for payment of the same, which money lent appeare in the last accompt   £5 10s. 0d.

Rentes resolutes

And of £22 16s.6d., *videlicet*, of £20 0s.0d. paid to John Jermyn, esquier, parcell of th'annuytie given by Edmunde Jermyn, esquier, disceased, for one whole yere whereof <*deletion*> two acquittaunces for this yere past were shewed at this accompt, and for other rentes paid owte of the aforesaid londes and tenementes, and for the receyvors fees, as by the rentall dothe appeare, which was shewed at this accompt, *in toto*   £22 16s. 6d.

Mynisters

And of £40 0s.0d. pade to Mr Doctor Mosse, preacher of St James parishe, for one whole yeres stipend endid at the feast of the birthe of Christ last past. And of £40 0s.0d. paid to Mr Lewis, preacher of St Maries, for a yeres stipend then endid, *in toto*,   £80   0s. 0d.

Poore and orphans

And of £34 10s.8d. paid and distributed this yere past to diverse and sondrie poore persons for their relief, and for the kepinge of poore children and orphans, as appeare by a bill of particulers shewed at this accompt   £34 10s. 8d.

Reparacions
And of £9 17s.2d. bestowed this yere in reparacions abowte
diverse almes howses and others, as by biles of particulers
shewed at this accompt do appeare   £9 17s. 2d.

Paymentes
And of £8 10s.2d. paid to John Man, for a dett to him due, as
appeare by the last accompt   £8 10s. 2d.

And of £4 0s.4d. paid to Sir Robert Jermyn, knight, due to him as
there appearithe   £4 0s. 4d.

Rent paid for Bridewell[173]
And of £4 0s.0d. paid to Thomas Short for a yeres rent and
dimidium of Bridewell howse endid at Michelmas last, 1597   £4 0s. 0d.

And of £1 3s.8d. paid to Mr Peede for a dett to him due   £1 3s. 8d.

And of £1 9s.10d. paid to Thomas Reade, due to him by the last
accompt   £1 9s.10d.

And of £1 0s.0d. paid to old Wretham for cures of certeine poore
diseasid persons   £1 0s. 0d.

Prisoners
And of £1 0s.0d. given in relief of the prisoners in the gaole   £1 0s. 0d.

The churches
And of £2 0s.0d. paid to the churche wardeins of the parisshes of
St James and St Maries   £2 0s. 0d.

And of £1 5s.0d. paid to the Widow Snowdon for half a yere for
kepinge of Bridewell   £1 5s. 0d.

And of 6s.0d. disbursed abowt a repl[*evin?*] and the bailiefes fee
et alia upon a suyte attemptid for the lynnen   6s. 0d.

And of £2 0s.0d. given to Mr Worton, mynister of the parishe of
St Maries, in respect of deteyning some churche dueties, and
for his further relief   £2 0s. 0d.

And of £3 0s.0d. given to Widow Snowdon, by order at the hall,
as a recompence for many losses, as she saieth, susteyned by
the kepinge of Bridewell howse   £3 0s. 0d.

And of £2 0s.0d. given to Christofer Johnson for washinge the
lynnen diverse yeres   £2 0s. 0d.

And of £1 10s.0d. paid to the keper of the sicke howse   £1 10s. 0d.

Money lent. Harper paid it, *patet in compoto '99*
And of £1 17s.0d. lent by this accomptaunt to certeine poore
persons by billes and promises, *videlicet*, to John Clitter, upon
a bill, 12s.0d., and to William Harper upon a bill, 5s.0d., and to
Thomas Glover, for which Mr Walker dothe promise payment,
£1 0s.0d.. Glover paid, *ut patet in compoto*   £1 17s. 0d.

Arrerages in super
And of £9 18s.8d. of old arrerages, not receyved above, in charge   £9 18s. 8d.

---

173   Bridewell was synonymous with the 'working house'. See Introduction, p.lxiv.

And of £3 19s.9d., parcell of £4 6s.5d., likewise arrerages mencioned in th'end of the last accompt \and in charge/, of which somme of £4 6s.5d. the somme of 6s.8d. was receyved by this accomptaunt for the rent of Robert Sparke, parcell of the supers of the last accompt, and for the rent of Crowder, beinge 16s.0d. there mencioned, he and one Hill have putt in bond for payment thereof. And of 16s.0d. more for the rent of Crowder for this yere past unpaid and conteyned in the same bond, which bond is now delivered into this howse upon this accompt. [*In another hand*] **This bond of Crowder paid as appeare in the accompt 99 in clothe**   £3 19s. 9d.

[*f. 42r.*]

Supers

And of 13s.4d. remayning in th'andes of John Cobbe for a yeres endid at Michelmas last, for an almes howse in the Colledge Streete. And of 4s.0d. for a yeres rent then endid for an almeshowse in Northegate Streete, wherein Widowe Aggas dwellithe. And of 6s.8d. and 4d. for a yeres rent, then endid, of an almes howse in Garlond Strete, wherein John Dister dwellith. *Ut patet in compoto Thomo Peede.* And of 3d. for the rent of another almes howse there, wherein Robinson and Buckenham dwell. And of 5s.0d. for a yeres rent then endid, of an almes howse there, wherein Widow Able late dwellid. And of 5s.0d. for a yeres rent then endid of a bearne in Westgate Strete in th'occupacion of the saltpeter man. And of 14s.0d. for a yeres rent then endid for a closse at Stanford Bridg in th'occupacion of Widowe Carre. **This dischargid with 6d., parcell of 2s.0d., in the next accompt for £1 0s.0d. due to Carre for the taske.** And of £3 0s.0d. for a yeres rent then endid of a tenemente late purchasid of Richard Collin lyinge by St James churche, which Collines wief claymeth to hold frelie for terme of hir lief. And of 2s.0d. for a yeres rent then endid, for a peece of ground in the Horse Markett in th'occupacion of John Landisdale. And of 6d. for a yeres rent then endid, of a void peece of ground in the occupacion of Anthony Payne, gentleman. And of 4s.0d. for a yeres rent then endid, for a stable in th'occupacion of Widowe Potter. **This 6d. and 4s.0d. answered in the next accompt.** And of £2 0s.0d. for a yeres rent then endid, of a messuage and gardeine in Guildhall Streete, late \in th'occupacion of/ Leder, and now to be paid by Mr Richard Heigham by vertue of a lease made to him. And of 5s.0d. for a yeres rent then endid, of a tenement and gardene in the Risbiegate Streete, in th'occupacion of William Heyward, gentleman. And of 8d. for a yeres rent of a messuage in Longe Brackelond in th'occupacion of William Johnson. And of £1 0s.0d. for half a yeres rent of a howse and closse in Westgate Streete, in the tenure of Symond Kinge, due at Michelmas last, *in toto*   £9 0s. 8d.

And of £8 18s.4¾d. for the half yeres rent of St Peters, paiable by Mr William Revell at the feast of the birthe of Christ or within

28 daies after, not yet receyved. **This answered *in proximo*** | £8 18s. 4¾d.
compoto

A gallon of wine

And of a gallon of wine spent at the dyner of this company at this | A gallon of
accompt | wine

> *Summa allocacionis* £220 9s.9¾d.,
> and a gallon of wine
> *Sic remanet* £22 19s.1½d., whereof

Charges of the dyner: provision for the poore

Paid for the charges of the dyner of this companye at th'accompt,
videlicet, £2 10s.0d./, and bestowed in victuals for the poore
and other thinges abowte the dyner, as appeare by a bill of
particulers, \£5 18s.4d., *in toto*/ | £8 8s. 4d.
Paid more for the clerkes fee | 3s. 4d.
Paid more to Alman for dressing the armour | 4s. 0d.

Poore

Paid more to Thomas Peade for appareling and in relief of diverse
poore, as appeare by a bill | £1 12s. 9d.
Paid more to John Man for the like, as appeare by a bill | £1 4s. 6d.
Paid to Ede. Lakers for taking Thomas Traye apprentize, beinge
of th'age of 15 yeres | £2 0s. 0d.
Paid more to the widow Glover for kepinge 2 of James Chapmans
children, as a full recompence untill this daye | 13s. 4d.
Paid more to John Gippes which he by request gave to John Coote
in relief | 2s. 0d.
Given more in relief to Kendals wief | 2s. 0d.
Given more to Cheynes wief for placing one of Wiberdes children | 5s. 0d.
Given to John Turnor ~~for~~ \to/ kepe *<deletion>* William Crowche
alias Gaunt | 10s. 0d.
Given to Smythes wief in relief. | 2s. 0d.
Given more to old Gillie in relief | 3s. 4d.
Given to \Rodes/ ?~~Bodles~~ wief for keping a poor child | 2s. 0d.

> *Summa solucionis* £15 12s.7d.
> *Sic remanet* £6 6s.6½d.

Onus

Edmond Inglethorppe dothe yeld his accompt for money by him
received for diners kept at the hall this yere | £2 10s. 0d.

> *Summa* £2 10s.0d.

And dothe demaund allowans for his wages for this yere past,
£2 0s.0d. and for other thinges to him due and laid owte abowte
this howse, as appeare by a bill shewed by him at this accompt,
18s.6d., *in toto* | £2 18s. 6d.

> *Summa* £2 18s.6d.
> And so due to him 8s.6d., which was now paid him by Mr Walker
> and so Mr Walker oweth upon his accompt £6 18s.0½d., which
> was now paid and delivered by him to Robert \Sparke nowe/
> chosen receyvor for the yere to come, to be answerid upon his
> accompt and *sic predictus Ricardus Walker quietus*

117

Roberte Jermyn Roger Barber William Cooke
Thomas Peade Thomas Hamond John Gillie
Wylliam Fayerclif

[f.42v.]   **1598**

Th'accompt of Robert Sparke, surveior and receyvor of all the mesuages, londes, tenementes and hereditamentes bilonginge to the towne of Bury St Edmunde, and the comon profitt of the same, sometymes John Smythes, esquier and others, made and taken the second daie of January in the one and fouretie yere of the reign of our soveraign Ladie Quene Elizabethe, and *anno Domini* **1598, for one whole yere nowe endid**

Arrerages

First the said accomptaunt dothe charge him silf with £9 18s.8d., old arrerages collectid owte of former accomptes, *ut patet in fine compoti* '96, and also in the last accompt, not received £9 18s. 8d.

And with £3 3s.9d., parcell of £3 19s.9d., likewise arrerages mencionid in the last accompt, 16s.0d. of which £3 19s.9d. is parcell of the bond next mencioned £3 3s. 9d.

And with £1 12s.0d. for Umfrey Crowders rent unpaid, mencionid in the supers of the last accompt. **By bond** £1 12s. 0d.

And with £9 0s.8d., likewise arrerages in super of the last accompt £9 0s. 8d.

And with £8 18s.4¾d. received for St Peteres being a super of the last accompt £8 18s. 4¾d.

Resceiptes

And with £6 18s.0½d. received upon the determynacion of the last accompt *ut patet per eundem* £6 18s. 0½d.

And with £20 0s.0d. received of the parishioners of St James towardes the payment of their preacher for this yere past, endid at this Christmas £20 0s. 0d.

And with £10 0s.0d. ~~£2 11s.0d.~~ received for suche purpose of the parishioners of St Maryes ~~£2 11s. 0d.~~
  £10 0s. 0d.

Money Lent

And with £5 10s.0d. and £1 17s.0d. for money lent to poore \men/ upon billes and promises wherewith this accomptaunt is charged, which sommes appeare in the 2 last accomptes £7 7s. 0d.

Yerelie revenues

And with £200 8s.6½d. being the whole yeres rent and fearme of the londes and tenementes aforesaid, as appeare by the rentall of the same shewed at this accompt £200 8s. 6½d.

And with a gallon of wyne, paiable by John Revell and his heires, for certeine londes in Bury fieldes, some tymes Jenkyn Barrettes A gallon of wyne

  Summa oneris <deletion> \£277 7s.0¾d./[174]
  and a gallon of wine, whereof

---

[174] This amount is given in both arabic and roman numerals.

Owt rentes

The said accomptaunt dothe praye allowans of £22 16s.6d., *vide-licet* of £20 0s.0d. paid to John Jermyn, esquier, parcell of th'annuitie given by Edmond Jermyn, esquier, disceasid, for one whole yere, whereof two acquittaunces for this yere past were shewed at this accompt, and for other rentes paid owte of th'aforesaid londes and tenementes, and for the receyvors fees, as by the rentall shewed at this accompt appeare £22 16s. 6d.

And of 3d. paid for an amerciament for not mending the strete bifore the Guildhall[175]   3d.

Mynisters

And of £30 0s.0d. paid to Doctor Mosse and Mr Ward, preachers of St James parishe, for thre quarters stipend endid at Michelmas last. And of £30 0s.0d. paid to Mr Lewis for his stipend for St Maries parishe for 3 quarters then endid. And to of £10 0s.0d. *<deletion>* \paid to/ Mr Estye for a quarters stipend for St Maries parishe, endid at Christmas last £70 0s. 0d.

Poore and orphans

And of £33 8s.4d. paid and distributed this yere past to diverse and sundrie poore persons, and for the kepinge of poore children and orphans, as appeare by a bill of particulers shewed at this accompt £33 8s. 4d.

Taske and Subsidie

And of £50 13s.4d. this yere for the taske and subsidie of this towne graunted at the last Parliament £50 13s. 4d.

Reparacions

And of £2 11s.8d. bestowed this yere in reparacions of parte of the premisses £2 11s. 8d.

Paymentes

And of 10s.0d. paid to Mr Richard Heigham[176] for measuringe lond at Hepworth. And of £2 0s.0d. given to Mr Worton. And of £1 5s.0d. paid to Widow Snowdon, for half yeres wages for the howse of correccion, *videlicet* Christmas and Our Ladie. And of £1 13s.8d. paid to Thomas Bendo for an old dett. And of 14s.6d. paid to Mr Lewis for a journey to Cambridg for Mr Esty. And of 4s.0d. paid to Thomas Michell for the like. And of £1 10s.2d. paid to Widowe Bright, for a dett due to hir husband for clothe. And of £1 10s.0d. paid to the keper of the sickehowse. **Prisoners.** And of £1 0s.0d. given to the prisoners in the gaole. **Churches.** And of £1 0s.0d. to the parishe of St Maryes. And of £1 0s.0d. to the parishe of St James. And of £2 12s.10d. paid to John Gilly for a dett due to him for money disbursed for the towne busynes. *in toto* And of £1 10s.0d. paid

---

[175] This one of a very few indications that the court leet was held between the dissolution of the abbey and the incorporation of the borough in 1606.

[176] If Richard Heigham was a professional surveyor, none of his work seems to have survived among the maps and surveys at the Bury Record Office.

to Wretham the surgion for curing diverse poore this yere, *in
toto* £16 10s. 2d.

And of £10 0s.0d. parcell of the £20 0s.0d. receyved of the parishioners of St James bifore in charge, repaid to Mr Heyward for
the same parishioners for their preacher for parte of the yere to
come. £10 0s. 0d.

**Money lent not received. Hereof £1 5s.0d. paid *ut patet in proximo
compoto***

And of £7 7s.0d. bifore in charge not receyved, for money lent to
poore men as appeare in the 2 former accomptes by billes and
promises and the billes now redelivered to this howse by this
accomptaunt £7 7s. 0d.

Supers old arrerages

And of £9 18s.8d. of old arrerages, above in charge, not receyved £9 18s. 8d.

And of £3 ?++ 3s.9d., parcell of £3 19s.9d. arrerages in super in
the last accompt, bifore in charge, not yet received £3 3s. 9d.

And of £1 12s.0d. by bond now delivered into this howse by this
accompt[*ant*], being bifore in charge, which bond was bifore
taken for payment of two yeres rent of Crowder, endid at
Michaelmas '97. **This answered in the next accompt in
clothe** £1 12s. 0d.
by bond

[*f.43r.*]
Supers

And of £8 16s.2d., parcell of £9 0s.8d. bifore in charge, being a
super of the last accompt for that yere not received, savinge
4s.0d. of the same £9 0s.8d. receyved of the Widow Potter for a
stable in Punche Lane And of 6d. of Mr Payne, *sic remanet non
receptum* £8 16s. 2d.

And of £8 18s.4¾d. for the half yeres rent of St Peters, paiable
twentie daies after Christmas, not yet received. **This answered
*in proximo compoto*** £8 18s. 4¾d.

And of 9d.[177] unpaid this yere past by Sir Robert Jermyn, knight,
for londes in Hepworthe. **3s.4d. parcell paid *ut patet in
proximo compoto.*** And of 13s.4d. unpaid by John Cobbe. And
of 16s.0d. unpaid by Umfry Crowder. **This 16s.0d. answered
in clothe, *ut patet in proximo compoto.*** And of 4s.0d. unpaid
by Widow Aggas. **Paid by Dister *Thomo Peede ut in
compoto.*** And of 3s.4d. and 3d. unpaid by John Dister. And of
3d. unpaid by Buckenham. And of 5s.0d. unpaid by Widowe
Shippe. **This 5s.0d. paid, *ut patet proximo compoto.*** And of
5s.0d. for a bearne in the Westgate Strete in th'occupacion of
the saltpeterman. And of 7s.0d. for the half yeres rent of
Widow Carre, due at Our Ladie last for a closse at Stanford
Bridge. **6s.0d. *inde* discharged with 14s.0d. *in compoto
predicto.*** And of 2s.0d. unpaid by John Landisdale. And of
£3 0s.0d. for Collins howse. And of 2d. unpaid by Roger

---

177 Here 'li' has been crudely altered to 'd'.

Wright for part of his howse next the Angell. And of 4s.0d.
unpaid this yere by Widow Potter for a stable in Punche Lane.
This 2d. and 4s.0d. answered *in proximo compoto.* And of
£2 0s.0d. unpaid by Mr Richard Heigham. And of 5s.0d.
unpaid by Mr Heyward. And of 8d. unpaid by William Johnson
for a tenement in the Longe Bracklond. **Paid *ut patet in***
***compoto* Thomas Peede.** And of 6d. unpaid by Henry Kent for
a tenement at the Northe Gate. **This 6d. paid *ut patet in***
proximo compoto. *In toto*   £8 7s. 3d.

A gallon of wyne
And of a gallon of wyne spent at the dyner of this company at this
accompt   A galon of wyne

> *Summa allocacionis* £256 13s.0d.
> £254 3s.5¾d. and a gallon of wyne
> *Sic remanet* £23 4s.7d. £25 14s.7d.
> £23 3s. 7d.[178] whereof

Charges of the dyner and provision for the poore
Laid owte more for the charge of the dyner for the company at the
taking of this accompt and provision for the poore for their
relief at that tyme and for helpe and other thinges necessarie, as
did appeare by billes of particulers then shewed   £12 19s. 5d.

> *Summa* £12 19s.5d., whereof for the companye
> £4 10s.8d. and for the poore £8 8s.9d.
> *Sic remanet* £11 5s.2d. £12 15s.2d. £10 4s. 2d.

Onus
Th'accompt of Edmunde Inglethorpe, *videlicet* for money by him
receyved for dyners kept at the hall this yere   £3 11s. 8d.

> *Summa* £3 11s.8d.

Allocacio
And he demaundethe the allowans for his wages this yere past
£2 0s.0d. And for other thinges by him laid owte abowte this
howse and other allowances, as by a bill of particulers shewed
at this accompt appeared 14s.8d., *in toto*   £2 14s. 8d.
More then allowed him for money then laid owte   1s. 0d.

> *Summa allocacionis* £2 15s.8d.
> So remayne due by him 16s.0d., which was presentlie paid to
> Robert Sparke now accomptaunt. So the same accomptant with
> the aforesaid sum of £10 12s.2d., *<deletion>* aforesaid somme
> of £10 4s.2d. owethe £11 *<deletion>* 0s.2d., whereof

Paid presentlie to the clerke for his paynes and fee   10s. 0d.
And for wine, sugar and cakes spent at the second meting for the
fynishing of this accompt   2s. 0d.

> *Summa* 12s.0d.
> So rest due by this accomptaunt £10 8s.2d., £10 9s.2d. *<deletion>*
> which somme was presentlie paid to John Gilly, receyvor for the

---

178 Again the amount is given in both roman and arabic numerals.

yere to come, together with a bond of Clementes and another of Harperes, another of Clitters, another of Hilles for Crowder, another of Talbottes and another of Freemans.

Et sic praedictus Robertus Sparke eque et quiete est.

Roger Barber	William Hayward	Wm.Cooke
Thomas Peade	Richard Walker	Robrte Spark
Thomas Gooderych the elder		

[*f. 43v.*]

1599

Th'accompt of John Gilly th'elder, surveior and receyvor of all the mesuages, londes \and/ tenementes bilonging to the common profitt of the towne of Bury St Edmunde, sometymes John Smythes, esquier, and others, made and taken the second daye of January in the two and fouretie yere of the reign of our soveraign Ladie Queene Elizabethe, *et anno Domini* 1599 [*1600*], for one whole yere now endid

Arrerages

First the said accomptaunt dothe charge him silf with £29 7s.5d. old arrerages, collectid owte of former accomptes untill and for the yere 1598, as appeare by two severall notes delivered to the same accomptaunt at the last accompt, to receive and answere at this accompt — £29 7s. 5d.

And with £8 18s.4¾d. receyved for St Peters, being a super of the last accompt — £8 18s. 4¾d.

And with £1 12s.0d. for two yeres rent of Umfrey Crowder endid at Michelmas '97, as appeare in the supers of the last accompt, for payment whereof a bond was made — £1 12s. 0d.

Money lent

And with £7 7s.0d. for money lent to poore men upon billes and promises, which somes appeare in the accompt '96 and '97 — £7 7s. 0d.

Receipts

And with £10 9s.2d. receyved upon the determynacion of the last accompt — £10 9s. 2d.

And with £36 0s.0d. receyved of Henry Hamond, delivered to him as appeare by the accompt '94 — £36 0s. 0d.

Yerelie revenues

And with £200 8s.6½d. being the whole yeres rent and fearme of the londes and tenementes aforesaid, as appeare by the rentall of the same, shewed at this accompt — £200 8s. 6½d.

A gallon of wyne

And with a gallon of wyne paiable by John Revell and his heires for certeine londes in Bury fieldes sometymes Jenkyn Barrettes — A gallon of wyne

Summa oneris £294 2s.6¼d. and a gallon of wine, whereof

Owtrentes

The said accomptaunt demaundethe allowans of £22 16s.6d.,

videlicet, of £20 0s.0d. paid to John Jermyn, esquier, percell of th'annuytie given by Edmunde Jermyn, esquier, disceasid, for one whole yere, whereof acquittauns was shewed at this accompt. And for other rentes paid owte of the aforesaid londes and tenementes. And for the receyvors fees, as by the rentall shewed at this accompt appearithe · · · · · · · · · · · · · · · · · · £22 16s. 6d.

And of £2 3s.6d. for a tenthe paid yerelie to the Queenes Majestie owte of St Peters, for foure yeres endid at Michelmas last, and for 4 severall acquittaunces for the same, *videlicet*, 10s.6d. for the tenthe of every yere and the residue for the acquittaunces · · · · · · · · · · £2 3s. 6d.

Rent paid for the howse of correcion

And of £5 6s.8d. paid for two yeres rent endid at Michelmas last for the howse of correccion · · · · · · · · · · · · · · · · · · £5 6s. 8d.

Mynisters

And of £20 0s.0d. paid to Mr Estye for his stipend, for one whole yere endid at the feaste of the birthe of Christ last, for St Maryes parishe · £20 0s. 0d.

And of £20 0s.0d. paid to Mr Newton, for his stipend for one whole yere then endid, for St James parishe · · · · · · · · · · · · £20 0s. 0d.

Poore

And of £26 0s.0d. paid to the collectors for the poore in bothe parishes, 52 wekes now endid, after the rate of 10s.0d. the weeke · £26 0s. 0d.

And of 6s.8d. paid to them for one weke left unpaid by the last receyvor · 6s. 8d.

And of £3 12s.10d. given to certeine poore folkes at the Guildhall upon the determynacion of the last accompt · · · · · · · · · · £3 12s. 10d.

Taske and Subsidie

And of £50 13s.4d. paid this yere for the second payment of the taske and subsidie of this towne graunted at the last Parliament · · £50 13s. 4d.

Reparacions

And of £4 11s.11d. bestowed this yere in reparacions of the premisses, and the howse of correccion, as appeare by particulers now shewed · £4 11s. 4d.

Paymentes

And of 16s.4d. paid for 14 paire of cardes for the howse of correccion. And of 5s.0d. for two paire of stock cardes for the same howse. And of 4s.0d. paid for dressing the towne armour the yere bifore. And of 5s.0d. for fryce to make the bedell a coat. And of £1 10s.0d. paid to the keper of the sicke howse. And of £1 10s.0d. paid to Wretham for curing diverse poore this yere. And of 10s.0d. paid to Ambrose Lichefield for healing of Palfrymans boy. **Prisoners** And of £1 0s.0d. given to the prisoners in the gaole this yere. **Churches** And of £1 0s.0d. paid to the parishe of St James. And of £1 0s.0d. paid to the parishe of St Maryes towardes the reparacions of the churches. And of 10s.0d. paid to the clerke for his fee, *in toto* · · £8 10s. 4d.

Money lent not yet received, whereof £1 0s.0d. paid *ut patet in proximo compoto*

And of £6 2s.0d., parcell of £7 7s.0d. bifore in charge, lent to poore men, of which £7 7s.0d. there is paid for parcell of Streetes det £1 0s.0d., and by William Harper 5s.0d., and the residue of the bondes delivered in this howse   £6 2s. 0d.

Supers. Old arrerages

And of £27 18s.5d. [?]16s.10d, parcell of £29 7s.5d. arrerages bifore in charg, of which £29 7s.5d. there is paid 3s.4d., parcell of Cobbes rent, being 13s.4d. due the last yere '98, and for Crowders rent then due, 16s.0d., and for Widowe Shippes then due 5s.0d., and for Roger Wrightes rent, then due, 2d. And for Potters rent, then due, 4s.0d. And for Kentes rent, then due, 6d. And so remaine of th'arrerages unpaid   £27 18s. 5d.

    Summa allocacionis £198 2s.2d. and a gallon of wine.

    Sic remanet £96 0s.4¼d. whereof

[*f. 44r.*]

Supers

There is in the handes of Sir Robert Jermyn, knight, for a yeres rent endid at the feast of St Michaell th'archaungell last past for londes in Hepworthe   9d.

And in the handes of Laurence Coldeham for half a yeres rent for londes there then due   1s. 0d.

And for an almes howse in Northegate Strete wherein Widowe Aggas dwelt   4s. 0d.

And for an other almes howse in Garlond Strete, wherein John Dister dwell   3d.

And for a bearne in Westgate Strete, late occupied by the saltpeterman   5s. 0d.

And in the handes of Sir Robert Jermyn, knight, for half yeres annuytie issuyng and going owte of the mannor of Torkesey, due the 20 day of July last past. **Paid *ut patet in proximo compoto***   £10 0s. 0d.

And for the rent of Collins howse, bifore in charge, not paiable duringe the lief of his wife   £3 0s. 0d.

And in the handes of William Revell, gentleman, for half yeres rent for St Peters, paiable at the feast of the birthe of Christ or within 20 daies after, not yet receyved. **Paid *ut patet in proximo compoto***   £8 18s. 4¾d.

And in the handes of John Landisdale for a yeres rent of a piece of ground in the Horse Market due at Michelmas last.   2s. 0d.

And in the handes of Richard Heigham, gentleman, parcell of £2 0s.0d. for a yeres rent of a howse in Chrchegate Strete, endid at Michelmas last   £1 6s. 8d.

And in the handes of William Heyward, gentleman, for a yeres rent of a tenemente in Risbiegate Strete and a gardein in the Teyven then endid   5s. 0d.

And in the handes of William Johnson for a yeres rent of a tenemente in Longe Brackelond then endid. ***Ut patet in compoto Tho. Peade***   8d.

Summa £24 3s.8¾d.

So remayne due by this accomptaunt £71 16s.7½d. whereof clothe delivered by this accomptaunt for 4 yeres rent of Crowder to the value of £3 4s.0d. and remayne due by the same accomptaunt in moneye £68 12s.7½d., whereof

The charge of the dyner and provision for the poore

Paid for the charge of the dyner \for the company/ at the takinge of
this accompt £2 19s.8d., and for provision for the poore for
their relief at that tyme, as did appeare by billes of particulers
then shewed, £8 11s.0d., *in toto* — £11 10s. 8d.

Paid more to Alman the cutler for dressinge of the towne armour
this yere — 4s. 0d.

Paid more to Thomas Michell for a winding \sheet/ and buriall of
a poore woman — 2s. 8d.

Paid more to John Man for 4 winding sheetes for 4 poore women — 6s. 1d.

Paid more to John Man for diverse journeys for getting Mr
Newton, preacher of St James churche[179] — 18s. 0d.

Given to Mr Peede for trymmynge the lynnen for the judges — 10s. 0d.

    Summa £13 11s.5d.

    Sic remanet £55 1s.2½d.

Onus

Edmunde Inglethorpe dothe yeld his accompt for ~~dynners~~ money
by him receyved for mariage dynners kept at the Guildhall this
yere, £3 5s.0d. — £3 5s. 0d.

    Summa £3 5s.0d.

Allocacio

And he demaundethe allowans for his wages this yere past, £2
0s.0d. And for other thinges by him laid owte for fire burnt
here, and other allowances as appeared by a bill of pariculers
shewed at this accompt 9s.4d., *in toto* — £2 9s. 4d.

    Summa £2 9s.4d.

    Sic debet 15s.8d., which was presentlie \paid/ to John Gilly,
now accomptaunt. So the said John Gilly, with the aforesaid
somme of £55 1s.2½d. *<deletion>* owethe £55 16s.10½d.,
whereof

Prisoners

Paid to Robert Sparke and John Man to distribute at tymes convenient to the poore prisoners in the gaoll of this towne for
arrerages past — £3 0s. 0d.

And to Thomas Michell for 2 coates for the 2 bedels to looke to
the good order of the poore, *videlicet*, Atherton and Foxgill — £1 10s. 0d.

    Summa £4 10s.0d.

    So remayne due clere by the said accomptaunt £51 6s.10½d.
and he hathe delivered clothe for £3 4s.0d. besides.

---

[179] For details of the expenditure when Mr Newton's successor was appointed, see Introduction, p.xlv.

[*f.44v.*]

1600

Th'accompt of Henry Collinge, gentleman, surveior and receyvor of all the mesuages, londes and tenementes bilonginge to the common profit of the towne of Bury St Edmunde, sometyme John Smythes, esquier, and others, made and taken the 30ⁱᵉ day of December 43° yere of the reign of our Soveraign Lady Queene Elizabethe *et anno Domini* 1600, for one whole yere nowe endid

Arrerages

First the said accomptaunt dothe charge himself with £19 1s.11d.
old arrerages collectid owt of former accomptes untill and for
the yere '98, as appeare by a note to him delivered, to receive
and answere at this accompt   £19   1s.   11d.

And with £21 3s.8¾d., a super in the last accompt, as appeare by
another note to him delivered, to receive and answere at this
accompt   £21   3s.   8¾d.

Money lent

And with £6 2s.0d. for money heretofore lent to poore men *ut*
patet per priores compotos et per billas   £6   2s.   0d.

Resceiptes

And with £51 6s.10½d. receyved upon the determynacion of the
last accompt   £51   6s.   10½d.

And with clothe valued \and taken/ at £3 4s.0d. remayninge upon
the last accompt, *ut patet ibi*   £3   4s.   0d.

Yerely revenues

And with £200 8s.6½d., beinge the whole yeres rent and fearme of
the londes and tenementes aforesaid, and other revenues as
appeare by the rentall of the same, shewed at this accompt   £200   8s.   6½d.

And with £5 0s.0d. receyved for the porcion of tithes in
Foxhearthe, given by Thomas Bright   £5   0s.   0d.

A gallon of wyne

And with a gallon of wine, paiable by John Revell and his heires,   A gallon of
for certeine londes in Bury fieldes, sometymes Jenkyn Barret   wyne
       Summa oneris £306 7s.0¾d.and a gallon of wyne, whereof

Owt rentes

The said accomptaunt demaundethe allowans of £22 16s.6d.,
videlicet, of £20 0s.0d. paid to John Jermyn, esquier, parcell of
th'anuytie given by Edmunde Jermyn, esquier, disceased, for
one whole yere, whereof acquittauns was shewed at this
accompt. And for other rentes paid owte of the aforesaid londes
and tenementes. And for the receyvors fees, as by the rentall
shewed at this accompt appearithe   £22   16s.   6d.

Rent paid for Bridewell

And of £2 13s.4d. paid to Thomas Short for a yeres rent endid at
Michelmas last for the howse of correcion   £2   13s.   4d.

Mynisters

And of £25 0s.0d. paid to Mr Esty, preacher of St Maryes parishe, for his whole yeres stipend, endid at the feast of the birthe of Christ now past — £25 0s. 0d.

And of £25 0s.0d. paid to Mr Newton, preacher of St James parishe, for his whole yeres stipend then endid — £25 0s. 0d.

Poore

And of £26 0s.0d. paid to the collectors for the poore in bothe parishes for 52 weekes now endid, after the rate of 10s.0d. the weeke, *in toto* — £26 0s. 0d.

And of 15s.2d. given in relief of the poore at sondry tymes, *ut patet* by particlers now shewed — 15s. 2d.

Taske and subsidie

And of £50 13s.4d. paid for the last payment of the taske and subsidy graunted at the last Parliament — £50 13s. 4d.

Reparacions

And of £2 13s.3d. bestowed in reparacions of the premisses, *ut patet* by particulers now shewed — £2 13s. 3d.

Paymentes

And of £1 0s.0d. paid for the charg of a Commission sued owt for the benefit of this towne.[180] And of 10s.0d. paid for the dyet of the commissioners. And of £2 10s.0d. paid to John Gilly, the last accomptaunt, chargid upon his accompt and promised to be repaid him. And of £1 10s.0d. paid to the keper of the sickehowse. And of £1 0s.6d. paid for a suger loaf bestowed for the benefit of this towne. And of £1 3s.4d. paid towards the Quenis provision in July last. **Churches** And of £1 0s.0d. paid to the churche of St Maryes and of £1 0s.0d. to the churche of St James, for the reparacions of the same churches. And of £1 10s.0d. paid to Wretham for curing diverse poore persons. And of 6s.8d. paid for settinge forthe of soldiers in July last. And of £3 0s.0d. delivered to Mr Walker, to disburse for charges of suyte the last terme. **Thomas Brights guift.** And of £1 0s.0d given to the parishe churche of St James, according to the will of Thomas Bright. And of £1 0s.0d. given to the churche of St Maryes for suche purpose. And of £1 0s.0d. to the poore in St James parishe. And of £1 0s.0d. to the poore in St Maryes parishe. **Prisoners.** And of £1 0s.0d. to the poore prisoners in the gaole, accordinge to the said will. And of £1 0s.0d. given to the same prisoners, paiable for the other revenues. And of £2 0s.0d. paid to Widow Snowdon, keper of the howse of correccion at 2 severall tymes. And of 8s.0d. paid for 7 paire of cardes for the same howse. And of £1 0s.0d. paid towardes a stocke for the same howse in May last. And of 10s.0d. paid more to the same howse. And of 6s.0d. for fryce for a coate for Inglethorpe, the porter. And of 10s.0d. for the

---

[180] The subject of this commission has not yet been discovered.

clerkes fee. And of 13s.4d. for drawinge and ingrosing the deede of feofement and the rentall to be renewed. And of 2s.0d. more to the Widowe Snowdon. And of 4s.0d. paid to Alman the cutler for dressinge the towne armour this yere past, *in toto*   £25 17s. 2d.

Arrerages not received
And of £19 1s.11d. old arrerages bifore in charge, not yet receyved   £19 1s. 11d.

And of £2 5s.4d., parcell of £21 3s.8¾d., bifore in charg, of which somme £10 0s.0d. is receyved for the half yeres anuytie owt of Torkesey, in super in the last accompt. And of £8 18s.4¾d. for Mr Revels rent for half a yere, likewise in super there, and so remayne not receyved   £2 5s. 4d.

Money lent but not received
And of £5 2s.0d., parcel of £6 2s.0d. bifore in charge, of which somme £1 0s.0d. is receyved for the det of Thomas Glover, and the residue remayne not receyved.[181]   £5 2s. 0d.

The cloathe bestowed
And of 14s.10d. paid towardes the buyinge of 2 coates for Foxgill and Britoll, the 2 bedels, to make up £1 10s.0d. for the same coates, paid upon sale of 13 yardes of the cloathe, above in charge for 15s.2d. And the rest of the cloathe, rated at £1 14s.0d., was bestowed at the howse of correccion, *in toto*   £3 4s. 0d.

> *Summa allocacionis* £211 2s.0d. and a gallon of wine
> *Sic remanet* £95 5s.0¾d., whereof

[*f.45r.*]
Supers
There remaine in the handes of Sir Robert Jermyn, knight, for a yeres rent endid at Michelmas last for londes in Hepworthe   9d.

And in the handes of the same Sir Robert for a yeres rent, then ended, for other londes there. **Paid, *ut patet in proximo compoto***   £1 10s. 0d.

And in the handes of Giles Barker for half yeres rent of a tenemente there   3d.

And in the handes of Cobb for half a yeres rent of an almes howse in the Colledg Stret   6s. 8d.

And in the handes of Umfrey Crowder, for a yeres rent of a tenemente there   16s. 0d.

And in the handes of Widdowe Aggas for a yeres rent of an almeshowse in Northegate Streete   4s. 0d.

And in the handes of Widowe Sutton, for half a yeres rent of an almes howse there   2s. 0d.

And in the handes of Dister, for a yeres rent of an almes howse in Garlonde Strete. **Paid *ut in compoto Tho. Peade***   3d.

And in the handes of Widow Shipp, for a yeres rent of an almeshowse there   5s. 0d.

And for a bearne in Westgate Strete, late occupied by the saltpeter man, and now fallen downe   5s. 0d.

---

[181] See above, f.40v.

And in the handes of Sir Robert Jermyn, knight, for half yeres anuytie owte of the mannor of Torkesey, due the 20 of July last past. **Paid** *ut patet in proximo compoto*   £10 0s. 0d.

And for the whole yeres rent of a tenemente nere St James steple, purchasid of Richard Collin, disceased, wherein his wief claymethe estate for hir lief   £3 0s. 0d.

And in the handes of William Jellowe, for a yeres rent endid at Michelmas last, for a stall in the market   2s. 0d.

And in the handes of Fraunces Pynner, for half yeres rent of St Peters, paiable at Christmas or within 28 dayes after, not yet receyved. **Paid** *ut patet in proximo compoto*   £8 18s. 4¾d.

And in the handes of John Landisdale, for a yeres rent of a peece of ground in the Horse Market, due at Michelmas last   2s. 0d.

And in th'andes of Robert Sparke, baker, for a yeres rent, then endid, for ground in Mr Andrews Strete   6s. 8d.

And in th'andes of Roger Wright for a yeres rent, then endid, for a peece of ground by the Angell. **Paid** *ut patet in proximo compoto*   2d.

And in th'andes of Widowe Potter for a yeres rent, then endid, for a garden in Punche Lane. **Paid** *ut patet in proximo compoto*   4s. 0d.

And in th'andes of Richard Heigham, gentleman, for a yeres rent then endid for a tenement in Churchegate Strete   £2 0s. 0d.

And in th'andes of William Heyward, gentleman, for a yeres rent then endid, for a tenemente and gardeine   5s. 0d.

And in th'andes of John Parker for a yeres rent then endid, for a tenement in Longe Bracklond   6d.

And in th'andes of Hughe Mathewe for a yeres rent, then endid, for a tenemente there, late William Johnsons. **Paid** *ut patet in proximo compoto*   8d.

    Summa £28 9s.3¾d.

    And so remayne due by this accomptaunt £66 15s.9d.

Onus

Edmond Inglethorpe yeldithe his accompt for money by him receyved for mariage dyners kept at the Guildhall this yere   £4 4s. 2d.

    Summa patet

Allocacio

And demaundithe allowans for his wages this yere past, £2 0s.0d. And for other thinges by him laid owte for mending thinges in the kitchin and for fier in the chamber and other allowances, 9s.2d., *in toto*   £2 9s. 2d.

    Summa patet

    Sic debet £1 15s.0d., which was presently paid to Mr Colling, now accomptaunt.

    So the said Henry Colling, with the abovesaid somme of £66 15s.9d. owithe £68 10s.9d., whereof

The charges of the dyner and provision for the poore and other payments

Paid for the charge of the dyner for the company at the taking of this accompt, £2 16s.4d. And for provision for the poore at that tyme, as appeare by a bill of particulers, £9 14s.3d., *in toto*   £12 10s. 7d.

Paid more to John Man, laid owt by him for apparell for poore	10s. 10d.

Paid more to Piper, for money by him disbursed upon an arrest to
appeare at the Sessions, upon an inditement against this towne ..... 10s. 0d.

Paid more as given here to a poore trayling soldier by pasport of
his captayne[182] ..... 6d.

Paid more to Wretham in respect of his cures of the poore this
yere past ..... 10s. 0d.

> *Summa* £14 1s.11d.
>
> *Sic debet* £54 8s.10d., which some the 10th of January *anno supradicto* was delivered to William Heyward, gentleman, receyvor for this yere to come, to be answerid upon his accompt.
>
> *Et sic predictus Henricus Colling eque*

[*f.45v.*]

1601

Th'accompt of William Heyward, gentleman, surveior and receyvor of all the mesuages, londes, tenementes and hereditamentes bilonginge to the comon profit of the towne of Bury St Edmunde, sometymes John Smythes, esquier, and others, made and taken the 29 daye of December in the 44 yere of the reign of our soveraigne Ladie Queene Elizabethe, *et anno Domini*, 1601, for one whole yere nowe endid

Arrerages

First the said accomptaunt dothe charge himsilf with £25 9s.3d., parcell of £28 9s.3¾d., beinge a super of the last accompt, as appeare there ..... £25 9s. 3¾d.

Resceiptes

And with £54 8s.10d. receyved upon the determynacion of the last accompt, *ut patet ibi* ..... £54 8s. 10d.

Dyners at the hall

And with £5 5s.0d. received for mariage dyners kept at the Guildhall this yere ..... £5 5s. 0d.

Revenues

And with £201 16s.2½d., beinge the whole yeres rent and fearme of the londes and tenementes aforesaid, and other revenues, as appeare by the rentall of the same now shewed ..... £201 16s. 2½d.

And with a gallon of wyne, paiable by John Revell and his heires, for certein londes in Bury fieldes, sometymes Jenkyn Barret ..... A gallon of wine

> *Summs oneris* £286 19s.4¼d. and a gallon of wine, whereof

Owt rentes

The said accomptaunt demaundithe allowans of £22 16s.6d., *videlicet*, of £20 0s.0d. paid to John Jermyn, esquier, parcell of th'annuytie given by Edmunde Jermyn, esquier, disceased, for

---

[182] The Elizabethan legislation for the militia provided that injured soldiers travelling home be given passports to entitle them to relief as they travelled from one place to the next.

one yere, whereof two acquittaunces were now shewed. And
for other rentes paid owte of th'aforesaid londes. And for the
receyvors fees, as by the rentall shewed at this accompt
appearithe   £22 16s. 6d.

Rent for Bridewell

And of £3 6s.*<deletion>*8d. paid to Thomas Short for a yeres rent,
endid at the feast of St Michaell th'archaungell last past, for the
house of correccion   £3 6s. 8d.

Mynisters

And of £40 0s.0d paid to Mr Newton, preacher of St James
parishe, for his stipend for a yere nowe endid. And of
£40 0s.0d. paid to Mr Estye, for half a yere and half a quarter,
and to Mr Bedell, for the rest of the yere, beinge preachers of
St Maries parishe, for the whole yeres stipend now endid   £80 0s. 0d.

Poore

And of £26 0s.0d. paid to the collectors for the poore, in bothe
parishes, for 52 weekes now endid, after the rate of 10s.0d. the
weeke, *in toto*   £26 0s. 0d.
And of £6 0s.0d. given and distributed to the poore in this towne,
by common consent, in their relief this present feast of the
birthe of Christ   £6 0s. 0d.
And of £1 8s.0d. given to diverse poore folkes, at sondry tymes, as
appeare by particlers now shewed   £1 8s. 0d.

Reparacions

And of £17 3s.1d. bestowed this yere in reparacions of the Guildhall, the mynisters howses, and almes howses and other the
premisses   £17 3s. 1d.

Paymentes

Thomas Brightes guift. And of £1 0s.0d. given to the parishe of
St James, according to the will of Thomas Bright. And of
£1 0s.0d. given to the churche of St Maries for such purpose.
And of £1 0s.0d. to the poore of St Maries parishe. And of
£1 0s.0d. to the poore in St James parishe. And of £1 0s.0d. to
the poore prisoners in the gaole according to the same will.
And of 5s.0d. for thre paire of stockardes and one of Duche
cardes, for the howse of correccion. And of 3s.6d. for thre paire
of stocke cardes more there. And of 2s.4d. for two paire of
Spanishe cardes there. And of £2 0s.0d. to Wretham, the
surgion, for cureing diverse poore folkes this yere. And of
£1 10s.0d. paid to the keper of the sicke howse. **Prisoners.**
And of £1 0s.0d. to the poore prisoners in the gaole, owte of
the towne revenues. And of 6s.0d. for Inglethorpe, the porter,
for a coate. And 10s.0d. paid towardes a stocke for the howse
of correccion. And of £10 0s.0d. given towardes the charg of
the suyte against this towne, for the liberties of th'inhabitauntes
in the market.[183] And of 5s.0d. towardes the provision of the

---

[183] On 16 January 1599 John Mann and Thomas Michell admitted to the company that the ancient

Navy. And of 8s.0d. towardes the provision of Hir Highnes howshold. And of 5s.0d. towardes the setting forthe of a horse and a man for the fraunchise.[184] And of 16s.8d. towarde the setting forthe of soldiors. And of 6s.8d., in 2 several sommes, for like purposes. And of 3s.4d. more for the provision of the navye. And of 10s.0d. more for setting forthe soldiors. And of £3 0s.0d. delivered to Mr Walker, to disburse in the suyte of Kemboldes legacie.[185] And of 10s.0d. more for the provision of Hir Highenes howshold. And of 10s.0d. paid towardes the charge of the muster. And of 10s.0d. for the clerkes fee. And of £1 10s.0d. for engrossing the rentall, and the feofement, twice newlie ingrossed by reason of alteracion of names.[186] And of 15s.0d. for a coate for Britoll, the bedell. And of 4s.0d. paid to the cutler, for dressing the towne armour. And of £2 12s.4d. paid to Inglethorpe, the porter, whereof £2 0s.0d. for his wages this yere past, and the rest for fiers in the chamber, mendinge the sincke, and other thinges done by him, and allowed to him. And of £2 11s.0d. paid for the charge of the dyner for the company at the takinge of this accompt, and for the attendauntes, *in toto* £35 13s. 10d.

[f. 46r.]

Arrerages not received

And of £4 16s.1d., percell of £25 9s.3¾d., bifore in charge, of which last somme is receyved for Sir Robert Jermyns lease rent in Hepworthe £1 10s.0d. And £10 0s.0d. for the half yeres annuytie owte of Torkesey. And of £8 18s.4¾d. for Pynners rent for St Peters. And 2d. for Roger Wrightes rent. And 8d. for Hughe Mathewes rent. And 4s.0d. for th'executors of the Widowe Potter. And so remayne not receyved of the super of the last accompt £4 16s. 1d.

> *Summa allocacionis* £197 4s.2d. and a gallon of wine spent at the dyner
>
> *Et sic remanet* £89 15s.2d., whereof *patet in proximo compoto*

There remayne in the handes of Sir Robert Jermyn, knight, for a yeres rent, due at Michelmas last, for londes in Hepworthe, letton to Edward Tailor, £1 10s.0d. **Paid *ut patet in compotum***

Letters Patent of the liberties of Bury St Edmunds were in their custody and would be brought in to the house [Guildhall] on reasonable demand, Minutes, H2/6/2.1, p.20. On 8 April that year the Letters Patent of Henry VIII confirming the liberties of the town, which now have the number A1/1/1 at SROB, were returned to Thomas Baker to show to the Clerk of the Green Cloth, in connection with the town's privileges for purveyance, Minutes, H2/6/2.1, p.20. For purveyance see Introduction, p.lxii, and for Thomas Baker and a probable consequence of this incident, see Introduction, p.xxv.

[184] That is for the Liberty of St Edmund, an area largely corresponding to the former administrative county of West Suffolk, which had its origins in Edward the Confessor's grant of it to the abbey of St Edmund. At this period quarter sessions were held for the Liberty by adjournment, and it was similarly an accepted administrative division within the county for financial or, as here, military matters.

[185] For Kembold's legacy see Appendix 8, *sub* 1590.

[186] No general refeoffment was made this year so this must refer to a conveyance which was altered.

Johannis Gippes **£1 10s.0d.** And also in his handes for a yeres rent then endid, for londes there, 9d. And in th'andes of Humfry Crowder for a yeres rent of an almes howse in the Colledg Streete, 16s.0d. And in th'handes of Widow Aggas, for a yeres rent of an almes howse in Garlond Streete, then endid, 4s.0d. And in th'andes of John Dister, for another almes howse there, 3d. And in th'andes of Robinson, for the rent of another almes howse there, 3d. **Paid *ut patet in proximo compoto.*** And in th'andes of Symond King, for half yeres rent due at Michelmas last, for a howse and close in Westgate Street, £1 0s.0d. **Paid *ut patet in proximo compoto.*** And in th'andes of Sir Robert Jermyn, knight, for half yeres annuytie, paiable owt of Torkesey, due the 20 day of July last, £10 0s.0d. And for half yeres rent due at Michelmas last for londes letton to Mrs Hamond, not received, £1 11s.2d. **Paid *ut patet in proximo compoto.*** And in the handes of Fraunces Pynner for half yeres rent of St Peters, paiable at the feast of the birthe of Christ or within 20 dayes after, not yet paid, £8 18s.4¾d. **Paid *ut patet in proximo compoto.*** And in th'andes of th'executors of Sparke, baker, for a yeres rent endid at Michelmas last, 6s.8d. And in th'andes of John Landisdale for a yeres rent of a peece of ground in Horse Market, then due, 2s.0d. And in th'andes of Richard Heigham, gentleman, for a yeres rent, then endid, for a tenemente in Churchegate Streete £1 0s.0d. And in th'handes of William Heyward, gentleman, for a yeres rent, then endid, for a tenemente and gardene, 5s.0d., *in toto*   £25 14s. 5¾d.

 Summa £25 14s.5¾d.

 So the said accomptaunt owethe clere £64 0s.8½d. Which £64 0s.0d. is now delivered to Thomas Peede, receyvor for the yere to come, to be answered upon his accompt, and the 8½d. given to poore people.

Old arrerages and money lent

Memorandum that there been old arrerages collectid owt of former accomptes, untill and for the yere 1599, amountinge to the somme of £21 7s. 3d. **Parte hereof paid.** £21 7s. 3d.

[*In a different hand*] \Theis arrerages are hereunto annexed that remaine unpaid *ut patet supra*/[187]

And money lent to poore men, as appeare by former accomptes, not yet paid, amounting to £5 2s. 0d.

Th'accompt of the overseers of the £300 0s.0d. given by Thomas Bright

Onus

The overseers of the stocke of £300 0s.0d. given by Thomas Bright, diseased, to and for the relief of the poore in Bury St Edmunde, doo yeld their accompt for one yere, endid at the feast of the birthe of Christ 1601, aswell for the same somme, as for suche benefite as have growen thereby for the relief of the poore, and doo acknowledg the same £300 0s.0d. to be in

---

[187] This list, which is pinned to f.46r., has been numbered 46a and is printed below.

the handes of George Boldero and William Faierclife, upon
bondes for repayment thereof, and doo charg them silves with
the profit thereof, to the somme of £27 0s. 0d.

unde

> *Summa patet*

Allocacio

They praye allowans of £21 15s.7d., laid owte in clothe and frice
for the clothing of many poore people in Bury aforesaid, and of
£5 4s.5d. paid to diverse tailors for making the same
garmentes, in toto £27 0s. 0d.

> *Summa patet*, and so evin

[*The following note now numbered 46a, is written on a piece of paper stitched to
f. 46r.*]

A note of arrerages of rentes unpaid, collected owte of the booke of accomptes untill
and for the yere 1599

Inprimis for a mesuage letton to Richard Heigham for 5 yeres
rent, *videlicet*, '94,'95,'96, '97,'98, at £2 0s.0d. per annum, and £13 2s. 0d.
one yere, *videlicet*, '93, 3s.4d., the rest being paid, and for the
yere '99, £1 6s.8d., *in toto*

Item of Laurence Coldham for half yeres rent, due at Michelmas
'99, for londes in Hepworthe 1s. 0d.

Item for a bearne, late in th'occupacion of the saltpeter man, at
5s.0d. *per annum*, *videlicet*, '91, '92, '93, '94, '95, '96, '97,
'98, '99 £2 5s. 0d.

Item for a tenemente and gardein in th'occupacion of Mr
Heywarde for 5 yeres, *videlicet*, '94, '95, '97, '98, '99 £1 5s. 0d.

Item for lond in Hepworthe in th'occupacion of Sir Robert
Jermyn, for 20 yeres endid '99, beginning to be behind '80, at
9d. *per annum* 15s. 0d.

Item for ground in th'occupacion of John Landisdale, for 20 yeres
beginnyng and ending as bifore, at 2s.0d. *per annum* £2 0s. 0d.

Item of Symond Kinge for half yeres rent of a close in Westgate
Strete, due at Michelmas '97 £1 0s. 0d.

Item for an almes howse in Northegate Strete, wherein the
Widowe Aggas dwelt, for a yeres rent endid at Michelmas '99 4s. 0d.

> *Summa* £20 12s.0d.

[f. 46v.]

1602

**Th'accompt of Thomas Peede, gentleman, surveior and receyvor of all the
mesuages, londes, tenementes and hereditamentes bilonging to the common
profit of the towne of Bury St Edmunde, sometimes John Smythes, esquier, and
others, made and taken the fourthe of January in the 45 yere of the reign of our
soveraign Ladye Queene Elizabethe, and *anno Domini* 1602[/3], for one whole
yere now endid**

134

Arrerages

First the said accomptaunt dothe charge himsilf with £25 14s.5¾d., being a super in the last accompt, as appearithe there £25 14s. 5¾d.

And with 1s.4d. received of Hughe Mathewe for old arrerages of a tenement in Long Brackelond. And of £1 0s.0d. received of Symond Kinge for arrerages of a howse in Westgate Strete, for half yeres rent due 1601. And with 10s.0d. received of John \Dister/ for arrerages of a tenemente in Garlond Strete £1 11s. 4d.

Resceiptes

And with £64 0s.0d. received upon the determynacion of the last accompt, *ut patet ibidem* £64 0s. 0d.

And of £1 0s.0d. received of yonge Hamond for a fyne of londes to him letton £1 0s. 0d.

And of £3 13s.4d. received of Inglethorpe for mariage dyners kept at the hall £3 13s. 4d.

Yerely revenues

And with £201 16s.2½d., being the whole \yeres/ rentes of the londes and tenementes aforesaid, and other revenues, as appeare by the rentall of the same £201 16s. 2½d.

And with a gallon of wyne of John Revell, for londes in Bury fieldes, late Jenkyn Barrettes A gallon of wyne

Summa oneris £297 15s.4¼d. and a gallon of wyne whereof

Owt rentes

The said accomptaunt demandethe allowans of £22 16s.6d., *videlicet*, of £20 0s.0d. paid to John Jermyn, esquier, parcell of th'anuytie given by Edmunde Jermyn, esquier, disceasid, for a whole yere, with 2 acquittaunces now shewed, and for other rentes and fees owt of the said londes, *ut patet per rentale* £22 16s. 6d.

Rent for Bridewell [*?In another hand*]

And of £5 13s.4d. paid to Short, for a yeres rent, endid at Michaelmas last, for the howse of correccion £5 13s. 4d.

Mynisters

And of £30 0s.0d. paid to Mr Bedle, preacher of St Maries parishe for his yeres stipend, now endid. And of £30 0s.0d. to Mr Newton, preacher of St James, parishe for his stipend £60 0s. 0d.

Poore

And of £26 0s.0d. paid to the collectors for the poore, in bothe parishes, for 52 weekes endid at Christmas last, after the rate of 10s.0d. the weeke £26 0s. 0d.

And of £1 14s.0d. given in relief to diverse poore folkes at sondry times, *ut patet per* particulers £1 14s. 0d.

And of 5s.0d. given to Widowe Lichefield to take Threders child into service 5s. 0d.

And of £6 0s.0d. now at this Christmas distributed to the poore in their relief £6 0s. 0d.

Reparacions

And of £10 <deletion> 6s.4d. bestowed this yere in reperacions of
the Guildhall, almes howses and other howses £10 6s. 4d.

Taske and subsidye

And of <deletion> £72 0s.0d. paid at 2 severall tymes for the taske
of this yere, and 8d. for 2 acquittaunces £72 0s. 8d.

And of 7s.6d. paid to the towne of Westley, for taske of londes in
Westley, parcell of St Peters 7s. 6d.

And of £5 6s.8d., paid at 3 severall tymes, for the subsidy of this
howse this yere £5 6s. 8d.

Paymentes

And of £1 0s.0d. given to the parishe churche of St James,
according to the will of Thomas Bright. And of £1 0s.0d. to the
parishe churche of St Maryes. And of £1 0s.0d. to the poore in
St James parishe. And of £1 0d.0d. to the poore in St Maryes
parishe. And of £1 0s.0d. to the poore prisoners in the gaole,
according to the same will. And of £1 0s.0d. to the reparacions
of the parishe churche of St Maryes. And of £1 0s.0d. to the
reparacions of St James churche. And of £1 0s.0d. to the poore
prisoners in the gaole. And of £6 0s.0d. for wasshinge the
lynnen for 5 yeres, after the rate of £1 4s.0d. the yere. And of
5s.0d. to Sharpes wief, for healinge a fistula in Leazauns
daughters face. And of 1s.0d. for healinge Thompsons hand.
And of 16s.0d. paid to Atkin, at 2 severall times, for healing
the poore. And of £2 0s.0d. to Wretham, the surgion, for his
yeres wages. And of 15s.0d. more to Atkin. And of £1 0s.0d.
paid to William Faiercliff, towardes a stocke to set the poore
on worke. And of 5s.0d. for the liverey of Foxgill. And of
£1 10s.0d. to the keper of the sickehowse. And of 7s.6d. for
settinge forthe of souldiors. And of £8 4s.0d. paid into
th'eschequer, ymposed for new measures of brasse.[188] And of
£5 0s.0d. delivered to Mr Walker, to disburse in the suyte of
Kemboldes legacie. And of £2 11s.4d. paid to Inglethorpe, the
porter, whereof for his wages this yere past, £2 0s.0d., and the
rest for fiers in the chamber and other thinges done by him, and
allowed to him. And of 6s.0d. for a coate for him. And of
10s.0d. for the clerkes fees. And of 10s.0d. for provision of Hir
Highnes howshold, and of the Navy, *in toto* £38 10s.10d.

[*f.47r.*]

Arerages not receyved

And of £5 4s.5d., parcell of £25 14s.5¾d., bifore in charge, of
which last some is received of Robinson 3d. And of Dister 3d.
And for the half yeres annuytie owt of Torkesey £10 0s.0d.
And for Mr Hamondes rent £1 11s.2d. And for Fraunces
Pynners rent for St Peters £8 18s.4¾d. And so remaine of the
supers of the last accompt, not yet receyved £5 4s. 5d.

---

[188] Although the feoffees had no legal responsibility for the market at this date, they are here seen
providing a standard weight required for its management.

Summa allocacionis £254 5s.3d. and a gallon of wyne spent at the dyner.
Sic remanet £43 10s.1¼d., whereof

Supers
Roger Wr' paid, *ut patet compoto Johannis Gippes*

There remaine in the handes of Sir Robert Jermyn, knight, for a yeres rent, endid at Michelmas last, for londes in Hepworthe, £1 10s.0d. And more of him for londes there, 9d. **Paid, *ut patet in compoto Johannis Gippes*** £1 10s.0d. And for a tenemente, late in th'occupacion of Widowe Aggas, 4s.0d. And for an almes howse in possession of Buckenham, 3d. And for another, in the possession of Widowe Shippe, 1s.8d. And of th'executors of William Jellowe for a stall, 2s.0d. And of John Landisdale for a peece of ground in the Horse Market, 2s.0d. And of Roger Wright, 2d. And of Richard Heigham, gentleman, £1 0s.0d. And of William Heyward, gentleman, 5s.0d. And of the heires of John Parker, 6d. And also there remayne in the handes of John Bedall, as parcell of his rent for londes in Hepworthe, £1 0s.0d. And of Fraunces Pynner for the half yeres rent of St Peters, paiable at Christmas or 20 dayes after, £8 18s.4¾d. **Paid *ut patet in compoto Johannis Gippes*, in toto**   £13 4s. 8¾d.

> *Summa* £13 4s.8¾d.
> *Sic remanet* \in toto/ £3 5s.4½d., whereof

The charges of the dyner and other paymentes

Paid to Christofer Johnson for the dyner for the company, and attendauntes	£2 6s.	8d.
And for wine, sugar and cakes	7s.	0d.
And to Alman, the cutler, for dressing the armour	4s.	0d.
And to Atkyn for certeine cures done to diverse poore folkes	£1 0s.	0d.
And for mending the chymney at the Guildhall	2s.	0d.
	<deletion>	
And for reparacions of an almes howse at the Risbi Gate	2s.	11d.
And for a windinge sheet for a poore man	1s.	8d.
And for a coate for Brytoll the bedle	15s.	0d.

> *Summa* £4 19s.3d.
> So the said accomptaunte owethe clere £25 6s.1½d.
> [*In a different ink*] Which is delivered to John Gippes, now receyvor, whereof in money £15 0s.7d., and upon a bill of Mr Mallowes, £2 0s.0d., and two acquittaunces for a quarter for the poore, £6 10s.0d., and upon a note for the tenth for 3 yeres, £1 15s.6d.

Money lent not received

Memorandum that there is money heretofore lent to poore men, not yet receyved, amounting to the some of   £5 2s. 0d.

The accompt of the overseers of the £300 0s.0d. given by Thomas Bright
Onus

The overseers of the stock of £300 0s.0d. given by Thomas Bright, disceased, to and for the relief of the poore in Bury St

Edmunde, doo yeld ther accompt, for one yere endid at Christmas last, *videlicet*, 1602, as well for the same somme as for suche benefite as have growen therby, for the relief of the poore, and doo acknowledge the same somme of £300 0s.0d. to be in the handes of George Boldero and William Faiercliff, upon bondes for repayment thereof, and do charge themsilves with the profit thereof to the somme of £27 0s. 0d., *unde*

    Summa patet

Allocacio

They pray allowans of £22 13s.5d. laid owte in frize for clothinge many poore people in Bury, as appeare by particulers, and of £4 65s.7d., paid to diverse tailors for makinge the same garmentes, *in toto* £27 0s. 0d.

    Summa patet, and so evin.

Jo. Heigham   Roger Barber   William Haywarde   William Cooke

[f.2r., old number 130]

1603

The accompte of John Gippes, surveyor and receyvor of all the mesuages, londes, tenementes and hereditamentes belonginge to the comon prophit of the towne of Bury St Edmunde, sometymes John Smithes, esquire, and others made and taken the third daye of Januarye in the yere of the reigne of our Soveraigne Lord James, kinge of Inglond *et cetera* **the first,** *et anno Domini* **1604[1] for one whole yere now ended**

Arrerages

Firste the said accomptant dothe charge him silfe with £13 4s.8¾d. being a super in the last accompte, *ut patet ibidem*	£13	4s.	8¾d.
And with £1 10s.0d. receyved of Sir Robert Jermyn, knight, for londes in Hepworthe leaton to Edward Taylor, parcell of a super *anno* 1601 beinge £4 16s.1d., the residue not yet receyved	£1	10s.	0d.

Receiptes

And withe £25 6s.1½d. a remainder of the last accompt, *ut patet ibidem*	£25	6s.	1½d.
And with £4 8s.4d. receyved of Inglethope for mariage dinners kept at the hall this yere	£4	8s.	4d.
And withe £10 0s.0d. receyved of Edmond Avis of a band payable at Our Ladye daye and Mychelmas last past[2]	£10	0s.	0d.

Yerely rentes

And with £201 15s.2½d. beinge the whole yeres rentes of the londes and tenementes aforesaid, and other revenewes, as appearethe by the rentall of the same	£201	16s.	2½d.
And with a gallon of wine of John Revell for londes in Bury fieldes, late Jenkyn Barrittes	A gallon of wine		

> *Summa oneris* £256 5s.4¾d.
> and a gallon of wine, whereof

Out rentes

The said accomptant prayethe allowans of £22 16s.6d., *videlicet*, of £20 0s.0d. payed to John Jermin, esquire, percell of the annuitye given by Edmunde Jermin, esquire, disceasid, for one whole yere, whereof two acquittances were now shewed, and for other rentes and fees out of the said londes, as appearethe by the rental[3]	£22 16s.		6d.
And of £6 0s.0d. payed to Thomas Short, senior, for one whole yeres rent due at Michelmas last paste for the howse of correccion	£6	0s.	0d.

---

[1] The 3 January in James VI and I's first year was the new style 1604. The numeral has been altered either from 3 to 4 or from 4 to 3. An old style 1603 was no doubt intended.

[2] For Kembold's legacy see Appendix 8, *sub* 1590. The £100 was left first to his wife, Margaret, and it was her executors who were to hand it over to the feoffees to buy land, IC500/2/41, f.370v. Edmund Avis, who might have been a son-in-law, was no doubt executor to both Peter and Margaret Kembold.

[3] In the original account, H2/3/4/6, it is clear that the receiver's fee of 15s. is included in this amount.

Mynisters

And of £30 0s.0d. payed to Mr Beadle, preacher of St Maryes
parishe, for one yere endid at Christmas last

£30 0s. 0d.

And of th £30 0s.0d. payed to Mr Newton, preacher of St James
parishe for one yere then ended

£30 0s. 0d.

And of 13s.4d delivered to John Man by Sir John Heigham and
Mr Barbers note for Mr Newton, and of £1 0s.0d. delivered to
Mr Barber for Mr Newton without bill, *in toto*

£1 13s. 4d.

And of twentye shillinges payed to Mr Juell, minister of St
Maryes parishe

£1 0s. 0d.

And of twentye shillings payed to Mr Buller, mynister of St James
parishe

£1 0s. 0d.

Poore

And of £6 10s.0d. payed by the last resceyvor to the collectors for
the poer for the quarter due at Our Ladye daye last paste, which
was before this accomptant did take upon him his receipt and is
parcell of the £25 6s.1½d. before in charge

£6 10s. 0d.

[*f. 2v.*]

And of £26 0s.0d. payed to the collectors for the poore for 52
weekes to be ended at Our Ladye daye next cominge, after the
rate of 10s.0d. the weeke

£26 0s. 0d.

And of 16s.6d. given to the reliefe of the pooer at sunderye tymes,
and towardes the buryall of the deade from the hospitall, and
others, as apperethe by particulers nowe shewed

16s. 6d.

And of 13s.4d. payed to Oriels wiefe for kepinge of a base childe

13s. 4d.

And of £5 0s.0d. given and distributed to the poore at this
Christmas by comon consent

£5 0s. 0d.

Repayracions

And of £10 1s.7d. bestowed this yere in reparacions of the Guildhall, Gurdens howse, almes howses in the Northgate Street,
Colledge Strete and Westgate Strete, and a well at the hospitall
and in the Northgate Streete, as appearthe by particulers nowe
shewed

£10 1s. 7d.

Taske and subsedye

And of £48 0s.0d. payed at two severall tymes for the taske of this
towne this yere and eyght pence for two acquitances

£48 0s. 8d.

And of £2 13s.4d. payed for the subsedye of this howse at two
severall tymes

£2 13s. 4d.

And of 5s.0d. payed to Frances Pinner for the taske of londes in
Westley fieldes belonginge to St Peters

5s. 0d.

Paymentes
[*In another hand*] The guift of Thomas Bright disceased, owt of Foxherthe tithes

And of £1 0s.0d. to the parishe churche of St James accordinge to
the will of Thomas Brighte and of £1 0s.0d. to the parishe
churche of St Maryes, for the reparacions of them. And of
£1 0s.0d. given to the poore of St James parishe. And £1 0s.0d.
to the poore of St Maries parishe. And £1 0s.0d. to the poore
prisoners of the gaole, accordinge to the same will. And of

£1 0s.0d. for the reparacions of the parishe churche of St Maryes. And of £1 0s.0d. for the reparacions of the parishe church of St James. And of £1 0s.0d. for the pooer prisoners in the gaole. And of £2 0s.0d. payed to Robert Wretham, the surgion, for his fee for curinge the poore. And of £1 10s.0d. payed to the keper of the hospital. And of 12s.0d. for 16 sackes of cole layed into the Guildhall for those that were sicke.[4] And of £2 15s.0d. payed to Thomas Burbage by comon consent for mending the market crosse, and for his scruses and shores lefte there to uphoulde the same[5] And of 2s.8d. payed to Cobbe for mendinge of foure water payles. And of £1 0s.0d. payed to the cunstables at severall tymes for the sicke that were compelled to kepe there howses. And of £2 13s.1d. payed to Inglethorpe, the porter, whereof £2 0s.0d. for his wages this yere paste, and 6s.0d. for his coate and the reste for fyers in the chamber, and other things doone by him, and allowed to him. And of 10s.0d. payed to the clerke for his fee, *in toto*   £19   2s.   9d.

Arerages not received
And of £2 16s.2d., parcell of £13 4s.8¾d., before in charge, of which last some there is resceived of Sir Robert Jermin, knight, for londes in Hepworthe £1 10s.0d. And of Roger Wright 2d. And of Francis Pinner for his halfe yeres rente for St Peters £8 18s.4¾d. And soe remayne not receyved of the super of the laste accompte   £2 16s.   2d.

[*f.3r.*]
Moneye not yet receyved
And of £2 0s.0d. not yet payed, lente to Mr Mallowes upon his bill for Clerke, a poore man, beinge parcell of the £25 6s.1½d. before in charge, lent by the laste receyvor before this accoun-tant did take upon him his resceipte. And of £1 15s.6d. payed by the last receyvor, likewise parcell of the said some of £26 6s.1½d. before in charge for the arrerages of a tenthe out of St Peters for diverse yeres paste   £3 15s.   6d.

And of a gallon of wine spent at the dynner   A gallon of wine

> *Summa allocacionis* £218 4s.8d.
> and a gallon of wine
> *Et sic remanet* £38 0s.8¾d. whereof

Supers
There remaynethe in the hands of Sir Robert Jermin, knight, for londs in Hepworthe 9d. **Of this 5s.0d. received *ut patet* in Mr Walkers accompt, and the rest allowed for londes in pos-session of Sir Robert Jermyn.** And in the hands of John Bedwall for londs there £1 0s.0d. And of Henrye Hill for a howse in the Northgate Strete 4s.0d. And of Robinson 3d. And

---

4   Several entries to be found below in this account show that an epidemic, probably plague, was about and that people were being shut up in their houses. While it is possible that the Guildhall was used as an isolation hospital, it seems much more likely that coal was being stored until it was delivered to those who needed it.

5   See Introduction, pp.xxxviii, lii, for the building and rebuilding of the Market Cross.

of Buckenham and Everad 3d. And of Widowe Shippe 5s.0d. And in the handes of Mr George Boulderowe for a howse and grownd in the Westgate Strete £2 0s.0d. **Allowed for reparations.** And of the executors of William Jellowe for a stall in the market 2s.0d. And of John Landesdale for grownde in the Horsemarket 2s.0d. **Answered by composicion** *ut patet* **in Mr Bolderoes accompt.** And of Mr Richarde Heigham for a house in the Churchgate Strete £1 0s.0d. And of Mr Heywarde 5s.0d. And of William Johnson for a tenemente late John Parkers in the Longe Braklond 6d. And of Hewe Mathewe for a tenemente there 8d. **Answered** *ut patet* **in Mr Bolderoes accompt**

£5 0s. 5d.

> *Summa* £5 0s.5d.
> *Sic remanet* £33 0s.3¾d., whereof

The charges of the dynner and other paymentes[6]

Payed to George Boyden for the dinner for the companye and attendantes	£2	5s.	0d.
More for wine, suger and cakes		7s.	3d.
Payed more to Adkens for diverse cures in bonesettinge and other things	£2	3s.	4d.
Payed more to John Man for windinge sheates for the poore	£1	16s.	5d.
Payed more to Brithall for his coate xv^s		15s.	0d.
Given to Alman for dressinge a corslet[7]		2s.	0d.
And payed more for fire at the daye of this accompte		1s.	4d.

> *Summa* £8 0s.4d.
> *Sic remanet* £24 19s.11¾d. which somme is nowe delivered

[*Below is written in two columns, each of three lines in the manuscript.*]
Memorandum that £10 0s.0d., parcell of the £24 19s.11¾d., remayne in the handes of Mr Gyppes \as receyved/ and is to be lente to Harroulde, the glover, upon bondes to be taken to Mr Thomas Peede, nowe appointed resceovor for the yere to come, with a bond of £2 0s.0d. of Mr Mallowes.

Onus
The accompt of the overseers of the £300 0s.0d. given by Thomas Bright
The overseers of the stocke of £300 0s.0d. given by Thomas Bright, disceasid, to and for the reliefe of the pooer in Bury St Edmunde doe yelde their accompt for one yere endid at Christmas laste, *videlicet* 1603, as well for the said somme as for suche benefite as have growne thereby for the reliefe of the poore, and doe acknowlege the same somme of £300 0s.0d. to be in the handes of George Bouldroe and William Fayrcliefe upon bandes for repaymente thereof, and doe charge themsilves with the profit thereof for this yere to the somme of £30 0s. 0d.,
unde

> *Summa patet*

---

6 In the original account, H2/3/4/6, all that follows is written in the hand of Thomas Bright.
7 In the original, the word cutler is given after Alman and continues 'which heretofore have kept a corselet and this yere have done nothing'.

They praye allowans of £24 17s.0d. layed out in frise for clothing manye poore people in Burye as appeare by perticulers, and of £5 3s.0d. payd to diverse taylors for makinge the garmentes for the poore, *in toto*   £30   0s.   0d.

    Summa patet and soe even

Roger Barber	Wm. Cooke	Thomas Peade
Willm. Hayward	Rico. Walker	Robrte Sparke[8]

[f. 3v.]

1604

Th'accompt of Thomas Peede, gentleman, surveyer and receyver of all the mesuages, londes, tenementes and hereditaments belonginge to the comone benifite of the towne of Burye St Edmunde, sometymes John Smithes, esquier, and others, made and taken the seconde daye of Januarye in the yere of the reign of our Soveraigne Lord James, kinge of Inglonde etc., the second, *et anno Domini* 1604 [*1605*] for one whole yere nowe ended

Arrerages

Firste the said accomptante dothe charge himsilfe with 2s.0d. \received of Lawrens Coldham/, parcell of £5 0s.5d, beinge a super of the laste accompte, the residue not beinge yet received   2s.   0d.

Receiptes

And with £20 0s.0d., parcell of a remaynder of the last accompte beinge £25 0s.0d. (foure bandes for five powndes residue made to John Gyppes nowe beinge delivered into this howse)   £20   0s.   0d.

And with £20 0s.0d. receyved of Mr Barber, parcell of Kembouldes legacye, payed to him by Edmunde Avis. And with £10 0s.0d. more receyved of the same Avis upon a bande, parcell of the same legacye, *in toto*   £30   0s.   0d.

And with £3 0s.0d. receyved of Inglethorpe for marriage diners kepte at the Guilde Hall this yere   £3   0s.   0d.

Yearlye rentes

And with £201 16s.2½d., being the whole yeres rent of the londes and tenementes aforesaid, and other revenues *ut patet per rentale*   £201 16s. 2½d.

And with £3 0s.0d. received of Rowge for a yeres rente ended at Michaelmas last past for the howse late Richard Collins   £3   0s.   0d.

And with a gallon of wine of John Revell for londes in Burye fieldes, late Jenkin Barrets   A gallon of wine

    Summa oneris £257 18s.2½d.
    and a gallon of wine, whereof

---

8   Although Thomas Bright was at the account, he did not sign. It is likely that some time must have elapsed between the audit and the entering of the account into the book. Those who signed need not necessarily have been at the account.

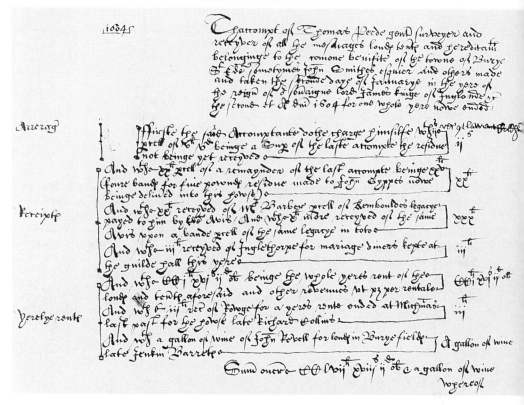

Plate 7. Part of Thomas Peed's account for 1604, showing the heading and passages recording payment of arrears, miscellaneous receipts and yearly rents (HD1150/2 f.3v.). Reproduced by permission of Suffolk Record Office.

Outrentes

The said accomptant dothe praye allowance of £22 16s.6d., *videlicet* of £20 0s.0d. payed to John Jermyn, esquier, parcel of th' annuytye given by Edmunde Jermyn, esquire, for one whole yere whereof two acquittances ware nowe shewed, and for other outrentes payed out of the said londes, and for the receyvors fee, *ut patet per rentale* £22 16s. 6d.

And of £6 0s.0d.payed to the Widowe Shorte for a yeres rente endid at Michlemas last past for the house of correccion £6 0s. 0d.

And of £1 1s.0d. payed for a tenthe due for two yeres out of St Peters endid at Michaelmas last, and of 1s.0d. for th'acquittance £1 2s. 0d.

Mynisters

And of £30 0s.0d. payed to Mr Beadle preacher of St Maryes parishe for his stipende for a yere nowe ended, and of £30 0s.0d. payed to Master Newton, preacher of St James parishe, for his stipend for a yere nowe likewise endid, *in toto* £60 0s. 0d.

144

And of £1 0s.0d. payed to Mr Jewell, mynister of St Maryes parishe, and of £1 0s.0d. payed to Mr Buller, mynister of St James parishe	£2 0s.	0d.

Poore

And of £19 10s.0d. payed to the collectors for the poore, for three quarters of a yere nowe ended, after the rate of 10s.0d. the weeke	£19 10s.	0d.
And of 13s.8d. given to diverse poore people at sunderye tymes	13s.	8d.
And of £5 5s.0d. given and distributed to the poore this Christmas by comon consente	£5 5s.	0d.

Reparaciones

And of £5 10s.5d. for reparacions doone at the Guildehall, and upon almes howses at th'ende of St Maryes churche and in the Colledge Streate	£5 10s.	5d.

Taske and subsedye

And of £48 0s.0d. payed this yere at two severall tymes for the taske, and of 8d. for two acquittances. And of £2 13s.4d payed for the subsedye at two severall tymes, *in toto*	£50 14s.	0d.

[*f. 4r.*]

Paymentes

[*In another hand*] **The guift of Thomas Bright disceased owt of Foxherthe tithes**

And of £1 0s.0d. given to the parishe churche of St James, and of £1 0s.0d. given to the parishe churche of St Maryes for the reparacions of them accordinge to the will of Thomas Bright. And of £1 0s.0d.given to the poore of St James parishe, and £1 0s.0d. to the poore of St Maryes parishe, and of £1 0s.0d. to the poore prisoners in the gaole accordinge to the same will.[9] And of £1 0s.0d. for the reparaciones of the parishe churche of St Maryes, and £1 0s.0d. for the reparacions of the parishe churche of St James, and £1 0s.0d. to the poore prisoners of the gaole, given out of this howse. And of £1 0s.0d. payed for composicion moneye[10] for the kinges household and for butter and chese. And of £2 10s.0d. payed to the cunstables at sonderye tymes for the poore howses infected in the tyme of the sickenes. And of £1 10s.0d. payed to the keper of the hospitall. And of £2 0s.0d. payed to Wretham, the surgion, for his yeres wages. And of £2 10s.0d. payed to Atken for curinge diverse poore folkes. And of £2 10s.0d. payed to William Scotte, by comon consente, towardes the charges of a suyte agaynste him for towles and customes in the market.[11] And of

---

9   Lines have been drawn beside and beneath the text relating to Thomas Bright's gift to mark this section off from the other payments.

10   See Introduction, p.lxii.

11   The account for 1608, p.174, makes it clear that Sir Nicholas Bacon II had brought a suit against William Scott for the tolls of the market. In addition to the payments made to William Scott in this year and in 1605 and 1608, the feoffees had agreed at a meeting on 3 January 1604 that when it could conveniently be done, John Mann was to be paid £30 at £5 a year towards 'a greate somme by him laid owte

2s.0d. for a newe booke of accomptes.[12] And of £1 10s.0d. for washinge the lynnen three tymes. And of £2 0s.0d. payed to Inglethorpe the porter for his wages this yere paste, and of 6s.0d. for his coate, and of 5s.6d. for other thinges done and layed out by him. And of 10s.0d. payed to the clerke for his fee, *in toto*   £24 13s.   6d.

Allowances

And of £10 0s.0d. allowed to Mr Walker toward the reparaciones of the howses at Katshall.[13] And of £4 0s.0d. allowed to Roger Reve and Roberte Reve, by comone consente, towardes the reparacions of the bearne without the Risbygate, *in toto*   £14   0s.   0d.

> *Summa allocacionis* £212 5s.1d.
> and a gallon of wine
> *Et sic remanet* £45 13s.1½d., whereof

There remaynethe in the handes of sir robert Jermyn, knight, for londes in Hepworthe 9d. **Of this 5s.0d. received *ut patet* in Mr Walkers accompt, and the rest allowed for 3 acres of lond in possession of Sir Robert Jermyn.** And of Bedwall for londes there £1 0s.0d.[14] And for an almes howse in the Northgate Streate, late Widdowe Aggas 4s.0d. And for parcel of the rente of another almes howse there, nowe Widowe Suttons 1s.0d. And of Buckenham and Everad for an almes howse in the Garlond Streate 3d. And of Harison for a howse there 6s.0d. And of the Widowe Shippe for a howse there 5s.0d. And of Mr George Bouldroe for a howse and closse in Westgate Streate £2 0s.0d. **Allowed for reparacions.** And of th'executors of William Jellowe for a stalle in the market 2s.0d. And in the handes of Fraunces Pinner for haulfe a yeres rente of St Peters, payable at Christmas or within 20 dayes after £8 18s.4¾d. **Paid *ut patet in proximo compoto*.** And of John Landisdaile 2s.0d. And of Mr Richard Heigham £1 0s.0d. And of Mr Heyward 5s.0d. And of William Johnson 6d. **Answered in Mr Boldroes accompt by composicion.** And of Hughe Mathewe 8d. **Answered by Mr Derby in Mr Boldroes accompt**, *in toto*   £14   5s.   6¾d.

> *Summa.* £14 5s.6¾d.
> *Et sic remanet.* £31 7s.6¾d., whereof

Payed to George Boydon for the dinner for the companye and attendantes   £2   5s.   0d.

---

abowte a suyte against the inhabitaunts of this towne for the tolls of the market'. Minutes, H2/6/2.1, p.25. See also Introduction, p.xliii.

[12] That is the book in which these accounts have been entered, HD1150/2.

[13] At a meeting on 3 January 1604 it appears that Mr Mallowes and his assignee, Smythe, were being urged to put Cattishall into good repair, but on 24 March that year it was reported that the repairs would cost £40 and that Walker, the new lessee and his assignee, were to be allowed £20 towards the cost, their rent being abated £5 each half year until the full amount had been paid, H2/6/2.1, pp.24 and 25. See also Introduction, p.liv.

[14] On 3 January 1604 it was agreed that if Bedwall did not pay his arrears, entry should be made into the land of which the rent had been withheld, Minutes, H2/6/2.1, p.24.

146

And for wine, cakes and fyer	7s.	0d.
And for Britall for his coate	15s.	0d.
Given to the wardes of Northe and Easte out of Kemboules legacye[15]	£1 0s.	0d.
And to Almon the cutler for dressinge corselettes	2s.	0d.

       Summa £4 9s.0d.

       Sic remanet £26 18s.6¾d. [*in the hand which made marginal notes above*] which is delivered to Mr Walker the receyvour for this yere to come

Roger Barber	Wm. Cooke	Thomas Peade
William Haward	Richard Walker	Robrte Sparke

verte

[*f. 4v.*]

Onus

Th'accompte of the overseers of the £300 0s.0d. given by Thomas Bright

The accompte of the overseers of the stocke of £300 0s.0d. given by Thomas Brighte, disceasid, to and for the releife of the poore in Burye St Edmunde, in which they charge themselves for one yeere ended at Christmas last, 1604,[16] as well for the said some as for suche benefite as have grown thereby for the releife of the poore, and doe acknowledge the same some of £300 0s.0d. to be in the handes of George Bouldroe, James Fayerclife, Sir John Pretiman and Henry Brighte, upon severall bandes taken for repaymente thereof, and doe also charge themselves with the profit thereof to the some of £30 0s.0d.   £30 0s. 0d.

unde

       Summa patet

Allocacio

They praye allowance of £25 6s.8d. layed out in frise and other thinges for clothinge manye poore people in Burye St Edmunde, as appearethe by particulers, and of £4 13s.4d. payed to divers taylors for makinge the garmentes for the poore, *in toto*   £30 0s. 0d.

       Summa patet and soe evin.

[*f. 4v.*]

1605

[*In another hand*] **Mr Walkers accompt**

Th'accompte of Richard Walker, gentleman, receyvor of all the messuages, londes, tenementes and hereditamentes belonginge to the comone benefite of the towne of Burye St Edmunde, sometyme John Smithes, esquire, and others, made and taken the second daye of January in the third yere of our soveraigne Lord, Kinge James, *et anno Domini* 1605 [*1606*] before Sir John Heigham,

---

[15] This was the first year in which payments were made under Kembold's legacy.

[16] This is one of several passages which suggest that the accounts which cover one of our calendar years may well have used Christmas as the accounting date.

147

knighte, and others, beinge feoffees of the londes and tenementes belonginge to the said towne of Burye in the presence of John Mallowes, John Boulderoe, George Boulderoe, John Hill, gentleman, and other of th'inhabitantes of Burye aforesaid, to the number of 12 of them at the least, for one whole yere nowe ended[17]

Arrerages

Firste the said accomptante dothe charge himsilfe with £8 18s.5d., parcell of £14 5s.6¾d., beinge a super of the last accompte receyved of Frances Pinner — £8 18s. 5d.

Arrerages

And with 15s.0d., parcell of £1 0s.0d., being parte of a super of the last accompte and beinge parcell of two like somes in two former accomptes restinge in supers, the residue of the same somes so in super beinge allowed to John Bedwall, by order, in allowance of three acres of grownde, parcell of his lease, detayned by Sir Robert Jermin, knighte — 15s. 0d.

Receiptes

And with £26 18s.6d. beinge the remaynder of the last accompte of Mr Peede — £26 18s. 6d.

And with £10 0s.0d. receyved of Edmunde Avis upon a band as parcell of Kembouldes legacye — £10 0s. 0d.

And with 10s.0d. receyved of Mr Mallowes as parcell of a more some due by his bill for Clerke the card maker[18] — 10s. 0d.

[f. 5r., old number 126]

Receiptes

And with £3 13s.4d. receyved of Inglethorpe for mariage dinners kept at the Guildhall this yere past — £3 13s. 4d.

Yerelye rentes

And with £3 0s.0d. receyved of Rowge for one yeres rente of a tenemente late purchased of Richard Collins — £3 0s. 0d.

And with £201 16s.2½d. beinge the yerelye rente and revenewe of the londes and tenementes aforsaid *ut patet per rentale* — £201 16s. 2½d.

And with a gallon of wine of John Revell for londes in Burye fieldes late Jenkin Barret — A gallon of wine

> *Summa oneris* £255 11s.5½d.
> and a gallon of wine, whereof

Outrentes

The said accomptant dothe praye allowance of £22 16s.6d., *videlicet* £20 0s.0d. allowed to John Jermin, esquire, parcell of th'annuity given by Edmunde Jermin, esquire, for one whole yere, and for other outrentes payed out of the said londes, and for the receyvors fee, *ut patet per rentale* — £22 16s. 6d.

---

[17] Members of the company who were not feoffees often attended the account, Introduction, p.xxix. However, this is the only account where the presence of inhabitants is mentioned at the audit. The four men named became feoffees in 1606. John Mallowes is known to have instigated the enquiry about the leases of Salter's land, and may well have been otherwise critical of the conduct of the remaining feoffees appointed in 1588.

[18] On 4 January 1604 it had been agreed that £1 10s.0d. should be lent to Clark, the cardmaker, and Mr Mallowes gave his word for repayment of this money, Minutes, H2/6/2.1, p.23.

And of £6 0s.0d. payed to Mr Howman for one yeres rente, ended at Michelmas last past, for the house of correccion	£6	0s.	0d.
And of 10s.6d. payed for a tenthe due at Michellmas last out of St Peters, and of 6d. for th'acquittance		11s.	0d.

Taske

And of £24 0s.0d. payed this yere for the last payment of the taske, and of 4d. for th'acquittance	£24	0s.	4d.

Poore

And of £26 0s.0d. payed to the collectors for the poore of bothe parishes for this yere past, endid at Christmas last	£26	0s.	0d.
And of £1 10s.10d. given at sudrye tymes in releife of ympotent persons and poore familyes	£1	10s.	10d.
And of £6 0s.0d. more distributed this Christmas tyme amongst the poore of boath parishes	£6	0s.	0d.

Ministers

And of £40 0s.0d. payed to Mr Beadle preacher of St Maryes parishe, for his yeres stipend out this howse, ended at Christmas last	£40	0s.	0d.
And of £10 0s.0d. payed to Mr Newton for a quarters stipend ended at th'Annunciacion last	£10	0s.	0d.
And of £2 0s.0d. payed to Mr Jewell and Mr Buller, ministers of boathe parishes	£2	0s.	0d.

Reparacions

And of £13 19s.9d. payed for reparacions this yeer at the Guild-hall and certayne almes howses as appearethe by a bill of perticulers	£13	0s.	0d.

Paymentes according to the will of Thomas Bright

And of £1 0s.0d. given to the parishe churche of St James, and of £1 0s.0d. given to the parishe churche of St Maries, for the reparacions of them accordinge to the will of Thomas Brighte. And of £1 0s.0d. given to the poore of St James parishe, and £1 0s.0d. to the poore of St Maries parishe, and of <deletion> £1 0s.0d. given to the poore prisoners in the gaole accordinge to the same will of the said Thomas Bright, *in toto*	£5	0s.	0d.

[*In another hand*] **The guift of Thomas Bright owt of Foxherthe tithes**

[*f. 5v.*]

Paymentes

And of £2 10s.0d. given to William Scotte towardes his charges in defence of a suyte for towles and customes in the market	£2	10s.	0d.
And of £1 13s.4d. payed to Thomas Bright for the third parte of the rente of the tithes of Brooke Hall[19]	£1	13s.	4d.

---

[19] It was agreed, probably on 2 January 1605, that Thomas Bright, during the time of the current lease of the tithes left by his father, should have £1 13s.4d. a year as he had agreed to release the arrears that had grown for these tithes, Minutes, H2/6/2.1, p.20. (Some entries in the Minute Book are out of order and dating can be doubtful.)

And of £1 0s.0d. payed to olde Wretham, for parte of his stipend for curinge divers poore folkes	£1	0s.	0d.
And of £1 5s.0d. payed to Atkin for parte of his allowance for diverse cuers doone by him this yere to the poore people	£1	5s.	0d.
And of £1 10s.0d. payed to the keper of the Hospitall	£1	10s.	0d.
And of £1 0s.0d. payed towardes the reparacons of the churche of St Maryes out of this house	£1	0s.	0d.
And of £1 0s.0d. payed towardes the reparacons of the churche of St James out of this howse	£1	0s.	0d.
And of £1 0s.0d. given to Sargant Hulbard for his opinion in some questions in lawe towching this howse	£1	0s.	0d.
And of £1 0s.0d. payed to William Fayerclife upon a taxacion towardes the reparacions of the church and steple of St Maries[20]	£1	0s.	0d.
And of 3s.4d. payed for the Kinges woodyard and Sudberye Bridge[21]		3s.	4d.
And of £1 0s.0d. payed out of this howse to the poore prisoners in the gaole	£1	0s.	0d.
And of £5 0s.0d. delivered to John Man for Mr Buller, by comone concente of the feoffees and of diverse inhabitantes, in supplyinge the place of Mr Newton since the feast of th'annunciation of the Virgine Marye last past upon the Sabothe daye[22]	£5	0s.	0d.
And of 15s.0d. allowed to John Bedwall, by order of the feoffees, for the rente of three acrees[sic] of londe, parcell of his lease, detayned by Sir Robert Jermin, knight[23]		15s.	0d.
And of £10 0s.0d. alowed, by order of the feoffees, out of the rent of Catshall towardes the reparacons of the howses there	£10	0s.	0d.
And of £2 19s.9d. allowed to Inglethorpe for his wages and other ordinarye allowances and charges at the Guildhall, as appearethe by his bill of ~~par~~ particulers nowe shewed	£2	19s.	9d.
And of 10s.0d. payed to the clerke for his fee		10s.	0d.
And of a gallon of wine spent at the dinner	A gallon of wine		

Summa allocacionis £190 4s.6d.
and a gallon of wine
Et sic remanet £65 5s.11½d., whereof

Supers

There remaynethe in the handes of Sir Robert Jermin, knighte, for the haulfe yeres anuitye out of the mannor of Torkeseye due the 20tie daye of Julye last. **Answered in Mr Nonnes accompt**	£10	0s.	0d.

[20] A church rate must have been levied to meet the cost of these repairs.
[21] The payment towards the cost of the king's woodyard was probably one of the charges for which purveyance was levied. Ballingdon Bridge which joins Suffolk and Essex at the hamlet of this name, which adjoins Sudbury, was in poor repair at this period. F.C.D. Sperling, *Hodson's History of the Borough of Sudbury* (Sudbury, 1896) p.214 noted that the municipal authorities were indicted at the borough quarter sessions for not keeping the bridge in repair. A county rate would have been levied to account for this payment.
[22] The reason for Mr Newton's suspension has not yet been discovered. It was probably in connection with Archbishop Bancroft's campaign against nonconforming ministers.
[23] Both Bedwall and Sir Robert leased land in Hepworth.

And for one yeres rente for a peice of londe in Hepworthe		9d.
And likewise for one yeres rente of certeyne londes in Hepworthe, due at Michelmas last, leaton to Edward Taylor	£1 10s.	0d.

[f. 6r., old number 20]

And in the handes of Frances Pinner for the haulfe yeres rente of St Peters, due at Christmas last or within 20^{tie} dayes after. *Solutum ut patet in proximo compoto*	£8 18s.	4½d.
And of £2 15s.0d. in the handes of Henrye Collinge for his halfe yeres rentes, due at Michelmas last. *Solutum ut patet in proximo compoto*	£2 15s.	0d
And in the handes of Marye Evans for hir haulfe yeres rent then due		12s. 0d.
And in the handes of William Gillye for his haulfe yeres rente then due for londes in Burye and Horningsherthe. *Solutum in proximo compoto*	£1 10s.	0d.
And for an almes howse in the Northegate Strete where the Widowe Aggas late dwelte		4s. 0d.
And for a howse in Garlond Streat where Harrison dwell		6s. 0d.
And for a howse where Widowe Shipp dwell there. **Allowed for reparacions**		5s. 0d.
And for 3 almes howses there		9d.
And in the handes of Mr George Boulderoe for the whole yeres rente of a howse and close in Westgate Streat. **Allowed for reparacions**	£2 0s.	0d.
And for a stalle in the Market, late in the tenure of William Jellowe		2s. 0d.
And for a peice of grownd in the Horse Market in th'occupacion of John Landisdale. *Solutum per composicionem ut patet* **in Mr Boldroes accompt**		2s. 0d.
And for a howse in the Churchegate Streat in th'occupacion of Mr Richard Heigham	£1 0s.	0d.
And for a howse and grownd in th'occupacion of Mr Heyward in the Risbygate Streat and Tayven. *Solutum in proximo compoto*		5s. 0d.
And of William Johnson for a howse		6d.
And of Hughe Mathewe for a howse. *Solutum ut patet* **in Mr Boldroes accompt**		8d.
And of th'executors of Sparke, baker, for a rent of a decayed tenemente in Mr Andrewes Streat. *Solutum in proximo compoto*		6s. 8d.
And of the heires of John Parker for the rent of a tenemente in Longe Braklond. *Solutum in proximo compoto*		6d.
And for the rente of a tenemente in Northegate Streat late in th'occupacion of Henry Kent		6d.
And for the rent of a gardine in the Eastgate Streat, late in the tenure of Frances Pinner. *Solutum in proximo compoto*		2s. 0d.
And for a quarters rent for a howse in Guildhall Strete, due at Christmas last, in th'occupacion of Gurden. *Solutum in proximo compoto*		5s. 10d.

     Summa £30 7s.6½d.

     Sic remanet in toto £34 19s.5d., whereof

Payed to Mr John Boulderoe for charges of suyte for the howse of correccion	5s.	6d.
Given to the keper of the howse of correccion in releife	5s.	0d.
Payed to John Man for windinge sheetes and appariling of two poore boyes	£1 19s.	0d.
Payed to Thomas Bright for haulfe yeres revenewe of the tithes of Brooke Hall which shalbe due at the feast of th'Annunciacion next cominge	16s.	8d.

[f. 6v.]

Payed to Baxter for the use of £30 0s.0d., parcell of Kemboldes legacye, to be distributed in the Northe and East wardes	£1 10s.	0d.
Delivered more to Thomas Bright for Mr Buller, minister of St James parishe, by the consent of those that ware present at this accompte	£5 0s.	0d.
Given to Robert Clare in releife	2s.	0d.
Given to olde Overin ~~in reliefe~~	5s.	0d.
Payed to Britall for his coate	16s.	0d.
Payed to Almond the cutler for dressinge two corselettes, and for a dagger and a gorget bought of him	6s.	0d.
Payed to George Boyton for charges of the dinner	£3 0s.	0d.
For wine and cakes the daye of accompte	9s.	0d.
For fire then	2s.	0d.
Payed more in discharge of two bills for nayles spent at the Guildhall in reparacions	14s.	0d.
Given to Smithe, the currier, in relief.	3s.	4d.
Payed to Harrison for worke done at the Widowe Suttons in the Northegate Streat	1s.	0d.
Payed to Atkens, the surgeon, in full discharge of his bill in cures done to the poore	£1 5s.	0d.
Payed to Lambard of Iclingam for kepinge of three poore children	£1 10s.	0d.
Payed more to Wretham the surgeon in discharge of his stipend	£1 0s.	0d.
Delivered to John Man for Marian Dickenson as money lent to hir, and to be answered at the next accompte, by the same John Man, after the rate of 4d. for everye weeke that shee shall live untill the same accompte, and he to retayne 4d. everye weeke of hir contribucion in the churche[24]	17s.	4d.

    Summa £20 7s.4d.

    Sic remanet £14 12s.1d.

    Which some is delivered to Robert Sparke, the new receyvor for the yere to come, to be answered upon his accompt.

Robte Jermyn   Roger Barber   Wm. Cooke   Robte Sparke

---

[24] The Book of Orders begun in 1571 indicates that materials for work were given out at church. See Introduction, p.xxxiii.

[f.7r., old number 25]
[This is written in the hand which copied up the account for 1606.]
1605
Onus. **The accompt of the overseers of the £300 0s.0d. given by Thomas Bright, disceased, in relief of the poore**

The overseers of the stocke of £300 0s.0d. given by Thomas
Bright, disceased, to and for the relief of the poore in Burye St
Edmunde, doe yeld their accompt for one yere ended at
Christmas 1605, aswell for the same somes as for suche
benifite as have growne this yere thereby, and doo acknowledge the same some of £300 0s.0d. to be in the handes of
George Boldroe, James Fayerclif, Sir John Pretiman, knight,
and Henrye Bright upon bandes for repayment thereof, and doe
charge themselves with the profitt thereof for this yere past to
the some of   £30   0s.   0d.
> *Summa patet*

Allocacio

And they doo praye allowance of £24 18s.11d. layed out by them
in frise for the clothing of manye poore people in Burye aforesaid, as appearethe by particulers, and of £5 1s.1d. payed to
divers taylors for making the garmentes for the poore there, *in
toto*   £30   0s.   0d.
> *Summa patet*, and so evin

[f. 7r.]   **1606**[25]
Th'accompt of Robert Sparke
The accompt of Robert Sparke receyvor of all the mesuages, londes, tenementes and hereditamentes belonging to the comone profitt and benefit of the Bur[ou]ghe[26] and towne of Burye St Edmunde, some tyme John Smithes, esquire, and others, made and taken the 30 daye of December in the fourthe yere of the reigne of our soveraigne Lord, King James of Inglonde *et cetera*, [*1606*] for one whole yere nowe ended

Receiptes

In primis the said accomptant dothe charge himsilfe with
£14 12s.1d. receyved upon the determinacion of the last
accompt   £14 12s.   1d.
And with 17s.4d. received of John Man, which he received as
appearethe in the last accompt   17s.   4d.
And with £10 0s.0d. received of Edmunde Avis upon a band,
parcell of Kemboldes legacy   £10   0s.   0d.
And with 3s.4d. received of Mr Cantrell for 20 rowf tiles   3s.   4d.
And with £5 5s.0d. received of Inglethorpe, the porter, for
mariage dinners kept at the Guildhall this yere   £5   5s.   0d.

---

[25] The original account has survived, H2/3/4/7.
[26] Bury St Edmunds was incorporated as a borough by Letters Patent dated 4 April 1606, D1/1/1.

Receiptes of Supers

And with £8 18s.4¾d. received of Francis Pinner as a super of the
    last accompt   £8 18s. 4¾d.

And with £2 15s.0d. received of Henrye Colling, gentleman, as a
    super of the same last account   £2 15s. 0d.

And with £1 10s.0d. received of William Gillye as a super of the
    same last accompte   £1 10s. 0d.

And with 5s.0d. received of William Heyward, gentleman, as a
    super of the same last accompte   5s. 0d.

And with 6s.8d. received of th'executors of Sparke, baker, as a
    super of the same last accompt   6s. 8d.

And with 6d. received of John Parker as a super of the same last
    accompt   6d.

And with ~~too~~ 2s.0d. received of John Bridon, late Francis Pinner,
    as a super of the same last accompt   2s. 0d.

And with 5s.10d. received of Gurden as a super of the last
    accompt   5s. 0d.

[*f. 7v.*]

Rentes newlye encreased[27]

And with £6 0s.0d. received of Nicholas Bell as an increased rent
    of the Angell for halfe a yere due and payed at and for
    Michelmas last   £6 0s. 0d.

And with £2 0s.0d. received of James Kent for a like increased
    rent, then due and payed for halfe a yere, for a howse in the
    Cooke Rowe late Roger Brunwins, clerke   £2 0s. 0d.

And with £5 13s.4d. received of William Ullet as an increased
    rent for londes late in th'occupacion of Mr Barber, for one
    whole yere ended at Michelmas last   £5 13s. 4d.

And with £2 5s.0d. received of Henrye Colling, gentleman, for an
    increased rent for the londes in his occupacion for halfe a yere
    ended at Michelmas last   £2 5s. 0d.

And with £3 5s.4d. received of th'executrix of Mr Barber for an
    increased rent for londes late in his occupacion in th'East
    fieldes for halfe a yere ended at Michelmas last   £3 5s. 4d.

Yerelye rentes

And with £204 16s.2½d. being the whole yeres rentes and
    revenewes of the londes and tenementes aforesaid ***ut patet per***
    rentale   £204 16s. 2½d.

And with a gallon of wine of John Revell for londes in Burye
    fieldes, late Jenkin Barrets   A gallon of wine

    Summa oneris £269 1s.0¼d.

    and a gallon of wine, whereof

Outrentes

This accomptant dothe praye allowance of £22 16s.6d., *videlicet*,
    £20 0s.0d. payed to John Jermin, esquire, or remayning in the
    handes of Sir Robert Jermin, knight, parcell of the annuitye

---

[27] These increased rents resulted from an enquiry by the Commissioners for Charitable Uses. See Introduction, p.xlvi.

given by Edmunde Jermin, esquire, disceased, for one whole yere ended in Julye last, and for other rentes payed out of the said londes and tenementes, and for the receyvors fee, *ut patet per rentale*	£22	16s.	6d.
And of 2s.6d. payed to Baylefe Reve for the halfe yeres rent of the Angell due at Michelmas last		2s.	6d.
And of £3 0s.0d. payed for the halfe yeres rent of the howse of correccion due at our Ladye daye last	£3	0s.	0d.

Taske and subsedye

And of £1 13s.4d. payed this yere for the subsedye of the towne stocke	£1	13s.	4d.
And of 1s.6d. payed for the taske of certeyne londes in Westleye this yere		1s.	6d.
And of £24 0s.0d. payed this yere for the first payment of the taske of the buroughe of Burye St Edmunde, as appearethe by the collectors acquittance	£24	0s.	0d.

Mynisters

And of £37 10s.0d. payed to Mr Beadle, preacher of St Maryes parishe, for three quarters of a yere of his stipend ended at Michelmas last	£37	10s.	0d.
And of £1 0s.0d. payed to Mr Jewell, minister of St Maryes parishe	£1	0s.	0d.
And of £1 0s.0d. payed to Mr Buller, minister of St James parishe	£1	0s.	0d.

[f. 8r., old number 44]

Poore

And of £26 0s.0d. payed to the collectors for the poore of boathe parishes for one whole yere nowe ended at Christmas	£26	0s.	0d.
And of £7 15s.6d. ᵽ given and distributed at sundrye tymes in relief of diverse poore, sicke, lame and impotent persons, and for the setting fourthe of poore children to service, as appearethe by particulers shewed at this accompt	£7	15s.	6d.

Reparacions

And of £31 16s.8½d. layed out this yere in reparacions of the Guildhall, the ministers howses, certeyne almes howses and the cage,[28] as appearethe by particulers shewed at this accompt	£31	16s.	8½d.
And of £5 0s.0d. lent to Andrewe Hargrave upon his band, with suertye for halfe a yere, at the request of Sir Robert Jermin, knight, due and not payed and nowe forborne for some tyme, by his request. **Paid as appearethe in Mr Nonnes accompt**	£5	0s.	0d.

Bestowed according to the will of Thomas Bright

And of £1 0s.0d. given to the parishe churche of St James, and £1 0s.0d. given to the parishe churche of St Maryes for the reparacions of them, according to the will of Thomas Bright. And of £1 0s.0d. given to the poor of St James parishe, and £1 0s.0d. to the poore of St Maryes parishe and £1 0s.0d. to the

---

[28] After the incorporation the feoffees continued to contribute to many things which had legally become the responsibility of the Corporation.

poore prisoners in the gaole, according to the same will of the said Thomas Bright bestowed this yere past, *in toto* £5 0s. 0d.

The guift of Thome Bright, disceased, owt of Foxherth tithes

Paymentes

And of £15 0s.0d. delivered to Mr Walker for the towne buisines, in Hillarye terme last, by the concent of diverse of the feoffees **Answered *ut patet* in Mallowes accompt** £15 0s. 0d.

And of 10s.0d. payed this yere for provision of the kings howseholde 10s. 0d.

And of £1 15s.0d. payed this yere at sundrye tymes for suche as ware shutt upp in their howses and other places in the tyme of the sicknes, and for the appareling of some of them £1 15s. 0d.

And of £1 10s.0d. payed to Atkens, the surgeon, for curing and helping of diverse poore folkes £1 10s. 0d.

And of 10s.0d. for writing the rentall of the londes and tenementes belonging to this towne 10s. 0d.

And of £5 0s.0d. for the diate of the comissioners upon the Statute of Charitable Uses £5 0s. 0d.

And of £1 10s.0d. payed to the keeper of the sicke howse £1 10s. 0d.

And of £1 0s.0d. payed towardes the reparacions of St Maryes churche out of this howse, and of £1 0s.0d. likewise payed out of this howse towardes the reparacions of St. James churche, *in toto* £2 0s. 0d.

And of £1 0s.0d. payed out of this howse to the poore prisoners in the gaole £1 0s. 0d.

[*f.8v.*]

Charges of suyte for Foxherthe tithes

And of £2 17s.10d. payed to Mathewe Teversam for charges of suyte in th'ecclesiasticall court for the tithes of the mannor of Brooke Hall in Foxherthe[29] £2 17s. 10d.

And of £1 0s.0d. payed to Lambertes wief of Iclingham in discharge of a bill of a greater some for the appareling of three children which she kepethe at the charge of this towne £1 0s. 0d.

And of £1 0s.0d. payed to <*deletion*> Wretham, the surgeon, for his halfe yeres wages for cuers done to the poore £1 0s. 0d.

And of 16s.8d. payed to Thomas Bright for halfe a yeres rent of the third parte of the tithes of Brooke Hall in Foxherthe 16s. 8d.

And of £2 11s.0d. payed for a dowsen of quisshens[30] for the Guildhall, and for lether to lyne them, and for fethers to stoppe them, and for the working of them £2 11s. 0d.

And of 2s.0d. payed to Dickensons wief for takinge in hand of a poore woman to hele hir of a fistula 2s. 0d.

And of £2 16s.0d. payed to Inglethorpe for his wages and other ordinarye allowances made unto him, and for his jorneye to Mr Ashfield[31] for his hand and seale to the general deed of

---

[29] The litigation about Foxearth tithes is discussed in the Introduction, p.li.

[30] Cushions. See Glossary.

[31] The feoffment was renewed in 1606, H1/1/37 and 52. Although he does not seem to have been very active, Robert Ashfield was a feoffee who lived at Stowlangtoft.

feoffement, as appeareth by his bill of particulers nowe shewed at this accompt	£2 16s.	0d.
And of 10s.0d. payed to the clerke for his fee	10s.	0d.

And of £2 0s.0d. for writing of two generall feoffementes[32] of the towne londes, whereof th'one from the ancient feoffees to two others, and th'other from the same two to the ancient and newe feoffees, with a schedule of the severall uses of the same londes, and 9 or 10 other severall deedes of feoffement, made and to be made, to th'use of the feoffees of certeyne londes and tenementes, newlye browght and reduced to the said feoffees by force of a comission directed to certeyne gentlemen upon the Statute of Charitable Uses, and for indentures to be made to lead the use of a Fine to be levied of parte of the same londes

and tenementes	£2 0s.	0d.
And a gallon of wine spent at the dinner	A gallon of wine	

> *Summa allocacionis* £209 4s.6½d.
> and a gallon of wine
> *Et sic remanet* £59 16s.5¾d., whereof

Supers

There remains in the handes of Sir Robert Jermin, knight, for the whole yeres anuitye out of the mannor of Torkeseye ended the 20 daye of Julye last. **Answered in Mr Nonnes accompt**	£20 0s.	0d.
And for one yeres rent of a pece of lond in Hepworth		9d.
And likewise for one yeres rent of certeyne londes there leaton to Edward Taylor, du at Michelmas last, remayning in the handes of the said Sir Robert Jermin	£1 10s.	0d.

[f. 9r., old number 50]

And in the handes of John Bedwall for halfe a yeres rent, due at Michelmas last, for certeyne londes in Hepworth aforesaid callid Brettes and Eashawghwoodd	£8 14s.	1d.
And alsoe in his handes for the halfe yeres rent of 43 acres of lond there due at Michelmas last	10s.	4d.
And more for the same londes upon a lease in revercion as a deead [*sic*] rent	£1 15s.	0d.
And also in his handes for halfe a yeres like rent due at Michelmas last for 10 acres of pasture in the possession of Mr Buckenham	10s.	0d.

John Parke

And also in his handes for londes in Hepworthe, leaton to him in revercion, nowe in the possession of Margerye Canham, for halfe a yere due at Michelmas last	2s.	2d.
And also in his handes for a like rent for londes in the possession of Giles Barker, due for halfe a yere at Michelmas last	2s.	2d.
And likewise in his handes for halfe a yeres rent then due for a pightle at Terrold Gappe[33]	1s.	3d.

---

32 This refers to the renewal of the feoffment in this year, while the nine or ten feoffments mentioned below reflect the impact of the Commissioners' enquiry into the sale of the Angel and various other matters.

33 In the original account, H2/3/4/7, the amount is given as 10d., not 1s.3d.

[*The items on f.9r. so far are bracketed together, and besides them is written*] **These somes paid** *ut patet in proximo compoto* **11–14–8**

And in the handes of Laurance Coldeham for a whole yeres rent of lond in Hepworthe to him leaton, due at Michelmas last	2s.	0d.
And in the handes of John Sporle for halfe a yeres rent due at Michelmas last for londes in the possession of John Deye lying in Hepworthe	15s.	2d.
And in the handes of Gurden for three quarters of a yeres rent for a howse in Guildhall Streat ended at Michelmas last	17s.	7½d.
And in the handes of Leonard Harrison for halfe a yeres rent of a howse in the Colledge Streat due at Michelmas last	8s.	0d.
And for a yeres rent due by Robinson at Michelmas last for a howse in the Garlond Streat		3d.
And for the yeres rent of a howse there wherein the Widowe Shippe dwellethe	5s.	0d.
And in the handes of Mr George Bolderoe for the yeres rent of a howse and close in the ~~Gal~~ Westgate Streat, due at Michelmas last: **Mr Mallowes to paie this by agreement 3 *Aprilis* 1606** *solutum ut patet* **in Mr Hills accompt**	£2 0s.	0d.
And in the handes of Francis Pinner for the halfe yeres rent of St Peters, payable at Christmas or within twentye dayes after: **Paid** *ut patet in proximo compoto*	£8 18s.	4¾d
And for the yeres rent of a stall in the market, late in the possession of Jellowe	2s.	0d.
And for a yeres rent of grownd in the possession of Mr Mowndeford or his assignes		6d.
And for the yeres rent of a peece of grownd in the possession of <*deletion*> Henrye[34] Landisdale lying in the Horsemarket *Solutum per composicionem ut patet* **in Mr Boldros accompt**	2s.	0d.
And for a yeres rent of a peece of grownd in Maydewater Lane in the possession of Mr George Bolderoe		6d.
And of Roger Write for parte of his howse in the Mustowe		2d.
And for a howse in the Churchegate Streat in the possession of Mr Richard Heigham	£1 0s.	0d.

[*f. 9v.*]

And of John Parker for a tenemente in Longe Braclond		6d.
And of Hughe Mathewe for the yeres rent of a tenemente there **Solutum ut patet** **in Mr Boldroes accompt**		8d.
And of William Grigges for the rent of a tenemente in the Northegate Streat, late in the occupacion of Henrye Kent		6d.

Summa   £47 18s.8¼d.
Sic remanet   £11 17s.9½d., whereof[35]

Payed upon the determinacion of this accompt to Mathewe Teversome for suyte for the tithes of Brooke Hall upon billes shewed at this accompt.	£3 9s.	9d.

[34] The original account reads John not Henry, *ibid.*
[35] The following passage is written in the hand of Thomas Bright in the original.

Payed more to Thomas Bright for the halfe yeres rent of the tithes of Brooke Hall aforesaid in Foxherthe	16s.	8d.
Payed more for the dinner	£4 10s.	0d.
And for wine and cakes	18s.	0d.
And for moneye payed to Sparrowe, the smithe, for worke done as by his bill appearethe	£1 6s.	0d.
And payed more to Inglethorpe for fier and kandle for three dayes before and at the accompt \and for other buisines at the hall/	4s.	11d.
Payed more to the armorer for keping and dressing of two corseletes, swordes and daggerdes	4s.	0d.

Summa £11 9s.4d.

Sic remanet 8s.5½d., which some is delivered to Mr Nonne, nowe appointed receyvor for the yere to come.[36] [*In a different hand*] With an obligacion of £10 0s.0d. for payment of £5 0s.0d. made by Andrew Hargrave with suretie made to Sir Robert Jermyn, knight, and others at a daye now past. [*Also in the same hand, but to the left of the foregoing*] Mr Nonne hath receyved an obligacion of £20 0s.0d. made by Edmunde Avis with suretie for payment of £5 0s.0d. at Our Ladie daie 1607 and £5 0s.0d. at Michelmas following.

At the tyme of this accompt made it was and is confessed and agreed that John Nonne, esquire, before this tyme, in performance of the decree in that behalfe made upon the Statue of Charitable Uses concerning the interest claymed by the towneshipp of and in some part of the howse and grownd which he purchased of Sir Robert Jermin, knight, did paye into the handes of John Mallowes, gentleman, thirtye powndes, which by the said decree was ordered to be paied for the same howse and grownd, by the said Sir Robert Jermin, and that the feoffees of the towne londes owght to make an absolute release unto the said John Nonne and his heires of and in the said howse and grownd, according as by the true meaning of the said order and decree ought to be done, unto the said Sir Robert Jermin, his heires and assignes. And it is also acknowledged that the said John Mallowes towardes the performance of the decree aforesaid hathe before this tyme imployed £10 0s.0d., parcell of the said £30 0s.0d., toward the purchase of the howse late Roger Brunwin, clerke, nowe in the occupacion of James Kent. And it is agreed that the said John Mallowes shall paye the other £20 0s.0d. residue unto William Gosling, gentleman, and Anne his wief, in parte of payment of the moneye which they are to have for the redemcion of the Angell to the use of the towne. And it is alsoe agreed that the feoffees shall save harmeles Mr Francis Pinner and the said John Mallowes agaynst the bandes wherein they stand bownd for the payment of £30 0s.0d. more to the said Roger Brunwin.[37] [*In a different hand*] The £30 0s.0d. abovesaid receyved of Mr Nonne by Mr Mallowes is discharged in Mr Mallowes accompt, 1608.

---

[36] At this point the original has the signatures of John Gippes, John Nonne, Thomas Bright, John Mallowes, George Boldero, Francis Pynner, Bennett Barker, John Boldero, John Man, Stephen Ashwell (who made his mark), John Revell, Charles Darby and Henry Gippes.

[37] In the original, this passage was written by John Mallowes and the following sentence does not occur there.

The accompt of the overseers of the £300 0s.0d. given by Thomas Bright, disceased, in reliefe of the poore
Onus

The overseers of the stocke of £300 0s.0d. given by Thomas Bright, disceased, to and for the relief of the poore in Burye St Edmunde doe yeld their accompt for one yere ended at Christmas 1606, as well for the same some, as for suche benifite as have growne this yere thereby and doe acknowledge the same some of £300 0s.0d. to be in the handes of George Boldroe, James Fayerclif, Henrye Bright and William Webbe of Ixworthe, gentleman, upon bandes for repayment thereof, and do charge themselves with the profit thereof for this yere past to the some of

      £30 0s. 0d.

      Summa patet

[f. 10r., old number 42]
Allocacio

And they doe praye allowance of £24 19s.0d. layed out by them in frise for the clothing of manye poore people in Burye aforesaid, as appearethe by particulers, and of £5 1s.0d. payed to diverse taylors for making the garmentes for the poore there, *in toto*

      £30 0s. 0d.

      Summa patet, and soe evin.

1607 Th'accompt of John Nonne, esquire

The accompt of John Nonne, esquier, receyver of all the mesuages, londes, tenementes and hereditamentes bilonging to the common profit and benefit of the towne and Burghe of Burie St Edmunde, sometimes John Smythes, esquier, and others, made and taken the 29° daie of December in the fift yere of the reign of our soveraigne Lord Kinge James of Inglond *et cetera*, and *Anno Domini* 1607, for one whole yere now endid

Inprimis the said accomptaunt dothe charge himsilf with 8s.6d. received upon the determynacion of the last accompt of Robert Sparke

      8s. 6d.

Torkesey

And with £40 0s.0d. received of Sir Robert Jermyn, knight, for this yeres anuytie owt of the mannor of Torkesey endid the 20 of Julie last, whereof Mr Mallowes received £20 0s.0d.

      £40 0s. 0d.

Arrerages

And with £10 0s.0d. for half yeres annuytie owt of the mannor of Torkesey, due the 20 daie of Julie 1605, being a super of Mr Walkers accompt

      £10 0s. 0d.

And of £20 0s.0d. for the whole yeres annuytie owt of the mannor of Torkesey, due the 20 daie of Julie 1606, beinge a super of th'accompt of Robert Sparke in the same yere

      £20 0s. 0d.

And with £8 18s.4¾d. beinge a super of the last accompt of Robert Sparke for half yeres rent of St Peters, paiable at Christmas or within 20 daies after

      £8 18s. 4¾d.

And with £19 0s.3½d., beinge the residue of the supers of the accompt of Robert Sparke, as appearithe there 1606   £19 0s. 3½d.

And with £10 12s.10d. receyved of John Bedwall for arrerages of his fearme, besides 15s.0d. allowed him for 3 acres deteyned from him by Sir Robert Jermyn, knight, and besides 6s.10d. allowed him for rent resolute paid by him for Hepworthe londes and now by him demaunded[38]   £10 12s. 10d.

And with 6s.10d. received of Robert Sparke, which he shuld have allowed to Bedwall for owt rentes for Hepworthe londes   6s. 10d.

Mariages, dettes

And withe £5 10s.0d. received of Inglethorpe for mariage dinners at the hall this yere   £5 10s. 0d.

And with £5 0s.0d. received of Hargrave upon a bond which was lent him   £5 0s. 0d.

And with £10 0s.0d. received of Avis upon a bond, part of Kemboldes legacie   £10 0s. 0d.

And £1 1s.11d. of Mr Sporle for woode at Hepworthe   £1 1s. 11d.

[f.10v.]

And with £70 0s.0d. receyved of John Man as lent to the feoffees, for which this accomptaunt gave his bill, and £13 15s.5d. more receyved of the same John Man by Mr Hill and Mr John Boldroe and ymployed towardes the reparacions of the Angell,[39] *in toto*   £83 15s. 5d.

Rentes
The yerelie rents and revenues

And with £20 0s.0d. received of William Webbe,[40] gentleman, for a yeres rent of Catshall in Barton. And with £6 10s.0d. received of Mistress Willowghbie for a yeres rent of Leyers in Rougham. And with £33 6s.8d. received of George Boldroe, gentleman, for his yeres rent of a bearne and diverse parcels of lond now in his possession. And with £10 0s.0d. received of Henry Collinge, gentleman, for a yeres rent of Salters londes and other londes in his possession. And with £1 4s.0d. received of Mary Evans, widowe, for 2 mesuages in Churchegate Streete. And with £1 3s.6d. received of Thomas Smythe for a mesuage by the Guildhall. And with 2s.0d. received of John Bridon for a peece of ground in th'Eastgate Strete. And with £52 2s.6d. received of Thomas Peake for the yeres rent of 104 acre of lond *et cetera* and 34 perches, after the rate of 10s.0d. the acre. And withe £2 14s.0d. received more reeof him for Easthawghe Woode, acres containing 10 acres 3 roodes and eight perches, after the rate of 5s.0d. the acre. And with £2 3s.4d. received of Sir Henry Buckenham, knight, for Wardes Woode containing 8 acres 3 roodes and 10 perches, and 2 acres and half by the Bower. And with 2s.4d. received

---

[38] See p.146, n.14 above.

[39] It seems likely that the Angel was improved as well as repaired.

[40] Richard Walker was the real tenant of Catishall, but, as he was one of the feoffees, Webbe's name was used in the lease. See Introduction, p.liii.

[*The yearly rents, continued*]

more of him for 10 acres of pasture in Weston. And with
£2 0s.0d. received of Mr Sporle for a yeres rent of Greate
Stubbinges. And with £2 0s.0d. received of John Deye for Litle
Atley, the Bower and Litle Stubbinges. And with £1 0s.0d.
received of Mr Leache for the rent where the scholemaster
dwellithe in Hepworthe. And with 2s.0d. received of Laurence
Coldham for an acre of lond. And with 10s.4d. received of Sir
Robert Jermyn, knight, for 21 acres and *dimidia* of lond in
Hepworthe, before leaton to Roger Berowgham.[41] And [*space*]
of him for londes letton to Edward Tailor and a peece called
the Russhies. And with 9d. more of him for the rent of londes
in Hepworthe. And with £6 0s.0d. received by Mr Mallowes of
Frost, fermor to the said Sir Robert Jermyn. And [*space*] of
him for Teroldgappe. And with 18s.0d. received of Humfrey
Linge for ground in Hepworthe. And with 8d. received of
Margerie Canham, widowe, for a tenemente and acre of ground
leton to Willys. And of 6d. received of Giles Barker for a
tenemente and ground there. And with 13s.4d. received of
Robert Kinge for an almes howse in the Colledge Streete. And
with 16s.0d. of Leonard Harrison for another almes howse
there. And with 4s.0d. for an almes howse in Northegate Strete,
late in the tenure of the Widowe Aggas. And with 4d. for
another almes howse there, where the Widowe Sutton dwelt.
And with 6s.8d. 3d.[42] [*sic*] of John Dister for an almes howse
in Garlond Strete. And with 3d. of Robinson for another almes
howse there. And with 3d. of Everard Buckenham for another
almes howse there. And with 3d of Dising for another there.
And with 6s.0d. of Harrison for another there. And with 5s.0d.
of Widowe Shippe for another. And with 5s.0d. of Robert
Sparke for a gardeine in Westgate Streete. And with £2 6s.8d.
received of John Cadge for a bearne and ortyard. And with
£2 0s.0d. more of Robert Sparke for a close at Stanford bridge.
And with £3 0s.0d. received of William Rowge for a mesuage
late Richard Collins adjoyning to St James steple \churche/.
And with a gallon of wine of John Revell for Barrettes londes.
And with £4 0s.0d. received of Thomas Hamond for londes in
the Sowthe Field. And with £10 0s.0d. received of William
Ullett for londes in the West Fieldes, late in the tenure of Mr
Barber. And with £14 14s.0d. received of th'executrix of Mr
Barber for thre [*f. 11r., old number 46*] **The yearlie rentes**
and revenues over and besides th'annuytie owt of
Torkeseye leases of londes in th'East and Sowthe Fieldes. And
with £4 0s.0d. received of William Gillie for 7 peeces of lond,
conteyning by estimacion 18 acres, lyinge in Burye and

---

[41] John Sutton (Jankin Smith's chantry priest) and the feoffees of the lands which endowed it, let Little
Attele, the Bower and a lay called Stubbing to Roger Borougham in 1533, H1/4/3/3, and also a further 30
acres in 9 pieces in Hepworth in the following year, 1534, H1/4/3/4.

[42] 6s.8d. and 3d. appears repeatedly in connection with this property. The 3d. was a small out-rent.

[The yearly rents, continued]

Horningeserthe. And with 2s.0d. for a stall in the Market, late Jellowes. And with £12 18s.0d. received of Thomas Turnor for the rent of a bearne in St Andrewes Streete and diverse peeces of lond in the Westfield. And with £17 16s.9½d. received of Fraunces Pynner for an annuitie by him graunted owt of St Peters. And with £8 0s.0d. received of Roger Reve and Robert Reve for an annuytie owt of the Risbiegate Graunge and St Peters. And with £1 0s.0d. received of Thomas Baker for a tenemente and ortyard in the Raingate Streete. And with 6d. received of Mr Fraunces Moundford for rent of a peece of ground nere the Horse Markett, late Doctor Woodes. And with 2s.0d. of Henry Landisdale for rent of ground sometyme builded in the Horse Market. And with 6d. received of Mr George Bolderoe for rent of a void peece of ground, now in parte inlcosid, next Maidewater Lane. And with 6s.8d. of th'executor of Robert Sparke, baker, for rent of a peece of ground in Mr Andrewes Streete. And with 4s.0d. received of Mr Walker for a howse and gardeine in Punche Lane. And with £1 0s.0d. of Mr Richard Heigham for a tenemente in Churchegate Streete. And with 5s.0d. received of Mr William Heyward for a tenemente in Risbiegate Streete and a garden nere the Teyven diche. And with 6d. of John Parker for a tenemente in the Long Brackelond. And with 8d. for a tenemente there, late William Johnsons, now Hughe Mathewes. And with 6d. of Margaret Grigges, widowe, for a tenemente in the Northegate Street, late Henry Kentes. And with £8 0s.0d. received for a porcion of tithes owt of the Mannor of Brooke Hall in Foxherthe in Essex, given by Thomas Bright, disceasid. **£8 0s.0d. received for Foxherthe tithes this yere with increase and last payment for them.** And with £17 0s.0d. receyved of Nicholas Bell for the rent of the Angell. And with £2 17s.4d. received of Henry Bright for tenementes in the Skinner Lane. And with £4 0s.0d. received of James Kent for a tenemente in the Cooke Rowe late Roger Brunwins, clerke. And with 3s.4d. received of Thomas Coell for parte of Roger Wrights howse. And with 2s.6d. of William Scott for ground nere his howse. And with 3s.4d. receyved of Oliver Ieon for an ortyard and a litle howse thereupon built in the Sowthegate Streete. And with £1 4s.0d. received of Thomas Overend for ground nere Hardewicke Heathe. And with 5s.0d. of Charles Derby for ground in the Northegate Streete. And with 1d. of Mrs Cotton for ground late built in Skynners Lane. And with 3s.4d. of Thomas Brunwyn for ground in Brentgovell Streete, *in toto*   £360 18s. 3½d.

   Summa oneris £474 10s.7d.
   and a gallon of wyne, whereof

Allowans extraordinarie

This accomptaunt dothe praie allowans of £20 0s.0d. given as a gratuitie bestowed for charges by Mr Newton in enterteyning

and appointing of preachers for the Wedinsdaie exercise after
his suspencion ~~and for the~~ and for Mr Bulwers extraordinarie
paynes in supplying the place of a precher[43] £20 0s. 0d.

[f.11v.]

Ministers

And of £112 10s.0d., *videlicet*, £12 10s.0d. for a quarter stipend to
Mr Bedle due at Christmas 1606, not paied by the former
receyvor, and £100 0s.0d. for a whole yeres stipend of bothe
preachers endid at Christmas last, *in toto* £112 10s. 0d.

And of £2 0s.0d. paied to the ministers of the 2 parishes

£2 0s. 0d.

Poore

And of £26 0s.0d. paied to the collectors for the poore in bothe
parishes, *videlicet* to eche of them quarterlie £3 5s.0d., *in toto* £26 0s. 0d.

Bestowed according to the will of Thomas Bright

And of £1 0s.0d. given towardes the reparacions of St James
churche, and £1 0s.0d. towardes the reparacions of St Maries
churche, according to the will of Thomas Bright, disceasid.
And of £1 0s.0d. given to the poore of St James parishe. And
£1 0s.0d. to the poore of St Maries parishe. And £1 0s.0d. to
the prisoners in the gaole, according to the same will.
Foxherthe tithes. *In toto* £5 0s. 0d.

Churches, reparacions and prisoners

And of £1 0s.0d. paid towardes the reparacions of St Maries
churche owt of this howse, and £1 0s.0d. likewise towardes the
reparacions of St James churche, and £1 0s.0d. to the prisoners
in the gaole, *in toto* £3 0s. 0d.

And of £1 0s.0d. paied to the churche wardens of St Maries
churche for the reparacions after the rate of 1s.0d. in the pound
owte of the hall taxed at £20 0s.0d.[44] ~~by yere~~ £1 0s. 0d.

Taske

And of £24 0s.0d. paied to Sir Robert Barker for the taske the 25
of Julye last, and 3s.0d. to his man for fees, *in toto*[45] £24 3s. 0d.

Composicion money

And of 10s.0d. paied to the constables for the hall for composicion
moneye 10s. 0d.

Subsidie and taske

And of £2 13s.4d. *videlicet* £1 0s.0d. to Mrs Boldero/ and
£1 13s.4d. paied to ~~the collectors~~ \Mr Mileson/ for 2 subsidies £2 13s. 4d.

And of 3s.0d. to Cropley for taske of londes in Westley at 2
payementes 3s. 0d.

[43] For the appointment of Mr Newton's successor, see Introduction, p.xlv.

[44] This is one of a number of instances in which either a church rate (as here) or some other tax was
payable on the Guildhall which was assessed along with other properties when rates and taxes were
levied in the town.

[45] [?]10s.0d. was deleted before 3s.

Owt rentes

And of £2 16s.6d. for owt rentes for the towne londes and for the
   receivors fee   £2 16s. 6d.

And of 5s.0d. paied for the rent of the Angell   5s. 0d.

The House of Correccion

And of £9 0s.0d. paied for a yere and half rent endid at Michelmas
   last for the howse of correccion, and £5 0s.0d. paied to the
   Widowe Snowden, the keper of the same howse, *in toto*   £14 0s. 0d.

Surgeons

And of £1 0s.0d. paied to old Wretham for cures, and £2 0s.0d.
   paied to Mr Perkins and Lichefield for cutting of Clerkes legg,
   in toto   £3 0s. 0d.

Reparacions of almes howses

And of £4 11s.1d. bestowed in reparacions of almes howses, and
   of 1s.6d. at the hall gardein wall, *in toto*   £4 12s. 7d.

Charges of suite [*and in another hand*] for Foxherthe tithes

And of £4 3s.0d. paied to Teverson and Mr Carter[46] for costes of
   suite abowt the tithes given by Thomas Bright, disceasid, owt
   of the mannor of Brooke Hall in Foxherthe   £4 3s. 0d.

Poore

And of £3 12s.8d. given at diverse times to diverse aged and
   ympotent persons and orphanes as appearithe by particulers
   now shewed   £3 12s. 8d.

Paymentes

And of 1s.6d. given to a messenger that went to Mildenhall
   abowte the affaires of the howse   [*sic*] 3s. 0d.

And of 10s.0d. for the clerkes fee   10s. 0d.

And of 6s.8d. paied to the constables for the houses visited with
   sickenes   6s. 8d.

Reparacions at the Angell

And of £88 15s.2d. paied and laied owt for brick and tile and
   cariage of timber,[47] and other cariage, and for wages of
   masons, carpenters, sawers and their men and other labourers,
   and for cleye, sand, lyme to stage with all splenting bondes and
   yrons used abowt the reparacions of the Angell as appeared by
   bills of particulers shewed at this accompt   £88 15s. 2d.

Inglethorpe

And of 15s. 0d. paied to Inglethorpe, the porter, for fires at the hall   15s. 0d.

And of £2 10s.0d. paied him for his wages and livery and for
   swepinge the doore   £2 10s. 0d.

Wyne at the dyner

And of 10s.9d. spent in wine at the dyner at the taking of this accompt   10s. 9d.

---

[46] Richard Carter was the farmer of Sir Nicholas Bacon's manor of Brookhall in Foxearth, H5/1/6.

[47] Only carriage of timber is mentioned here, and further on the cost of felling the timber is recorded, but as the timber required was from the feoffees' estates there is no charge for it as such.

The dressing of armour
And of 14s.0d. to Alman for kening the corselettes and heading
the spikes

14s. 0d.

Poore
And of 6s.0d. paid to Inglethorpe for making of apparell for poore
men

6s. 0d.

And of £1 0s.\10d./ paid to Henry Gippes for certeine wares delivered to the bedels

£1 0s. 10d.

And of 6s.8d. allowed to Christofer Johnson by[48] consent which is
before in charge and was to be for his daughters mariage
dynner kept at the Guildhall

6s. 8d.

[f. 12r., old number 20]
Charges of the dyner
And of £3 10s.0d. paied to Mr Bell for the charges of the dyner of
the feoffees at the taking of this accompte

£3 10s. 0d.

Charges abowt the Angell
And of £44 \5s.10d./ of victuals allowed to Mr Bell spent abowt
the reparacions of the Angell and some affaires of the towne
and for nayles, yrons, plancks, boardes and leade and worke
done at the Angell

£44 5s. 10d.

Charges at th'execution of the commission
And of £5 2s.0d. paied to George Fisson for the charge of the diet
of the Commissioners at th'execution of the last Commission
for Charitable Uses

£5 2s. 0d.

Arrerages before in charg not received
And of £10 0s.0d. before in charge for half yeres annuytie owt of
the mannor of Torkesey due the 20 July 1605, not yet received

£10 0s. 0d.

And of £20 0s.0d. before in charge for a whole yeres annuytie owt
of the said mannor due the 20 of Julie 1606, not yet received

£20 0s. 0d.

Received by Mr Mallowes and he is to answer it
And of £20 0s.0d. before in charge for the half yeres annuytie owt
of the said Mannor beinge now so muche due for the half yere
by the deathe of John Jermyn, esquier, for this present yere
endid the 20 July last past, which said £20 0s.0d. was received
by Mr John Mallowes and he is to answer the same, and is
parcell of the £40 0s.0d. before in charge for the whole yeres
annuytie as appearithe in the beginninge of this accompt.
Answerid in Mr Mallowes accompt

£5 2s. 0d.

Arrerages before in charge not received
And of £19 0s.3½d. before in charge beinge the residue of the
supers of th'accompt of Robert Sparke not yet received by this
accomptaunt

£19 0s. 3½d.

A gallon of wine
And of a gallon of wyne spent at the dynner

gallon of wyne

---

[48] The word 'by' has been altered and it is impossible to see what was originally written. There is no explanation in the Minute Book why this refund was made.

Summa allocationis £447 3s.9½d. and a gallon of wyne
Et sic remanet £27 6s.9d., whereof

Supers

There remayntethe in the handes of Sir Robert Jermyn, knight, for 21 acres *dimidia* of lond in Hepworthe before letton to Roger Berowgham for a yeres rent due at Michelmas last	10s.	4d.
And for a yeres rent of a peece of lond ther then due		9d.
And in the handes of Mary Evans, widowe, for a yeres rent of 2 mesuages in the Churchegate Streete then due	1s.	0d.
And of Leonard Harrison for an almes howse in the Colledge Streete. **Answered in Mr Mallowes accompt, allowed for worke done by him**	16s.	0d.
And for an almes howse in the Northegate strete where the Widowe Aggas late dwelt	4s.	0d.
And for another almes howse next to the sam	4s.	0d.
And of John Dister for an almes howse in the Garland Strete	6s.	8d.
		3d.
And for 3 almes howses thereunto next adjoyning either of them 3d., *in toto*		9d.
And of Harrison for the rent of an almes howse in the same streete	6s.	0d.
And of the Widowe Shippe for an almes howse there	5s.	0d.
And in th'handes of Robert Sparke for a yeres rent of a close at Stanford Bridg due at Michelmas last	£2 0s.	0d.
And of him for a yeres rent then due for a gardene in the Westgate Streete	5s.	0d.
And for a stall in the market \late/ in the occupacion of William Jellowe	2s.	0d.
And of Henry Landisdale for a peece of ground nere the Horse Market. *Solutum per composicionem ut patet* **in Mr Boldroes accompt**		
And of Richard \Heigham/ for a howse in the Churchegate Streete	£1 0s.	0d.

[*f. 12v.*]

And of John Parker for rent of a tenemente in the Longe Brackelond. *Solutum ut patet* **in Mr Boldroes accompt**		6d.
And of Hughe Mathew for rent of a tenemente there		8d.
And of Thomas Coell for rent of parcell of Roger Wrights howse	3s.	4d.
And of William Scott for rent of a gardeine plott by his howse	2s.	6d.
And of Charles Derbye for rent of ground in the Northegate Strete	5s.	0d.
And of Johane Cotton, widowe, for rent of a peece of ground lately \builded/ in Skinners Row		1d.
And of John Mallowes, gentleman, for rent receyved of Frost, Sir Robert Jermyns fermor, for londes in Hepworthe, or of Frost. **In charge in the next accompt**	£5 0s.	0d.
And of Giles Barker for rent of a tenemente and ground in Hepworthe		6d.
And of Franuces Pynner for the half yeres rent of St Peters paiable at Christmas last or within 20 daies after. **This £8 18s. 4¾d. is in charge in the next accompt**	£8 18s.	4¾d.

Summa £22 5s.8¾d.

Sic remanet clare £5 1s.0¾d. which said some of £5 1s.0¾d. Mr John Mallowes, now receyvor for the yere to come hathe received, with an obligacion of Edmunde Avis for the payment of £10 0s.0d. this yere *videlicet* £5 0s.0d. at Our Ladie daie and £5 0s.0d. at Michelmas followinge.

[*f. 13r., old number 48*]

1608 The accompte of John Mallowes, gentleman.

The accompt of John Mallowes, gentleman, receyvour of the rentes and revenewes belonging to the comon use of the towne of Bury St Edmunde made and yelded up the third daye of January in the sixte yere of the reigne of our soveraign Lord King James, *Anno Domini* **1608, [*1609*] for one whole yere then ended**

Onus

Inprimis the said accomptant chargeth himsilfe with £5 1s.0¾d. by him receyved of John Nonne, esquire, the last receyvour of the rentes and revenewes aforesaid upon the determinacion of his accompt as appeareth in the foote of the same accompt

£5 1s. 0¾d.

Yerely revenews

And with £263 4s.11½d., one boore, one coombe of rye and a gallon of wine, being the whole yerely rentes and revenewes of the said towne (over and besides th'annuitie of fourty powndes *per annum* given by Edmunde Jermin, esquire, and £10 0s.0d., parcell of the legacie of Peter Kembold)[49] as appearethe by the perticuler rentall thereof

£263 4s. 11½d.[50]
one boore, one coombe of rye and a gallon of wine

Mariage dinners

And with £6 13s. 4d. by him receyved of Edmond Inglethorp, the keper of the hall, for dinners kept there this yere, as by the particulers thereof sett downe in a bill by him in that behalfe delivered at this accompt appeareth

£6 13s. 4d.

Bourd

And with 400 *dimidia* 27 foote of bourd delivered into the hall by the executor of Mr Roger Barber, diseased, as so muche by him taken from thence in his liefe tyme[51]

400 *dimidia*
27 foot of bourd

Rent

And with £2 0s.0d. by him receyved of Thomas Read for the rent for one of the howses wherein the Ministers dwell, due for

---

[49] The bracket was not closed in the manuscript, but presumably should be placed here.

[50] A final 'j' before 'ob', which would have given the reading 12, has been crudely altered to 'd'.

[51] At a meeting on 30 December 4 James 1 [*1606*] the feoffees agreed that 500 boards taken from the Guildhall 'long since' were to be demanded of Mr Barber's executrix. The word 'redelivered' has been added at the end of this entry, Minutes, H2/6/2.1, p.28, though it seems that only 477 feet was actually received. Building materials were often stored at the Guildhall.

halfe a yere ended at the feast of the Nativitie of Our Lord God
last past within the tyme of this accompt   £2   0s.   0d.

Money borrowed

And with £100 0s.0d. borrowed at interest, by concent of the
feoffees, to paye the debtes of the howse for which Mr John
Hill, nowe alderman, and this accomptant doe stand bownd to
Mr William Cropley of whom the said £100 0s.0d. was
borrowed[52]   £100   0s.   0d.

Arrerages

And with £21 18s.2¾d. for divers supers upon the accompt of the
said Mr John Nonne, the last receyvor, as appeareth by the
same   £21 18s.   2¾d.

Receiptes

And with £15 0s.0d. by him receyved of Mr Richard Walker, as so
muche by him receyved before the tyme of this accompt of Mr
Robert Sparke, whilest he was receyvor *anno Domini* 1606, to
be imployed abowt the towne buisines   £15   0s.   0d.

And with £30 0s.0d. by him receyved of John Nonne, esquire,
anno Domini 1606, before the tyme of this accompte, as so
muche ordered by the Comissioners for Charitable Uses to be
payed for the extinguishement of the interest claymed by the
towne in parte of the howse which he purchased of Sir Robert
Jermin knight   £30   0s.   0d.

Arrerages of the annuitie of Torkeseye

And with £20 0s.0d. by him received of Sir Robert Jermin, knight,
before this accompt, as parcell of the arrerages of the annuitie
out of Torkesey given by Edmond Jermin, esquire, as
appeareth in the accompt of the said Mr Nonne, the last
receiver   £20   0s.   0d.

[f.13v.]

Receiptes

And with £1 0s.0d. by him reveyved of Mr Sporle, parson of
Hepworthe, for certeyne old trees \sold to him/ by consent of
diverse of the feoffees before the tyme of this accompte, being
cut downe in Brettes in Hepworthe by Bedwell whilst he was
fearmor there   £1   0s.   0d.

Peeter Kembold

And with £10 0s.0d. by him receyved of Avis upon an obligacion
made for parte of the £100 0s.0d. given by the last will of
Peeter Kembold   £10   0s.   0d.

> *Summa oneris* £475 4s.[?]6d., one boore, one coombe
> of rye and a gallon of wine, whereof

---

[52] An entry has been stuck into the Minute Book which stated that the feoffees were in debt to the sum
of £100 or more and had no immediate means of payment out of the revenues, so the money had to be
borrowed from Mr Cropley. Extraordinary payments were made at this time in connection with the fire
and the second charter which was granted in this year. See Introduction, p.xlviii.

Allocacionis [sic]

This accomptant prayeth allowance as followethe *videlicet, Inprimis* of 5s.4d. by him payed to the keeper of the hall for fiers which had beene spent in the tyme whilst Mr Nonne was receivor, and by him left unpayed   5s.   4d.

Taske

And of £24 0s.0d. for the taske of the towne payed to Sir Henry Warner, collector of the third taske, due in the tyme of Mr Nonne, the last receyvor, and by him lefte unpayed   £24   0s.   0d.

And of 6d. given to his clerke for an acquittance   6d.

Out rentes

And of £1 19s.3d. for certeyne rentes resolute payed out of the said possessions within the tyme of this accompt, *videlicet* of 18s.3d. payed to His Majestie for landmoll rent.[53] And of 6d. paid to His Majestie for a bearne without the Sowthe gate. And of 1s.1½d. payed to His Majestie for rent out of Leyers in Rowgham. And to His Majestie for two tenementes in the Churchgate Streat 2s.6d. And to his Majestie for a tenemente by the Guildhall 3s.6d. And to the Baylief of the hundred of Thedwardestree for Leyers 6d. And to the Manor of Forneham Alseintes for Sheere Hall Yard at Catshall 1½d.[54] And to His Majestie for foure tenementes in Garland Streat 1s.0d. And to His Majestie for the ministers howses 5s.6d. And to His Majestie for the tenementes late Mr Tassells 1s.1d. And to His Majestie for parte of the Angell 5s.0d., *in toto*   £1 19s.   3d.

And of 10s.6d. payed to His Majesties Receyvor Generall for a tenth going out of St Peters and 4d. for his acquittance, and 4d. to the receyvors door keper, *in toto*   11s.   2d.

Taske

And of 3s.0d. payed to the constable of Westley for the taske   3s.   0d.

Reparacions, Angell in parte[55]

And of £41 7s.1¾d. by him layed out about diverse reperacions this yere, done at the Angell, at the ministers howses, at <*dele-tion*> certeyne almes howses and at the Guildhall, as by bills of particulers shewed at this accompt appeareth   £41   7s.   1¾d.

And of 3s.0d. payed to Rabye for three loades of cley to the bourded howses   3s.   0d.

---

[53] See Glossary for landmoll rent.

[54] Before the old monastic school became the Shire House, assizes and other royal courts sat outside the town. Two places where the courts sat before then are known, the first of which was Cattishall Heath. The heath was at the junction of the parishes of St James's, Bury, Great Barton and Fornham St Martin. Justices are known to have sat here from 1186 to 1187, if not earlier. However, in 1304–5 Henowe Heath was named the place where the abbot's hall of pleas was established and the courts came to be held there. This area, just beyond the North Gate of the town, came to be known as Shire House Heath; it extended into the parishes of Westley and Fornham All Saints. See Gage, *Thingoe*, p.xi.

[55] The continued refurbishment of the Angel would have also added to the feoffees' financial burden.

Bourd, Angell in parte
And of 434 foote of bourd spent in the making of doores,
windowes and other thinges at the Angell, and in making of
penthowses at the ministers howses and almes howses[56]   434 foote

Reparacions
And of £1 18s.8d. allowed to Mr Pinner for reparacions done at St
Peters   £1 18s.   8d.

A Boore
And of one boore delivered to Mr Alderman Hill[57]   a boore

Fees
And of 10s.0d. payed to the clerke of the hall for his fee   10s.   0d.
And of 15s.0d. payed to the receyvor of the revenewes for his fee   15s.   0d.
[f.14r., old number 30]
Inglethorpe
And of £2 10s.0d. payed to the keeper of the hall for his wages
and his liverye   £2 10s.   0d.
And of £1 7s.7d.[58] payed to the hall keeper as so muche layed out
by him for fiers and other thinges and for some reparacions
done there, as by his bill appearethe   £1 3s.   7d.

Ministers
And of £100 0s.0d. payed to Mr Heley and Mr Sothersby,
preachers, for their allowance given unto them this yere   £100 0s.   0d.
And of £2 0s.0d. given to Mr Juell and Mr Bulwar, ministers   £2 0s.   0d.

Reparacions of the Church
And of £1 0s.0d. g delivered to the church wardens of St Maries
parishe towardes the reparacions of the churche   £1 0s.   0d.

Taske and Subsedy
And of £24 0s.0d. payed to Sir William Waldgrave, knight,
collector of the \fourth/ taske due to His Majestie within the
tyme of this accompte, and of 6d. given to his clerke for
acquitance   £24 0s.   6d.
And of £1 0s.0d. payed to Thomas Cleydon, collector of the
second payment of the second subsedye for this towne   £1 0s.   0d.

Paymentes
Gostling Angell
And of £20 0s.0d. payed to Mr Gostling in parte of payment of the
money awarded by the Commissioners for Charitable Uses, to
be payed unto him for the redemcion of the Angell   £20 0s.   0d.

Brunwin
And of £10 0s.0d. payed to Roger Brunwin, clerke, in parte of
payment of the money awarded by the Commissioners for

---

[56] No doubt some of the board returned by Mrs Barber was used. Board remaining at the end of this year
is recorded f.14v., p.173.
[57] From this year until the Charity Commissioners' scheme of 1842 was implemented, a boar was given
each year to the alderman.
[58] Note the discrepancy between the amount in the text and in the amounts column.

Charitable Uses, to be payed unto him for the redemcion of the howse in th'occupacion of James Kent	£10	0s.	0d.

Poore

And of £6 ~~ten~~ 10s.0d. given towards the relief of the poore in boathe parishes	£6	10s.	0d.
And of 5s.9d. given to Mother Shilling and other poore folke at diverse tymes in extremitie		5s.	9d.

Quayle

And of £1 10s.0d. given to Moother Quayle, governes of the Spittle howse, for hir allowance for this yere	£1	10s.	0d.

Paymentes

And of £1 9s.10d. for suyng out the fine[59] for the Angell and Mr Brunwins howse and Thomas Overendes lond and Henry Brightes howse, recovered by the Comission of Charitable Uses, and 5s.0d. for altering the ded potem,[60] for that Mr Derbye wold not joyne in the same. And 10s.0d. for the post fine, *in toto* — £2 4s. 10d.

And also £1 0s.0d. payed to Mr Brunwin his wief for hir good wil to joyne in the said fine — £1 0s. 0d

And of 10s.0d. for a searche in the towre[61] concerning the porcion of tithes in Foxherthe. And of 1s.0d. given to a messenger which came from Carter, the fearmor there. And of 1s.4d. given to Harrold to goe to Foxherthe with a lettre. And of 5s.0d. given to Robert Inglishe for his charges for 2 days at Foxherthe about the towne buisines there concerning the porcion of tithes, and of 2s.6d. given to George Fourd for traveling to find out proofe concerning the said tithes. **Charges abowt Foxerthe tithes** — 19s. 10d.

And of 17s.0d. payed for exchange for the ould guild pott,[62] being broken, for another very fayer sownd pott — 17s. 0d.

[f.14v.]

Mr Pinner

And of £4 8s.8d. allowed to Mr Pinner for two partes of the charges of planshering and other thinges done at St Peeters by Sir John Heigham, and answered to the same Sir John by Mr Pinner, and are there to be left by Mr Pinner in th'ende of his terme — £4 8s. 8d.

Paymentes

And of £3 8s.8d. payed to William Hawsted for wine by him and Roger Write delivered to the judges, *videlicet,* to Mr Justice

---

59 The redemption of the Angel is discussed in the Introduction, p.xlvii.

60 For this and other legal terms see Glossary.

61 The tower might mean the room above the Guildhall porch, but is more likely to mean the Tower of London, which was for a long time used as a record repository. The suit for Foxearth tithes is discussed in the Introduction, p.li.

62 This was a brewing vessel, nothing to do with a guild. See Glossary.

Daniell, 19 *Marcii*, 1606, one rundlet £1 12s.8d. and to my
Lord Cooke,[63] 13 *Julii*, 1607, one rundlet £1 16s.0d.   £3   8s.   8d.

Bourd
And of six bourdes conteyning 53 foote delivered backe agayne
to the Guildhall upon the finishing of this accompt   53 foot of bourd

A gallon of wine
And of a gallon of wine spent at the feoffees dinner in the tyme of
this accompte   A gallon of wine

Charges of the dinner
And of £6 7s.7d. for the charges of the feoffees dinner at the tyme
of this accompte   £6   7s.   7d.
And of 2s.0d. payed to Inglethorpe for fyer and kandle at the tyme
of this accompte   2s.   0d.

Corslettes
And of 4s.0d. to the armorer for scouring the corsletes   4s.   0d.

Reparacions
And of £1 12s.0d. allowed to Leonard Harrison for reparacions by
him done at certeyne almes howses, as by his bill expressing a
further charge at large appearethe   £1 12s.   0d.

Angell
And of £4 9s.0d. allowed to Nicholas Bell, fearmour of the
Angell, for certeyne reparacions by him done there, as by his
bill appearethe   £4   9s.   0d.

Paymentes
And of £1 0s.0d. by him given to Mr Sucklin, Secrytary to the late
Lord Treasurer, for procuring a warrant from the said Lord
Treasurer for a searche and a particuler from the Auditor
towching the towne londes before the tyme of this accompte[64]   £1   0s.   0d.
And of £1 0s.0d. by him given to the Auditor for the same searche
and particuler before the tyme of this accompt   £1   0s.   0d.

Gostling Angell [*In a different hand*] Due when Mr Nonne was Accomptant 1607[65]
And of £20 0s.0d. by him payed to Mr Gostling, before the tyme
of this accompt, in parte of payment of the money ordered by
the Comissioners for Charitable Uses to be payed to him for
the redemcion of the Angell, and £2 0s.0d. for the forbearing of
the same £20 0s.0d. for that it was not paid by the space of one
yere after it was due, *in toto*   £22   0s.   0d.

---

[63] This refers to Sir Edward Coke who had been appointed Chief Justice of the Common Pleas in 1606. He and William Daniel were on the Norfolk circuit together 1607–10, J.S. Cockburn, *A History of English Assizes* (Cambridge 1972), pp.268–9.

[64] Perhaps an attempt had been made to obtain an assurance of the town lands which was eventually granted in the 1614 charter.

[65] Yet another cause of heavy expenditure was the redemption of the Angel and other properties following the hearing by the Commissioners for Charitable Uses. See Introduction, p.xlvii.

Brunwin [*In a different hand*] **Due before this accompt**

And of £20 0s.0d. by him payed to Roger Brunwin, clerke, before
the tyme of this accompt, for the two first payes due unto him
by the decree of the Comissioners for Charitable Uses for the
redemcion of the howse wherein James Kent dwelleth. And of
£1 4s.2d. layed out for a deed potem to take the knowledge of a
fine from the said Mr Gostling and Mr Brunwin and their
wieves, of the same howses, and of £1 4s.2d. more layed out
for one other deed potem to take the knowledg of them and of
Mr Derby, Henry Bright, and Thomas Overend, and their
wieves, concerning the howses and growndes recovered to
th'use of the towne by the Comission of Charitable Uses before
the tyme of this accompte   £2   8s.   4d.

[f.15r., old number 39]

And of 2s.6d. layed out to a messenger which went to Aye for Mr
Sheene,[66] the survayor, and to Thomas Peake about the
survay[n]g of Hepworthe londes, and of £1 10s.0d. given to the
said Mr Sheen for measuring, booking and plotting certeyne of
the same londes, and of 5s.0d. given to his sonne which did
helpe him to measure the said londes before the tyme of this
accompt, *in toto*   £1   17s.   6d.

And of 6s.6d. given to the children and servantes at Mr Sporls at
divers tymes when certeyne of the feoffes ware there about
the dispache of the towne buisines, before the tyme of this
accompt   6s.   6d.

Angell

And of 15s.9d. payed for cutting downe of the timber at
Hepworthe, which was imployed for the repayring of the
Angell, before the tyme of this accompte[67]   15s.   9d.

And of £4 0s.6d. layed out before the tyme of this accompt about
the suyte for Foxherthe, over and besides the charges layed out
by Mathew Teversom, as by the particuler bill appearethe. [*In
a different hand*] **Charg of suyt for Foxherthe tithes**   £4   0s.   6d.

And of £5 0s.10d. by him layed out before the tyme of this
accompte in the suyte browght in the excheacour, in the name
of Sir Nicholas Bacon, agaynst William Scott towching the
libertyes of the townsmen in the markettes and fayers as by the
bills appeareth   £5   0s.   10d.

Paymentes, John Man

And of £83 15s.5d. by him payed to Mr John Hill, nowe alderman,
as so muche by him payed to the executrix of John Man,[68]
disceased, for money owing by the towne to the said John Man.
And of £11 12s.4d. by him payed to the said Mr Hill, as so

---

66 There are no plans or surveys by Mr Sheene at the Bury Record Office.

67 The cost of repairs must often have been reduced because timber was available from the feoffees'
own estates.

68 John Man was probably buried 19 November 1607, Hervey, *St James' Registers, Burials*, pp.45 and
435.

muche by him payed to John Cocksage for worke done for the towne. And of £3 11s.2d. by him payed to the said Mr Hill, as so much by him payed to Crumwell, the smithe, for iron worke taken of him for the use of the towne. And of £1 1s.6d. by him payed to the said Mr Hill as so much by him payed to Bartram, the smithe, for iron worke taken of him for the use of the towne, as by the particuler billes of the persons aforesaid appearethe, *in toto*	£100	0s.	5d.
And of 10s.0d. payed for repayring of the towne cromes[69]		10s.	0d.

Angell[70]

And of £5 12s.0d. by him payed to Roger Miller for 16 chalder of lyme by him delivered in at the Angell, in the yere of Our Lord 1607, before the tyme of this accompt	£5	12s.	0d.
And of £2 19s.8d. payed to Richard Frithe, mason, for worke by him done at the Angell *anno Domini* 1607, before the tyme of this accompt, as by his bill appearethe	£2	19s.	8d.
And of £3 0s.4d. by him payed to John Cocksage, carpenter, for worke for him done at the Angell *Anno Domini* 1607, before the tyme of this accompt, as by his bill appearethe	£3	0s.	4d.
And of £2 0s.0d. payed to Mr Heley, preacher of St James churche, for the rent of the howse wherein Mr Bulwar dwelt for the halfe yere ended at the feast of the Nativitie of Our Lord, before the tyme of this accompt	£2	0s.	0d.

[*f.15v.*]

And of £1 0s.0d. by him allowed to Mr Richard Walker as so muche by him layed out to Mr Godfrye for his cownsell in the affaires of the towne before the tyme of this accompte	£1	0s.	0d.

Kembold

And of £3 0s.0d. payed to the handes of Mr Charles Derbye to be distributed amongest the poore people of the east and north wardes, according to the will of Peter Kembold, disceased	£3	0s.	0d.

> *Summa allocacionis* £444 4s.11¾d., one
> coombe of rye, a boore and a gallon of wine
> So there resteth due to the howse upon this
> accompte £31 19s.3¼d., whereof

Supers *de antiquo*

There remaynethe in the handes of the severall persons here under named as so muche owing by them at the tyme of the finishing of Mr Nonnes accompte, the last receyvor, and still resting unpayed as followeth *videlicet*			
Sir Robert Jermin, knight, for 21 acres *dimidia* of lond in Hepworthe leaton to Roger Berowgham		10s.	4d.
The same Sir Robert for other londes in Hepworth			9d.

---

[69] The repairs to the town cromes (hooks with which burning thatch could be pulled from roofs) were needed after their use in fighting the great fire of April 1608. It is very probable that the payments to Cocksage, Crumwell and Bartram were also made in the wake of the fire. See Introduction, p.xlviii.

[70] There was another marginal heading 'Angel' a few lines above this which has been ignored.

Anthony Bumpstead for halfe yeres rent of two mesuages in the Churchgate Streat	12s.	0d.
An almes \howse/ in Northgate Streat where the Widow Aggas dwelt	4s.	0d.
For an other almes howse there next the same	4s.	0d.
John Dister for an almes howse in the Garlond Streat	6s.	8d.
		3d.
And for three almes howses thereto next adjoyning, eyther of them 3d., *in toto*		9d.
Harrison for an almes howse in the same streat	6s.	0d.
The Widowe Shipp for an almes howse in the same streat	5s.	0d.
Robert Sparke for a yeres rent for the close at Standforde Bridge	£2 0s.	0d.
The same Robert for a gardein in the Westgate Streat	5s.	0d.
Jellowe for a stall in the market	2s.	0d.
Henry Landisdall for a peece of grownd nere the Horsemarket	2s.	0d.
[*In another hand*] **Solutum per composicionem**		
Richard Heigham for a howse in Churchgate Streat	£1 0s.	0d.
John Parker for a tenemente in Long Bracklond		6d.
Hughe Mathewe for a tenemente there		8d.
[*The last two entries are bracketed together and beside them*] **solutum per composicionem**		
Thomas Coell for parcell of Roger Wrightes howse	3s.	4d.
William Scott for a garden plott by his howse	2s.	6d.
Charl[e]s Derby for grownd in Northgate Streat	5s.	0d.
Johanne Cotton, widowe, for a peece of grownd in Skinner Rowe		1d.
Giles Barker for a tenenmente and lond in Hepworth		6d.

Supers *de novo*

More in super upon the severall persons herunder named as so muche owing by them for the rentes incurred within the tyme of this accompt and yet remayning unpayd as followeth *videlicet*		
Henry Colling, gentleman, for one yeres rent of Salters londes and a close and other londes neere Standford Bridge	£10 0s.	0d.
[*f.16r., old number 31*]		
John Bridon for a gardein in the Eastgate Streat upon Sparrow Hill	2s.	0d.
Sir Robert Jermin, knight, for 21 acres *dimidia* of lond in Hepworthe, parcell of the londes antiently dimised to Roger Berrowham	10s.	4d.
The same Sir Robert for other londes in Hepworthe		9d.
Giles Barker for a tenemente and peece of grownd there leaton to John Brundishe		6d.
For an almes howse in the Northgate Streat late Widowe Agges	4s.	0d.
For another almes howse there late Widdow Sutton	4s.	0d.
[*The next six entries are bracketed together*] **These howses ware burnt before the rent due**[71]		
John Dister for an Almes howse in Garlond Streat	6s.	8d.
		3d.

---

[71] This is the most direct of several references in this account to the fire of April 1608. These seem to have been the only properties owned by the feoffees that were destroyed.

Robbinson for an other almes howse there		3d.
Bukkenham and Everard for an other almes howse there		3d.
Dizyng for an other almes howse there		3d.
Harrison for an other almes howse there	6s.	0d.
Widowe Shippe for an other almes howse there	5s.	0d.
Thomas Rose for parte of his rent of the howse and grownd by the Spittle Howse	£1 0s.	0d.
For the rent of a stall in the Markett, late in the occupacion of William Jellow	2s.	0d.
Henry Landisdale for a peece of grownd nere the Horse Markett	2s.	0d.

[*In another hand*] **Solutum per composicionem ut patet in compotem Mr Boldero**

Oliver Ieon for his halfe yere rent due at Michelmas last, 1608	1s.	8d.
Richard Heigham, gentleman, for a tenemente in Churchgate Streat	£1 0s.	0d.
John Parker for a tenemente in the Long Bracklond		6d.
Hughe Mathewe for a tenemente there late William Johnsons		8d.

[*The last two items are bracketed and, in an other hand*] **solutum ut patet** in **Mr Boldroes accompt**

Margaret Grigges, widowe, for a howse ~~by~~ in the Northgate Streat, late Kentes		6d.
Thomas Coell for parte of a tenemente callid the Castle, late Roger Writes	3s.	4d.
William Scott for grownd nere his howse	2s.	6d.
Charl[e]s Derby for grownd in the Northgate Streat	5s.	0d.
Johan Cotton, widowe, for grownd late builded in Skinners Lane		1d.
Thomas Brunwin for grownde in Brentgovell Streat	3s.	4d.
Francis Pinner for the halfe yeres rent of St Peeters due to be payed at the feast of the Nativitie of Our Lord God last past or within twenty dayes after, which tyme is not come. [*In another hand*] **Answerid in the next accompt**	£8 18s.	4¾d.

Summa of all the supers £30 13s.4¾d.

And so remayneth cleere upon this accompte as appeareth on the other side of this leafe

[f.16v.]

There remaynethe due to the howse by the accomptant, all allowances made

7s. 8½d.
and a coombe
of rye

<Deletion>

Which \money/ this accomptant upon the finishing of this accomp hath delivered into the handes of Mr Hill, alderman, now chosen to be receyvor for the next yere to come

And by him delivered to John Nonne, esquire, deputy receyvor to Mr Alderman Hill, with one obligacion for payment of £10 0s.0d. by Avis a parcell of the £100 0s. 0d. given by Peeter Kembold

John Hill 1609[72]

Th'accompt of John Hill, gentleman, receyvor of the rentes and revenues belonginge to the common use of the towne of Burie St Edmunde, made and yeldid upp the third daie of Januarie in the sevinthe yere of the reign of our soveraign Lord, Kinge James of England *et cetera, et anno Domini* **1609 [*1610*] for one whole year then endid**

Onus

Inprimis the said accomptaunt dothe charge himsilf with 7s.8½d. by him receyved of John Mallowes, gentleman, the last receyvour, upon the determynacion of his accompt as appearithe in the foote of the same accompte   7s. 8½d.

Yearlie revenues

And with £262 3s.5d., beinge the whole yerelie rentes and revenues of the said towne (over and besides £40 0s.0d. *per annum* of annuytie given by Edmunde Jermyn, esquier, disceasid, not receyved by this accomptaunt, but is ymployed other wise for and towardes a stocke to set the poore on worke within the towne of Bury aforesaid) as appearithe by the rentall thereof   £262 3s. 5d.

Mariages

And withe £8 0s.0d. receyved of Edmunde Inglethorpe, the keper of the hall, for for [*sic*] diverse mariage dynners kept there this yere past   £8 0s. 0d.

Kembold

And with £10 0s.0d. receyved of Emunde Avis for parte of Peter Kemboldes legacie   £10 0s. 0d.
\And with 18s. received of Fuller for barke sold at Hepworthe   18s. 0d./

Arrerages

And withe £2 0s.0d. receyved of th'arrerages due by Mr George Boldero for a yeres rent of a howse and close in the Westgate Strete, due at Michaelmas 1606, and paid by Mr John Mallowes   £2 0s. 0d.
And with £1 0s.0d. received of Mr Mallowes for the half yeres profit of the same close, 1607   £1 0s. 0d.

Rentes

And with a combe \of rye/ of William Ullet for parte of his rent   A combe of rye
And with a fat boare of Thomas Peake for parte of his rent   A boare
And with a gallon of wyne of John Revell   A gallon of wine

Supers

And with £30 13s. ~~summa oneris~~ 4¾d. for diverse supers upon th'accompte of Mr Mallowes, the last receyvor, as appearithe by the same   £30 13s. 4¾d.
     Summa oneris £315 2s.6¼d., a combe of rye, a boare, a gallon of wine, whereof

---

[72] The original account from which this was copied into the account book has survived and is H2/3/4/8.

[f.17r., old number 38]
Allocaciones, Brunwin

The said accomptant dothe praie allowans of £10 0s.0d. paied to
Mr Roger Brunwin of Barton, being the last payment of the
purchase of the howse wherein James Kent dwellithe in the
Cooke Rowe   £10   0s.   0d.

Reparacions

And of 3s.4d. for five bunches of ralles[73] for mendinge the Shere
House[74]   3s.   4d.
And of 11s.0d. for a loade of strawe for the same Shire Howse[75]   11s.   0d.
And of 4d. paied to two laborers to carie in the same strawe   4d.
And of 8d. for 2 bunches of strawe more and fetchinge it   8d.
And of 11s.0d. paied to Silvester and Abbot for five daies and
halfe worke in thatchinge of the Shire Howse   11s.   0d.

Paymentes

And of £1 0s.2d. paied[76] for a runlet of sacke given to the judges
at Lent assises last   £1   0s.   2d.
And of 16s.0d. for a caulf and 11s.0d. for half a dozen of capons
given to the judges at the same assises   £1   7s.   0d.
And of 11s.8d. paied to Thomas Reade for mendinge the sincke in
the Churcheyarde   11s.   8d.
And of 10s.8d. paied to Thurston for bringing 15 loades of gravell
and carying awaye the mener[77] owt of the Churcheyarde   10s.   8d.
And of 2s.6d. paied to Jellowe for the same gravell and digging it   2s.   6d.

Poore

And of 2s.6d. given to Goulty havinge his wief and children sicke   2s.   6d.
And of 2s.0d. given for the buryall of Mother Glover[78]   2s.   0d.

Paymentes

And of 1s.2d. paied for a pen knife, ynck and paper for the hall   1s.   2d.
And of 4s.0d. paied for fier and candle at the hall   4s.   0d.
And of 4s.0d. paied to Alman, the cutler, for scouring the harneys   4s.   0d.
And of £1 13s.4d. for a kegge of sturgion and a freshe salmon
given to the judges at sommer assises last   £1 13s.   4d.

Poore

And of 1s.0d. given to Bendoes wief, for relief of hir husband, sicke 1s.   0d.
And of 1s.0d. given to[79] Ullettes wief, having 3 childres sicke   1s.   0d.
And of 1s.0d. given to Ingoldes wief, having 2 children verie sicke[80] 1s.   0d.

---

[73] In the original this reads 'roddes' quite clearly, H2/3/4/8.
[74] For the acquisition of the Shire House, see Appendix 8, *sub* 1578.
[75] The original account states that this was paid to Mrs Gyppes, H2/3/4/8.
[76] The original adds that this payment was made to Mr Gippes, H2/3/4/8.
[77] This word means manure or compost, see Glossary. The Great Churchyard was in private hands and may not have been kept as well as the town governors thought desirable. If the Shire Hall had fallen into disrepair, there may even have been a fear that Bury would be dropped from the judges' circuit. This alone could have made the authorities take steps to improve the Shire House and its surroundings.
[78] In the original account there is the additional information that this was paid by consent of Mr Richard Walker, *ibid.*
[79] The Christian name John is given in the original, *ibid.*
[80] In the original the words 'of the smale pox' are added, H2/3/4/8.

Paymentes, Aide[81]

And of 6s.7d. paied to Robert Reve in allowans of the Kinges aide	6s.	7d.
And of £10 0s.0d. paied to Mr William Cropley for the loane of £100 0s.0d., for which Mr Mallowes and this accomptant stand bound for payment thereof	£10 0s.	0d.
And of 3s.4d. paied to Mr Pynner in allowans of the ~~Kinges~~ \Princes/ aide for St Peters	3s.	4d.

Angell, reparacions

And of £10 1s.0d. paied in part of the charges of reparacions of Mr Helies howse and Juelles howse, as by the bill thereof appearithe	£10 1s.	0d.
And of £5 0s.0d. paied to Mr Bennet Barker in parte of William Meycros[82] bill for glasing the Angell, as by the bill thereof appearithe	£5 0s.	0d.
And of £14 10s.0d. paied to Cockesedge for worke at the ministers howses, as appearithe by the bill thereof	£14 10s.	0d.

Reparacions

And of 6d. given to Welham to carie a lettre to Sir John Heigham to give him notice of the daie of th'accompt		6d.
And of 10s.0d. paied to the constables of the west ward for the Kinges provision for the yere[83]	10s.	0d.
And of £2 10s.0d. paied to Inglethorpe, the keper of the Hall, for his wages	£2 0s.	0d.
And for 13s.8d. paied him for fier and reparacions of the hall	13s.	8d.

Angell

And of £13 2s.2d. paied to Mr Derby, in parte of payment of the reparacions of the Angell, as appearithe by his billes thereof	£13 2s.	2d.

[f.17v.]

Receyvors fee

And of 15s.0d. for the recyvors fee	15s.	0d.

Wine

And of a gallon of wine of John Revell spent at the dyner	A gallon of wine

Charges of the dyner

And of £4 9s.7d. for the charge of the dyner at the accompt	£4 9s.	7d.
And of 11s.6d. spent in wine at the same dyner[84]	11s.	6d.

A boare

And of a boare delivered to Mr Alderman Bright	A boare

Clerkes fee

And of 10s.0d. for the clerkes fee	10s.	0d.

---

[81] See Glossary.

[82] The original account reads Meyer, not Meycro, H2/3/4/8.

[83] The Guildhall was in the West Ward. The constable was the parish official who normally collected payments for purveyance.

[84] The figures denoting the cost of the dinner and the wine were added in a different hand in the original account, H2/3/4/8.

Aide

And of 2s.0d. paied for the ~~Kinges~~ \Princes/ aide for the Angell[85] 2s. 0d.

Poore

And of 1s.4d. given to Mabornes wief to buy wollen wheles 1s. 4d.

And of 3s.0d. given to Dunkons wief havinge many children 3s. 0d.

Paymentes

And of 1s.0d. paied to Slowman for mending a locke and keye 1s. 0d.

And of 10s.0d. paied for a post fine[86] for the Angell 10s. 0d.

Owt rentes

And of £3 0s.0d. paied to Mr Howman for haulf yeres rent of the howse of correccion, due at th'annunciation of Our Ladie last £3 0s. 0d.

And of 19s.4½d. paied for half yeres rent due to the Kinges Majestie at the same feast[87] 19s. 4½d.

Gostlinge

And of £20 0s.0d. paied to Mr Gostlinge for parte of the purchase of the Angell £20 0s. 0d.

Taske and subsidie

And of £24 0s.0d. paied for the taske of this towne[88] £24 0s. 0d.

And of 1s.6d. paied for taske to Westley 1s. 6d.

And of £1 13s.4d. paied for the subside of the towne stocke[89] £1 13s. 4d.

Poore

And of ~~2s.6d.~~\1s.0d./ paied given to Mabournes wief to buye cards ~~2s.6d.~~ 1s. 0d.

And of 2s.6d. given to Mother Thompson hurt with falling of a wall 2s. 6d.

And of 1s.0d. given to a poore woman for relief of 2 sick children[90] 1s. 0d.

Reparacions

And of £2 7s.3d. paied to Mr Pynner for thinges used in the reparacions of Mr Helies howse £2 7s. 3d.

And of 6s.7d. for the curbe \and/ mending of the decaied well before the Angell[91] 6s. 7d.

Angell

And of 8s.0d. paied for a windowe at the Angell 8s. 0d.

Owt rentes

And of 18s.1½d. paied for haulf yeres rent due to the Kinges[92] Majestie at the feast of St Michaell th'archaungell last 18s. 1½d.

And of 1s.0d. paied to Sir Robert Drury, knight, for 2 yeres rent for Leyers 1s. 0d.

---

85 The original adds that it was paid to Bell, the landlord of the Angel, H2/3/4/8.
86 See Glossary.
87 This rent was paid to Christopher Johnson, original account, H2/3/4/8.
88 Paid to Sir Anthony Felton's deputy, *ibid.*
89 Paid to Mr Adames, *ibid.*
90 In the original these children were said to be sick of the pox.
91 This is the first of several records of the feoffees repairing common wells.
92 Paid to Christopher Johnson, H2/3/4/8.

Mynisters

And of £2 0s.0d. paied to Mr Corder and Mr Jewell, mynisters, for
a yere, given by Mr Tassell — £2 0s. 0d.

And of £100 paied to Mr Helye and Mr Sotherby, preachers of the
parishes of St Maries and St James, for their yeres stipend — £100 0s. 0d.

Reparacions of St Maries churche

And of £1 0s.0d. paied to Robert Hynes, churche warden, for the
reparacions of St Maries churche — £1 0s. 0d.

Paymentes

And of £23 7s.11d. paied to Mr Mallowes for money by him
disbursed in the affaires of the towne as appearithe by diverse
billes shewed at this accompt — £23 7s. 0d.[93]

Old Supers

And of £21 15s.0d., parcell of £30 13s.4¾d., beinge the supers of
the last accompt, ~~being~~ before in charge and not receyved by
this accomptaunt — £21 15s. 0d.

> *Summa allocacionum* £283 12s.7d.,
> a boare and a gallon of wine
> *Sic debet* £31 9s.6¼d., whereof

[f.18r., old number 33]

Supers

There remaynethe in the handes of Henry Colling, gentleman, for
a yeres rent of Salters landes, and a close nere Stanford Bridge,
and other landes in the West Fieldes of Bury, due at Michelmas
last — £10 0s. 0d.

And in the handes of John Bridon for a garden upon Sparrow
Hill[94] — 2s. 0d.

And in the handes of Sir Robert Jermyn, knight, for 21 acres
dimidia lande in Hepworthe, parcell of the landes auncientlie
demised to Roger Berowham — 10s. 4d.

And of him for other landes in Hepworthe — 9d.

And in the handes of Giles Barker for a tenemente and landes in
Hepworthe, leaton to John Brundishe — 6d.

And for an almes howse in the Northegate Strete, late Widowe
Aggas — 4s. 0d.

And for another almes howse there, late Wydowe Sutton — 4s. 0d.

All theis are burnt downe [*This relates to the next four items.*]

And for an almes howse in the Garlond Strete where Dister dwelt — 6s. 8d
3d.

And for 3 other almes howses thereunto adjoyning, everie one
3d.,[95] *in toto* — 9d.

And for another almes howse there, where Harryson dwelt — 6s. 0d.

And for another almes howse there, where Widowe Shippe dwelt — 5s. 0d.

And in the handes of Thomas Rose for a yeres rent of a howse and
close by the Spittle Howse, due at Michelmas last — £2 10s. 0d.

---

[93] The v in vij^s. has been altered, and it is impossible to read what was originally written here.
[94] The words 'in the Eastgate Street' are added in H2/3/4/8.
[95] The tenants were identified as Robinson, Buckenham and Everad, and Dising, *ibid.*

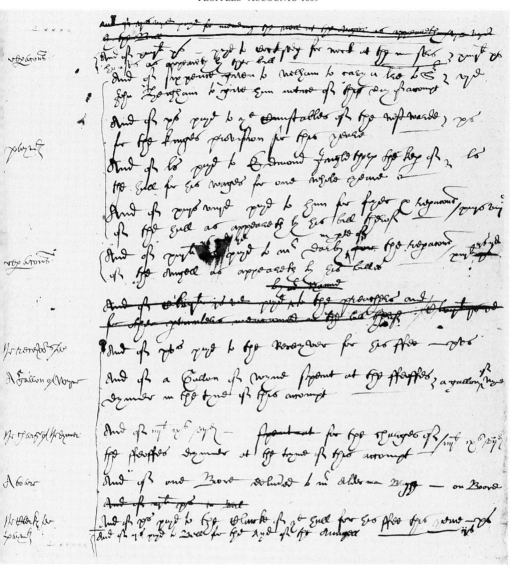

Plate 8. Part of the original account for 1609. Although this section is relatively neat, it shows how the rough accounts were altered. Clerks who made copies in the account book must sometimes have found it difficult to decipher some entries. (H2/3/4/8). Reproduced by permission of the Guildhall Feoffees.

And for the rent of a stall in the market, late William Jellowe		2s.	0d.
And for a yeres rent for ground in the Horsemarket, occupied by Landisdale *Solutum in proximo compoto*		2s.	0d.
And for a howse in Churchgate Strete, wherein Richard Heigham dwelle	£1	0s.	0d.
And for a tenemente in Longe Bracklond, occupied by John Parker		6s.	0d.

183

And for a tenemente there, late Hughe Mathewes and Johnsons		8d.

[*The last two entries are bracketed together and beside them is written*] **Solutum in proximo compoto**

And for the half yeres rent of a tenemente in Skynner Row, late Henry Bright **Solutum in proximo compoto** — £1 8s. 8d.

And for a tenemente in Northgate Strete, occupied by Grigges,[96] late Kentes — 6d.

And in th'andes of Thomas Coell, gentleman, for parte of the tenemente called the Castle, occupied by Roger Wright, due at Michelmas last — 3s. 4d.

And for a peece of ground in Skynners Rowe, occupied by Mrs Cotton — 1d.

And of [*space*] Ravens for a peece of ground in Brentgovell \Strete/, late Brunwins — 3s. 4d.

And in the handes of Fraunces Pynner, for the half yeres rent of St Peters, paiable at the feast of the Birthe of Christ[97], or within 20 daies after, which tyme is not yet come **Answered in proximo compoto** — £8 18s. 4¾d.

And of Thomas Smythe for the half yeres rent of a tenement by[98] the Guildhall, due at Michelmas last **Solutum in proximo compoto** — 11s. 9d.

And of Leonard Harryson for a yeres rent of a howse in Colledge Strete **Solutum in proximo compoto** — 16s. 0d.

And of Thomas Coell, gentleman, for half yeres rent of 18 acres land in Bury and Horningeserthe, late William Gillies, due at th'annunciacion last — £2 0s. 0d.

Of James Smythe, esquire, for a peece of ground in the Horsemarket — 6d.

Mrs [99]Heyward for a tenemente in Risbeigate Strete and a garden at the Teyfen — 5s. 0d.

And of Mary[100] Canham for a tenemente and acre of ground in Hepworthe, leaton to Willys — 8d.

Of William Scot for ground nere his howse — 2s. 6d.

And of Charles Derby for a peece of ground in Northegate Strete — 5s. 0d.

Summa of the supers £30 11s.1¾d.

Sic debet 18s.9¾d. and a combe of rye not delivered by him.[101]

Which was delivered to John Boldero, gentleman, recyvor for the year following, to be answered upon his accompt.

---

96 The original adds the Christian name Margarett, H2/3/4/8.
97 The writer of the original was content to write Christmas, *ibid*.
98 The clerk began to write 'f', but changed the letter to 'b'.
99 The Christian name Elizabeth and the description 'widow' are in the original, H2/3/4/8.
100 The original reads Margery, not Mary, *ibid*.
101 The original concludes at this point apart from some rough calculations and the signatures of William Cooke, Bennett Barker, Francis Pynner, John Revell, Charles Darby, John Boldero, Thomas Bright and Henry Gippes, H2/3/4/8.

[*f.18v.*]

John Boldero 1610[102]

The accompt of John Boldero, gentleman, receyvor of the rentes and revenues belonginge to the common use of the towne of Bury St Edmunde made and and yelded upp the second daie of Januarie in the, eight yere of the reign of our soveraign Lord, Kinge James of England *etcetera, annoque Domini* 1610 [*1611*] for one whole yere then endid

Onus[103]

Inprimis the said accomptaunt dothe charge himsilf with 18s.9¾d. receyved of Mr Hill, the last receyvor, upon the determynacion of his accompt, as appearithe in the foote of the same accompt   18s.   9¾d.

Old Supers

And with £7 6s.8d. receyved of John King for the yeres rent of~~of~~ certeine londes, late in Mr Collinges occupacion, *anno Domini* 1609   £7   6s.   8d.

And with 6s.0d. received of Thomas Smythe, furrier. And withe 12s.0d. received of Leonard Harryson, parcell of 16s.0d. in super in Mr Hilles accompt. And with £8 18s.4¾d. received of Mr Pynner, as a super there. And with 2s.0d. of Henry Landisdale. And with 8d. of Mr Derbye for a howse in the Long Bracklond. And with 6d. for Parkers house there. And with £1 8s.8d. received of Smythe and Spinke for the howse late Henry Brightes. All which sommes are parcell of the supers in Mr Hilles accompte   £11   8s.   2¾d.

Compounded for all former arrerages

And with 6s.0d. of Henry Landisdale. And with 8d. of Mr Derby for the said howse in the Long Bracklond, late ~~Johnsons~~ \Hugh Mathew/. And withe 6d. for Parkers howse there, being supers of former accomptes   7s.   2d.

And with £19 2s.11d. for the residue \of the supers/ in Mr Hilles accompt, not receyved   £19   2s.   11d.

Yerelie rentes

And with £1 0s.0d. received of Thomas Peake, for parcell of his rent not conteyned in the rentall   £1   0s.   0d.

And with £261 16s.5½d. for the whole yeres rent and revenues of the towne landes, as appearithe by the rentall thereof   [104]£261 16s.   5½d.

Encreased rentes

And with £1 13s.4d. received of John Kinge, as an increased rent for land late in possession of Mr Collinge   £1 13s.   4d.

Mariages

And withe £6 3s.4d. receyved of James Wright, keper of the Guildhall, for mariage dynners kept there   £6   3s.   4d.

---

[102] The original account survives and is H2/3/4/9.

[103] The person who wrote the original account preferred the vernacular and wrote 'The Chardge', H2/3/4/9.

[104] In the original this total is given as £261 18s.5½d., H2/3/4/9.

Rent

And with £10 0s.0d. receyved of Mr Nicholas Bell by waie of
antecipacion for his half yeres rent of the Angell, to be due at
the feast of the Annunciacion of the Virgin Marie next, to be
bestowed upon reparacions there | £10 | 0s. | 0d.

Guift Mr Gippes

And of £20 0s.0d. given by Mr John Gippes for a stocke to set the
poore on worke[105] | £20 | 0s. | 0d.

Rent boare, rye, wine

And with a fat boare of Thomas Peake, parcell of his rent — A boare
And with a combe of rye of William Ullet, parcell of his rent — A combe of rye
And with a gallon of wine of John Revell — A gallon of wine

> Summa oneris £339 18s.11d., a boare, a combe
> of rye and a gallon of wine whereof

Poore

The said accomptant dothe praie allowans of 10s.0d., given to
Hargrave in relief in the tyme of his sickenes, at Mr Walkers
request | 10s. | 0d.

Reparacions

And of 2s.9d. for nayles, and for removinge the table in the
Guildhall | 2s. | 9d.
And of 15s.1d. paied to [106]Mayhewe for bricke, lyme and masons
worke abowt the table[107] in the Guildhall | 15s. | 1d.

Aide

And of 3s.4d. for the Princes aide for St Peters, \paied to the
constable/ | 3s. | 4d.

Paymentes

And of 2s.0d. given to a woman that kept the hangman, for his
buryall | 2s. | 0d.
And of 3s.4d. paied to Welham for making the sincke[108] in the
Churcheyard | 3s. | 4d.
And of £100 0s.0d. paied to Mr Helye and Mr Sotherby for their
yeres stipend, as preachers of the 2 parishes in Bury, endid at
Christmas last | £100 | 0s. | 0d.
And of £1 0s.0d. to Mr Jewell for his yeres stipend as mynister of
St Maries parishe | £1 | 0s. | 0d.

---

[105] See Appendix 8, *sub* 1610.
[106] The Christian name William is given in the original account, H2/3/4/9.
[107] I think this must be the table with the feoffees' names mentioned in the Candlemas guild accounts, where 2s.9d. was spent in the account for the year ending Michaelmas 1524 for the table with the feoffees' names hanging in the hall, Bodl. MS Suff. b.1, f.13v., photostat copy of this at the SROB, Acc. 515.
[108] The word 'cleane' is written between 'making' and 'the' in the original account, H2/3/4/9.

Plate I. Jankin Smith, d.1481. Bought by the feoffees in 1616, and possibly painted by Fenn. It is at least possible that an original fifteenth-century portrait was copied in 1616. Photo Graham Portlock; reproduced by kind permission of St Edmundsbury Museum Services.

Thomas Bright sometime draper of this Towne a worthy Benefactor whoe gaue for the
benefit of the towne the Inheritance of a portion of Tythes worthe ₤ lb p anum and an equall
part of his goods as much as he gaue any of his children whith amounted to /CCC. ₤.
1587

Plate II. Thomas Bright the elder, died 1587. Bought by the feoffees in 1616, and
perhaps painted by Fenn. Bright gave tithes in Foxearth, Essex, and £300 to the
feoffees. Photo Graham Portlock; reproduced by kind permission of St
Edmundsbury Museum Services.

Plate III. King James I, 1566–1625. Shows the three charters he granted to Bury St Edmunds on the table beside him. Bought by the feoffees in 1616 from Mr Fenn. Photo Graham Portlock; reproduced by kind permission of St Edmundsbury Museum Services.

Plate IV. Arms of James I. Bought by the feoffees in 1616 from Mr Newman of Cambridge. At some later date, the 'I' for James was altered to 'C'. Photo Graham Portlock; reproduced by kind permission of St Edmundsbury Museum Services.

Plate V. Edmund Jermyn of Denham, d.1573. Gave an annuity of £40 a year out of the manor of Torksey in Lincolnshire. The portrait, by an unknown artist, shows him dressed in the height of fashion. Photo Graham Portlock; reproduced by kind permission of St Edmundsbury Museum Services.

Plate VI. Sir Nicholas Bacon, 1509–79. Born in Suffolk, Sir Nicholas had many interests in the town. He was Lord Keeper of the Great Seal from 1558 until his death. This portrait, by an unknown artist, shows the embroidered purse in which the Great Seal of England was kept. By courtesy of the National Portrait Gallery, London.

Plate VII. Sir Thomas Kitson of Hengrave, 1540–1602. This portrait was painted
by Gower, 1573, when Kitson was active as a feoffee. Because of his recusancy his
name was not included in the general feoffments after 1582. Copyright Tate,
London 2002.

Plate VIII. Thomas Bright the younger, d.1626. This picture is not named, but the date, 1624, is the year in which he made a handsome gift of property in the Market Place. He took the lead in gaining the incorporation of Bury St Edmunds as a borough. Photo Graham Portlock; reproduced by kind permission of St Edmundsbury Museum Services.

[f.19r. old number 36]

Bedwalles anuytie

And of £51 5s.0d. paied to John Bedwall for arrerages of rent
incurred, assigned by the Comissioners upon the Statute of
Charitable Uses[109]

£51 5s. 0d.

And of £8 0s.0d. paied him for his half yeres annuytie, paiable at
the feast of th'annunciacion of the Virgin Marie last past

£8 0s. 0d.

Receivors fee

And of 15s.0d. for the receyvors fee

15s. 0d.

Taske

And of £24 0s.0d. paied for the taske of this towne \in Maye last/

£24 0s. 0d.

And of 5s.0d. paied for taske to Westley for St Peters

5s. 0d.

And of 1s.6d. for taske to Westley, for landes in Robert Reves
occupacion

1s. 6d.

Paymentes

And of £1 10s.0d. given to Mr Richardson[110] for a fee for a
mocion in the Chauncerie in Mr Collings suyte there, against
the feoffees

£1 10s. 0d.

Reparacions

And of £1 6s.6d. for reparacions of certeine almes howses in the
Northegate Strete, Short Brackelond and abowte Foxgilles
Howse

£1 6s. 6d.

Angell

And of £1 3s.4d. paied to John Kinge for casementes abowt the
Angell

£1 3s. 4d.
[altered]

Paymentes

And of £1 9s.0d. in a guift given to the justices of assises by Mr
Bright, as appearithe by his note

£1 9s. 0d.

Poore

And of £3 0s.10d. given by Mr Bright to certeine poore folkes, as
appearethe by his note, and paied him by this receyvor

£3 0s. 10d.

Quayle

And of 15s.0d. paied to the keper of the Spittil howse

15s. 0d.

Rent

And of 8d. paied to the bailief of Thedwestre for ~~taske~~ \rent/ for
Leyers in Rowgham

8d.

And of 3d. paied to the bailiefe of Forneham All Seinctes for
Sherehall yard at Catshall for 2 yeres rent endid at Michelmas
last

3d.

---

[109] On 3 January 1610 the feoffees noted that John Bedwall had been granted a rent charge of £16 a year
out of Brettes in Hepworth by the Commissioners. Three years had passed since the order was made, but
no payment had been made and it was agreed that a further £2 should be paid him for forbearing the
payment, Minutes H2/6/2.1, p.32.

[110] In the original Mr Richardson was identified as the Recorder of Bury St Edmunds, H2/3/4/9. See
Notes on People for (Sir) Thomas Richardson.

Reparacions

And of ł £2 2s.6d. paied to Mr Barker for reparacions, as by a note
under the handes of Mr Bright, Mr Gippes and Mr Derby
appearithe   £2   2s.   6d.

And of £1 12s.0d. paied to Mr Pynner for reparacions done at St
Peters   £1 12s.   0d.

Taske

And of £24 0s.0d. paied for[111] the taske of this towne in
November last   £24   0s.   0d.

Paymentes

And of 4s.0d. for a writt for Mr Barker against Wragge, for money
due to the towne[112]   4s.   0d.

Gostling

And of £20 0s.0d. paied to Mr Gostling for parte of the purchase
of the Angell[113]   £20   0s.   0d.

Paymentes

And of 7d.[114] for paper left in the hall   7d.

And of £10 0s.0d. paied to Mr William Cropley for the loane of
£100 0s.0d.   £10   0s.   0d.

Wright

And of £1 5s.0d. paied to James Wright, keper of the Guildhall,
for his half yeres wages endid at Michelmas last   £1   5s.   0d.

And of 3s.4d. paied to him for candle and woode spent at the hall   3s.   4d.

Paymentes

And of 1s.0d. given him to ride to Sir John Heigham, knight to
give him notice of the daie of the accompt   1s.   0d.

Clerkes fee

And of 10s.0d. paied to the clerke[115] of the hall for his fee   10s.   0d.

Prisoners

And of £1 0s.0d. given to the prisoners in the gaole in biefe and
breade   £1   0s.   0d.

Poore

And of 2s.6d. given to Welham, being sicke   2s.   6d.

And of 1s.0d. given to John Compton, beinge sicke   1s.   0d.

Reparacions of churches

And of £1 0s.0d. paied to the churche wardens of St Maries
churche for reparacions of the same   £1   0s.   0d.

---

[111] In the original account, instead of 'paied for' there was written 'which I left with Mr Pynner,
Alderman, to discharge', H2/3/4/9.

[112] The word 'bidell', beadle, follows 'town' in the original account, H2/3/4/9.

[113] The information that the money was left with Mr Nonne to pay to Mr Gostling is given in the original account, H2/3/4/9.

[114] Here the original reads 2d., but at the end another entry relates to 4d. for a quire of paper, H2/3/4/9.

[115] The original makes it clear that Mr Cooke was the clerk, H2/3/4/9.

And of £1 0s.0d. paied to the churche wardens of St James
churches [*sic*] for the reparacions of the same   £1   0s.   0d.

Angell reparacions

And of £3 6s.9d. for reparacions done at the Angell, as appearithe
by Mr Revels bill   £3   6s.   9d.

Armour

And of 4s.0d. paied to Alman, the cutler, for skowringe the
armour this yere   4s.   0d.

[*f.19v.*]

Charges of the dynner

And of £5 4s.6d for the charges of the dynner at th'accompt   £5   4s.   6d.

And of 11s.0d. paied for wine spent at the same accompt   11s.   0d.

Paymentes

And of 5s.0d. allowed to Mr Hill, the last receyvor, for a
surplusage in his accompt, more than the rentall   5s.   0d.

Old supers

And of £19 2s.11d. being the supers of the last accompt, before in
charge, and not receyved by this accomptant   £19   2s.   11d.

A gallon of wine

And of a gallon of wine spent at the dynner   A gallon of wine

A boare

And of a boare delivered to Mr Alderman Pynner   A boare

       Summa allocacionis £288 3s.10d., a gallon of wine and a boare

       Sic debet £51 15s.1d. and a combe of rye whereof

Supers *de novo*

There remeynethe in the handes of Nicholas Bell for the yeres rent
of the Angell ended at Michelmas last. **Discharged *ut patet in
proximo compoto***   £17   0s.   0d.

And in the handes of Mr Pynner for the half yeres rent of St
Peters, paiable at the feast of the birthe of Christ[116] or within 20
daies after **Satisfied *ut patet* in Mr Brights and Mr Barkers
accomptes**   £8 18s.   5d.

And in the handes of Mr Henry Collinge for a yeres rent of Salters
land endid at Michelmas last   £5   0d.   0d.

And of John Bridon for a gardeine at Sparowe Hill   2s.   0d.

And in the handes of Sir Robert Jermyn, knight, for the yeres rent
of 21 acres *et dimidia* of land in Hepworthe endid at
Michelmas last   10s.   4d.

And of him for a peece of land there callid Russhes   9d.

And for an almes howse in the Northegate Strete, late Siggers   4s.   0d.

And of Giles Barker for a yeres rent of a cotage in Hepworthe due
at Michelmas last **Letton to Sporle *ideo vacat***   6d.

And of Leonard Harryson for an almes howse in Colledge Strete   16s.   0d.
   Paid in *proximo compoto*

---

116   The writer of the original account was content to write Christmas, H2/3/4/9.

Supers

And for an almes howse in Northegate Strete, late Widowe Chittinges	4s.	0d.
And for 6[117] almes howses in the Garlond Strete, now burnt downe	18s.	8d.
And in the handes of Mr Mallowes, for a yeres rent of a howse, gardeine and close in the Westgate Strete, endid at the feast of St Michaell th'archaungell last. **Answered in *proximo compoto***	£3 5s.	0d.
And of Thomas Rose for ~~the~~ \part of his/ rent for a yere of a howse and close in the Risbygate Strete, then endid **£1 10s.0d. *unde* paied Mr Barkers accompt**	£1 15s.	0d.
And ~~of~~ for the haulf yeres rent of landes, late in th'occupacion of Mr Hamond, due at Michelmas last	£2 0s.	0d.
And of James Smythe, esquire, for a piece of ground in Horse Market[118]		6d.
And for a stall in the market, late occupied by William Jellowe	2s.	0d.
And of Mr Thomas Coell for the yeres rent of a howse, called the Castle, in Roger Wrights occupacion	3s.	4d.
And of Widowe Grigges for the rent of a howse in Northegate Strete		6d.
And of William Scott for ground nere his howse	2s.	6d.
And of John Shawe for a gardeine in the Sowthegate Strete, late in the possession of Oliver Ions	3s.	4d.
And of Robert Mans for a peece of ground in Skynners Lane, nere his howse, late in the possession of Mrs Cotton		1d.

[f.20r. old number 68]

Supers

And of Mr Raven for a peece of ground in Brentgovell Streete, late Thomas Brunwines	3s.	4d.
And of th'executors of Robert Sparke, baker, for ground in Mr Andrewes street	6s.	8d.
And of Richard Heigham for a howse in the Churchegate Strete	£1 0s.	0d.
And of Charles Derby for ground in the Northegate Streete	5s.	0d.

Summa of the supers £46[119] 1s.11d.

Sic debet clare £8 13s.2d. and a combe of rye not delivered by him. **Which £8 13s.2d. was delivered to Mr Thomas Bright, the receyvor for the yere to come, with an obligacion made by Avis with a suretie \for payment/ of £10 0s.0d., parcell of Kemboldes legacie, to be answered upon his accompt.**[120]

---

[117] The original account has the 6 altered to 7 and has the additional information 'which were but foure ~~new built~~ and two other not built', H2/3/4/9.

[118] The words 'late Mr Mountford' are in the original account, H2/3/4/9.

[119] This was altered from £43 in H2/3/4/9.

[120] The original account was signed by William Cooke, Francis Pynner, John Hill, Thomas Bright and Bennet Barker, H2/3/4/9. At the end of the third page of the original account an entry relating to payment of subsidy was deleted: ~~And for the subsedye payd to Mr Skirre for the townehall xxs.~~

[f. 20v.]

Mr Thomas Bright, 1611[121]

The accompt of Mr Thomas Bright, receyvor of the rentes and revenues belonginge to the common use and benefit of the towne of Burie St Edmunde, \made/ and yelded upp the last daye of December in the ninethe yere of the reign of our soveraign lord Kinge James, [*1611*] for one whole yere then endid

Onus
Inprimis the said accomptant chargithe himsilf with £8 13s.2d. by him received of Mr John Boldero, the last receyvor, upon the determynacion of his accompt as appeare in the foot of the same accompt

£8 13s. 2d.

Old Supers
And withe £43 1s.11d., beinge the whole somme of the supers upon diverse men particulerlie named in th'accompt of Mr John Boldero, the last receyvor

£43 1s. 11d.

Kembold
And with £10 0s.0d. by him receyved of Edmunde Avis, by the handes of Mr Mallowes, as parcell of £100 0s.0d., and the last payment thereof, given by Peter Kembold and due in the yere of Our Lord 1610

£10 0s. 0d.

Arrerages of rent
And with 1s.0d. by him received of John Brydon,[122] by waie of composicion for certein arrerages of rent due by him for a small peece of ground at Sparrowe Hill, letton to him for the yerelie rent of 2s.0d., over and besides 2s.0d. likewise receyved by him as a super in the last accompt

1s. 0d.

The yerelie revenues
And with £262 3s.5½d., a gallon of wine, \a combe of rye/ and a boare, beinge the whole yeres rent and revenue of the towne lande, as by the rentall thereof appearithe

£262 3s. 5½d.
a gallon of wine,
a combe of rye
and a boare

And with £5 6s.8d. by him received of the occupiers of the londes late in the tenure of Mr Collinge, over and besides £10 0s.0d. conteyned in the rentall

£5 6s. 8d.

Mariages
And with £2 16s.8d. by him received of Mr Fraunces Pynner, late alderman,[123] for dyvers mariages at the Guildhall this yere

£2 16s. 8d.

---

121 Mr Bright himself entered his account into the account book.
122 On 14 July 1610 the feoffees agreed to enter a garden plot at Sparrow Hill for which John Bridon refused to pay the rent, and to lease it to someone else. Afterwards, however, it was agreed that John Bridon should lease it for eleven years at 2s. a year, and leave it fenced, Minute Book H2/6/2.1, p.32.
123 This entry suggests that the alderman still retained his ancient rights in the Guildhall.

Sale of Woode

And with 16s.0d. by him received for certene wood sold to Mr
Sporle upon the towne londes lying in Hepworthe   16s.   0d.
> *Summa oneris* £332 18s.10½d., a boare, a gallon
> of wyne and a combe of rye, whereof

Allocaciones

The said accomptaunt dothe praie allowans of theis
disbursementes and somes of money followinge, *videlicet*

Owtrentes and the tenthe of St Peters, due 1610 to the kinge

Of £1 18s.5½d. by him paied to Mr Mallowes, for rentes due to
the Kinges Majestie for certein of the towne londes, being
behind for one whole yere endid at Michelmas 1610, when Mr
Boldero was receyvor[124]   £1 18s. 5½d.

And of 10s.6d. for the tenthe due to His Majestie for St Peters.
And 4d. for the receyvor his acquittauns. And 4d. to his
doorekeper, laied owt by Mr Mallowes in the same yere, when
Mr Boldero was receyvor, and now paied againe to the said Mr
Mallowes by this accomptaunt   11s.   2d.

[f.21r., old number 56]

Bedwall, 1610

And of £9 0s.0d. by him paied to John Bedwall, whereof £8
0s.0d.in arrerage for his haulf yers anuytie due in the yere
whilest Mr Boldero was receyvor, and £1 0s.0d. for forbearing
the same and for his travell[125]   £9   0s.   0d.

Charges of suite in Chancerie, 1610

And of £2 15s.10d. by him paied to Mr Mallowes for divers
charges of suyte by him laied owte in the suyte brought against
the feoffees by Mr Colling in the Chauncerie, and due in the
yere whilest the said Mr Boldero was receyvor, as by the bill of
charges appearithe   £2 15s. 10d.

And of 5s.0d. paied to Mr Mallowes for 2 *sub poenaes*[sic] in the
same suite   5s.   0d.

Out rentes, 1610

And of 6d. paied by him to the bailiefe of the mannor of
Rowgham for the rent of parte of Leyers. And to the bailief of
the mannor of Forneham All Seintes for the rent of Shirehall
Yard at Catshall, due for one whole yere endid at Michelmas
1610, when Mr Boldero was receyvor   7½d.

Guift to the justices of assise, 1610

And of \£1 0s.0d. for/ 2 fatt lambes bought of Woode, the butcher,
and of 12s.0d. for six fat capons given to the judges at Lent
assises, when Mr Boldero was receyvor, and provided by Mr
Mallowes   £1 12s. 0d.

---

[124] Many things recorded in this account were paid for while Mr Boldero was accountant, but so far no
explanation for their omission from his account can be made.
[125] See n.109 above.

Clothing of the poore, 1610

And of £20 0s.0d., by him paied to Mr Mallowes, as so muche laid owt by him in the yere 1610, whilest Mr Boldero was receyvor, for the clothing of the poore according to the guift of Mr Thomas Bright th'elder, deceased, being agreid by the feoffees of the towne londes that for as muche as the £300 0s.0d. given by the said Thomas Bright was laied owt for the charges of obteyning the fee fearme of the Elemozyners Bearnes, and other thinges given by His Majestie, and which in tyme shall come to the generall benefit of this towne, that therefore yerelie, untill the said somme of £300 0s.0d. maie be raised againe of the rentes and profittes of the said towne londes, there shalbe allowed owt of the revenues of the same londes the yerelie some of £24 0s.0d. for the performans of the will of the said Thomas Bright[126]   £20   0s.   0d.

And of £3 6s.3d. laied owt in the same yere, 1610, for making of the coates of the same poore folke   £3   6s.   3d.

Mr Corder, mynister, 1610

And of £1 0s.0d. by him paied to Mr Boldero, the last accomptaunt, as so muche laied owt by the same Mr Boldero to Mr Corder, mynister of St James parishe, and omytted in his accompt   £1   0s.   0d.

Owt rentes

And of £1 18s.5½d. paied by this accomptaunt for the rentes due to the Kinges Majestie for one yere endid at Michelmas last   £1 18s. 5½d.

And of 10s.6d. paied by this accomptaunt for the tenthe of St Peters, due at Michelmas last, withe 4d. for the receyvors acquittauns and 4d. to his doore keper   11s.   2d.

And of 6d. paied to the bailye of the mannor of Rowgham for the rent of parte of Leyers, due for a yere endid at Michelmas last   6d.

And of 8d. paied to the bailie of the hundred of Thedwestre for the rent of some other parte of Leyers, due for one whole yere endid at Michelmas last   8d.

And of 1½d., paied to the bailie of the mannor of Forneham All Seinctes, for the rent of Shirehall Yard at Catshall, for one yere then ended   1½d.

[f.21v.]
Charge of suyte

And of £2 9s.8d. by him paied to Mr Mallowes for charges of suyte against Mr Colling expendid this yere   £2   9s.   8d.

Gostling

And of £20 0s.0d. by him paied to Mr Gostling for the redempcion of the Angell, according to the order of the Commissioners upon the Statute of Charitable Uses   £20   0s.   0d.

126   For discussion of the use of Thomas Bright's £300, see Introduction, p.xlviii.

Bedwall

And of £16 0s.0d. by him paied to Bedwall for one yeres anuytie
in regard of surrendring the lease he had of Hepworthe londes,
accordinge to the same Commissioners order   £16 0s.   0d.

Cropley

And of £10 0s.0d. by him paied for the use of £100 0s.0d.
borowed of Cropley   £10 0s.   0d.

Reparacions, Boyton

And of £22 18s.9d. by him paied to George Boyton and Edwarde
Boyton, plommers, for worke done by them at the Guildhall,
and for leade and sowder as by the billes of \Mr Henry Gippes/,
one of the surveiors[127] appointed this yere appearethe   £22 8s.   9d.

Reparacions

And of 17s.6d. paied to William Rowge for reparacions, done at
the howse wherein he dwelt, before the tyme of this accompt   17s.   6d.

And of £6 5s.7d. paied by this accomptaunt to the same surveyor,
and by his direcion at divers severall times, for reparacions and
worke done at Mr Helyes howse, and other howses belonging
to the towne, as by the particulers appeare   £6   5s.   7d.

Angell

And of £1 17s.6d. for 3 loades of white bricke to pave the hall at
the Angell, and of 4s.0d. for 3 loades of claye and one loade of
sand bought for that use, *in toto*   £2   1s.   6d.

And of 4s.0d. by him paide to Rose, the cleyer, for foure daies
worke done at the Angell   4s.   0d.

Preachers and Mynisters

And of £100 0s.0d. by him paied to Mr Bedell and Mr Helye,
preachers, for this yeres allowans   £100 0s.   0d.

And of £2 0s.0d. paied to Mr Jewell and Mr Corder mynisters of
Є the churches of St Maries and St James   £2   0s.   0d.

Reparacions of the churches

And of £2 0s.0d. paied to the churchewardens of the parishe
churches of St Marie and St James towardes the repayring of
the same churches   £2   0s.   0d.

Clothing of the poore

And of £19 16s.0d. for 22 dozens of greye bought for clothing of
the poore this present yere, according to the guift of the said
Mr Bright, deceased. And of £3 6s.1d. for making the same
clothes. And of £1 4s.8d. paied to Mr Robert Hynes for
lyninges and other thinges to fynishe the same clothes for the
poore. And of 6s.9d. paied to Mr Anthony Smithe for lyninges
and other thinges to fynishe the same clothes for the poore, *in
toto*   £24 13s.   6d.

---

[127] No such appointments are recorded in the Minute Book.

Quayle

And of £1 10s.0d. paied to Mother Quayle, governes of the Spittle
Howse, for hir wages due for this present yere, 1611 .... £1 10s. 0d.

Poore

And of £2 16s.8d. given at divers tymes to divers poore and nedie
persons for their relief in tymes of their sicknes, wantes and
necessities .... £2 16s. 8d.

And of £1 6s.8d. given to the overseers of the 2 parishes, for two
weekes to end the 4 of Januarie next, by the agreament of the
feoffees, to be so contynued for the winter quarter .... £1 6s. 8d.

Wages, Bradishe

And of £1 0s.0d. given to Robert Bradishe, the late hall keper, for
part of his yeres wages. And of 10s.0d. given to his wief, by
consent, to bury him. And of 10s.6d. for 7 yardes of ~~frise~~ gray
to clothe 3 of his litle children, *in toto* .... £2 0s. 6d.

[f.22r., old number [6]
Paymentes

And of 13s.6d. for the dynner of Mr Paman and others when the
metinge was by the arbitrators, for the hearing and ending of
the cause betwene the feoffees and Mr Colling, for Salters
land, in contraversie .... 13s. 6d.

Judges

And of £1 12s.0d. for a wether sheepe and 6 capons, given to the
judges at the assises in the time of the Lent last past .... £1 12s. 0d.

And of £1 13s.4d. for a wether sheepe and a salmon, given to the
judges at sommer assises laste .... £1 13s. 4d.

Paymentes

And of 1s.0d. given to a messenger sent to Sir Henry Buckenham
abowte the woodes in his occupacion .... 1s. 0d.

And of £2 18s.7d. for 2 suger loves and 2 dozen of quailes given
to His Majesties Atturney Generall at his being in Suffolk this
last sommer, and for the hier of a horse to send those things .... £2 18s. 7d.

The clerkes fee

And of 10s.0d. paied to the clerke of the entring this accompt .... 10s. 0d.

The receyvors fee

And of 15s.0d. for the fee of the receyvor, for collecting the rentes
within his charge .... 15s. 0d.

Reparacions

And of 3s.4d. paid to Meyer for worke in glasing at the Guildhall .... 3s. 4d.

The dynner

And of £6 3s.11d. for the expences of the feoffees at the tyme of
the taking of this accompt .... £6 3s. 11d.

A gallon of wine

And of a gallon of wine spent at the taking of this accompt .... A gallon of wyne

A boare

And of a boare given to Mr Revell, now alderman

   Summa allocacionum ~~£58 3s.7½d.~~ £274 15s.4d.,

   a boare and gallon of wyne

   Et sic debet £58 3s.7½d., and a combe of rye, whereof

A boare

Super *de antiquo*

[The notes beside this paragraph are in another hand]

There remaynethe of the old supers of Mr Boldero his accompt as

 followethe, *videlicet*

Bell discharged. Nicholas Bell £17 0s.0d. **Colling discharged by order of the Comissioners for Charitable Uses and of all other former arrerages.** Mr Colling £5 0s.0d. Sir Robert Jermyn 10s.4d. The same Sir Robert 9d. Giles Barker 6d. **Barker leaton to Sporle *ideo vacat.*** For the almes howses in the Northegate Strete and Garlond Strete £1 6s.8d. **Rose £1 10s.0d. inde paid *ut patet in compoto* Mr Barker by bond made for that and more by him, *videlicet* £4 5s.0d. for arrearages of his rent, *sic remanet* £2 15s.0d.** Thomas Rose £1 15s.0d. Mr James Smythe 6d. For a stall 2s.0d. Mr Thomas Coell 3s.4d. William Scott 2s.6d. Mr John Ravens 3s.4d. Th'executors of Robert Sparke 6s.8d. Richard Heigham £1 0s.0d. And Mr Charles Derby 5s.0d., *in toto*

£27 16s.   7d.

Super *de novo*

And there remaynethe ~~in the~~ unreceyved by this accomptaunt of the rentes conteyned in the rentall due for this yere, within the tyme of this accomptaunt, upon theis severall persons as followethe, *videlicet*

Discharged First £10 0s.0d. ~~due by~~ \of/ Nicholas Bell for his half yeres rent due at th'annunciacion of the Blessed Virgin Marie last past, and receyved by Mr John Boldero by waie of anticipacion, as appearithe by his accompt. **This receyved by Mr John Boldero *ut patet* in his accompt and by his entree and so discharged**

£10 0s.   0d.

And in th'andes of Mr Fraunces Pynner for part of his haulf yeres rent of St Peters land due at midsomer last, and remayning unpaied. **Paied *ut patet proximo compoto***

£4 10s.   0d.

The other moytie discharged upon the said composicion

And in th'andes of the same Mr Pynner for his haulf yeres rent to be due within 20 daies after the feast of the birthe of our Saviour Christ. **Answered by payment of £4 9s.3d., being the moytie by composicion upon surrender of his lease of St Peters, *ut patet in proximo compoto***

£8 18s.   5d.

[f.22v.]

And in the handes of Sir Robert Jermyn, knight, for his rent of 21 acres and haulf of lond in Hepworthe, due for one yere endid at Michelmas last

10s.   4d.

And in the handes of the same Sir Robert for a peece of land there callid the Russhes for the like tyme

9d.

And in th'andes of the occupiers of the almoyse howses in the Northegate Strete and Garlond Strete	£1	6s.	8d.
And in the handes of Giles Barker for his cotage in Hepworthe.			6d.
Leaton to Sporle *ideo vacat hic*			
And in the handes of Mr James Smythe for a peece of ground in the Horse Markett			6d.
And in th'andes of Henry Landisdale for a peece of ground there		2s.	0d.
Paied *ut patet* in Mr Pynners accompt			
And for a stall in the markett place		2s.	0d.
And in the handes of Mr Thomas Coell for parte of the howse callid the Castell		3s.	4d.
And in th'andes of William Scott for a peece of ground nere his howse		2s.	6d.
And in th'andes of Mr John Ravens for a peece of ground in Brentgovell Strete, late Thomas Brunwins		3s.	4d.
And in the handes of [*space*] Bridgeman, clerke, for a peece of ground in Mr Andrewes Strete, late Robert Sparkes		6s.	8d.
And in the handes of Richard Heigham for a howse in the Churchegate Strete	£1	0s.	0d.
And in the handes of Mr Charles Derby for a peece of ground in the Northegate Strete, which is within the general some of the rentall, thowghe stricken owt in the particuler of the same rentall		5s.	0d.

> *Summa* £26 9s.0d.
>
> *Summa* of all the supers £55 7s.7d.
>
> *Et sic debet de claro* £2 16s.0½d., which some was delivered to Mr Bennett Barker, receyvor for the yere now followinge, to be answered upon his accompt. And there remaynethe in Mr Brightes handes a combe of rye [*in another hand*] not delivered by him.

[*f.23r., old number 65*]

Mr Bennet Barker 1612

The accompt of Mr Bennet Barker, receyvor of the rentes and revenues belonging to the common use and benefit of the towne of Bury St Edmunde, made and yelded upp the fift daie of January in the tenthe yere of the reign of our soveraigne Lord Kinge James of England *etcetera* for one whole [*yere*] then endid, *anno Domini* 1612 [*1613*]

Onus

First the said accomptaunt dothe charge himsilf with £2 16s.0d. receyved by him of Mr Thomas Bright, the last receyvor, upon the determynacion of his accompt *ut patet in pede compoti sui*	£2 16s.		0d.

Arrerages

And with £4 10s.0d. receyved of Mr Pynner for arrerages of St Peters, due in Mr Brights accompt	£4 10s.		0d.
And with £4 9s.3d. receyved more of him for the fourthe part of the yeres rent of St Peters, then due as appearithe in the same accompt	£4 9s.		3d.

197

And with 6d. receyved of Mr Inman for a yeres rent for a peece of ground lyinge by Maide Water Lane, late Mr George Bolderoes — 6d.

And with £1 10s.0d. receyved of Thomas Rose, parcell of his dett for the arrerages of rent of a tenemente and close by the Spittlehowse, due by bond made for payment of £4 5s.0d. — £1 10s. 0d.

Receipt
And with £2 0s.0d. <deletion> receyved of Sir Henry Buckenham, knight, by Mr Alman for standes cut downe in Wardes Woode in Hepworthe — £2 0s. 0d.

Mariages
And with £7 0s.0d. received for mariage dynners in the Guildhall this yere — £7 0s. 0d.

Receipt
And with 10s.0d. received of Mr Firmyn[128] for parte of the charge of the Comission at the Angell in Bury for Foxherthe tithes — 10s. 0d.

Sale of woode
And with £11 12s.4d. received for part of the woode sold at Hepworthe this yere — £11 12s. 4d.

And with £17 15s.4d. more for woode sold there to Thomas Peake — £17 15s. 4d.

Receipt
And with 5s.0d. received of Thomas Golding, junior, for parte of reparacions done upon mending the waye throwghe the Sowthe Gate — 5s. 0d.

Old Supers
And with £55 7s.7d., being the whole supers in Mr Brights accompt, the last receyvor, bothe old and new there — £55 7s. 7d.

Yerelie rentes Bury, Barton and Rowgham
And with £20 0s.0d. received of Mr Webbe for the whole yeres rent of Cattishall endid at Michelmas last — £20 0s. 0d.

And with £6 10s.0d. received of Mrs Willowghbye for the yeres rent of Leyers, then due — £6 10s. 0d.

And with £33 6s.8d. received of Mrs Inman for a bearne and landes in the Sowthe fieldes et cetera — £33 6s. 8d.

And with £15 6s.8d. received of th'occupiers of the landes callid Salters landes and the landes, parcell of the new purchased landes, late in th'occupacion of Mr Collinges — £15 6s. 8d.

And with £3 6s.8d. received of Anthony Bumpsted for 2 tenementes in the Churchgate Strete — £3 6s. 8d.

And with 11s.9d. received of received of the Widowe Bradishe for the half yeres rent of the tenemente by the Guildhall, endid at Michelmas last — 11s. 9d.

And with 2s.0d. received of John Bridon for a plot of ground at Sparowe Hill — 2s. 0d.

---

128 Mr Firmyn was the parson at Foxearth who had been persuaded to claim a right to tithes which had been given to the feoffees by Thomas Bright the elder. See Introduction, p.li.

Hepworthe yerelie rentes

And with £53 6s.6d. received of Thomas Peake for landes in
  Hepworthe

£53 6s. 6d.
and a boare

And with £2 3s.4d. received of Sir Henry Buckenham, knight, for
  woode ground there

£2 3s. 4d.

And with 2s.4d. received more of him for landes and pasture

2s. 4d.

And with £6 0s.0d. received of Mr Sporle for Greate Stubbings,
  Larkes tenemente and Lomes Land there

£6 0s. 0d.

And with £2 0s.0d. received of John Deye for landes in
  Hepworthe

£2 0s. 0d.

And with 2s.0d. received of Lawrence Coldham for landes there

2s. 0d.

And with 10s.4d. received of Sir Robert Jermyn, knight, for
  landes there

10s. 4d.

And with 9d. more of him

9d.

And with £5 12s.6d. received of Frost for landes there

£5 12s. 6d.

And with £2 0s.0d. reveived of Humfrey Linge for landes there

£2 0s. 0d.

And with 8d. received of Stepin [sic] Parkyns for a howse and
  ground there

8d.

Burye

And with 13s.4d. received of Robert King for a tenement in Bury
  in Colledg Strete

13s. 4d.

And with 16s.0d. of the Widowe Harryson for a tenement there

16s. 0d.

Almeshowses

And with 8s.0d. for 2 tenementes in Northegate Strete, in the
  occupacion of the Widowe Syger, Chittinge and Seaman

8s. 0d.

And with 1s.0d. of John Baylys for half yeres rent due at
  Michelmas last for one of the new erected almes howses in
  Garlond Strete

1s. 0d.

And with 6d. of the Widowe Shippe for half yeres rent then due
  for another of the same new almes howses there

6d.

[f.23v]

And with 2s.6d. of Stephin Eagle for half yeres rent then due for
  another of the same new almes howses there

2s. 6d.

And with 1s.0d. of Dodd for half yeres rent for another of the
  same new almes howses

1s. 0d.

Yerelie rentes

And with £3 5s.0d. received of Mr John Mallowes for a
  tenemente, close and gardene in the Westgate Strete

£3 5s. 0d.

And with £2 6s.8d. for parte of an ortyard in Mr Andrewe Strete
  received of th'executors of John Cadge

£2 6s. 8d.

And with £2 6s.8d. received of William Ullet for a bearne and the
  residue of the same ortyard

£2 6s. 8d.

And with £4 0s.0d. and a combe of rye received more of him for
  close at Stamford Bridge

£4 0s. 0d.
a combe of rye

And with £2 10s.0d. of Thomas Rose for a cotage by the hospitall
  and the hospitall close

£2 10s. 0d.

[The yearly rents, continued]

And with £3 0s.0d. received of William Rowge for a tenemente by St James churche	£3	0s.	0d.
And with a gallon of wine of Mr John Revell	A gallon of wyne		
And with £4 0s.0d. of Mr Hamond for landes in th'occupacion of Baker in Sowthe Field	£4	0s.	0d.
And with £14 14s.0d. received of Mr Blagge for landes \late/ in th'occupacion of Mr Barber in th'East Field	£14	14s.	0d.
And with £10 0s.0d. received of William Ullet for landes in the West Field, late in th'occupacion of Mr Barber	£10	0s.	0d.
And with £4 0s.0d. received of William Gilly for landes in the fields of Horningeserthe in Wyardes possession	£4	0s.	0d.
And with 2s.0d. for a stall in the market, late in th'occupacion of William Jellowe		2s.	0d.
And with £12 18s.0d. received of Thomas Turnor for landes in his occupacion	£12	18s.	0d.
And with £8 0s.0d. received of Mr Robert Reve for the Grange landes and bearne in his occupacion	£8	0s.	0d.
And with £1 0s.0d. received of Thomas Baker for a howse and ortyard in the Rainegate Strete	£1	0s.	0d.
And with 6d. of Mr James Smythe for ground by the ~~How~~ Horse Markett			6d.
And with 2s.0d. of Henry Landisdale for ground there		2s.	0d.
And with 6d. received of Mr Inman for a peece of ground by Maidewater Lane			6d.
And with 6s.8d. of Mr Bridgeman for ground in Mr Andrewes Strete		6s.	8d.
And with 4s.0d. received of Mr Walker for a howse and ground in Punche Lane		4s.	0d.
And with £1 0s.0d. of Richard Heigham for a howse in Churchegate Strete	£1	0s.	0d.
And with 5s.0d. of Mrs Heyward for a tenemente nere hir howse and a peece of ground nere the Teyvene		5s.	0d.
And with 6d. of John Parker for a tenemente in Longe Brackelonde			6d.
And with 8d. of Mr Charles Derby for a tenemente there, late Hughe Mathewes			8d.
And with 6d. of Margaret Grigges for a tenemente nere the Northe Gate			6d.
And with £20 0s.0d. received of Mr Nicholas Bell for the Angell	£20	0s.	0d.
And with £2 17s.4d. received of Mr Cole, the husband of Henry Brightes widowe, for tenementes in Skynners Lane	£2	17s.	4d.
And with £6 0s.0d. received of James Kent, 2 capons and a gallon of wyne for a tenemente in Cooke Rowe	£6	0s.	0d. and 2s.0d. for the capons
And with 3s.4d. of Mr Thomas Coell for the Castle		3s.	4d.
And with 2s.6d. of William Scott for ground nere his howse		2s.	6d.
And with 3s.4d. of John Shawe for a gardene in Sowthegate Strete, late Oliver Ions		3s.	4d.

And with £1 4s.0d. of Mr Bridgeman for landes late in the tenure of Thomas Overend	£1 4s.	0d.
And with 1d. of Robert Mance for a peece of ground in Skynners Lane, late in the occupacion of Mrs Cotton, lying by his howse there		1d.
And with 3s.4d. of Mr Ravens for ground lying by Brentgovell Streete, late in th'occupacion of Thomas Brunwyn	3s.	4d.
And with 1s.0d. of Mr Darcy for ground in his tenure in Northegate Strete	1s.	0d.

Summa oneris £366 0s.1d., a boare, 2 gallons of wyne and a combe of rye, whereof

[f.24r., old number 54]

Paimentes, tenthe and outrentes

The said accomptaunt praiethe allowans of 10s.6d. for the tenthe of St Peters, paied to the Kings Majestie for this yere, and 4d. for th'acquitauns, and 4d. to the dore keper, *in toto*	11s.	2d.
And of 8d. paied for the rent of Leyers to the Bailief of the hundred of Thedwistrye		8d.
And of 6d. to Sir Robert Drury, knight, for rent to the Mannor of Rowgham		6d.
And of £1 18s.5½d. paied to Mr Mallowes for the Kinges Majesties rentes in Bury, and for Leyers in Rowgham	£1 18s.	5½d.

Reparacions

And of 1s.8d. paied to John Coxsedge, due the last yere, for a longrayle and two postes upon th'Eastgate Bridge	1s.	8d.

Angell

And of 3s.6d. to him then for planckes for the Angell stable	3s.	6d.
And of 3s.6d. for bourd and makinge of the stayers in the hall at the Angell	3s.	6d.
And of 2s.8d. paied to Godderd for a short rayle and post and settinge them on th'Eastgate Bridge	2s.	8d.
And of 8d. for a locke for the same		8d.

Foxerthe tithes

And of 1s.0d. paied for conveying a lettre to Teversham abowt Foxherthe tythes	1s.	0d.
And of 14s.7d. given to Mr Sporle and his servauntes for Mr Bright and Mr Mallowes and this accomptaunt, \beinge/ there sondrie tymes, and for there horsemeate	14s.	7d.

Paymentes

And of £1 17s.0d. paied for a calf and wether to Sellond, the butcher, for the Lord Cook[129]	£1 17s.	0d.
And of £1 16s.0d. paied to Harrold for two swans and a freshe salmon	£1 16s.	0d.
And of 5s.0d. given to Inglishe for his horse hire to Hepworthe, and for measureing the ground in Linges occupacion	5s.	0d.
And of 12s.0d. paied for a booke of Statutes	12s.	0d.

---

[129] Once again a present is given to Sir Edward Coke, Chief Justice of the Common Pleas.

Mynisters and preachers

And of £100 0s.0d. paied to Mr Bedle and Mr Helye, preachers in
the two parishes, for their whole yeres stipend, now endid £100 0s. 0d.

And of £4 0s.0d. paied to Mr Corder and Mr Jeoll, as their
allowans owt of Mr Tassels \guift/ and towardes their
dwelling[130] £4 0s. 0d.

Paymentes Quayle

And of 15s.0d. paied to the Widowe Quayle for hir half yeres
wages for the sicke howse 15s. 0d.

Clothing of the poore, Mr Brightes guift

And of £20 15s.0d, paied for 24 dozens for the clothing of the
poore by Mr Brights guift £20 15s. 0d.

And of £4 4s.8d. paied for making of the apparell as appearithe by
the billes £4 4s. 8d.

And of £1 0s.6d. for lyning for them, as by the billes appearithe £1 0s. 6d.

Paymentes

And of 1s.6d. paied to old Frogge for Mr Pamans charges at the
Beare when he came abowt the towne affaiers 1s. 6d.

Paymentes, Foxherthe tithes,[131] Gostling

And of 3s.4d. paied to Inglishe when he servid the *subpoena* upon
Mr Firmyn and Mr Carter for Foxherthe tithes 3s. 4d.

And of £20 0s.0d. paied to Mr Coell and Mr Tillot for Mr
Gostling for the Angell £20 0s. 0d.

And of 5s.0d. paied to the clerk for part of the charge of the
writing of the feofement from Scot, and the lease made to him
by assent of the Feoffees 5s. 0d.

Bowman

And of 16s.3d. for a yard and half \an ell/ of ~~clothe~~ broad clothe
for the porters livery 16s. 3d.

And of 7s.0d. paied for his cognizauns[132] 7s. 0d.

And of £2 10s.0d. paied to him for his yeres wages £2 10s. 0d.

Paymentes

And of 5s.10d. paied to Cobbe for mending of fier buckettes of
lether 5s. 10d.

And of 4d. paied for a quayer of paper 4d.

Collinge

And of 4s.0d. given to Cole for caryinge the Lord Cookes warrant
to Mr Colling to appeare at th'assises 4s. 0d.

~~Foxerthe tithes~~

And of £1 14s.8d. paied to Mr Revels man upon Rabyes and
Cromwells bill from[*sic*] making the pillarye £1 14s. 8d.

---

[130] On 31 December 1611, it was agreed that the preachers should live in the houses by St James's
church and that the ministers should each have £1 a year in recompense of any interest that they might
have in these houses, Minutes H2/6/2.1, p.33.

[131] See Introduction, p.li.

[132] This was a badge. See Glossary.

And of 1s.2d. given to Cole for carying a lettre to Sir George Waldgrave, knight | 1s. | 2d.

Foxerthe tithes
And of 2s.6d. given to Cole for carying a lettre to Mr Tillot, and to serve the Commissioners warrant upon George Ford at Disse abowt the tithes of Foxherthe | 2s. | 6d.

Collinge[133]
And of 4s.0d. paied to the bailief for warning the jurye abowt Mr Collinges lease | 4s. | 0d.

And of 7s.0d. given to the jurye when they gave in their verditt | 7s. | 0d.

And of 2s.0d. paied to Sir John Heighams and Mr Pamans horsemen the daie before the metinge | 2s. | 0d.

And of £1 10s.0d. given to Inglishe for warninge diverse witnesses and giving them 1s.0d. a peece towards their charges | £1 10s. | 0d.

Paymentes
And of 4d. paied more for a quaire of paper | 4d.

And of £7 0s.0d. paied to Mr Bell for the dynners and horsemeat of Sir Robert Gardener, Sir Robert Jermyn, Sir John Heigham, Sir Henry Warner, Mr Tillot and Mr Paman, and the jury at severall tymes, as appearith by his bill | £7 0s. | 0d.

And of 14s.10d. paied to Robert Glover for the charge of Mr Recorder at that tyme, as appearithe by his bill | 14s. | 10d.

[f.24v.]

Paymentes, Foxherthe tithes
And of £3 16s.10d. paied for parte of the charge of the dynner, breakefast and horsemeate of the Comissioners, at Long Melford, abowt the tythes of Foxherthe and the charges of the witnesses, as by bill appearethe | £3 16s. | 10d.

And of 8s.0d. paied to the clerke for entring of 4 deposicions of 4 deponentes | 8s. | 0d.

And of £1 4s.4d. paied for the charge of the Comissioners, and their horsemeate, at the Whight Horse in Bury, 5 *Octobris*, abowt the said tithes | £1 4s. | 4d.

And of 8s.0d. more for th'entring of 4 deposicions of 4 deponentes given to the clerkes | 8s. | 0d.

Bedwall
And of £16 0s.0d. paied to Bedwall for his yeres annuytie due at Michelmas last | £16 0s. | 0d.

Poore
And of 10s.0d. paied to Gager in parte of £1 0s.0d. for healing of Quayles sore legg | 10s. | 0d.

And of 3s.2d. paied for repayring the Cage | 3s. | 2d.

And of 1s.6d. paied for a bucket for the Guildhall well | 1s. | 6d.

And of 8s.7d. paied for mendinge of the chanell nere the Abbeygate, and for [?]foure stones setting against the churche doore | 8s. | 7d.

---

133 See Introduction, p.xlvi.

And of £1 14s.10d. paied to Mr Pynner, upon the note of Mr
  Mallowes   £1 14s. 10d.

Woode makinge at Hepworthe[134]

And of 18s.2d. paied to Mr Sporle for making of 900 of woode
  and 15 fagottes   18s.   2d.
And of 13s.0d. paied to Frost for making of 680 faggottes   13s.   0d.
And of 311 faggottes for tithe
And of £17 15s.4d. as money still in the handes \of/ Thomas
  Peake for 22 hundred and 27 fagottes   £17 15s.   4d.

Churchwardens

And of £2 0s.0d. paied to the churchewardens of the two parishe
  churches in Burye   £2   0s.   0d.

Clerkes fee

And of 10s.0d. paied to the clerke for his fee   10s.   0d.

Receyvors fee

And of 15s.0d. for the receyvors fee   15s.   0d.
And of 3s.2d. given to Cole for caryinge a lettre to Cambridge to
  Mr Barrowe   3s.   2d.
And of 6d. to him for carying a lettre to Sir John Heigham to
  aquaint him with the daie of the accompt   6d.

Reparacions at the Angell

And of 13s.8d. paied to Mayer, the glasier, as money due to him
  longe since for worke done at the Angell   13s.   8d.
And of 7s.0d. paied to Stere for laying of the brickes at the Angell,
  when Mr Bright was receyvor   7s.   0d.
And with 3s.4d. paied to Milles for 3 combes, 2 busshels of lyme
  for that worke   3s.   4d.
And of 1s.0d. for a loade of sand   1s.   0d.
And of 13s.8d. more for other worke done at the Angell, as by bill
  appearithe   13s.   8d.
And of £1 18s.10d. paied to Disborowghe for making a new
  greate gate on the backe side of the Angell, and for a greate
  post, hookes, hingels and other thinges, *ut patet per billa*   £1 18s.   10d.
And of 1s.2d. to Wixe for nayles for the gates   1s.   2d.
And of £2 17s.4d. for repayring the howse of office, at the request
  of Sir John Heigham and other feoffees, and for mending the
  entry thereto, and for studdes, sparres, groundsels and staires,
  as by bill appearithe   £2 17s.   4d.
And of £2 5s.0d. for 3 loodes of tyle for covering the entrye and
  mending the howse   £2   5s.   0d.
And of 4s.6d. for carying awaie 9 loades of rubbishe of the
  chimney, fallen into the celler   4s.   6d.
And of 12s.0d. for 6 loades of sand and 6 loades of cleye for
  repayring the walles of the entrye, for pynnyng the celler, and
  making up the chymney, which was in part fallen downe   12s.   0d.

---

[134] The woods at Hepworth provided part of the feoffees' income as well as timber for building and repairs.

Plate 9. The Angel, as depicted on the first state of Kendall's print of Angel Hill, 1785. Reproduced by permission of Suffolk Record Office.

And of 15s.0d. for 15 combes of lyme, as by bill appearethe	15s.	0d.
And of £4 6s.8d. paied to the masons for their worke, dawbers, splentes, splent yarne and bricke, as by bill appearithe	£4 6s.	8d.
And of 16s.11d. paied to Bourne for lathe nayles, lathe and tyle pynne	16s.	11d.
And of 7s.2d. paied to Wixe for dogges and boltes of yron, *ut patet per billam*	7s.	2d.

Reparacions at Mr Helies howse

And of 19s.10d. paied to Mr Helye for reparacions done at his howse, *ut patet per billam*	19s.	10d.
And of £3 0s.6d. paied to Dister for 20 yerdes *dimidia* of sealing at 3s.0d. the yard	£3 0s.	6d.
And of 1s.10d. paied to him for quarters to staye the seeling	1s.	10d.

[*f. 25r., old number 63*]

Reparacions at Mr Heleys, Rowge, Bradishe, reparacions at Mr Juells howse

And of 9s.2d. paied to Slowman for joyntes, hengelles and latches, as by bill appearithe	9s.	2d.
And of 6s.0d. paied for bricke, morter, tyle and tyle pynne ~~em~~ bestowed at Mr Helyes howse, *ut patet per billam*	6s.	0d.
And of 4s.6d. for reparacions done at Rowges howse, *ut patet per billam*	4s.	6d.

205

And of 6s.0d. for reparacions done at the Widowe Bradishe howse *ut patet per billam*	6s.	0d.
And of 6s.8d. paied to Mr Juell for reparacions done abowt his howse, *ut patet per billam*	6s.	8d.
And of £2 2s.4d. paied for the repayring of his howse upon the fall of a chymney in the tempest, as by his bill appearithe	£2 2s.	4d.
And of £1 12s.0d. paied to Welham for makinge a well for Mr Jewell at 6s.0d. the fadame	£1 12s.	0d.
And of 6s.0d. paied for carying awaie the meynor	6s.	0d.

Reparacions

And of 1s.0d. paied for candle	1s.	0d.
And of 1d. for a basket to carie awaie the meynor		1d.
And of 6s.0d. paied for a curble of elme for the bottome of the well	6s.	0d.
And of 10s.0d. paied to Fraunces for a curble to drawe upp the water, *ut patet per billam*	10s.	0d.
And of 14s.0d. for 14 combes of lyme for the making of the well and pynnyng the howse	14s.	0d.
And of 4s.0d. for foure loades of sand	4s.	0d.
And of 6s.8d. for a barrell, bucket and winche and rope	6s.	8d.
And of £1 14s.0d. for 6 ħ loades of brick endes, and for one loade of whole brickes, and for caryage, to pynne the well	£1 14s.	0d.
And of 2s.6d. paied to Richard Ward for a loade of flynt, and the caryage, for the well	2s.	6d.

Reparacions

And of 1s.6d. for two loades of cleye for the Spittle Howse	1s.	6d.
And of 10s.8d. paied to Rabye for grounselling and other worke there done, *ut patet per billam*	10s.	8d.
And of 15s.0d. for a loade of tyle for repayring the new almes howses	15s.	0d.
And of 1s.7d. for mending [*?*]some casementes at the Guildhall	1s.	7d.
And of 3s.0d. paied to Miller for lyme to amend the floare	3s.	0d.
And of 8s.0d. to Stele for tyling and tyle pynne for repayring the new almes howses	8s.	0d.
And of 1s.6d. paied for lyme for the tyling	1s.	6d.
And of 1s.0d. for a loade of sand	1s.	0d.

Reparacions

And of 17s.0d. for brick, morter, sand and 3 loades of gravell, and for wor[k]manshipp, to Coe for mending the Sowthe Gate passage throwghe it	17s.	0d.
And of 5s.6d. to Younges for mending the glasse in the Guildhall	5s.	6d.
And of £1 0s.0d. paied to Cropley for mending one of the arches under the almes howse upon the Eastgate bridge[135]	£1 0s.	0d.

Foxherthe tithes paymentes

And of 10s.1d. given to Inglishe for serving of a subpoena upon Mr Felgate and Mr Sidaye of Bures, and giving knowledge to Mr Firmyn and Mr Carter of the Commission	10s.	1d.

---

[135] This is shown on Godfrey's print of the East Gate.

Poore

And of 19s.5d. given to diverse poore people this yere	19s.	5d.
And of £1 9s.6d. given to divers poore people in th'east and northe wardes, in part of Kemboldes guift	£1 9s.	6d.

Paymentes, Foxherthe tithes

And of £15 0s.0d. paied to Mr Mallowes for money paied by the assignment of diverse of the feoffees, for the towne busynes	£15	0s.	0d.
And of £10 0s.0d. paied to Mr Cropley for use money	£10	0s.	0d.
And of £9 16s.2d. paied to Mr Mallowes for charges of suyt for Foxherthe tithes, *ut patet per billam*	£9 16s.		2d.
And of £1 15s.4d. paied to Mr Bright for charges of suyte by him layed owt abowt Foxherthe tythes	£1 15s.		4d.
And of 12s.0d. given to Cole for going to Redgrave, and from thens to Mr Felgates howse, and from thens to Norwich to serve a *subpena* upon him, and for his examynacion for Foxherthe tithes and for Felgates charges	12s.		0d.
And of £1 3s.2d. paied for the charges of the Commissioners dynner and horsemeate, at the Angell, for those tithes	£1 3s.		2d.

The dynner

And of £6 11s.7d. for the charges of the dynner at the taking of this accompt	£6 11s.	7d.
And for wyne, suger and cakes then spent	11s.	0d.
And for beere spent the night of the same accompt		6d.
And of 10s.4d. paied to Bowman, the hall keper, for fire this accompt, and at sundry tymes besides, in the hall, this yere	10s.	4d.

2 gallons of wine

And of 2 gallons of wyne, *videlicet*, one of Mr Revell, and another of James Kent, reserved upon his lease, spent at the taking of this accompte	Two gallons of wyne

A boare

And of a boare given to Mr Boldero, now alderman	A boare
And of 5s.0d. given to a Grecyan upon the Bisshop of Norwich his lettres, towardes the building of a Colledg in Bohemia[136]	5s. 0d.

> *Summa allocacionis* £307 8s.10½d., a boare and
> 2 gallons of wyne
> *Et sic debet* £58 11s.2½d. and a combe of rye,
> whereof

---

[136] The bishop of Norwich must have issued an appeal for funds for establishing a protestant college in Bohemia; freedom in religious matters had been granted in Bohemia in 1609. Such letters, known as church briefs, were read out in church to encourage donations to good causes of all kinds – one was issued by the Crown to help the people of Bury who had suffered loss in the fire of 1608. This, and another instance in 1617, when Grecians were collecting on the bishop's behalf, is also perplexing. It may possibly refer to a Greek Orthodox priest in England for training as it is known that some of them spent some time in Norwich diocese. In 1604 money was collected for a Greek called Tryphon, Thomas F. Barton (ed.) *The Registrum Vagum of Anthony Harrison*, p.116. A possible identification in this case may be Christophoros Angelos, see W.S.B. Patterson, 'Educating the Greeks', pp.227–38.

[f.25v.]

Old supers received

The said accomptaunt praiethe allowans of £55 7s.7d. of the supers in \Mr/ Brightes accompt, old and new, before in charge, parte whereof, *videlicet*, £10 9s.9d. receyved by this accomptaunt of Mr Pynner, Mr Inman and Thomas Rose and answerid by him as appearithe in the beginnyng of this accompt ..... £10 9s. 9d.

Not received

And of diverse sommes of money remayninge in the handes of diverse persons particulerlye mencioned in Mr Brightes accompt, old and newe, not receyved by this accomptaunt, before in charge, *videlicet*, of the old supers there. Of Sir Robert Jermyn, knight, 10s.3d., and more of him 9d. And for the almes howses in the Northegate Strete and Garlond Stret £1 6s.8d. **Rose *solutus inde* 10s.0d. *in compoto* Mr Pynner.** And of Thomas Rose £2 15s.0d. And of Mr Smythe 6d. And for a stall 2s.0d. And of Mr Coell 3s.4d. And of William Scot 2s.6d. And of Mr Ravens 3s.4d. And of th'executors of Sparke 6s.8d. And of Richard Heigham £1 0s.0d. And of Mr Derbye 5s.0d. And of new there: Of Sir Robert Jermyn 10s.4d., and more of him 9d. And for the almes howses in the Northegate Street and Garlond Street £1 6s.8d. Of Mr Smythe 6d. Of Landisdale[137] 2s.0d. *Solutum in proximo compoto*. For a stall in the market 2s.0d. Of Mr Coell 3s.4d. Of William Scot 2s.6d. Of Mr Ravens 3s.4d. Of Mr Bridgeman 6s.8d. Of Richard Heigham £1 0s.0d. And of Mr Derby 5s.0d., *in toto* ..... £10 19s. 2d.

Dischargid

And of £33 18s.8d. set upon diverse persons in Mr Brightes accompt, which are dischardid since the same accompt, as appearithe upon the same accompt ..... £33 18s. 8d.

~~And there~~   *Summa* £60 7s.7d.

Supers *de novo*

And there \remayneth not/ receyved by this accomptaunt of the rentes due for this yere, within the tyme of this accompt, upon theis severall persons as followithe, *videlicet:*

There remaynethe in the handes of Sir Robert Jermyn, knight, for lands in Hepworthe	10s.	4d.
And more of him for lands there		9d.
And in the handes of the Widowe Harrison for an almes howse in the Colledge Strete \for [?]~~yeres~~ half yeres rent/	8s.	0d.
And in the handes of Widowe Seger for an almes howse in the Northegate Stret	4s.	0d.
And for another almes howse there in the possession of the Widowe Seman	4s.	0d.
And in [sic] for a stall in the market, late in the possession of William Jellowe	2s.	0d.

---

[137] So in the manuscript.

And of Mr James Smythe for ground nere the Horse Market		6d.
And of Henry Landisdale for a peece of ground there	2s.	0d.
And for a tenement late in th'occupacion of Richard Heigham in the Churchegate Strete	£1 0s.	0d.
And of Mr Thomas Coell for part of Roger Wrightes howse	3s.	4d.

Solutum in proximo compoto

And of Mr Darcy for ground in the Northegate Strete	1s.	0d.
And of Robert Mance for a peece of ground in Skynners lane, late Mrs Cottons. *Solutum in proximo compoto*		1d.
And of Mr Ravens for ground in Brentgovell Strete, late Thomas Brunwyns	3s.	4d.
And of John Parker for a tenemente in Longe Brackeland		6d.

Summa £2 19s.10d.

Summa of all the supers, new and old, not paied £13 19s.0d.

Et sic debet clare 3s.3½d., which some is delivered to Mr Fraunces Pynner, receyvor for the yere now followinge, to be answered upon \his/ accompt. And there remaynethe in Mr Barkers handes a combe of rye not delivered by him upon this accompt.

[f.26r., old number 70]

Mr Fraunces Pynner 1613

Th'accompt of Mr Fraunces Pynner, receyvor of the rentes and revenues belonginge to the common use and benefite of the towne of Bury St Edmunde, made and yelded upp the fourthe daie of January in the elevinthe yere of the reign of our soveraigne King James of England *et cetera*, for one whole yere then endid, *anno Domini* 1613 [*1614*]

Onus

First the said accomptaunt dothe charge him silf with 3s.3½d. receyved of Mr Bennet Barker, the last receyvour, *ut patet in pede compoti sui*	3s.	3½d.

Arrerages

And with 2s.0d. receyved of Henry Landisdale for arrerages, parcell of £10 19s.2d. in Mr Barkers accompt	2s.	0d.
And with 2s.0d. more receyved of him for arrerages, parcell of £2 19s.10d., likewise in Mr Barkers accompt	2s.	0d.
And with 1d. receyved of Robert Mance for arrerages, parcell of the same £2 19s.10d.		1d.
And with 10s.0d. receyved of Thomas Rose, parcell of £2 15s.0d. due by him, by bond, taken for rent parcell of the said £10 19s.2d. mencioned in Mr Barkers accompt	10s.	0d.
And with 4d. receyved of Stephin Parkins for rent due for a tenemente in Hepworthe upon an old lease endid and determyned		4d.

Northefield

And with 10s.0d. receyved of Mr Northefield for haulf yeres rent due at Our Ladie daie last, for the Shirehowse	10s.	0d.

209

And with £2 0s.0d. receyved of him, by composicion, for the Shire Howse — £2 0s. 0d.

And with £1 0s.0d., parcell of £1 10s.0d., receyved, due by byll for the same howse — £1 0s. 0d.

Peake for woode

And with £15 0s.0d., parcell of £17 15s.4d., receyved of Thomas Peake for ₵₵ two and twentie hundred and 27 faggottes of woode, sold to him as appearithe in Mr Barkers accompt, the rest allowed to him for the making *et cetera*. — £15 0s. 0d.

Firmyn

And with £12 0s.0d. received of Mr Firmyn, for Mr Carter, for costes of suyte awarded against him in the Chauncerie abowt the suite there for the tythes of Brookehall in Foxhearthe — £12 0s. 0d.

Mariage dynners

And with £5 10s.0d. received this yere for mariage dyners at the Guildhall — £5 10s. 0d.

Old supers

And with £13 4s.11d., parcell of £13 19s.0d., being the supers in Mr Barkers accompt, old and newe, deducting the 13s.1d. as appearithe before, receyved of Henry Landisdale, Robert Mance and Thomas Rose — £13 4s. 11d.

Yerelie rentes, Bury, Barton, Rowgham

And with £20 0s.0d. received of Mr William Webbe for the wholeyeres rent of Catshall, endid at Michelmas last — £20 0s. 0d.

And with £6 10s.0d. receyved of Mrs Willowghby for a yeres rent of Leyers then endid — £6 10s. 0d.

And with £33 6s.8d. receyved of Robert Smythe for a yeres rent of a bearne and landes in the Sowthegate Fieldes then endid — £33 6s. 8d.

And with £5 0s.0d. received of Thomas Godfrey for the yeres rent of ten acres of Salters land — £5 0s. 0d.

And with £1 12s.0d. received of John Rolff for the rent of foure acres of the same landes — £1 12s. 0d.

And with £3 12s.0d. received of Robert Cropley for rent of 9 acres of the same land — £3 12s. 0d.

And with £7 6s.8d. received of John King for the landes called the new purchased landes — £7 6s. 8d.

And with £3 6s.8d. received of Anthony Bumpsted for 2 tenementes in the Churchegate Street — £3 6s. 8d.

And with £1 3s.6d. received of Widowe Bradishe for a tenemente by the Guildhall — £1 3s. 6d.

And with 2s.0d. received of John Bridon for a peece of ground lying at Sparowe Hill — 2s. 0d.

Hepworthe yerelie rentes

And with £53 6s.6d. received of Thomas Peake for a yeres rent of land in Hepworthe — £53 6s. 6d.
and a boare

And with £2 3s.4d. received of Sir Henry Buckenham, knight, for woode ground there — £2 3s. 4d.

[The yearly rents, continued]

And with 2s.4d. received more of him for pasture ground there	2s.	4d.
And with £6 0s.0d. received of John Sporle \for/ Greate Stubbubbinges[*sic*], Larkes tenement and Lombes land there	£6 0s.	0d.
And with £2 0s.0d. received of John Deye for the rent of land in Hepworthe	£2 0s.	0d.
And with 10s.4d. of Sir Robert Jermyn, knight, of 21 acres *dimidia* of land there	10s.	4d.
And with 9d. more of him for land there		9d.
And with £5 12s.6d. received of John Frost for the rent of land there	£5 12s.	6d.
And with £2 0s.0d. received of Humfrey Linge for rente of ground there	£2 0s.	0d.
And with £1 0s.0d. received of Stephin Parkyn for haulf yeres rent of an acre of ground and a cotage in Hepworthe, due at Michelmas last	£1 0s.	0d.
And with 10s.0d. received of Samuell Reve for haulf yeres rent of a tenemente and yeard then due	10s.	0d.
And with 15s.0d. received of John Clere for *dimidia* yeres rent of 2 acres of pasture at Hendall then due	15s.	0d.

[*f.26v.*]

Bury yerelie rentes

And with 13s.4d. receyved of Robert Kinge for the yeres rent of a howse in the Colledg Strete	13s.	4d.
And with 16s.0d. of the Widowe Haryson for another howse there	16s.	0d.

Almes howses

And with 4s.0d. of the Widowe Siger for an almes howse in the Northegate Strete	4s.	0d.
And with 4s.0d. of the Widowe Chitting and the Widowe Seman for another there	4s.	0d.
And with 2s.0d. of John Baylys for an almes howse in the Garlond Strete	2s.	0d.
And with 1s.0d. of the Widowe Shippe for another there	1s.	0d.
And with 5s.0d. of Stephin Egle for another there	5s.	0d.
And with 2s.0d. of the Widowe Doddes for another there	2s.	0d.

Yerelie rentes

And with £3 5s.0d. received of Mr Mallowes for a howse, gardein and close in the Westgate Strete	£3 5s.	0d.
And with £2 6s.8d. received of th'executors of John Cadge for part of an ortyard in Mr Andrewes Strete	£2 6s.	8d.
And with £2 6s.8d. received of William Ullet for a bearne and the other parte of the same ortyarde	£2 6s.	8d.
And with £4 0s.0d. received of the same William Ullet for a close at Stanford Bridge	£4 0s.	0d.
	a combe of rye	
And with £2 10s.0d. received of Thomas Rose for a close and cotage by the hospitall	£2 10s.	0d.
And with £3 0s.0d. received of William Rowge for a mesuage by St James Churche	£3 0s.	0d.
And with a gallon of wyne received of Mr John Revell for landes late Mr Barrettes	A gallon of wyne	

[The yearly rents, continued]

And with £4 0s.0d. received of Mr Hamond for land in the Sowthe
Field, in th'occupacion of George Baker   £4   0s.   0d.

And with £14 14s.0d. of Henry Blagge, esquire, for land late in
th'occupacion of Mr Barber   £14   14s.   0d.

And with £10 0s.0d. received of William Ullet for land in the
Westgate Field   £10   0s.   0d.

And with £4 0s.0d. received of William Gillye for land in
th'occupacion of Wyard   £4   0s.   0d.

And with £25 16s.0d. received of John Hawsted for land late in
th'occupacion of Thomas Turnour   £25   16s.   0d.

And with £1 0s.0d. received of Christofer Coxe for the ground
whereon the barne was built, late Turnours   £1   0s.   0d.

And with 2s.6d. received of Samuell Jellowe for the haulf yeres
rent of a stall in the market   2s.   6d.

Yerlie rentes, St Peters

And with £19 4s.0d. received of Thomas Godfrey for 37 acres of
St Peters land and a pightell at th'end of St Peters chappell   £19   4s.   0d.

And with £5 0s.0d. received of Adam Gillam for the parte of the
howse in his occupaction, and the ortyard and gardein within
the wall, and a peece of ground at the west end of the ortyard   £5   0s.   0d.

And with £1 10s.0d. received of Mr Bennet Barker for the bearne
at St Peters   £1   10s.   0d.

And with £10 0s.0d. received of Mr Hill for the tithes belonging to
St Peters   £10   0s.   0d.

And with 8s.0d. of Mr Rockit for the dove howse there   8s.   0d.

And with £4 0s.0d. of Mr Derby for St Peters Pittes   £4   0s.   0d.

And with £8 0s.0d. received of Robert Reve for the bearne and
graunge landes, leaton to him and Roger Reve   £8   0s.   0d.

Yerelie rentes

And of £1 0s.0d. received of Thomas Baker for a tenemente and
gardein in the Raingate Strete   £1   0s.   0d.

And with 6d. of Mr James Smythe for ground nere the Horse
Market   6d.

And with 2s.0d. received of Henry Landisdale for ground there
nere   2s.   0d.

And with 6d. received of Mr Inman for ground lying by Maide
Water Lane   6d.

And with 6s.8d. of Mr Bridgeman for ground in Mr Andrewes
Strete   6s.   0d.

And with 10s.0d. received of James Faiercliff for ground by his
howse nere the Horse Market   10s.   0d.

And with 4s.0d. received of Mr Henry Walker for a stable and
gardein in Punche Lane   4s.   0d.

And with 5s.0d. received of Mrs Heyward for a tenemente nere hir
howse, and a peece of ground nere the Teyven   5s.   0d.

And with 6d. of John Parker for a tenemente in the Longe
Brackeland   6d.

And with 8d. of Mr Derby for a tenemente there, late Hughe
Mathewes, before William Johnsons   8d.

212

[The yearly rents, continued]

And with 6d. received of Margaret Grigges, widowe, for a
    tenemente at the Northe Gate   6d.

And with £15 0s.0d. received of Mr Nicholas \Bell/ for the rent of
    the Angell this yere   £15   0s.   0d.

And with £10 0s.0d. received for the tithes of Brooke Hall in
    Foxhearthe this yere   £10   0s.   0d.

And with £2 17s.4d. received of Mr Cole, the husband of Henry
    Brights widowe, for tenementes in the Marketsteade   £2 17s.   4d.

And with £6 0s.0d. receyved of James Kent for a tenemente in the
    Cooke Rowe, late in the occupacion of Roger Brunwyn, with 2
    capons and a gallon of wyne reserved upon his lease   £6   0s.   0d.
                                                                    2 capons and a
                                                                   gallon of wine

And with 3s.4d. of Mr Thomas Coell for the rent of parte of the
    Castle   3s.   4d.

And with 2s.6d. received of William Scott for ground nere his
    howse in Brentgovell Strete, which he hathe in lease   2s.   6d.

[f.27r., old number 71]

Yerelie rentes

And with 3s.4d. received of John Shaw for a gardeine in the
    Sowthegate Strete, late Oliver Ions   3s.   4d.

And with £1 4s.0d. received of Mr Bridgeman, assignee of
    Thomas Overend, for land   £1   4s.   0d.

And with 1d. received of Robert Mance for ground in Skynners
    Lane, late Mrs Cottons   1d.

And with 3s.4d. of Mr Ravens for ground nere Brentgovell Streete   3s.   4d.

And with 1s.0d. of Eustace Darcy, esquire, for a peece of ground
    in Northegate Strete   1s.   0d.

        Summa oneris £371 18s.3½d., a boare, 2 gallons of wyne,
        2 capons and a combe of rye, whereof

Allowances

Owtrentes

The said accomptaunt dothe praye allowans of 11s.6d. paied to Mr
    Osborne for the arrerages of the rent of 1s.6½d. *per annum* due
    for diverse yeres past to the mannour of Wattisfield Hall, endid
    at our Ladie daie last past *videlicet* 1613   11s.   6d.

And of 9½d. paied to him for haulf yeres rent due to the same
    mannor at Michelmas last   9½d.

And of 1½d. paied to the mannor of Forneham All Saints for a
    yeres rent   1½d.

And of 8d. paied to the bailief of the hundred of Thedwestrye for
    Leyers   8d.

And of £1 18s.5½d. paied Mr Mallowes for the Kinges Majesties
    rent   £1 18s. 5½d.

And of 6d. paied to the baileife of the Mannor of Rowgham   6d.

Tenthe for St Peters

And of 10s.6d. paied for the tenthe of St Peters, and of 4d. for
    th'acquittauns, and of 4d. to the dore keper, *in toto*   11s.   2d.

And for £5 9s.10½d. paied to the governours of the Free Grammer
\Schole/ for St Peters and the Graunge landes £5 9s. 10½d.

Annuyties

And of £5 0s.0d. paied to Mr Collins for an annuytie to him
graunted for certeine yeres £5 0s. 0d.

And of £10 0s.0d. to Mr Pynner for an annuytie to him graunted
for certeine yeres £10 0s. 0d.

And of £16 0s.0d. paied to John Bedwall for an annuytie to him
graunted for yeres £16 0s. 0d.

Preachers and mynisters

And of £50 0s.0d. paied to Mr Beadle for his stipend for this yere
now endid, as preacher in St Maries parishe £50 0s. 0d.

And of £50 0s.0d. paied to Mr Helye, preacher in St James parishe
for his yeres stipend nowe endid £50 0s. 0d.

And of £4 0s.0d. paied to Mr Jewell and Mr Newstubs, mynisters
of the two parisshes, as their allowans owt of Mr Tassels guift,
and towardes theire dwelling £4 0s. 0d.

Aide *pro file marier*[sic]

And of 13s.2d. paied for aide towardes the mariage of the Kinges
Majesties daughter[138] 13s. 2d.

Paymentes

And of 1s.0d. for incke and paper 1s. 0d.

Gostlinge

And of £20 0s.0d. paied to Mr Gostlinge for the purchace of the
Angell £20 0s. 0d.

Craddocke

And of £5 0s.0d. paied to Mr Craddocke, parcell of £30 0s.0d. due
to John Man, disceased, to be paied £5 0s.0d. by the yere,
whereof this is the first payment £5 0s. 0d.

Armour

And of £8 3s.4d. paied to Mr Boldero, the last alderman, for
corselettes and other armour, which he bought for this towne £8 3s. 4d.

Paymentes

And of £2 2s.0d. paied for a dynner at the Angell for Sir John
Heigham, knight, and the Muster Master, upon the shewe of
Arms £5 0s. 0d.

Armour

And of 10s.4d. paied the cutler for trymyng 2 corselettes and
swordes 10s. 4d.

And of 4s.0d. paied to sixe poore men for trayning with the towne
corselettes 4s. 0d.

And of 3s.8d. paied for girdles and hangers 3s. 8d.

Paymentes

And of £1 10s.0d. to Robert Inglishe for going to London abowte
Foxhearthe tithes £1 10s. 0d.

---

[138] This payment is for the marriage of Princess Elizabeth to the Elector of Bohemia.

And of 10s.0d. paied to Liston, for Bowmans going upp and
coming downe from London, in his wagon, abowt those tithes | 10s. | 0d.
And of 9s.0d. paied to Bowman for his expences in going to
London, and coming from thence, and his being there | 9s. | 0d.
And of 6s.8d. paied to Bowman for his journey to London | 6s. | 8d.
And of 10s.0d. to the clerke for writing the rentall, and for
drawing the confirmacion, made by Sir Robert Jermyn, knight,.
for Torkesey annuytie[139] | 10s. | 0d.

Sir Henry Buckenhams paymentes
And of £16 15s.0d. paied to Sir Henry Buckenham, knight, for the
purchace of the woode ground bought of him at Hepworthe | £16 15s. | 0d.
And of 2s.0d. for charges at the assuerauns of the same ground | 2s. | 0d.
And of 3s.4d. to the clerke for drawing John Byes lease | 3s. | 4d.
[*f.27v.*]
Paymentes
And of 11s.6d. for a dynner at the Angell when the [?]Coroner
was sent for | 11s. | 6d.
And of £1 0s.0d. paied to Adkyns for loking to Parlyes legg thre
tymes | £1 0s. | 0d.

Poore
And of £21 8s.0d. for the poores clothing, of the guift of Mr
Bright, disceasid | £21 8s. | 0d.
And of 2s.0d. for binding | 2s. | 0d.

Clothing of the poore Mr Brightes guift
And of £1 13s.10d. for making the poores apparell in St James
parishe | £1 13s. | 10d.
And of £1 16s.2d. for making their apparell in St Maries parishe | £1 16s. | 2d.
And of £1 7s.3d. for lyning and other necessaries for the same | £1 7s. | 3d.

Poore to the churches
And of £1 19s.0d. paied to the poore in St Maries parishe, for thre
quarters of a yere, in the churche,[140] endid at Christmas last | £1 19s. | 0d.
And of £1 6s.0d. paied in the churche of St James, for the poore in
that parishe, for two quarters then endid | £1 6s. | 0d.

Poore for Kemboldes guift
And of £2 6s.8d. paied Mr Derby and Mr Grigges, for the poore in
the Northe Warde, for Kemboldes guift | £2 6s. | 8d.
And of 13s.4d. paied to John Bridon and Ambrose Bridon, for the
poore in the'East Ward, for the same guift | 13s. | 4d.
And of 18s.6d. given to diverse poore folkes at sondrie tymes | 18s. | 6d.

[139] The feoffees conveyed the Torkesey annuity to the governors in 1576, H1/5/8/1 and Woodward's Register, p.188. The governors reconveyed to the feoffees in 1609, Woodward's Register, p.194, but Sir Robert Jermyn's confirmation does not seem to have survived in any form. On 31 December 1611 the feoffees had agreed that the £40 a year annuity was to be used to feed, clothe and train poor children. See also Introduction, p.l.
[140] Once again it is made clear that payments were made to the poor in church.

Reparacions

And of 3s.10d. for cleye, and cariage of rubbishe from the Guild-hall, for making the oven	3s.	10d.
And of 1s.0d. for charges of nealing the oven	1s.	0d.
And of 14s.8d. for making the greate oven at the Guildhall	14s.	8d.
And of 3s.6d. for lyme for making the oven there and mending the hearthe	3s.	6d.
And of 5s.2d. to Botye and Glover for worke at the almes howse of Widowe Harrison, grounselling, and studding a wall and two bourdes	5s.	2d.
And of 10s.3d. for claye, nailes, lyme, sand, splentes and workemanship abowte the same wall	10s.	3d.
And of 13s.0d. for haulf a loade of brickes and haulf a loade of tile for the Guildhall	13s.	0d.
And of 6d. to Traye for mending the railes at the Sowthe Gate		6d.
And of £1 0s.4d. for reparacions done at Mr Helyes howse	£1 0s.	4d.
And of £1 5s.0d. for reparacions done at Mr Jewels howse	£1 5s.	0d.

Reparacions

And of 4s.0d. for worke in pynnyng done at an almes howse	4s.	0d.
And of 6s.8d. for 300 tyles, wanting ten tiles	6s.	8d.
And of 1s.4d. for lyme, sand, lathe and nayles	1s.	4d.
And of £3 5s.2d. for reparacions done at the Spittle Howse	£3 5s.	2d.
And of £1 14s.0d. to Boydon for leade, sowder and worke done at the Guildhall	£1 14s.	0d.

Paymentes

And of 9d. paied to the ratt ketcher for the Guildhall	9d.

Guiftes

And of £14 3s.1d. for gratuities upon the judges and others for the common benefite of the towne	£14 3s.	1d.
And of £1 16s.9d. for postes set upp, and mending, at the Sowthe Gate	£1 16s.	9d.

Paymentes, suytes

And of £1 1s.3d. for clothe for a coate for Foxgill, the bedell	£1 1s.	3d.

Interest, Cropley

And of £9 10s.0d. paied for interest for £100 0s.0d., th'accomptaunt receyving 10\s.0d. of £10 0s.0d./ towardes the finishing of the Crosse	£10 0s.	0d.

Colling

And of £10 1s.6d. paied for the suyte of Mr Collinges leases, left unpaid by Mr Barker	£10 1s.	6d.

Foxhearthe tithes

And of £31 3s.6d. paied for suyte of Foxhearthe tithes	£31 3s.	6d.

Fine, Sir Henry Buckenham

And of £2 14s.10d. for the knowledge and suyinge owte of the fyne for Sir Henry Buckenhams woode	£2 14s.	10d.

Plate 10. The Market Place *c.*1700. Shows the Market Cross rebuilt after the fire of 1608. The terrace of early seventeenth-century houses on the left also illustrates rebuilding after the fire (K511/405). Reproduced by permission of Suffolk Record Office.

And of 4s.6d. paied to Bowman for candle and fiers, left unpaied by Mr Barker	4s.	6d.
And of 14s.8d. paied more to him for fier and candle for this yere, and keping the dore cleane	14s.	8d.
And of 10s.0d. paied to Oliver Tebold for healing of Andrewes boye, being diseasid	10s.	0d.

Paymentes

And of 13s.4d. to Alexander Gent for writing \the deede from Mr Gold,/ Mr Havers lease, and ingrossing the confirmacion made by Sir Robert Jermyn for th'annuytie of Mr Edmunde Jermyn owt of Torkesey	13s.	4d.
And of 5s.6d. to Mr Sporle for the charge of Mr Bright, Mr Revell and this accomptaunt, lying at his howse at Hepworthe one night abowt the towne busynes	5s.	6d.
And of 4s.0d. paied to the constables of the West Ward for composicion money for the Guildhall	4s.	0d.

Bowman, wages

And of £2 10s.0d. to Bowman for his wages for this yere	£2 10s.	0d.

The receyvours fee

And of 15s.0d. for the receyvours fee	15s.	0d.

The clerkes fee

And of 10s.0d. for the clerkes fee	10s.	0d.

[f. 28r., old number 35]

The dynner

And of £5 7s.1d. paied to Boydon for the dynner of the feoffees at the taking of this accompt, and for cakes, wyne and suger, *in toto* .... £5 7s. 1d.

And of a gallon of wyne of Mr John Revell, spent at the same dynner .... A gallon of wyne

And of a boare bestowed upon Mr Smythe, now alderman .... A boare

> *Summa allocationis* £329 3s.0d.
> *Et sic debet* £41 15s.3½d., and a combe of rye, whereof

Old supers

This accomptaunt praiethe allowans of £13 4s.11d., parcell of £13 19s.0d., being the supers in Mr Barkers accompt, old and newe, before in charge, part whereof are receyved by this accomptaunt of Henry Landisdale, Robert Mance, Thomas Rose and answerid by him, as appearithe in the beginnyng of this accompt, *videlicet*, 14s.1d., and the rest not receyved remaynyng in the handes of diverse persons is to be allowed this accomptaunt .... £13 4s. 11d.

Supers *de novo*

And there remaynethe in the handes of the persons herunder written, due for this yere, within the tyme of this accompt, not receyved as followethe *videlicet*,

First in the handes of John Roulf for haulf yeres rent for parcell of Salters land .... 16s. 0d.

And in the handes of Sir Robert Jermyn, knight, for a yeres rent for 21 acres *dimidia* of land in Hepworthe .... 10s. 4d.

And more of him for landes there .... 9d.

And in th'andes of Widowe Harrison for a yeres rent of an almes howse in the Colledg Stret .... 16s. 0d.

And in th'andes of Widowe Siger for a yeres rent of an almes howse in the Northegate Stret .... 4s. 0d.

And of the Widowe Chitting and the Widowe Seman for another almes howse there .... 4s. 0d.

And in the handes of Ambrose Blagge, esquire, for haulf yeres rent, due at Michelmas last, for Mr Barbers landes .... £7 7s. 0d.

And in th'andes of Mr Charles Derby for the yeres rent of St Peters Pittes .... £4 0s. 0d.

And in th'andes of Mr Rockit for the yeres rent of the dove howse at St Peters .... 8s. 0d.

And in th'andes of Mr James Smythe for a yeres rent of a peece of ground by the Horse Market .... 6d.

And in th'andes of Mr Bridgeman for ground in Mr Andrewes Strete .... 6s. 8d.

And in th'andes of John Parker for a tenemente in the Long Brackelond .... 6d.

And in th'andes of Mr Charles Derby for a tenemente there, late Mathewes, before Hoye and after Johnsons .... 8d.

And in the handes of James Kent for a mesuage in the Cooke
  Rowe

          2 capons and a
          gallon of wyne

And in th'andes of Mr Thomas Coell for parte of the Castle, late
  in possession of Roger Wright   3s.   4d.

And in th'andes of Mr Ravens for ground nere Brentgovell Strete,
  late in possession of Thomas Brunwyn   3s.   4d.

And in th'andes of Ewstace Dracy, esquire, for a peece of ground
  in the Northegate Strete   1s.   0d.

> Sum of the supers old and newe £28 7s.0d.
> *Sic debet de clare* £14 8s.3½d. and a combe of rye,
> which rye remayneth not delivered by him.

[f.28v.]

1614 Mr John Revell

**The accompt of Mr John Revell, receivour of the towne revenues *et cetera* taken
the fourth day of January *anno duodecimo Jacobi regis Anglie et cetera*, for the
yeare ended at Christmas last *anno Domini* ~~1615~~ 1614 [*1615*]**

Onus

~~This~~ First the said accomptaunt dothe charge himself with
£14 8s.3½d. by him received of Mr Pynner, the last receivour,
remayninge due by him as appere in the foote of his accompt   £14   8s.   3½d.

Arrerages

And with £3 0s.0d. received of Robert Gilbert of Hopton as part of
th'arrerages of Sir Roberte Jermyn, knight, for landes in
Hepworth occupied by the same Robert Gilbert   £3   0s.   0d.

Arrerages

And with 2 combes of rye received of William Walker, due at
  Christmas 1613   2 combes of rye
And with one combe of rye received of Mr Pinner, due by him
  upon his accompt, 1613   one combe of rye

Supers old

And with £13 13s.11d. beinge the supers in Mr Barkers accompt,
  old and new, *ut patet* in Mr Pinners accompt   £13 13s.   11d.
And with ~~supers~~ £15 2s.1d. being the new supers in Mr Pynners
  accompt   £15   2s.   1d.
And with 10s.0d. received of John Deye for certen trees sold to
  him at Hepworthe   10s.   0d.

Legacie

And with ~~xli~~ £40 0s.0d. received of Mr Henry Walker for a
legacie given by the last will of Mr Richard Walker,[141] his
father   £40   0s.   0d.

---

141   For Richard Walker's gift see Introduction, p.liii.

Sale of woode

And with £2 10s.0d. received of Mr Sporle for 300 of one binde
woode solde to him at Hepworthe .... £2 10s. 0d.

Maryage dinners

And with £5 2s.0d. received this yere for mariage dinners at the
Guildhall .... £5 2s. 0d.

And with two capons and a gallon wine due by James Kent in Mr
[*Pinners*] accompt, 1613 .... 2 capons and
a gallon of wine

> Summa £93 17s.3½d., 3 combes of rye,
> 2 capons and a gallon of wine

Yearlie rentes
Barton

And with £20 0s.0d. received of Mr Henry Walker for a yeares
rent ended at Michaelmas for Catshall in Barton .... £20 0s. 0d.

Rowgham

And with £6 10s.0d. received of Mrs Willoughbie for Leyers in
Rougham, *per annum* .... £6 10s. 0d.

Bury

And with £33 6s.8d. of Mr Thomas Claydon, assignee of Robert
Smyth, of a barne withowt the South Gate, and landes in the
Southe Feild, late in the possession of Mr George Boldero, *per
annum* .... £33 6s. 8d.

And with £5 0s.0d. received of John Godfrey, junior, for 10 acres
of Salters land, late in the possession of Mr Collyn, *per annum* £5 0s. 0d.

And with £6 4s.0d. received of John Kinge for 3 acres of the said
land, sometyme Salters, *per annum* .... £6 4s. 0d.

And with £9 0s.0d. and 2 combes of rye received of William
Walker for the new purchased land, late in possession of Mr
Collyn, *per annum* .... £9 0s. 0d.
and 2 combs of
rye at Christmas

And with £3 6s.8d. received of Anthony Bumpsted for 2
tenementes in Churchgate Streete, *per annum*/ .... £3 6s. 8d.

And with £1 3s.6d. received of Widowe Bradishe for a tenement
by the Guildhall, *per annum* .... £1 3s. 6d.

And with 2s.0d. received of John Bridon for a peece of ground at
Sparrow Hill, *per annum* .... 2s. 0d.

Hepworth

And with £53 6s.6d. and a boare received of Thomas Peake for
land and pasture in Hepworth, *per annum* .... £53 6s. 6d.
and a boare

And with £6 0s.0d. received of John Sporle for the tenement
Larkes, Great Stubbings and Lomes land, *per annum* .... £6 0s. 0d.

And with £2 0s.0d. received of John Deye for Litle Atley, Litle
Stubbings and the Bower, *per annum* .... £2 0s. 0d.

And with ~~six po~~ £6 8s.9d. received of the same John Daye for
eight acres of pasture and woode at the Hendall in Weston and
Ward Woode and 2 acres and half of woode grownd in two

220

[*The yearly rents, continued*]

peeces, and 3 acres and a roode of woode ground purchased of Sir H. ~~Boke~~ Buckenham, knight	£6 8s.	9d.
And with 10s.4d. of Sir Thomas Jermyn, knight, for 21 acres and half of land there, *per annum*	10s.	4d.
And with 9d. more of ~~or~~ him for land there		9d.
And with £5 12s.6d. received of John Frost for land there, *per annum*	£5 12s.	6d.
And with £2 0s.0d. received of Humfry Linge for groundes there, nere his howse, *per annum*	£2 0s.	0d.
And with £2 0s.0d. received of William Perkin for an acre of grownd ~~of~~ \in/ Hepworth, with a cotage ther upon built, *per annum*	£2 0s.	0d.
And with £1 0s.0d. received of Samuell Reve for a mesuage, and a yard to it, in Hepworth, *per annum*	£1 0s.	0d.
And with £1 13s.4d. received of John Cleere, of Weston, for two acres of pasture at Hendall, *per annum*[142]	£1 13s.	4d.

Summa £163 5s.0d., 2 combs of rye and a boare

[*f.29r., old number 69*]

Bury

And with 13s.4d. received of Robert Kinge for an howse in the Colledge Streete, *per annum*	13s.	4d.
And with 16s.0d. of [*space*] Milbye for an other howse there next unto it, *per annum*	16s.	0d.
And with 4s.0d. of Widowe Siger ~~fe~~ \for/ an almes howse in Northgate Streete	4s.	0d.
And with 4s.0d. of Widowe Chittinge and Widowe Seman for an other howse there	4s.	0d.
And with 2s.0d. received of John Baylie for one of the new erected almes howses in the Garlond Street	2s.	0d.
And with 1s.0d. of the Widowe Shipp for an other there of the same	1s.	0d.
And with 5s.0d. of Stephen Eagle for an other of the same howses	5s.	0d.
And with 2s.0d. of [*space*] Dodd for an other there of the same howses	2s.	0d.
And with £3 5s.0d. received of John Mallowes, gentleman, for a howse, garden and close in the Westgate Streete, *per annum*	£3 5s.	0d.
And with £2 6s.8d. received of th'executors of John ~~Claydon~~ Cadge for part of an orchard in Mr Andrewes Streete, *per annum*	£2 6s.	8d.
And with £2 6s.8d. received of William Ullett for a barne and the residue of the same ortyard, *per annum*	£2 6s.	8d.
And with £4 0s.0d. and a combe of \rye/ received of the same William Ullett for a close at Stanford Bridge, *per annum*	£4 0s. and a combe of rye	0d.

---

142 Although it is undoubtedly part of the feoffees' archive, a draft of the lease from the feoffees to John Clere or Cleere of Weston has survived and it is to be found under the reference G1/3. The pightle called Little Hendall contained 2 acres pasture and is fully abuttalled. The lease was to run for eleven years at a rent of £1 13s.4d. with a covenant forbidding the tenant to plough.

[*The yearly rents, continued*]

And with £2 10s.0d. received of Thomas [*Rose*] for a cotage by the[143] hospitall, and the close adioyning to it, *per annum*	£2 10s.	0d.
And with £3 0s.0d. received of William Rowge for a mesuage by St James church, purchased of Rychard Collyn, *per annum*	£3 0s.	0d.
And with a gallon of wine received of Mr John Revell	A gallon of wine	
And with £4 0s.0d. received of Mr Hammond for lands withowt the Southgate, in the occupacion of George Baker, *per annum*	£4 0s.	0d.
And with £14 14s.0d. received of Ambrose Blage, esquire, for lands in th'eastefeild of Bury, late three leases, and late in th'occupacion of Mr Barber, *per annum*	£14 14s.	0d.
And with £10 0s.0d. received of William Ullett for lands in the West Feild, late in th'occupacion of Mr Barber, *per annum*	£10 0s.	0d.
And with £4 0s.0d. received of William Gilley for land in the same feild, occupied by Wyard, *per annum*	£4 0s.	0d.
And with 5s.0d. received of Samuell Jellowe for a stale in the markett, late in the occupacion of William Jellowe, *per annum*	5s.	0d.
And with £25 16s.0d. received of John Hawstede for land, late in th'occupacion of Thomas Turnour, *per annum*	£25 16s.	0d.
And with £1 0s.0d. received of Christofer Cox for the ground, wher upon the barne was built, late in th'occupacion of the said Thomas Turnour, *per annum*	£1 0s.	0d.
And with £19 4s.0d. received of Thomas Godfrey, junior,[144] for 37 acres of St Peters land, and one pightell at th'east end of St Peters chappell, late in th'occupacion of Mr Pynner, *per annum*	£1 0s.	0d.
And with £5 0s.0d. received of Adam <..> Gillam for the howse now in his occupacion, and the ortyard and ground within the wall, and one peece of ground at the west end of the ortyard, parcell of St Peters	£5 0s.	0d.
And with £3 0s.0d. received of Mr Bennett Barker for the barne and stable there, *per annum*	£3 0s.	0d.
And with £10 0s.0d. received of the same Mr Barker for the tythes belonging to St Peters, *per annum*	£10 0s.	0d.
And with 8s.0d. of Mr Rockett for the dovehowse there	8s.	0d.
And with £4 0s.0d. received of Henry Cropley for St Peters Pittes, *per annum*	£4 0s.	0d.
And with £8 0s.0d. received of Mr Roberte Reve for the barne and landes leatten to him and Roger Reve, deceased, parcell of the Grainge landes, withowt the Risby Gate, *per annum*	£8 0s.	0d.

Summa £129 2s.8d., a combe of rye
and a gallon of wyne

Bury

And with £1 0s.0d. received of Thomas Baker for a tenement, late three tenementes, and a gardine in the Raingate Street, *per annum*	£1 0s.	0d.

---

143 Only two instances have been noted in these accounts in which the contraction 'ye' was used instead of 'the', though from time to time 'yt' was used for 'that'. The 'y' is derived from the Old English thorn.
144 The draft lease to Thomas Godfrey, junior, has survived and gives a detailed description of the St Peter's Hospital property, G1/3.

[The yearly rents, continued]

And with 6d. of Mr James Smyth for ground by the Horse Markett		6d.
And with 2s.0d. received of Henry Landsdale for ground there by his howse	2s.	0d.
And with 6d. of Mr Inman for ground nere Maid Water Lane, late in the possession of Mr George Boldero		6d.
And with 6s.8d. of Mr Bridgman for ground in Mr Andrewes Streete	6s.	8d.
And with 10s.0d. received of James Fayrecliff for ground by his howse nere the Horse Market, *per annum*	10s.	0d.
And with 13s.4d. received of Henry Coe for a tenemente in the Churchgate Streete, wherein Richard Heigham late dwelt, *per annum*	13s.	4d.
And with 4s.0d. received of Mr Henry Walker for a howse and gardin in Punch \Lane/, *per annum*	4s.	0d.
And with 5s.0d. received of Mrs Heyward for a tenemente nere her howse in the Risbygate Streete, and a peece of ground nere the Teyven	5s.	0d.
And with 6d. of John Parker for a tenemente in the Long Bracklond		6d.

[*f.29v.*]

And with 8d. of Mr Charles Darby for a tenement there, late Hughe Mathewes, before Hoyes and William Johnsons		8d.
And with 6d. received of Margarett Griggs, widowe, for a tenemente at the North Gate		6d.
And with £16 13s.4d. of Mr Nicholas Bell for the Angell, *per annum*	£16 13s.	4d.
And with £2 17s.4d. received of Mr Cole, the husband of the widowe of Henry Bright, for tenementes in the Market Steade and Skyners Lane, late leatten for yeares to Thomas Bright the yonger, the sonne of the same Henry Bright, *per annum*	£2 17s.	4d.
And with £6 0s.0d., 2 capons and a gallon of wine received of James Kent for a mesuage in the Cooke Rowe, late in the possession of Roger Brunwyn, clerke, *per annum*	£6 0s. 2 capons and a gallon of wine	0d.
And with 3s.4d. received of Mr Thomas Havers, of London, for part of the Castle, late in the occupacion of Roger Wright, *per annum*	3s.	4d.
And with 2s.6d. received of William Scott for ground neere his howse in the Brentgovell Streete, *per annum*	2s.	6d.
And with 3s.4d. received of John Shawe for a gardine in the Southgate Streete, *per annum*	3s.	4d.
And with £1 4s.0d. received of Mr Bridgman, asignee of Thomas Overend, for land neere Hardwick Heath	£1 4s.	0d.
And with 1d. received of Robert Mance for a peece of ground in Skinners Lane, by his howse, late Mrs Cottons		1d.
And with 3s.4d. received of Mr Ravens for ground in Brentgovell Streete, late in the possession of Thomas Brunwyn	3s.	4d.
And with 1s.0d. received of Mr Eustace Darcy for a peece of ground in the Northgate Street	1s.	0d.

And with £2 0s.0d. received for the half yeares rent due at Michaelmas last for the tenements in the Churchgate Streete,

which Mr Richard Walker, deceased, gave to this towne by his
last will and testament   £2   0s.   0d.

The tythes in Foxherth
And with £10 0s.0d. received of Mathew Teversham for the tythes
of Brookehall in Foxherth, given by Thomas Bright, deceased,
per annum   £10   0s.   0d.
> *Summa* £42 11s.11d., 2 capons and a gallon of wine[145]
> *Summa oneris* £429 16s.10½d., 6 combs rie, a boare,
> 4 capons and 3 gallons of wine

Allowauns
The said accomptaunt prayeth allowance of 1s.6½d. paid to Mr
Osborne for rent due to the manour of Wattlisfeild Hall, *per
annum*   1s.   6½d.

Owtrents
And of 6d. paid to Sir Robert Drury, knight, for rent due to the
manour of Rougham, *per annum*   6d.
And of 1½d. paid to the manour of Fornham All S[ain]cts for
Shire Hall Yard at Catshall, *per annum*   1½d.
And of £1 18s.5½d. paid to Mr Mallowes for the kinges rent *per
annum*   £1   18s.   5½d.

The tenth of St Peters
And of 11s.2d. ~~viz~~ *videlicet*, 10s.6d. for the tenemente of St
Peters, and for the receivours fee, acquitaunces and
doorekeeper, 8d., *in toto*   11s.   2d.

Owt rents
And of 8d. ~~rec of~~ \paid to/ the baylief of the hundred of
Thedwistrie for Leyers in Rougham, *per annum*   8d.
And of £5 9s.10½d. paid to the governours of the Free Gramer
Schole in Bury for St Peters lands, late in occupacion of Mr
Francis Pynner or his assignes   £5   9s.10½d.

Annuities
And of £16 0s.0d. paid to John Bedwall for his annuitie for a
yeare ended at Michaelmas last   £16   0s.   0d.
And of £10 0s.0d. paid to Mr Francis Pinner for his annuity for a
yeare then ended   £10   0s.   0d.
And of £5 0s.0d. paid to Mr Henry Collins for his annuitie for a
yeare then endid[146]   £5   0s.   0d.

Preachers and mynisters
And of £50 0s.0d. paid to Mr Bedell, preacher of St Maries
parishe, for his yeers stipend, ended at Christmas last   £50   0s.   0d.
And of £50 0s.0d. paid to Mr Helie, precher of St James his
parishe, for his yeares stipend then ended   £50   0s.   0d.

---

[145] This may well be the total of the sheet in the original which the clerk has copied here.
[146] All three annuities were awarded as compensation by the Commissioners when they deprived these tenants of leases which had been granted to them at very low rents.

And of £2 0s.0d. paid to Mr Juell, mynister of St Maries parishe,
for a yere ended at Christmas last ... £2 0s. 0d.

And of £2 0s.0d. paid to Mr Newstubs, mynister of St James
parishe, for a yeare then ended ... £2 0s. 0d.

Craddock payments

And of £5 0s.0d. paid to Mr Craddock, part of £30 0s.0d. due to
John Man, deceased, to be paid by £5 0s.0d. the yeare, wherof
this is the second payment ... £5 0s. 0d.

Cropley

And of £8 0s.0d. paid Mr Cropley, of Shelland, for the use of
£100 0s.0d. lent to the feoffees ... £8 0s. 0d.

And of 11s.8d. paid for the charges of the clerke of the markett for
the kings houshold[147] ... 11s. 8d.

Payments

And of 5s.0d. paid for the kinges caryages to Edward Bourne ... 5s. 0d.

And of 5s.0d. paid for the kings provision ... 5s. 0d.

And of £60 0s.0d. paid and delivered to Mr Mallowes by consent
of the feoffes for the obteyninge of the kinges graunt, under the
great seale of England, for the clearinge all titles and questions
in the towne lands[148] ... £60 0s. 0d.

And of 10s.0d. to the clerke for writinge the rentall by consent ... 10s. 0d.

[f.30r., old number 72][149]

Poore

And of £1 10s.0d. paid to Oliver Tebold for healinge the feete of
the daughter of the Widowe Bowghton ... £1 10s. 0d.

And of 10s.0d. paid to Ambrose Lichefeild for healinge of a poore
womans legg, sore hurt with a boare ... 10s. 0d.

And of 10s.0d. given to John Bartlet in relief of him and his
howsehould, being sick, by the hands of Mr Bright ... 10s. 0d.

And of 4s.0d. given to Johnson, a poore man, in relief, that went
to the Bathe[150] ... 4s. 0d.

And of 4s.0d. given to the poore in the worke howse in relief ... 4s. 0d.

And of 8s.2d. more given to the poore in bread ther, in relief ... 8s. 2d.

And of 2s.0d. paid for burying of *[space]* Hynard, Walletts sister,
at the hospitall ... 2s. 0d.

For the clothing of the poore by Mr Brights guift

And of £20 0s.0d. for clothe for the poore clothings of Mr Brights
guift, deceased ... £20 0s. 0d.

And of £1 13s.6½d. for lynninge for the same apparell ... £1 13s. 6½d.

And of £1 15s.8d. for makeing of part of the apparell for the poore ... £1 15s. 8d.

And of £1 14s.2d. for makeing the residue of the same apparell ... £1 14s. 2d.

And of £12 8s.6d. for gratuities upon the judges and others for the
common benefitt of the towne ... £12 8s. 6d.

---

147 This and the next two items were paid in connection with the collection of the composition for purveyance. See Introduction, p.lxii.

148 For the 1614 charter see Introduction, p.li.

149 The corner of this page was torn off before the old number was written.

150 A visit to Bath as part of a cure seems to have been allowed by the authorities in this case.

And of £1 13s.4d. more to the judges [?]a at Lent assizes, before
this accompt was finished   £1 13s.   4d.

And of £9 14s.0d. paid to Mr Bright for clothe for Foxgills coate,
Davyes and Copcies cootes, and for 2 sargents gownes, *anno*
1611   £9 14s.   0d.

And of £5 4s.0d. paid this yeere, now ended at Christmas, to the
overseers for the poore in bothe parishes   £5   4s.   0d.

And of 13s.0d. more to the overseers of St James parishe for the
poore, for the quarter to end at Our Lady, 1615   13s.   0d.

And of £1 5s.0d. paid to the Coroner[151] for a dynner for the
Muster Master at the Angell   £1   5s.   0d.

And of £2 0s.0d. given to the Kings Majesties trumpeters   £2   0s.   0d.

And of 6s.0d. paid to two workeman for their day worke in
opening the lockes of the chist in the tower of the Guildhall[152] 6s.   0d.

Mr Bright £5 0s.0d. owt of the tythes of Foxhearth

And of £2 0s.0d. paid to the church wardens of St Maryes parishe
for the poore, and towards the reparacions of the same church,
by Mr Brights guift   £2   0s.   0d.

And of £2 0s.0d. to the churche wardens of St James parishe for
the poore, and towards the reparacions of the same church, by
the same guift   £2   0s.   0d.

And of £1 0s.0d. to the towne gaole by the same guift   £1   0s.   0d.

Kembold

And of £3 0s.0d. paid to Mr Darby, for the poore in the North and
East Wards, for the guift of Peter Kembold   £3   0s.   0d.

Reparacions

And of £6 13s.4d. for reparacions done at the ~~Guildh~~ Guildhall,
and almes howse, the howse which Mr Walker gave to the
towne, the howse of Mr Hely, the howse of Mr Jewell, St
Peters and Stanford Bridge   £6 13s.   4d.

And of 1s.2d. for a buckett for a common well in the Northgate
Streete   1s.   2d.

Summa £294 3s.9½d.[153]

And of 15s.0d. for the receivours fee   15s.   0d.

And of 10s.0d. for the clerks fee   10s.   0d.

And of £1 0s.0d. for the clerke for drawinge the two deeds for
renewing the feoffament of the towne lands[154]   £1   0s.   0d.

And of £2 10s.0d. paid to Bowman for his yeares wages   £2 10s.   0d.

---

151 The office of coroner had been granted to the corporation by the charter of 1614.

152 This probably refers to the hutch or coffer in the wall of the Evidence House, above the thirteenth-century doorway into the Guildhall. See Introduction, p.xxiii and frontispiece.

153 Here again the sheet total from the original account appears to have been copied into the account book.

154 The feoffment was not renewed until 1617. Perhaps this entry refers to the preparation of preliminary draft deeds, or deeds which were not executed for some time to come. On 15 March 1616, when the release had already been signed by Sir John Heigham, William Cooke, John Mallowes and Francis Pinner, Thomas Baker refused to sign, demanding to be reimbursed for money he had laid out about sixteen years before. See Introduction, p.xxx.

And of £1 3s.4d. paid more to him for woode, coale and candle, and for [*space*] the carpet, and for attendinge upon the carpenters and masons at the Guildhall, and other things, and keeping the hall doore cleane, *ut patet per billam* — £1 3s. 4d.

[*f.30v.*]

The charge of the dynner

And of £5 6s.8d. paid for the dynner at the takeing of the accompt to Thomas Reade — £5 6s. 8d.

And of 10s.0d. for wine and suger spent at the dynner, and for wine and cakes — 10s. 0d.

[*The next two items are bracketed together, but have no heading*]

And of 8s.0d. for horse hire for Mr Pynner and this accomptaunt and of 4s.0d. for hyringe of a man to ride with them for two dayes, *in toto* — 12s. 0d.

And of 16s.0d. for their charges — 16s. 0d.

And of 2s.0d. for ryding to Hepworth by this accomptaunt to sell the wood — 2s. 0d.

And of £1 0s.3d., for 2 yards quarter of broade blewe, paid to Mr Bright for a coatt for Foxgill — £1 0s. 3d.

And of 15s.7d., for a yard 3 quarters of broad blew, paide to Roger Lowdall for a coate for Bowman — 15s. 7d.

And of £1 0s.0d., for 2 yards of blew, paide to Mrs Chapman, 1613, for a coate for Robert Astinge — £1 0s. 0d.

And of 2 combes of rye, before in charge, received of William Walker, and a combe of rye received of Mr Pynner, likewise before in charge, with a combe of rye received this yeare of William Ullett, by this accomptaunt, and baked and bestowed in bread upon the poore — 4 combes of rye

And of 5s.0d. for the bakeing of the same bread — 5s. 0d.

And of 2s.6d. for grynding the corne — 2s. 6d.

And of 4d. for a quire of paper — 4d.

Supers old

And of £13 4s.11d. before in charge, beinge the supers in Mr Barkers accompt, *ut patet* in Mr Pynners accompt — £13 4s. 11d.

And of £16 2s.1d., before in charge, beinge the new supers in Mr Pynners accompt — £16 2s. 1d.
2 capons and a gallon of wine

A boare

And of a boare bestowed upon Mr Alderman Gippes — A boare

A gallon of wyne

And of a gallon of wine of this accomptaunts[155] spent at the dinner — A gallon of wyne

Summa £44 15s.8d., 4 combes rye, a boare, 2 capons and 2 gallons of wyne
Summa allocacionis £338 19s.5½d., 4 combes rye, a boare 2 capons and two gallons of wine

---

[155] For many years the gallon of wine out of land held by John Revell had been accounted for.

Et sic debet £90 18s.5d., 2 combes rye, 2 capons and one gallon of wine

New supers

And in the hands of William Walker for the new purchased lands late in the occupacion of Mr Colling		2 combes of rye
And in the hands of Sir Robert Jermyn, knight, for 21 acres *dimidia* of land in Hepworth	10s.	4d.
And more in his hands for lands there		9d.
And of [*space*] Milby for an almes howse in the Colledge Streete	16s.	0d.
And of Widowe Siger for ann [*sic*] almes howse in the Northgate Streete	4s.	0d.
And of Widowe Chittinge and Widowe Seman for an other there	4s.	0d.
And of Mr Rockett for the dovehowse at St Peters	8s.	0d.
And of Mr James Smyth for ground nere the Horse Market		6d.
And of Mr Bridgeman for ground in Mr Andrewes Streete	6s.	8d.
And of Mr John Parker for a tenement in the Longe Bracklond		6d.
And of Mr Charles Darby for a tenement there, late Hughe Mathews, before Hoyes and Johnsons		8d.
And of James Kent for a mesuage in the Cooke Rowe, late in the possession of Roger Brownwyn, clerke	3s.	4d.
And of Mr Thomas Havers, of London, for parte of the Castle late in the possession of Roger Wright	3s.	4d.
And of Mr Ravens for ground neere Brentgovell Streete, late in the possession of Thomas Brunwyn	3s.	4d.

> *Summa* £2 18s.1d. 2 combes rye, 2 capons, a gallon of wine
> *Et sic debet clare* £88 0s.4d.

[f.31r., old number 68]

1615

The accompt of Mr Henry Gippes, receivour of the towne revenues taken the [*space*] daye of January *anno tercio decimo Jacobi Regis Anglie et cetera*, for the yeare endid at Christmas last, *anno Domini* 1615 [*16*]

First the saide accomptant doth charge himself with £88 0s.4d. by him received of Mr John Revell, the last receivour, and remayninge due to be payde by him as appereth upon the foote of his accompt	£88	0s.	4d.

Item the saide accomptant chargeth himself with the wholl yeares rentes and revenues of the mesuages, landes, tenementes and hereditamentes belonging to the common profict of the towne of Bury aforesaid, conteyned in the rentall thereof made, the particulers whereof are hereunder expressed, *videlicet*

With £20 0s.0d. due by Henry Walker, gentleman, for Catshall farme in Great Barton	£20	0s.	0d.
And with £6 10s.0d. due by Mrs Willoughby for Layers farme in Rugham	£6	10s.	0d.
And with £33 6s.8d. [156]of \due/ by Mr Claydon for landes lately demysed to George Boldero, gentleman	£33	6s.	8d.

---

[156] Here and in several other instances the clerk has had to correct 'of' into 'due by' which shows that the sums shown here are those which ought to be paid, not those which were received.

[The yearly rents, continued]

And with £5 0s.0d. due by Thomas Godfrey for tenn acres of
lande, late Salters, and late in the possession of Mr Collinge — £5 0s. 0d.

And with £5 4s.0d. due by John Kinge for 13 acres of the saide
lande, late Salters — £5 4s. 0d.

And with £9 0s.0d. and two combes of rye, due by William
Walker for the new purchased lande, late in the possession of
Mr Collinge — £9 0s. 0d.
2 combes rye

And with £3 6s.8d. due by Anthony Bompsted for two tenementes
in Churchgate Streete — £3 6s. 8d.

And with £1 3s.6d. due by the Widowe Bradishe for a tenement in
Guildhal Streete — £1 3s. 6d.

And with 2s.0d. due by John Brydon for a peece of ground at
Sparrow hill — 2s. 0d.

And with £53 6s.8d. and a bore due by Thomas Peeke for landes
and pasture ground in Hepworth — £53 6s. 8d.
and a bore

And with £6 0s.0d. due by John Sporle for the tenement Larkes,
Great Stubbinges and Lomes Lande — £6 0s. 0d.

And with £2 0s.0d. due by John Dey for Litle Atlyes, Litle
Stubbinges and the Bower — £2 0s. 0d.

And with £6 8s.9d. due by the saide John Dey for divers peeces of
pasture and wood groundes lying in Hepworth and Weston — £6 8s. 9d.

And with 10s.4d. ~~of~~ \due by/ Sir Thomas Jermyn, knight, for 21
acres and an halfe of lande — 10s. 4d.

And with 9d. due by the saide Sir Thomas for lande — 9d.

And with £5 12s.6d. due by John Frost for lande — £5 12s. 6d.

And with £2 0s.0d. due by Humfrey Lynge for groundes lying
nere his howse — £2 0s. 0d.

And with £2 0s.0d. due by William Parkyns for an acre of ground,
with an howse thereupon built, lying and being in Hepworth — £2 0s. 0d.

And with £1 0s.0d. due by Samuell Reve for a mesuage and a
yarde — £1 0s. 0d.

And with £1 3s.4d. due by John Clere, of Weston, for two acres of
pasture lying at the Hendall — £1 3s. 4d.

And with 13s.4d. due by the Widowe Kinge for a tenemente in
Colledg Streete — 13s. 4d.

And with 16s.0d. due by Edmund Milbye for another tenenemente
lying next thereunto — 16s. 0d.

And with 4s.0d. due by the Widowe Siger for an almose howse
lying in the Northgate Strete — 4s. 0d.

And with 4s.0d. due by the Widowe Chitting and the Widowe
Soman for another almose howse there — 4s. 0d.

And with 2s.0d. due by John Baylye for one of the new erected
almose howses in the Garlond Streete — 2s. 0d.

And with 1s.0d. due by Elizabeth Shipp, widowe, for another
almose howse there — 1s. 0d.

And with 5s.0d. due by Roberte Cowper for another almose
howse there — 5s. 0d.

[*The yearly rents, continued*]

And with 2s.0d. due by the Widowe Dodd for another almose
howse there   2s.   0d.

[*f.31v.*]

And with £3 5s.0d. ~~of Joh~~ due by John Mallowes, gentleman, for a
tenemente, gardin and close lying and being in Westgate
Streete   £3   5s.   0d.

And with £2 6s.8d. due by Rafe Adams for parte of an ortyard in
Mr Andrew Streete   £2   6s.   8d.

And with £4 0s.0d. and a combe of rye at Christmas due by
William Ullett for a close at Stanford Bridge   £4   0s.   0d.
   and 1 combe rye

And with £2 6s.8d. due by ~~by~~ the saide William Ullett for a barne
and the residue of the saide ortyard lying in Mr Andrew Streete   £2   6s.   8d.

And with £2 10s.0d. due by Thomas Rose for a cotage and a close
at the Spitlehowse   £2 10s.   0d.

And with £3 0s.0d. due by William Rowge for a mesuage nere St
James church   £3   0s.   0d.

And with a gallon of wyne due by Mr John Revell   A gallon of wyne

And with £4 0s.0d. due by George Baker for landes withowt the
South Gate, lately demysed to Mr Hamond   £4   0s.   0d.

And with £14 14s.0d. due by Mr Ambrose Blagge for landes lying
in the Eastfeildes, lately demysed to Roger Barber, gentleman   £14 14s.   0d.

And with £10 0s.0d. due by William Ullet for landes lying in the
West Feildes, lately demysed to the saide Roger Barber   £10   0s.   0d.

And with £4 0s.0d. due by William Gillye for landes lying in the
saide feildes in the occupacion of [*space*] Wyard of
Horningsherth   £4   0s.   0d.

And with 5s.0d. ~~of~~ \due by/ Samuell Jellowe for a stall in the
Great Markett   5s.   0d.

And with £25 16s.0d. ~~of~~ due by John Hawsted for lande late in the
occupacion of Thomas Turner   £25 16s.   0d.

And with £1 0s.0d. ~~of~~ due by Christofer Cox for a peece of
ground, whereupon a barne was built, and late in the
occupacion of the saide Thomas Turner   £1   0s.   0d.

And with £9 4s.0d. due by Thomas Godfrey for 37 acres of ~~lande~~
St Peters landes and one pightell at the east end of the chappell,
late in the occupacion of Mr Francis Pynner   £19   4s.   0d.

And with 10s.0d. ~~of~~ \due by/ James Fayerclif for a peece of
ground lying in Horse Markett   10s.   0d.

And with £5 0s.0d. due by Adam Gillam for a howse and the
ortyard within the walles at St Peters, and one peece of ground
at the west end of the saide ortyard   £5   0s.   0d.

And with £3 0s.0d. ~~of~~ due by Mr Bennett Barker for a barne and a
stable there   £3   0s.   0d.

And with £10 0s.0d. due by the saide Mr Barker for tythes
belonging to St Peters   £10   0s.   0d.

And with £4 0s.0d. due by Mr Henry Cropley for St Peters Pittes   £4   0s.   0d.

And with £8 0s.0d. due by Mr Roberte Reve for a barne and
landes, demysed to him and Mr Roger Reve, being parcell of
the grange landes without the Risby Gate   £8   0s.   0d.

[The yearly rents, continued]

And with £1 0s.0d. due by Thomas Baker for a tenement, late
   three tenementes, and a gardine in the Raynegate Streete   £1   0s.   0d.

And with 6d. due by Mr James Smyth for ground lying nere the
   Horse Markett   6d.

And with 2s.0d. due by Henry Lansdale for a parcell of ground
   lying there   2s.   0d.

And with 6d. ~~of~~ due by Mr John Inman for a peece of ground
   lying nere Mayde Water Lane   6d.

And with 6s.8d. due by Mr Bridgman for ground lying in Mr
   Andrew Streete   6s.   8d.

And with £1 6s.8d. due by Henry Coe for a tenement in
   Churchgate Streete, late in the occupacion of Richard
   Heigham, gentleman   £1   6s.   8d.

And with 4s.0d. due by Mr Henry Walker for a howse and gardein
   in Pounch Lane   4s.   0d.

And with 5s.0d. due by Mrs Heyward for a tenemente nere her
   dwelling howse in the Risbygate Streete, and a peece of ground
   nere the Teyfen   5s.   0d.

And with 6d. ~~of~~ due by Mr John Parker for a tenemente in Long
   Brakelond   6d.

And with 8d. due by Mr Charles Darby for a tenemente there, late
   Hughe Mathewes   8d.

And with 6d. due by Margaret Grigges, widowe, for a tenemente
   at the North Gate   6d.

And with £16 13s.4d. due by Nicholas Bell, gentleman, for the
   Angell   £16 13s.   4d.

And with £2 17s.4d. due by Mr \William/ Cole for tenementes
   scituate in the Great Markett and Skynners Rowe, demysed to
   Henry Bright the yonger   £2 17s.   4d.

And with £6 0s.0d., 2 capons and a gallon of wyne for a
   tenemente in the Cooke Rowe demysed to James Kent   £6   0s.   0d.
    2 capons, a
    gallon of wyne

[f.32r., old number 67]

And with 3s.4d. due by Mr Thomas Havers for parte of the
   mesuage, sometyme called the Castle, and now in the
   occupacion of Mr Anthony Adams   3s.   0d.

And with 2s.6d. due by William Scott for a peece of ground lying
   nere his howse in Brentgovell Streete   2s.   6d.

And with 3s.4d. due by John Shawe for a gardin in the Southgate
   Streete   3s.   4d.

And with £1 4s.0d. due by Mr Bridgman for lande lying nere
   Hardwick Heathe, late Thomas Overyndes   £1   4s.   0d.

And with 1d. due by Roberte Mance for a peece of ground lying
   next unto his mesuage in Skynners Rowe   1d.

And with 3s.4d. due by Mr Doctor Raven for ground lying in
   Brentgovell Streete, late Thomas Brunwyns   3s.   4d.

And with 1s.0d. due by Eustace Darcy, esquire, for a peece of
   ground in Northgate Streete   1s.   0d.

And with £10 0s.0d. due by Mathew Teversham for the tythes of
Brookehall in Foxheathe in Essex   £10   0s.   0d.

And with £2 10s.0d. due by Henry Bompsted for parte of a
tenemente, given by Mr Richard Walker, scituate in the
Churchegate Strete   £2   10s.   0d.

And with £1 10s.0d. due by [*space*] Maninge, glover, for th'other
parte of the saide tenement   £1   10s.   0d.

And with £4 8s.0d. due by Roberte Bowman, as so much receyved
by him for mariage dynners

[*In another hand*] And with £1 0s.0d. due by John Northfeild for
the Shire Howse   £1   0s.   0d.

> Summa annualium redditum[157]

And with £4 8s.0d. received this yeare for divers marriage
dynners in the Gyldehall   £4   8s.   0d.

> Summa oneris £430 13s.3d.

Allocaciones

The saide accomptant prayethe allowance of theis thinges
following, *videlicet*

Of £1 18s.11½d. by him paide for the free rentes due to His
Majestie for divers landes and tenementes holden of His
Majestie[158]   £1 18s.11½d.

And with 10s.6d. payde to His Majestie for the tenth of St Peters,
and for the receivour his acquitance, and dorekeper 8d., *in toto*   11s.   2d.

And of 1s.6½d. payde to the manour of Wattisfeld for one wholl
yeares rent   1s. 6½d.

And of certen other rentes payde, *videlicet*, 8d. to the hundred and
6d. to Sir Roberte Drury for Layers   1s.   2d.

And of 1½d. to the manour of Fornham All Saincts for Shirehall
Yard at Catshall   1½d.

And of £50 0s.0d. payde to Mr Bedell, preacher of St Maries
church, for this yeare   £50   0s.   0d.

And of £50 0s.0d. payd to Mr Heiley, preacher of St James
church, for this yeare   £50   0s.   0d.

And of £2 0s.0d. payde to Mr Jewell, minister of St Maries church   £2   0s.   0d.

And of £2 0s.0d. payde to Mr Knewstubb, minister of St James
church   £2   0s.   0d.

And of £2 0s.0d. payde to Henry Coe, churchwarden of St Maries   £2   0s.   0d.

Mr Bright his gift

And of £5 0s.0d. bestowed according to Mr Bright his gyft, *videlicet*, to the reparacions of St Maries church £1 0s.0d., to the
reparacions of St James church, £1 0s.0d., to the poore of St
Maries parishe £1 0s.0d., to the poore of St James parishe
£1 0s.0d., to the prisoners in the towne gaole £1 0s.0d., *in toto*   £5   0s.   0d.

---

[157] No amount is given here.

[158] The 1614 charter required the corporation to collect some ancient small rents which had once been
paid to obedientiaries of the abbey, and after the dissolution had been collected for the Crown. These
rents, which came to be called fee farm rents (probably because they provided income with which the
Corporation could pay its fee farm rent to the Crown) were only extinguished in 1963, Borough Council
Minutes, EE500/1/66, p.308.

And of £24 0s.0d. for cloth for the poore, in recompence of the profict of Mr Brightes money, and £2 9s.10d. for makeing the cotes for the poore	£26	9s.	10d.
And of £3 0s.0d. delyvered to Mr Charles Darby and William Grigg for Peter Kymboldes gyft	£3	0s.	0d.
And of £2 12s.0d. to the overseers of the poore of St Maries	£2 12s.		0d.
And of £1 19s.0d. to the overseers of the poore of St James	£1 19s.		0d.
And to of £2 12s.0d. towardes the raysing of a stock to sett the poore on worke, *videlicet*, to either parishe, £1 6s.0d., *in toto*	£2 12s.		0d.
And of 4 combes rye baked owt for the poore at Christmas[159]	4 combes rye		
And of 6s.8d. payde to John Sharpe for bakeinge the same bread for the poore		6s.	8d.
And of 5s.0d. given for healing Priestes girle scald head		5s.	0d.
And of 10s.0d. payde to John Adkyn for curinge of divers poore people		10s.	0d.

[*f.32v.*]

The Poore

And of 10s.0d. given to Rafe Winter to relieve him, his wief and children in the tyme of their sicknes		10s.	0d.
And of £1 0s.0d. given to Oliver Tebold, for healing Henry Allen, which was hurt at the fire at Simon Humfreys howse	£1	0s.	0d.
And of 4s.0d. payd towardes the healing of Gurdons wiefes legg		4s.	0d.
And of 2s.7d. for a sheete and threde to bury old Ingold		2s.	7d.

Officers wages and liveries

And of £1 12s.0d. payde to Roberte Astyn, one of the bedelles, remayning unpayde by Mr Revell, the last accomptant, \for part of his last yeares wages/	£1 12s.		0d.
And of £2 12s.0d. payde to the said Roberte Astyn for this yeares wages	£2 12s.		0d.
And of £2 12s.0d. payde to Roberte Foxgill, the other bedell, for his wages	£2 12s.		0d.
And of £2 10s.0d. payde to Roberte Bowman, the bedell of the Gyldhall, for his wages	£2 10s.		0d.
And of 15s.0d. payde to Roger Lowedale for clothe for a livery for the said Austyn		15s.	0d.
And of 18s.0d. payde to Thomas Sandwith for cloth for a livery for the said Foxgill		18s.	0d.
And of 14s.0d. payde to Mr Bright for clothe for a livry for the said Bowman		14s.	0d.
And of 4s.10d. for faceing for Astyn and Foxgilles cotes		4s.	0d.

[?]*Data*

And of £100 0s.0d. disbursed by consent towardes the shortning of the debt for the purchase of the Ampners Barnes[160]	£100	0s.	0d.
And of £30 0s.0d., borrowed by Mr Goodrich, alderman, Mr Barker and this accomptant, to be imployed towardes the obteyning of His Majesties *lettres patentes* for the better			

---

[159] This reads 'Xpas'.
[160] See Introduction, p.l.

assurance of the churches, the towne landes, and other good uses for the benefitt of the towne[161]	£30	0s.	0d.
And of £7 10s.0d. payde for use of that money where it was borrowed	£7	10s.	0d.
And of £10 0s.0d. payde to Mr Bright, as so much lent by him also for that use	£10	0s.	0d.
And of £10 0s.0d. payde to the Corporacion as so much owing, as appereth by former accompts[162]	£10	0s.	0d.
And of 5s.4d. payde to Bowman for wyne spent as by the bill appereth		5s.	4d.
And of £2 3s.0d. payde to Mrs Bell for a sessions dynner	£2	3s.	0d.
And of £3 7s.2d. payde to Thomas Reade for an other sessions dynner	£3	7s.	2d.
And of £16 0s.0d. payde to John Bedwall for his yeares annuitie	£16	0s.	0d.
And of £10 0s.0d. payde to Mr Pynner for his yeares annuitie	£10	0s.	0d.
And of £5 0s.0d. payde to Mr Collynge for his yeares annuitie	£5	0s.	0d.
And of £5 0s.0d. payde to Mr Cradock for part of the £30 0s.0d. owing to John Man, being the third payment	£5	0s.	0d.
\And of £13 0s.0d. [sic] payde to Mr Cropley for the use of £100 0s.0d. borrowed by the hall	£5	0s.	0d./
And of £3 0s.0d. payde by consent for the [?]rent fine of the Bell Meadowe[163]	£3	0s.	0d.
And of £1 12s.0d. payde to Thomas Wright for two muttons given to the judges	£1	12s.	0d.
And of £1 12s.0d. payde by him for 32 elles of narrow holland for table napkyns for the judges	£1	12s.	0d.
And of £7 2s.0d. payde for the towne aunciante[164]	£7	2s.	0d.
And of 1s.0d. payde to the caryer for bringing home the saide aunciante		1s.	0d.
And of 1s.4d. payde for an ell of buckeram for a case for the aunciante		1s.	4d.
And of divers summes of money layde owt this yeare for reparacions and other nesessaries, *videlicet*			
Of £1 17s.8d. payde to Mr Helye for reparacions done at the howse wherein he dwelleth, as appereth by two billes	£1	17s.	8d.
And of 7s.10d. payde to Edward Whyte for reparacions done at Stamford Bridge		7s.	10d.
And of £2 14s.10d. payde to Thomas Goddard, carpenter, for a wall and worke done at the howse in the Garlond Streete where the Widowe Cage dwelleth	£2	14s.	10d.
And of 10s.0d. payde to Sweeting and Boyton for fyve dayes worke there		10s.	0d.
And of 4s.4d. payde to Mascall for stone and pynning the wall there		4s.	4d.

---

161 This money was used to meet part of the cost of obtaining the charter of 1614.

162 Some of the Corporation chamberlains' accounts which have survived show items marked 'the town' which were regarded as the responsibility of the feoffees.

163 See HD1150/1, f.28r., p.65, n.130 above. Bell Meadow was copyhold land and new feoffees would have been admitted as tenants.

164 See Glossary. This was a banner or ensign with the arms of the borough of Bury St Edmunds upon it.

And of 3s.0d. payde to Hunt for three loades of claye spent there	3s.	0d.
And of 6d. payde for splent bynd used at the saide howse		6d.
And of 1s.9d. payde to Roger Myller for lyme spent there	1s.	9d.
And of £1 13s.8d. payde for worke and stuff at the Guihald [*sic*] as by the bill appereth	£1 13s.	4d. [*sic*]
And of 3s.2d. payde to Olyver Theobold for ~~th~~ mending the glasse there	3s.	2d.
And of £2 19s.2d. payde for repayringe of four welles, one in the Westgate street, one at the almose howses next St Maryes church, one in the Garlond Streete and one against Henry Neales	£2 19s.	2d.
And of 18s.0d. payde to Mr Claydon for reparacions by him done at the South Gate	18s.	0d.

[*f.33r., old number 74*]

And of 7s.9d. payde to William Rowge for reparacions done by him at his howse	7s.	9d.
And of 2s.4d. payde to Thomas Goddard for bourde, nayles and worke done at St Peters	2s.	4d.
And of 2s.0d. payde to Thomas Rose for two dayes worke in clayinge there	2s.	0d.
And of 3s.10d. payde to Henry Steele for lyme, tyles and worke done at St Peters and the Spitlehowse	3s.	10d.
And of 4s.2d. payde to Mawnde for ~~worke~~ glasing worke done at St Peters	4s.	2d.
And of 16s.9d. payde for reparacions done at the ministers howses, as appereth by the bill	16s.	9d.
And of 6d. for two bushelles of lyme used at the almose howse where John Baylye dwelleth		6d.
And of 12s.1d. payde to Roberte Bowman for worke and bere as appereth by his bill	12s.	1d.
And of ~~2s.6d.~~ £1 12s.0d. payde to William Cobb for 8 leather buckettes for the Guildhald[165]	£1 12s.	0d.
And of £1 12s.0d. payde to Henry Sweeting and Isaacc Harrold for repayringe the iron worke of the two towne cromes	£1 12s.	0d.
And of 2s.6d. gyven to fyve men that did ware the towne coslettes at the view of armor	2s.	6d.
And of 7s.8d. layde owt for wyne and cakes at the election of the new alderman	7s.	8d.
And of £6 5s.2d. for the charges of the dynner ~~taken~~ at the tyme of this accompt taking	£6 5s.	2d.
And of 15s.0d. for the receivors fee	10s.	0d. [*sic*]
And of 5s.0d. for the clerks fee	5s.	0d.
And of one bore given to the alderman		1 bore
Summa allocacionum [*No amount is given*]		
Et sic debet [*No amount given*]		

---

[165] These buckets were to be used for fire-fighting. In the inventory of 11 January 1585, pinned into the first of these account books, twelve leather buckets marked with a sheaf of arrows were listed as being in the chamber, HD1150/1, 23a. The cromes mentioned in the next entry were also for fire-fighting.

And there remayne in the handes of the persons under written theis sums of money and other thinges, parcell of ~~the year~~ their yearly rentes, due within the tyme of this accompt, as followeth, not received by this accomptant, *videlicet*

In the handes of Sir Thomas Jermyn, knight, for certein landes in Hepworth	10s.	4d.
And in his handes for certen other landes there		9d.
And in the handes of William Parkyn for a cotage and an acre of ground in Hepworth	£1 0s.	0d.
And in the handes of Thomas Peeke for parte of his rent for certen landes in Hepworthe	£11 0s.	0d.
And in the handes of Edmund Milby for a tenement in Colledge Streete	16s.	0d.
And in the handes of [space] Siger, widowe, for a tenement in the Northgate Streete	4s.	0d.
And in the handes of [space] Chitting, widowe, for a tenement there	4s.	0d.
And in the handes of James Smythe, esquire, for a peece of ground nere the Horse Markett		6d.
And in the handes of John Parker for a tenement in the Long Brakelond		6d.
And in the handes of Mr Charles Darby for a tenement, late Hughe Mathewes		8d.
And in the handes of Margaret Grigges, widowe, for a tenement at the North Gate		6d.
And in the handes of Mr Havers, of London, for parte of the tenement called the Castle, in the occupacion of Mr Anthony Adams	3s.	4d.
And in the handes of John Shawe for a gardin in the Southgate Streete	3s.	4d.
And in the handes of Roberte Mance for a peece of ground in Skynners Rowe		1d.
And ~~of~~ in the handes of Eustace Darcy, esquire, for a peece of ground in Northgate Streete	1s.	0d.

[*f.33v.*]

And in the handes of Mr Doctor Raven for a peece of ground, late Thomas Brunwyns, nere Brentgovell Streete	3s.	4d.
And in the handes of Thomas Rose for parte of his rent for the howse and close nere the Spitlehowse	5s.	0d.
And in the handes of James Kent, a gallon of wyne	a gallon of wyne	
And in the handes of [space] Manninge, glover, for parte of his rent for the howse given by Mr Walker	15s.	0d.
And in the handes of Samuell Jellowe for parte of his rent for a stall in the Great Markett	2s.	6d.

    Summa

    Summa totalis allocacionum £426 10s.8½d.,

    1 bore, 1 gallon of wyne and three combes of rye

    And soe there remayneth good in the hand of this accomptant £3 9s. 8½d. which summe he hathe delyvered over to John Mallowes, chosen for the next receivour

[f.34r., old number 66]

1616

The accompt of John Mallowes, gentleman, receivor of the rentes and revenues belonging to the common use and benefitt of the towne of Bury St Edmund, made and yealded upp the second day of January in the fourtenth yeare of the reigne of Our Soveraigne Lorde Kinge James, [*1617*] for one wholl yeare then endid.

Onus

Inprimis the saide accomptant dothe charge himself with £3 9s.8½d. by him received of Mr Henry Gippes, the last receivor, remayninge good in his handes upon the determinacion of his accompt, as by the foote of his accompt appereth £3   9s. 8½d.

And with 10s.2d. by him received of divers persons for arrerages left in super upon former accomptes, *videlicet,*

With 6s.8d. for parte of the arrerages due by Mr Havers of London for parte of the mesuage aunciently called the Castle, now used with the howse in the occuupacion of Mr Anthony Adams. And with 1s.0d. received of Mr Eustace Darcye for his rent due in the tyme of Mr Gipps, the last accomptant. And with 2s.6d. received of Samuell Jellowe for his half yeares rent arrere in the tyme of the saide Mr Gipps, the last accomptant, *in toto* 10s.   2d.

And with three hundred fourtye <*deletion*> poundes, ~~six~~ \tenn/shillinges ~~eleven~~ \and six/ pence, one bore, two capons, two gallons of wyne and three combes of rye, being the certein yearly rentes and revenues of this howse particularly expressed in the rentall thereof made, as by the same rentall appereth £340 10s. 11d.[166]

1 bore, 2 capons,
2 gallons of wyne,
3 combes of rye

And with £4 4s.0d. \received this yeare/ for mariage dynners kept in the Gyldehall £4   4s.   0d.

Summa oneris ~~£349 10s.9½d.~~ \£348 14s.4½d./[167]
one bore, two capons, two gallons of wyne
and three combes of rye.

Allocaciones
Out Rentes and Tenthes

Inprimis the saide accomptant dothe praye allowaunce of £1 18s.11½d. by him payde for the rentes due to His Majestie for divers landes and tenementes holden of His Majestie £1 18s.11½d.

And of 10s.6d. payde to His Majesties Receiver Generall for the tenthe of St Peters, and for the receivor his acquittance, 4d., and to his dore keper 4d. 11s.   2d.

And of 1s.6½d. payde to the manor of Wattisfeild for one wholl yeres rent 1s. 6½d.

And of 1½d. payde to the manor of Fornham All Sainctes for a yeres rent 1½d.

---

166 The numerals forming these amounts have been much altered.
167 This amount is also given in arabic numerals.

And of 6d. payde to the manor of Rougham for a yeres rent   6d.

And of 8d. payde to the bailief of the hundred of Thedwardstree
for Layers   8d.

The Free Schole

And of £5 9s.10d. by him payde to the Governors of the Free
Gramer Schole for St Peters and the Grange landes   £5 9s. 10d.

Preachers

And of £50 0s.0d. payde to Mr Heily, preacher of St James, for his
yeres allowance owt of this howse   £50 0s. 0d.

And of £12 10s.0d. payde to Mr Bedell, late preacher of St
Maryes, for one quarter endid at the Annunciacion, 1616   £12 10s. 0d.

And of £5 0s.0d. more given to Mr Bedell towardes his paynes in
preachinge and mayneteyninge the Fryday exercise whilest the
parishe hathe been destitute of a preacher   £5 0s. 0d.

And of £12 10s.0d. payde to Mr Gybbon, preacher of St Maryes,
for the quarter betwene Michaelmas and Christmas last   £12 10s. 0d.

And of £5 0s.0d. given to Mr Jewell, minister of St Maryes, for
divers sermons by him preached there whilest the place was
destitute of a preacher   £5 0s. 0d.

93–2–9 *ob*[168]

[*f.34v.*]

Preachers

And of £18 6s.9d. given to divers preachers which supplyed the
place upon divers Sabothe dayes, after the departure of Mr
Bedell and untill the coming of Mr Gybbon, and for the
expenses of them and their horses at the tymes of their being
here at common inns, and for the expenses of Mr Alderman
Gooderich, Mr Bedell, Mr Heily and divers others travelling
sundry tymes to Cambridge and other places to provide a
preacher for St Maries parishe as by the billes of particuler
appereth   £18 6s. 9d.

Annuities

And of £10 0s.0d. payde to Mr Pynner for his annuitie for this
yeare   £10 0s. 0d.

And of £5 0s.0d. payde to Mr Colling for his annuitie for this yeare   £5 0s. 0d.

And of £16 0s.0d. payde to John Bedwall for his annuitie for this
yeare   £16 0s. 0d.

And of £5 0s.0d. payde to Mr Cradock in parte of payment of the
£30 0s.0d. owinge to John Man, deceased, this being the 4th
payment at £5 0s.0d. *per annum*   £5 0s. 0d.

And of £8 0s.0d. payde to Mr Raineberd for one yeres use of £100
0s.0d. borrowed of him by the Company   £8 0s. 0d.

And of 4d. for paper and 6d. for waxe   10d.

And of 5s.0d. payde towardes the provision of His Majesties
houshold   5s. 0d.

---

[168] Here and elsewhere an intermediate total, probably taken from the original account, is given.

And of 6s.8d. payde towardes the charges of the generall muster and trayninge	6s.	8d.
And of £8 0s.0d. payde to Newman, the paynter, of Cambridge for the kinges armes[169]	£8 0s.	0d.
And of £11 0s.0d. payde to Mr Fenn, the paynter, for the kinges picture for the hall[170]	£11 0s.	0d.
And of 7s.8d. for other charges layde owt abowt the same picture	7s.	8d.
And of £3 6s.8d. for the picture of Jankyn Smyth and Mr Thomas Bright, two of our worthy benefactors[171]	£3 6s.	8d.
And of £2 0s.0d. payde for a parte of Doctor Perse his will, and afterwardes for a copy of the wholl will	£2 0s.	0d.
\And of 19s.6d. spent at Cambridge the first tyme when divers of the Company rode abowt Dr Perse his gift[172]	19s.	6d./

Pencions

And of £5 0s.0d. given to Mr William Cooke, one of this company, for one yeres pencion for his paynes taken in former tymes[173]	£5 0s.	0d.

Mr Brightes gyft

And of £5 0s.0d. bestowed according to Mr Brightes will, *videlicet*, to the reparacions of St Maries church £1 0s.0d., to the reparacions of St James church £1 0s.0d., to the poore of St Maries parishe £1 0s.0d., to the poore of St James parishe £1 0s.0d., to the prisoners of the towne gaole £1 0s.0d., *in toto*	£5 0s.	0d.
For 20 dosen of grayes to clothe the poore accordinge to Mr Brights gyft £20 4s.0d. Payde to Mr Henry Gipps for lyninges, thred and other thinges to make upp those clothes as by his bill appereth, £1 10s.8d. And payde to divers taylers for making upp that apparell as by Mr Brightes bill appereth, £3 8s.4d., *in toto*	£26 3s.	3d.

The Ministers and Churches

And of £2 0s.0d. payde to Mr Jewell, minister of St Maries	£2 0s.	0d.
And of £2 0s.0d. payde to Mr Knewstubbe, minister of St James	£2 0s.	0d.
And of £1 0s.0d. payde towardes the reparacions of St Maries churche	£1 0s.	0d.
And of £1 0s.0d. payde towardes the reparacions of St James churche	£1 0s.	0d.

---

169 These arms are in the Court Room at the Guildhall, the initial I for James having later been altered to C. The date 1616 is still legible on the frame, but the rest of the inscription is obscured by many coats of varnish.

170 The portrait of James I also hangs in the Court Room.

171 These portraits are now hung in the Banqueting Room. See Introduction, p.liii.

172 Dr Perse's bequest was left to the Corporation so expenditure about it should not have been found here but in the Corporation books. This is another instance of the feoffees helping out the Corporation. For Dr Perse, see Notes on People.

173 On 3 January 1616 William Cooke was granted a pension of £5 a year for life, being ill and infirm and unfit to serve the office of clerk to the company any longer, Minutes H2/6/2.1, p.43. Cooke had already been granted another pension of £5 a year by the governors of the Grammar School on 12 August 1615, when it was said that although he had poor sight and hearing, his advice was still valued, Governors' Minutes, E5/9/202.1, p.72.

The Judges

And of £2 0s.0d. for a calf and a wether given to the judges at Lent assises	£2 0s.	0d.
And for a calf, a wether and 6 fatt turkyes given to the judges at somer assises	£1 12s.	0d.
And of 3s.0d. payde for makeing of 3 dosen of napkyns bought for the judges in the tyme of Mr Gippes, the last receivor	3s.	0d.

The Poore

And of £1 0s.0d. given to John Adkyn for bone setting and divers cures done to divers poore people, as by his bill appereth	£1 0s.	0d.
To Ambrose Litchfeild for chirurgery upon Townesendes wief, a poore woman haveing a grievous sore brest	10s.	0d.
To the overseers of the poore of St Maryes parishe	£2 12s.	0d.
To the overseers of the poore of St James parishe	£2 12s.	0d.
To divers poore folke at sundry tymes	12s.	0d.
To Samuell Stanton upon his bill for thinges delivered for the poore	4s.	0d.
For a shette and two shirtes for Cornishe, a poore creature	7s.	8d.
To the poore prisoners in the gaole in wood, according to Mrs Odehams gyft	10s.	0d.
Three combes rye baked for the poore against Christmas	3 combes rye	
For grynding and bakeing the same	8s.	0d.
To the poore in the East and Northe wardes according to Peter Kembolds gyft	£3 0s.	0d.

147–7–0

[f.35r, old number 94]

Officers wages and lyveries

To Robert Bowman, the bedell of the hall, for his yeares wages	£2 10s.	0d.
To Mr Lowdale for a cote clothe for a lyvery for him	15s.	9d.
To Foxgill, one of the towne bedelles, for his yeares wages	£2 12s.	0d.
To Mr Bright for a cote clothe for a lyvery for him	£1 2s.	6d.
To Roberte Austyn, th'other towne bedell, for his yeres wages	£2 12s.	0d.
To Mr Bright for a cote clothe for a lyvery for him	16s.	0d.
To Mr Gipps for trymming for Allingtons cote	2s.	4d.

Ministers howses

And of divers summes of money layde owt this yeare for reparacions, *videlicet*

For postes, rayles and pales sett at the ministers howses, and for carpenters wages, as by the carpenters bill appereth	11s.	10d.
To the stone setter for amending the broken places there		4d.
To Mr ~~Jewell~~ Heiley for reparacions done at his howse, as by his bill appereth	19s.	0d.
\To Mr Jewell for reparacions done at his howse, as by his bill apperethe	4s.	3d./

St Peters

To Seaman, the smyth, for great nayles fetched by the Widowe Snowden		6d.
For strawe for thatchinge	9s.	0d.
For thatchinge stuff	2s.	0d.

240

To Silvester for thatchinge	6s.	8d.
For claye	1s.	0d.
To Rose for two dayes worke in clayinge	2s.	0d.
To the smyth for mending three lockes there	1s.	0d.
For makeing a new hollowe key	1s.	0d.
For bourding upp a place decayed in the chapell chamber	1s.	1d.
To Mr Barker, farmor of the barne there, for reperacions done by him as appereth by his bill	11s.	0d.
For setting of postes by the waye side to kepe cartes from the fense	3s.	9d.
For setting postes and rayles for a fense against the broken place there	5s.	0d.

Reperacions

Payde to Mr Claydon, receivor of the rentes of the Ampners Barnes, upon a bill of debt made by William Francis to that company, £3 15s.0d., which bill I toke in for that William Francis had agreed with the feoffees to worke owt that debt in new floringe and repayreing the inner chamber at the Gyldehall, but after he had done some parte thereof, he left the worke, and so the bill resteth good to be recorded by this company[174]	£3	15s.	0d.
Payde to Bowman, 6° *Julii*, upon his bill for plombers worke and carpenters worke done at the Gylldehall		11s.	0d.
For 50 *libre* solder	£1	17s.	6d.
To Prigge, the plomber, for worke done there		8s.	9d.
To Gyles Howes, carpenter, upon his bill, 13° *Julii*, for worke done there		19s.	6d.
To a smyth for opening the lock of the great chest			3d.
To Edward Bourne for iron for the dogges in the kitchen chimmney, 3 q[*uarte*]rs 2 *libre*		13s.	6d.
To the smyth for workemanshipp		3s.	4d.
To the mason for setting the same and makeing the harthe and a place to sett dishes from hande		2s.	4d.
For 227 foote of bourd for planchering in the new chamber there	£1	2s.	3d.
For 72 of bourd for benches and backes		7s.	0d.
For a plancke to amend the well		1s.	0d.
To Balles, the mason, upon his bill for worke and stuff 18° *Julii*	£1	13s.	10d.
To Bowman then upon his bill		16s.	8d.
For two loades of brick layde in there		15s.	0d.
For a loade of tyles layde in there		16s.	0d.
For casting the menure owt of the sinke in the yarde		1s.	4d.
For a grate of iron to laye over that synke		2s.	4d.
For leade to fastne the same			6d.
To Cromwell, the smyth, for spickyns and nayles		6s.	2d.
For bourde and ledges for the dore going upp to the garrett		2s.	4d.
\For makeing the same dore		1s.	0d./

---

[174] The feoffees' relations with the purchasers of Almoners Barns and the Corporation were close. The feoffees had taken over a debt due to the purchasers and had hoped to recover it by having work done to the same value.

To Gyles upon his bill, 20 *Julii*	6s.	3d.
To Cromwell for hookes, hingells and nayles, 26 *Julii*	1s.	9d.
For a planke for a dresser bourde in the kitchin	7s.	0d.
For feete, bourd and nayles to make upp the same dresser, and to Giles for workmanshipp, as by his bill appereth	6s.	3d.
For a grate of iron ~~in the~~ to laye over the sinke in the kitchin and for leade and workemanshipp to fastne the same	3s.	0d.

30–16–1

[f.35v.]

For stuff and workmanshipp for the new table in the inner chamber		19s.	0d.
To Adam Bull for a casement for the new windowe in the inner chamber		2s.	6d.
For a large sheete of leade to lay before the chimney to catche the dripping wayinge 166½ *libre*[175]	£1	7s.	0d.
To Prigg for stuff and workmanshipp in glasing there	£1	3s.	4d.
To Kinge for a loade of sande layde in there		1s.	0d.
More to Prigg for glasinge there		1s.	2d.
To Balles, the mason, upon his bill, for stuff and workemanshipp at the almose howses in the Crowne Streete	£1	8s.	6d.
For a loade of claye		1s.	0d.
For claying, splentes and splentbynde		6s.	3d.
For a loade of sande		1s.	0d.
To Gyles for stuff and workmanshipp there, and at Roopers howse \and St Peters/ 4° *Januarii* as by his bill appereth	£1	18s.	11d.
To Gyles Howes for stuff and workmanshipp at the almose howses in the Scholehall Streete, by St Maries churche, as by his bill appereth, 7° *Octobris*	£1	18s.	1d.
To a laborer to pluck e downe and carry away the thatch there		2s.	4d.
To Giles Howes for stuff and workmanshipp at those almose howses, and at Roopers howse, as by his bill appere, 13° *Octobris*	£1	15s.	0d.
To Prigge, the plomber, for leade, solder and workemanshipp at those almose howses in the Scholehall Streete, as by his bill appereth	£3	4s.	10d.
For four loades of tyles layde in at those almose howses	£3	0s.	0d.
To Balles, the mason, upon his bill, 19 *Octobris*, for stuff and workmanshipp there	£1	6s.	6d.
To Roger Myller, 1° November, for lyme delivered to the almose howses as appereth by his bill		6s.	6d.
For two loades of sande		2s.	0d.
To Edward Bourne, upon his bill for nayles		6s.	6d.
To Adam Bull for 2 keyes and mending the lockes there		1s.	0d.
To Butler, the mason, upon his bill, 4° *Novembris*, for stuff and workmanshipp at Roopers howse		12s.	2d.
For three dayes worke of two clayers there		6s.	0d.
For two loades of claye there		2s.	0d.
To Prigg, the glasyer, for stuff and workmanshipp \there/ as by his bill appereth	£1	12s.	6d.

---

[175] The text reads '*C di xvj li di*'.

To Giles Howes for stuff and workmanshipp in makeing upp the decayed well in the Short Braklond	£1 3s.	0d.
To Roberte Bowman upon his bill, 2° *Januarii*, for divers thinges by him done and layde owt, as by his bill appereth	£1 7s.	6d.
To Mr Christofer Cox for a wellrope for the Spitlehowse	1s.	4d.
Payde to Edward Whyte for reperacions done at Stamford Bridge	2s.	10d.
Payde fo Edward Bourne for three firr poles to make towne ladders, 10s.0d., and for the cariage of them 2s.3d.	12s.	3d.
Payde for finishinge one of the towne cromes	2s.	4d.

Charges of sute

Layde owt in prosecuting against Thomas Baker, one of the feoffees, upon the Commission of Charitable Uses, for that he obstinately refused to joyne with the rest of the feoffees in renewing the Feoffment of the Towne Landes, according to the will of Jankyn Smyth, *videlicet*,[176]

For parte of the charges of the Commission		6s.	8d.		
For drawing the inquisicion		6s.	8d.		
To Sir George Waldegraves clerke for ingrossing the same		5s.	0d.		
To Mr Bell for parte of the commissioners and jurors charges	£2	0s.	0d.		
To the Baily towardes the summoning of the jury		2s.	0d.		
For drawing the decree against him, and to the clerke for ingrossing the same		10s.	0d.		
For filinge the same in the Petty Bagg Office		2s.	0d.		
The writ of execucion thereupon		13s.	10d.		
For two attachmentes against him for disobeying the decree		5s.	0d.		
Given to a messenger which went to Nichlas Heyward to summon him to appere at the same Commission <*deletion*>		1s.	0d.	£4 11s.	2d.

28–19–0

[f.36r., old number 95]

Layde owt in defense of two sutes brought by Nicholas Heyward and Walston for parte of the howse and ground in Gyldehall Strete, late in the tenure of Mr Richard Heigham, and now demysed to Henry Coe, as by the particular bill of charges appereth[177]	£2 4s.	6d.
Layde owt in prosecutinge an other action against Walston, which came to tryall, for the same howse and ground, as by the bill of particulers appereth	£5 6s.	3d.
To Henry Coe for so much layde owt by him to witnesses and otherwise at those two sutes, and at the Commission of Charitable Uses, as by his bill appereth	14s.	6d.

---

176 This is discussed in the Introduction, p.xxxi.

177 Richard Heigham lived in the house on the corner of Churchgate Street and Guildhall Street which was part of Tassell's gift. On 15 March 1616 John Mallowes was instructed to prosecute before the Commissioners for Charitable Uses for lands and tenements unjustly withheld or held without lease, Minutes, H2/6/2.1, p.44. It is not yet clear whether this litigation arose from this decision.

Spent in a supper at in Holborne, 3° *Maii* 1616, upon \when/ Mr Goldsmith, Mr Hill, Mr Boldero, Mr Claydon and myself mett in conference with Nicholas Heyward for the ending of theis sutes and questions	12s.	0d.
For entring the two accomptes of Mr Revell and Mr Gipps, the two last receivors, before the tyme of this receivor, the same being left unentred by Mr Cooke, the last clerke of this company	10s.	0d.
For makeing a new rentall for the next receivor	3s.	4d.
For drawing and ingrossing the bonde and release concerninge the Angell	5s.	0d.
The receivors fee	15s.	0d.
The clerkes fee	10s.	0d.
For makeing the new feoffment and two releases	10s.	0d.
The charges of the dynner at the tyme of this accompt makeing	£10 10s.	5d.
Delyvered to Mr Alderman, by consent, a bore		1 bore
Layde owt by consent for wyne at the election of the new alderman	£1 0s.	0d.
To Roberte Bowman, the bedell of the hall, upon his bill delivered at the tyme of the fynishing of this accompt, for divers thinges layde owt and done by him this yeare at the hall, as by his bill of particulers appereth	£1 7s.	6d.
To him for a lock for the chamber dore goinge upp to the garrett	1s.	0d.

24–9–

Summa totalis allocacionum £323 12s.10d.

And there remayne in super in the handes of the persons undernamed theis summs of money and other thinges of their yearly rentes due within the tyme of this accompt, and not received by this accomptant, as followeth, *videlicet*

Supers

Sir Thomas Jermyn, knight, for certen landes in Hepworthe	10s.	4d.
The same Sir Thomas Jermyn for other landes in Hepworth		9d.
Thomas Peake for divers landes and groundes in Hepworth	£53 6s.	6d.
William Perkyns for a cotage and an acre of ground in Hepworth	£2 0s.	0d.
Lawrence Coldham for an acre of grounde lande in Barningham	2s.	0d.
Edmund Milby for a howse in Colledge Streete	16s.	0d.
The Widowe Sparrowe for an howse in the Northgate Streete	4s.	0d.
The Widowe Chitting for an howse there	4s.	0d.
The Widowe Dodd for an howse in the Garlond Streete	2s.	0d.
Thomas Rose for the half \yeare/ for the cotage and close by the Spitlehowse	£1 5s.	0d.
Mr James Smyth for a peece of ground by the Horse Markett		6d.
Mr James Fayerclif for a peece of ground by the Horse Markett	10s.	0d.
Mr John Parker for a tenement in the Long Brakelond		6d.
Mr Charles Darby for a tenement there, late Hughe Mathewes		8d.
Margaret Grigges, widowe, for parcell of a tenement at the North Gate		6d.
Roberte Mance for a peece of ground in Skynners Lane		1d.
Mr D[r] Raven for a peece of ground, late in the possession of Thomas Brunwyn, in Brentgovell Streete	3s.	4d.

[*f.36v.*]
John Northfeild for the Shire howse[178] and a gardine plott thereto
    adjoyninge   £1   0s.   0d.
Henry Bompsted for ~~the~~ his half yeres rent   £1   5s.   0d.
William Manninge, glover, for his half yeares rent   15s.   0d.
Mr John Revell a gallon of wyne   A gallon of wyne
James Kent a gallon of wyne and 2 capons   A gallon of wyne
                                and two capons

        Summa £62 6s.2d., two capons and two gallons of wyne
        Summa totalis allocacionum £386 <deletion> 4d.
        one bore, two capons, two gallons of wyne and
        three combes of rye.
        Soe this accomptant is in surplus to be answered unto him
        by the next Receivor ~~£36 9s.~~ <deletion> ~~6½d.~~ £37 5s.11½d.
37–5–11 *obulus*

[*f.37r.*, old number *93*]

1617

The accompt of John Hill, gentleman, receivor of the rentes and revenues belonging to the towne use and benefitt of the towne of Bury St Edmundes, made and yealded upp the 6th day of Januarye, in the fiftenth yeare of the reigne of our Soveraigne Lord, Kinge James, [*1618*] for one wholl yeare then ended

Onus

Of the remainder of the last accompt *nulla f*or that the last
    accomptant was in surplus, *ut patet in precedenti compoto*
But this accomptant doth charge himself with divers summes of
    money by him received of divers persons for arrerages of
    rentes left in super upon former accomptes, *videlicet*, of
    Thomas Peake £64 6s.6d., and of Laurence Coldham, gentle-
    man, £1 6s.8d., *in toto*   £65 13s.   2d.
And with 5s.4d. by him received by consent of the company for 4
    capons, in super upon James Kent, parcell of his rent arrere   5s.   4d.
And with £340 10s.6d., one boare, two capons, two gallons of
    wyne and three combes of rye beinge the certen yearely rentes
    and revenues of this house, for this yeare, particularly
    expressed in the rentall thereof made, as by the same rentall
    appeareth   £340 10s.   6d.
                                    one boare, two
                                    capons, two
                               gallons of wyne
                           and three combes
                                of rye
And with five poundes received this yeare for mariage dynners   £5   0s.   0d.
And with ten poundes received of Mr Bright, for the legacye of
    Mr Esty, late preacher of the towne[179]   £10   0s.   0d.

---

[178] There is a blot over the words which appear to read 'for the Shire howse'.
[179] For Mr Esty's gift see Appendix 8, *sub* 1617 and Notes on People.

~~Summa oneris £421 9s.0d., one boare, 2 capons,~~
~~2 gallons of wyne and 3 combes of rye~~

And with £6 15s.0d. by him received for wood cutt downe and solde this yere at Hepworth, *videlicet*, £4 10s.0d. received of Mr Sporle, and £2 0s.0d. received of Samuel Pott, *in toto*   £6 15s.   0d.

  Summa oneris £428 4s.0d., one boare, two capons,
  two gallons of wyne, and three combes of rye.

Allocaciones

Inprimis the said accomptant doth pray allowance of £1 18s.11½d. by him paide for the rentes due to His Majestie, for divers landes and tenementes holden of His Majestie, for one whole yeare ended at the feast of St Michaell th'arcangell last past   £1 18s. 11½d.

And of ten shillinges six pence paide to His Majesties Receivor Generall for the tenth of St Peters, and for the receivors acquitance 4d., and to his dore keeper, 4d.   11s.   2d.

And of 1s.6½d. paide to the manor of Watisfeilde for one wholl yeares rent   1s. 6½d.

And of 3d. paide to the mannor of Forneham All Sainctes for two yeares rent ended at the feast of St Michaell last past   3d.

And of 6d. paide to the manor of Rougham for one wholl yeares rent then due   6d.

And of 9d. paide to John Frost for the wholl yeares hallymot rent due at St Michaell last   9d.

And of 8d. paide to the bayly of the hundred of Thedwastree for one wholl yeares rent then due   8d.

And of 6d. payde for one wholl yeares rent then due for the mannor of Rushalles   6d.

And of £5 9s.10½d. paide to the Governors of the Free Grammer Schole for St Peters and the Graunge landes   £5 9s. 10½d.

And of £50 0s.0d. paide to Mr Heiley, preacher of St James his parish, for his yeares allowance out of this howse   £50 0s.   0d.

And of £50 0s.0d. paid to Mr Gibbon, preacher of St
Maries ħ parish, for his yeares allowance owt of this howse   £50 0s.   0d.

And of £2 0s.0d. paide to Mr Jewell, minister of St Maries parish   £2 0s.   0d.

And of £2 0s.0d. paide to Mr Knewstubb, minister of St James parish   £2 0s.   0d.

And of £10 0s.0d. paide to Mr Pynner for his annuitye for this yeare   £10 0s.   0d.

And of £5 0s.0d. paide to Mr Henry Collinge for his annuitie for this yeare   £5 0s.   0d.

And of £16 0s.0d. paide to John Bedwell for his annuitye for this yeare   £16 0s.   0d.

And of £5 0s.0d. paide to Mr Craddocke, in parte of payment of £30 0s.0d. owinge to John Mann, deceased, this beinge the fift payment at £5 0s.0d. *per annum*   £5 0s.   0d.

And of £8 0s.0d. payde to Mr Rainberde for one yeares use of £100 0s.0d. borrowed of him by the Company   £8 0s.   0d.

[*f.37v.*]
And of £5 0s.0d. given to Mr William Cooke, one of this

company, for one yeares pencion for his paines in former tymes	£5	0s.	0d.

And of £5 0s.0d. bestowed accordinge to Mr Brightes will, *videlicet*, towardes the reparacions of St Maries church £1 0s.0d., towardes the reparacions of St James church £1 0s.0d., to the poore of St Maries parish £1 0s.0d., to the poore of St James parish £1 0s.0d., to the prisoners in the towne gaole £1 0s.0d., *in toto* — £5 0s. 0d.

And of 24 dozen of grayes to cloath the poore accordinge to Mr Brights gift, £23 8s.2d., and £2 6s.11d. payde to Mr Henry Gipps for lynings, thredd and other things to make upp those cloathes, as by his bill appeareth, and for faceinge of the beadelles coates, and to divers taylors for making upp the apparrell, as appeareth by their billes, for St James his parish and likewise for the makeinge of them for the poore of St Maries parish £4 4s.2d., and of 7s.2d. payde to Mr Bright for more lynings and more cloth — £30 6s. 5d.

And of £1 0s.0d. payde to William Manninge, churchwarden of St Maries, and £1 0s.0d. paide to Roger Sharpe, churchwarden of St James parish, towardes the reparacions of both churches — £2 0s. 0d.

And of £1 11s.6d. for a veale and a weather given to the judges at Lent assises — £1 11s. 6d.

And of £1 18s.0d. for a weather, a veale and a lambe given to the judges at sommer assises — £1 18s. 0d.

And of £2 12s.0d. given to the overseers of the poore of St Maries parish — £2 12s. 0d.

And of £2 12s.0d. given to the overseers of the poore of St James parish — £2 0s. 0d.

And of 6d. given to a poore woman that traveled thoroughe the towne with her children, beinge sent accordinge to the Statute — 6d.

And of £1 6s.0d. more paide to the overseers of St James his parish upon raisinge the Guildhall 2s.0d. a weeke from Michaelmas last[180] — £1 6s. 0d.

And of 3s.6d. given to the Widowe Preist towardes her losse by fier — 3s. 6d.

And of 2s.4d. given at severall tymes to Mawnde, in the tyme of his sicknes — 2s. 4d.

And of 4d. given to the widowe Smith in prison — 4d.

And of 2s.0d. given to John Atkin for healing Mother Dodsons legg — 2s. 0d.

And of 10s.0d. given upon Easter daye last to a Grecian, because he shold not gather in the churches, by the appointment of Mr Alderman Browne, Mr Mallowes and other of the Feoffees then present[181] — 10s. 0d.

And of 1s.0d. given to Bradley, the cooke, for his wief, beinge sick in childbedd — 1s. 0d.

---

180 The Guildhall's assessment for rates had been increased.

181 This is the second instance in these accounts where a Grecian visited the town to collect money. It can be assumed that now, as in 1612, he was collecting under the authority of a letter, a 'church brief' from the bishop of Norwich. See above, p.207, n.136.

And of 4d. given to a poore travelor, beinge sick			4d.
And of 2s.0d. given to the Widowe Dodds, beinge sicke, by the handes of Mr Gipps		2s.	0d.
And of 2s.0d. given to Riches wief, beinge sicke, and her husband gone, she haveinge four children		2s.	0d.
And of 5s.0d. gyven to the overseers of St Maryes parish for the releif of Dysters wief, beinge very sick, and her husband gone		5s.	0d.
And of 3 combes of rye baked for the poore		3 combes of rye	
And of 9s.0d. for grindinge and bakinge the same		9s.	0d.
And of 10s.0d. given to the poore prisoners in wood, accordinge to Mrs Odams will		10s.	0d.
And of £3 0s.0d. given to the poore of the East and North Wardes, accordinge to Peter Kembolds will	£3	0s.	0d.
And of 1s.0d. given to Richard Hunt, beinge poore		1s.	0d.
And of 6d. given to Edward Avys, beinge poore			6d.
And of 1s.0d. given to Mother Shipp, towards the buyinge of [space] for two poore children		1s.	0d.
And of £2 10s.0d. paide to Roberte Bowman for his yeares wages	£2	0s.	0d.
And of £2 12s.0d. paide to Roberte Allington, beadell of St James parish, for his yeares wages	£2	12s.	0d.
And of £2 12s.0d. payde to Roberte Austen, beadell of St Maryes parish, for his yeares wages	£2	12s.	0d.
And of £2 16s.6d. payde for three liveries for the three beadelles to Mr Bright	£2	16s.	0d.
And of 15s.0d. to the receivor for his fee		15s.	0d.
And of 10s.0d. to the clerke for his fee		10s.	0d.

[f.38r., old number 96]

And of £5 16s.1d. for the reparacions of one of the ministers howses, wherein Mr Jewell dwelleth, as appeareth by Mr Jewelles severall billes thereof	£5	16s.	1d.
And of £1 12s.0d. for the reparacion of Mr Heily, his howse, as appeareth by his bill therof	£1	12s.	0d.
And of 1s.4d. paide to Thomas Brooke for two bunches of thatchinge roddes for St Peters		1s.	4d.
And of 7s.0d. paide to Silverston, the thatcher, for three dayes worke of himself, a man and a boy		7s.	0d.
And of 8d. paide to Henry Allen for a bunch of thatchinge roddes			8d.
And of 14s.0d. paide more to Silverston for 6 dayes worke for himself, a man and a boy		14s.	0d.
And of £1 7s.0d. paide to Mr Bennett Barker for three loades of strawe for thatchinge St Peters	£1	7s.	0d.
And of 4d. for 1 *libra* of nayles for St Peters			4d.
And of 5d. for makinge a pannell, and for nayles there			5d.
And of 5s.2d. for glasiers worke done there		5s.	2d.
And of 4s.5d. payde to Edmund Raby for penthowsinge windowes at St Peters, as appeareth by his bill		4s.	5d.
And of 9d. for raynbarrs and nayles for St Peters			9d.
And of 6s.10d. for other worke done by Raby there, as appeareth by his bill		6s.	10d.
And of 4s.0d. for three loade of claye and a loade of deade lyme for the walles there		4s.	0d.

And of 4s.10d. paide for carpenters worke done by Duisburghe in the howse of correcion	4s.	10d.
And of 8s.5d. payde to Marmaduke and Rowlande for 4 dayes worke, splent bonde, nayles and splent	8s.	5d.
And of 10s.0d. paide to John Marshall for makeinge and staveinge 3 towne longe ladders[182]	10s.	0d.
And of 1s.0d. payde to Roberte Bowman for hanginge the towne ladders, and mending the Guildhall buttery	1s.	0d.
And of £1 6s.8d. payde to Pricke, the carpenter, for the repayringe Stanforde Bridge	£1 6s.	8d.
And of 4d. paide to Bull, the smith, for mendinge the locke of the Guildhall doore		4d.
And of 4s.2d. paide for the buckett and rope of the well at the Spitlehowse	4s.	2d.
And of 6s.0d. for three candlesticks for this howse	6s.	0d.
And of £1 7s.6d. paide to Sparke, the carpenter, for a new kirble, and new covering the well in the Chequer,[183] as appeareth by his bill	£1 7s.	6d.
And of £1 4s.6d. payde to the beadell of the hall upon his bill for scouringe armour and doinge other necessary thinges abowte this howse, as appeareth by his bill	£1 4s.	6d.
And of 8d. paide to John Baily, that keepeth a towne childe, to buy a paire of shooes for the childe		8d.
And of 5s.0d. paide to the constables for the Kings provision	5s.	0d.
And of £5 18s.0d. payde for the charges of severall journeyes to Cambridge abowt Doctor Perce his money[184]	£5 18s.	0d.
And of 2d. paid for inke		2d.
And of 8d. for a booke to write this accompt		8d.
And of 4d. for a quier of paper for the hall		4d.
And of £2 11s.4d. for two corsletts for the towne, for a hamper, cord, porter and the bringing downe	£2 11s.	4d.
And of 2s.6d. paide to Mr Bright and Mr John Bridon for their charges when they went to Hepworth	2s.	6d.
And of 6s.8d. paide towardes the charges of the Muster Master	6s.	8d.

[f. 38v.]

And of 12s.0d. paid for wine at the Guildhall when Alderman Davy was elected	12s.	0d.
And of £1 0s.0d. for wine and musicke when Mr Alderman Davy did take his oath	£1 0s.	0d.
And of £16 17s.8d. spent upon the dinner, and for provision of 80[185] messe of bread and beefe for the poore	£16 17s.	8d.
And of £104 0s.0d. paide to Mr Rainebirde for a debt due to him from this howse, and for the use thereof due at Candlemas	£104 0s.	0d.

---

[182] These town ladders would, of course, have been used by the feoffees and the Corporation, and may also have been lent out to others who needed them.

[183] John Baret, who made his will in 1463, ordered that the well in front of his house in Chequer Square should be repaired and that, with the advice of Thomas Ide, his executors should erect timber work with four posts and a cross above it 'as it is at Eye, or ellys bettyr', Tymms, *Wills*, p.20.

[184] See above, p.239, n.172.

[185] This was written as four score, i.e., iiij[xx].

And of £36 5s.11½d. paide to Mr Mallowes for the surplus of his
accompt for the last yeare   £36   5s. 11½d.

And of £16 13s.4d. paide to Stephen Ashwell for a debt due to
him for money borrowed by the feoffees   £16 13s.   4d.

And of £2 9s.6d. for 3 dozen napkins, and the makeinge of them
for the judges   £2   9s.   0d.

[*In another hand. The supers below seem also to be written in this
hand.*]

And of one bore, given to Mr Alderman by consent, and of three
combes rye, bakd and given to the poore, and two capons spent
at the dynner   one bore,
    3 combes rye,
    2 capons

      Summa allocacionum £430 16s.8½d., one bore
      3 combes rye and 2 capons

£430 16s.8½d.

And there remayneth in super in the handes of the persons under
named theis summs of money, and other thinges, of their yearly
rentes and reservacions, due within the tyme of this accompt, and
not received by this accomptant, *videlicet*

Super

Sir Thomas Jermyn for certen landes in Hepworth   10s.   4d.

Of the saide Sir Thomas for other landes in Hepworthe   9d.

Ө Samuell Reve for his yeares rent   £1 0s.   0d.

Edmund Milby for his yeares rent   15s.   0d.

The tenantes of the two almose howses in the Northgate Streete   8s.   0d.

Samuell Jellowe for his yeares rent of the market stall   5s.   0d.

John Northfeild for his yeares rent of the Shere Howse, with the
peece of ground thereto adjoyning   £1 0s.   0d.

Nicholas Bell for his rent of the Angell, for the halfe yeare due at
Michaelmas, 1617   £8 6s.   8d.

John Shawe for the yeares rent of the ground in the Southgate
Strete, leatton to Oliver Ion   3s.   4d.

James Smyth, esquire, for his yeares rent   6d.

Henry Landesdale for his ~~halfe~~ \wholl/ yeares rent   2s.   0d.

Roberte Mance for his yeares rent   1d.

John Raven, Doctor of Phisick, for the peece of ground in
Brent[g]ovell Streete, late Thomas Brunwyns \for his yeares
rent/   3s.   4d.

John Parker for a tenement in Longe Brackland, for his yeares rent   6d.

Mr Charles Darby for his yeares rent   ~~7d.~~   8d.

Margaret Grigges, widowe, for a tenemente at the Northgate   6d.

John Baker £6 0s.0d. and Thomas Noble £1 0s.0d. for ~~parte of~~ the
remainder of £64 6s.6d. in super upon Thomas Peake, as
appereth in the last accompt   £7 0s.   0d.

Elizabeth Shipp, widdowe, for her [*space*] rent   1s.   0d.

Widowe Dodd for hir half yeares rent due at [*no date given*]   1s.   0d.

John Revell a gallon of wyne, and James Kent a gallon of wyne   two gallons of
    wyne

      Summa £19 18s.8d., two gallons of wyne

19–18–8

450–15–4 *obolus*

> *Summa allocacionum* and in super £450 ~~16s.~~ 15s.4½d.
> one bore, 3 combes rye, two capons, 2 gallons of wyne

> Soe this accomptant is in surplus, to be answered
> unto him by the next receivor £22 11s.4½d.

[*f.39r., old number 92*]

1618

The accompt of John Boldero, gentleman, receivor of the rentes and revenues belonging to the common use and benefitt of the towne of Bury St Edmond, made and yealded upp at the Gyldehall the [*space*] day of January, in the sixtenth yeare of the reigne of Our Soveraigne Lord, Kinge James, *[1619]* for one wholl yeare then last past

Onus

The sayde accomptant is not to be charged with any remainder of the last accompt, for that the last accomptant was in suplus, as appereth in the foote of the last accompt, and so of the remainder the last accompt   *nulla*

But this accomptant dothe charge himself with £9 6s.8d. by him received of Mr Nicolas Bell and Samuell Reve, left upon them in super and due in the tyme of Mr John Hill, the last receivor, *videlicet*, of Mr Bell £8 6s.8d., and of Samuell Reve £1 0s.0d., *in toto*   £9   6s.   8d.

And with £340 10s.6d., one boare, two capons, two gallons of wyne and five combes of rye, being the certen yearely rentes and revenues for this howse, for this yeare, particularly expressed in the rentall thereof made, as by the same rentall appereth   £340 10s.   6d.,

one boare, two capons,
two gallons of wyne
and five combes rye

And with £3 8s.0d. by him received of Roberte Bowman, the bedell of the hall, for divers marriage dynners kept in the Gyldehall this yeare   £3   8s.   0d.

And with £4 7s.9d. received of Mr John Inman, one of the feoffes, for wood cutt downe upon Layers in Rougham, and by him soe solde this yeare[186]   £4   7s.   9d.

Allocaciones

Inprimis the saide accomptant dothe praye allowance of £1 18s.11½d. by him paide for the rentes due to his Majestie, for divers landes and tenementes holden of his Majestie   £1 18s. 11½d.

---

[186]   No total including the last two sums is given.

Owt rentes and tenthes

And of 10s.6d. paide to His Majesties Receivor Generall for the tenth of St Peters, and for the receivors acquitance 4d., and to his dore keper 4d., *in toto*   11s.   2d.

And of 9½d. paide for rent to the manor of Watisfeild   9½d.

And of 8d. for rent to the hundred of Thedwastree   8d.

And of 1½d. for rent to the manor of Forneham All Saincts   1½d.

And of 6d. for rent to the manor of Rougham   6d.

The Free Schole

And of £5 9s.10½d. paide to the governors of the Free Gramer Schole, for the part to them belonging, for St Peters and the graunge landes   £5   9s. 10½d.

Preachers and Ministers

And of £50 0s.0d. paide to Mr Heilye, preacher of St James parishe, for his yeares allowance owt of this howse   £50   0s.   0d.

And of £50 0s.0d. paide to Mr Guibon, preacher of St Maryes parishe, for his yeares allowance owt of this howse   £50   0s.   0d.

And of £2 0s.0d. paide to Mr Jewell, minister of St Maries churche   £2   0s.   0d.

And of £2 0s.0d. paide to Mr Crossman, minister of St James churche   £2   0s.   0d.

Reparacions of churches

And of £1 0s.0d. paide to the churchwardens of St Maries parishe, towardes the reparacion of the churche there, and of £1 0s.0d. paide to the church wardens of St James parishe, towardes the reparacions of that church, *in toto*   £2   0s.   0d.

[*f. 39v.*]

Mr Brightes gift

And of £5 0s.0d. bestowed according to Mr Brights will, *videlicet,*

To the reparacion of St Maries churche	£1 0s.0d.	
To the reparacion of St James churche	£1 0s.0d.	
To the poore of St Maries parishe	£1 0s.0d.	
To the poore of St James parishe	£1 0s.0d.	
To the poore prisoners in the towne gaole	£1 0s.0d.	£5 0s. 0d.
And for cloath for coates to the poore	£22 0s.0d.	
And for makeing the coates of the poore in St Maries parishe	£2 18s.6d.	
And for makeing the coates of the poore in St James parishe	£2 4s.0d.	£27 2s. 6d.

Mrs Odehams gift

And of £1 6s.0d. paide to Disburghe, the carpenter, for stuff and workemanshipp, for the makeing of the pulpitt at the gaole, for divine service to be saide, and other dueties to be performed to the prisoners there, towardes the performance of the will of Mrs Margarett Odeham[187]   £1   6s.   0d.

---

[187] For Margaret Odeham's gift, see Appendix 8, *sub* 1478. Here is the protestant interpretation of her intentions.

And of 10s.6d. paide to Bales, for workemanshipp and other things abowt the same pulpitt	10s.	6d.
And of 1s.0d. paide to Mr Heily for a Catachisme to instruct the prisoneres	1s.	0d.
And of £4 10s.0d. paide to Mr Heily for instructing the prisoners three quarters of a yeare, accordinge to the allowance of Mrs Odeham	£4 10s.	0d.
And of £2 10s.0d. paide to Mr Inman for five loades of wood for the comfort of the prisoners in the gaole	£2 10s.	0d.

Peter Kembolds gift

And of £3 0s.0d. delivered to Ambrose Brydon for relief of the poore in the north and east wardes, according to the will of Peter Kembold	£3 0s.	0d.

The Poore

And of divers summs of money paide for the releif of the poore, *videlicet*		
To the overseers of St James parishe for a quarter ended at Christmas, 1617	£1 6s.	0d.
And to the overseers of St James for a yeare ended at Michaelmas, 1618	£5 17s.	0d.
To the overseers of St James for the workehowse for a quarter ended at Michaelmas, 1618[188]	£1 19s.	0d.
To the overseers of St Maries for Christmas quarter	[*no amount*]	
To the overseers of St Maries for three quarters ended at Michaelmas, 1618	£5 17s.	0d.
To the overseers of St Maries for the workehowse, for a quarter ended at Michaelmas, 1618	£1 19s.	0d.
Given to Parkers wief lying in the gaole		6d.
To Johan Parker haveing broken her legg	1s.	0d.
To Atkin, the surgen, for dressing Copsies legg	1s.	0d.
To Atkin for cures done in Mr Hilles tyme	£1 0s.	0d.
To Turner for releif of him self and his wief	1s.	0d.
To the widowe Winter	1s.	0d.
To Jesopp, the surgeon, for healinge Pounsabies eye	£2 13s.	4d.
To a poore man that releived his mother, at Mr Hilles request	3s.	0d.
To an old woman nere St Maries churche	1s.	0d.
To Edmund Avis, at Mr Hilles request	1s.	6d.
To old Farrowe, upon Mr Hilles lettre	5s.	0d.
To Hewett, haveing a sore legg		6d.
To old Rabye	2s.	0d.
To Richard Hunt, at Mr Gooderiches request	1s.	0d.
To a poore woman, at the request of Mr Brydon and Edward Bourne		6d.
To Rushes wief, being in travell	1s.	0d.
To Mother Shipp, for cloathing the poore children in her custodye	6s.	8d.
For the buriall of the widowe Till	2s.	0d.

---

[188] It is clear from this and three entries later that there were workhouses in both parishes at this date.

To the overseers of St James parishe, for sheetes for Johan Harrolde and others	4s.	4d.
For a sheete for Johnsons daughter	1s.	10d.
For a sheete for Spitlehowse	2s.	6d.
For a sheete for one that dyed in Bridwell[189]	2s.	6d.
For a sheete for Hazard	2s.	6d.
For a sheete for Maund	2s.	6d.
For removeing the stuff of a poore man that lay over against the Angell	1s.	2d.
For a sheete for Osborne	2s.	6d.
To Oliver Tebold for healinge Butteries daughter of the falling sicknes	£1 10s.	0d.

[f.40r., old number 97]

Annuities

And of £10 0s.0d. paide to Mr Pynner for his annuity for this yeare	£10 0s.	0d.
And of £5 0s.0d. paide to Mr Henry Collyn for his annuitye	£5 0s.	0d.
And of £16 0s.0d. paide to Mr John Bidwell for his annuitye	£16 0s.	0d.

Wages and fees

And of £2 10s.0d. paide to Bowman, the beadell of the hall, for his wages	£2 10s.	0d.
And of £2 12s.0d. paide to Austen, beadell of St Maries parishe, for his wages	£2 12s.	0d.
And of £2 12s.0d. paide to Allington, beadell of St James parishe for his wages	£2 12s.	0d.
And of 15s.0d. for the receivors fee	15s.	0d.
And of 10s.0d. for the clerks fee	10s.	0d.

Liveries

Item paide for cloath for the livery coates for the three beadelles, and of Rooper and Ilger	£5 6s.	4d.
And for the livery coate of Edmund Davye	16s.	7d.
And for three nayles of taffetye for faceinge for Bowmans coate	2s.	4d.

Benevolence

And of £2 10s.0d. given to Mr Cooke, a decayed feoffee, for benevolence for half a yeare ended at Midsomer, 1618	£2 10s.	0d.

Judges

And of £4 5s.0d. bestowed in gratueties given to the judges at the two assisses	£4 5s.	0d.

Reparacions

Paide to Mr Heily for reparacions done at his howse	1s.	10d.
Paide to Mr Jewell, minister of St Maries, for reparacions by him done abowte the howse wherein he dwelleth	6s.	4d.
For a barrell at the well at the Spitilhowse	1s.	4d.
For mending the chaine of the buckett there		8d.
To Greene for a cheyne at the well in the Spittlehowse Close	1s.	0d.
For a wellrope at the howse of correccion	4s.	0d.

---

[189] This term is interchangeable with House of Correction. See Glossary.

To Balles, the mason, for mending the oven there	1s.	0d.
To the keeper of the howse for mending the lockes and keys there	2s.	0d.
For two loades of tyle to repaire the Almes howses in the Colledge Street	£1 9s.	0d.
For two loades of sand	2s.	4d.
For five combes of lime	5s.	0d.
To Balles, the mason, for 12 dayes worke, tile pines, lath, ewesborde and ruff tiles	£1 17s.	9d.
More for ewesbord and nayles	5s.	1d.
For two loades of clay	2s.	4d.
To Perceivall for splentes, splentburd, nayles and workemanshipp there	6s.	10d.
And of 3s.4d. to given [sic] to Yonges for feying the well at Bridewell	3s.	4d.
And of 11s.10d. paide for makeinge of an oven there, and for brick and workemanshipp	11s.	10d.
And for two combes of lyme spent there	2s.	0d.
And for a load of tyle for repayring of Foxgilles howse	13s.	4d.
To Scolfeild, the carpenter, for worke done there		6d.
To William Myller for lyme	3s.	0d.
To Edward Bourne for lathe and nayles	9s.	6d.
To the mason	11s.	8d.
For 3 combes of lyme for the almose howses in the North Streete	3s.	0d.
To the mason for worke done there	4s.	8d.
For strawe, splentes, thatching stuff and other thinges for the repayringe of the almose howses in the Westgate Streete, and for workemanshipp	£4 5s.	10d.
For a lattice for one of the Gyldehall windowes		8d.
For a load of tyles used there	14s.	6d.
For lyme used there	2s.	6d.
For a dogg of iron for the well howse there	1s.	6d.
For sand used there	2s.	8d.
For nayles and tyle pyns	5s.	5d.
For workemanshipp done by the mason	9s.	4d.
For carrying a loade of rubbishe from thence		6d.

Woodmaking

And of 2s.0d. paide to Mr Inman, as so much by him to Farrowe, for the cutting downe of wood at Leyers in Rougham	2s.	0d.
And of £1 17s.9d. paide to Mr Inman for the makeing and carying of the wood there	£1 17s.	9d.

[*f. 40v.*]

Debtes paide

And of £5 0s.0d. paide to Mr Cradock for the remainder of the debt owing to John Man whilest he lived, this being the last paye	£5 0s.	0d.
And of £7 0s.0d. paide to Mr Henry Gippes, as so much owing to him by this howse	£7 0s.	0d.
And of £21 11s.4½d. paid to Mr Hill, as so much owing unto him by this howse for the surplus of his accompt for the yeare last past	£21 1s.	4½d.

Extraordinary charges

And of £2 10s.0d. paide to Mr Alderman for necessary charges by him laid owt for the towne	£2 10s.	0d.
And of £3 10s.0d. paid unto for [*sic*] provision of wheate for His Majesties honourable howsholde	£3 10s.	0d.
And of 5s.0d. paid more towardes the provision of His Majesties howsholde	5s.	0d.
And of 8s.0d. paid to Harbert and Ullett towardes the charges of the Musters	8s.	0d.
And of 5s.0d. paid to Roberte Bowman for arming the pikes	5s.	0d.
And of 9s.4d. for a load of wood for fier at the Gyldehall, and for carying in the same 2d.	9s.	6d.
And of £1 3s.0d. paid to Bowman, the beadell of the hall, for fier coale, candle, and other thinges bought and done by him for the howse this yeare, as by his bill appereth	£1 3s.	0d.
And of £3 6s.0d. paide to Mr Alderman Davy, as so much laide owt by him for a cookqueanestole[190]	£3 6s.	0d.
And of 19s.0d. paide to Mr Mallowes for 4 elles of fine holland for pillowbeers for the judges	19s.	0d.
And of 1s.0d. paide for makeing the same pillowbeeres	1s.	0d.
And of £2 5s.0d. given to Mr Guibon for his charges in procureing a licence to preache[191]	£2 5s.	0d.

Aldermans gift

And of one boare delivered to Mr Alderman Davy by consent	A boare

The dynner and reief to the poore

And of £12 12s.8d. laide owt by this accomptant for the charges of the dynner of the feoffees and others at the tyme of this accompt makeing, and for releif given to the poore upon this daye, according to the will of Mr Richard Walker	£12 12s.	8d.
And of six combes rye baked and given owt to the poore this day	Rye 6 combes	
And of 16s.4d. paide for the grynding and bakeing of the same rye	16s.	4d.
And of [*space*] rent wyne and [*space*] rent capons expended this daye, besides the charges aforesaide	wyne	capons

Purchase

And of £25 0s.0d. paide to Mr Mallowes, by consent of the feoffees, towardes the purchase of the ground at Rotten Rowe[192]	£25 0s.	0d.

> [*In another hand*]
> *Summa allocacionum* £340 8s.8d.,
> one boare and [*space*] combes rye

---

[190] An eccentric spelling for 'cucking stool'. A seventeenth-century cucking stool from Ipswich has survived and is in Christchurch Mansion. See photograph, Webb, *The Town Finances of Elizabethan Ipswich*, Plate 1.

[191] Mr Gibbon was first paid his stipend in 1616 and it might have been thought that he would have had a licence to preach before he was appointed.

[192] The buildings in Rotten Row had been badly damaged if not utterly destroyed in the fire in 1608 and were never rebuilt. John Mallowes, on behalf of the feoffees, bought up the sites of these buildings, H1/2/9/1–6. See also Introduction, p.lii.

And he is allowed as so much in super, remayning in the handes
of the persons undernamed, theis particuler sums of money and
other thinges of their yearely rentes, due within the tyme of this
accompt and not received by this accomptant, *videlicet,*

Supers

Sir Thomas Jermyn for his wholl yeares rent	11s.	1d.
Anthony Bumstede for his half yeares rent, due at Michaelmas now last past	£1 13s.	4d.
Roberte Roper for part of his yeares rent	£1 10s.	0d.
John Northfeild for his half yeares rent due at th'annunciacion laste	10s.	0d.
Samuell Reve for his half yeares rent due at Michaelmas last	10s.	0d.
John Shawe, assignee of Oliver Ion, for his wholl yeares rent	3s.	4d.
Mr James Smith for his wholl yeares rent		6d.
Henry Landesdale for his wholl yeares rent	2s.	0d.
The assignes of Mr Havers, for the wholl yeares rent of the tenemente in the occupacion of Mr Anthony Adames	3s.	4d.
The assignees of Roberte Mance for their wholl yeares rent		1d.

[f. 41r., old number 91]

Dr Ravens for the gardine, late Mr Thomas Brunwyns, for the wholl yeare	3s.	4d.
The assignees of Mr John Parker for the wholl yeare		6d.
Mr Charles Darby for the wholl yeare		8d.
Margarett Grigges for the wholl yeare		6d.
Edmund Milby for the wholl yeare	16s.	0d.
The tenantes of the two poore houses in the Northgate Streete	8s.	0d.
Widowe Shippe	1s.	0d.
Widowe Dodd	2s.	0d.
Samuell Jelowe	5s.	0d.
John Curtis for a wholl yeare	£2 0s.	0d.
Mr John Revell for his wholl yeares rent	A gallon of wyne	
James Kent for part of his yeares rent	Two capons and a gallon of wyne	
William Walker for part of his yeares rent	A combe of rye	
William Ullett for part of his yeares rent	A combe of rye	

Summa £9 8s.0d., two gallons of wyne,
two capons and two combes rye.

Summa totalis omnium allocacionum £359 16s.8d.,
two galons of wyne, two capons and two combes rye
And soe there remaineth good in the hands of
this accomptant £7 16s.3d.

[f.41v.]

1619

The accompt of Mr Thomas Bright, receivor of the rentes and revenues belonging to the common use and benefitt of the towne of Bury St Edmunde, made and yealded upp at the Guildhall there, the 16th day of January in the 17th yere of the reigne of Our Soveraigne Lorde, Kinge James *et cetera*, [*1620*] for one wholl yere ~~paste~~ then last paste.

Onus

Inprimis the saide accomptant dothe charge himself with [*space*]
    by him received of Mr John Boldero, the last receivor,
    remayninge good in his handes upon the determyncacion of his
    accompt, as by the foote of his accompt appereth   [*no amount*]

And with £5 9s.0d. received of Mr Roberte Gilbert by the handes
    of John Mallowes, gentleman, for the arrearages of his rent for
    certen pasture groundes, conteyninge by estimacion three
    acres, lying in Hepworth, in the occupacion of the said
    Roberte, incurred before and at the feast of St Michaell
    th'archangell, now laste paste   £5   9s.   0d.

And with £8 0s.0d. received of the saide Roberte Gilbert, by the
    handes of the saide John Mallowes, for one acre of ground
    lying in the length of four furlonges in Easthawe Close in
    Hepworth, in the occupacion of the saide Roberte, and which
    by the Commissioners for Charitable Uses was ordered to be
    solde by the feoffees of the towne landes to the saide Roberte
    Gilbert and his heires, for that the same could not easely be
    discerned and sett owt from the groundes of the saide Roberte
    Gilbert lying there   £8   0s.   0d.

And with £341 7s.2d., one boare, two capons, two gallons of
    wyne six combes of rye, being the certen yerely rentes and
    revenues of this howse for this yeare, particularly expressed in
    the rental thereof made, as by the same rental appereth   £341   7s.   2d.
                                    one boare, two
                          capons, two gallons
                          of wyne and six
                          combes of rye

And with £5 18s.0d. by him received for divers mariage dynners
    kept in the Gyldehall this yeare   £5 18s.   0d.

And with £3 2s.6d. by him received of John Frost for woode solde
    at Hepworthe   £3   2s.   6d.

And with £20 0s.0d. received for a stock of rye sold, whereof
    £10 0s.0d. was of the gyft of Mr Butler of London, and £10
    0s.0d. of the gyft of Mr Barber at the lottery[193]   £20   0s.   0d.

And with £2 0s.0d. received of Mr Hamond, by the handes of
    George Baker, for a forfeyture in not delyvering a terrar   £2   0s.   0d.
            Summa oneris £385 16s.8d., one boare, two capons,
            two gallons of ~~rye~~ wyne and six combes of rye,
            besides the money in Mr Bolderoes handes

---

[193] In 1567 a lottery, authorised by Letters Patent, was held to raise money for repairing harbours. During the reign of James I two lotteries were held to raise funds for the Virginia Company, one in 1612, another in 1614, *Lotteries in the City of London* (Corporation of London Record Office, 1994). Meanwhile, in Bury, the governors were authorised by Queen Elizabeth to hold a lottery 'for the honest recreation of our loyal subjects' to raise funds for the school. The undated document authorising this remains in the school archive, E5/9/102. (Another school which raised funds by lottery was the Bogaerden School in Bruges. Pieter Pourbus designed a lottery ticket which included a bird's eye view of the school with the pupils and their masters. This was exhibited in the *Memling to Pourbus* exhibition in Bruges in 1998.) Nothing more has been found about the lottery, or lotteries, mentioned here and below, p.261.

Allocaciones
Owt rentes and tenthes

Inprimis the saide accomptant dothe pray allowance of
£1 18s.11½d. by him payde for the rentes due to His Majestie
for divers landes and tenementes holden of His Majestie

£1 18s. 11½d.

And of 10s.6d. payde to His Majesties Receivor Generall for the
tenth of St Peters, and for the receivors aquittance 4d., and to
his dore keper 4d., *in toto*

11s. 2d.

And of 1s.6½d. payde to the manor of Wattesfeild

1s. 6½d.

And of 6d. payde to the manor of Rougham

6d.

And of 8d. payde to the hundred of Thedwardstree

8d.

The free schole

And of £5 9s.10½d. payde to the Governors of the free gramer
schole, for the parte to them belonging, for St Peters and the
Grange landes

£5 9s. 10½d.

Preachers and Ministers

And of £50 0s.0d. payde to Mr Heiley, preacher of St James
parishe for his yeares allowance

£50 0s. 0d.

And of £50 0s.0d. payde to Mr Guybon, preacher of St Maries, for
his yeres allowance owt of this howse

£50 0s. 0d.

And of £2 0s.0d. payde to Mr Jewell, minister of St. Maries
church

£2 0s. 0d.

And of £2 0s.0d. payde to Mr Crossman, minister of St James
church

£2 0s. 0d.

And of £6 0s.0d. given to Mr Heiley which hathe redd service and
preached to the prisoners in the gaole, according to the will of
Mrs Margaret Odeham, for this yeare

£6 0s. 0d.

And of £1 0s.0d. given to Mr Cary which preached here upon
probacion

£1 0s. 0d.

[*f. 42r., old number 98*]
Reparacions of churches

And of £1 0s.0d. payde to James Fayercliffe, church warden of St
Maries parishe, towardes the reparacion of the church there.
And of £1 0s.0d. payde to Edward Bourne, churchwarden of St
James parishe, towardes the reparacion of that church, *in toto*

£2 0s. 0d.

Mr Brightes gyft

And of £5 0s.0d. bestowed according to Mr Brightes will,
videlicet,

To the reparacions of St Maries church	£1 0s.0d.	
To the reparacion of St James church	£1 0s.0d.	
To the poore of St Maries parishe	£1 0s.0d.	
To the poore of St James parishe	£1 0s.0d.	
To the prisoners in the towne gaole	£1 0s.0d.	£5 0s. 0d.

And for 22 dozen of grey clothe, for the clothinge of the poore
according to Mr Brightes gyft, £20 18s.0d. And for making the
same cotes for the poore in the parishe of St Mary, and to Mr
Gipps for lyning for the same £2 16s.1½d. And for makeing
the cotes for the poore in St James parishe, and to Christopher

Cox for lyninges for the same, and for makeing the same, £1 15s.1d., *in toto*	£25	9s.	2½d.

Peter Kembold his gyft

And of £2 0s.0d. payde to Mr Charles Darby for the poore of the North Ward, and to Mr John Brydon £1 0s.0d. for the poore of the East Ward, to be distributed according to the will of Peter Kembold	£3	0s.	0d.

The Poore

And of £5 4s.0d. given owt of this howse towardes the weekely contribucion to the poore, *videlicet*, to the overseers of the poore in St Maries parishe, £2 12s.0d., and to the overseers of the poore in St James parishe, £2 12s.0d., *in toto*	£5	4s.	0d.
And of 2s.6d. given to Richard Hunt, a poore man, for his relief		2s.	6d.
And of 5s.0d. given to 15 poore men which did helpe to quenche the fyer at Frostes howse		5s.	0d.
And of £2 8s.4d. payde for woode bought, and given to the poore prisoners accordinge to the will of Mrs Odeham	£2	8s.	4d.
And of £2 10s.0d. given to Olyver Tebold for chirurgery upon Anne Milby, a poore woman	£2 10s.		0d.
And of £1 16s.8d. payde towardes the healing of fyve poore, diseased folke	£1 16s.		8d.
And of 11s.4d. payde to Mr Gipps for sheetes to bury certen poore *et cetera*		11s.	4d.
And of £1 3s.1d. payde to [*space*] Moodye, 7° *Maii*, 1619, for sheettes to bury the poore	£1	3s.	1d.
And of 2s.6d. payde to Thomas Smyth, and of 2s.3d. payde to Mr Gipps, for sheetes to bury the poore		4s.	9d.

Annuities

And of £10 0s.0d. payde to Mr Pynner for his annuitie for this yeare	£10	0s.	0d.
And of £5 0s.0d. payde to Mr Henry Collinge for his annuitie	£5	0s.	0d.
And of £16 0s.0d. payde to John Bidwell for his annuitie	£16	0s.	0d.

Wages and fees

And of £2 10s.0d. payde to Roberte Bowman, beadell of the hall, for his wages	£2 10s.		0d.
And of £2 12s.0d. payde to Astyn, beadell of St Maries parishe, for his wages	£2 12s.		0d.
And of £2 12s.0d. payde to Alington, beadell of St James parishe, for his yeres wages	£2 12s.		0d.
And of 15s.0d. for the receivors fee		15s.	0d.
And of 10s.0d. for the clerkes fee		10s.	0d.
And of 10s.0d. payde to Roberte Studd for half a yere for aydeing and wypinge the bookes in the library[194]		10s.	0d.

---

[194] See Appendix 8, *sub.* 1612 for Baxter's gift for repairing the library. For the library see Introduction, p.xli.

Liveries

And 18s.6d. for a yarde and three quarters of broade blewe for a
coate for Bowman, the bedell of the hall — 18s. 6d.

And of £1 16s.3d. for three yardes and half an ell of broade blewe
for liveryes for the other two bedelles — £1 16s. 3d.

Judges

And of £1 19s.0d. for provision given to the judges at Lent
assises.

And of £1 13s.4d. for provision given to the judges at sommer
assises last, *in toto* — £3 12s. 4d.

Reparacions

And of 3s.11d. payde for mending the stockes for the bushell at
the Crosse, and a clogge — 3s. 11d.

And of £1 6s.6d. payde to George Kirby as so much layde owt by
him for repayringe a well in the Almose Rowe — £1 6s. 6d.

And of 3s.0d. for fayinge of a well at the almose howses in the
College Rowe — 3s. 0d.

And of £1 1s.2d. payde to George Kirby as so much layde owt by
him for repayringe the common well in the Crowne Streete — £1 1s. 2d.

[*f. 42v.*]

Reparacions

And of £2 4s.4d. payde to Mr Roberte Davy as so much layde owt
by him for bricke, free stone, sand, lyme and workmanshipp
makeing the bridge against the well with two pumps — £2 4s. 4d.

And of 1s.9d. payde for the caryage of free stone which came of
the stone stall broken downe in the Markett Place, and for
helpe to laye upp the same at the Gyldehall — 1s. 9d.

And of £4 4s.4d. layde owt about the repayringe of the Markett
Crosse, over and above the £2 0s.0d. given to that use by Mr
Barber at the lotterye[195] — £4 4s. 4d.

Towne beames and scales[196]

And of £5 18s.0d. payde for four beames and four payre of scales,
bought for the common use of the towne and country,
according to the Statute made for weight and measures — £5 18s. 0d.

And of two shillinges payde to Bull, the smyth, for workmanshipp
of the irons to hang the great beames on, to trye the great
weightes — 2s. 0d.

And to Edward Bourne for iron for those uses — 8s. 4d.

Kinges picture

And of £2 18s.10d. for taffeta for the curteine for the Kinges
picture, and for makeing the same curteyne[197] — £2 18s. 10d.

And of 2s.6d. payde to Bull, the smyth, for the curten rodd and
irons for the same — 2s. 6d.

---

195 See p.258, n.193 above.
196 It seems that the feoffees were providing these for the Liberty of St Edmund as well as the borough itself. Much later standard weights which are exhibited at Moyses Hall Museum are inscribed 'The Liberty of St Edmund'.
197 At this period portraits were often covered with a coloured, sometimes striped, curtain. See Jacob Simon, *The Art of the Picture Frame*, pp.13–14, where a detail of a picture showing a portrait partially concealed by a curtain is reproduced.

Extraordinary charges

And of 5s.0d. payde for watcheing of the gunnpowder, whilest the same did lye at the Markett Crosse, and for removeing the poulder and matche from the Crosse to the Gildehall, and from the Gyldehall to the dove howse in the Abbye[198]		5s.	0d.
And of £1 0s.0d. given to the late Quenes players, to send them owt of towne, when they came to playe at an unfittinge tyme[199]	£1	0s.	0d.
And of £1 0s.0d. given to messengers which brought His Majesties proclamacions to the towne	£1	0s.	0d.
And of £1 0s.0d. given to Mr Turner, the messenger, for coming to levy the fee farmes[200] of the towne, due in the yere whilest Mr Browne was alderman		5s.	0d.
And of £8 10s.8d. payde to Mr Mallowes as so much layde owt by him in defense of the peticion prefered to His Majestie by Thomas Baker against the towne[201]	£8	10s.	8d.
And of £4 17s.10d. payde to Mr Mallowes as so much payde and due to him for charges in defence of the sute brought against divers of the feoffees by the saide Thomas Baker in the Court of Requestes	£4	17s.	10d.
And of £20 0s.0d. payde to His Majestie for the fee farme in the yeare whilest Mr Davy was alderman	£20	0s.	0d.
And of £11 0s.0d. payde in this Michaelmas Terme, 1619, towardes the fee farme due to His Majestie for this yere	£11	0s.	0d.
And of £2 3s.0d. layde owt for the charges of the dynner at the Towne Sessions holden in January 1619	£2	3s.	0d.
And of £3 10s.0d. payde to John Brydon and Ambrose Brydon, heynors of the feast when this accomptant was elected alderman, for wyne and towardes the other charges	£3	10s.	0d.
And of £1 0s.0d. payde to James Fayercliff and Richard Maltyward, heynors of the feast when this accomptant did take his oath of alderman, towardes the charges of the wyne	£1	0s.	0d.
And of 10s.0d. given to John Grene, the musitian, at that tyme		10s.	0d.
And of £4 1s.6d. payde to Bowman, the beadell, for coale, woode, candell and other necessaries used at the Gyldehall this yeare, as by his bill of particulers appereth	£4	1s.	6d.
And of one boare delivered to Mr Alderman Pynner by consent			A boare
And of £11 0s.10d. layde owt by this accomptant for the charges of the dynner of the feoffees and others at the tyme of this accompt making. And £4 0s.0d. in provision for relief given to the poore upon this daye according to the will of Mr Richard Walker	£15	0s.	10d.

[198] The dovehouse can still be seen in the Abbey Gardens. It is one of two towers, which originally marked the corners of the abbot's garden on the bank of the River Linnet, which then joined the River Lark at the Abbot's Bridge. The nesting boxes were not an original feature of the tower, A.B. Whittingham, 'Bury St Edmunds Abbey', p.87.

[199] The only reference in these books to travelling players visiting the town. But for the 'unfittinge tyme' we should not have been aware of this visit.

[200] The fee farms were paid by the Corporation to the Crown for various privileges granted by the three charters. See Glossary.

[201] See Introduction, p.xxx.

And of fyve combes rye baked and given owt to the poore this daye	fyve combes rye	
And for bakeing the same rye	13s.	8d.
[f. 43r., old number 90]		
And of 4s.0d. payde for the gryndinge of the same rye	4s.	0d.
And of two rent capons expended this day, besides the charges aforesaide	two capons	
And of £2 0s.0d. lent to Adam Bull, to be repayde upon his bonde 26 December next	£2 0s.	0d.
And of £20 0s.0d. which was received for the stock of rye solde and the money now lent to the purchasors of the Amners Barnes towardes the shortninge of the towne debt	£20 0s.	0d.
And of £25 0s.0d. payde to Mr Mallowes, by consent of the feoffees, towardes the purchase of the ground at Rotten Rowe[202]	£25 0s.	0d.
~~And of £2 0s.0d. lent to Adam lent to Adam B[sic] by Mr Bright to be repaid by bond~~	~~£2 0s.~~	~~0d.~~
And of £12 10s.0d. paide to Mr Roberte Browne in part payment of the moneys by him laide owt to the use of the towne	£12 10s.	0d.
~~And of £20 0s.0d. which was received for the stock of rye sold and the money now lent to the purchasers of the tythes et cetera towardes the shortning of the towne debt~~	~~£20 0s.~~	~~0d.~~

> *Summa allocacionum* £370 11s.11d., one boare,
> two capons and fyve combes rye.

And he is allowed as so much in super remaining in the handes of the persons undernamed, theis particuler summes of money and other thinges remayning unpaide of their yearly rentes, due within the tyme of his accompt, and not received by this accomptant, *videlicet*

Supers

Sir Thomas Jermyn for his wholl yeares rent \of certen lands in Hepworth/	10s.	4d.
~~Of~~ the said Sir Thomas for certen other lands there		9d.
Abraham Greene for his yeares rent	£2 10s.	0d.
Adam Gillam for his yeares rent	£5 0s.	0d.
John Brydon for his yeares rent	2s.	0d.
Roberte Wynter for his half yeares rent due at Michaelmas last	10s.	0d.
Mr James Smyth for his yeares rent ~~due at~~		6d.
The assignes of Mr Thomas Havers for his yeares rent	3s.	4d.
Francis Parker, widowe, for her yeares rent		6d.
William Grigges for his yeares rent		6d.
Charles Darby for his yeares rent		8d.
The heir of Thomas Brunwyn for his yeares rent	3s.	4d.
Edmund Milby for his yeares rent	16s.	0d.
The tenantes of the two almose howses in the Northgate Streete	8s.	0d.
The widowe Dode	1s.	4d.
Samuell Jellowe for his yeares rent for the stall in the Market	5s.	0d.

---

[202] See above, p.256, n.192.

Roberte Roper for his rent	£2 10s.	0d.
Anthony Bumsted for his yeares rent	£3 6s.	8d.
Roberte Fuller for his half yeares rent for the Shire Howse	10s.	0d.

    Summa allocacionum in super £16 <..>7s.9d.

    Summa totalis omnium allocacionum £386 9s.0d.

    And soe this accomptant is in surplus 13s.1d.

    Which is to be answered unto him by the next receivor

Memorandum that Mr Bright paid to John Mallowes but £15 0s.0d. towardes the moneys laide owt by the saide John Mallowes for the purchase of Rotten Rowe, and Mr Bright in this accompt hathe demanded allowance of £25 0s.0d., soe that Mr Bright standeth still chargeable to the feoffees for £10 0s.0d. as so much demaunded more then he paide.

[f.43v.]

1620

The accompt of Mr Francis Pynner Receivor of the rentes and revenues belonging to the common use and benefitt of the towne of Bury St Edmunds, made and yealded upp at the Guildhall there, the third day of January in the eightenth yeare of the Reigne of our Soveraigne Lord King James *et cetera* [*1621*] for one wholl yeare then last paste

Onus

Inprimis the said accomptant is not charged with any remainder of the last accompt, for that Mr Thomas Bright, the last accomptant, upon the yealding upp of his accompt, was in surplus 13s.1d.   *nulla*

But this accomptant doth charge himself with three hundred fourty one poundes, seaventene shillinges, two pence, one bore, two capons, two gallons of wine and six combes of rye, being the certeine yearely rents and revenues of this howse for this yeare, particularly expressed in the rentall thereof made, as by the same rentall appeareth   £340 17s. 2d.
            one bore, two capons, two gallons of wine and six combes of rye

And with 8s.0d. by him received of Stephen Peck for wood cutt downe at Hepworth this yeare, and solde to the said Stephen for   8s. 0d.

And with four poundes two shillinges and eight pence by him received for divers mariage dynners kept in the Guildhall this yeare   £4 2s. 8d.

And with £3 6s.8d. by him received of Anthony Bumpsted as so much in super upon him for the arrerages of rent due in the yeare wherein Mr Thomas Bright was receivor   £3 6s. 8d.

And with twenty poundes by him received as a legacy given by his owne sonne, Mr Francis Pynner the younger, by his last will and testament, towardes the provision and entertaynement

of the preachers which doe keepe the Mondayes exercise in this towne[203]	£20	0s.	0d.
And with 10s.0d. received of of Mr Ward of Livermere, and five shillings received of Edmund Hynard, towardes the finishing of the Markett Crosse		15s.	0d.
And with £18 0s.0d. remayning good in the handes of this accomptant upon other accomptes wherewith he was chargeable[204]	£18	0s.	0d.
And with £12 0s.0d. by him received of William Hewes, farmor of the Angell, at his first entry into the said howse at Michaelmas last, beinge his half yeares rent paid before hand, and to be abated unto him at the last half yeare of his terme[205]	£12	0s.	0d.

> *Summa oneris* £412 19s.6d., one bore, two capons, two gallons of wyne and six combes rye

Allocaciones

Inprimis the said accomptant doth praye allowance of thirty eight shillings eleaven pence *obolus* by him paide for the rents due to His Majestie for divers landes and tenementes holden of his Majestie

£1 18s. 11½d.

Out rents ~~and tithes~~ and tenthes[206]

And of 10s.6d. paide to his Majesties Receivor Generall for the tenth of St Peters, and for the receivors acquitance 4d., and to his dorekeeper 4d., *in toto*	11s.	2d.
And of 1s.6½d. paide to the manor of Watisfelld	1s.	6½d.
And of 6d. paide to the manor of Rougham		6d.
And of 8d. paide to the ~~manor~~ \hundred/ of Thedwastree		8d.

The free schoole

And of £5 9s.10½d. paide to the governors of the Free Gramer School, for the part to them belonginge, for St Peters and the Grange

£5 9s.10½d.

Preachers and Ministers

And of £50 0s.0d. paide to Mr Walbanck, preacher of St James parish, for his yeares allowance out of this howse[207]	£50	0s.	0d.
And of £50 0s.0d. paide to Mr Cary, preacher of St Maries parish, for his ~~his~~ yeares allowance out of this howse	£50	0s.	0d.

---

[203] For the gift of Francis Pinner, junior, see Appendix 8, *sub.* 1618.

[204] Entries such as this show that these accounts are not the full record of the feoffees' affairs that we would like to have.

[205] The lease made to William Hewes of the Angel is recorded in the Minute Book on 26 August 1620. It was to run from the following Michaelmas for eleven years at an annual rent of £24, of which £12 was to be paid before the sealing of the lease, Minutes, H2/6/2.1, p.47.

[206] Out-rents and other regular payments made by the feoffees at this period are best studied in the rental made 1 October 1621, printed as Appendix 3.

[207] Mr Walbank did not resign his benefice at Gretworth, Northamptonshire. On 9 January 1623 – the day on which the last account in these books was audited – it was reported that most of the 'better sort' in St James's parish found this unsatisfactory. After due consideration the feoffees decided that as Mr Walbank's allowance was not of right but paid out of courtesy, he should be paid for the quarter ended at Christmas 1622 and no more, applying himself thereafter to his cure at Gretworth, Minutes, H2/6/2.1, p.47.

And of £2 0s.0d. paide to Mr Jewell, minister of St Maries parish	£2	0s.	0d.
And of £2 0s.0d. paide to Mr Crossman, minister of St James parish	£2	0s.	0d.
And of £6 0s.0d. given to Mr Crossman, who hath read service and preached to the prisoners in the gaole, accordinge to the will of Mrs Margaret Odeham for this yeare	£6	0s.	0d.
And of 9s.0d. delivered to Mr Barker, now alderman, towardes the provision of the preachers that kepe the Mondaye exercise, allowed out of the profict of the £20 0s.0d. given by Mr Francis Pynner, junior, besides the allowance given by this receivor whilest he was alderman		9s.	0d.

[f. 44r., old number 99]

Reparacions of Churches

And of £1 0s.0d. paide to Mr Kirby, churchwarden of St Maries parish, towardes the reparacion of the church there, and of £1 0s.0d. paide to Mr Driver, churchwarden of St James parish, toward the reparacion of that church, *in toto*	£2	0s.	0d.

And of £5 0s.0d. bestowed according to Mr Brights will, *videlicet,*

To the reparacion of St Maries p church	£1 0s.0d.			
To the reparacion of St James church	£1 0s.0d.			
To the poore of St Maries parish	£1 0s.0d.			
To the poore of St James parish	£1 0s.0d.			
To the prisoners in the towne gaole	£1 0s.0d.	£5	0s.	0d.

And for 21 dozen *dimidia* of grey cloth for the clothinge of the poore, according to Mr Brights gift, £21 18s.0d., and for the making of the same cotes for the same poore, in both parishes, £5 1s.9d.	£26	19s.	9d.
And of £3 0s.0d. paide to [*space*] for the poor of the north and east wardes, to be distributed according to the will of Peter Kembold	£3	0s.	0d.
And of ~~iij^s~~ \£5 4s.0d./ given out of this house towardes the weekely contribution to the poore, *videlicet* £2 12s.0d. to the overseers of the poore of St Maries parish, and £2 12s.0d. to the overseers of the poore of St James parish, *in toto*	£5	4s.	0d.
And of £1 1s.8d. paide for wood bought and given to the poore prisoners, according to the will of Mrs Odeham	£1	1s.	8d.
And of £1 0s.0d. given by consent of the feoffees to Edward Bartlett, in releif, when he promised to leave the towne and to travell into Nottinghamshere[208]	£1	0s.	0d.
And of 6s.8d. paide to the overseers of the workehowse		6s.	8d.
And of £10 0s.0d. reteyned by the said Mr Francis Pynner, the present receivor, for his annuitie graunted by the feoffees	£10	0s.	0d.
And of £16 0s.0d. paide to John Bedwall for his annuity	£16	0s.	0d.
And of £5 0s.0d. paide to Mr Henry Colling for his annuity	£5	0s.	0d.
And of £1 0s.0d. [*sic*] paide to the receivor for his fee	~~xx~~^{s}	15s.	0d.

---

[208] The Introduction, p.xxxiii, cites instances where poor people were required to return to their place of birth or last settlement. This seems to be the sole instance recorded in these accounts where the feoffees gave financial assistance to such a person. Normally any assistance towards travelling expenses would have been met from parish funds.

And of £2 0s.0d. paide to the clarke of the company for his fee	£2	0s.	0d.
And of £2 10s.0d. paide to Roberte Bowman, beadell of the hall, for his wages	£2	10s.	0d.
And of £2 12s.0d. paide to Roberte Allington, one of the beadells of the towne, for his wages	£2	12s.	0d.
And of 10s.0d. paide to Purdy, the beadell, for his wages during the tyme he served		10s.	0d.
And of £1 0s.0d. paide to Studd, for his wages for keepinge the library	£1	0s.	0d.
And of £4 5s.6d. paide to Samuell Moody for 8 y[ard]es and *dimidia* of blew cloth for liveries for Rooper, Ilger, Davy, Bowman and Alington	£4	5s.	6d.
And of 17s.10d. paide to Mr Henry Gippes for faceinge for the liveries, and for buttons and silke		17s.	10d.
And of £2 10s.0d. for one veale, one mutton and certeine fowles given to the judges at Lent assisses, and of £2 9s.4d. for one veale and one mutton, and certeine capons given to the judges at somer asisses	£4	19s.	4d.
And of £4 1s.0d. for six loves of suger given to the Lord Bishopp of Norwich, and for the charges of cariage of them[209]	£4	1s.	0d.
And of £1 5s.9d. for 2 suger loaves given to Sir John Heigham at new yeares time	£1	5s.	9d.
And of 6d. laide out for mending the copeinge where the Kinges picture hangeth at the Guildhall			6d.
And with 6d. for fetching the towne lader from St James church to the Market Crosse			6d.
And of £1 4s.1d. paide to Booty, the carpenter, for bourd, tymber and other charges expended in reparacions at the almose howses in the Colledge Strete	£1	4s.	1d.
And of 3s.9d. paide to Booty for bord, ledges, claye and worke done at St Peters		3s.	9d.
And of 11s.3d. paide to Booty for worke about the Guildhall		11s.	3d.
[f.44v.]			
And of £2 6s.11d. paide to Edward Bourne for worke and stuff done by him, as surveyor, at St Peters	£2	6s.	11d.
And of 19s.1d. paide more to Edward Bourne for more worke done ther		19s.	1d.
And 2s.4d. for \two/ well ropes to Bridewell		2s.	4d.

---

[209] Such a present for the Bishop of Norwich suggests that there was a problem concerning one or both of the parish churches. What this was is not known with any certainty, but one of the periodic lists of the documents which John Mallowes either returned (or first deposited) in the Evidence House, contains all the documents relating to the sale of the church plate and the subsequent purchase of the new purchased lands, Minutes, H2/6/2.1, p.46. William Payne, for one, considered that more money should be spent by the feoffees on church repairs, which would mean that church rates need not be levied, see Introduction, p.liv. Sir John Heigham, as a long-serving feoffee, might well have been asked for advice or to use his influence had such a question been raised, which could explain why he was given a present. Although sometimes frustrating when nothing can be found about some item which nowadays would have been minuted, the feoffees' Minute Book at this period acted as both an accession register for items deposited in the Evidence House, and as a temporary loans book when they were removed for use in connection with the feoffees' business and legal affairs.

And of 3s.2d. paide for a cheine and an iron for half a hundred weight sent to Bridewell	3s.	2d.
And of 1s.0d. paide to Adam Bull for removeing the Kinges armes[210]	1s.	0d.
And of 10s.4d. paide for a paire of gould waightes and for the bakers 1d. weightes, bought for the use of the towne[211]	10s.	4d.
And of £1 10s.0d. paide to pursivantes for 12 proclamacions brought this yeare	£1 10s.	0d.
And of £1 17s.0d. paide for the Statutes at Large, in two volumes, bought for the common use of the towne[212]	£1 17s.	0d.
And of 2s.6d. given to Stephen Peck, of Hepworth, for coming to towne divers tymes about buisines betweene the towne and Mr Gilbert	2s.	6d.
And of £21 0s.0d. paide, by consent, for discharge of the fee farmes due to His Majestie[213]	£21 0s.	0d.
~~And of £18 5s.0d. paide to Mr Roberte Browne as so much laide out by him to the use of the towne~~	~~£18 5s.~~	~~0d.~~
And of £3 9s.6d. paide to Mr Roberte Davy, as so much laid out by him to the use of the towne	£3 9s.	6d.
And of £30 0s.0d. paide to John Mallowes, the Towne Clarke, for the defense and prosequution of the sutes against Sir Nicholas Bacon and against Thomas Baker[214]	£30 0s.	0d.
And of £1 0s.0d. paide for the dinners of the comissioners and witnesses, and for wyne, at the first sitting upon the comission, in the sute betwene Mr Thomas Baker and the towne	£1 0s.	0d.
And of 16s.0d. paide to Mr Masons clarke, and Mr Bolderoes sonne, for writing the deposicions at that comission	16s.	0d.
And of £1 15s.8d. for grocery and wine expended at the feast when the Erle of Suffolk sent a buck to the towne[215]	£1 15s.	8d.
And of £1 0s.0d. paide for wine and musick at the eleccion of Mr Alderman Barker	£1 0s.	0d.
And of 14s.3d. paide for wine and musick when Mr Alderman Barker did take his place	14s.	3d.
And of £1 0s.0d. paide to Wyett, the free mason, for his charges in travelling to this towne to view the decayed bridges, and twice in to Northamptonshire to buy stone for the bridges, and towardes the losse which he had by turning the said stone into his handes	£1 0s.	0d.
And of 6d. given to Frith, the bricklayer, for viewing the Eastgate Bridge		6d.

[210] The royal arms were very likely displayed on the Market Cross as well as in whichever part of the Guildhall was used for the borough courts.

[211] Provision of standard weights and measures must always have been important in a market town. This seems to have been an area in which the feoffees helped out the Corporation.

[212] The surviving law books from the Guildhall are all later than this two-volume edition of the *Statutes at Large*. Another book of statutes was bought in 1612, f.24r.

[213] The fee farms paid by the Corporation in return for the privileges granted by charter are here paid by the feoffees.

[214] See Introduction, pp.xxx and li.

[215] Thomas Howard, Earl of Suffolk, was Lord Lieutenant of Suffolk and held the office of Lord High Treasurer 1614–1618. He was fined and imprisoned for embezzlement in 1619, *DNB*.

And of £31 12s.7d. laide out in repairing the Eastgate Bridge, as by the particulers therof appeareth	£31 12s.	7d.
And of £50 18s.2d. layde out towardes the finishing of the Markett Crosse, as by the bills of particulers appeareth	£50 18s.	2d.
And of £4 7s.8d. laide out for setting the streete before the Guildhall	£4 7s.	8d.
And of 2s.6d. laide out by this accomptant for setting the way from the Abby Gate[216] to the Church Gate, over and besides what was collected	2s.	6d.
And of £1 4s.0d. paide to Bowman, the beadell of the hall, for wood, cole, candell and other necessaries, expended at the hall this yeare, as by his bill appeareth	£1 4s.	0d.
And of 1s.0d. laide out for paper, penns, inke and a glasse to putt it in, for the use of the company this yeare	1s.	0d.

[f. 45r., old number 88]

And of one bore allowed to the alderman this yeare	A boore
And of six combes rye, baked out and given to the poore at the tyme of this accompt	six combes rye
And of £12 2s.7d. expended for the charges of the dynner of the feoffees, preachers and others, at the time of this accompt makeing, with £4 0s.0d. in provision for the releif of the poore, given unto them this daye, according to the will of Mr Richard Walker	£12 2s. 7d.
And of two rent capons expended at the same dynner, besides the charges aforesaid	two capons

> *Summa allocacionum* £370 x6s.11d.,
> one bore, two capons, six combes rye.

And he is allowed theis particuler summes of money and other thinges, remayning unpaide of the aforesaid yearely rentes and revenues, specified in the said rentall, and due within the tyme of this accompt and not received by him, but sett in super upon the severall persons by whom the same are still owinge, *videlicet*

Supers

Sir Thomas Jermyn, knight, for his yeares rent of certen landes in Hepworth	10s.	4d.
The said Sir Thomas Jermyn for his yeares rent for certeine other landes in Hepworth		9d.
Mr Bennett Barker for part of his rent	£7 0s.	0d.
Mr Robert Davy for the Elemosinars Barnes, for half a yeares rent for the tithes belonginge to St Peters[217]	£5 0s.	0d.
Anthony Bumpstede for his yeares rent	£3 3s.	8d.
William Walker for part of his rent	£2 0s.	0d.

[216] This is an early instance of the use of 'Abbey Gate' for the gate into the court of the abbey of St Edmund. 'Norman Tower' replaced 'Church Gate' only much more recently.

[217] In 1618 there was a dispute between the feoffees, the purchasers and Francis Pynner which had to be referred to men agreeable to all parties for settlement, School Minutes, E5/9/201.1, p.76. This controversy is not mentioned in the feoffees' Minute Book. It seems here that the purchasers of the Almoner's Barns had collected the tithes, and then handed on to the feoffees those tithes payable for the St Peter's estate.

John King for part of his rent	£2	0s.	0d.
~~John~~ Adam Gillam for part of his rent	£1	0s.	0d.
Abraham Greene for part of his rent	£1	10s.	0d.
Robert Rooper for part of his yeares rent	£2	10s.	0d.
James Smith, esquire, for his yeares rent			6d.
Roberte Wynter for his yeares rent	£1	0s.	0d.
The assignes of Mr Thomas Havers for his yeares rent		3s.	4d.
Amy Mance for her yeares rent			1d.
The heire of Thomas Brunwyn for his yeares rent		3s.	4d.
Mr Charles Darby for his yeares rent			8d.
Mr William Grigges for his yeares rent			6d.
Edmund Milby for his yeares rent		16s.	0d.
The tenantes of the two almose howses in the Northgate Strete		8s.	0d.
Roberte Fuller for his yeares rent	£1	0s.	0d.
Mr Laurence Coldham for halfe a yeares rent		3s.	4d.
Mr John Revell	A gallon of wyne		
James Kent	A gallon of wyne		

Summa £28 0s.2d., and two galons of wyne
Summa totalis allocacionum ~~£429 4s.~~
\£428 19s.11½d./ one bore, two capons, two
galons of wyne, and six combes rye
~~Soe this accomptant is in surplus, to be answered
unto him by the next receyvor £26 <deletion>s. 5½d.~~

1621

The accompt of Mr Roberte Browne, receivor of the rentes and revenues belonging to the common use and benefitt of the towne of Bury St Edmunde, made and yealded upp at the Gyldehall there, the second day of January in the nynetenth yeare of the reigne of Our Soveraigne Lorde, Kinge James, *et cetera* [*1622*] for one wholl yeare then last past.

Onus

Inprimis the saide accomptant is not charged with any remaynder of the last accompt, for that Mr Francis Pynner, the last receivor, upon the yealding upp of his accompt was in surplus, as appeareth by the same account   *nulla*

But this accomptant dothe charge himself with £348 9s.1d., one bore, two capons, two gallons of wyne and six combes of rye, being the certein yerely rentes and revenues of this howse for this yere, particularly expressed in the rentall thereof made, as by the same rentall appereth   £348 9s. 1d.
one bore, 2 capons,
2 gallons of wyne
and six combes rye

And with £2 10s.0d. by him received for divers arrerages behinde and in super upon divers severall persons in the [*sic*] in the precedent yeare wherein the saide Mr Francis Pynner was receivor, *videlicet*, of the saide Mr Francis Pynner for part of John Kinge his arrerages, 10s.0d., of John Raynham for part of William Walker his arrerages, £2 0s.0d.   £2 10s. 0d.

And with 8s.8½d. by him received of the saide Mr Pynner, for
money left of the moneys levied for the kings cariages   8s. 8½d.

And with £1 2s.6d. by him received of John Frost for certen
woode by him cutt downe and solde at Hepworth   £1 2s. 6d.

And with £3 18s.0d. by him received of Roberte Bowman, the
bedell of the Hall, for divers mariage dynners kept there this
yeare   £3 18s. 0d.

And with 1s.4d. by him received of Thomas Maplett toward the
repayring of the well in the Churchgate Streete   1s. 4d.

Allocaciones

Inprimis the saide accomptant dothe pray allowance of
£1 18s.11½d. by him paid for the rentes due to His Majestie for
divers of the towne landes holden of His Majestie   £1 18s.11½d.

Rentes resolute

And of 10s.6d. payde to His Majesties Receivor Generall for the
tenth of St Peters, and for the receivors acquittance and doore
keper, 8d.   11s. 2d.

And of 1s.6½d. payde to the manor of Wattisfeild   1s. 6½d.

And of 6d. payde to the manor of Rougham   6d.

And of 8d. payde to the hundred of Thedwastree   8d.

And of 1½d. payde to the manor of Fornham All Saincts   1½d.

The Schole

And of £5 9s.10½d. paide to the Governors of the Fre Gramer
Schole for the part of to them belonging for St Peters and the
graunge   £5 9s.10½d.

Preachers

And of £50 0s.0d. paide to Mr Carey, preacher of St Maries
parishe, for his yeres allowance owt of this howse   £50 0s. 0d.

And of £50 0s.0d. paide to Mr Walbanck, preacher of St James
parishe, for his yeres allowance owt of this howse   £50 0s. 0d.

Ministers

And of £2 0s.0d. paide to Mr Juell, minister of St Maries parishe   £2 0s. 0d.

And of £2 0s. 0d. payde to Mr Crossman, minister of St James
parishe   £2 0s. 0d.

Mrs Odeham her gift

And of £6 0s.0d. paide to Mr Crossman for reading service and
preaching to the prisoners in the gaole, according to the will of
Mrs Odeham   £6 0s. 0d.

And of £1 15s.0d. paide for 184 fagottes bought and given to the
poore prisoners in gaoles,[218] according to the will of Mrs
Odeham   £1 15s. 0d.

---

[218] The use of the plural must mean that fuel was provided for both borough and county (Liberty) gaols.
Note too that Bright's gift for prisoners was specified as paid to the town gaol. The feoffees did not buy
Moyse's Hall for a borough gaol, house of correction and workhouse until 1626, but it is likely that the
Corporation had used part of it, at least, ever since 1606, when they not only paid rent for it but spent
money on repairs, chamberlain's account, D6/4/1.

[*f. 46r., old number 89*]

Mr Brightes gyft

And of £5 0s.0d. bestowed according to the will of Mr Thomas
  Bright, *videlicet*

To the reparacions of St Maries church	£1 0s.0d.			
To the reparacions of St James church	£1 0s.0d.			
To the poore of St Maries parishe	£1 0s.0d.			
To the poore of St James parishe	£1 0s.0d.			
To the prisoners in the towne gaole	£1 0s.0d.	£5	0s.	0d.

And of 22 dosen of medlies and greys bought to clothe the poore
  according to the gyft of the saide Mr Bright, £21 0s.0d., and for
  makeing and finishinge the same clothes, £6 6s.4d., as by the
  particulers thereof appereth   £27 6s. 4d.

Peter Kembold

And of £3 0s.0d. payde to ~~the poore~~ John Brydon for the poore of
  the North and East Wardes to be distributed according to the
  will of Peter Kembold   £3 0s. 0d.

Mr Walker

And of £4 0s.0d. layde owt in provision for the poore, according
  to the will of Mr Richard Walker   £4 0s. 0d.

Mr Pynner

And of [*space*] paid to the preachers that have kept the Monday
  exercise [*according*] to the will of Mr Francis Pynner the
  yonger   [*no amount given*]

Churches

And of £1 0s.0d. payde to Roberte Glover, churchwarden of St
  Maries, toward the reparacions of that church   £1 0s. 0d.

And of £1 0s.0d. paide to Richard Maltyward and Thomas
  Godfrey churchwardens of St James, towardes the reparacion
  of that church   £1 0s. 0d.

Judges

And of ~~£5 4s.0d. given owt of this house~~ £2 0s.0d. for a veale and
  a mutton, given to the judges at Lent assises, and £2 4s.0d. for
  a veale, a mutton and six capons given to the judges at somer
  assisses, *in toto*   £4 4s. 0d.

The Poore

And of £5 4s.0d. given owt of this howse towardes the weekely
  contribution to the poore, *videlicet*, £2 12s.0d. to the overseers
  of the poore in St Maries parishe, and £2 12s.0d. to the
  overseers of the poore of St James parishe   £5 4s. 0d.

And of 1s.3d. paide for a payre of wooll cardes given to the
  Widowe Colly   1s. 3d.

And of 1s.2d. paide for a payre of wooll cardes given to the
  Widowe Mann   1s. 2d.

And of 10s.0d. given to the Germaine doctor for cutting Lyles boy
  of a rupture   10s. 0d.

And of £1 0s.0d. paide to Oliver Theobald for divers cures done

272

by him upon poore folke in the tyme whilest Mr Pynner was receivor	£1	0s.	0d.

And of £1 0s.0d. more paide to the saide Olyver for cures done by him this yere upon the poore, as by his billes appereth   £1   0s.   0d.

And of 6s.8d. paide to Abraham Wright, apothecarie, for things by him done and delivered for the cure of diseased poore, as by his bill appereth   6s.   8d.

And of 5s.6d. by him given at divers tymes to the Widowe Dawson, the Widowe Hardy and the Widowe Percyvall, being in great want   5s.   6d.

And of 6d. by him given to old Farrowe for going to Rougham to view what woode was cutt downe by Mr Springe, the tenant at Layers   6d.

And of £1 0s.0d. lent to Elizabeth Cowper upon John Chaunter bill   £1   0s.   0d.

Reparacions

And of £45 0s.0d. by him laide owt for reparacions by him done at the Angell this yere, as by the bill of particulers appereth   £45   0s.   0d.

And of £3 5s.5d. for reparacions by him done at the almose howses next St Maries church, as by the bill of particulers appereth   £3   5s.   5d.

And of £7 11s.7d. by him layde owt for makeing the particion at the Markett Crosse, and for reparactions done there, as by the bill of particulers appereth[219]   £7   11s.   7d.

And of £6 3s.2d. for setting upp a new pumpe in the Mustowe, and for the reparacions done there, as by the bill of particulers appereth   £6   3s.   2d.

And of 10s.0d. for reparacions done by him at the Gyldehall, as by the bill of particulers appereth   10s.   0d.

And of £1 4s.1d. for repayringe the well in the Churchgate Streete, as by the bill of particulers apereth   £1   4s.   1d.

And of 3s.6d. paide for a post sett upp at the Eastgate Bridge, and for workmanshipp   3s.   6d.

And of 2s.10d. for reparacions done at the almose howse wherein the Widowe Foxgill dwelleth. And of 3s.0d. for reparacions done at the almose howse wherein Aggas dwelleth. And of 5s.0d. for reparacions done at the howse wherein William Rowge dwelleth, *in toto*   10s.   10d.

And of £1 4s.2d. layde owt for divers reparacions done at the Bridewell howse, as by the particulers appereth   £1   4s.   2d.

And of £1 0s.0d. paide to the surveyors[220] towardes the paveing and amending of the streete before the ministers dores   £1   0s.   0d.

---

[219] There is no clue to the nature of this partition. A cobbler's shop existed there, for which £1 3s.8d. was laid out on 9 July 1625, miscellaneous papers (among the Corporation records, but some undoubtedly forming part of the feoffees' archive) D11/2/3.

[220] It is not clear whether the feoffees had been assessed for this sum as their highway rate or whether they had made a special arrangement for repairing the road near the ministers' houses by St James's church.

[*f. 46v.*]

A brasse pot bought

And of 18s.0d. paide for the exchaunge of an old brasse pott for a better and a bigger brasse pott, for the use of the Gyldehall	18s.	0d.

Fees, wages and liveries

And of 15s.0d. due to this accomptant for his fee	15s.	0d.
And of £2 0s.0d. allowed to Mr Mallowes, the clerke of this company, for his fee and for drawing and entring this accompt and makeing the rentall	£2 0s.	0d.
And of £2 10s.0d. paide to Roberte Bowman, the bedell of the hall, for his yeres wages	£2 10s.	0d.
And of £2 12s.0d. paide to Roberte Allington, the common bedell and cryer of the towne, for his wages this yere	£2 12s.	0d.
And of £1 0s.0d. payde to Roberte Studd, for his yeres wages for kepeing the library	£1 0s.	0d.
And of £4 0s.0d. for 10 yardes of blewe clothe for 5 liveries *videlicet* for Rooper, Ilger and Harryson, 3 of the serjauntes, and for Bowman and Allington, the bedells, at 8s.0d. the yard	£4 0s.	0d.
And of 12s.4d. payde to Mr Gippes for faceing those 5 liveries	12s.	4d.

Annuities

And of £10 0s.0d. paide to Mr Francis Pynner for his annuitie due this yere, and from hence forth to cease, being expired	£10 0s.	0d.
And of £5 0s.0d. paide to Mr Henry Collynge for his annuitie for this yere	£5 0s.	0d.
And of £16 0s.0d. paide to John Bedwall for his annuitie for this yere	£16 0s.	0d.
And of [*space*] paide to Mr Francis Pynner, the last accomptant, being the money which was owinge unto him, as in surplus upon the determynacion of th his accompt, as appereth in the foote of the same accompt	[*no amount given*]	
And of £2 4s.0d. paide for the Commissioners at the Angell at the assessement of the first subsedy	£2 4s.	0d.
And of 5s.10d. paide to John Petchey for charges of certen commissioners in the towne affaires	5s.	10d.
And of £1 7s.11d. paide for wyne spent at the Gyldehall, at the election of Mr Anthony Smythe, alderman	£1 7s.	11d.
And of £1 19s.0d. paide to Mr Hughes for charges at the Gyldehall at the same election, more then was allowed by the Company	£1 19s.	0d.
And of 10s.0d. given to Greene for musick then	10s.	0d.
And of 6s.6d. given then to the ringers[221]	6s.	6d.
And of 5s.10d. paide to Mr Hughes for expenses, more than was allowed to him by the company, when Mr Alderman Smyth toke his oathe	5s.	10d.
And of 6s.0d. paide to William Hawsted for wyne spent then	6s.	0d.
And of one boare given to Mr Alderman by consent	one boare	
And of six combes of rye, baked and given to the poore	6 combes rye	

---

[221] The only reference to bell ringing in these accounts.

And of 4s.0d. paide for grinding the same rye   4s.   0d.

And of [space] for the charges of the dynner of the feoffes and others, at the tyme of this accompt, and in provision for the poore, as by the bill of particulers apereth   [no amount given]

And of 19s.0d. payde to Bowman, the bedell of the hall, for fyer, candell and other provisions for the feoffees at the tymes of their assemblies, as by his bill of particulers appereth   19s.   0d.

[f. 47r. old number 80]

1622

The accompt of Mr John Gooderich, receivor of the rentes and revenues belonging to the common use and benefitt of the towne of Bury St Edmund, made and yealded upp at the Guildhall there, the ninth daye of January in the twentith yeare of the reigne of our soveraigne lord, King James *et cetera*, [1623] for one wholl yeare then last past

Onus

Inprimis the said accomptant doth charge himself with [space] due by Mr Roberte Browne, the last receivor, uppon the determinacion of his accompt, as appeareth by the foote of the same accompt   [no amount given]

And with £29 1s.3d. by him received for divers arrerages behinde and in super upon divers severall persons, in divers precedent yeares, as appeareth in divers former accomptes and in the booke of arrerages,[222] *videlicet* Of Sir Thomas Jermyn, knight, for all arrerages rune in the time of Sir Roberte Jermyn, knight, now deceased, the father of the said Sir Thomas Jermyn, and in the time of the said Sir Thomas Jermyn, for divers parcelles of the towne groundes, heretofore in the occupacion of the said Sir Roberte and Sir Thomas Jermyn and of their assignes, lyinge in Hepworth, so agreed upon by composicion untill the feast of St Michaell th'archangell in the yeare of Our Lord, 1621, £15 12s.6d. And of Roberte Wynter for the wholl arrerages of the rent of a gardine or peece of ground, with a small building thereupon, in the Southgate Streete, late in the tenure of Oliver Ion, by composicion £1 10s.0d. And of John Daye, of Hepworthe, for his arrerage of part of his rent incurd in the time of the said Mr Roberte Browne, the last receivor, £5 8s.9d. And of Samuel Reve for part of his arrerages, mencioned in the saide booke of arrerages, for a tenement in Hepworth £1 0s.0d. And of John Curtis, by the handes of Mr John Boldero, one of the feoffees, for his arrerage due in *anno* 1618, for a tenemente in Hepworth, £2 0s.0d. And of Mr Anthony Adams, assignee of Mr Thomas Havers, deceased, for part of the Angell, occupied with the howse wherein the saide Mr Adams now dwelleth, for his arrerage for the yeares 1618, 1619, 1620 at 3s.4d. *per annum*, 10s.0d. And of Mr Bennett

222   This has survived and is H2/3/4/10.

Barker for St Peters Barne, for one wholl yeare ended at Micaelmas, 1621, £3 0s.0d.   £29 1s.   3d.

And with £386 8s.10d., one boare, two capons, two gallons of wyne and seaven combes of rye, being the certeine yearely rentes and revenues of this howse for this yeare, particularly expressed in the rentall thereof made, as by the same rentall appeareth, besides Mr Shawbery his rent, for certeine landes in Hepworth, which is not yet certeinely agreed upon   £386 8s. 10d., one boare, seaven combes rye, two capons, two gallons wyne

And with ten poundes by him received of Mr Shawbery in part paiment of his yeares rent due for the landes in Hepworth, in the occupacion of his assignes   £10 0s.   0d.

And with £4 2s.0d. by him received of Roberte Bowman, the beadell of the hall, for divers mariage dinners kept there this yeare, and by him paide over to this accomptant   £4 2s.   0d.

And with £33 17s.6d. by him received of divers severall persons for wood by him cutt downe at Hepworth this yeare, *videlicet*, Of Rose of Weston for wood cutt downe in Little Attelly £10 0s.0d. Of John Tye of Hepworth 15s.0d. Of Humfry Ling of Hepworth for wood cutt downe in Laye Meadowe £5 13s.0d. Of the same Humfry Ling for tymber[223] cutt downe in Brettes £2 0s.0d. Of the same Humfry Ling for 17 loades and *dimidia* of wood cutt downe in Brettes £4 10s.2d. Of the same Humfry Ling for more wood solde to him £6 10s.4d. Of Miles Scott for six loades of wood cutt downe in Brettes, £1 19s.0d. And of Richard Foster of Hepworth for 12 loades of wood £3 0s.0d., *in toto*   £33 17s.   6d.

And with £1 5s.0d. by him received for muck cast out of the privye howses belonging to the almose howses in the Colledge Streete   £1 5s.   0d.

[*f.47v.*]

Allocaciones

Out rentes

Inprimis the said accomptant doth praye allowance of £1 18s.11½d. by him paide for the rentes due to His Majestie for divers of the towne landes holden of His Majestie   £1 18s. 11½d.

And of 10s.6d. paide to His Majesties Receiver Generall for the tenth of St Peters, due to His Majestie and of 8d. paide for the receivors acquitance, and to his dorekeeper, *in toto*   11s.   2d.

And of 1s.6½d. paide to the manor of Watisfeild   1s. 6½d.

And of 9d. paide for Hallymott rent   9d.

Free Schoole

And of £5 9s.10½d. paide to the governors of the Free Gramer Schoole, for the part to them belonging for St Peters and the Graunge   £5 9s. 10½d.

---

223   Timber for building was distinguished from wood for firewood and suchlike uses.

Preachers

And of £50 0s.0d. paide to Mr Carey, preacher of St Maries
parish, for his yeares allowance out of this howse   £50   0s.   0d.

And of £50 0s.0d. paide to Mr Walbanck, preacher of St James
parish, for his yeares allowance out of this howse   £50   0s.   0d.

Ministers

And of £2 0s.0d. paide to Mr Jewell, minister of St Maries parish   £2   0s.   0d.

And of £2 0s.0d. paide to Mr Crossman, minister of St James
parish   £2   0s.   0d.

Mrs Odehams gift

And of £6 0s.0d. paide to Mr Crossman for reading service and
preachinge to the prisoners in the gaole, accordinge to the will
of Mrs Odeham   £6   0s.   0d.

And of £1 5s.0d. paide for wood bought and given to the poore
prisoners in the gaoles, according to the will of Mrs Odeham   £1   5s.   0d.

Mr Bright his gift

And of £5 0s.0d. bestowed according to the will of Mr Thomas
Bright, *videlicet,*

To the reparacions of St Maries church	£1 0s.0d.			
To the reparacions of St James church	£1 0s.0d.			
To the poore of St Maries parishe	£1 0s.0d.			
To the poore of St James parish	£1 0s.0d.			
To the prisoners of the towne gaole	£1 0s.0d.	£5	0s.	0d.

And of £22 2s.8d. for 27 dozen and 9 yardes of medlies and
grayes, bought to cloth the poore, according to the gift of the
said Mr Bright. And of £8 9s.5d. for making and finishing the
same clothes, as by the bill of particulers appeareth, *in toto*   £30   12s.   1d.

Peter Kembold

And of £3 0s.0d. paide to Peter Linge for the poore of the north
and east wardes, to be distributed according to the will of Peter
Kembold   £3   0s.   0d.

Mr Richard Walker

And of £4 0s.0d. laide out in provision given to the poore,
according to the will of Mr Richard Walker   £4   0s.   0d.

Churches

And of £1 0s.0d. paide to Thomas Browne, churchwarden of St
Maries, towardes the reparacions of that church   £1   0s.   0d.

And of £1 0s.0d. paide to Thomas Godfrey, senior, churchwarden
of St James, towardes the reparacions of that church   £1   0s.   0d.

Judges

And of £2 5s.8d. for a weather, and a calf, and six capons, given to
the judges at Lent assises. And £2 5s.0d. for a weather, and a
calf, and six capons, given to the judges at somer assises, *in
toto*   £4   10s.   8d.

Poore

And of £5 4s.0d. given out of this howse towardes the weekely contribucion to the poore *videlicet*, £2 12s.0d. to the overseers of St Maries parish, and £2 12s.0d. to the overseers of St James parish, *in toto*	£5	4s.	0d.
And of 2s.6d. paide for a sheete to burye old Hanson		2s.	6d.
And of 2s.6d. paide for a sheete to burye Johnsons wief		2s.	6d.
And of 1s.2d. paide for two paire of old cardes for Mother Coolye		1s.	2d.
And of 1s.0d. paide to an old wooman for keeping the sick wooment[*sic*] in the almose howses		1s.	0d.
And of £1 0s.0d. distributed amongest divers poore men that did help at the fier at Wallys howse in the Northgate Streete	£1	0s.	0d.
And of 2s.0d. paide for the releif of a poore childe that was found sick and allmost dead in a hoggescoate in the Westgate Streete[224]		2s.	0d.
And of 6s.0d. given to John Atkin in the time of his sickenes		6s.	0d.
And of 2s.0d. given to Mother Snowden for keeping Prattes wief beinge much distrempred in her sences[225]		2s.	0d.
And of 1s.0d. given to the Widowe Snowden towardes the healing of the head of Manies sonne		1s.	0d.

[*f.48r., old number 78*]

And of £1 0s.0d. paide to Oliver Teobald for healing the legge of Emme Pondes sonne	£1	0s.	0d.
And of five combes rye, being parcell of the rent corne mencioned in the rentall, whereof was made 106 dozen of bread, given and distributed to the poore of both parishes. 16 *Decembris*, 1622	five combes rye		
And of 3s.4d. for grinding the same rye		3s.	4d.
And of 15s.0d. paide for baking the same rye		15s.	0d.
And of £4 19s.2d. given to the poore for their releif at the same time	£4 19s.		2d.
And of two combes rye, being the remainder of the 7 combes rent rye, baked out in bread and given to the poore the 8th of Januarye	two combes rye		
And of 1s.4d. paide for grinding the same two combes rye		1s.	4d.
And of 6s.0d. paide for baking the same two combes rye		6s.	0d.
And of £2 18s.8d. paide to Thurston, the miller, for four combes rye bought of him, and baked and given to the poore the same eight daye of Januarye, and for grinding the same	£2 18s.		8d.
And of 12s.0d. paide for bakinge the same four combes rye		12s.	0d.
And of £3 0s.0d. given to the poore in money the same daye	£3	0s.	0d.
And of 11s.5d. paide for bord and workemanshipp for <*deletion*> a bing at the Markett Crosse to putt in meale to serve the poore		11s.	5d.
And of £1 0s.0d. given to the poore in the towne gaole	£1	0s.	0d.
And of £2 12s.11d. paide to Joseph Alexander and Clement Chaplyn for wood, given to the two gaoles in the yeare when Mr Roberte Browne was Receivor	£2 12s.		11d.

---

[224] This is the only instance in these account books of a child being abandoned. The near famine conditions at this time may have made some family unable to feed the child.
[225] This is the only reference to mental illness in these books.

Reparacions

And of 8s.0d. paide to Mr John Bridon, one of the feoffees, for tyle that he bought towardes the repairinge of the Eastgate Bridge, when Mr Pynner was Receivor | 8s. | 0d.

And of £3 4s.8d. paide to Mr Christofer Cox as so much laide out by him, in the time when Mr Roberte Browne was receivor, for reparacions done at the howse allowed to Mr Walbanck, lecturer of St James church | £3 | 4s. | 8d.

And of £27 16s.4d. for reparacions done at the howse in the Churchgate Streete, given by Mr Walker, now repaired and made fitt for the common workehowse, as by the booke of particulars appeareth[226] | £27 16s. | 4d.

And of £4 2s.6d. for divers reparacions done at the almose howses and spitle howses,[227] as by the bill of particulers appeareth | £4 | 2s. | 6d.

And of £4 7s.4d. for divers reparacions done at the Angell this yeare, as by the bill of particulers appeareth | £4 | 7s. | 4d.

And of £3 11s.11d. for divers reparacions done at the towne howse wherein William Rowge dwelleth, and at the Markett Crosse, as appeareth by the same bill of particulers | £3 11s. | 11d.

And of £5 7s.4d. for divers reparacions done at the towne howse wherein Abraham Greene dwelleth, in the Risbygate Streete, as by the booke of particulers appeareth | £5 | 7s. | 4d.

And of £1 7s.3d. for divers reparacions done at St Peters, being now imploied for the howse of correcion[228] | £1 | 6s. | 3d.

And of 2s.0d. paide to Mosse, the mason, for mending the foote bridge over against the well with two pumps | 2s. | 0d.

And of 1s.0d. laide out for mending the lock at the Cage | 1s. | 0d.

And of 6s.9d. for repairinge the common well in the Old Baxter Streete, and 1s.0d. for repairinge the well against the Angell | 7s. | 9d.

And of 12s.6d. paide to Prigge, the plumber, for melting the weightes and for worke done by him at the Crosse, when Mr Bright was alderman[229] | 12s. | 6d.

Annuities

And of £5 0s.0d. paide to Mr Colling, for his annuitie for this yeare | £5 0s. | 0d.

And of £16 0s.0d. paide to John Bedwall, for his annuitie for this yeare | £16 0s. | 0d.

Fees, wages and liveries

And of 15s.0d. due to this accomptant for his fee | 15s. | 0d.

And of fourty shillinges paide to Mr Mallowes, the clerke of this company, for his fee, and for drawinge and entring the accompt and makinge a new rentall[230] | £2 0s. | 0d.

---

[226] See Introduction, p.liv.

[227] The use of the plural here indicates that by this date there was somewhere other than St Peter's Hospital used for the sick.

[228] See Introduction, p.lxiv.

[229] Perhaps the weights were melted down because they had been found to be inaccurate.

[230] This has survived (H2/3/4/11) and is printed as Appendix 3.

[f. 48v.]

And of £2 10s.0d. paide to Roberte Bowman, the beadell of this company, for his wages	£2 10s.	0d.
And of £2 12s.0d. paide to Roberte Allington, the common beadell and cryer of this towne, for his wages for this yeare	£2 12s.	0d.
And of £1 0s.0d. paide to Roberte Studd for his yeares wages for tendinge the library	£1 0s.	0d.
And of 13s.4d. paide to Dockinge for his wages for tending the markett clock[231]	13s.	4d.
And of £3 7s.0d. paide to Mr Bright for 7 yardes of blew cloth at 9s.0d. the yard for liveries for the towne waytes, in the tyme when Mr Roberte Browne was receiver	£3 7s.	0d.
And of £4 12s.6d. paide to Mr Bright for blew cloth for 5 liveries for the towne officers, *videlicet*, for Roper, Ilger, Harrison, three of the sarjauntes at mace,[232] and for Bowman, the beadell of the hall, and for Allington, the beadell and cryer of the towne	£4 12s.	6d.
And of 12s.6d. paide to Mr Gippes for facing, buttons and sowinge silke for those liveries	12s.	6d.
And of £2 14s.6d. paide to the goldsmith for the silver cognizaunces for the waites of the towne	£2 14s.	6d.
And of 10s.0d. given to Roberte Roper, by consent of the feoffees, towardes his howse rent for one quarter ended at the feast of the Nativety of Our Lord, [16]22	10s.	0d.
And of £1 0s.0d. paide to Roberte Bowman, the beadell of the hall for fieringe, candell and other thinges, laide out by him for the use of the feoffees at their meetinges about the busines of the towne	£1 0s.	0d.
And of 3s.0d. laide out for two chamber pottes to be used at the Guildhall	3s.	0d.
And of £1 4s.0d. paide to Cobb, the botle maker, for six new buckettes of lether, made and bought for the use of the towne	£1 4s.	0d.
And of 9d. paide to the churchwardens, as so much rate upon the workehowse, towardes the reparacions of St Maries church[233]		9d.
And of 13s.0d. paide to the overseers of the two parishes, for half a quarter, rated upon the towne landes, towardes the maintenance of the workehowse	13s.	0d.
And of £20 0s.0d. paide to Mr Mallowes in part of paiment of the money due to him for the purchase of the ground at Rotten Rowe	£20 0s.	0d.
And of £5 0s.0d. paide to John Morse for the rent of his howse in the Whiting Streete, where the workehowse was kept for half a yeare ended at the Annunciacion, 1622	£5 0s.	0d.

231 C. Morris (ed.) *The Journeys of Celia Fiennes*, p.151 noted the dial on the Market Cross when she visited Bury in 1698. Downing's map of 1740, and Warren's of 1747, both show the Market Cross with a clock.
232 Note that the feoffees were paying for the liveries of these essentially Corporation servants. The Corporation had been granted the right to have four sergeants (instead of the original two) in the 1614 Letters Patent, D1/1/3.
233 This is another instance of a church rate being levied. The house in Churchgate Street which was given by Richard Walker and used as a workhouse was in St Mary's parish.

And of £25 0s.0d. paide to Mr Mathewe Lancaster, overseer of the workehowse[234]	£25	0s.	0d.
And of £10 0s.0d. paide to Mr William Grigges, overseer of the house of correccion	£10	0s.	0d.
And of £4 6s.0d. laide out for felling and making the wood and trees that were cutt downe and solde at Hepworth this yeare	£4	6s.	0d.
And of 4s.4d. expended by this accomptant and other of the feoffees at such times as they rode to Hepworth about the cuttinge downe and sellinge of the same wood		4s.	4d.
And of 2s.0d. paide for a pottell of sack given to the Comissioners Compounders for His Majesties provisions and cariages		2s.	0d.
And of £1 16s.6d. for a fresh salmon and two suger loaves given to Sir Albertus Mourton, Clerke of the Counsell,[235] when he laye in towne	£1	16s.	6d.
And of £4 17s.0d. laide out for the charges of the Comissioners and others, in the sute that was betwene Sir Nicholas Bacon and the towne	£4	17s.	0d.
And of £18 13s.5d. laide out for the charges of the four Knightes Commissioners and others in the sute that was betwene Mr Thomas Baker and the towne	£18	13s.	5d.
And of £20 0s.0d. paide to Mr Mallowes towardes the charges of those two sutes, and other busines of the towne and to be accompted for by the said Mr Mallowes	£20	0s.	0d.
And of 2s.0d. given to Foxgill for caryinge a lettre to Sir Roger North		2s.	0d.
And of £5 8s.4d. <deletion> expended by Mr Alderman Smith, Mr Barker, this accomptant and Roberte Roper when they travelled to London about the defense of theis sutes, and busines for the towne	£5	8s.	4d.
And of 2s.0d. given to Mr Callowe, Sir John Heighams clerke, for writing a lettre touching the composicion money		2s.	0d.

[f. 49r., old number 76]

And of 2s.0d. given to a scrivener for writing a lettre that was sent to the Lordes of the Counsell for certificat of their proceedinge, touching the abatinge of the prices of corne[236]		2s.	0d.
And of £2 0s.0d. paide to Thomas Cropley towardes the charges of the dinner at the Guildhall at Mr Aldermans election	£2	0s.	0d.
And of 13s.10d. laide out for wyne and suger at the time of the same eleccion		13s.	10d.

[234] See Introduction, p.xl, for the workhouse and the house of correction.

[235] Sir Albertus Morton, as well as holding a high office which would in any case merit a present on his coming to the town, must have known William Bedell, for many years the preacher of St Mary's and at this date rector of Horringer. Sir Albertus had accompanied his uncle, Sir Henry Wotton, on his embassy to Venice in 1604. William Bedell was Sir Henry's chaplain. See *DNB* and Gordon Rupp, *William Bedell*.

[236] This letter calendared in *CSPD* cxxxvii, 1619–1623, p.484, explained how the magistrates and Corporation had restrained the maltsters from malting as frequently as usual and, to avoid trouble, had ventured to abate the price of corn against the orders of the council. This is yet another instance of the feoffees making a payment which might have been expected to fall on the Corporation.

And of 15s.0d. laide out for wyne and suger at the time of the alderman taking his oath	15s.	0d.
And of ten shillinges given to the towne waytes at both those dynners	10s.	0d.
And of 2s.2d. paide for two paper bookes to enter the receiptes and paymentes of this accomptant[237]	2s.	2d.
And of one boare, beinge parcell of the revenues of this howse, given to the alderman by consent of the feoffees	A boare	
And of £6 18s.3d. for the charges of the dynner of the feoffees and others upon the Commemoracion daye,[238] and at the time of the taking of this accompt, as by the particulers in the booke appeareth	£6 18s.	3d.

And of £7 10s.0d. by him paide to Mr Bennett Barker, as so much, and 9s.5d. more, laide out by the said Mr Barker for the affaires of the towne in the yeare when he was alderman *videlicet*

To pursivantes for bringing 11 proclamacions	£1 7s.6d.	
To Foxgill for caryinge lettres to the Lord Chauncellor concerning a Burgesse of Parliament for the towne[239]	15s.0d.	
For the charges of one dynner at the towne sessions	£2 6s.8d.	~~£7 0s. 0d.~~
To pursivantes for bringing downe the two commissions and bookes for the subsidies	10s.0d.	
To the preachers which kept the Mondaye exercise in this towne, according to the will of Mr Francis Pynner the younger	~~£1 16s.0d.~~	
For the charges of the dynner of the Muster Master and others at the trayninge of soldiors, above that which was collected	£1 1s.3d.	
To a pursivant for bringing the Counselles lettres touchinge the composicion of cariages	2s.0d.	
To a messenger for bringing a brief touching the suppressing of unlawfull games	1s.0d.	£7 10s. 0d.

But by agreement betweene the feoffees and the saide Mr Barker the said Mr Barker was content to accept of £7 10s.0d. in satisfaccion of all the said disbursementes amounting to £7 19s.5d.

And of £3 6s.0d. paide to Mr John Mallowes as so much laide out by him for a sute of diaper, by him bought, for the use of the towne in the entertainement of the judges at the assises, *videlicet*, for a long table cloth, a square bord cloth, a cupbord cloth and two dozen of napkins
£3 6s. 0d.

---

[237] This and the previous account are only drafts of which fair copies would have been entered into these new books.
[238] This is the earliest reference known of the use of this term, which is still used today. See Glossary.
[239] For parliamentary representation in Bury see Introduction, p.li. There was in fact no Lord Chancellor at this period, but Bishop John Williams had been appointed Lord Keeper of the Great Seal in 1621, *DNB*.

Appendix 1

Will of John Smith, 1477, and Bidding Prayer from the Book of Benefactors, H1/2/1

This is a small parchment book, written *c.*1500, which also contains English versions of Margaret Odeham's will, and an exhortation to pray for the soul of John Baret. Some lines have been scored out. While it is possible to make out the words erased from the bidding prayer, more than two lines of the five-line exhortation are illegible. The rest of the book contains terriers of lands given by John Smith and Margaret Odeham. At the end of Margaret Odeham's terrier are the signatures of Robert Jermyn, Robert Ashfield and Thomas Poley. Both Ashfield and Jermyn became feoffees in 1588, but their signatures here no doubt indicate that the book had been examined during one of the many late sixteenth- and early seventeenth-century enquiries into the feoffees' lands and actions.

Where words or phrases were emphasised by heavy inking in the original, these have been printed in **bold**.

[f.1r.]

John Smyth
Copia testamenti ac ultime voluntatis Johannis Smyth armigeri de Bury

In the name of God, Amen. This present wrytyng tripartite indentyd mad at Bury Saynt Edmund in the 10 day of the moneth of Aprile in the yer of Oure Lord a thowsand fowre hundred seventy and sevyn, in the yer of the reigne of Kyng Edward the 4te after the conquest of Inglond seventene, wytnesseth that this is the sur', perfect and perpetuall wyll of me John Smyth of Bury Seynt Edmund in the Counte of Suffolke, esquyer, nevir to be revokyd by me of alle the meses, landes, tenementes, rentes and services wyth alle there pertinences in the townys and feldes of Berton besyde Bury, Fornham Saint Martyn and in the feldys of Bury forsaid called Estfelde, Southfelde and Vinefeldes. Also in the townys of Nowton and Rougham, the which meses, landes, tenementes, rentes and services with their pertinences Robert Gardener, alderman of the same town of Bury, John Aylward, Thomas Brett, William Thwyate, Herry Banyard, Clement Drury, John Forster, William Buntyng, Andrue Scarbott, John Furssney, Thomas Bunnyng, John Reggeman, Symon Clerk, Robert Roose, Robert Burges, Water Thurston, John Mey, Thomas Emmys, John Gowty, Wylliam **[f.1v.]** Copyng, Edmund Lorymer, Laurens Smyth, Robert Cryppyng and John Salman have of the gift amd feffement off me the forsaid John Smyth by a dede tripartite indentyd in the 10 day of Septembyr in the yere of the reigne of the said kyng Edward the 10, yoven and made at Berton forsaid. Also of a nothir mese in the town of Rougham and of 18 peces off arabyll land, 1 pece of medow and 1 pec[e] off bosc' with liberte of foldes and alle othir pertinences in the said town of Rougham. The which meses, londes, medowe, bosc' with liberte of foldes and other pertinences in the said toun of Rougham John Forster, thanne aldyrman of Bury, Robert Gardener, John Aylward, Thomas Brett, William Thwyete, Clement Drury, William Buntyng, Andrue Scarbott, John Furssney, Thomas Bunnyng, John Reggeman, Symon Clerk, Robert Roose, Robert

Burges, Water Thurston, John Meye, Thomas Emmys, John Gouty, William Copynger, Laurens Smyth, Robert Cryppyng and John Salman have of the gyfte and fefement of me the said John Smyth, by a nothir dede tripartite also indentid yoven and made the 20^{ti} day off July in the yere of the reigne of sayd kyng the 13^{ti} att Rougham forsaid, for that intent to execute deuly and to fulfille my last wyll in all thynges as it is wretyn and conteynyd in this present wrytyng folowynge *et cetera.* **[f.2r.] Fyrst** in to the laude and honour of almyghty God and his most glorious modir and mayde, Oure Lady Saynt Mary and of the gloryous kyng and martir Seynt Edmund and unto the releve and helpe of the Aldirman, burgeyses and of alle the commynalte and poore inhabitantes of the sayd toun of Bury and unto the supportacion of the chargis dayly lying over them, that they theire eyres and successours may specyally pray evermore for the helth of my soule and for the soule of Anne now late my wyff, also for the soules of my fadyr and modir and my benefactours and for alle christen soules. I wyll that I the forsaid John Smyth have and receyve duryng the terme of my lyff alle issues and profites of all the forsaid meses, londes, tenementes, medowes, pastures, bosc' with liberte of foldes with all and syngler pertinences aforesaid comyng and growyng of the same withoute any man geynseying. **And aftyr** my decess I will that the said alderman, burgesses and feoffes have and receyve fully alle the issues and profytes of alle and syngler mesuages, londes, tenementes, medowes, bosc' with liberte of foldys and odyr pertinences a for said for evermore to this intent, that the said alderman, burgeysses and feoffes, or the sayd burgeysses and feoffes in the stede of alderman faylyng, which shalbe for the tyme every yere alway schall [*?*]solenny and devoutly do kepe my yere day and Anne my **[f.2v.]** wyffes in the parich churche of oure lady in Bury for my soule and for the soules of the seyd Anne, our faderis and moderis, oure benefactors and for alle Cristen soules with priestes and clerkys, that is seyn in the vigile off the said myn annyversary they shall synge and sey devoutly ***Placebo*** and ***Dirige*** and in the day of the said myn anniversary a messe of **Requiem** solenny by note with othir suffragiis and prayers wont to be doon in swich obsequiis. **And I wyll** and require the said alderman, burgeyses and feoffes that they kepe my said annyversary every yere perpetually in the same day of the moneth that it happith me to deye in, but iff a lawfull cause come that it may not be thanne, I wyll it schalbe doon sum day a forn or after as sone as it may. **Also I wyll** that residue and overpluse of the issues and profites of the said mes[*suages*], londes, tenementes, medowys, bosc', rentes, services and of all the premisses with the pertinences be reservyd and kepyd savely and suerly by the said alderman, burges and feoffes for the tyme beyng to that entent that whansovever and howoftsoever in tymes to come the abbey of Bury Seynt Edmund schalbe vacant of an abbot be the deth off the abbot, and a new abbot theire after his deth schall lawfully be chosyn, I wyll thanne that of the sayd issues and profites be payd to the sayd newe abbot for the tyme beyng as moche as may be reservyd and kepyd therof in to a satisfaccyon and a recompensacion of a certeyn summe off mony **[f.3r.]** wont of custom to be payd to the newe abbot by the inhabitantes of the sayd toun of Bury Seynt Edmund. And so as often as it happyth ony new abbot ther to be chosyn and prefect after the deth of any abbot for evermore. **Also yf any** thyng therof remayne over the said charges I wyll that it be applyed and disposid to the paymentes of tenthis and fyftens, taxis, tallagys and of alle odir maner charges the which shalbe exact and put to the burges and comynalte of the sayd toun in to the releve and discharge of the burges and comynalte of the sayd toun off alle and syngler forsayd chargys. **Moreovyr** I wyll that whanne the sayd 24 feoffes decess and dye outtake 14 of them at the lest ovyrlevyng, that thanne or afor if it be nedefull and expedient, 12 of the sayd 14 feoffes or moo yff they overleve schall relese alway for them and theire eyrys to 2 off the oldest cofeoffes al their cleyme, interess and demaundes the which they have by any maner reson of and in the sayd meses, londes, tenementes, medowes, pasturys, boskys with liberte of foldes, rentes and servyces and othir pertynences to have and to hold to them too their heyrys and theire assignes for evermore of the cheff lordes of the fees by the servyces off due and custom. Which too feoffes so put in full and peasyble possessyon off the sayd meses, londes and tenementes and othir premisses with theire pertinences shall feoffe ageyn the [f.3v.] sayd 12 feoffyd afore with them or mo levyng over, yff case requyre, with othir off the moost sufficient men of the burges and inhabitauntes of the said town unto the full nowmbyr of 24 or moo feoffes in alle the which be namyd chosyn and assigned to the sayd overlyvers by the aldirman and burgeys of the sayd town for the tyme beyng or by the said 12 feoffes and burges of the same toun for the tyme being in the stede of an alderman faylyng. To have and to hold to them and to theire eyris and assignes perpetually of the cheff lordes by the servyce forsayd to fulfylle this my last wyll in forme a forn said. **And so as often** in tyme to come as it fortuneth the feoffes in and of the said meses, londes, tenementes, rentes and othir premisses with theire portynaunces oute take 14 of them at the lest ovyre levyng, as it is foresaid, to decess and deye, that thanne or afore as it is afore said, if it seme nedefull and expedient to the said feoffes, 12 of them 14 or moo overlyvyng shal remit and reless in forme forsaid alwey for them and theire eyres to too of the sadder senyours of the said feoffes all there tytyll, clayme, interess and demaundes which they shall have or may have by ony reson of and in the said meses, londes, tenementes, medowes, pasturys, buskys with liberte of fooldes, rentes and services and [f.4r.] odir pertinences to have and to hold to them there eyris and theire assignes for ever more. The which 2 feoffes thus beyng in full and peasyble possessyon of the said meses, londys, tenementis and othir premisses with theire portenaunces schall feoffe ageyn the sayd 12 or moo the which lyve over with them feoffed afor with odir of most suffycient men of the burgeys and inhabitantes of the sayd toun of Bury unto the said full nowmbre off 24 feoffes in alle, the which schalbe chosyn namyd and associat to the said for feoffyd by the alderman and burges of the sayd toun or be the sayd feoffes survyvyng and burges of the same toun for the tyme beyng in the stede off an alderman faylyng. To have and to hold to them theire eyris and there assignes in forme aforsaid for ever-more to fulfylle ever lyke wyse this myn laste wyll. **And for asmoch as** my said feoffes are sworn upon the holy evangeli wele and truely to execute and fulfylle all the premysses in every articull. **So I wyll** that [?]hosomever in tyme to come shalbe feoffed in the said meses, londes, and tenementes, rentes, services and othir premysses with the portenaunces shall also swere upon the holy gospell by fore the alderman and burges of the said toun for the tyme beyng in the stede of an alderman faylyng, to fulfylle in forme a fore sayd all and syngler thynges content and specyfyed in this my last wyll. **Also I wyll** that after my decess [f.4v.] every yere alway 4 provyd men and abyll of the sayd feoffes for the tyme beyng be chosyn be the alderman and burges of the same town for the tyme beyng, or ellys be the said feoffes and burges for the tyme beyng in the stede of an alderman faylyng, **The whych** 4 abyll men fro yere in to yere chosyn in forme a forn rehersyd schal have supervysyon and governauce of alle the sayd meses, londes, tenementes, medowes, pastures, bosc' with lyberte of fooldes, rentes, services and almaner othir portenaunces. **And they** shall take and receyve all issues and profytes theroff in the name of the sayd feoffes for the tyme beyng to fulfylle al a fore rehersyd yerly for evermore. **And they schall** make every yere a dwe and a trewe account therof to the alderman and burges of the said town for the tyme beyng or to the residue of the cofeffes a fore sayd, and burges for the tyme beyng in the stede of an alderman faylyng. **Also I wyll** that the mony theroff every yere clerely receyvyd be put and reservid in a hooche or in a nothir convenyent place after the discrecion of the said alderman and burges and feoffes for the tyme beyng in the stede of an alderman faylyng, **So that** that[*sic*] it be turned ne putt to non odyr use but over to the execucyon and fulfyllyng of this my [*f.5r.*] last wyll as they wyll answere afore the jugement of Our Lord Jhu Crist at the day of dome *et cetera*. **In to the feyth** and testymony off all these thynges and syngler and that this present wrytyng indentyd in 3 partyes off my last wyll may have strength all way to abyde and known openly to alle men, I have sealed it and every part theroff and subscribed it with myn owne signe manuell in the day, place and yeere aforesaid. **Wittnessyng** the ryght reverent fadyr in God Richard abbot of the monastery of seynt Edmund in Bury[1] and Thomas, prior of the same place,[2] wyth many mo *et cetera*.

John Smyth

The which John this lyvelode hath yoven passid to God he is
On the Peter's evyn at midsomer as godys wyll is.
In the yere of Our Lord M[l] CCCCLXXX and oon.[3]
Late us all of charite [4]pray for the soule of John.
We put yow in remembraunce that ye [?]shall not misse
The kepyng of his dirige and also of his messe.
On the Peter's evyn is whyn the dirige shal be seed,
And on the Peter's evyn the messe with many a good beed
We put yow in remembraunce all the othe hav maad
To come to the dirige and the messe the soules for to glaad[5]
All th'enhabitauntes of this town arn bound to do the same.
To pray for the soul of John and Anne, ell thei be to blame.
The which John a fore rehersyd to this toun hath be full kynde
CCC marces for this toun hath payd, no peny on payd behynde.
[f.5v.]
Now we have informyd you off John Smythis wyll in wrytyng as it is,
And off the grett gyftes that he hath govyn God bryng his soule to blys.
Amen.

---

1   Richard of Hingham was abbot of St Edmund's, 1475–9, A. Goodwin, *The Abbey of St Edmundsbury*, p.82.
2   Thomas, prior of St Edmund's, also witnessed an indenture, dated 12 January 1478, which formed part of Margaret Odeham's will which was proved in 1492, Tymms, *Wills*, p.81.
3   That is, 28 June 1481.
4   The passage which has been erased begins here.
5   The erased passage ends here.

Appendix 2

Rentals of Feoffment Properties and Related Papers, 1587, H1/1/59

These documents are here transcribed from a file of receiver's papers. The first is a rental of the new purchased land and William Tassell's lands. The second is a rental which begins with the lands which had formerly been John Smyth's, Margaret Odeham's and Ellen Fish's. The third document is a list of rents actually received. The pages are not numbered but have been given page numbers here. It is unfortunate that these documents must have been stored for a long time at the bottom of a metal deed box on a damp floor. The resulting rust stains and mould damage have made some parts difficult, where not impossible, to read.

Wherever possible the donor, or other source from which the feoffees acquired a property, has been identified, usually with a reference to Appendix 8. Where properties in the town can be identified, they have been given a number on the map of Bury St Edmunds, p.300. These numbers are given at some convenient place in the text, in brackets and in bold type. Woodward's Register, H1/6/1, was invaluable in the attempt to identify properties and in many cases the full reference will be found in footnotes to the Introduction.

A true and perfyght rental of all such [*?*]rentes and fearmes as ben in and at this daie leviable for lo[*ndes*] and tenementes callid the newe purchasid londes bilonging to the towne of Burie St Edmunde, made and ren[*?ewed*] the 13th daie of Januarie in the 29th yere [*of*] the reign of our soveraigne ladie Quene Elizabeth and *anno Domini* [*1587*]

In primis of Thomas Coxsedge \nowe Margaret Coxsededg/ late in the fearme of John Osborne foure peeces of arrable londe lyinge in the Sowthe fieldes of Burie St Edmunde letten to him by indenture[1]	£1	0s.	0d.
Item of Roger Barber, gentleman, \nowe [*space*] Barber/ for nine peeces of lond conteyninge by estimacion 27 acres lyinge in the fieldes of Burie, Muche Horingeserthe and Westly, to him letton by indenture[2]	£4	3s.	4d.
Item of Henry Collinge, gentleman, \nowe Henry Colling the younger/ late John Holtes gentleman, disceased, for the fearme of foure peces of londe conteyninge nineteen acres 11 perches lyinge in the West [*f*]elde [*several words lost*] conteyninge two acres lyinge at Stanford [*?Bridge to*] him letten by indenture[3]	£3	6s.	8d.

---

[1]   See Appendix 8, *sub* 1478 and 1549. The land contained sixteen acres.
[2]   Appendix 8, *sub* 1478.
[3]   Appendix 8, *sub*. 1503 and Introduction, p.xlvi. John Salter gave only two acres in the Risbygate field, but by this date what was called Salter's land included other land given by either Jankin Smith or, more likely, Margaret Odeham. Twenty-three acres in the Westfield given by Margaret Odeham, which were included in Edward VI's grant, are not accounted for elsewhere in the rental.

Item of Raulff Adames for the fearme of nine pieces of lond late in th'occupacion of John Smythe conteyninge by estimacion 31 acres lyinge in th'East and Sowthe fieldes of Burie, to him letton by indenture bearinge date the sixt daie of October in 23th yere of the [*reign*] of our soveraign ladie Quene Elizabeth [*1581*] [*for the terme*] of 21 yeres from the feast of St Michael th'archaungel then last past yerelie ~~payable~~ for the said nine peeces[4] £1 13s. 4d.

Item of Robert Leache for 7 peeces of lond conteyning by estimacion 18 acres lyinge in the fieldes of Burie and Muche Horningeserthe, late in the fearme of and occupacion of William Godfrey and John Godfrey, letton to fearme to the said Robert Leache for 21 yeares by indenture bearinge date *et cetera*[5] 16s. 0d.

Item of Walter Brooke for 6 peeces of lond cont[*aining*] by estimacion 22 acres late in th'occupacion of John Hubberd lying in th'East feldes of Burie, late letton to John Heathe by indenture[6] £1 10s. 0d.

Item of Thomas Overyn for the fearme of one close conteyning 7 acres thre roodes and 18 pooles and thre acres 27 pooles of lond late letten to John Powle by indenture bearinge date the [*space*] of in the [*space*] yere of the reign of our soveraign ladie Quene Elizabeth for 21 yeres from Michaelmas next bifore the date of the same indenture £1 4s. 0d.

[*Page 2*]

Item of John Keale for thre parcelles of lond conteyning by estimacion eight acres late in th'occupacion of Robert Cheston, lyinge in th'East field of Burie letton to him by indenture bearing date the second daie of October the 23º yere of the reign of our said soveraign ladie Quene Elizabeth [*1581*] for 21 yeres from Michaelmas then last past[7] 13s. 4d.

Item of William Jellowe for a stall in the Greate Markett letton to him by indenture bearinge date the 14 daie of Jaunuarie in the 13th yere of the reign of our soveraign ladie Quene Elizabethe [*1571*] for 21 yeres from Michaelmas bifore[8] 2s. 0d.

Item of Thomas Goderiche th'elder \nowe Edward Goderiche/ for eight peeces of lond lyinge in severall parcelles in the fieldes of Burie, late in the occupacion of Johane Horseman, widowe, to him letton by indenture *et cetera* £3 0s. 0d.

Item of Thomas Carre for a bearne in St Andrewes Strete without the Risbiegate with diverse <*deletion*> peeces of lond in the West fieldes of Burie late in the occupacion of Richard Coppinge, letton to the said Richard Copping by indenture dated the last daie of Januarie in the 12th yere of the reign of our soveraign ladie Quene Elizabeth [*1570*] for 21 yeres from

---

4   Appendix 8, *sub* 1478.
5   *Ibid.*
6   *Ibid.*
7   Appendix 8, *sub* 1549, the Morrow Mass priest in St James's church.
8   *Ibid.*

Michaelmas then next folowinge, and for non payment of the rent by the space of 7° weekes to rente[*?*] r[*e-enter?*]	£3 18s.	8d.
Item a [*?newe*] rent paiable by the governors of the free grammer skole in Burie goinge owte of St Peters and the Risbiegate londes £29 18s. 0d.	£23 0s.	0d.

Summa totalis £51 5s.4d. £44 7s.4d., whereof

Paid to the Quenis Majestie for a yerelie rent owte of the mesuage next to St James steple where the mynisters nowe dwell[9]	5s.	6d.

And so resteth clere £50?? £44 1s.10d.[10]

Mr Tasselles rentes[11]

In primis of Roger Potter \nowe Cutbert Smyths/ for the fearme of thre tenementes with gardenis thereunto lyinge with theyr appurtenanuces in the Rainegate Strete sometyme in the occupacion of Thomas Shippen, dymised to Thomas Langthorne by indenture	10s.	0d.
Item of Thomas Woode, doctor of phisicke \nowe William Alman/ for a yerlie rent goinge owt of a void peece of ground late William Bakers, before Thomas Michams, to him dimised by indenture[12]		6d.
Item of John Lansdale for a yerelie rent goinge owt of a peece of ground sometyme builded and nowe whollie decaied, sometyme Andrewe Reves, after Roger Linges, nowe the said John Lansdales, lying by the strete callid the Horse Markett,[13] betwene the ortyard sometyme Spurlings and nowe or late William Tassell, gentleman, on th'east parte and the mesuage of the said John Lansdale on the west parte, the sowthe hedd thereof abbuttithe upon the Horse Markett aforesaid and the northe hedd upon the ortyard nowe or late the said William Tassell, gentleman	2s.	0d.

[*Page 3*]

Item of Anthonie Payne, gentleman, for the fearme of a void peece of ground now enclosid with a pale and joyninge to his p[*astu*]re or closse on th'east parte and next to Maydewater[14] [*Lan*]e on the west part, and it hathe the forme of a bow[*?*] on the east part which he holdithe at will and paiethe yerelie		6d.
Item of Robert Spar[*ke*], baker, for a yerelie rent goinge owte of a howse latelie builded and nowe wholie wasted lyinge \in Mr Andrewes stret/[15] betwene the ground nowe Henry Horningolds, late parcell of the late Colledge, on the north		

---

[9] This does not seem to correspond with any of the new purchased lands, but is a good match for the house next to the Great Churchyard given by William Tassell. This and references in earlier rentals suggests that both ministers lived here at this time. As Woodward noted, it was sold before his time; a reply to William Payne's petition, K1/3, shows that it was considered unsuitable as a clergy residence because of the noise of constant bell ringing.

[10] Here a '*v*' seems to have been altered to an '*i*' for the shillings.

[11] Appendix 8, *sub* 1557, for all the properties in this section.

[12] I cannot identify this or the following property in the conveyance of Tassell's lands, Woodward's Register, H1/6/1, p.125. For the identity of Dr Wood, see Notes on People.

[13] Now St Mary's Square.

[14] Now Mainwater Lane.

[15] Now Bridewell Lane.

parte and the said ground of the said Roberte Sparke on [*the*] sowthe parte, th'east hedd thereof abbuttithe upon the [*f*]oresaid stret   6s.   8d.

Item of James Wright, gentleman, for the rent of a mesuage builded with a peece of ground joyned thereunto in Burie St Edmunde in the strete callid Mustowe[16] betwixt the mesuage callid the Angell on the sowthe parte and me[*s*]uage and tenemente of the said James Wright on the north part[17] **(14)**   2d.

[*The next two items are much stained with rust, and a large hole has utterly destroyed part of the text.*]

Item of Roger [*Potter*] for the ferme of a [*illegible word*][18] or stable with th'appurtenances in Punch[*e Lane*][19] for the ferme of a [*space*] [*formerlie*] in th'occupacion of G[*eorge*] Watton to him letton by indent[*ure*]   4s.   0d.

[*Word(s) illegible*] Leader latelie disceased \nowe Ro[*bert Le*]ader/ [*word(s) illegible*] lyinge in the Churchegate Strete [*word(s) illegible*] graunted by the A[*bbot*] and Co[*nv*]ent of [*word(s) illegible*] [*i*]ndenture dated the first daie of Maye [*fo*]r 99[20] yeres from the feast of St [*Michael the*] archaungell next before the date thereof [*pa*]y[*in*]g yerelie[21] **(7)**   4s.   4d.

Item of William Heyward, gentleman, for the fearme of a tenemente lyinge in the Risbiegate Strete and also for one garden lyinge nighe the Teyffen diche and the gardeine of the said William Heyward[22]   5s.   0d.

Item of John Parker, draper, for a yerelie rent of a tenemente, late Bartimewe Dallisons lyinge in the strete callid Longe Brackelond[23] betwene a mesuag or tenemente nowe John Waldingefields on the sowthe parte and a mesuage or tenemente late Symond Cage, nowe Richard Edgars in the right of his wief towardes the northe, the west hedd thereof abbuttithe upon the said strete and th'east hedd upon the gardeine or ground of Thomas Brunwyn **(24)**   6d.

Item of Edmond Hoye, \nowe William Johnson/ for a yerelie rent goinge owte of a mesuage or tenemente in Longe Brackelond aforesaid betwene the mesuage or tenemente of the same Edmunde on the sowthe parte and the ground or pasture of Robert Cage, in the right of his wief, on the northe parte, th'east hedd thereof abbutithe upon the said strete and the west hedd thereof [*upon the*] closse or pasture of William Heyward   8d.

---

16 Now Angel Hill.

17 This is identified as the Boar's Head in the conveyance, Woodward's Register, H1/6/1, p.125.

18 From other sources this word is likely to be 'stall'.

19 Now Athenaeum Lane.

20 Expressed as iiii ˣˣ xix.

21 This property was on the south corner of Churchgate Street and Guildhall Street.

22 Woodward noted a 99-year lease of these properties by Abbot Coddington to John Heyward dated 12 February 1502, Woodward's Register, H1/6/1, p.164.

23 Although there is still a street called Long Brackland, much of what was Long Brackland is now called St John's Street.

[*Page 4*]

[*Three lines are illegible apart from the last word*] Cages, scituat
and adjoyning [*hole in paper*] highe waye of the said stret the
north hedd thereof abbuttithe upon the stone wall adjoyninge to
the tower of the North Gate and the [*sou*]th hed upon the
mesuage nowe the [*? said*] [*?h, followed by some illegible
letters*]ylent   6d.

Item for the yerelie rent for a litle howse at the [*almost two full
lines are illegible*] latelie purchased by the feoffees of this
howse[24]   [*illegible*]

    Summa totalis 39 [*?li*] , whereof

Paid yerelie to the Quene [*word(s) illegible*] for the said
tenementes and [*only odd words words legible*] as appearethe
in the [*many words illegible*] whereof abate for St Peters rent   [*illegible*]
~~And so restith £45 15s.1d.~~[25]

    Summa totalis of this rental to be paid into the howse
    by the receyvors with the abetement aforesaid   £45 15s. 7d.
    Summa totalis whereof the recevor is to accompt of
    this rentall   £46 7s. 2d.

[*Words illegible*] **of all suche rentes and fearmes of the mesuages [*word(s) illegible*] by John Smyth[e] or Jenkyn Smythe, Margaret Odeham [*Ellen*] Fisshe
[*many words illegible*]**

[*Word(s) illegible*] \Henry Muskett late/ [*illegible passage*] lands
containing by estimacion [*illegible passage*]

Item of John [*?*]Trist \~~Edward~~ Roger Hempson late Edmund/
[*illegible*]

Item of \John Gouche late/ Edward Ubanke for the fearme of a
parcell of lond conteyninge by estimacion [*?*]4 acres thre
pooles in th'East and Sowthe fieldes of [*a number of words
illegible*] of the same towne late in the fearme [*a number of
words illegible*] dymised to the said Edward Ubank [*a few
words illegible*]

Item of Raulf Adams for x[*rest of numeral illegible*] acres [*words
illegible*] by estimacion 46 acres lyinge in the sout[*h*] [*words
illegible*] and in the fields of Nowton sometime in the ferme
and [*?tenure*] of William Wiffyn and Nicholas Avis and after
of [*word illegible*] Fissher latelie dymised to the said Raulf
Ad[*ams by*] indenture

Item of John Evans for the ferme of two mesuages or
[*?tenementes*] with their appurtennces sett and beinge in Burie
in the strete there callid Churchegate Strete to him letton by
indenture[26] **(9)**

Item of Henry Collinge, gentleman, late John Holtes, gentleman,
for the fearme of 11 yeares [*?recte pieces*]of lond conteyninge

---

[24] This is almost certainly the stone chapel in the Risby Gate which the feoffees purchased in 1583. See
p.46, and n.117.
[25] This reading is uncertain.
[26] See Appendix 8, *sub* 1478. These houses were never surrendered to the Crown.

by estimacion 25^tie acres *dimidia* late John Salter's lyinge in the Risbiegate and Northegate fieldes and in Forneham All Sainctes to him letton by indenture[27]	£2	0s.	0d.
Item of Thomas Shorte for the fearme of [*?*]a mesuage or tenement next unto the sowthe end of the Guildhall to him dimised by indenture[28] **(8)**	[*?*]8s.		0d.
Item of Barbara Cheston nowe the wife of John [*?*]Realdoff for one gardein or ortyard in th'Eastgate Strete dymised to hir by indenture[29]		2s.	0d.

> *Summa totalis* £29 3s.2d.[*?*]

Rentes [*?*]reserved and other [*?*]charges

Inprimis paid to Bailief Skott for [*word(s) illegible*]		3s.	4d.
Item to the same bailief for the rent of a barne withowt the Southgate	[*?*]6s.		0d.
Item to the same bailief for the rent of Leyers			[*?*]½d.
Item to the same bailief for a tenemente in Churchegate Strete in the fearme of John Evans **(7)**		2s.	6d.
Item to the bailief of the hundred of Thedwesrie for the tenemente of Leyers			8d.
Item to Robert ~~Dure~~ Drurie, esquier, or to the manor of [*space*]			6d.
Item to the surveior and receyvor for his fee		5s.	0d.
Item to the said bailief Scott [*for a r*]ent paid yerelie owte of the house in th'occupaction of Thomas Short adjoyninge to the sowthe end of the Guildhall **(8)**		3s.	6d.

> *Summa totalis* £1 12s.0½d.
>
> And so restithe clere £27 11s.1½d.

The rentall of all suche rentes and fearmes of the mesuages, londes and tenementes sometime the said John Smythe, esquier, latelie bought ~~and~~ for better assuerauns as concealed londes for the relief of the poore and defrayinge of other charges as taxes and tallages paiable at eny tyme by th'inhabitauntes of the towne of Burie St Edmund to the Quenis Majestie hir heires and successors, which rental was ~~rewer~~ renewed the daie and yere aforesaid[30]

In primis of Stephen Muryell for a pasture callid Brettes in Hepworth and two parcelles of pasture called Pudding Yard and Brettes Entree, late in the fearme of John Futter and William Futter, nowe dymised to the said Stephen Muriell by indenture	£4	4s.	2d.
Item of the same Stephen for the fearme of a woode callid Estowghe Woode in Hepworthe conteyninge by estimacion 12			

---

27 See p.287, n.3 above.

28 At Michaelmas 1550, 8s. from this property and a further shilling for the garden on the south and east sides of the Hall was paid to the keeper. At this date the house was occupied by Robert Dykeman during pleasure with repairs being made by the brethren. No doubt he was the caretaker, beadle or working keeper of the Guildhall, Note of rents payable to the keeper of the Guildhall, H1/1/15.

29 This cannot be matched with any of the rents specified in the 1550 note, but the Cheston's rent was included in the receipts of the keeper of the Guildhall for a few years, no doubt until a new rental was written which included it, HD1150/1, fos. 2v., 4r., 6r. and 10r.

30 Appendix 8, *sub* 1569 and Introduction, p.xxxviii.

acres and also for a closse callid Greate Atley in Hepworthe
aforesaid with one acre of woode within the same closse, late
in the fearme of William Muryell and Margarett his wief and
nowe dymised to the said Stephen Muryell by indenture   £1 4s. 0d.

Item of \George Nunne, gentleman, late/ Valentine Rose for the
fearme of two peeces of woode conteyninge two acres and
dimidia and of one other woode or grove lyinge in Weston
conteyninge by estimacion 11 acres *dimidia* and of two peeces
of arrable lond lying in Barningham conteyninge one acre of
lond to him dymised by indenture   7s. 9d.

Item of \William Hodgekyn, late/ Roger Barham now \after/ in
th'occupacion of William Brundishe for 9 peeces of lond,
meadowe and pasture conteyninge 30tie acres and foure peeces
of lond conteyninge 13 acres dimised to the said Roger Barham
by indenture   £1 0s. 8d.

Item of \John Daye, late/ Robert Braham ~~nowe~~ \after/ the said
William Brundishe for a pasture inclosed callid Litle Atley, a
pasture callid the Bower and a leye callid Stubbinges in
Hepworthe aforesaid, dimised to the said Robert Barham by
indenture   9s. 8½d.

[*Page 3*]

Item of \John Rust, the sonne of/ Giles Rust, for the ferme of ten
parcelles of meadowe lyinge in the towne meadowe and foure
acres of lond at Osmond Crowche and two acres and one roode
of leyes lyinge in Russhe Leyes to him dymised by indenture   7s. 7d.

Item of \George Nunne, gentleman, late/ John Deynes for the
fearme of ten acres of pasture lyinge in Weston dimised to him
by indenture   2s. 4d.

Item of Robert Astye for the fearme of two peeces of lond and one
parcell of lond dimised to him by indenture   3s. 0d.

Item of Sir Robert Jermyn, knight, late Sir Ambrose Jermyn, his
father, disceasid, for the fearme of parcell of the premisses in
th'occupacion of the fermor of the manor of Brettes in
Hepworthe holden at will   9d.

Item of \Margery Canham, widowe, sometyme wife of/ Symon
Perkyn ~~nowe~~ \and after of Michaell/ Cavenham for the fearme
of \a little pightell callid/ Terroldes Gappe containing *dimidia*
acre for the fearme of parcell of the premisses   10d.

Item of \Giles Barker, late/ Stephen Barker for the fearme of a
parcell of ground nowe builded with a howse, sometyme in
th'occupacion of the aforesaid William Barker, dissceased, by
indenture   6d.

Item of Margery Canham, \widowe, late wife of Michaell
Canham, before wife of Symon Parkyn/ for a mesuage and one
acre of errable lond in Hepworthe dimised to Robert Wyllys
and Ede Wyllys by indenture \bearinge date the fiftene/ daie of
Januarye *anno* 34to *Henrici Octavi* [*1543*] for 69 yeres from the
daie of th'indenture at 8d. rent with clause of re-entry for the
rent behinde eight daies   8d.

    Summa totalis £8 1s.11½d.

Rentes resolutes and other charges

Only 2s.0d. is for the sute and the residue is of the farmer's liberality

Inprimis to the bailief of the hundred of Blackebourne for
<*deletion*> \respecte of/ suyte to the generall court of the same
hundred   2s.   6d.

This rent was never paid to the lorde but is a wronge allowance concealed by your fermer

Item to the manor of Stanton Hall yerelie for rent and suyte   2s.   2d.
Item to the manor of Wattisfield Hall yerelie for rent and suyte   1s.   6½d.
Item to the manor of Giffordes for rent and suite yerelie   1s.   6d.
Item paid for hall mote rent yerelie   9d.
Item to the manor of Bardewell Hall for castleward rent, *videlicet*,
at everie 20^{ti} weekes end 2¾d., and so for the hoole   7d.
Item to the surveyor and receyvour for the fee   5s.   0d.

       Summa totalis 14s.0½d.
       And so restithe clere £7 7s.11d.

[*Page 4*]

Rentes in Burie with th'annuytie of Sir Robert Jermyn, knight, and the almes houses in the same towne for the herboyer and relief of the poore people there, renewed the daie and yere aforesaid

The Risbiegate Strete

In primis the hospital havinge in it one hall with a chymney, a
butterye, a litle garden and fyve severall chambers, whereof
two have chymneys[31]   *nulla*

The Crowne Stret on the west wall of the Greate Churcheyard[32] in
th'occupacion of Adrye Hoore, widowe, rented by yere **(17)**   *nulla*
In th'occupacion of John Britton, rented by yere   *nulla*
In th'occupacion of Alis Hill and Agnes Edmond, widowes   *nulla*
In th'occupacion of Alis Darbye, widowe   *nulla*
In th'occupacion of William Crosbye and Mawde his wief   *nulla*
In th'occupacion of Jane Rondes, widowe   *nulla*
In th'occupacion of Katherine Yewle, widowe   *nulla*
In th'occupacion of Christyen Bateman, widowe   *nulla*
In th'occupacion of William Rose and [*space*] his wief   *nulla*

The Colledge Strete[33] **(6)**

The Maryegold in th'occupacion of Roger Pitcher and Mother
Swetinge   *nulla*
The Boradge Flower in th'occupacion of Father Tuffild and
[*space*] his wief   *nulla*
The Flower de Luce in th'occupacion of Thomas Taylor   *nulla*
The Rose in th'occupacion of Father Anthonye and his wief   *nulla*

---

[31] See Introduction, p.xxxvii.
[32] Appendix 8, *sub* 1564. No other almshouses in Bury were given names.
[33] See Appendix 8, *sub* 1570.

Westgate Strete nighe the lane callid Maide Water Lane[34]

In th'occupacion of John Leder and his wief	*nulla*
In th'occupacion of Mathewe Burnebye and his wief	*nulla*
In th'occupacion of John Underwoode and his wief	*nulla*
In th'occupacion of Rose Randes, widowe	*nulla*

Burmans Lane[35] **(23)**

In th'occupacion of ~~Katherine Jeneway~~ Thomas Skelton	*nulla*
In th'occupacion of Johane Deswicke	*nulla*
In th'occupacion of Thomas Thriste	*nulla*

[*Page 5*]

Northegate Streate on th'east parte of the same streate

In th'occupacion of Katherine Jenewaie and Marion Browne	*nulla*
In th'occupacion of Hughe Caster	*nulla*
In th'occupacion of Widowe Pinchebacke	*nulla*
In th'occupacion of Widowe Stringer and Cicillie Rockett	*nulla*
In th'occupacion of Ketherine Jellowe and Cicillie Beare	*nulla*
In th'occupacion of Dombe Anne	*nulla*

Shorte Brackelond[36] **(?25)**

In th'occupacion of Ralf Johnson and Mother Nuttman	*nulla*
In th'occupacion of Thomas Milbye	*nulla*

    Summa totalis of almes howses rent free,
    beside the Hospitall afore said 28

The Colledge Strete[37] **(6)**

The Woodebyn or Suckelin in th'occupacion of John Cobbe, next adjoyninge to the tenemente nowe Henry Horningold on the north parte, and paiethe by yere	13s.	4d.
The Pomegranate in th'occupacion of Humfrey Crowder next adjoyninge to the same, and paiethe yerelie	16s.	0d.

Northegate Strete on th'east side of the same strete

In th'occupacion of Widowe Haggas rented by yere	4s.	0d.
In th'occupacion of Widowe Sutton rented by yere	4s.	0d.

Garlond Streate on the west parte[38] **(22)**

In th'occupacion of John Dyster rented by yere	6s.	11d.
In th'occupacion of \Robertson, late of/ Christian Mitchell		3d.
In th'occupacion of \Buckenham and Evered, late of/ Agnes Chanter and Johane Wolman, widowes		3d.
In th'occupacion of Christofer Disinge		3d.
In th'occupacion of ~~Christof~~ Thomas Harryson on th'east parte of the same streat[39]	6s.	0d.

[34] The origin of these almshouses has not been discovered.

[35] Now Pump Lane.

[36] Part of Short Brackland is now known as Cannon Street, but these almshouses may well have been on the site in Short Brackland on which the Guildhall Feoffment Girls' School was later built.

[37] See n.32 above. These two of the six College Street almshouses were let to provide for repairing the other four.

[38] Appendix 8, *sub* 1558.

[39] Appendix 8, *sub* 1527. The feoffees sold this property long ago and in 1834 the Baptist Chapel was built on the site.

In th'occupacion of Roger Abelye, next to Burmans Lane	5s.	0d.
Of Richard Collin for a mesuage late purchased of him scituate of the northe side of St James's churche and letton again to him[40] **(15)**	£3 0s.	0d.

[*Page 6*]

Westgate Streat

Item \of the adminystrators of John Bennytt for/ a bearne and a meadowe ground or pasture \late graunted/ in lease to Anthony Payne, gentleman, for certeine yeres yet to come, payinge yerelie by evin porcions — £2 0s. 0d.

Item \of Thomas Parker for/ one barne late in the'occupacion of Jefferey Smythe and nowe dymised to Robert Skott, taylor, by indenture dated the 4th of November *Anno* 23 *Elizabethe regine* [*1581*] paying yerelie — 5s. 0d.

Mr Andrewes Strete

Item one bearne with certeine ortyardes thereunto adjoyning in the tenure of John Cadge for certeine yeres yet to come, paying yerelie by evin porcions[41] — £2 0s. 0d.

Withowte the West Gate

Item of Thomas Carre for one pightle or closse containing by estimacion two acres lying at Stanford Bridge withowt the Westgate of Burie by the Quenis highe waye on the sowthe parte and the common water \course/ there on the northe part by indenture to him made \dated/ the last daie of Aprill in the 19[ti] yere of the reign of Quene Elizabethe [*1577*] for 21 yeres from the feast of th'annuciacion of Our Ladie then last paste payinge yerelie — 14s. 0d.

Item of Nicholas Rabye for a pasture and ground next adjoyning or bilonging to the hospitall in the Risbiegate Strete and a litle howse or bearne within the said pasture nowe dymised to him by Indenture late in the fearme and occupacion of Robert Careles — £1 10s. 0d.

Item of Sir Robert Jermyn, knight, for a yerelie rent owte of the mannor of Torkeseye and other londes in the counties of Lincoln and Yorke paiable at Rusbroke in the countie of Suffolk the 20[tie] daie of Julie and the 20tie daie of Januarie, and for non payment thereof at the same dayes to forfeit for everie daie after that it shalbe unpaid 6d. for a payne — £40 0s. 0d.

> *Summa totalis* of the said rentes £49 5s.0d. £52 0s.0d., whereof

Paid yerelie to the Quenis Majestie for the foure tenementes in the Garlond Streete, *videlicet* for everie one of theym severallie, 3d. an so in all yerelie **(22)** — 1s. 0d.

---

[40] Appendix 8, *sub* 1584.
[41] Tassell's gift included a messuage or tenement in Mr Andrews Street but it may be rash to identify this property positively, Woodward's Register, H1/6/1, p.125.

Item paid yerelie to John Jermyn of Debden in the countie of Suffolk, esquire, duringe his naturall lief[42]	£20	0s.	0d.
Summa totalis of the said owte rentes and charges	£20	1s.	0d.
And so remaynethe clere ~~£29 4s.0d.~~	£32	4s.	0d.
Summa totalis of theis rentalles clere besides			
the owte rentes and other allowances	£67	3s.	0½d.

[*In another hand*]

The total sume of the whole revenue conteyned in this rentall is *per annum*	£89	10s.	1½d.
Whereof laide owte yerelye in owte rentes for the landes in Hepworth, 9s.0½d. And in out rentes for the landes in Burye, £1 7s.0½d. And more in Bury the out rentes of 4 tenementes in the Garlond Street at 3d. a pece, 1s.0d. And the receavors' fees, 10s.0d. And Mr Edmunde Jermyn his annuytie *per annum* £20 0s.0d.	£22	7s.	1d.
So rest *de claro per annum* £67 3s.0½d.			

Item of John Revell and his heires for certeyne landes lienge in Bury fieldes ~~last~~ somtyme parcell of Jenkyn Barrett, esquyer, \yerely/[43]	One galon of wyne

[*Page 9*]

In the charge of Thomas Goodriche

A note of arrerages of rent [*page torn*] apperithe by the booke of accompes made the 21 daie of January 1587 [*1588*]

In primis of Sir Robert Jermyn, knight, for the rent of londes in Hepworthe, not paid by the space of 8 yers nowe past, *videlicet* for the yere 1580 and so untill and for this yere 1587, everie yere 9d. **Received**	6s.	0d.
~~Item for thre yeres rent of lond in Hepworthe, late Wyllys, \everie yere, 8d./, videlicet 1585, '86,'87~~	~~2s.~~	~~0d.~~

Mr George Nune

Item for the half yere rent of londes in Hepworth, late Valentine Rose, due at Michelmas last	3s.	10½d.

[*Some illegible marks in margin*]

Item for the half yeres rent of londes in Hepworthe, late John Deynes, due at Michelmas last	1s.	2d.
Item for two yeres rent and *dimidia* of the Widowe Haggas received by William Baker everie yere, \4s.0d./ 1585, '86, '87	10s.	0d.

Received of William Yonge £3 0s.0d.

Item for the hoole yere's rent of a tenemente by St James' churche, late purchasid of Collin, due at Michelmas last past[44]		
(15)	£3	0s.	0d.

Received 6s.0d.

---

42 See Introduction, p.xxxviii.

43 John Baret, whose will was made in 1463 and proved in 1467, gave a gallon of wine, or 8d. in lieu of it, to the alderman and brethren of Candlemas guild to drink at their customary dinner or drinking on Candlemas Day, Tymms, *Wills*, p.30.

44 After the feoffees had bought this property it was found that Collin's wife was entitled to dower in it, and it was rented back to him for the rest of her lifetime. See Index for references.

Item for the hole yere's rent for a tenemente in th'occupacion of
Thomas Harryson due at Michelmas last   6s.   0d.
Received 2s.6d.
Item for half yere's rent of a tenemente in th'occupacion of Roger
Abelye due at Michelmas last   2s.   6d.
Item of Henry Garrard for the residue of £4 0s.0d. due by
obligacion made to Thomas Godriche and Henry Hornigold \as
appeare in the booke of accomptes, '84/[45]   10s.   0d.
Item for the half yere's rent due at Michelmas 1585 of a closse in
Westgate Strete late in the occupacion of Anthonye Payne,
gentleman, and nowe of John Bennett, £1 0s.0d., and for the
[*wh*]ole yere's rent of the same closse due at Michelmas 1586,
£2 0s.0d.   £3   0s.   0d.

A Rentall of Bury Landes[46]

[*Page 1*]
Received of Mr Futter for hole yere rent	£4	4s.	2d.
Received of William Moryell for his hole yere rent	£18	0s.	0d.
Received of William Brundishe for his hole yere rent	£1	10s.	5d.
Received of Rafe Robarde for his hole yere rent		5s.	0d.
Received of Giles Rust for his hole yere rent	£7	7s.	0d.
Received of the Widowe Deyne for hir hole yere rent		2s.	4d.
Received of William Moryell for his hole yere rent for a woode that is called Estaugh Wood		6s.	0d.
Received of Robart Astye for his hole yere rent		3s.	0d.
Received of Simon Parkyne his hole yeres			10d.
Received of John Coldham his hole yere rent			8d.
Received of Stephene [*?*]Baker his hole yere rent			6d.
Received of Valentine Roose for his hole yere rent		1s.	3d.

         Summa £3 <*deletion*> 9d.

Received of Roger Potter rente for the Angell[47] **(14)**	£6	0s.	0d.
Received of the sayd Roger Potter *pro* [*?*]Anne Mason			[*illegible*]

[*One line illegible*]
Received of the sayd Roger Potter for [*rest illegible, but may
include the word* stable.]
Received of [*illegible*]

Received of [*illegible*] Cole his hole yere's rent for a stall and the gardinge on Punche Lane	[*?*]2s.	0d.
Received of John Leadere hys hole yere rent		[*illegible*]

Received of [*?*] George [*or Gregory*] Bartlet for a house that was
the Widowe [*?*]Shires
[*An illegible passage*]

---

[45] Henry Garrard was paying for a house in Lavenham which he had bought from the feoffees. See
Index *sub* Garrard.

[46] Whereas so far the rental has been used for a theoretical account of rents which were due, here it is
used in the sense of an account of rents actually received. The heading denotes lands belonging to the
town of Bury.

[47] The feoffees had sold the Angel to Roger Potter on 23 January 1582. He was making annual
payments of the purchase price. See Index *sub* Potter.

Received of Robart [?]Parker for a house with [?]certyne [*word(s) illegible*] adjoyninge — 6s. 8d.

Received of the widowe Dalisone by the hands of [?]Yatte the glover — 6d.

Received of the Widowe Hoye in the Longbracklond **(?24)** — 8d.

Received of Mr [?]Orne rent for a parcell of ground on the Horsemarket — [*illegible*]

Received more for the rent for rent of a tenement in the same streate — [?]4d.

Received of Mr Peyton at the North Gate his rent — 6d.

[*Page 2*]

Received of John Cutteres by the handes of John Bright for a hole yer rent for Catesshall in Barton — £6 13s. 4d.

Received of John Clare the hole yere rente for the Leyers in Rougham — £4 0s. 0d.

Received of Mr Anthony Payne gott by the hands of the Goodman Moosse and Goodman Frogge the hole yere rente — £4 15s. 0d.

Received of the Goodman Smythe at the Southegate for his hole yere rente — £2 6s. 8d.

Received of John Evans in the Churche Gate streat for his hole yere rent **(9)** — 12s. 0d.

Received of Goodman [?]Broninge for a shope in the fish markite for his hole yere rent **(10)** — 8s. 0d.

Received of Mr Collyne for his hole yere rente — £1 0s. 0d.

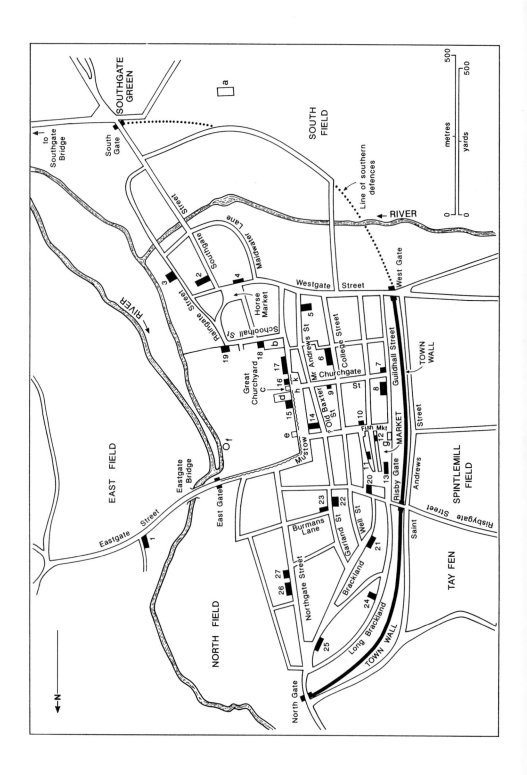

Bury St Edmunds c.1621

Property owned by the feoffees, and names of donors where known

1   The Grammar School
2   Garden in Southgate Street, Tassell
3   Tenements in Raingate Street, probably Tassell
4   John Hill's almshouses
5   Orchard in Mr Andrews Street
6   The College or William Barnaby's almshouses
7   House at corner of Guildhall Street and Churchgate Street, Tassell
8   The Guildhall and adjacent properties
9   Houses in Churchgate Street, Odeham
10 House in Fishmarket, Odeham
11 Tenements in Market Place, Thomas Bright the younger
12 Tenements in Skinner Row and the Market Place, Odeham
13 Market Cross
14 The Angel and adjacent properties, Tassell
15 House next St James's church, Markant
16 House next St James's steeple, ?Tassell
17 Bartholemew Brocklesby's almshouses
18 Almshouses
19 The Shire House
20 Moyses Hall, bought 1626
21 House in Short Brackland, Tassell
22 Thomas Browse's almshouses
23 Bereve's almshouses
24 Long Brackland, Tassell
25 Almshouses
26 John Parker's and Francis Boldero's almshouses
27 John Parker's and Francis Boldero's almshouses

Other features mentioned in the text

a   Almoner's Barns
b   St Mary's church
c   The Church Gate or St James's steeple
d   St James's church
e   Abbey Gate
f   Dovecote
g   Gaol for the Liberty of St Edmund
h   Punch Lane
k   The Chequer

Note that the names of the rivers on the map – the Lark and the Linnet – were not used in the period covered by the documents edited in this volume.

301

Appendix 3

A Rental of all Feoffment Properties made 1 October 1621,
H2/3/4/11

This document was written by John Mallows, the feoffees' clerk. The pages are not numbered but have been given page numbers here. The many marks in the margins have generally been ignored, but some which were intelligible have been transcribed in bold before or after the passage to which they refer. This rental was drawn up after the Angel and other properties which had been sold had been bought back, and after some leases for long terms or at low rents had been revoked and replaced by new ones on more reasonable terms. It ends with an invaluable list of payments for which the feoffees were responsible.

Primo die Octobris anno xix° Jacobi regis 1621

Bury St Edmund

A rentall of the landes, tenementes and revenues of the towne of Bury St Edmund in the County of Suffolk in the charge of the feoffees of trust of the same towne, made and renewed the first daye of October in the nynetenth yeare of the reigne of Our Soveraigne Lord Kinge James *et cetera anno Domini* **1621, for one wholl yeare then following.**

Within the towne and feildes of Bury St Edmund

Thomas Claydon, gentleman, for a barne withowt the Southgate, and for certen landes in the feildes hertofore demysed to Mr George Boldero[1]	£33	6s.	8d.
Mr Thomas Hamond for landes withowt the Southgate in the occupacion of George Baker	£4	0s.	0d.
Henry Wyard for landes late in the occupacion of Gilly	£4	0s.	0d.
Henry Baker for a tenemente late 3 tenementes and a gardine in Raingate Strete[2] **(3)**	£1	0s.	0d.
Robert Winter for a gardine in the Southgate Strete[3] **(2)**	£1	0s.	0d.
Mr John ~~Wynter~~ \Inman/ for a parcell of ground nere Maidewater Lane[4]			6d.
James Smyth, \esquire/, for a parcell of grounde in the Horsemarkett			6d.
Henry Landesdale for a parcell of ground nere to the Horsemarkett and Scholehall Strete		2s.	0d.

---

[1] See Appendix 8, *sub* 1478.
[2] See Appendix 8, *sub* 1557.
[3] *Ibid.* The feoffees still own this site on which the almshouses now known as Long Row, Southgate Street, were built in 1811.
[4] *Ibid.*

Robert Fuller for the Sherehowse with a gardine therto adjoyninge[5] **(19)**   £1   0s.   0d.

£44 9s. 8d.[6]

[*Page 2*]

The assignees of John Mallowes for the howse sometime called the Saltpeter Howse with a garedine and a close therto adjoyning in the Westgate Streete being part of the tenementes late in the occupacion of Elizabeth Hovell, widowe, and now in th'occupacion of [*space*] Crysall   £3   5s.   0d.

John Rayneham for certen landes parcell of the new purchased landes late in th'occupacion of William Walker   £9   0s.   0d
                   two combes
                   of rye

Mr James Bridgeman, clerk, for certen landes nere Hardwich Heathe lately demysed to Thomas Overend[7]   £1   4s.   0d.

Of the saide James for a peece of void grounde in Mr Andrewes Strete   6s.   8d.

William Ullet for landes in the Westfeld £10 0s.0d. and four combes rye at Christmas. And for a close at Stamford Bridge £4 0s.0d. and a combe of rye at Christmas. And for a barne and parte of an ortyard in Mr Adrews Streete £2 6s.8d.   £16   6s.   8d
               and five combs
                   of rye

Margarett Adams, widowe, for the rest of the same ortyard in Mr Andrewes Streete   £2   6s.   8d.

Roberte Rooper for \part of/ a tenemente in the Churchgate Streete late Mr Richard Walker's[8]   £2 10s.   0d.

[*Space*] Mannynge, widowe, for the one other part of the same tenemente   £1 10s.   0d.

Mr Henry Walker for a gardine and a howse in Punch Lane late in the in the tenure of Mr Henry Richard Walker[9]   4s.   0d.

The two preachers' howses. They have them withowt paying any rent.[10]

William Rowge for a mesuage by St James' churche payde[11] **(15)**   £3   0s.   0d.

34–13–0

---

5   See Appendix 8, *sub* 1578.

6   This and similar sums in the margin gives the total rents for the page.

7   A deed to declare the uses of a Fine, dated 20 March 1607, included the close and twelve acres of land near Stamford Bridge which had been leased and then sold to Thomas Overend for £110; it was said to have been part of Odeham's gift, Woodward's Register, H1/6/1, p.156.

8   Appendix 8, *sub* 1610. These might have been on the site where the Queen's Head is now in Churchgate Street. The feoffees owned the inn for many years and Walker's gift could be how the site came into their hands.

9   Appendix 8, *sub* 1557. This was formerly described as a stall or stable, and the area was sometimes called Les Rowes, PRO E178/2228, f.9v. The use of the word 'house' here may well indicate that what had formerly been ground used for commercial stalls was being built over. The Athenaeum now stands on this site.

10   From the papers relating to Payne's complaint, K1/3, it is known that the house on the south side of the Norman Tower, which had been used by the preacher of St Mary's, had been sold because it was thought that excessive bell ringing made it unsuitable for a clergy residence.

11   If this refers to the house provided for the preacher of St James's, perhaps it had also been deemed unsuitable and let, but it should be remembered that affairs at St James's at this point were complicated

[Page 3]

Mr William Hewes for the Angell[12] **(14)**	£24	0s.	0d.

Mr Anthony Adams as leasee or assignee to Mr Thomas Havers
for part of the mesuage late called ~~Angell~~ Castell and now
occupyed with the mesuage in the tenure of the saide Anthony

Adams[13] **(14)**		3s.	4d.

Resayed of [*?*]Cantner for the tenement of Bumsted £1 13s.4d. poste[*?a*]

Anthony Bumstede for two tenementes in the Churchgate Strete[14]

(9)	£3	6s.	8d.
Henry Coe for a tenemente in the Gildehall Strete and Churchgate Strete[15] **(7)**	£1	6s.	8d.
The widowe Clarke for a temente by the Gyldehall[16] **(8)**	£1	10s.	0d.
The widowe Kinge for a howse in the College Strete		13s.	4d.

<deletion>

The widowe of James Kent for a mesuage in the Cooke

Rowe[17] **(10)**	£6	0s.	0d.
			two capons
			and
			a gallon of
			wine

<deletion>

Samuell Moody for certen tenementes in the Marketstede and Skynners Lane late in the tenure of Thomas Bright[18]	£2	17s.	4d.
Amy Mance, widowe, for a peece of ground in Skynners Lane by her house late Mrs Cottons[19]			1d.
[Space] for a stall in the market place late in the tenure of Samuell Jellowe[20]		5s.	0d.
William Scott for a parcel of ground nere his howse in Brentgovell Strete[21]		2s.	6d.
Christopher Cox, for a peece of ground in St Andrewes Strete whereupon a barne was lately built, sometyme in the tenure of Thomas Turner	£1	0s.	0d.
The widowe of John Hawstede for divers landes in the feildes late in the occupacion of the saide Thomas Turner	£25	16s.	0d.

67–0–11

[Page 4]

Thomas Godfrey, junior, for tenn acres of the landes sometyme
Salters, late in the occupacion of Mr Collinge, £5 0s.0d.[22] And

because their preacher insisted on retaining his living in Northamptonshire. See Notes on People, *sub*
Waldebanks.

[12] See Appendix 8, *sub* 1557. The Angel had been sold in 1582.
[13] See Appendix 8, *sub* 1557. This property had been sold in 1565.
[14] See Appendix 8, *sub* 1478. These tenements were successfully concealed.
[15] See Appendix 8, *sub* 1557.
[16] See Appendix 8, *sub* 1569 and Appendix 2, n.28. It formed part of the Guildhall curtilage and was often used as the hall keeper's residence.
[17] See Appendix 8, *sub* 1478.
[18] Appendix 8, *sub* 1478.
[19] *Ibid.*
[20] Appendix 8, *sub* 1549, Morrow Mass priest.
[21] Appendix 8, *sub* 1557.
[22] For Collin's leases of Salter's lands see Introduction, p.xlvi.

for 37 acres of St Peter's landes and one pightell at the east end
of St Peter's chappell late in the occupacion of Mr Francis
Pynner £19 4s.0d., *in toto*[23]   £24   4s.   0d.
The purchasers of the Ampners Barnes for the tythes belonging to
St Peter's   £10   0s.   0d.

P[aid]

Mr Bennett Barker for the barne and stable at St Peter's
<deletion>   £3   0s.   0d.

P[aid] in partt

Adam Marcus *alias* Gillam for certen parcelles of the howse and
scite of St Peters in his occupacion   £5   0s.   0d.

Paid in partt

John Peck for the groundes called St Peter's Pittes[24]   £4   0s.   0d.
Abraham Grene for a cotage and a close in the Risbygate Strete   £2   10s.   0d.
Mrs Elizabeth Heyward, widowe, for a howse in the Risbygate
Strete, and a peece of ground nere the Teyfen[25]   5s.   0d.
Richard Chandler and Alice his wief, late the wief of Mr Robert
Reve for a barne and certen landes late parcell of the Grange
landes without the Risbygate   £8   0s.   0d.
Francis Parker, widowe, for a tenemente in the Longe Brackland   6d.
Mr Charles Darby for a tenemente late ~~Mr Charles~~ Hughe
Mathewes before that Hoyes and Johnson's   8d.
William Grigges for a tenemente at the North Gate   6d.
Mr Ewstace Darcy for a peece of ground in the ~~Eastgate Strete~~
Northgate Strete sometyme in the tenure of Ede Darby   1s.   0d.
John Kinge for 13 acres of lande late Salter[26]   £5   4s.   0d.

64–2–8

[*Page 5*]

[*Space*] for an almshouse in the Northgate Streete   4s.   0d.
Widowe Cheting for another almose howse there   4s.   0d.
John Baily for one of the new almose howses in the Garlond
Streete[27] **(22)**   2s.   0d.
The widowe Cowper for another of those howses   5s.   0d.
[*Space*] for another of those howses   2s.   0d.
The widowe Shipp for another of those howses   1s.   0d.
Thomas West for diverse landes late in the tenure of Mr Roger
Barber   £14   14s.   0d.
John Brydon for a peece of ground at Sparrowe Hill[28]   2s.   0d.

---

[23] Appendix 8, *sub* 1583 and Introduction, p.xlviii. The hospital was in Out Risbygate and the St Peter's
Nursing Home now stands on the site.

[24] St Peter's Pits are almost opposite the site of the hospital in Out Risbygate. At this date they were
used for burials in time of plague, but are now a play area for children.

[25] Appendix 8, *sub* 1557.

[26] John King is mentioned in the papers relating to Collin's leases. He was a local husbandman, and
John Mallowes and others thought that he would be a good tenant who would cultivate the land well,
H3/1/1.

[27] Appendix 8, *sub* 1558 and above, p.190, for their rebuilding after the fire of 1608.

[28] Appendix 8, *sub* 1569. This was one of the properties which provided an income for repairing the
Guildhall.

John Tillott of Rougham for a peece of lande late in the tenure of
    Mr John Revell[29]   A gallon of wyne

The heir of Thomas Brunwyn \Henry Brunwyn/ for a gardine in
    Brentgovell Streete[30]   3s.   4d.

Moneys to be received by the bedell for mariage dynners at the
    Gyldehall

Barton
\Mr Henry Walker/ payed for Catshall farme[31]   £20   0s.   0d.

Rougham
Mr Thomas Springe for Layers farme late in the tenure of Mrs
    Willoughby[32]   £20   0d.   0d.

Foxherth in Essex
Mathew Teversham for the porcion of tythes given by Mr Bright   £10   0s.   0d.

52–7–4 beside mariage dynners[33]

[Page 5]

Hepworth and Weston[34]
William Mason, esquier, for divers ~~parcell~~ landes meadowes
    pastures and woodgroundes   £58   3s.   6d.
                                          and a boare[35]

Mr John Shawbery for divers landes meadowes and pastures
    conteyning together by estimacion *[space]* late in the severall
    occupacions of Sir Thomas Jermyn and John Frost   *[No amount given]*

John Sporle for certen landes   £6   0s.   0d.

John Day for divers landes in divers leases   £8   8s.   9d.

Humphrey Lynge for certen parcelles of ground nere his dwelling
    house   £2   0s.   0d.

Stephen Peck for an acre of ground with a cotage thereupon built
    wherein he now dwelleth, and two acres of ground adjoyning
    to Great Bromskott   £3   0s.   0d.

Samuell Reve for a mesuage and a yard   £1   0s.   0d.

John Clere for two acres of ~~lande~~ pasture at Hendall   £1 13s.   4d.

Barningham
Mr Lawrence Coldham for an acre of lande in two peeces   6s.   8d.

Torkesey[36]
Sir Thomas Jermyn, knight, for a rent charge given by Edmund
    Jermyn, esquire, owt of the manor of Torkesey payable upon
    the 20th daye of January and the 20th daye of July by even
    porcions   £40   0s.   0d.

---

[29] For John Baret's bequest to the alderman and dye of Candlemas guild, see Introduction, pp.lviii, lvix and n.277.

[30] Appendix 8, *sub* 1557. This part of Tassell's gift was alienated, but the conveyance by which it came back to the feoffees has not yet been found.

[31] Appendix 8, *sub* 1470.

[32] Appendix 8, *sub* 1473.

[33] Appendix 8, *sub* 1587.

[34] Appendix 8, *sub* 1569.

[35] This was struck out, but has *stet* written beside it in the margin.

[36] Appendix 8, *sub* 1573.

Summa totalis £386 8s.10d., one boare, 7 combs
rye, two capons, two gallons of ~~rye~~ wyne besides
Mr Shawberries rent and the mariage dynners.

120–12–3 besides Mr Shawberyes rent
[*Page 6*]

Out rentes payable to divers lordes

To the corporacion of Bury for the rentes due to His Majestie for divers landes and tenementes with the towne of Bury	£1	18s.	11½d.
To His Majestie's receivor generall for the tenth of St Peter's 10s.6d. and for the receivor's acquitance and dorekeper 8d.		11s.	8d.
To the bailief of Thedwarstre hundred for Layers			8d.
To the manor of Rougham			6d.
To the manor of Forneham All Sainctes			1½d.
To the bailief of Blackborne hundred		2s.	6d.
To the manor of Wattisfeld		1s.	6½d.
To the manor of Giffordes		1s.	6d.
The hallimot rent			9d.
To the manor of Bardwell for the castleward rent at 2¾d. for every 20 weekes, *in toto*			7d.

Summa [No amount given]

Annuities graunted owt of the towne landes

To John Bedwall for certen yeares to come[37]	£16	0s.	0d.
To Mr Henry Colling for certen yeares	£5	0s.	0d.
There is to be paid to the Governors of the free schole in Bury for their part in St Peter's landes[38]	£5	9s.	10½d.

Divers other paymentes fees and allowances
to be paide by the receivor

To His Majestie for the taske when any is graunted			
To His Majestie for the subsidy when any is graunted			
To the preacher of St Marie's parishe	£50	0s.0d.	
To the minister of the same parishe	£2	0s.0d.	
To the churchwardens towardes the reparacions of the church, £1 0s.0d., and £1 0s.0d. more of Mr Bright's gift	£2	0s.0d.	
£1 0s.0d. more of Mr Bright's gift			
To the overseers of the poore of that parishe	£2	12s.0d.	
		£56 12s.	0d.
The like for St James' parishe		£56 12s.	0d.
To the clerke of St James for tending the library		£1 0s.	0d.

---

[37] John Bedwall and Henry Collin were paid annuities as recompense for leases which had been revoked. They were first paid to Bedwall in 1610, HD1150/2, f.21r. and to Collin in 1614, HD1150/2, f.29v. A similar annuity had been paid to Francis Pinner in connection with the lease which he had held of St Peter's, but this payment had ceased by this date.

[38] St Peter's became part of the Grammar School estate, in exchange for the Broomes in Bradfield Combust, in 1632, E5/9/305.4.

To a minister to saye service and preache to the prisoners in the gaole according to Mrs Odeham's will	£6	0s.	0d.

[*Page 7*]

Wood is to be given in the cold tyme of wynter to the poore prysoners in the gaole according to Mrs Odeham's will

Mr Bright's gift

There is to be bestowed in clothing of the poore according to Mr Bright's will	£24	0s.	0d.
The poore of St Maries parishe	£1	0s.	0d.
The poore of St James parishe	£1	0s.	0d.
The poore prisoners in the towne gaole	£1	0s.	0d.
To the East and North Wardes towardes the relief of the poore of Peter Kemboldes gift	£3	0s.	0d.
Giftes to the judges at the two assises			
The receivor his fee		15s.	0d.
The clerkes fee and for wryting the rentalls and accomptes	£2	0s.	0d.
The bedell of the hall for his wages	£2	10s.	0d.
The bedell of the towne for his wages	£2	12s.	0d.
The two bedelles liveries			
Liveries for the waytes of the towne			
The chirurgion for the poore			
Some relief in breade and bief to be given to the poore upon the accompte daye according to Mr Walker's will			
The rye reserved for rent is to be baked owt ~~for them~~ and distributed to the poore at that tyme			
The charges of grinding and bakeing that rye			
The charges of the feoffees dynner at the tyme of the accompt			
To the howse of correction	£10	0s.	0d.
To the worke howse			
Such howses as the tenantes thereof have not covenanted to repayre are to be repayred by the receivor			
The Bridges and the Market Crosse			
Fyer and candle at such tymes as the feoffees shall meete abowt busynes of the towne			

[*Page 8*]

The receivor is to add to his receites all such moneys as he shall receive for arrerages of rentes unpaide and which were left ~~unpaide~~ in super upon any former accompt and as yet not received

All such money as he shall receive for wood sales

Remembraunces

[*The reciever*] is to be at the Gildehall in the later part of the 24th daie of Aprill and the 19th daye of October and to take the bedell and one or two more witnesses to him,[39] [*a*]nd there in the name of all [*th*]e feoffees of the towne londes to demaund all the rentes then due of every of the tenantes and [*f*]armors thereof [*?and*] so to contynue therein demand[*?ing ther*]of so longe as [*t*]h[*ey c*]an see to tell money by [*d*]aylight.

---

[39] The rental has been repaired and a few letters are missing but could be supplied without too much difficulty.

Appendix 4

Schedule of Uses of the New Purchased Lands, 1555,
from John Woodward's register of evidences,
compiled 1657–9, H1/6/1, pp.105–107

Bold writing and underlinings are used in this transcript as in the original.

Memorandum that in this schedule tripartite indented be conteyned aswell what Godly and charitable acts the rents, farmes and profitts comeing growing and renewing of the chantereis, gildes, lands, tenements and hereditaments contained and specifyed in the deeds tripartite indented, whereunto this shedile is annexed, shall bee yearely expended, ymployed and bestowed, as alsoe the manner and forme of the ordering and disposicion of the same.

1. That the feoffees of the said lands and tenements and hereditaments for the tyme being shall yerely once in the yere (that is to say) in the second Sunday of December make the assemblie within the Guildhall in Bury St Edmunde and there have a convenient repast provided for them, to [*be*] borne of the yssues and profitts of the lands and tenements aforesaid.

2. *Item* at the same assemblie the said feoffees or the more parte of them to name and chose 2 of themselves to be supervisors of the saide lands, tenements and hereditaments and receyvers of the yssues, rents, farmes and profitts of the same, whereof the one to be of the parishe of Saint Maryes and the other of the parish of Saint James for one whole yeare then next followinge, which shall employ and bestowe the same in and about such things as be hereafter expressed. And that the same surveyors soe chosen shall then before the rest of the feoffees there assembled make a **corporall oath** to yeld a true **accompt** at their next assemblie that tyme twelve moneths of the said yssues, rents, farmes and profitts to bee employed and bestowed as hereafter is declared.

[*Page 106*]
1. First that the said surveyors shall with such reasonable porcions of the said revenues and profitts as shall seeme to them convenient make and prepare the said dyet and repast for the said assemblie.

2. *Item* the said surveyors shall alsoe with such other parte or porcion of the same yssues, revenues and profitts as shall seeme to them reasonable beare the reparations of the said lands, tenements and hereditaments and pay such quit rents and other charges wherewith the same lands, tenements and other the premises shall be charged, so alwayes as the howses and buildings belonging to the same shall be from tyme to tyme susteyned and kept in good and sufficient reparacions.

3. *Item* the said surveyors shall alsoe with such other parte and porcion of the said issues, rents, farmes and profitts as shall seeme to them convenient beare and susteyne some parte of such taxes and *quindecims* as shall happen to fall with[*in*] the said towne of Bury. And alsoe with some other parte of the same yssues, rents and farmes <u>relieve</u> the <u>poore</u>, lame and impotent <u>persons</u> dwelling within the said towne.

309

And likewise with some other parte of the same yssues, rents, revenues and profitts to releive and help the <u>prisoners</u> within the Kinges Gayle in Bury aforesaid in such sort as shall alwaies seeme good and convenient to the said surveyors.

4. *Item* the same surveyors upon the determinacion of their accompt shall yeild and pay unto the rest and residue of the said feoffees all such sommes of money as shall happen to remaine in their hands unbestowed and not laid out about the premisses.

5. *Item* that for the safe keeping of the same surplusage and arrerages there shalbe provided by the said surveyors <u>a chest</u> with 3 lockes and 3 keyes to be always in the custody of the said surveyers for the tyme being. And the third key to remaine with one of the said feoffees by the appointment of the company. All which summes of money comeing of every such accompt to remaine in the said chest to be bestowed and employed to [*page 107*] such uses and intents as the said feoffees or the more parte of them shall from tyme to tyme appoynt.

6. And for the better continuance of the premisses it is agreed aswell by the feoffees as the feoffees named in the said deed herunto annexed that whensoever the same feoffees shall happen to decease to the number of 12 persons that then a new feoff- ment to be made to two other honest persons of the towne of Bury to the use of the same 12 persons and 12 more of the most discreet and substantiall persons of both the said parishes, soe as upon every new feoffment there shall be 24 feoffees whereof 12 to be of the parish of St James and the other 12 of the parish of Our Blessed Lady, and thus have a continuance for ever.

Appendix 5

The Schedule of Uses annexed to the re-feoffment made 19 September 1606, H1/1/52

Decimo nono die Septembris Anno quarto Jacobi regis et anno Domini 1606

A scedule conteyning the severall uses of the mannours, mesuages, annuities, rentes, tithes, porcions of tithes and hereditamentes severallie given and convayed by John Smithe, esquire, and others to and for the benefite of the inhabitants of Burye St Edmunde conteyned and specified in the deede of feoffement whereunto this scedule is annexed, howe the same and the rentes and other profites yerelie coming, arising and renewing of the same are to be yerely expended, imployed, bestowed and ordered, it is agreed shalbe as followethe, that is to seye

The uses of the landes late John Smithe esquier[1]

First concerning the mannours, messuages, londes, tenementes and hereditamentes sometime of the said John Smithe, esquier, conteyned in the deede whereunto this scedule is annexed, it is ment and intended betwene all the parties named in the said deede of feoffement hereunto annexed, and fullie agreed upon to and[*sic*] betwene all the same parties, that the rentes, fearmes and other profites yerelie coming, growing or other wise receyved of and for the same, shall yerelie from time to time be disposed, bestowed and imployed to the payment of fiftenes, taxes, tallages and other imposicions, burthens and charges whats[o]ever at all times hereafter to be layed and imposed upon the burgeses and comonaltie of the towne and burrowghe of Burye St Edmunde, their heires and successors in relief and discharge of the same burgeses and commonaltie for ever

> **And as** concerninge the londes, tenementes and hereditamentes given by William Tassell, gentleman, also mencioned in the said deede of feoffement, it is likewise by like consent agreed, that the rentes, fearmes and profites yerelie coming, growing and arising of the same, shall yerely from time to time for ever hereafter be disposed, bestowed and imployed in maner and fourme following, that is to sey

The uses of Mr Tasselles londes

First there shalbe bestowed yerelie towardes the reparacions of the churche of St Maries in Burye St Edmunde twentie shillinges. And towardes the reparacions of the churche of St James there other twentie shillings.

Item, that some suche other porcion of the rentes, revenewes and profites of the same mesuages, londes and tenementes as shalbe thowght good by the feoffees named in the said deede of feoffement, shalbe imployed and bestowed by the discretion of the same feoffees or the greater parte of them for the time beinge towardes

---

[1] A mark which looks like an arabic 2 is placed above and between the marginal note and the first paragraph.

311

the setting fourthe of souldiers which shalbe set fourthe at the generall charge of the towne and borowghe of Burye aforesaid, and also towardes the payment of suche taxes and imposicions as shalbe set and imposed in and upon the generall charge of the same towneshippe, for the ease and relief of the inhabitantes there.

Item that some other porcion of the same rentes and profites shalbe by the discretion of the said feoffees given and bestowed upon the curates of eyther of the said churches for the time beinge.

Item that the residue of the said rentes, revenewes and profites of the same mesuages, londes and tenementes shalbe bestowed upon the reparacions of the same mesuages and tenementes.

[2]And as concerning the rentes and profites yerelie coming, arising and growing of the mesuages, landes and tenementes calid the newe purchased landes likewise conteyned in the deede of feoffement whereunto this scedule is annexed, and likewise in a deede tripartite indented bearing date the fourthe daye of September in the second and third yeres of the reignes of Kinge Philip and Queene Marye it is agreed by like mutuall consent as aforesaid that the same rentes and profites shalbe from time to time hereafter yerelye imployed and bestowed in maner and fourme following, that is to seye,

The uses of the new purchased londes, late chaunteries etc.

Firste that there shalbe yerelye prepared by the receyvors of the rentes and profites of the same londes and tenementes and hereditaments conteyned in the said deede of feoffement whereunto this schedule is annexed, a convenient dinner for the said feoffees at the daye of the generall accompt to be taken for the same londes and tenementes according to the true intent of a scedule indented and annexed to the aforesaid deede tripartite bearing date the fourthe daye of September in the second and third yeres abovesaid, saving that the said accompt and dinner are ment to be taken and holden at the discretion of the same feoffees.

Item that some other porcion of the rentes and profites of the same londes and tenementes callid the newe purchased londes shalbe bestowed and imployed about the reparacions of the mesuages and buildinges belonging to the same for the suffi-cient mayntenance of them, and to paye suche quit rentes and other charges where-with the same londes and tenementes are and shalbe charged.

Item some other parte and porcion of the same rentes and profites shalbe bestowed and imployed towardes the payment of suche parte of suche taxes and fiftenes as shall happen to be within the burroughe and towne of Burye aforesaid \for the ease and relief of the inhabitanntes there/. And some other parte of the same rentes and profites shalbe bestowed yerely towardes the relief of poore, lame and impotent persons dwelling within the same towne. And some other parte shalbe imployed yerely towardes the relief of the poore prisoners within the gaole of the boroughe of Burye aforesaid. And the rest of the same rentes and profites to be yerelie imployed and bestowed to suche intentes and purposes as the feoffees of the said landes and tenementes or the greater parte of them for the time being shall thinke fit and convenient.

---

2 This passage is indented and beside it to the left is an arabic 4.

Spittlehouse[3]

The rentes and profites of a close lying next to the spitlehowse, and of a close nere Stanford Bridge conteyning about two acres given by the will of [*space*] Frence is to be bestowed yerelie upon the leprous people in the Spittle Howse by the same will.

Guildhall and Schoolehall

The Guildhall and schoolehall mencionid in the deede whereunto this scedule is annexed shalbe and remayne to and for the uses and purposes for which they are nowe used.

> The rents and profites of the porcion of tithes \which/ shall yerelie growe, arise and renewe out of the manor of Brooke Hall in Foxherthe given by the last will and testament of Thomas Bright, draper, disceasid, it is agreed by like consent, that the same shalbe yerely imployed and bestowed according to the true intent and meaning of the same last will and testament, that is to sey

The uses of the porcion of tithes

The somme of five powndes thereof shalbe thus yerely disposed, *videlicet*, towardes the reparacions of the parishe churche of St James in Burye aforesaid, twentie shillinges. And towardes the reparacions of the parishe churche of St Maryes there twentie shillinges. And to the poore people of the parishe of St James in Burye aforesaid twenty shillinges. And to the poor people of the parishe of St Maryes there twentie shillinges And to the poore prisoners in the gaole there twentie shillinges according to the last will and testament of the said Thomas Bright. And if anye further profites maye be made or arise of the said tithes over and above the said severall sumes assigned to the severall uses aforesaid, then suche profites of the same tithes over and above the said severall sommes so assigned to the several uses aforesaid, then such profites of the same tithes over and above the said sommes so assigned shalbe converted, imployed and bestowed to suche other godly and charitable uses as shalbe thought best by the the greater nomber of the feoffees of the londes and tenementes belonging to the towne of Burye aforesaid for the tyme being according to the said last will and testament of the said Thomas Bright.

The londes *et cetera* whereof noe special uses are limited[4]

The residue of the rentes and profites of the londes and tenementes, annuities, rentes and hereditamentes conteyned in the deede whereunto this scedule is annexed, whereof noe speciall use is herein limitted and appoynted, it is agreed by like mutuall consent as is aforesaid, that the same shalbe yerely imployed and bestowed according to the discrecion of the foeffees of the said londes and tenementes, or the greater part of them for the time being, and as it shalbe thought fit for the comon good and benefit of the burgeses and inhabitantes of the towne and burroughe of Burye aforesaid, and in reliefe of the poore there.

---

3 Above this marginal heading is an arabic 5.
4 Above this marginal heading is an arabic 6.

Appendix 6

Tables of feoffees, 1555–1617

From the earliest benefactions until 1545, although the same feoffees usually acted for all the charities, and the feoffments were renewed in the same years, the feoffees of each charity were appointed individually. There seems to have been some uncertainty in the immediate post-Reformation period. The feoffees of the new purchased lands were a new creation. For the others, it seems likely that the feoffees appointed in 1545 continued, but the names of those enfeoffed before 1572 show that some feoffees were concerned with some of the new properties, but not with others. The general feoffment of 1572 may well be the first document by which the same men were enfeoffed with all the feoffees' property.

For Table 6(a), which covers the period before 1572, the names of feoffees have been taken from copies of deeds in John Woodward's Register. An asterisk marks those feoffees who served in 1572 and later. The numbers indicate the position in which a man's name appears in the list of feoffees. The documents consulted are as follows:

Feoffment of the new purchased land, 14 September 1555, Woodward's Register, H1/6/1, pp.103–4
Feoffment of Tassell's gift, 18 December 1557, *ibid.*, pp.125–6
Feoffment of Browse's gift, 30 August 1558, *ibid.*, p.167
Feoffment of Katherine Cage's gift, 19 April 1563, *ibid.*, p.166
Bartholemew Brockesby's gift of the poor men's rents, 1564, *ibid.*, pp.169–70
Sale by Sir Nicholas Bacon and others of a messuage next the Angel, 4 January 1565, *ibid.*, p.143.
The conveyance of the Guildhall and other concealed lands, 7 July 1569, *ibid.*, p.114

Table 6(a): Feoffees 1555–69, and their position in the lists

Name	1555	1557	1558	1563	1564	1565	1569
Andrews, Thos.	9	10	11	9	7	7	8*
Annable, John	18	15	15				
Axton, William	23		19	13	17	14	18*
Bacon, John			8				
Bacon, Nicholas				1	1	1	1*
Badby, Thomas				17	5	6	5*
Baker, William			18	17	11	15	12*
Barber, Roger	1	11	12	4*			
Becham, James	14	12	13	5	13	8	14*
Boldero, Francis							10*
Boldero, John				22			20*
Brown, Thomas				20	19	19	13*
Browning, Robt.				21		20	16*

Name	1555	1557	1558	1563	1564	1565	1569
Browse, Thomas	17	17		8			
Bullock, John	8						
Buttery, John	10						
Cage, John	11	14					
Cage, Thomas	13		14	6	14	9	15*
Cheston, Wm.	12						
Chetham, John				19	10	18	11*
Cocksage, Thos.	19		20	14	18	15	
Croft, John		4					
Cutteras, John					21	21	19*
Drury, William		1					
Eyer, John		5	3				
Fairfax, Willliam	22						
Hawkin, Edward	2					10	
Hayward, Steph.			10	7	8		9*
Heigham, Clemt.		2	1	2	2	2	2*
Holt, John	6	9	6		6	5	7
Horningold, Hen.	15		18	12	16	13	17*
Jermyn, Amb.		3	2	3	3	3	3*
Kitson, Thomas							4*
Lucas, Henry	5	8	7				
Park, William	3						
Payne, Anthony				18	12	17	
Payne, Henry	4	6	4		4	4	
Peyton, Christr.		7	5				
Rikard, William	24						
Rought, John	20	13					
Sharp, Robert	21						
Smith, William				16	20	16	
Stacy, Thos.,sen.	16	16	16				
Tassell, William	7		9	10	9	11	6*
Wright, James				15	11		12*

Table 6(b) gives the names of those enfeoffed between 1572 and 1617. The column headed 1571 gives the name of those who attended 'common conference' in that year on behalf of the two parishes. Those nominated for St Mary's parish are marked 'M'; those for St James's, 'J'. An asterisk marks those feoffees who had served before the general refeoffment of 1572. The names in the column headed 1582 which are marked + were described as deceased in the deeds relating to the 1588 general refeoffment. The numbers indicate the position in which a man's name appears in the list of feoffees. These names are taken from the following deeds of general refeoffment: 1572 H1/1/51(d); 1582 and 1588 H1/1/51(a), (b) and (c); 1606 H1/1/52; 1617 H1/1/40.

Table 6(b). Feoffees 1571–1617 and their position in the lists

Name	1571	1572	1582	1588	1606	1617
Andrews, Thomas*	J	6	14			
Ashfield, Robert				15	4	
Ashwell, Stephen					26	10
Axton, William*		20				
Bacon, Nicholas*		1				
Badby, Thomas*	J	5	13			
Baker, Thomas					22	
Baker, William*			9	9		
Barber, Roger*			5	5		
Barker, Bennet					21	7
Blagge, Henry				16		
Boldero, Francis*	J	10				
Boldero, George					15	
Boldero, John*		16	16+			
Boldero, John					13	
Bourne, Edward						25
Bridon, John						20
Bright, Thomas, senior	J		18+			
Bright, Thomas, junior					19	
Brook, Walter				23		
Brown, Robert						12
Brown, Thomas*		9				
Browning, Robert*	J	18				
Cage, Thomas	M	15				
Carles, Robert	M	23				
Chetham, John*		12	23			
Cocksage, Thomas*	J	22	10	10		
Collin, Henry	M	3	3			
Cook, Erasmus			25			
Cook, William			4	4	10	2
Cutteris, John		21	24			
Darby, Charles					23	8
Davy, Robert						17
Drury, William				13		
Faircliff, James						22
Faircliff, William				24		
Gilly, John	M			26		
Gippes, Henry					27	11
Gippes, John				22	16	
Gippes, Thomas			12	12		

Name	1571	1572	1582	1588	1606	1617
Godfrey, Richard, junior						24
Golding, Robert			22		5	
Goodrich, John						16
Goodrich, Thomas, senior	M	24	11	11	17	
Goodrich, Thomas, junior				18		
Groom, Robert				19		
Hayward, Stephen*	J	11				
Hayward, William				17	9	
Higham, John		4	1	1	3	1
Hill, John					12	4
Hill, William	M	19	17+			
Horningold, Henry*	M	17	8	8		
Hinds, Robert						21
Inman, John						19
Jermyn, Ambrose*		2				
Jermyn, Robert				14	2	
Kitson, Thomas*		3	20			
Lancaster, Matthew						23
Lowdale, Roger						18
Mallowes, John					11	3
Mann, John					25	
Mawe, Robert					6	
Nunn, John					7	
Payne, Anthony*	M	14	2	2	8	
Pead, Thomas					7	14
Peyton, Thomas	M	7	21			
Pinner, Francis					20	6
Potter, Roger	M		19+			
Revell, John					24	9
Revell, William						14
Rockett, Thomas				20	13	
Smith, Anthony						15
Sparke, Robert				28	18	5
Tassell, William*		8	15+			
Ubank, Edward			7	7		
Walker, Richard				20	1	
Wright, James*	M	13	6	6		
Withers, John	J			27		

Appendix 7

Payments to the Town Clergy recorded in the Feoffees' Accounts

Year	St Mary's	St James's
1586	Minister £9 0s.0d.	Minister £12 0s.0d.
1587	Minister £26 0s.0d.	Minister £18 0s.0d
1588	Mr Morgan, minister, £16 0s.0d.	Mr Hill £8 0s.0d.for serving the cure Mr Moss, minister, £29 0s.0d.
1589	Mr Lewis, minister, £40 0s.0d.	Mr Moss, minister, £33 0s.11d.
1590	Mr Lewis, minister, £40 0s.0d.	Mr Moss, minister, £40 0s.0d.
1591[1]	Mr Lewis, minister £30 0s.0d (for three quarters only)	Mr Moss, minister, £30 0s.0d. (for three quarters only)
1592	Mr Lewis, £40 0s.0d.	Mr Moss, minister, £40 0s.0d
1593	Mr Lewis, preacher, £30 0s.0d. (for three quarters only)	Mr Moss, minister, £30 0s.0d. (for three quarters only)
1594	Mr Lewis, preacher, £40 0s.0d. (included £10 0s.0d. arrears)	Mr Moss, preacher, £50 0s.0d. (included £10 0s.0d. arrears)
1595	Mr Lewis, preacher, £50 0s.0d. (included £10 0s.0d. in advance)	Mr Moss, preacher, £50 0s.0d. (included £10 0s.0d. in advance)
1596	Mr Lewis, preacher, £40 0s.0d.	Mr Moss, preacher, £40 0s.0d.
1597	Mr Lewis, preacher, £40 0s.0d.	Mr Moss, preacher, £40 0s.0d.
1598	Mr Lewis, preacher, £30 0s.0d. Mr Esty, £10 0s.0d.	Mr Moss and Mr Ward, preachers, £30 0s.0d. for three quarters.
1599	Mr Esty, £10 0s.0d.	Mr Newton, £20 0s.0d
1600	Mr Esty, preacher, £25 0s.0d.	Mr Newton, preacher, £40 0s.0d.
1601	Mr Esty, preacher, for 32 weeks and Mr Bedell, preacher, for the remainder of the year, £40 0s.0d.	Mr Newton, preacher, £40 0s.0d.
1602	Mr Bedell, preacher, £30 0s.0d.	Mr Newton, preacher, £30 0s.0d.
1603	Mr Bedell, preacher, £30 0s.0d. Mr Jewell, minister, £1 0s.0d.	Mr Newton, preacher, £30 0s.0d. Mr Buller, minister, £1 0s.0d.
1604	Mr Bedell, preacher, £30 0s.0d. Mr Jewell, minister, £1 0s.0d.	Mr Newton, preacher, £30 0s.0d. Mr Buller, minister, £1 0s.0d.
1605	Mr Bedell, preacher, £40 0s.0d. Mr Jewell, minister, £1 0s.0d.	Mr Newton, £10 0s.0d. for one quarter Mr Buller, £1 0s.0d. plus £5 0s.od. extra for filling Mr Newton's place since 25 March

[1] In this year £5 was paid to Mr Hill, described as 'minister' in the Minute Book, H2/6/2.1 p.2. Neither the accounts nor the minutes give the parish in which he worked. Tymms, *St Mary's*, citing the feoffees' accounts as his authority, described him as curate of St Mary's.

Year	St Mary's	St James's
1606	Mr Bedell, £37 10s.0d. for three quarters Mr Jewell, minister, £1 0s.0d.	Mr Buller, minister, £1 0s.0d.
1607	Mr Bedell, £12 0s.0d. for arrear Preacher, £50 0s.od. Minister, £1 0s.0d.	Preacher, £50 0s.0d. Minister, £1 0s.0d.
1608	Mr Sotheby, £50 0s.0d. Mr Jewell, £1 0s.0d.	Mr Healey, £50 0s.0d. Mr Buller, minister, £1 0s.0d.
1609	Mr Sotheby, preacher, £50 0s.0d. Mr Jewell, minister, £1 0s.0d.	Mr Healey, preacher, £50 0s.0d. Mr Corder, minister, £1 0s.0d.
1610	Mr Sotheby, preacher, £50 0s.0d. Mr Jewell, minister, £1 0s.0d.	Mr Healey, preacher, £50 0s.0d
1611	Mr Bedell, preacher, £50 0s.0d. Mr Jewell, minister, £1 0s.0d.	Mr Healey, preacher, £50 0s.0d. Mr Corder, minister, £1 0s.0d. including £1 0s.0d. omitted from last account
1612	Mr Bedell, preacher, £50 0s.0d. Mr Jewell, minister, £2 0s.0d.	Mr Healey, preacher, £50 0s.0d. Mr Corder, minister, £2 0s.0d.
1613	Mr Bedell, preacher, £50 0s.0d. Mr Jewell, minister, £2 0s.0d.	Mr Healey, preacher, £50 0s.0d. Mr Knewstubbs, minister, £2 0s.0d.
1614	Mr Bedell, preacher, £50 0s.0d. Mr Jewell, minister, £2 0s.0d.	Mr Healey, preacher, £50 0s.0d. Mr Knewstubbs, minister, £2 0s.0d.
1615	Mr Bedell, preacher, £50 0s.0d. Mr Jewell, minister, £2 0s.0d.	Mr Healey, preacher, £50 0s.0d. Mr Knewstubbs, minister, £2 0s.0d.
1616	Mr Bedell, preacher, £12 0s.0d. for quarter ended 25 March. Mr Bedell £5 0s.0d. for maintaining Friday exercise during vacancy. Mr Gibbon, preacher, for quarter from Michaelmas to Christmas. Mr Jewell £5 0s.0d. for sermons he preached during vacancy. £18 6s.9d. for providing Sunday preachers during vacancy. Mr Jewell, minister, £2 0s.0d.	Mr Healey, preacher, £50 0s.0d. Mr Knewstubbs, minister, £2 0s.0d.
1617	Mr Gibbon, preacher, £50 0s.0d. Mr Jewell, minister, £2 0s.0d.	Mr Healey, preacher, £50 0s.0d. Mr Knewstubbs, minister, £5 0s.0d.
1618	Mr Gibbon, preacher, £50 0s.0d. Mr Jewell, minister, £2 0s.0d.	Mr Healey, preacher, £50 0s.0d. Mr Crossman, minister, £2 0s.0d.
1619	Mr Gibbon, preacher, £50 0s.0d. Mr Jewell, minister, £2 0s.0d. Mr Cary, who preached on probation, £1 0s.0d.	Mr Healey, preacher, £50 0s.0d. Mr Crossman, minister, £2 0s.0d. Mr Healey, for the gaol, £6 0s.0d.
1620	Mr Cary, preacher, £50 0s.0d. Mr Jewell, minister, £2 0s.0d.	Mr Wallbank, preacher, £50 0s.0d. Mr Crossman, minister, £2 0s.0d. Mr Crossman, the gaol, £6 0s.0d. 9s.0d. for preachers at the Monday Exercise

1621	Mr Cary, preacher, £50 0s.0d. Mr Jewell, minister, £2 0s.0d.	Mr Wallbank, preacher, £50 0s.0d. Mr Crossman, minister, £2 0s.0d. [*space*] for Monday Exercise
1622	Mr Cary, preacher, £50 0s.0d. Mr Jewell, minister, £2 0s.0d.	Mr Wallbank, preacher, £50 0s.0d. Mr Crossman, minister, £2 0s.0d. Mr Crossman, the gaol, £6 0s.0d.

In 1609 the sum of £1 0s.0d. then paid to the minister of each parish was said to be the gift of Mr Tassell. The additional sum of £1 0s.0d. paid to the ministers from 1611 was the gift of Thomas Bright the elder, while the 9s.0d. paid in 1620 for the Monday Exercise was the gift of Francis Pinner, junior.

Appendix 8

Land and money acquired by the feoffees, with a note of major purchases, 1481–1639

Except where otherwise indicated, this table is based on information taken from Woodward's Register, H1/6/1, which is largely arranged in chronological order.

Date	Name of donor	Description of property	Purposes of gift
1481	John Smith	1470: Messuage called Reycyes; an ac. of land called Sheepcote on which a sheep fold had been erected; 15 pieces containing 80 acres in Gt Barton and Fornham St Martin; a messuage in Gt Barton; 7 pieces of arable containing 12½ ac. in Barton fields; 7 pieces of arable in Bury and Nowton; 16 ac in 6 pieces in South field of Bury; all other land which he had in fields of Bury called Vine field , Eastgate fields, Southgate field, and also in the fields of Gt Barton, Nowton and Fornham St Martin (except his land called Redcastle in Gt Barton); 1½ ac. in Rougham called Les Firres.	Payment of the abbot's cope, fifteenths, tenths and other taxes.
		1473: Messuage, 16 pieces of arable; a piece of meadow, a wood and a fold course in Rougham.	As above, provision of his *obit*.
1492	Margaret Odeham	House in Skinner Row; land in the East, South and West fields of Bury; land in the fields of Nowton, Gt and Lt. Horringer and Westley. Two tenements in Churchgate St and property in the Market Place.	To find a lamp before the holy sacrament and a chantry priest at the altar of St Lawrence in St James's church; the chantry priest also to say mass in the chapel of the gaol; to provide wood for the prisoners. For the friars of Babwell to say *placebo* and *dirige*, and to have a requiem mass annually for her and her family.
1495	Margaret Drury	Two houses in Short Brackland.	To be used as almshouses.
1498	Reginald Church	Three small tenements in Raingate St.	To be used as almshouses.

Date	Name of donor	Description of property	Purposes of gift
1499	William Fish	Tenement called Loundes near Southgate Bridge; 2 pieces of land in East field of Bury; 2 pieces in South field near road from Rothebridge to Eldo; 4 ac. in East field abutting on Shakersway; 2 ac. in East field; 2ac.3r. in South field.	For payment of the abbot's cope and provision of an *obit*.
1502	John Frenze	2 ac. at Stamford Bridge and a pightle in Spintlemill field.	For the relief of lepers.
1503	John Salter	Tenement in Northgate St; 2 ac. in Risbygate field.	To be used according to the will of John Smith.
1521	Feoffees of Adam Newhawe	51 ac. arable and 1½ ac. pasture in fields of Bury, Rushbrook and Nowton.	Originally given to the guild of the Holy Name of Jesus in the College, but now, if not earlier, transferred to the feoffees and administered with Smith's gift.
1527	Thomas Bereve	Two houses in Garland St on the corner of Burmans (now Pump) Lane.	Used as almshouses.
1548	William Parke	A shop in Spicer Row or the Fish Market, now Abbeygate St.	Formerly part of Odeham's bequest to the friars of Babwell.
1549	Former chantries bought from Robert Bedes and Giles Levet, who had bought them from the Crown for £358 5s.4d.	Odeham's: 16 ac. without the South Gate; 17 ac. in Bury, Westley and Gt Horringer; 18 ac. in Bury, Gt and Lt. Horringer; 22 ac. in East field of Bury; arable in East and South fields; 15 ac. in West field and other lands in fields of Bury; shops in Skinner Row. Beckett's chantry in St James's church: 44½ ac. in Gt Horringer; 18 ac. in East field of Bury; tenement in Rotten Row with a chamber (*cubiculum*); messuage in Bury; 2 messuages in Baxter St; a dovehouse and a small pightle outside the North Gate; a barn and a garden without the Risby Gate. Morrow Mass priest in St James's church: 8 ac. in East field; barn in Northgate St; stall in the Gt Market; messuage in Northgate St. Smith's anniversary: out of land in Rougham. St Nicholas guild: 6 messuages in Bury. St Botolph's guild: a messuage in Garland St.	These were known as the new purchased lands, and the schedule of uses is printed in Appendix 4.
1557	Francis Boldero and William Parker	5 small tenements in High (Northgate) St, which had been given by Edmund King, grocer, to endow a chantry in 1483.	Used as almshouses.

Year	Name	Property	Purpose
1557	William Tassell	The Angel, The Castle and The Boar's Head all in Mustowe (Angel Hill); a stable with a garden in Punch (Athenaeum) Lane; messuage in Crown St; messuage in Mr Andrew's Street (Bridwell Lane); messuage and garden in Southgate St; messuage in Churchgate St; land in Maidwater (Mainwater) Lane; messuage and a stable or tenement with a garden in Brentgovel St; messuage in Schoolhall St (Honey Hill); 3 messuages and a garden in Raingate St; 3 messuages in Long Brackland; land in Northgate St; messuage in Risbygate St; orchard or garden near the Tayfen.	The schedule of uses of Tassell's land is printed in Appendix 5.
1558	Thomas Browse	4 tenements in Garland St.	To be used as almshouses.
1563	Katherine Cage	A [?rent charge out of] a messuage in Crown St; a piece of ground in Mr Andrew's St; a messuage in Westgate St; pasture and meadow called Tenter Close in Westgate St; a barn, stable and yard in Mr Andrew's St; an orchard or root ground in Mr Andrew's St.	For the relief of the poor.
1564	Bartholemew Brockesby and John Walker	Almshouses or poor men's rents next to the stone wall of the Gt Churchyard which they had purchased of Wm Grice, servant of the queen, and Anthony Forster of Cumnor.	For the consolation and relief of the honest poor people of Bury.
1569	Concealed lands bought from Edward Grimston and William le Grys	Messuage and grange, barn and garden in Eastgate St, formerly the hall of the guilds of St Thomas the Martyr, the Assumption of the Blessed Virgin Mary and St Peter the Apostle. Messuages, cottages, lands etc. in Hepworth, Barningham and (Coney) Weston which had belonged to Smith's chantry in St Mary's church. The Guildhall in Guildhall Street.	Had been used since 1550 as the Grammar School. For the relief and support of the poor of Bury. For considering matters of concern to the town of Bury.
1570	William Barnaby	6 messuages called the College almshouses in College Street.	4 used as almshouses, the other 2 let to pay for repairs.
1573	Edmund Jermyn	An annuity of £40 a year out of the manor of Torkesey in Lincolnshire.	To provide work for the poor.
1574	Robert Browning	£4 0s.0d.	For the relief of the poor.
1578	Thomas Badby, from benevolence and for £10.	The Shire House	For the welfare of the people of Bury.
1579	Thomas Brown	£30 0s.0d.	To provide a stock for the poor.

Date	Name of donor	Description of property	Purposes of gift
1580	Sir Nicholas Bacon	£14 0s.0d.	To relieve prisoners.
1580	John Boldero	£5 16s.0d.	
1580	E[dward] R[ookwood]	£15 0s.0d.	
1581	John Boldero	£4 0s.0d.	
1581	E[dward] R[ookwood]	£29 18s.0d.	
1581	Edmund Markant of Colchester[1]	£13 0s.0d.	
1582	Purchase, in conjunction with governors[2]	St Peter's Hospital and the Grange lands	See Introduction, p.xxxvii.
1583	William Hill	£4 0s.0d.	
1583	Sir Thomas Jermyn, died 1552	£30 0s.0d., part of his legacy taken from the coffer.	Used to build the Market Cross.
1583	William Page	£5	For the relief of the poor.
1584	William Markant	£30; a further £30, making up the £60 he left, was received in 1590.	
1587	Thomas Bright the elder	£300	For clothing the poor.
		A portion of tithes out of the manor of Brook Hall in Foxearth, Essex.	Payments to the ministers; repairing the churches; relief of the poor in each parish; relief of prisoners.
1590	Peter Kembold	£100 to buy land.	Relief of the poor in North and East wards.
1595	Francis Boldero	£40	

1 Account book, HD1150/1, f.19r.
2 See Introduction, p.xxxviii, for the purchase of St Peter's.

Year	Name	Amount	Description
1595	Martha Heigham	£10	
1602	Sir Thomas Kitson	£40[3]	
1610	John Gipps[4]	£20	To provide work for the poor.
1612	James Baxter	An acre in Spintlemill field.	Repairing the library in St James's church.
1613	Richard Walker	£40 and two messuages in Churchgate St.	For relief of the poor.
1617	George Esty	£10	Fuel for the poor.
1618	Francis Pinner, junior	£20	Towards the cost of the Monday Exercise.
1624	Charles Darby	£6	For the poor, £4 to be given in the Northgate ward which he considered to be in greatest need.
1624	Stephen Ashwell	£200; almshouses in Southgate Street.	The money to be used for clothing the poor.
1625	Thomas Bright the younger	Two messuages in the Butter Market.	£5 a year for apprenticing; £1 a year to each church for repairs; £1 a year for prisoners in the county gaol and 3s.4d. a year for cakes and wine at the annual account meeting.[5]
1625	Lady Kitson	Rent charge out of the manor of Lackford.	For food, clothing, fuel and other relief for the poor.
1627	Peter Ling	Two houses in Short Brackland and a house in Westgate Street.	The rents to be used for clothing the poor.

3   Sir John Cullum's copy of the Book of Benefactors says that Sir Thomas gave £40 for a stock for the poor; this must have been a gift *inter vivos* as the abstract of his will in Gage, *Thingoe*, mentions only £5 to be distributed to the poor.
4   Account Book, HD1150/2, f.18v.
5   J.B. Bright, *The Brights of Suffolk*, p.66.

Date	Name of donor	Description of property	Purposes of gift
1632	John Sharpe	£200	Each year £1 to prisoners in the town gaol; £1 to prisoners in the county gaol; 10s. each to poor in Bridewell and Spittle House; remainder to be divided between poor in North and East wards.
1634	Edward Darby	£300	Catechising poor people in St James's parish.
1635	John Hill	4 small tenements in Westgate Street near the Horse Market (St Mary's Square).	For housing poor of St Mary's parish.
?1636	Lady Cary	£100 with which Jeekes tenement in Hepworth was bought.	Relief of poor widows.
1637	Edward Bourne	£8 to be distributed in bread at the Guildhall within a week of his death (which happened while the plague was raging in 1637).	
		£20	To provide a stock of wool for clothing the poor in Bridewell (Moyses Hall).
		Three tenements in Westgate St.	To be used as almshouses for widows over 50.
		An orchard in Hepworth.	For apprenticing 2 boys from each parish every year.
1639	Francis Pinner, senior	House in Whiting Street.	To clothe 80 poor people in St Mary's parish each November; also to provide bread on last Friday of each month to poor who were catechised in St Mary's, the minister having £1 and any surplus to provide horn books and primers to children in St Mary's parish.
		Unexpired leases of 4 houses in Mustowe.	To provide bread for poor who attended church on Sundays; apprenticing poor children from St Mary's parish, preference being given to those from the workhouse.
		£40 to pipe water to the Market Place and provide a cistern of water there.	To be used in case of fire.

Glossary

The best way of getting at the present-day equivalent of unfamiliar words in these accounts is to say the word aloud. Many words, such as 'bill' and 'byll', show that 'i' and 'y' were used interchangeably. Letters were often doubled where today they are single, and *vice versa*. A 'w' was often used instead of 'u' in words such as 'house' and 'south'. Plural forms often end with -es, e.g. 'bondes', 'landes'. The conjugation of some verbs was somewhat different at this period, for example 'shewde' for 'showed'; 'apperith' for 'appears'; 'dothe' for 'does'; 'dwellethe' for 'dwells'; and 'leaton' or 'letten' for 'let'. An aspirate may sometimes be found where it would not be used nowadays, as in 'hable' for 'able'. Words beginning with a vowel following 'the' were often elided, for instance 'thalderman'.

Latin words and phrases commonly appear in the accounts, often embedded in English sentences. In this glossary they are printed in italic. Nouns and adjectives are first given in their nominative forms, and verbs in the infinitive, followed by the principal variants which appear in the accounts.

The *Oxford English Dictionary* has been the main source of definitions for English words. In a few instances C.T. Onions (revised by Robert D. Eagleson) *A Shakespeare Glossary* (Oxford, 1986) has also been useful, as have E.A. Livingstone (ed.) *Concise Oxford Dictionary of the Christian Church* (1977); Rosemary Milward, *A Glossary of Household, Farming and Trade Terms from Probate Inventories* (Chesterfield, 1982); and Eric Gee, *A Glossary of Building Terms used in England from the Conquest to c.1550* (Frome, 1984). Works on specific subjects, which have been consulted for English words, are Eric Kerridge, *Textile Manufactures in Early Modern England* (Manchester University Press, 1985); Lindsay Boyton, *The Elizabethan Militia, 1558–1638* (1967); Santina M. Levey, *An Elizabethan Inheritance: the Hardwick Hall Textiles* (1998); John B. Saunders (ed.) *Mozley and Whiteley's Law Dictionary* (1977); L.F. Salzman, *Building in England down to 1540: a Documentary History* (Oxford, 1992); Oliver Rackham, *Trees and Woodland in the British Landscape* (1976).

Most of the Latin words have been found in R.E. Latham, *Revised Medieval Latin Word List* (1983). W.H. Maigne d'Arnis, *Lexicon manuale ad scriptores mediæ et infimæ Latinitatis . . .* (Paris, 1866) contains one or two words not found in Latham. A large proportion of the Latin words are included in the word-list in Eileen A. Gooder, *Latin for Local History: an Introduction* (1961).

acquittance, acquittaunce, acquittauns, acquytaunce: acquittance, receipt; a writing providing evidence that a sum had been paid.
adhuc: to this place, thus far.
afore: before, previously.
ageinst: against; **agenest fier:** to be used in the event of fire.
aide: aid or **subsidy** (*q.v.*), a tax granted to the king for an extraordinary purpose.
alderman: this word was used in the twelfth century in the sense of headman or governor of the guild merchant in York, and could have been used of the head of the guild merchant in Bury St Edmunds from the same period. Later it was used of the head of the Candlemas guild and, after the dissolution of guilds, the company or fellowship which produced these accounts also elected an alderman as their head or chairman. Apart from a few years at the end of the seventeenth century, Bury St Edmunds did not have a mayor (in the usual sense) until after the Municipal Corporations Act of 1835. In the charter of incorporation of 1606, the chief magistrate was still called the alderman, the equivalent of the mayor in most incorporated towns.
alius: other; *alia:* other things.

alienacion, alienation: transfer of property; a licence of alienation was required before property could be conveyed to a body or person in perpetuity. The Crown lost income from land held by the church, charities or other institutions who never died and would never pay dues on the death of the holder. Fees were payable to the Crown for a licence to alienate land for ever.

almain rivets, almaine rivetes: almain rivets; light, flexible body armour of German origin; considered obsolete by the mid-sixteenth century and superseded by the corslet (see **corseletes**).

allmoes, almoise, almose, almoyse: alms; **almoise howses:** almshouses

allocacio: allowance, payment; *allocaciones:* payments; *allocacionum:* of payments, as in the phrase *summa allocationum predictorum:* total of aforesaid allowances.

allocare: to allow; *allocata:* allowed; *allocatur:* it is allowed, as in the phrase *adhuc allocata:* allowances made so far.

allowance, allowans, allowauns: allowances, payments.

amend: repair.

Ampners: the Almoner's; pertaining to the office of Almoner of Bury abbey; used in the phrase 'Ampners Barnes', an estate which formerly belonged to the Almoner (see also **Elemozyner's Bearnes**).

amerciament: amercement, an arbitrary fine.

andirons, andyrons: fire dogs, used to support logs in a large open fireplace.

annus: year; *anno:* in the year: *anno Domini:* in the year of the Lord; *anno predicto:* in the aforesaid year; *anno supradicto:* in the abovesaid year.

annualis, annuales: yearly

annuity, annuytie, annuytye: annual payment of a fixed sum. Might be part of the revenue of an estate, or annual payments made to tenants whose leases had been cancelled at the behest of the Commissioners for Charitable Uses.

Annunciation (of Our Lady): feast of the Annunciation of Our Lady, 25 March.

answer, to be answered: often means to account for a sum of money.

anticipacion: a sum paid or received before the due date.

antiently: anciently, a long time ago.

apparell: clothing.

apparailing(e), apparelling, appariling: the provision of clothing.

appothecarie: apothecary or pharmacist; one who prepared and sold drugs.

apprentize: apprentice; **apprentizeshippe:** apprenticeship.

arbitrators: men, in this instance JPs, appointed by the Privy Council to settle a dispute.

armiger: esquire. At this period 'esquire' and *armiger* were used only of those entitled to coats of arms.

arming (pikes): repair of the metal spikes on pikes. Pikemen were divided into those armed who wore body armour, and those unarmed who wore leather jacks.

armorer: armourer; one who made and repaired armour. In many instances, however, a cutler repaired the town armour.

arreragia: arrears; *arreragia nulla:* no arrears; *arreragia patent:* the arrears are shown; *cum arreragia:* with arrears.

articles: individual clauses of a document.

ashe: ash tree.

asignee, assignee, assignes, assisgnees: person or persons to whom something had been transferred; usually used in a lease.

assignment: a) transfer of a lease from the original lessee to another person; b) the authority of feoffees.

assises, assisses, assizes: sessions held in each county by judges acting under a special commission, to hear both criminal and civil cases. Assize judges usually sat in Bury St Edmunds during Lent and at Midsummer.

assuerance, assuerauns, assurance: deed or deeds by which the title to a property was assured.

attachmentes: (writs of) attachment whereby a person or property is taken into the custody of the law.

attendantes, attendauntes: servants, waiters.

augmentacion, augmentation: the process of making greater, used of rents.

aunciante: ancient, a flag or ensign. In this case the ancient no doubt carried some or all of the charges in the arms granted to Bury St Edmunds in November 1606. The arms had a blue ground on which were three crowns with crossed arrows. Long before the incorporation, fire buckets stored in the Guildhall were marked with crossed arrows. St Edmund was said to have been killed by the arrows of invading Vikings (see **cognizaunces**).

band, bandes: see **bond**.

barke: bark of trees, used in both dyeing and tanning.

base childe: illegitimate child.

bailie, baily, baylief(e), baylieff, baylif(f), bayly(e): bailiff; a local official, often of a **hundred** (*q.v.*), who had administrative authority and duties within that area.

barrell: barrel or revolving cylinder around which a rope or chain was wound to raise and lower a well-bucket.

beadell, beadell(e)s, beadle, bedell, bedelles, bedels, bedle: beadle; (a) used instead of **porter** (*q.v.*) for the caretaker of the Guildhall (not to be confused with the 'keeper' of the Guildhall in the earliest accounts); (b) a parish officer with responsibility for poor relief; (c) common beadle and cryer of the town, after incorporation, who made announcements of public importance.

beame(s): (a) beam or large timber used in building work; (b) a balance consisting of a beam and scales.

bearers: persons who helped to carry a corpse to burial.

bearne: barn.

behinde: in arrear (before this account).

benevolence, beneveolence: voluntary gift or grant of money.

bestowed: dedicated for a specified purpose.

biforehand: in advance.

billa: bill, bond.

bill, billes: (a) an account for things bought; (b) a weapon used by infantry consisting of a metal head on a long wooden pole; (c) see **bond**, for which it was sometimes used as an synonym, as in the phrase 'by billes and promises'.

bind: bind a boy as apprentice by means of an indenture, to a master who would train him in his trade or craft.

binding: binding or strengthening raw edges of cloth with other pieces; perhaps it also referred to braid used to trim livery coats.

bing: bin (dialect).

blew, blew(e) cloth: blue cloth, as made locally, using woad as the principal dye. Medieval clothmen of Bury frequently mentioned the 'woad house'.

board cloth: table cloth.

booking: entering into a book; included the compiling of a field-book to accompany a drawn plan.

boore, bore: boar.

boltes: (a) bolts or pins of iron for fastening; (b) moveable parts of locks.

bond(e), bondes: document(s) in English law whereby one person binds himself and his heirs to pay a sum of money to another person on a specified day, usually with penalties should payment not be made.

bonesettinge: setting a fractured limb.

botle maker: leather worker who made vessels for holding liquid. These would now be of glass.

bourd (e): (a) wooden board used in building; (b) a table.

bourded houses: houses boarded up during epidemics, to prevent comings and goings.

bourding upp: boarding up houses infected with disease.

bownde: bound by means of a bond for the payment of a sum of money.

brasse: brass (metal) and objects made of brass.

bredrye: brethren.

brick endes: broken bricks, part of a brick; sometimes distinguished from whole bricks.

brideales, brydall(e)s: bride-ales, a wedding feast.

broad clothe: cloth woven on looms up to two yards or so in width; **broad(e) blew:** blue cloth woven on such a loom.

buckeling: repair or replacement of buckles on town armour.

buckeram: buckram, a type of linen fabric.

buckettes of leather: (a) buckets for a well; (b) buckets for public use in case of fire.

bushell, busshel(l)es: bushel, a measure of capacity holding eight gallons.

buttery: originally a room where liquor was stored, but later a room where provisions were kept.

cage: a lock-up or prison for petty offenders.

Candlemas: feast of the Purification of Our Lady, popularly called Candlemas because the day's ritual included a procession with lighted candles.

capons: castrated cocks.

cardes, cards: wooden implements with handles and wire teeth, used in the preparation of wool before spinning (see **stockardes**). **Duche cardes** and **Spanishe cardes** appear in these accounts but their significance has not been discovered.

card maker: one who made cards for the preparation of wool (see **cardes**).

carpet: cloth covering a table.

cariages, carriages, caryages (kinges): transporting of provisions for the royal household (see **provision**).

casementes: casement windows, whose frames are attached by hinges.

castleward rent: imposition on those living in certain properties to maintain a particular castle and its garrison.

causes: subjects of litigation, matters to be decided.

chalder: chaldron, a measure for coal and lime, varying between 32 and 40 bushels depending on whether the measure was heaped or level.

chamber: upstairs room, in this instance where the feoffees and corporation held meetings. The 'inner chamber' seems to have been a smaller room, probably used when only the alderman and chief burgesses, or other small groups, met.

chanell: gutter to remove surface-water from a street.

charg(e), charges: charge(s), signifying income collected by the accountant or receiver; equivalent of the Latin word *onus* (*q.v.*). The accountant was said to **chardge himself** with the receipt of various sums.

charged, chargid: charged or responsible for accounting for some amount due.

charged to be levyed: charged for sums which had to be collected.

charges of suyt(e): costs of a suit at law.

chirurgery: surgery.

chist: chest or coffer (see **cofer**).

Christmas quarter: period between Christmas and Lady Day, 25 March.

church graces: occasional services of the church. In 1593 Henry Horningold deposed that in the past offerings and payments for 'christenings, marriages and other graces of the church' were always paid to the priest who served the cure.

citation: summons to an ecclesiastical court.

clare: clearly, net (in accounts); as in *et sic debet clare:* and thus he owes clearly.

claye, cley(e): clay or plaster used in building work.

clayers, cleyer: dauber(s), who applied clay to a building.

claying: daubing, the application of clay to the walls of a building.

clerke: the feoffees' clerk was responsible for routine administration, keeping accounts and sometimes undertaking legal work on their behalf.

clogg: a large block of wood, perhaps part of a tree trunk.

close, closse: enclosure, an enclosed piece of land.

clothier: entrepreneur who co-ordinated and financed the various processes involved in making woollen cloth.

cobirons, cobyrons: irons supporting a spit in front of a fire.

cofer, coffer: coffer or safe where money belonging to the town was kept, in an upper chamber of the Guildhall porch or 'tower' (see **treasury**).

cognizaunces, cognizauns: cognizances or silver badges worn by officers such as the sergeants-at-mace and town waits. Today mace-bearers wear badges showing the wolf guarding St Edmund's severed head, which was the crest of the borough's arms (see **aunciante**).

colleccion: money collected for the poor, probably by what was later called a rate.

collectors for the poore: officers who collected contributions for the poor.

combe(s), combs, coombe: a dry measure equal to four bushels or half a quarter.

commodytie: the profit arising from letting out the Guildhall, largely for marriage dinners.

common, comone: (a) not private, e.g. 'common inns' and 'common profit'; (b) usual to a particular group, e.g. 'common hall' and 'common dinner'.

company(e): this word with 'fellowship' was used to describe the residual Candlemas guild after its dissolution.

composicio: composition, payment (often a sum agreed between parties to clear off arrears.)

composicion, composicion money(e): payment agreed upon, either (a) to wipe out accumulated arrears, or (b) in lieu of providing food for the royal household (see **provision**).

compounded: the act of arranging a composition.

compotus: account; thus *vide in compoto '91*: see the account for [15]91.

computans: accountant; *per computantem:* through or by the accountant.

contynuall stocke: see **stock**.

contribucion in the churche: perhaps refers the payment of poor relief in church on Sunday. The Book of Orders makes it clear that many aspects of poor relief were dealt with after Sunday service.

cookqeanestole: cuckingstool, a chair in which offenders were fastened, exposed to public abuse and ducked in water.

copeinge: coping or top course of masonry.

copi(e)hold, copyhold: customary land held by copy of court roll; admittance to a property was entered into the manorial court roll, while the tenant (i.e. copyholder) had a copy of that entry as his title-deed.

coroner: a royal officer who enquired into sudden or unusual deaths. Before 1614, the county coroner had to be summoned if an inquest was required; after that date the immediate past alderman held the office of coroner for the borough of Bury.

corselet(t)es, corsletes, corsletts, coslettes: corslets; armour worn by pikemen to protect the upper half of the body.

costes: costs of a legal action which, by direction of the court, were paid by the losers.

cote clothe for a lyvery: a length of cloth sufficient to make a livery coat.

country: county, one's home district.

covenants: clauses in a lease setting out the obligations of both landlord and tenant.

cownsell: counsel, legal advisers.

crome(s): long-handled hook(s) used to pull burning thatch from the roofs of burning houses. These were usually provided by the community.

craves: asks for, requests.

cryer (of this towne): town cryer, a post filled by one of the beadles (see **beadell**).

cum: with; *cum arreragia:* with the arrears.

cunstable: constable. Usually a parish officer, but in Bury each of the five wards had a constable or constables whose prime function was to keep the peace and collect taxes.

cupbord: a board or table on which cups and other vessels were set out; forerunner of the modern sideboard.

cupbord cloth: a cloth to cover a such a cupboard.

curate: see **mynister**.

curble: a curving edge or border; often used for the circular wooden framework under the brickwork of a well.

currier: one who cured and dyed leather.

cutler: a person who made knives and other cutting instruments; was sometimes employed by the feoffees to maintain the town armour.

daggerdes: daggers, short edged and pointed weapons for thrusting and stabbing.

dawbers: daubers of walls; plasterers or **clayers**.

day of the due thereof: the day on which a payment was due to be made.

de: of, from; *de antiquo*, from an earlier time. Arrears were sometimes split into those which had arisen in the current year and those brought forward.

dead lyme: deadlime, as opposed to quicklime: made inactive by burning.

debere: to owe; *debent:* they owe; *debentur:* they [e.g. debts] are owed; *debet:* he owes, it is necessary; *debetur, debitur:* it is owed, there is owed. *Debet* may also have been used as an English noun, thus 'debt'.

debitum: debt; *debita:* debts; *debiti:* of debt.

debyte: the quotation from Margaret Odeham's will on p.xxii requires the word to mean a person who adheres strictly to the terms of his contract.

decaied, decayed: decreased (rent of a house).

Decembris: of December.

decree: (a) sentence of the court of Chancery, corresponding to a judgement in other courts; (b) the document in which the sentence was written out.

ded, deead: deed.

de(e)d potem: a deed used in the process of levying a fine.

dee: clearly used in these accounts to describe the officer responsible for arranging the company's feast on the account day; 'steward' might be a modern equivalent; origin of the word obscure.

deforciant(s): person(s) who deprived others of land; usually defendant in a process by which a fine of land (a final concord) was levied to assure the title.

demised, demysed, dimised, dymised: demised; used of land transferred by will or lease.

denarius: penny; normally used in plural *denarii:* pence, money.

depending *in super*: awaiting payment, overdue, in arrears.

deponentes: deponents; persons who made statements on oath in a legal suit.

deposicions: depositions, written statements given under oath to be read out in court.

determyned: determined, concluded, ended.

determinatio: determination, conclusion; the closing of an account after audit.

determinacion, determination, determynacion: conclusion, completion, of an account after being audited and found correct.

deu: due.

diaper: a linen fabric with a small woven pattern; used at this date for all patterned linen (damask), not just for small geometrical patterns as today.

diate, diet: diet, food.

dimidia: a half.

dimidius: half.

dirige: dirge; the morning office of the dead, from the antiphon *Dirige Domine Deus* (see also *placebo*).

disbursed: paid, expended.

discharged: waived, forgiven; used when an expected payment was forgiven after further consideration.

dispache: conduct, management of the town's business.

distempred (in her sences): distempered, mentally unbalanced or ill.

distresses: seizures of goods to force their owners to pay a debt or to make recompense for some wrong.

divers(e), dyvers: divers, various; several different kinds.

diversus: divers, various; usually in form *diversis*.

dogges (of yron): dogs, stays, metal straps, e.g. for the kitchen chimney.

dominus: lord; *domini:* of the lord; used in these accounts for year 'of Our Lord'.

dossen, dowsen, dozens: dozen(s) of cloth; ?cloths a dozen yards long.

draper: dealer in cloth.

drawing, drawinge: drawing up, composing (legal documents).

dresse, dressinge the meat: prepare, preparing food; **dressing(e) a corslet:** cleaning and maintaining armour.

dresser bourde: board or table on which food was prepared.

drie fattes: dry vats; ?for the storage of dry goods, as opposed to liquids.

due: the day on which payment was due.

due by bill, due to him by bond: payable under the terms of a bond.

durge: see **dirige**.

dwelling: house, residence.

Elemozyner's Bearnes: Almoner's barns (see also **Ampners**).

Elizabetha: Elizabeth (Queen).

ell, elles: ell, measure of length; an English ell was 45 inches, though by the late sixteenth century it was being replaced by the yard. In Flanders only 27 inches.

elmes: elm trees; **curble of elme:** edge or border of elm wood; frequently used for the curving timber base supporting the brickwork of a well.

engross, ingrosse: engross, write a fair copy in due legal form (literally, to write out in large letters).

entree, entry: gate, door or porch of a building.

eodem: by the same.

equus: even, equal, balanced (of accounts); usually in form *eque*.

esquier, esquire, esquyer: esquire; at this date used only of gentlemen entitled to bear coats of arms; a translation of the Latin word *armiger*.

et: and.

et cetera: and the others; and the rest.

et sic: and thus.

eundem: the same.

ewesbord(e): eavesbord, fixed at the edges of a roof.

examinatur: it is examined, checked [*at the end of accounts*].

examynacion: examination, formally, of an accused person.

excheacour, exchequer: exchequer, court of; originally dealt with matters of revenue, although its jurisdiction was later extended.

executrix: female executor of a will, often a widow.

exercise: a market-day sermon given by one of a rota of preachers, and then discussed by other clergy. Lay people attended and ocassionally contributed to discussion. In the late seventeenth and eighteenth centuries, such sermons became the Wednesday Lectures.

exhibited: shown.

exhibicion: exhibition; the sum paid by the Crown out of the property of the former abbey of St Edmund towards the stipends of the town clergymen.

extent, extenthe: extent, survey.

extinguishement: extinguishment, putting an end to something.

faceinge, facing: facings on clothing, such as collars and cuffs; used in the accounts with reference to the officers' livery coats.

fadame: fathom; a measure of 6 feet, usually used for lengths of rope and soundings.

faggottes, fagottes: faggots, bundles of sticks tied together for firewood.

falling sicknes: epilepsy (*OED*).

fattes: vats; **drie fattes:** dry measure of 8 bushels.

fayinge, feyinge: faying, cleaning, sweeping.

fearme, ferme (rent): farm, rent; paid annually in money or in kind.

fearmor, fearmour, fermer, fermor: farmer, one who rents or leases a property.

feast of the birthe of Christ, of the nativitie of Our Lord God: Christmas. Some of those who copied up these accounts were reluctant to use the word 'Christmas'.

feast of St John Baptiste: 29 August.

fee farme(s), fee fearme: (a) the tenure of land in fee simple, subject to the payment of a perpetual fixed rent; (b) more often, the rent paid for such land.

fellowship(pe), feloweship: fellowship; used, with **company**, for the post-dissolution organisation which developed out of Candlemas guild.

feoda: fees.

feoffees: people to whom land had been conveyed by a deed of feoffment, to enable them to do something or pay something on behalf of others; a form of trusteeship.

feofement, feoffement: feoffment, (a) body of feoffees; or (b) the deed by which land was conveyed to feoffees.

fier: fire; **fier buckettes:** fire buckets (of leather); **fier sholve:** fire shovel.

fift: fifth.

findinge: finding, providing.

fine(s), fyne(s): fine(s); (a) sum of money paid on entering into a lease, or when the remaining years of a lease were assigned to another person; (b) sum paid when new feoffees were admitted to copyhold lands; (c) a type of conveyance known as a fine or final concord, used to strengthen a legal title to land; see also **deforciant** and **playnant**.

finis: the end, as in the phrase *fine (huius) compoti:* at the end of (this) account.

firr poles: wood from fir trees generally used to make scaffolding poles and ladders.

fistula: (medical) an abnormal passage connecting the cavity of one organ with another, or connecting such a cavity with the surface of the body. It can result from disease, surgical error or, occasionally, neglected injury during childbirth.

flynt: flint, a local building stone, often gathered on the surface of fields.

foote: foot, end (of account).

forbearing(e): allowing time for payment after a sum became due.

fraunchise: franchise; royal prerogatives granted to an individual or corporation. The eight and a half hundreds of western Suffolk were given to Bury abbey by Edward the Confessor, and survived as an administrative area after the Dissolution.

free mason: mason working with free stone or ashlar.

free stone: fine-grained, good-quality limestone or sandstone, easy to cut, saw and shape.

freeses, frice, frieses, friezes, frise(s), frize, fryce, fryse(s): frieze, a hard-wearing fabric regularly used for clothing the poor during winter. Edmund Spenser wrote of 'winter clothed all in frize'.

Frenche pockes: French pox, a venereal disease.

furlonges: a furlong was a measurement of length equivalent to 220 yards.

gentleman: man of some local distinction, but not entitled to bear a coat-of-arms.

girdles: belts on which items could be hung, part of the town armour.

gorget: armour for protecting the throat.

gould waightes (pair of): weights for gold and other precious metals.

governes: governess or keeper of the hospital.

grainge, graunge (landes): lands which formerly belonged to St Peter's Hospital at Bury.

gratueties, gratuitie: gratuities; frequently used of presents given to assize judges.

grate of iron: grating over a drain.

gray, grayes, grey(e), grey cloth(e): perhaps Colchester greys, a cheaper kind of cloth in which the weft included noils; often used to clothe the poor.

grocery: provisions such as spices, dried fruit and sugar imported from abroad.

groundsels: groundsells; the lowest horizontal timbers on which a timber-framed building rests; **grounselling:** placing or replacing a decayed groundsell.

guild pott: gyle pot or vat, for fermenting wort in the making of beer.

gunnpowder: gunpowder; explosive mixture of saltpeter, sulphur and charcoal used in guns (see **saltpeter man**).

hangers: loops or straps on sword belts, from which weapons hung.

hanginges: hangings, tapestries around walls of rooms; often painted or embroidered.

hallymot(t) rent: hallmote rent; paid to the lord of a manor, originally at his hall.

harneis, harness, harneys: body armour for a foot soldier.

heading the pikes: renewing the metal spikes on pikes.

hengelles, hingel(l)s: hinges.

herboyer: harbour, shelter; used in the sense of providing the necessities of life.

hereditaments: real property, which could be inherited by the heirs of an owner without any testamentary disposition.

herse with five lights: a funeral herse bearing five candles or torches.

heyle: hail (well).

heynors (of the feast): after the incorporation, persons responsible for organising the annual dinner or feast, after the election and swearing in of the alderman; of unknown origin but clearly the equivalent of **dee** (*q.v.*).

hic: here.

Hil(l)arye terme: a period when courts of law sat; named after the feast of St Hilary, 13 January.

hogeshedde, hogshead: liquid measure of 63 wine gallons; equivalent of 32½ imperial gallons.

holland: linen cloth, sometimes described as 'fine'; could cost as much as 6s. an **ell** (*q.v.*).

hollowe key: a key with a hollow shank.

holy bread: bread consecrated at Holy Communion.

holy water: water blessed and used when the Mass was said in the prison chapel on Sundays and feast days, by the terms of Margaret Odeham's will.

hooch: hutch, chest.

horsemeat(e): meat in the general sense of food; hence, food for horses.

howse of office: a privy.

huius: of this.

hundred: sub-division of a county, which held its own courts and appointed its own constables and bailiffs.

hundred weight (half a): 112 pounds or 8 stones in weight, so half a hundredweight was 56 pounds or 4 stones.

hyre (of his howse): rent.

ibi: there.

ibidem: in the same place.

ideo: therefore.

inclosid: enclosed (land), surrounded by hedges and ditches.

inde: therefrom, out of which.

indenture: a deed created by writing two or more copies on a single skin of parchment and cutting them up with an indented or wavy line. This was for security; the parts laid together made up the whole skin.

inditement: indictment, a formal written accusation.

infeoffed: (person) granted the fee simple of land.

ingrosing, ingrossing: see **engross**.

inprimis, in primis: in the first place, firstly.

in super: (sum of money) left over, not paid when the account was closed.

in service: in service of the cook, that is those who assisted the cook at the dinner.

in suspens: not being executed or paid (found mainly in legal documents).

inquisicion: (a) inquisition, official enquiry; (b) the document recording the enquiry and final decision.

in travell: in travail, in labour, childbirth.

issues: profits; often found in the phrase 'issues and profits'. In the phrase **issues lost in th'exchequier** the word referred to points in dispute between parties.

item: also.

Januarii: of January.

Julii: of July.

justices of assise: judges who rode around the country hearing criminal and civil cases in each county.

kegge: keg, a small barrel or cask which normally did not hold more than 10 gallons.

kening: sharpening, maintaining (weapons and armour).

kepers: keepers, nurses.

king's aide: see **aide**.

kirble: see **curble**.

knight: rank conferred by the sovereign, in recognition of personal merit or services.

know(e)ledge and passinge of a fyne; knowledge and suyinge owte of the fyne: refers to a document in which the parties acknowledge the title to land.

lame: weak or disabled (often as a result of injury to a limb).

land moll, landmoll rent: an ancient rent dating back to the foundation of the borough, paid to the sacrist of the abbey at 2d. an acre. After the Dissolution, these rents were paid first to the crown and then, after 1606, to the new corporation; they were extinguished in 1963.

lath, lathe: thin pieces of riven, not sawn, oak; used to support roofing materials and in walls to support plaster.

lattice: a latice, made from pieces of wood or metal crossing each other and fastened together; often refers to an unglazed window.

leades: leads, particularly the lead roof of the Guildhall.

lecturer: see **preacher**.

Lent: period of forty days between Ash Wednesday and Easter, during which the **Lent assis(s)es** were often held in Bury St Edmunds.

letting: putting money out at interest.

levying: the process involved in a fictitious lawsuit brought by the would-be puchaser of an estate, claiming that the vendor held the land unlawfully. This led to the issue of a document known as a fine or final concord, hence the phrase 'levying a fine'.

libertyes (of th'inhabitauntes in the market): rights and privileges when trading in the town's market, which the abbot and convent had obtained from the Crown.

libra: a pound in either (a) weight or (b) money.

licence (to alyen his lease), lycence of alienacion: licence needed by tenant wishing to transfer property to another person, in leases granted by the feoffees.

lifelode: livelihood.

liver(e)y, liveries, lyv(e)ry: coat(s) forming part of the remuneration of the porter or hall keeper, beadles and sergeants-at-mace. Also **livery coates**.

livery cupboard, liverye cupborde: originally a board or table on which food for doles was set out, but probably used here in the sense of a buffet or sideboard.

lyme to stage: 'to stage' could mean to set up a platform or scaffolding; it is not clear how lime was used.

lynnen: linen, variously described as fine, holland and coarse.

lyvinge: living or stipend of a minister of religion.

Maii: of May.

maimed, maymed: maimed, disabled.

making of 900 of woode: cutting and trimming 900 bundles of firewood.

mannour, manor, manour: estate of a lord who held courts both for the transfer of land and also, in many cases, for petty offenders.

Marcii: of March.

mark, markes: two-thirds of a pound, 13s.4d. A unit of accounting, but never a coin.

Master of the Rolls: a judge in the court of Chancery who also kept its rolls and records.

match: a device made of wick and a piece of cord or rope, which lit easily and burnt steadily; used to fire cannons and other guns. Often appears in the phrase **powder and match**.

meadowe: meadow, hay field.

measuring: in sense of surveying land.

medlies: broad cloth in which wool of various colours had been blended.

memorandum: it is to be remembered.

mener, menure, meynor: manure, compost.

mercer, merser: a merchant who sold goods other than food and bulky heavy wares: specially associated with luxury goods.

messe: a portion of food.

messuage, mesuag(e), mesuages: (a) site on which a dwelling house, garden and ancilliary buildings were erected; (b) such a house and its adjuncts.

Michaelmas: the feast of St Michael the Archangel, 29 September.

Michaelmas quarter: the period from Michaelmas, 29 September, until Christmas.

miles: a **knight** (*q.v.*).

ministri: of the minister, usually meaning the accountant in these accounts (see *computans* and **mynister**).

mocion in the Chauncerie: motion or application to the court of Chancery or a judge to obtain a rule or order.

moitie, moytie: moiety, a half (in legal documents).

moother: mother, used as a term of respect of a woman of the lesser sort.

more: greater, e.g. a **more sum** means a greater sum.

morowe, morrow: the day after.

morter: mortar, the mixture of sand, lime and water used in stone and brick walls.

muster: an assembly, with inspection, of men liable for military service, aged between sixteen and sixty.

muster master: the officer who inspected those attending a muster.

mutton, muttons: lamb or sheep prepared for eating.

mynister: minister of religion; from 1593 until the 1840s, each of the two Bury churches had two clergymen, one called the minister or curate, and the other called the preacher or lecturer (see Introduction, pp.xxxix, xlvii).

nayles: a nail was a measurement, 2¼ inches; used when silk fabric was purchased for a beadle's coat.

nealing: annealing, tempering, firing of an oven as it was constructed.

nulla: literally 'no things', nothing.

nurse children: foster children.

nurssing: fostering, caring for and bringing up orphan children who were the town's responsibility.

obit: commemoration of, and thanksgiving for, a dead person

obligacion, obligation: bond, usually to secure re-payment of money on loan.

obolus: a half penny.

Octobris: of October.

offringes, offrings: contributions towards the stipends of the town clergy. These contributions were probably not voluntary but assessed at so much per house.

okes: oak trees.

omnes: all; *omnium*: of all.

onus: load or burden, used of rents and other sums which the accountant had to collect during his year (in English the **charge**); *onere compoti:* in the charge of the account; *oneris predicti:* of the aforesaid charge; *adhuc onus:* the charge thus far.

ordinary: a set meal; in an inn the equivalent of a *table de hôte* meal. In relation to the feoffees' dinner, it may have implied some optional extras as well as a 'set meal'.

otemeale: oatmeal.

otemeale woode: ?perhaps the straw of oats, possibly used for bedding for the poor.

Our Ladie daie, Our Ladye daye: the feast of the Annunciation of the Blessed Virgin Mary, 25 March.

oute rentes, out rent, owt rentes: rents paid by the holder, either to the Crown or some other lord.

pales: paling, wooden fence.

parcell(es), percell: sometimes used to indicate items on a bill for building work.

parish clerke: a parish officer, usually appointed by incumbent, who had various duties in church, including leading the responses. The parish clerk of St James's was also responsible for the library.

pardonare: to pardon; *pardonantur:* (they) are pardoned; e.g. in the phrase *pardonantur arreragia:* arrears are pardoned; *pardonatur:* (it or he) is pardoned; e.g. *pardonatur pro pauperetate:* pardoned on account of poverty.

particuler: detail, as in a bill.

pasport (of his captayne): a permit authorising a discharged soldier to travel to a given destination, if necessary begging as he went.

pasture: area of grass for grazing, less valuable than meadow.

patet: it appears; often *ut patet:* as it appears.

pauper: poor person (could be Latin or English).

pauperitas: poverty; *pauperitate, pauperetate:* through or by poverty.

payes: payments, used when a large sum was paid by instalments.

paynes: pains, effort and care taken in performing a task.

pes: foot, end; as in the phrase *in pede compoti:* at the foot of the account.

Pentecost: Whitsunday, the seventh Sunday after Easter.

penthowses: sloping projections to deflect rain from windows or doors; canopies or porches; also **penthowsinge windowes**.

per: by or through; *per annum:* by the year, yearly; *per composicionem:* by composition, by an agreed sum; *per computantem:* by the accountant; *per rentale:* by the rental.

perch(es): a measure of length and area, with many localised variants; the standard length of a perch was 5½ yards.

perticuler(s): see **particuler**.

Doctor of Phisick: the university degree taken by a medical man or doctor.

pightell, pightle: a small field or enclosure.

pikes: weapons with iron or steel heads on long poles (up to 16 or 18 feet long); used by infantry.

pillory, pillarye: an instrument of punishment which secured an offender by the neck and arms in a standing position.

pillowbeer(e)s: pillow cases.

placebo: name for the Vespers of the Dead, recited in church on the night before a funeral, so called because of the word with which the office opened. The *placebo* and *dirige* formed part of Jankin Smith's anniversary.

placing: apprenticing (a boy).

plagge: plague.

planchering, planshering: planking, boarding; often used for boarding floors or panelling walls. In *Measure for Measure* Shakespeare wrote of a 'planched' gate to the vineyard.

plea, plea in th'exchequer: a law suit in the Court of Exchequer.

playnant, pleynants: complainant, plaintiff; in connection with a **fine** (*q.v.*), the plainant sought to strengthen his title to disputed land.

plomber, plommer, ploomer: plumber, one who worked lead.

plotting: making a map, plan or diagram.

pollards: trees of which the heads were regularly cut, at some height above the ground, to encourage the new growth of straight branches.

pooles: poles of tents, for housing those infected with plague.

porter: an officer of the company who acted as cleaner and caretaker of the Guildhall, kept and trained bloodhounds for apprehending malefactors, and carried messages to members about deaths.

postea: afterwards.

post fine, post fyne: a duty paid to the Crown for licence to levy a fine.

pottell (of claret wine) (of sack): pottle, a liquid measure equivalent to four pints or half a gallon.

poulder, powder and match: powder and match; gunpowder, and the means of firing it (see **match**).

praye allowance: a phrase often used by accountants when requesting reimbursement for an item of expenditure.

preacher: from 1593 until the 1840s, each Bury church had a preacher or lecturer, as well as a minister or curate (see Introduction, pp.xxxix, xlvii).

precedent yeare: the previous year.

precedens: preceding; *precedentis:* of the preceding (year).

predictus: aforesaid.

prefect: chosen, elected.

prentise: apprentice.

presentlie: shortly.

Prince's aide: see **aide**.

priores: former.

probacion: used of preachers on trial for their fitness to be appointed one of the town preachers.

proces(s): the word used to describe all the proceedings in a legal action; also **cease proces:** abandon a case (f.24r).

proclamacions: formal orders from the Crown, either announced by a herald or posted in a public place.

prohibere: to prohibit; *prohibitur per concensum:* it is forbidden by agreement.

pro: for.

prosecutinge, proseqution: the carrying out or carrying through of a law suit.

provision (of Hir Highenes howsold) (Kings): the requisitioning and collection of provisions and other things necessary for the royal household, at a price fixed by an official called a purveyor; it also involved the taking of horses and carts necessary to carry these goods. Also **provision of the navy:** collection of money or foodstuffs for the navy.

proximus: next; *proximo:* at or in the next; *proximo compoto:* in the next account.

pursivantes: pursuivants, royal or state messengers.

putt (in bond): to obtain a bond from a person to ensure that a payment would be made or a task performed.

pynne: (a) to pin, to fasten with pegs or nails; (b) to underpin, as in phrases such as **pynne the well** and **pynnyng the wall**.

quaire, quayer, quier: quire of paper, four sheets of paper doubled to give eight leaves.

quarter: (a) a quarter of beef, one of the four quarters of the animal, each with a limb; (b) a quarter of a **hundredweight** (*q.v.*) or 2 stones; (c) upright studs for supporting panelling and partitions, as in the phrase **quarters to staye the seeling**.

-que: suffix meaning 'and'; e.g. *annoque:* 'and in the year'.

quenche: to extinguish (a fire).

quia: because, on account of; as in the phrase *quia in manibus ministri:* because [it is] in the hands of the official [accountant].

quietus: quit, settled.

quindecims: fifteenths, a tax.

quisshens: cushions.

rakes, a pair of: part of the equipment provided to set the poor to work (with spinning wheels and cards).

raising (the Guildhall 2s.0d. a weeke): probably means that the Guildhall had been assessed at that sum each week.

ralles, rayle(s): rails, bars of wood fixed horizontally.

raynbarrs: probably the same as **penthowses** (*q.v.*).

re-entry: resuming possession of lands or tenements which had been sold or let to another person.

receipt: often used of money received from rents on specified days.

receiver, receivor(s), receyver, receyvor(s), receyvour, recyvors, resceover: the feoffees' financial officer, still used in the phrase 'Clerk and Receiver'. In earlier accounts it was used alongside **surveyor** (see **survayor**).

recited: given, mentioned, e.g. **the same some [sum] last recited**.

reckoning, reckonning: calculation, computation.

receptus: received; often in the form of *recepto*.

recte: correctly.

redditus: rent; *redditus resolutus:* rents paid out, out-rents; used for rents paid by the feoffees to others, sometimes called **rent resolute**.

redeme: redeem, buy back.

redinge post: riding post, that is, 'at great speed'. During Queen Elizabeth's progress through the eastern counties, men rode out to carry official messages.

redemcion: redemption, buying back, by order of the Commissioners for Charitable Uses, of properties which had formerly been sold improperly.

regina: queen; *reginae:* to or of the queen.

release: disclaimer by a person who had a right or interest in lands. Also **absolute release**.

remaining on his head: meaning that the tenant still owed rent.

remanere: to remain; *remanet:* there or it remains; *remanet clare:* there remains clear; *remanet computanto:* there remains to the accountant; *remanet non receptum:* there remains not received.

remaynder: money remaining at the end of an accounting period.

remembraunces: remembrances, matters to be considered or things to be done; a favourite word of John Mallowes.

rentale: rental, rent-book.

rental(l), rentalles: document(s) recording the rents due from an estate during a year;

sometimes annotated to show those rents actually received, or to serve as a draft for the next year, indicating any changes in tenants or rents to be paid.

rent resolute, rents resolutes: rents paid out, out-rents; used for rents which the feoffees paid to the Crown or to some other lord.

reparaciones: repairs; *reparacionibus:* to or for repairs.

reparacions, repayracions, reperacions: repairs.

replegiamentum: replevin; redelivery to the owner of property pledged as security.

requiem: a mass offered for the dead.

resceipte: see **receipt**.

reservacions: in sense of covenants or conditions under which a lease was granted; used especially of rights reserved to the lessor, perhaps that of felling timber or digging brick earth. Also **reserved upon his lease**.

respite: postponement of the day on which payment was to be made.

rest due to: remains owing to.

resteth: remains.

revercion: reversion, the return either to the grantor or to a new grantee on the completion of an existing term.

reyny: rainy (weather).

ringers: bell ringers.

roages: rogues.

roode(s): a measurement of area, equivalent to one quarter of an acre.

rowf tiles, ruff tiles: roof tiles.

rundlet: runlet, a container for liquid, varying in size from as little as a pint to 18½ gallons.

Sabothe: Sabboth, Sunday.

sack: white wine imported from Spain and the Canary Islands.

St Michaell th'archangell: feast of St Michael or Michaelmas, 29 September, a quarter day when rent was usually paid and when the accounting year often ended.

saltpeter man: saltpetre man; authorised to enter property to seek for and remove nitrogenous matter which could be made into saltpetre, which was the main ingredient of gunpowder and was also used medicinally.

sangred: originally a weekly reading of the bede-roll to invite prayers for the souls of the dead; East Anglian equivalent of a 'certain'. Mentioned in Margaret Odeham's will.

sargant, sargent, serjauntes: (a) sergeant-at-law, barrister; (b) also used, after 1606, for the sergeants of mace or mace-bearers of the borough.

satisfaccion: satisfaction, payment of a debt in full.

sawers: sawyers, those who sawed wood.

scituat: situated, located.

scouring: cleaning (armour which belonged to the town).

scovels: shovels.

scrivener: a professional writer; employed by those who could not write, or for drafting formal documents where special legal knowledge was required.

scruses: screws, as in the phrase 'shores and scruses' when the Market Cross was shored up and scaffolded (see **shores**).

sealing, seelinge: making ceilings.

seised: seized, in possession of land.

seke: sick.

seller: cellar.

serten: certain.

service: refers to placing of apprentices, often by indenture, to work for a master.

sessions: Quarter Sessions; **sessions dynner:** a dinner held at the time of Quarter Sessions.

set on work: find employment (for the poor).

sett owt: make a survey or plan (of land); sometimes used for marking the boundaries of land when a lease was drawn up.

setting forth: providing and equipping a man for military service.

setting the streete; setting the way: repairing the surface of a road.

severall, severallie: individual, individually.

sexten, sextyn: sexton, an officer who cared for the church and churchyard.

sheetes: (a) sheets or bed linen provided for the assize judges; (b) the winding sheets or shrouds used for burying the poor.

sherman: shearman, one who sheared woollen cloth in the finishing stages of making broadcloth.

shewe of armes: show of arms, muster, when armour and weapons were inspected.

sholve: shovel.

shores: in sense of props, pieces of timber or iron used to prop up a building in danger of collapsing.

shortning: reducing (a debt).

sic: thus.

sick(e) howse: sickhouse, hospital; St Peter's Hospital in Bury.

sickenes, sicknes: sickness, illness; often refers to plague, but also to infectious diseases such as smallpox.

signum: sign or mark of a person who did not make a full signature.

sincke, sinke, synke: drain.

skalt: scalded.

skoring, skowringe: scouring, cleaning (armour provided by the feoffees).

solucio: payment; used on a few occasions instead of *allocacio*. Always abbreviated, so the true reading may be *soluciones*.

soluciones: payments; *solucionum:* of payments.

solutus: paid; *soluti aldermanno:* paid to the alderman; *solutus in proximo compoto:* paid in the next account; *solutus ut patet:* paid as appears.

somer assises, sommer asisses: summer assizes.

sonderye, sondrie, sondry: sundry, various.

sore: painfully.

sowder: solder, an alloy used to join pieces of metal, e.g. in lead roofs.

sparres: spars, poles or pieces of timber; possibly a roof rafter.

spickyns: spikings, spike nails. Salzman cites their use to fix corner tiles.

spyttes: spits, pointed rods of metal on which meat was turned over an open fire.

spitlehowse, spittell, spittil, spittle (howse): hospital (without its first syllable).

spent: in sense of used or consumed, e.g. of wine.

splent(es), splentburd: splints, laths; thin, flexible lengths of riven, not sawn, wood.

splent bonde, splent bynd(e), splenting bondes: string or cord used to fasten laths or splints. Also **splente yarne.**

spone: spoon.

stalle: stall, probably for trading; for example in Punch (now Athenaeum) Lane in Bury which was one side of an open space called les Rowes.

stand bound, stand bownd, standeth bounde, stonde bownde, stoode bound: used of a person who had entered into a bond to do or to pay something.

standes: stands, trees left to grow and to provide large timber.

staveinge: fitting staves or rungs into ladders.

staye: stay, stop or delay; as when an item in an account was queried and its payment was stayed or held up.

stipende, stypend: salary paid to the town clergy.

stock, stocke: (a) stock of money or capital, on which the feoffees were assessed for taxation; (b) money given or raised to buy materials for the poor to work on; a **contynuall stocke** was a sum of money used e.g. to buy wool, which the poor would spin and weave into cloth, and from the sale of which more wool could be bought and the process repeated.

stockes (for the bushell): ?a wooden frame supporting the official bushell measure.

stockardes, stock cards: cards set in a wooden stock or handle (see **cardes**).

stone setter: a builder who worked with stone but was inferior to a stone mason.

stool, stoolles: pew(s) or other seat(s) in church.

stoppe: (a) to stop or block up; (b) to stuff or fill (cushions).

studdes: studs, vertical posts in walling.

studding: the setting up of studs.

sturgion: sturgeon, a large 'royal' fish (specimens washed onshore belonged to the sovereign), prized as food and as a source of caviar.

subpena, subpoena, sub poenaes: subpoena; at this date a writ under which people were called upon to appear and answer a bill of complaint in Chancery.

subsedy, subsedye, subside, subsidie, subsidy: a tax granted to the sovereign by parliament.

sued owt: to have taken legal action.

suger: sugar.

sugar loaf, sugar loaves, suger loffe, suger loves: cone(s) of hard, refined white sugar.

sui: his.

suit, sute, suyte: an action at law.

summa: sum, total; *summa allocacionum:* total of the amounts expended; *summa annualium redditum:* total of annual rents; *summa debiti:* total of debt; *summa oneris:* total of the charge; *summa patet:* the total is shown; *summa solucionum:* the total of payments. *summa totalis:* sum total.

sondrie, sunderye, sundrie, sundry: sundry, various.

super: upon, over, above.

super, supers: shortened form of **in super**, meaning the balance left over; used regularly of rents which were due, but not paid, during the period of the account.

super(s) *de antiquo:* old arrear(s), carried forward from previous years.

super(s) *de novo:* arrear(s) due in the current account.

suretie: surety, security; given to ensure that a payment would be made or some action carried out, e.g. that a person would appear in court on a given day.

surgen, surgion: surgeon.

surplusage: deficit; the receiver was said to be in surplusage when he had spent more than he had received from rents, etc.

surplusagium: surplusage, deficit; hence *in surplusagio:* in deficit.

surrendring: giving up property or tenures, e.g. a lease before its term had ended.

survayor, surveior(s), surveyer, surveyor: (a) the person who supervised the feoffees' estates; (b) occasionally used of one who mapped or described the estate.

suspencion: prohibition from carrying out an office, e.g. from preaching in one of the churches.

suyinge owte of the fyne, suyng out the fine: taking legal action to obtain a final concord.

sweeping the dore: presumably means cleaning the approach to the Guildhall door.

sythens: since.

table (in the Guildhall): in 1610 was used in the sense of a table on which the names of the feoffees were painted. Such a table was provided in 1523–4 (compare the surviving example in the hall of the Great Hospital in Norwich).

taffeta, taffetye: taffeta, a plain woven glossy silk; a very expensive fabric, for 2s.4d was paid for 3 nails (6¾ inches) in 1618.

taske: consistently used of the tax usually known as the tenths and fifteenths; originally assessed on a tenth and a fifteenth respectively of a person's personal property, but the sums involved had by this period long been fixed.

taxacion: often used of a rate levied for poor relief or church repair.

tempest: a violent storm.

tenement(e), tenementes: used of any property, but often referring to a dwelling house.

tenth(e), tenths: (a) tax of the tenths and fifteenths, see **taske** above; (b) the yearly tenth was a fixed annual payment to the Crown from ecclesiastical livings.

tenure: the holding of property.

terrar: terrier, document in which land was described, usually by means of abuttals.

term(e) of St Michaell: one of the four legal terms during which courts sat; took its name from the feast of St Michael, 29 September.

testament: document disposing of real property (as opposed to a will).

thatchinge roddes: rods used in fixing thatch to a roof.

thred, thredd: almost certainly sewing thread; may be assumed to be of linen, unless specified as silk thread.

tile pines, tile pynne, tyle pynne, tyle pyns: nails used to fix tiles.

timber, tymber: large pieces of wood used in buildings, in contrast to smaller pieces used for firewood, hand-tools, etc.

tithe, tithes: tenth part of the produce of agriculture originally set aside to support the parish clergy. After the dissolution of the monasteries, tithes which had been appropriated by monastic houses came into the hands of lay people.

title of supers: list of those in arrears with their rent (see **super**).

tonges: fire tongs.

to take the knowledg: to acknowledge the title to land.

totus: all; *in toto*: in all; *in toto debet:* in all he owes.

towchinge: touching, in the sense of concerning, in connection with.

towles and customes: tolls and other payments made by market traders.

town, towneship, towneshipp: a town or other community which had not been incorporated as a borough.

town: used adjectivally of the town's possessions, e.g. **armour**.

town house: (a) a house which belonged to the feoffees; (b) sometimes a synonym for the Guildhall.

trayling: travelling.

treasury, treash', treshry: used of the metal 'safe' in which the town's money was kept; set into a wall in the room over the Guildhall's porch.

trimming, trymmynge, trymyng: (a) cleaning, putting into good repair (armour); (b) **trymming for Allingtons cote:** special embellishments on a livery coat.

tyle pynne, tyle pyns: see **tile pines**.

unde: whence, out of which.

uphoulde: support, prop up.

use money: interest, payment received in return for a loan of money.

ut: as; *ut in compoto:* as [shown] in the account; *ut patet:* as it appears.

vacare: to be vacant; *vacat:* it is vacant.

veale: veal, calf prepared for eating.

verte: turn over (page).

victuals: food, provisions.

videre: to see; *vide:* see, look for (command); *vide in finem proximi compoti:* see at the end of the following account.

videlicet: that is to say, namely. The modern 'viz' or 'vizt.' is an abbreviated form of this word.

view: an inspection of armour at a **muster**.

visited with: infected with, struck down (by an infectious disease).

void: unoccupied, uninhabited.

ware: were.

ward, wardes: a sub-division of a town and city. Bury had five wards: the high or Risbygate ward, the north ward and the east ward were in St James's parish, and the south and west wards were in St Mary's. The official normally associated with each ward was its constable; in 1594, in the first reference so far found, several overseers were appointed for each of the wards.

warrant: permission, authority to do something

watching the gates: keeping a watch on those who came into or left the town, especially so that grain was not taken away in time of famine.

wateringe, watering place: a place where cattle could drink water.

wax, waxe: sealing wax.

waytes: waits, musicians, usually players of wind instruments, retained by the town.

Wedinsdaie exercise: see **exercise**.

wench: a girl.

weather, wether, wether sheep: a castrated ram.

wheles, wollen wheles: spinning wheels.

white bricks: bricks made from clay found in a number of places near Bury (notably at Woolpit).

wiefe, wieves, wife: wife, wives.

winche: ?a well wheel for drawing up water.

windinge sheete(s), winding sheates, winding sheet: see **sheets** above.

wood: thin branches used for light building work or firewood, as opposed to **timber** which was larger and used for structural purposes. A number of words are used in connection with wood. 'Making' means cutting and trimming in preparation for transporting. 'Two hundred and a half of wood' may, it is suggested, mean two hundred and fifty bundles. The meaning of '**one bind woode**' has not been discovered.

woode making: cutting and trimming firewood.

writ(t): a legal document commanding that something should be done in the course of a legal action.

wyned: ?wainscotted, panelled (of forms).

Notes on People

The names of feoffees for the earlier period covered by these account books are taken from Woodward's Register; the page references have already been given in Appendix 6. From 1572 the deeds of general refeoffment, which are also set out there, have been used. The feoffees' Minute Book, H2/6/2.1, has provided additional information. The Grammar School charter, E5/9/101.1, names the governors in 1550. The Minute Book of the governors of the Grammar School, E5/9/202.1, has been especially helpful as governors were replaced as soon as a vacancy occurred; sometimes the date of death is given, or at least there is a date before which a man had died. These books also helped to provide information about the Corporation members from 1606. There are no Corporation minutes before 1652, so many sources have been used to reconstitute the membership of the Corporation in its earliest years. Lists of Corporation members are given in the three charters, D1/1/1, D1/2/1 and D1/3/1. Those who worked to obtain the incorporation are named in both Thomas Bright's chamberlain's account for 1606–7, D6/4/1, and in the memoranda he made in a book containing a survey of the manor of Brettes in Hepworth, H1/4/16.

This basic information has been augmented by information from any other source that has come to hand: assignment of lease of the toll house, 1610, D7/4/1; licence granted to Francis Pinner by the alderman and burgesses to use a rebuilt house as a common inn, 22 August 1611, SROI HD1538/170/24; order inviting foreign weavers to introduce their craft into the town, 26 October 1622, D11/2/3; lease of Horne Meadow, 1613, D7/7/2; chamberlain's patents 1 April 1616 and 12 April 1632, D11/1/1 and 2; chamberlain's notifications, 1 April 1616 and 20 March 1628, D11/1/1/6 and 7; the conveyance of the Almoner's Barns estate in 1609, C7/2/3, for the occupations of men who (if described at all) were usually called 'gentleman': indenture for the return of a member of Parliament, 1621, D13/1/2; coroner's inquests, 1621–87, D11/11/1.

A number of other documents have provided information about individuals: Bartholemew Brokesby's account of charges for the purchase of the concealed lands, 1569, H1/1/9; letter from Lord Keeper Bacon to his son, 1573, Joseph Regenstein Library, Chicago University, Redgrave Bacon Letter 4127; agreement between the inhabitants and the feoffees, 1585, C2/2; memorandum of election to the company, 1582, H2/1/1(b); almshouse regulations, 1582, H2/1/1(a); William Baker's release of his interest in the town lands, 1590, H1/1/1; deponents who gave evidence in the tithe cause in 1593 gave their age and place of birth, which has been an added bonus in preparing these notes, C7/2/9; papers relating to Dr Perse's bequest, D2/3/1.3; conveyance of a house in Hatter Street to John Mallowes, 1597, HB502/2/6; deed of land in Hartest to which John Mallowes was a party, 1599, E3/10/68.1; minutes of the Corporation, 1652–91, D4/1/2.

Wills have been extensively used. Probate records for the court of the Archdeacon of Sudbury are listed as IC500; the registered copies of wills which have generally been used are IC500/2, followed by the number of the register and folio concerned. In a few cases original wills, listed under IC500/1 followed by the number denoting the annual bundle, were pressed into service. Also invaluable were the photographic copies of wills of Bury residents proved in the Prerogative Court of Canterbury at SROB, 1406–1584, Acc. 1652, and 1585–1604, Acc. 1765. Photographic copies of wills of Bury people proved at Norwich during the seventeenth century are also available at Bury, Acc. 2043. In these notes, the court in which a will was proved is indicated at the end of each note.

Persons are assumed to be of Bury St Edmunds unless otherwise stated. There was often more than one person of the same name, so it is possible that some have been confused. Details of the gifts of those described as benefactors will be found in Appendix 8 under the year indicated.

Printed sources used in preparing these notes are:

Bright, J.B., *The Brights of Suffolk* (Boston, Mass., 1858)

Anonymous, 'Condition of the Archdeaconry of Sudbury 1603', *PSIA* xi (1901)

Corder, Joan, *A Dictionary of Suffolk Arms*, SRS, vii (1965)

Corder, Joan (ed) *The Visitation of Suffolk, 1561*, 2 vols., Harleian Society's Publications, new series, ii (1981), iii (1984)

Craig, John S., *Reformation, Politics and Polemics: the Growth of Protestantism in East Anglian Market Towns, 1500–1610* (Aldershot, 2001)

Davis, W.G., *The Ancestry of Mary Isaac* (Portland, Maine, 1955)

Dictionary of National Biography

Dovey, Zillah, *An Elizabethan Progress: the Queen's Journey into East Anglia 1578* (Stroud, 1996)

Ford, J.C., Aldermen and Mayors of Bury St Edmunds, 1302–1896 (n.d.) (a compilation of manuscript notes and press cuttings, at SROB on open shelves)

Foss, Edward, *A Biographical Dictionary of the Judges of England . . .1066–1870* (1870)

Gage, John, *The History and Antiquities of Hengrave in Suffolk* (1822)

Gage, John, *The History and Antiquities of Suffolk: Thingoe Hundred* (1838)

Gipps, Bryan, *History of the Gipps Family* (privately printed, n.d.)

Hasler, P.W. (ed.) *The History of Parliament: the House of Commons 1558–1603*, ii, *Members D–L* (1981)

Hervey, S.H.A. *Biographical List of Boys educated at King Edward VI Free Grammar School . . .* (Bury St Edmunds, 1908)

Hervey, S.H.A. (ed.) *Suffolk in 1524: being a return for a subsidy granted in 1523* (Woodbridge, 1910)

Hervey, S.H.A. (ed.) *Suffolk in 1568: being the return for a subsidy granted in 1566* (Bury St Edmunds, 1909)

Hervey, S.H.A. (ed.) *Rushbrooke Parish Registers, 1567–1850, with Jermyn and Davers Annals*, Suffolk Green Books, vi (Woodbridge, 1903)

Hervey, S.H.A., *Denham Parish Registers, 1539–1850* (Bury St Edmunds, 1904)

Lobel, M.D., 'A list of the Aldermen and Bailiffs of Bury St Edmunds from the twelfth to the sixteenth century', *PSIA*, xxii (1934)

MacCulloch, Diarmaid (ed.) 'Henry Chitting's Suffolk Collections', *PSIA*, xxxiv (1978)

MacCulloch, Diarmaid, *Suffolk and the Tudors: Politics and Religion in an English County, 1500–1600* (Oxford, 1986)

Martin, G., *The Story of Colchester* (1959)

Metcalfe, Walter C. (ed.) *The Visitations of Suffolk . . .1561, 1577 and 1612* (Exeter, 1882)

Muskett, Joseph James, *Suffolk Manorial Families . . .*, 3 vols (privately printed, 1900, 1908)

Northeast, Peter (ed.) *Wills of the Archdeaconry of Sudbury, 1439–1474*, vol. 1, SRS, xliv (2001)

Rupp, Gordon, *William Bedell, 1571–1642* (Cambridge, 1972)

Smith, A.H., *County and Court: government and politics in Norfolk 1558–1603* (Oxford, 1974)

Smith, A.H. and Baker, G.M. (eds.) *The Papers of Nathaniel Bacon of Stiffkey*, Norfolk Record Society, xlvi (1979)

Statham, Margaret, 'John Baret of Bury' in Livia Visser-Fuchs (ed.) *The Ricardian*, xiii (2003, forthcoming)

Tittler, Robert, *Nicholas Bacon: the making of a Tudor Statesman* (1976)

'Transcription of the Parish Registers of St Mary's church, Bury St Edmunds' (typescript, n.d., at SROB on open shelves)

Tymms, Samuel, *Wills and Inventories from the Registers of the Commissary of Bury St Edmunds and the Archdeacon of Sudbury*, Camden Society, xlix (1850)

Tymms, Samuel, *An Architectural and Historical Account of the Church of St Mary, Bury St Edmunds* (Bury St Edmunds, 1854)

Venn, J. and J.A. (eds.) *Alumni Cantabrigienses. Part I, from the earliest times to 1751*, 4 vols. (Cambridge, 1922–4)

Walton, Issak, 'Life of Sir Henry Wotton' in *Lives by Isaak Walton* (Oxford, World's Classics, 1940)

Abbreviations

ac.	acre(s)	exec.	executor
adm.	admitted	*fl.*	*floruit*, flourished
admon.	letters of administration.	governor	governor of the Grammar School
b.	born	incorp.	incorporated
bap.	baptised	IPM	Inquisition *post mortem*
BCC	burgess of the common council	J	baptised, married or buried at
bur.	buried		St James's church
c.	*circa*	m.	married
Cambs.	Cambridgeshire	M	baptised, married or buried at
Ches.	Cheshire		St Mary's church
CB	chief or capital burgess	Nfk	Norfolk
crt	court	p.	priest
d.	died	pr.	proved
dcn	deacon	R.	Rector
dau.	daughter	s.	son
dep.	deputy	V.	Vicar
DNB	*Dictionary of National*	w.	wife
	Biography	wo.	widow
educ.	educated	ygr	younger

ADAMS, Anthony: *fl. c.*1615–22; lessee of part of the Angel/Castle; governor from 16 Dec. 1625.

ALMAN, William: gentleman, notary public; d. 2 Dec. and bur. M 5 Dec.1595; member of the company 1590; governor from 31 Dec. 1589; presumably either the brother or cousin of that name, both of Bury, mentioned by William Alman, clerk of the peace for Suffolk, 1582–5, in his will pr. 1585; gave book to library.

ANDREWS, Thomas: yeoman 1550, but usually esquire; s. of Thomas Andrews (also feoffee *c.*1517–46) and Amy, dau. of Thomas Hewer of Oxborough, Nfk (see also Boldero, John); educ. three years at Oxford and four at Cambridge, B.Civ. Law, 1541–2; adm. Middle Temple 11 May 1558; m. Susan Allen of London; bur. J 20 Jan. 1585; feoffee 1555–85; receiver of Smith's 1570, 1571, all properties 1579, 1580; before 1584 had given four shovels and two great cromes against fire; signed almshouse regulations, 1582; governor, 1550–85; gave 116 books to school library – of those which survive one has a handsome hand-painted heraldic book plate and another appears to have the signature of Martin Bucer in it; MP for Sudbury 1563; often acted on behalf of the Lord Keeper, and was seal-bearer in Sir Nicholas's funeral procession; feodary and under-steward of the Liberty of St Edmund; clerk of the Western Assize circuit 1560–9; from 1578 solicitor to the University of Cambridge; resident justice in the town, moderate in religious matters, at times opposed the Puritan justices of West Suffolk; had brother Edmund not had issue, his estate would have gone to the governors; Edward Hewer, the earliest person to endow exhibitions for the school was a member of his mother's family; wills of this period give the impression that Thomas Andrews was often chosen as godfather, executor or supervisor by his friends and colleagues; PCC will not executed, admon. issued.

ANNABLE, John: porter or beadle of the hall 1582–9; beadle of the school 26 Feb. 1591; ?J A £2 in lands, West Ward, 1568 subsidy.

ASHFIELD, Robert: knight of Stowlangtoft; d.1613; feoffee 1588–1613; influential Puritan JP in the Bury area; sometimes appointed commissioner to investigate allegations of shortcomings of feoffees – this is no doubt why his fine italic signature is to be found in the benefactors' book, H1/2/1; gave book to library.

ASHWELL, Stephen: maltster, a benefactor, Appendix 8, *sub* 1624; bur. M 11 November

1624, capital burgess; feoffee 1606–24; capital burgess 1606–24; in 1617 the feoffees paid him £16 13s.4d. interest on a loan he had made to them.

ATHERTON, George: bur. M 4 Mar. 1600; 'a servaunte of the house' 1574–5; beadle, 1599.

ATKINS, John: surgeon; *fl.* 1596–1622.

AUSTIN, Robert: bur. M 6 Jan. 1620, the beadle; beadle of St Mary's parish, 1613–19.

AVIS, Edmund: of Bradfield St Clare; *fl.* 1603–11; executor of Peter Kembold, *q.v.*; a man of this name was given relief of 1s.6d. in 1618.

AXTON, William: clothier; bur. M 21 July 1579; feoffee 1569–79; keeper of the Guildhall and alderman 1571; accountant, Smith's etc. 1572 , 1573; PCC will.

BACON, Nicholas: knight, lawyer, Lord Keeper of Great Seal, benefactor, see Appendix 8, *sub* 1580; b. 1509; s. of Robert Bacon and Isabel, dau. of John Cage of Pakenham; d. 1579; feoffee *c.*1564–79; keeper of Guildhall and alderman 1573, when James Wright, *q.v.*, acted as his deputy; entertained on Henow Heath, summer 1573; Lord Keeper of Great Seal from 1558; distinguished lawyer who, despite great involvement with matters of state, maintained many interests in the town; from time to time appointed to enquire into the conduct of fellow feoffees; in *DNB*.

BACON, Nicholas, jun: knight, baronet of Redgrave; b. *c.*1543, eldest s. of Sir Nicholas, *q.v.*; d. 1624; knighted at Norwich 22 August 1578 during Elizabeth's progress through the Eastern counties; one of puritan JPs removed from bench, 1583; opposed incorporation; created baronet, 1611; involved in litigation against feoffees and corporation; in *DNB*.

BACON, Thomas: citizen and salter of London; eldest s. of Robert Bacon and Isabel, dau. of John Cage of Pakenham; elder brother of Sir Nicholas, *q.v.*; member of Salters' Company before 1536; elected MP for London, 1545; his wife d. 1563, after which he seems to have retired and lived quietly until his death, sometime after 1573 on the evidence of these accounts; had entered land formerly belonging to Nicholas Platt, and which had been conveyed to the feoffees by William Tassell, under an extent for the recovery of debts, 1571–3.

BADBY, Thomas: esquire; m. J 3 Dec. 1562 to Mary dau. of John Eyer; d. 1583; feoffee from *c.*1569 until death; alderman 1575; accountant of the Hepworth land, Smith's and others, and Tassell's 1574; in following year of these and also Jermyn's annuity; said to have given the Shire House to the feoffees, but £10 was paid for it 1580; signed almshouse regulations, 1582; one of Puritan JPs removed from bench, 1583; lived in the house John Eyer had made out of abbey buildings – shown in early oil painting in Manor House Museum; it was in this house that he entertained the Queen during her 1578 progress.

BAKER, Thomas: *fl.* ?1594, 1606–24; perhaps TB bur. M 14 Aug. 1637 of the plague, baker; one of this name was overseer, South Ward, 1594; feoffee 1606–15; CB 1606; removed from that office 1624; in 1600 the feoffees lent him the charter of the liberties of Bury to take to London in connection with the collection of purveyance in the town; when the feoffment was being renewed in 1615, refused to sign, alleging that the feoffees owed him large sums of money – see Introduction, p.xxx.

BAKER, William: clothier; d. 8 Dec. and bur. J 10 December 1590; feoffee 1545–90; governor from 1550; in 1583 was the last survivor of governors named in the charter; the feoffees brought a suit in Chancery against him in 1590 whereon he relinquished his interest in the town lands – see Introduction, p.xxx.

BARBER, Roger: esquire; m. J 9 Apr. 1572 Mary Boldero; d. 20 and bur. J 21 June 1606; signed account for 1579; feoffee 1582–1606; accountant of profits belonging to the township, 1582 and 1583; accountant of new purchased land and Tassell's 1588 and 1594; alderman 1587; governor 1589–1606; signed almshouse regulations, 1582; gave book to library; opposed incorporation; a wealthy man, who, in his will of 1605 gave the governors responsibility for seeing that his wishes were carried out; Bury will.

BARET, John: esquire; b. *c.*1390, m. Elizabeth Drury, will pr. 1467; a member of the household of abbot of Bury; left to the alderman, dye and brethren of Candlemas guild a gallon of wine each year for them to drink at their feast; Bury will.

BARKER, Benedict: beer brewer, gentleman; b. at Hopton, m. J 2 Feb.1592 Katherine, sister of Thomas Bright the younger; will pr. 25 Aug. 1632; feoffee 1606–32; receiver 1612;

involved in obtaining the corporation; CB 1606; alderman 1607–8. and 1620–1; governor from 23 Oct. 1607; Bury will.

BARKER, Robert: knight; ? of Trimley St Martin, PCC will 1618; collector of task in 1607.

BARNABY, William: esquire, of Great Saxham, benefactor, see Appendix 8, *sub* 1570; m. Frances, dau. of Sir Thos. Kitson d. 1540 (and sister of TK d. 1602 *q.v.*) and wo. of John Bourchier, Lord Fitzwarren, *c.*1557; d. before his w. whose will was pr. 1585.

BARROW, Philip: gentleman, surgeon and medical writer; s. of John B of Suffolk; licensed as surgeon by Cambridge University 1559; physician 1572; his wife bur. at Wicken, Cambs; bur. M 5 Apr. 1599; his name only occurs when he made the first payment of Edmund Jermyn's annuity to Thomas Badby 10 October 1573; in *DNB*, where it was assumed he practised in London, but described as of Bury St Edmunds in his PCC will.

BAXTER, James: baker, benefactor, see Appendix 8, *sub* 1612; bur. J 12 Aug.1612; involved in obtaining the corporation; BCC 1606; first payment from his bequest received in 1619; it was used for dusting ('wiping') the books, but later in the century it was used for book purchases.

BEACHAM, James: apothecary/grocer; will pr. 2 Mar. 1570; feoffee 1542–70; PCC will.

BEARCHAM, John: *fl.* 1575; paid for providing medical care; might be son of James Beacham, *q.v.*, whose elder son was John.

BEDELL, William: clergyman: bapt. 25 Dec. 1571, s. of John B of Black Notley, Essex, yeoman; educ. at Braintree; adm. to Emmanuel College, Cambridge 1584, an early student under Laurence Chaderton, the first master; BA 1588–9; MA 1592; Fellow 1593; ordained p. at Colchester, 10 Jan. 1597; m. Leah (née L'Estrange) wo. of Robert Mawe, *q.v.*, 1611; d. 7 Feb. 1642; preacher of St Mary's 1601–7 and 1611–16; chaplain to Sir Henry Wotton, ambassador to Venice, 1602–10; returned to Bury until 1616; R. of Horringer, 1616–27; Provost of Trinity College, Dublin, 1627–9; bishop of Kilmore and Ardagh, 1629–42; in Venice became interested in gardening; afterwards tried to do some digging every day; noted as a linguist and wrote a most elegant italic hand (*see* Plate 11); a strict prayer-book man; great worker for religious reconciliation; in *DNB*; PCC will.

BELL, Nicholas: gentleman; *fl. c.*1606–1618; tenant of the Angel.

BEREVE, Thomas: clothmaker, benefactor, see Appendix 8, *sub* 1527; will pr. Feb. 1527; member of Candlemas guild; left to Candlemas guild 13s.4d. for paying the king's tax and the same sum for repairing the Guildhall; intended his almshouses to be administerd by his family, but they were conveyed to Candlemas guild because his family was dying out; Bury will.

BLAGGE, Henry: esquire; bur. M 22 April 1596; signed account, 1586 and 1587; feoffee 1588–96; member of almshouse committee 1590; gave books to library.

BOARDMAN, Andrew: clergyman; a Lancashire man; BA 1571–2; Fellow of St John's College, Cambridge, 1573; MA 1575; BD 1582; university preacher 1582; bur. 1639; minister of St Mary's 1582 to *c.*1585; V. of St Mary's, Norwich, 1591–1639; DD 1594; author of religious works; William Alman, clerk of the peace, left him 10s. in 1585, when he was described as minister.

BOLDERO, Edmund: gentleman; son of John B, *q.v.*; m. Eliz; will pr. 1602; described as Thomas Andrews' man, presumably acting as his clerk; Thomas and Edward Andrews were his cousins.

BOLDERO, Francis: esquire, benefactor, see Appendix 8, *sub* 1557 and 1595; of [?]Fornham All Saints; eldest son of Edmund Boldero of Fornham All Saints; educ. Cambridge and Gray's Inn; m. Bridget Chitting; will pr. 7 Oct. 1580; feodary for the Liberty of St Edmund; tenant of Sir Nicholas Bacon's manor of Ingham; feoffee 1557–80; accountant, new purchased lands 1572 and 1573 and of Hepworth, Smith's, Tassell's and Jermyn's annuity 1577; Bury will.

BOLDERO, George: gentleman of Babwell; 4th son of John Boldero of Fornham All Saints; mar. Margaret dau. of . . . Faircliff; d. 7 Nov. and bur. M 11 Nov. 1609; ?overseer, South Ward, 1594; feoffee, 1606–9; CB 1606; alderman at time of death; inherited Babwell Friary (now the Priory Hotel); gave book to library.

BOLDERO, Henry: gentleman; b. *c.*1556; sold St Nicholas Chapel, 1587–8; went abroad, returned to this country and d. after 1595; executor of will of father Francis; he and Thomas Harwell agreed to pay the costs of the suit brought to obtain this legacy in 1595.

349

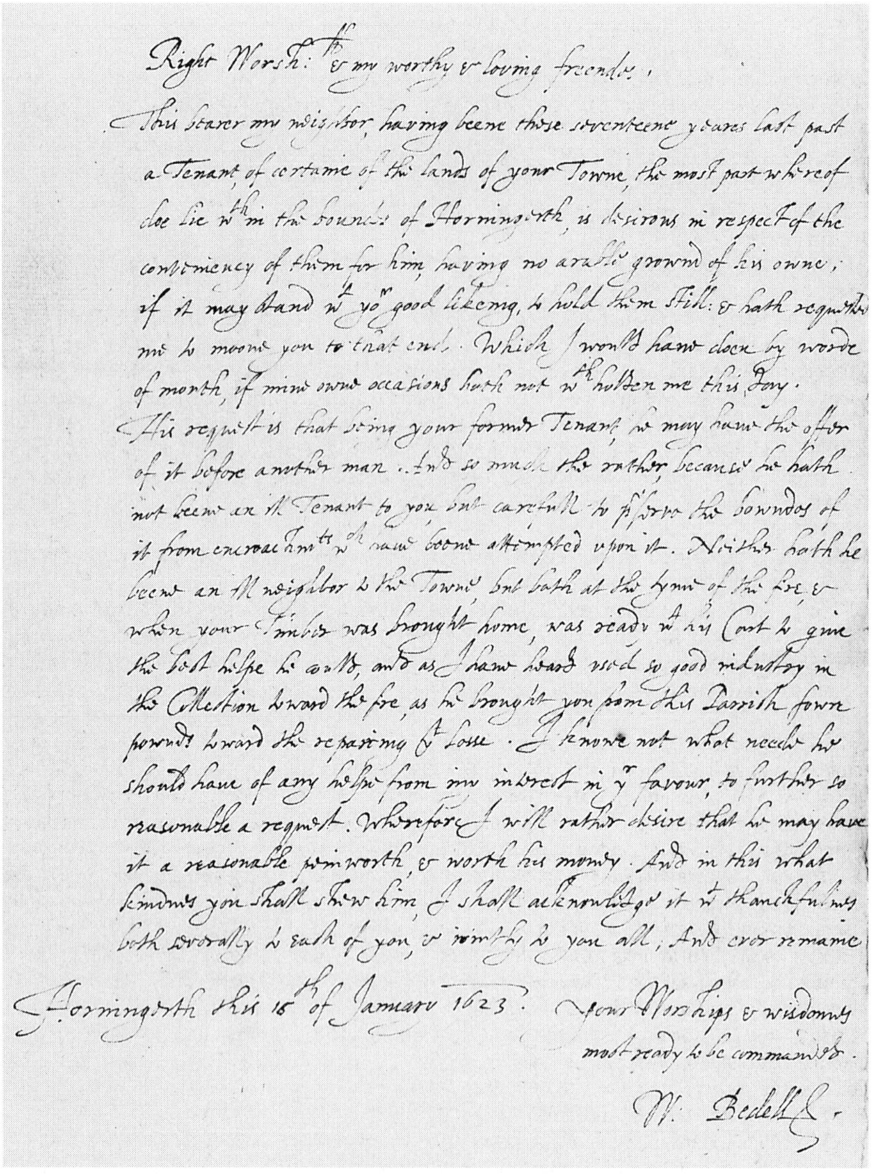
Right Worsh:ll & my worthy & loving friends,

This bearer my neighbor, having beene these seventeene yeares last past a Tenant of certaine of the lands of your Towne, the most part whereof doe lie wthin the bounds of Horningerth, is desirous in respect of the convenience of them for him, having no arable ground of his owne, if it may stand wth yor good liking, to hold them still: & hath requested me to moove you to that end. Which I would have doen by worde of mouth, if mine owne occasions hath not wthholden me this day. His request is that being your former Tenant he may have the offer of it before another man. And so much the rather, because he hath not been an ill Tenant to you but carefull to preserve the boundes of it from encroachments wch have beene attempted upon it. Neither hath he beene an ill neighbor to the Towne, but both at the tyme of the fire, & when your Timber was brought home, was ready wth his Cart to give the best helpe he could, and as I have heard used so good industry in the Collection toward the fire, as he brought you from this Parrish fowre poundes toward the repairing of losse. I know not what neede he should have of any helpe from my interest in yr favour, to further so reasonable a request. Wherefore I will rather desire that he may have it a reasonable penniworth, & worth his money. And in this what kindness you shall shew him, I shall acknowledge it wth thankfulness both severally to each of you, & jointly to you all; And ever remaine

Horningerth this 16th of January 1623. Your Worships & wisdoms most ready to be commanded.

W. Bedell.

Plate 11. Letter from William Bedell, rector of Horringer, to the feoffees supporting a parishioner's request that his lease be renewed, 16 January 1624 (D11/2/3). Reproduced by permission of St Edmundsbury Council.

BOLDERO, John: of Fornham St Martin and Babwell; b. *c.* 1517; m. (1) Anne Nunn of Tostock 12 Sept. 1541 and (2) Margaret, dau. of Thos. Hewer of Oxborough, Nfk, 21 June 1546; will pr. 10 July 1584; probably brother of Francis B *q.v.*; feoffee 1549–84; signed account 1579; exec. of Catherine Cage, *q.v.*; Thomas Andrews his brother-in-law; PCC will.

BOLDERO, John: b. 1560, eldest s. of Thomas B of Fornham St Martin; d. 1633 and bur. at Fornham St Martin; feoffee 1606; receiver 1610 and 1618; CB 1606; alderman 1612–13; governor from 13 Jan. 1613.

BOURNE, Edward: ironmonger, a benefactor, see Appendix 8, *sub* 1637; bur. M 12 July 1637 – where the parish register entry states that he did not have the plague; feoffee 1617–37; corporation member by 1616; chamberlain 1619–22; alderman 1633–4; governor from 16 Dec. 1625; his tombstone near the tower of St Mary's church is the oldest in the Great Churchyard; Bury will.

BOWMAN, Robert: bur. J 1 Sept. 1638; beadle, 1612–22.

BRADISH, Robert: bur. M 1 Dec. 1611; late hall keeper, 1611.

BRIDGEMAN, James: clerk; tenant, 1612–14; a Richard B bur. M 22 Nov. 1623; no likely person has been found in Venn.

BRIDON, Ambrose: glover; ?bur. J 2 Aug. 1604; one of distributors for poor and orphans, 1588; overseer, North Ward, 1594; PCC will.

BRIDON, Ambrose: ?haberdasher; *fl.* 1613–19; prob. bur. M 26 June 1640; a CB; prepared feast when Thomas Bright became alderman in 1618; two men of this name served on the Corporation in 1616; one of them alderman on 12 March 1636; governor from 1636; if correctly identified, will gives details of shop and business papers; also mentions having the town arms and a Suffolk map in his house; Bury will.

BRIDON, Gregory: bur. J 1 April 1613; one of those, not feoffees, to whom William Baker, *q.v.*, released his interest in town lands in 1590; took lease of land at Sparrow Hill in 1595.

BRIDON, John: maltster; ?bapt. J 1572, son of Ambrose Bridon; bur. J 15 July 1640; feoffee 1617–40; BCC 1606; chamberlain 1616.

BRIGHT, John: clothier; s. of Thomas Bright the elder; m. Alice Walot in 1544; bur. M 10 Aug. 1593; bought land and timber from the feoffees.

BRIGHT, Thomas the elder: draper, a benefactor, see Appendix 8, *sub* 1587, and Introduction, p.xxxvi; m. 27 July 1554 Margaret Peyton; bur. J 1 Sept. 1587; feoffee 1582–7; accountant of profits belonging to the town, 1583, 1584; according to *The Brights of Suffolk*, he held the office of alderman, but no date is given; name in margin of almshouse regulations, 1582; PCC will.

BRIGHT, Thomas, the younger: draper, a benefactor, see Appendix 8, *sub* 1625; b. before 1560; m. (1) Margaret Kemp 11 July 1577 and (2) Margaret Beton, and ?(3) Mary 4 Sept. 1625; bur. M 13 Jul. 1626; feoffee 1606–17; receiver 1611 and 1619; took lead in obtaining charter of incorporation for Bury St Edmunds in the years immediately before 1606 and spent £8 in seven journeys to London and one to Royston about the business; on one of these visits to the court was away from Bury for ten days at a stretch; CB 1606; first chamberlain of the corporation, from April 1606 until perhaps July 1607; alderman in 1609–10 and 1618–19; inscription on his tombstone, which no longer survives but was recorded by J.C. Ford, said that he was the first to hold this office for two terms; in 1616 William Camden, Clarenceux, granted him arms: sable, a fess argent between 3 escallops or; described as alderman 1599 when son, Walter, admitted to Caius College, Cambridge, 10 April 1599; employed Dr Miles Mosse as Walter's private tutor; the 3s.4d. he gave for cakes and wine at the feoffees' annual meeting continues as the cake and ale ceremony held in the Guildhall after the Commemoration Service each year; appears to have died intestate.

BRITTAL, . . .: *fl.* 1600–5; a beadle.

BROCKESBY, Bartholomew: gentleman, ?lawyer of London; benefactor, see Appendix 8, *sub* 1564; *fl.* 1564–69; a bill among the feoffees' archives shows he laid out £68 9s.0d for legal work in connection with the purchase of the concealed lands in 1569; had connections with Thomas Andrews and Thomas Brown, *q.v.*

BROOKE, Walter: yeoman; bur. J 4 July 1589; elected into fellowship or company 20 Dec. 1582; enfeoffed 1588; PCC will.

BROWN, Robert: will pr. 25 June 1644; feoffee 1617–*c.*1644; receiver 1621; BCC by 22 August 1611; must have become CB before 1616; alderman 1616–17 and 1625–6; governor from 16 Dec. 1625; in his will forgave the corporation the money owed to him for dinners when he was last alderman – they were to use the money to apprentice poor children, two every year; Bury will.

BROWN, Thomas: citizen and merchant tailor of London, benefactor, see Appendix 8, *sub* 1579; will pr. 20 July 1579; in addition to bequest to feoffees he made a number of gifts for charitable purposes in London, including £20 to Christ's Hospital and £6 13s.4d. each to St

Bartholomew's and St Thomas's Hospitals; also gifts for poor scholars at Oxford and Cambridge; bequests to those with Bury connections include Bartholomew Brockesby, *q.v.* and to Edmund and Thomas Andrews, *q.v.*, the latter being one of his supervisors and a witness of his will; PCC will.

BROWN, Mr [*William*]: physician; bur. J 20 Mar. 1576 'apoticary'; given £1 relief in year ending 1575.

BROWNING or BRUNWYN, Robert: mercer; bur. J 7 June 1579, draper; feoffee by 1569; accountant of new purchased lands 1570; of Hepworth, Smith's, Tassell's and Jermyn's annuity 1575 and 1576; 1568 subsidy, £15 in goods, Risby Ward; bought property in Brentgovel Street of Henry Horn and feoffees and in Fish Market of Robert Park and fellow feoffees, which was left to son Roger, *q.v.*; this was later recovered; in will explained that son Robert was 'sometimes greved with infirmity' and he left an annuity out of the property bequeathed to his son Thomas 'to his loving friend' Thomas Andrews, *q.v.*, and the rest of the feoffees to provide for Robert during his lifetime; the feoffees to receive 6s.8d. yearly for caring for Robert, to be used for relief of the poor at Guildhall on account day; such a payment is recorded in the account for 1579; Mr Handson, the minister of St James's whose dismissal led to the 'Bury stirs', requested to preach his funeral sermon; PCC will.

BROWSE, Thomas: yeoman; benefactor, see Appendix 8, *sub* 1558; will pr. 31 Jan. 1564; his will indicates that he had bought a house and garden from the feoffees, in which his servant lived; Bury will.

BRUNWYN, Roger: clergyman; b. *c.*1554, s. of Robert Browning, *q.v.*; educated for five years at Bury school; BA Caius College, Cambridge, 1575; d. 1623; V. of Great Barton from 1583 until his death; received payments when the feoffees redeemed the property his father purchased 1606–9.

BRUNWYN, Thomas: *fl.* 1607, 1608, perhaps brother of Roger; occupied ground in Brentgovel Street.

BULLER or BULWER, Christopher: clergyman; minister of St James's, 1603–8.

CAGE, Katherine: benefactor; see Appendix 8, *sub* 1563; made will 21 April 1557.

CAGE, Simon: draper, clothier; bur. M 6 Oct. 1581, sen.; probably feoffee from 1545; signed account for 1579; 1568 subsidy £30, West Ward; Thomas Andrews, *q.v.*, and William Cook, *q.v.*, were supervisors of his will and one of its witnesses was the benefactor, Peter Kembold, *q.v.*; PCC will.

CAGE, Thomas: cloth maker; m. more than once, his last wife being Margaret Burnham; bur. M 20 July 1574, senior; feoffee 1545–74; receiver of Smith's, Hepworth, Odeham's and Tassell's lands 1570; as churchwarden of St Mary's, involved in sale of church plate and subsequent purchase of former chantry lands; 5s. for bread given to the poor at his death 1575; 1524 subsidy, TC and John Awngell together assessed for £5, North Ward; 1568 subsidy, TC alone £20 in lands, West Ward; Thomas Andrews, godfather to his son, to advise the boy at 14 whether he should 'contynew still in lerninge'; PCC will.

CARELES, Robert: ?miller; his mother's maiden name was Levett, perhaps connected to Giles Levett who was much involved in the purchase of the chantry lands; bur. M 26 Sept. 1582; admitted to the company 1570; feoffee 1572–82; accountant of new purchased land 1574, 1575; of Jermyn's annuity,1574; of Guildhall 1574–76; profits belonging to the township, 1578; 1568 subsidy £25 in goods, West Ward; PCC will.

CARY, . . .: clergyman; preacher of St Mary's, 1619–22 and possibly later.

CHETHAM, John: gentleman, of Bury St Edmunds and Great Livermere; buried, Gt. Livermere, 1588; feoffee 1565–88; 1568 subsidy, £20 in lands, East Ward.

CHURCH, Reginald: burgess and bell founder; benefactor, see Appendix 8, *sub* 1498; will pr. 24 Feb. 1499; member of Candlemas guild, to which he left £1; Bury will.

CLAYDON, Thomas: of St Pernell's [the former St Petronilla's hospital]; will pr. 23 Apr. 1639; a tenant; governor from 13 Jan. 1613; collector of subsidy, 1608; receiver of Almoners Barns 1616.

COCKSEDGE, Thomas: at least two men of this name belonged to the company in the early years covered by the accounts; both signature and mark of TC in accounts for 1575–78; in accounts from 1578–82 a TC signed, but the signature quite unlike that in earlier account.

COCKSEDGE, Thomas the elder: bur. J 13 Feb. 1589; probably feoffee 1572–89; collector of Smith's, keeper of the Guildhall and alderman 1572; collector of Smith's 1573; name in margin of almshouse regulations, 1582; also probably governor 1550–89, who with Thomas Andrews and William Baker, but in the absence of William Tassell (these being the surviving governors appointed in 1550) appointed additional governors, 21 Jan. 1583.

COCKSEDGE, Thomas: bur. M 15 April 1600; in the absence of further evidence it is assumed that this TC was a member of the company.

COKE, Sir Edward: (1552–1634) a well known judge, called Lord Cook in these accounts; in *DNB*.

COLDHAM, Laurence: clerk to Mr George Kempe; tenant of ground in Barningham, 1591–c.1621.

COLLIN, Henry, senior: gentleman; d. before 6 July 1611; feoffee 1572–1606; accountant, profits belonging to the township, 1578, 1580, 1581; new purchased land, 1585, 1586, 1593; of all profits belonging to common benefit of town, 1600; alderman 1585; signed almshouse regulations, 1582; the account of 1574 notes that a silver spoon which he had given on admission to the company had been placed in the coffer or treasury; became governor between 21 Jan. 1583 and 31 Dec. 1589; family moved to Wendling, Nfk.; Collin fraudulently obtained long leases of lands which were the subject of much litigation.

COLLIN, Henry, junior: gentleman, of Wendling, Norfolk; involved in the litigation to recover lands of which he and his father had fraudulently obtained long leases; the feoffees alleged that he intended to sub-let the land at a profit and to appropriate at least some of it for his own use.

COLLIN, Richard: bur. M 19 Nov. 1587; in 1583–6 the feoffees bought from him the house on the north side of St James's church to use as one of the ministers' houses.

COLLIN, Robert: *fl.* 1579–86; keeper of house of correction 1579–80; keeper of the hospital, 1586.

COOK, Erasmus: goldsmith; d.1590; one of his daughters m. Robert Hyndes, *q.v.*; feoffee 1588–90; accountant of the new purchased land, 1589, and his executors accounted for this in 1590; left almshouses to his son, Simon; 1568 subsidy, £10 in goods, West Ward; PCC will.

COOK, William: lawyer; bur. M 11 Aug 1618; feoffee 1582–1618; mentioned as clerk 1589; receiver of profits belonging to the township, 1581, 1582; of new purchased land, 1586, 1587; alderman 1586; signed almshouse regulations, 1582; signed agreement between inhabitants and feoffees, 1585; member of almshouse committee 1590; governor from 21 Jan. 1583; awarded a pension of £5 *per annum* in 1616; also awarded a pension by the governors, whose minute book said that his advice was valued despite his poor sight and hearing; Henry Payne left him law books in 1568; Bury will.

COPPING, Richard: servant of William Barnaby, *q.v.*; bur. J 25 Aug. 1571; at time of his death he and Thomas Carr had money on bond from the feoffees; Norwich will.

COPPINGER, Henry: m. Barbara, dau. of Robert Brunwyn; bur. J 4 Aug. 1618; member of the company to whom William Baker made his release in 1590.

CORDELL, William: knight, of Long Melford; bur. Long Melford, 19 June 1581; Master of the Rolls; bought land in Long Melford from the feoffees; in *DNB*.

CORDER, ...: minister of St James's, 1609–1612; possibly John C, BA Cant. 1602–3; MA 1606; R. of Timworth, 1612.

COTTON, Robert: gentleman; could be second s. of George C of Gt Barton; m. Katherine, dau. of Roger Potter, *q.v.*; will pr. 3 Dec. 1597; distributor for the poor and orphans, 1590; PCC will.

CRADDOCK, ...: received money owed to John Man, *q.v.*; not named an executor in Man's will.

CROSSMAN, ...: clergyman; minister of St James's, 1618–22 and possibly later; (perhaps Samuel C, sizar, Christ's College, Cambridge, 1606; BA 1609–10; ord. p. (Norwich) Dec. 1612; R. of Bradfield St George, 1633–44; R. of Bradfield St Clare, 1644–61, ejected; parish registrar 1654.)

CUTTERAS, John: will pr. 20 Dec. 1597; feoffee 1565–88; receiver of new purchased lands 1569–71; signed accounts for 1570, 1571, 1573, 1577 and 1578; his will, made 1555, not proved until 1597, was very conservative and his sole executor was William Tassell, *q.v.*; PCC will.

DANIEL, William: judge; ygr. s. of Daniels of Over-Tabley, Ches.; entered Gray's Inn, 1556; dep. recorder of London, 1584; sergeant-at-law, 1594; judge of crt of common pleas, 1604; d. 1610; given a runlet of wine in 1608; in the previous year was one of the judges who approved the corporation's book of by-laws; in describing one of his jocular sayings a brother judge, recording the incident in a mixture of Latin, law French and English, used the oft-quoted phrase 'a brickbat que narrowly mist'.

DARBY, Charles: gentleman; benefactor, see Appendix 8, *sub* 1624; bur. J 6 Aug. 1624; overseer, North Ward, 1594; feoffee 1606–24; chamberlain, 1609–10, but no evidence that he was ever a member of the corporation; governor from 23 Oct. 1607; lived in Northgate Street and probably his family gave name to Darby (now Schoolhall) lane.

DAVY, Edmund: ?bur. J 2 Oct. 1637; probably a beadle, 1614 and 1618–20.

DAVY, Robert: ?m. J Agnes Reuse 24 May 1593; bur. J 12 Nov 1633; feoffee 1617–33; BCC 1606; must have been CB by 1617; alderman 1617–18.

DAVY, Thomas: bur. J 15 Nov. 1605; distributor for poor and orphans, 1591; on 2 Jan 1594 it was ordered that an old debt of £4 18s.8d. was to be paid to him; overseer, Risby Ward, 1594.

DAY, John: *fl.* 1590; tenant of the Bower and Lt. Atley at Hepworth; ordered not to fell trees unless marked by the clerk and surveyors, 20 Mar. 1590.

DAYNES, John: clergyman; of Corpus Christi College, Cambridge, BA 1584–5; ord. p. (Norwich) 1588; V. of Flixton by Bungay, 1588–90; in trouble with the diocesan authorities, 1597 and 1602 because of nonconformity; an unsuccessful candidate for the post of preacher of St James's in 1606.

DISBOROUGH, Thomas: carpenter; will pr. 27 Nov. 1615; made the great gate for the back of the Angel in 1612 and, perhaps, a pulpit for the gaol in 1618; his will includes a bequest to his elder brother, Mr Anthony Disborough, preacher of God's word; Norwich will.

DRURY, Margaret: widow; will pr. 8 Aug. 1495; benefactor, see Appendix 8, *sub* 1495; widow of Clement Drury, burgess; sister of Ralph Duke, one of Jankin Smith's executors; Bury will.

DRURY, Robert: knight; m. Anne, dau. of Sir Nicholas Bacon; will pr. 27 Nov. 1615; granted lease of the tithes, churches, advowsons, right of presentation, markets, fairs, Almoners barns, etc. by James I in 1604; reversion of virtually all these properties bought by a group of corporation members, usually called collectively the purchasers, in the years following 1608; see Introduction, p.l.

DRURY, William: d.1589; petitioned for the grant of the concealed land to be made to the feoffees in 1569.

ESTY, George: clergyman, theological writer; benefactor, see Appendix 8, *sub* 1617; b.1566; Emmanuel College, Cambridge, BA 1581; fellow, MA 1584; BD 1591; will pr. 3 Oct.1601; monument M; preacher of St Mary's, 1598–1601; had many unpublished manuscripts at time of his death, including sermons preached at Bury; PCC will.

FAIRCLIFF, James: d. after 1639; feoffee 1617 until his death; BCC by 1622.

FAIRCLIFF, William, the elder: clothier; bur. M 26 Mar. 1601; distributor for poor and orphans, 1587; feoffee from 1588–1601; accountant of Smith's, 1589, 1590; accountant for all lands belonging to Bury St Edmunds 1595; governor from 28 Dec. 1596; Geo. Esty, *q.v.*, was his son-in-law; 1568 subsidy, £3 in goods, South Ward.

FENN, Mr: painter; *fl.* 1616; painted, for £11, portrait of King James I, which now hangs in the court room at the Guildhall; he may also have made the copies of portraits of Jankin Smith and Thomas Bright the elder, for which £3 6s.8d. was paid in the same year – these now hang in the banqueting room at the Guildhall.

FISH, Ellen: widow; benefactor, see Appendix 8, *sub* 1499; d. after 1503; by deed dated 10 February 1503, declared the uses of land left by her husband, William, and provided for a sangred for William and Ellen Fish and their benefactors in both parish churches; after Ellen's death, an *obit* was to be kept for their souls in St Mary's.

FISH, William: benefactor, see Appendix 8, *sub* 1499; will pr. 17 Sept. 1499; because his wife, Ellen, confirmed his gift, her name rather than his sometimes occurs as the benefactor; Bury will.

FOXGILL, Robert: perhaps RF who died of plague, bur. J 8 Aug. 1637; beadle, *fl.* 1600–1 and 1610–22; could be two men of this name.

FRENZE, John: priest; master of St Peter's hospital; benefactor, see Appendix 8 *sub* 1502; will pr. 8 Oct. 1505.

GARDINER, Robert: knight, of Pakenham; will pr. 1620, bur. at Elmswell; a meal bought for him during the course of negotiations about Collin's leases.

GARDINER, Stephen: bishop; son of John, clothmaker, d. 1506; educ. Trinity Hall, Cambridge; B.Civ.L., 1517–18, D.Civ.L. 1520, D.Can.L. 1521, incorp. at Oxford, 1531; d. 12 Nov. 1555; bishop of Winchester 1531–51 and 1553–5 and Lord Chancellor 1553–5; audited accounts of Candlemas guild 1529; feoffee 1531–55; in *DNB*.

GIBBON, [*?John*]: clergyman; if identification correct, b. at Bury *c.*1586; BA 1602–3; MA Jesus College, Cambridge, 1606; ord. p. (London) 19 Mar. 1609; ?curate of Halstead, Essex; preacher of St Mary's 1616–19; reimbursed the cost of his licence to preach 1618; perhaps R. of Wordwell 1619–29.

GILLY, John: tanner; bur. M 17 Sept. 1604; feoffee 1588–1604; accountant of new purchased land and Tassell's, 1591, 1592; of lands belonging to Bury St Edmunds 1599; overseer, South Ward, 1594.

GIPPS, Henry: son of Thomas Gipps, *q.v.*; bur. M 20 Feb. 1625, described as old man; feoffee from 1606–25; accountant, 1615; CB 1606; alderman, 1614; governor from 1 April 1608.

GIPPS, John: gentleman of Gt Whelnetham; s. of Richard Gipps, who m. Joan, dau. of Edmund Boldero; married (1) Annes, daughter of Henry Horningold (*q.v.*) who died before her father made his will in 1594, and (2) Lucy Borage; bur. M 27 Sept. 1607; elected into the fellowship 20 Dec. 1582; signed accounts from 1584–5; feoffee 1588–1607; accountant of Smith's, 1587, 1591; land belonging to Bury St Edmunds 1596, 1603; overseer, West Ward, 1594; governor from 8 Jan. 1601; CB 1606; alderman 1606–7; gave communion cup to Gt Whelnetham church; son Richard was author of *Antiquitates Suffolciensis*, and governor from 19 March 1635.

GIPPS, Thomas: mercer; will pr. 14 May 1590; signed accounts from 1578–9; feoffee 1582–89; accountant, Smith's, 1585, 1586; name in margin of almshouse regulations, 1582; governor from 21 Jan. 1583; 1568 subsidy, £5 in goods, South Ward; PCC will.

GODFREY, Richard, jun: bur. M 24 October 1646; 'Master'; feoffee from 1617 to death; BCC 1616.

GOLDING, Robert: esquire; bur. J 1 Mar.1611; feoffee 1582–88 and 1606–11; signed almshouse regulations, 1582; ?two men or a gap in service; governor of the school from 21 Jan. 1583; Norwich will.

GOLDSMITH, Mr: perhaps Henry Goldsmith, a borough JP 1611; in 1616 Mr Goldsmith was at a supper in Holborn in the City of London to settle the dispute about the house on the corner of Guildhall and Churchgate Streets which had been bought by Nicholas Heyward.

GOODRICH, John: gentleman, haberdasher in 1609 and clothier in his will; dead before 16 Dec. 1625; feoffee from 1617; receiver, 1622; BCC 1606; CB by 1611; alderman, 1615–16; governor from 21 Dec. 1611; Bury will.

GOODRICH, Thomas, senior: tailor; b. *c.*1522 at Felsham; bur. M 23 Oct. 1607; admitted to the company 1570; feoffee 1572–1607; accountant, Smith's, 1588; new purchased land, [?]1575, [?]1576, 1585; profits belonging to township of Bury St Edmunds, 1579, 1580, 1584; the accountant in 1582–3 might be his son; distributor for poor and orphans, 1586; became governor between 21 Jan. 1583 and 31 Dec. 1589; 1568 subsidy, £6 in goods, West Ward.

GOODRICH, Thomas, junior: of Clifford's Inn, London; d. in Clifford's Inn, 26 Oct. 1597; feoffee 1588–97; accountant, Smith's, 1589; acted for feoffees in connection with Salter's lands 1585; governor from 31 Dec. 1589; gave book to library; PCC will.

GOSLING, William: received purchase money for Angel when feoffees bought it back at the behest of the Commissioners for Charitable Uses, 1606; presumably m. a grand daughter of Roger Potter.

GREEN John: musician; bur. J 27 Dec. 1621, 'musition for the town'; payments made to him in connection with the town waits who performed at feasts.

GRICE (le Grice) William: of Gt Yarmouth, Nfk, and Milk Street, St Bride's London; d. 1593; as an attorney frequently represented Gt. Yarmouth; represented Gt. Yarmouth in Parliament 1565, 1571, 1578, 1584 and 1586; a follower of the Earl of Leicester; through Leicester's influence he no doubt received considerable grants of concealed lands between 1564 and 1566 – see Introduction, p.xxviii.

GRIGGS, William: yeoman; d. c.1634; overseer, North Ward, 1594; BCC 1606; chamberlain, 1609–10; alderman 1628; Bury will.

GRIMSTON, Edward, of Rishangles: c.1508–1600; entered royal service under Henry VIII, who left him lands in Suffolk; remained in favour under Edward VI; appointed comptroller of Calais, 1555; member of parliament for Ipswich 1563, 1571, 1572; for Eye 1589; for Orford 1593 (when he was 85); he was involved with William le Grice in the purchase of the concealed lands in 1569; See Introduction, p.xxviii.

GROOM, Robert: feoffee from 1588, but not re-enfeoffed in 1606.

HAMMOND, Thomas: dead by 29 Dec. 1597; member of the company; signed accounts from 1593–6; governor from 5 Jan. 1594.

HAYWARD, Stephen: gentleman; bur. J 21 Dec. [?]1580; feoffee from [?]1545; accountant, Smith's 1570; of profits belonging to township, 1579, 1580; 1568 subsidy, £40 in goods, Risby Ward; died intestate.

HAYWARD, William: gentleman; bur. J 5 June 1608, *generosus*; feoffee from 1588; accountant, all properties, 1593, 1601; governor from 31 Dec. 1589, but did not attend meetings and was asked to resign on 28 Dec. 1596; Bury will.

HEALEY, John: clergyman; bur. Rushbrooke, 4 Apr. 1633; Emmanuel College, Cambridge, Nov. 1586; ordained d. and p. 1603; preacher of St James's, 1606–13; R of Rushbrooke 1618–33 and of Gt Whelneltham 1619–33; PCC will.

HIGHAM, Clement: knight, of Barrow; d. 1570, bur. Barrow; feoffee from 1557; Privy Councillor and Speaker of the House of Commons under Queen Mary; in *DNB*.

HIGHAM, John: knight, of Barrow; b. c.1540, seventh child and son and heir of Sir Clement Heigham, *q.v.*, and Anne Waldegrave, his second wife; married (1) Anne, daughter and co-heir of Edmund Wright of Bradfield, 9 December 1562; and (2) Anne, daughter of William Poley of Boxted; d. and bur. at Barrow, 1626; admitted to the company 1571; non-payment of admission fee was probably a protest against the lingering pre-Reformation traditions of Candlemas guild; feoffee from 1572–1626; signed almshouse regulations, 1582; signed agreement which ended dispute between feoffees and inhabitants, 1585; active protestant JP in West Suffolk (one of those removed from the bench in 1583); MP Sudbury, 1563, Ipswich 1585; knighted 1579; knight of the shire 1586 and 1603; sheriff 1577; (?entertained Elizabeth I at Barrow Hall, 1578 according to Gage only); commanded one of Suffolk bands of infantry at Tilbury 1588; opposed incorporation; William Bedell, *q.v.*, of Horringer to preach his funeral sermon; Norwich will.

HIGHAM, Martha: gentlewoman, of Denham; b. c.1520, dau. of Sir Thomas Jermyn and his first wife, Ann Spring of Lavenham; sister of Edmund Jermyn, *q.v.*; m. Thomas Higham, 1548; bur. recorded at Denham June 1594, but from the evidence of her will and IPM she must have died in 1593; among many charitable gifts, including £100 to found a scholarship at Emmanuel College, Cambridge, left £10 to the poor of Bury; from the minutes it seems Sir Robert Jermyn had to use his influence to secure payment of this legacy.

HIGHAM, Richard: gentleman; *fl.* 1586–1612; bur. M 2 April 1612; member of the company who signed account 4 Jan. 1586; tenant of the house on the south corner of Guildhall and Churchgate Streets c.1593–1612; overseer, West Ward, 1594; employed to survey feoffees' estate in Hepworth, 1598.

HILL, James: signed account, 1577–8.

HILL, John: clergyman; Trinity College, Cambridge, 1577; BA 1581–2; MA 1585; according to Venn preacher at St Mary's until 1590 when he was suspended for nonconformity; paid for serving the cure at St Mary's, Christmas quarter in 1588; a minute dated 15 Jan. 1590 stated that he was owed £5, which was to be paid if no further order was made.

HILL, John: gentleman; bur. M 2 Sept. 1635; feoffee from 1606; receiver 1609 (John Nunn his deputy) and 1617; CB 1606; alderman, 1608–9; borough JP, 1611; governor from 1605.

HILL, William: mercer; benefactor, see Appendix 8, *sub* 1583; s. of Margaret Browse; d.

1582/3; signed account, 1571, 1572; feoffee from 1572; accountant, new purchased land, 1573, and, with Jermyn's annuity, 1574; all properties, 1577, 1578; left St Robert's Hall in Hatter Street to son James, possibly James H above; 1568 subsidy, £20 in goods, West Ward; PCC will.

HOLT, John: gentleman; s. of JH whose will pr. 1539; m. Anne dau. of William Rope or Ropp of Cheshire; bur. M 23 Mar 1570; feoffee 1542–70; 5s. bestowed on bread for the poor on his death in 1570; owned the almshouses at the east end of St Mary's church which he left to his daughter Anne and his son-in-law, Henry Collin, *q.v.*; these came to the feoffees not long after his death; subsidy, 1568, £20 in lands, West Ward; PCC will.

HORNINGHOLD, Henry: b. *c.*1511 at Fornham St Martin; bur. M 9 Apr. 1597; feoffee from 1569; alderman and keeper of the Guildhall, 1570; accountant of Smith's, 1571, 1572, 1573, profits belonging to the township, 1581, 1582, 1583; signed almshouse regulations, 1582; a very active feoffee whose distinctive HH mark is to be found at the end of many accounts; governor from 21 Jan. 1583; 1568 subsidy, £30 in lands, West Ward; Bury will.

HOWGRAVE, . . .: clergyman; probably Henry: adm. King's College, Cambridge, 1593; BA 1597–8; MA 1601; ord. p. (London) 1603; R. of Horstead and Coltishall, Norfolk, 1619; chaplain to the Bishop of Lincoln; d.1646; considered as potential preacher of St James's in 1606.

HUBANK, Edward: *fl.* 1582–1601; feoffee from 1582; accountant, all property, 1586; name in margin of almshouse regulations, 1582; governor 1589 until his resignation before 8 Jan. 1601.

HYNARD, Edmund: *fl.* ?1611–20; gave 5s. towards finishing the Market Cross, 1620; probably the EH who was BCC in 1611.

HYNDES, Robert: goldsmith; bur. J 14 Aug 1631; feoffee 1617–31; BCC from *c.*1611.

INGLETHORPE, Edmund: *fl.* 1592–1609; (s. of EI, b. at Bury St Edmunds *c.*1523; brought up among priests in the College of Jesus before the suppression, was parish clerk of St Mary's when he gave evidence in a tithe cause in 1593 and bur. J 18 Sept. 1594) beadle or porter of the Guildhall 1592–1609.

INMAN, John: merchant; seems to have been married first to a Boldero; bur. M 21 Oct. 1625; feoffee from 1617; BCC by 1616; governor from 12 Aug. 1615; among other things left his two hall 'goundes', presumably his civic dress; Bury will.

JERMYN, Ambrose: knight, of Rushbrook; eldest s. of Sir Thomas; aged over 40 when his father d. in 1552; d. ?1577; feoffee 1557–77; accountant of Smyth's 1570, and 1571.

JERMYN, Edmund: esquire of Denham, benefactor, see Appendix 8, *sub* 1573; second s. of Sir Thomas; perhaps 'Edward' Jermyn admitted to Gray's Inn, 1535; d. 1572; PCC will.

JERMYN, John: s. of Sir Thomas by his second w. Ann, dau. of Sir Robert Drury of Hawstead and wo. of George Waldegrave of Smallbridge; m. Mary, dau. of Lionel Tollemache of Helmingham and had nine children between 1556 and 1566; bur. Depden, 28 Nov. 1606; from 1573 until his death the feoffees paid him £20 a year out the annuity given by Edmund Jermyn.

JERMYN, Robert: knight, of Rushbrook; b. *c.*1540, s. of Sir Thomas, knighted at Bury St Edmunds by Elizabeth I in course of her progress through Suffolk in 1578; d. 1614; feoffee 1588–1614; see Introduction for his involvement with the house of correction, p.xli; a leading puritan JP in West Suffolk; returned to Parliament, 1587; in the Low Countries with Leicester; gave handsomely bound edition of the works of Calvin to the library in 1595; the books have his arms in gilt on the front and backboards and were at one time chained; in 1606 was asked to return 6 corslets and furniture to the Guildhall; in his will said that when the corporation of Bury had provided a house and stock to set the poor and youth to work his son, Sir Thomas, was to give them £20 within 6 months after they had so governed their youth and poor; PCC will.

JERMYN, Thomas: knight of Rushbrooke; d. 1552; feoffee 1545–52; part of his legacy to the town was used to build the Market Cross in 1583.

JESSOP, . . .: surgeon; paid £2 13s.4d. for healing Pounsabie's eye, 1618.

JEWELL, John: clergyman; s. of Robert J of Carleton Rode, Nfk.; ed. Palgrave under Mr More; admitted Caius College, Cambridge, 1586; BA 1596–7; MA 1600; ordained p.

(Norwich) 1593; m. Mary White at Rushbrook 24 Apr. 1623. d. *c.*1650; minister of St Mary's from 1603 until after 1627; PCC will.

KELLAM, William: distributor for poor and orphans, 1590.

KEMBOLD, Peter: maltster, benefactor, see Appendix 8, *sub* 1590; will pr. 1 Oct. 1590; had no immediate heirs; whether land was bought with the money he left is not clear; Bury will.

KITSON, Thomas: knight, of Hengrave; benefactor, see Appendix 8 *sub* 1602; posthumous s. of Sir Thomas Kitson the merchant, b. 9 Oct. 1540; m. Elizabeth Cornwallis, 15 Jan. 1560; knighted at Bury by Elizabeth I during her progress through Suffolk, 1 Aug. 1578; d. 1602; entertained the queen at Hengrave on her way back from Norwich, 1578; feoffee from 1569 but was not re-enfeoffed in 1588, presumably because of his recusancy; accountant, new purchased land, 1572; 1568 subsidy, £200 in lands, Hengrave; portraits of Sir Thomas and his wife by George Gower, now in the Tate Gallery, were painted in 1573; PCC will.

KNEWSTUBBS, Richard: clergyman; bur. J 19 Aug. 1618; minister of St James's 1613–17; gave a book to library.

LANCASTER, Matthew: mercer; b. *c.*1579; m. Margaret ?. . . .; bur. M 28 Oct. 1634; feoffee 1617–34; BCC by 1616; CB by 1628; governor from 3 June 1618.

LANDISDALE, John: clothier; *fl.* 1580–1605; asked to be buried in the village of his birth, Kelvedon, Essex; tenant of small piece of land in St Mary's Square, often in arrears; overseer, South Ward, 1594; gave book to library; PCC will.

LEWIS, Robert: clergyman; b. *c.* 1550, s. of John L of Lydd, Kent; at Colchester school; BA St John's College, Cambridge, 1571–2; MA Caius College, Cambridge, 1575; prob. ord. p. (Rochester) 17 Feb. 1573; V. of St Peter's, Colchester, 1578–89; 1581 confined to Newgate for nonconformity; minister of St Mary's, 1589–93, and preacher until 1598; R. of Rushbrooke, 1598–1618.

LICHFIELD, . . .: surgeon; early references may be to Richard L who made his will in 1593; later references are found to two of his sons, Ambrose and Richard; PCC will.

LICHFIELD, Ambrose: surgeon.

LICHFIELD, Richard: surgeon; d. 3 Feb. 1627; either he or his father was granted an annual retainer of £3 6s.8d. for curing the sick, 21 Jan. 1591.

LOWDALE, Roger: woollen draper; bur. M 5 May 1618; feoffee 1617–18; BCC 1606; governor from 12 Aug. 1615.

MALLOWES, John: gentleman, described as of Inner Temple, London, 1599, but seems to have been living in Bury from about that time; he bought a 'mansion house' in Hatter Street, extending to Angel Lane, with a coach house and garden house, 1597 from the widow of Thomas Goodrich, junior, *q.v.*; bur. M 11 Nov. 1637; feoffee 1606–37; probably became clerk in 1616 on retirement of William Cook, but had done much legal work for the feoffees before then; receiver, 1608, 1616; governor from 8 Jan. 1605; clerk to the governors on the death of Thomas Rockett, 1625; town clerk 1606–37; gave book to library; died during Bury's great plague, but whether of the plague or some other cause is not known.

MALTYWARD, Richard: bur. J 23 Aug. 1622; 'heynor' of the feast when Thomas Bright was sworn as alderman in 1619; churchwarden of St James's, 1621.

MANN, John: mercer; bur. J 19 Nov. 1607; described himself as 'crased in body' when he made his will in 1603; feoffee 1606; distributor for poor and orphans, 1592; an old debt of £20 ordered to be paid to him 2 Jan. 1594; overseer, Risby Ward, 1594; gave book to library and was one of the churchwardens who drew up the 1599 library inventory; in January 1604 he was paid £30 towards a great sum which he had laid out in connection with a suit which had been brought against the town for tolls of the market; though not a feoffee until the last year of his life, was very active in town affairs before then.

MARKANT, Edmund, of Colchester: benefactor, see Appendix 8, *sub* 1581; probably brother of William, *q.v.*

MARKANT, William: b. in Bury St Edmunds; benefactor, see Appendix 8, *sub* 1584; a member of the household of the recorder of Colchester, Sir Thomas Lucas, of St John's abbey, Colchester; will pr. 7 Feb. 1583; made bequests similar to that to the poor of Bury to the poor and prisoners of Colchester; also left £40 each to the two universities to provide divinity students with Tremellius Bibles or other approved texts.

MAWE, Robert: esquire; bur. M 1 June 1609 – his widow, Leah, née L'Estrange, married

William Bedell, *q.v.*, in 1611; governor of the school from 29 Dec. 1597; opposed incorporation; recorder of Bury St Edmunds 1606–9; gave a book to library.

MILES [Mlyes], Robert: signed account for 1570–1.

MICHELL, Thomas: baker; bur. M 9 Aug. 1601; distributor for poor and orphans, 1589; overseer, West Ward, 1594.

MORE, Richard: ?bur. J 17 June 1593, described as grocer; distributor for poor and orphans, 1586; one of those to whom William Baker released his interest in the town lands, 1590.

MORGAN, . . .: clergyman; minister of St Mary's, year ending 1588.

MOSS, Miles: clergyman, theological writer; b. *c.*1558, s. of Miles, of Chevington; educ. Bury school; adm. Caius College, Cambridge, 14 Apr. 1575; BA 1578–9; MA 1582; BD 1583; DD 1595; ord. p. at Lincoln, 7 Oct. 1583. bur. Combes, 13 Sept. 1615; minister of St James's 1588–93; preacher there 1593–8; author of numerous theological works; library founded in 1595, almost certainly at his instigation; gave several volumes of which at least three survive; acted as private tutor to Walter, son of Thomas Bright the younger.

MOTTE, . . .: surgeon; *fl.* 1591.

MOUNTFORD, Francis: ?bur. 22 Mar. 1614; two men had this name in Bury around 1600; Margaret, wife of Francis Mountford, gentleman, was listed as a recusant in 1604; it seems more likely that the FM who refused to pay a rate to provide stipends for the clergy was the recusant, rather than the FM who was the archdeacon of Sudbury's official.

MURELL, Stephen: *fl.* 1582–4, 1590, 1594; tenant at Hepworth; bought wood and timber; minute dated 20 Mar 1590 agreed that he could buy 30 timber trees on midsummer day for £13, and to take his lease for the years to come on same terms as before except that the feoffees should have liberty to fell trees at Atley, apart from the 27 he was allowed to buy; agreed to lease lands at an increased rent, 2 Jan. 1594.

MURELL, William: father of Stephen; tenant at Hepworth 1570 when he was granted a lease of Easthaugh Wood and Great Atley.

NEWHAWE, Adam: burgess; benefactor, see Appendix 8, *sub* 1521 and Introduction, p.xxiv; will made 20 June, 1496; one of Jankin Smith's executors; appointed Ralph Duke (also one of Smith's executors) to undertake this office for him; his bequest originally for the College of Jesus; Bury will.

NEWHAWE, Margaret: widow of Adam, *q.v.* who confirmed his charitable gift.

NEWMAN, . . .: painter, of Cambridge; *fl.* 1616; painted royal arms now in Court Room at Guildhall.

NEWTON, Mr: clergyman; preacher of St James's, 1599–1605 when he was suspended; still living in the town when Richard Walker made his will in 1610, when he was described as 'late preacher of the word'.

NORTH, Roger: knight; a letter sent to him, 1622; not certainly identified.

NORTHFIELD, . . .: mentioned in connection with the Shire House rent; not clerk of the peace; ?under sheriff.

NUNN, George: *fl.* 1591–3; granted lease of land he already occupied, 21 Jan. 1591; on 3 Jan. 1592 agreed that 14 ac. wood he was to have was to be viewed; the accounts show that this was wood ground in Hepworth.

NUNN, John; esquire: s. of George Nunn of Tostock and his wife Ann, daughter of William Page of Hessett, esquire; m. Elizabeth dau. of . . . Wootton of N. Tuddenham, Nfk; d. 1613; feoffee 1606–13; receiver, 1607; borough JP 22 Aug. 1611; governor from 2 Sept. 1606; gave £100 and lent a further £500 towards purchasing Sir Robert Drury's lease.

ODEHAM, Margaret: widow, benefactor, see Appendix 8, *sub* 1492; 3rd wife of John Odeham, draper; outlived her daughters; their dau. Margaret may have been apprenticed as a silk woman to Isabel Frowicke, wife of Henry Frowick, twice Lord Mayor of London, in 1464; will pr. 8 Nov. 1492; Bury will.

OLIVER, Margaret: see STONE.

OVEREND, Thomas: woollen draper; bur. M 28 Aug. 1604; distributor for poor and orphans, 1592; bought 11 ac. of land from the feoffees, 1594; overseer, West Ward, 1594.

PAGE, William: 'the parsone' late of Hessett; benefactor, see Appendix 8, *sub* 1583; not certainly identified; no induction recorded in Archdeaconry of Sudbury register of inductions;

George Nunn of Tostock, father of John N, *q.v.*, married a daughter of William Page of Hessett, esquire.

PARKER, John, senior, shoemaker: ?bur. J 23 Nov. 1600; given money allowed for the hospital, 1584–5; distributor for poor and orphans, 1587; member of the company to whom William Baker released his interest in the town lands, 1590; overseer, North Ward, 1594.

PAYNE, Anthony: gentleman of Nowton; s. of William and brother of Henry who d. 25 July 1568; as Henry had no children, he settled his manor of Nowton on Anthony; d. 3 Mar. 1606; feoffee 1572–1606; accountant of Brettes, Smith's and Tassell's, 1574; of Hepworth, Smith's and Jermyn's annuity, 1575; all properties, 1581, 1582; alderman, 1576; signed almshouse regulations, 1582; governor 21 Jan. 1583; emerges as 'the wicked feoffee' in the papers relating to a compaint about the feoffees and corporation which was brought by his son William in the 1630s; 1568 subsidy, £10 in lands, South Ward; PCC will.

PAYNE, Walter: *fl.* 1570, nephew of Anthony and Henry, whose heir he was and son of their late brother, John; Henry Payne left him property in College Street; reimbursed for repairs made to the College Street almshouses before they entered the feoffees' hands.

PAYNE, William: third s. of Anthony Payne; m. Eliz. dau. of John Sparrow of Stansfield; d. after 1637; 5 Jan. 1594 proposed terms for a new lease of St Peter's, but on 20 July the governors agreed to make an entry into the St Peter's lands for non-payment of rent; lease continued, but it was then found that he had concealed the tithes of 7 or 8 ac. when the last lease was drawn; they were offered to the farmer of St Peter's for one fat swan; in 1633 (aged about 68) made allegations of maladministration against the feoffees and the corporation which were heard, and dismissed, by the Commissioners for Charitable Uses.

PEAD, Thomas: registrar of the Archdeacon of Sudbury; prob. d. before 5 May 1614; signed account 2 Jan. 1587; feoffee from 1588; governor from 8 Jan. 1601; leased a barn in Westgate Street at 10s. a year from 21 July 1592 for 21 years; overseer, Risby Ward, 1594.

PERKINS, . . .: surgeon; *fl.* 1607; perhaps Thomas, bur. M 26 Dec.1630, physician.

PERSE, Stephen: Doctor of Physic, Fellow of Gonville and Caius College, Cambridge; 1548–1615; had an extensive medical practice throughout East Anglia; by his will gave £1000 to the corporation of Bury St Edmunds (among other towns) to lend to honest young tradesmen on good security, not taking interest of more than 5% each year; the interest to be paid annually to his executors or supervisors in the hall of Caius College, Cambridge, at Michaelmas and Lady Day in even portions.

PEYTON, Christopher: gentleman; benefactor, see Appendix 8, *sub* 1584; *fl.* 1551–*c*.1584; with John Eyer, Christopher Peyton successfully petitioned Edward VI for money to finish building St James's church and for the establishment of the Grammar School.

PEYTON, Thomas: said to have been the customer of Plymouth; s. of Christopher; m. 17 Jul. 1561 Lady Cecil, dau. of John Bourchier, Earl of Bath; admitted to fellowship 1571, but his admission fee was noted as unpaid in this and the two following accounts; feoffee 1572–82, when he was re-enfeoffed; not noted as deceased when feoffment renewed 1588; accountant, all property, 1578; signed each account until 1576; ?recusant.

PINNER, Francis, junior: bur. J 3 July 1618, Mr; benefactor, see Appendix 8, *sub* 1618.

PINNER, Francis, sen: grocer, vintner and inn keeper; benefactor, see Appendix 8, *sub* 1639; bur. M 5 Aug. 1639; feoffee 1606–39; receiver, 1613, 1620; CB 1606; alderman, 1610–11 and 1619–20; made it a condition of his will that the feoffment should be renewed within four months of his death, but it was in fact renewed shortly before he died and his name was included in the new feoffment; suffered greatly in the fire of 1608; his will contains a moving account of his and his wife's sufferings when they both had plague in 1637 and almost all their friends and relatives deserted them; on 22 Aug. 1611, when he was alderman, the corporation granted him a licence to rebuild a common inn which had been destroyed by fire in 1608 – almost certainly the Greyhound, which he owned at his death and which later became the Suffolk Hotel.

POTTER, Roger: landlord of the Angel; bur. M 24 Feb. 1588; feoffee 1572–88; receiver, all properties, 1584, 1585; name in margin of almshouse regulations, 1582; a papist sympathiser; bought Angel from feoffees for which he paid £20 in each year from 1581–6.

PRETIMAN, Sir John: m. Dorothy, dau. of Sir Robert Drury; d. 1638; in 1604 and 1605 part of the capital of Bright's gift was lent to him at interest.

RAVENS, John: physician; b. at Hadleigh, son of John R, Richmond Herald; scholar of Trinity College, Cambridge, 1602; BA 1603–4; MA 1607; MD 1614; licensed to practise medicine, 1610; FRCP 1616; censor; anatomy reader; bur. Hadleigh 5 Oct.1636, having left London to escape the plague; physician to Anne of Denmark, wife of James I; rented a garden in Brentgovel Street, 1609–21; PCC will.

REVE, Edward: s. of Edward, s. of Roger Reve, clothmaker and brother of John Reve, the last abbot of St Edmunds; bur. M 20 Aug. 1598; left his lease lands to his daughter Dorothy who was to pay the rent to the brothers of Candlemas guild, showing that the company was still thought of as Candlemas guild in the last years of the sixteenth century; the feoffees and governors bought St Peter's from him; 1568 subsidy, £15 in goods, Risby Ward; Bury will.

REVE, Robert: s. of Edward; bur. J 6 Feb. 1616; gentleman; a tenant.

REVE, Roger: s. of Robert ; d. 1672; a tenant.

REVELL, John: tanner; bur. J 18 Feb. 1631; one of those to whom William Baker released his interest in 1590; overseer, Risby Ward, 1594; feoffee 1606; receiver 1614; CB 1606; alderman 1611–12.

REVELL, William: prob. bur. J 30 Aug. 1639, Mr; feoffee 1617; governor from 5 May 1614 until his resignation on 11 Jan. 1632 on grounds of age and inability to attend meetings.

RICHARDSON, Thomas: judge; 1569–1635; recorder of Bury St Edmunds by August 1611 until 1623 or later; speaker of the House of Commons 1621; his refusal to allow torture to induce a confession, 1628, a landmark in history of criminal jurisprudence; monument in Westminster Abbey; in *DNB*.

ROCKETT, Thomas: gentleman; d. 1625 according to governors' minutes; no doubt the Mr Thomas Rockell bur. J 24 Apr. 1625; unless two men of the same name are involved, TR was one of those to whom William Baker released his interest in 1590; feoffee from 1617; governor from 31 Dec. 1589, and their clerk at the time of his death; member of the corporation, probably, by 1609; borough JP and CB 1611; Bury will.

RODES, Mr: was paid for a sermon, 1584.

R[OOKWOOD] E[dward]: gentleman; benefactor, see Appendix 8, *sub* 1580 and 1581; Dr Craig has identified 'E R gentleman a frinde' as Edward Rookwood of Euston; Queen Elizabeth visited Euston on her way to Norwich in the course of her progress in 1578; image of the Virgin Mary was found in a hay loft and Rookwood was taken to Norwich for examination before the bishop for his Catholic recusancy.

SALTER, John: will pr. 12 Oct. 1503; benefactor, see Appendix 8, *sub* 1503; feoffee from 1477–1503; lands he left (probably augmented by some of those left by Margaret Odeham) had been leased by Henry Collin and his son, and their recovery is charted in these accounts; Bury will.

SCOTT, William: in 1604, 1605 and 1608, the feoffees contributed towards the costs of a suit brought against him by Sir Nicholas Bacon II for the tolls and customs of the market; BCC 1611.

SHARP, Roger: maltster; bur. J 21 Jan. 1631; BCC by 1611; CB by 1630; churchwarden of St James's 1617.

SHAWBERRY, John: ?bur. M 18 Feb. 1638; tenant; almost certainly JS who was BCC 1606; CB by 1622; alderman 1630–1; coroner 1631–2.

SHORT, Thomas: bur. J 3 Jan. 1604, senior; one to whom Baker released his interest in 1590; governor, but was asked to resign on 28 Dec. 1596 as he did not attend meetings; on 21 July 1592 Thomas Short and his wife were living in a house next to the Guildhall; in a list of recusants in Bury in 1604 there were Thomas Short and his wife.

SMITH, Anthony: mercer, 1609, gentleman, 1617; bur. M 11 Apr. 1644; feoffee 1617–44; BCC 1606; CB before 1613; receiver of corporation revenues, 1617; alderman, 1613–14 and 1621; governor from 12 March 1636.

SMITH, John: esquire; founder and benefactor, see Appendix 8, *sub* 1481; b. late 14th cent., s. of John and Hawise; mar. Anne Roach (surname assumed from the arms formerly on monument); had s. John, who had no children living when his father died; dau. Rose, married (2nd husband) Richard Yaxley, Suffolk JP from 1465; Rose, alive 20 April 1459 when her mother-in-law made her will but probably died soon after, for as his 2nd w. Richard m. Alice Lyard, d. in 1474; all Rose's children were of age when their grandfather died; made generous provision for children of his dau. Rose by Richard Yaxley and they started a new branch of the Yaxley family at Mellis; Smith used the arms formerly used by the family of Brett of Hepworth: azure, a bend between seven billets or; d. 28 June 1481, bur. St Mary's; brass now in sanctuary of Lady chapel; alderman of Bury St Edmunds at least 7 times between 1424 and 1481; built chancel aisles and sanctuary of St Mary's church before 1470; in will provided for perpetual chantries for him and his family in both St Mary's (endowed with the manor of Bretts in Hepworth) and in the College of Jesus, to which he gave the manor of Swifts in Preston and insisted that his execs. obtained its incorporation – possibly its second founder. See also Introduction, p.xix.

SMITHY, John: *fl.* 1578–9; porter or hall keeper.

SMITH or Smithis, William: d. 1570; feoffee 1564–70; 5s. spent on a dole of bread at his death and recorded in the first account.

SOTHEBY, Samuel: clergyman; at Emmanuel College, Cambridge, 1591; acted as preacher of St Mary's, 1608, 1609 while William Bedell, *q.v.*, was acting as chaplain to Sir Henry Wotton's embassy to Venice; perhaps R. of Stanton All Saints 1613; Stanton St John 1615; V. of Outragh, Kilmore, 1638.

SOTHERBY, John: lawyer; 3rd s. of Thomas S of Combes, clerk; adm. Emmanuel College, Cambridge, 1631; adm. Gray's Inn, 1637; barrister-at-law; m. Eliz. dau. of Sir William Castleton of Bury: probably d. c.1689, when Joseph Weld was appointed recorder; post-Restoration recorder of Bury, *c.*1660–*c.*1689; feoffee 1657–death; paid to sort records of feoffees and corporation 1664; made a speech to newly appointed feoffees, 1682, in which he outlined the trust's history and particularly mentioned the benefit received from the involvement of those holding high offices of state.

SPARKE, Robert: skinner, furrier; bur. M 16 Feb. 1625; feoffee from 1588; accountant, all property, 1591, 1592, 1598, 1606; distributor for poor and orphans, 1586, 1589; governor from 31 Dec. 1589; BCC 1606; CB by 1611.

SPORLE, John: clergyman; *fl.* 1606–16; parson at Hepworth.

STERNE, John: distributor of poor and orphans, 1591.

STONE, *alias* OLIVER, Margaret: surgeon; bur. J 28 March 1577; paid 10s. in 1573–4 for healing Bekon's daughter; her will mentions her tools, instruments and boxes belonging to the surgeon's or apothecary's art which she left to her elder son Thomas, an old boy of the school, who practiced as a physician in Bury St Edmunds from before 1597 until his death in 1610; Thomas published works on medicine and mathematics and is in *DNB*; her will also reveals that she managed her late husband's goldsmith's business, and left his tools and equipment to her younger son.

TASSELL, William: gentleman, benefactor, see Appendix 8, *sub* 1557; son of William Tassell and his wife Alice Jermyn of Rushbrooke, daughter of Thomas and sister of Sir Thomas Jermyn; m. (1) Margaret, dau. of Roger Reve, brother of the last abbot and (2) in 1561, Margery Downes, wo. dau. of Roger Barber; d. after 11 Jan. 1585 and before 1588; feoffee from 1545; accountant, Smith's, 1571, 1572; governor from 1550.

TAYLOR, Edward: *fl.* 1592–*c.*1606; tenant of land in Hepworth, which had formerly been occupied by Rust, leased to him for £1 10s.0d. a year; in 1607 Sir Robert Jermyn paid the rent of a piece of land formerly occupied by him.

UBANK: see HUBANK

WALDEBANKS (Wallbank) James: clergyman; adm. Emmanuel College, Cambridge, 1593; BA 1596–7; MA 1600; BD 1607; fellow 1600–11; V. of Greatworth, Northants, 1610–47; bur. at Greatworth 7 Feb.1648; preacher of St James's, 1620–3; removed from office as he refused to reside in Bury.

WALKER, Henry: gentleman; s. of Richard; d. 1644; signed account, 1595; tenant of land at Catishall and in Bury, 1614, 1615; paid legacy left by his father, 1614; governor from 16 Dec. 1625, and became clerk to governors, 17 March 1638, on the death of John Mallowes, *q.v.*; Bury will.

WALKER, Richard: gentleman; bur. J 13 May 1610; benefactor, see Appendix 8, *sub* 1613 and also Introduction, p.li; feoffee 1588–1610; accountant, new purchased land and Tassell's, 1591; for all property, 1597, 1605; governor from 28 Dec. 1596; named as first alderman of the newly incorporated borough 1606; left bequests to ten ministers and preachers living in

Bury; John Nunn, *q.v.*, and William Webb, *q.v.*, were executors; bequest of £6 13s.4d. to his worshipful friend Sir John Higham, *q.v.*

WARD, John: clergyman; preacher of St James's 1598; his monument at Haverhill is not dated, but it may be conjectured that the sole payment in the accounts indicates that he died soon after his appointment.

WEBB, William: gentleman of Ixworth; exec. of Richard Walker; had part of Bright's £300 at interest in 1606.

WITHERS, John sen.: feoffee from 1588.

WOOD, Thomas: physician; d. ?1595; tenant of ground in street from Horsemarket to Shire House, i.e. modern Swan Lane; at Trinity College, Cambridge 1561; BA 1564–5; MA 1568; licensed to practise medicine from Jesus College, Cambridge, 1575; MD 1576; Fellow of Jesus College, Cambridge, 1566–7; ?PCC will where described as of Ipswich.

WOODWARD, John: *fl.* 1635–*c.*1661; feoffee 1639 until death; clerk for a number of years, perhaps as early as 1641; in March 1661 the feoffees paid £4 to his son Francis, for the salary owed to him; during 1650s made copies of many documents no longer surviving; without Woodward's Register it would have been difficult, if not impossible, to work out the history of the feoffees; governor from 19 March 1635.

WORTON, . . .: clergyman; minister of St Mary's, 1597, 1598.

WRETHAM, Robert: surgeon; will pr. 15 Mar. 1610; town surgeon 1595–1606.

WRIGHT, James: vintner; m. (1) Thomasin, dau. of John Cage and (2) Clemens Killam, wo; d. 6 Feb.1592; feoffee from 1569; accountant, Smith's and keeper of the Guildhall, 1573; as deputy to Lord Keeper Bacon, alderman, 1573; accountant, Brettes 1574; alderman, 1574; accountant for all property, 1583, 1584; signed almshouse regulations, 1582; member of committee to review almshouses and remove residents, 1590; governor 1589; among other bequests mentioned his cockpits and tennis courts and also the bowling alley that he had built on the Palace Garden, part of the abbey site on N. side of St James's Church; to Richard Lichefield the elder of Bury (*q.v.*) he left a gelding or nag or else £3 6s.8d; a letter from Lord Keeper Bacon to his son contains a request that Wright should provide wine for the Lord Keeper's forthcoming visit to Suffolk.

Bibliography

Manuscript Sources

HD1150/1, 2, account books of Bury town feoffees, 1569–1622.

From the archive of the Guildhall Feoffees
These records have recently been re-classified as GB500. However, while a new arrangement of the records has been made, the 'H' numbers have been retained for documents to which they had already been assigned. The section of the new catalogue in which items can be found is indicated in these notes.

Two items were of outstanding importance in preparing this edition. H1/6/1 (catalogued under GB500/3) is a register of evidences compiled by John Woodward, the feoffees' clerk, *c.*1657–9. Many of the documents he copied into this register no longer exist. From 1590, the first minute book of the feoffees, H2/6/2.1, 1590–1776 (GB500/5) provided additional information which often makes clear obscure entries in the accounts.

Other documents cited include: Title deeds, H1/3/5, 6; H1/5/6/1–7; H1/5/8/1; H1/5/23/1–18; H1/7/2; and H1/2/9/1–6. H1/5/33 is the licence to alienate St Peter's Hospital in mortmain (GB500/1).

Many feoffments and deeds relating to all feoffment properties have been used, especially in determining the names of those who had a legal interest in the land with which the town charities were endowed. Reference numbers are given in the introduction to Appendix 6 (GB500/2).

H2/1/1 is a pre-Reformation book about Jankin Smith and Margaret Odeham. The English version of the part of John Smith's will which gave land to provide for the payment of town taxes and the pre-Reformation bidding prayer, are printed in Appendix 1. A photocopy of a similar book, of rather later date, GB500/3/1, has provided a few lines quoted in the Introduction, p.xix. Also in this section is Bartholomew Brockesby's receipt for the legal costs of the purchase of concealed lands in 1569 (GB500/3).

H1/3/4/8, 9, 15 and H1/4/3, 4 are counterpart leases (GB500/4).

H2/6/2.3, minutes, 1822–36 (GB500/5).

H3/1/1–3 and H3/1/6 are legal case papers, while H2/4/1 is one version of the speech John Sotheby made to new feoffees, 1682 (GB500/6).

Original accounts, which were copied into the account books here edited, are H2/3/4/1–9, while H2/3/4/11, also described as a receiver's account, is the new rental made in 1621, printed in Appendix 3 (GB500/7).

H1/1/15 is a note of rents payable to the keeper of the Guildhall, 1550. H1/4/16, as well as a survey of Hepworth, contains Thomas Bright's memoranda about obtaining the corporation and other matters not concerned with the feoffees, including a draft of his account as the corporation's first chamberlain, April 1606 to ?July 1607. H1/2/7, memoranda and correspondence about the Great Barton copyholds, also contains valuable information about the workhouse, 1618–19. H2/3/4/10 is the book of arrears taken from HD1150/2 in 1622. A more recent accession, GB500/8/17, is the particulars of sale held on 22 August 1918 (GB500/8).

H2/1/1(a) is a set of orders for the conduct of almshouse residents, but H2/1/1(b) is a memorandum of an election to the company or fellowship which succeeded Candlemas guild (GB500/9).

From the archives of the Borough of Bury St Edmunds
The borough records have recently been re-classified as EE500, but the old catalogue numbers beginning 'A', 'C' and 'D' have been retained and the detailed catalogue of the earlier material is on cards in the search room. The following items have been cited:

Inspeximus charter of Henry VIII to the abbot confirming the liberties of Bury St Edmunds, 20 Nov. 1516, A1/1.

Book of Orders, 1571–5, C2/1; agreement between townsmen and feoffees, 1585, C2/2; letter from Sir Nicholas Bacon to Sir Clement Higham and others about incorporation, 1562, C4/1; papers in tithe cause, 1591–3, C7/2/9; conveyance of Almoner's Barns estate, 1609, C7/2/3.

Letters patent of James I incorporating the borough of Bury St Edmunds in 1606 and increasing its privileges in 1608 and 1614, D1/1/1, D1/2/1, D1/3/1; papers relating to the bequest of Dr Stephen Perse, D2/3/1, 3; minutes of corporation, 1652–91, D4/1/2; first chamberlain's account, D6/4/1; lease of Toll House, 1610, D7/4/1; leases of parts of the Almoner's Barns estate, 1613–19, D7/7/1, 2; accounts of the receivers of Almoner's Barns *c.*1612–28, D7/7/4; counterpart conveyances of parts of Almoner's Barns estate sold *c.*1617–22, to which the governors of the grammar school were a party, D7/10/1; papers relating to Sir Nicholas Bacon II's complaint against the alderman and burgesses, 1620, D10/1, D10/6; draft decree in chancery, Thomas Baker *v.* corporation, 1624, D10/5/1; chamberlains' patents, 1616 and 1632, D11/1/1, 2; chamberlains' notifications, 1616 and 1628, D11/1/6, 7; a version of John Sotheby's speech to the new feoffees, 1682, and a letter from William Bedell recommending that a tenant's lease should be renewed, 1624, D11/2/3; the letter from Sir John Higham and Thomas Andrews appealing for funds to build the Market Cross, 1583, memoranda about the purchase of St Peter's, costs (paid by feoffees) incurred by lessees of Almoner's Barns against Smith, 1612, a note of sums laid out about a cobbler's shop under the Market Cross, 1615, purveyance petition, n.d., after 1618, order of the corporation with a list of members, 1622 and a receipt for the 'pension' paid to the ministers of the town, 1630, are to be found in Town Clerk's papers miscellaneous, D11/3/2; coroners' inquests, 1621–87, D11/11/1; a further copy of the purveyance petition, after 1618, D11/11/3; indenture for the return of a member of parliament, 1621, D13/1/2; by-laws made 1607 and later, D14/2/1; Borough Council Minutes, 1962–3, EE500/1/66.

Although class G is said to relate to the affairs of the trustees of the town lands (the purchasers) all the documents in fact relate to relations between the feoffees and the governors of the grammar school. There are drafts relating to St Peter's, G1/3, and John Goldbold's proposals for ending the dispute between the two bodies about the value of St Peter's and the Brooms in Bradfield Combust, G1/4. The papers about the work of the commissioners for charitable uses seem to have survived because the town clerk of Bury, John Mallowes, was also the commissioners' clerk. The papers relating to William Payne's petition alleging maladministration by the feoffees and the corporation, 1630–3, are K1/3.

Archive of the grammar school founded by King Edward VI, 1550
As soon as the feoffees and the governors each had their own minute books, the governors' records were removed from the Guildhall to the Schoolhall. The catalogue for these is now to be found under GD502, but the references with E5/9 have been retained.

Grammar school charter, 1550, E5/9/101.1; licence to hold a lottery, n.d., 1567–1603, E5/9/102; governors' minute book, beginning 1589, E5/9/202.1; governors' accounts, 1623, E5/9/203.18; lease of St Peter's, 1545, E5/9/305.7; conveyance of St Peter's to the governors, 1582, E5/9/305.9.

Other documents
Wills proved in the court of the Archdeacon of Sudbury are classed as IC500. The registered copies which have normally been used are IC500/2 followed by the number of the volume and page. In a few instances an original will has been used, IC500/1 followed by the number of the annual bundle and the individual will. See also photographic copies, below.

Other documents used were the conveyance of a house in Hatter Street to John Mallowes, 1597, HB502/2/6; a deed relating to land in Hartest to which John Mallowes was a party, 1599, E3/10/68.1; Sir James Burrough's *Collectanea Buriensia* FL541/13/4; Archdeacon of Sudbury's Faculty Book, *c.*1634–98, E14/1/13; Archdeacon of Sudbury's Induction Book (1537)–1641, E14/5/1; letter formerly owned by W.T. Jackson, Acc. 406/1.

Photographs at SROB of documents elsewhere
P755 comprises the unpublished parts of Yates' *History of Bury St Edmunds*. The original is
  BL MS Eger. 2372–4.
Acc. 515, accounts of Candlemas guild, 1520–33. The original is Bodl. MS Suffolk b.1, fos.
  8–28v.
Acc. 829, orders for the house of correction, 1589. The original is BL MS Harl. 364, fos.
  144–52.
Acc. 1055, sacrist's rental, 1433. The original is BL MS Harl. 58.
Acc. 1652 and 1765, wills of Bury people proved in the Prerogative Court of Canterbury,
  1406–1604. The originals are now at the Public Record Office, Kew, London.
Acc. 2043, wills of Bury residents proved in the Norwich Consistory Court, 1370–1730.

Documents not in the Bury Record Office
BL MS Harl. 4626, statutes of Candlemas guild.
Joseph Regenstein Library, University of Chicago, Redgrave Bacon Letters 4059 and 4127.
Vatican MS Reg. Lat. 12, the Bury St Edmunds Psalter with a calendar giving the date of the
  foundation of the abbey of St Edmund.
SROI HD1538/170/24, licence to Francis Pinner to use a house as a common inn, 1611.

Printed Sources

Except where otherwise stated, the place of publication is London.
Abbo of Fleury, *Passio Sancti Eadmundi* in Michael Winterbottom (ed.) *Three Lives of
  English Saints* (Toronto, 1972)
Alsop, J.D., 'The Theory and Practice of Tudor Taxation', *EHR*, xcvii (1982)
Alsop, J.D., 'Innovation in Tudor Taxation', *EHR*, xcix (1984)
Anonymous 'Condition of the Archdeaconry of Sudbury 1603', *PSIA*, xi (1901)
Barton, Thomas F. (ed.) *The Registrum Vagum of Anthony Harrison* (Norfolk Record
  Society, 1963)
Blake, E.O. (ed.) *Liber Eliensis*, Camden Society, 3rd series, xcii (1962)
Boynton, Lindsay, *The Elizabethan Militia, 1558–1638* (1967)
Bright, J.B., *The Brights of Suffolk* (Boston, Mass., 1858)
Briquet, C.M., *Les Filigranes* (ed. Allan Stevenson) Jubilee edition, 4 vols. (Amsterdam,
  1968)
Butler, H.E. (ed.) *The Chronicle of Jocelin of Brakelond* (Nelson's Medieval Classics, 1949)
Calendar of the Manuscripts of the Marquis of Salisbury XI (Historic Manuscripts Commis-
  sion, 1883–1976)
Calendars of State Papers Domestic
Cheney, C.R. (ed.) *Handbook of Dates for students of English History* (Cambridge, 2000)
Cockburn, J.S., *A History of English Assizes 1588–1714* (Cambridge, 1972)
Collinson, Patrick, *The Elizabethan Puritan Movement* (Oxford, 1990)
Copinger, W.A., *County of Suffolk: its history disclosed by existing records and other docu-
  ments, being materials for the history of Suffolk*, 5 vols. (1904–05)
Copsey, Tony, *Book Distribution and Printing in Suffolk, 1534–1850* (Ipswich, 1994)
Corder, Joan, *A Dictionary of Suffolk Arms*, SRS, vii (1965)
Corder, Joan (ed.) *The Visitation of Suffolk, 1561*, 2 vols., Harleian Society's Publications,
  new series, ii (1981), iii (1984)
Craig, John S., *Reformation, Politics and Polemics: the growth of Protestantism in East
  Anglian market towns, 1500–1610* (Aldershot, 2001)

Davis, W.G., *The Ancestry of Mary Isaac* (Portland, Maine, 1955)

Dawson, Giles E. and Laetitia Kennedy-Skipton, *Elizabethan Handwriting, 1500–1650* (Chichester, 1981)

Dictionary of National Biography

Douglas, C.D. (ed.) *Feudal Documents from the Abbey of Bury St Edmunds*, British Academy Records of Social and Economic History, viii (Oxford, 1932)

Dovey, Zillah, *An Elizabethan Progress: the Queen's Journey into East Anglia 1578* (Stroud, 1996)

Duffy, Eamon, *The Stripping of the Altars: Traditional Religion in England, c.1400–c.1580* (New Haven and London, 1992)

Dugdale, W., *Monasticon Anglicanum*, ed. J. Caley, H. Ellis and B. Bandinel, 8 vols. (1817–30)

Dymond, David, 'God's Disputed Acre', *Journal of Ecclesiastical History*, L (1999)

Eagle, F.K., *Catalogue of the Library of St James's Church, Bury St Edmunds, now deposited in the Guildhall* (Bury St Edmunds, 1847)

Ford, J.C., Aldermen and Mayors of Bury St Edmunds, 1302–1896 (n.d.); this is a compilation of manuscript notes and press cuttings: on open shelves at SROB

Foss, Edward, *A Biographical Dictionary of the Judges of England . . . 1066–1870* (1870)

Fox, Sally (ed.) *The Medieval Woman: an illuminated book of days* (1985)

Gage, John, *The History and Antiquities of Hengrave in Suffolk* (Bury St Edmunds, 1822)

Gage, John, *The History and Antiquities of Suffolk: Thingoe Hundred* (1838)

Gauthiez, Bernard, 'The Planning of the Town of Bury St Edmunds: a probable Norman origin', in Antonia Gransden (ed.) *Bury St Edmunds, Medieval Art, Architecture and Economy*, BAA Conference Proceedings, xx (1998)

Gee, Eric, *A Glossary of Building Terms used in England from the Conquest to c.1550* (Frome, 1984)

Gipps, Bryan, *History of the Gipps Family* (privately printed, n.d.)

Gooder, Eileen A., *Latin for Local History: an introduction* (1961)

Goodwin, A., *The Abbey of St Edmundsbury* (Oxford, 1931)

Gottfried, Robert, *Bury St Edmunds and the Urban Crisis: 1290–1539* (Princeton, 1982)

Gransden, Antonia (ed.) *Bury St Edmunds, Medieval Art, Architecture and Economy*, BAA Conference Proceedings, xx (1998)

Gunnis, Rupert, *Dictionary of British Sculptors, 1660–1851* (new revised edition, n.d.)

Harper-Bill, C. (ed.) *Charters of the Medieval Hospitals of Bury St Edmunds*, SRS, Suffolk Charters, xi (Woodbridge, 1994)

Hasler, P.W. (ed.) *The History of Parliament: the House of Commons 1558–1603*, ii, *Members D–L* (1981)

Hervey, Lord Francis (ed.) *Suffolk in the XVIIth Century: the Breviary of Suffolk by Robert Reyce, 1618* (1902)

Hervey, S.H.A. (ed.) *Letter Books of John, First Earl of Bristol*, Suffolk Green Books, i (1894)

Hervey, S.H.A. (ed.) *Rushbrooke Parish Registers, 1567–1850, with Jermyn and Davers Annals*, Suffolk Green Books, vi (Woodbridge, 1903)

Hervey, S.H.A. (ed.) *Denham Parish Registers, 1539–1850* (Bury St Edmunds, 1904)

Hervey, S.H.A., *Biographical List of Boys educated at King Edward VI Free Grammar School, Bury St Edmunds, from 1550 to 1900*, Suffolk Green Books, xiii (Bury St Edmunds 1908)

Hervey, S.H.A. (ed.) *Suffolk in 1568: being the return for a subsidy granted in 1566* (Bury St Edmunds, 1909)

Hervey, S.H.A. (ed.) *Suffolk in 1524: being a return for a subsidy granted in 1523* (Woodbridge, 1910)

Hervey, S.H.A, *Bury St Edmunds: St James Parish Registers*, Suffolk Green Books, xvii, 3 vols. (Bury St Edmunds, 1915–16)

Kerridge, Eric, *Textile Manufactures in Early Modern Britain* (Manchester, 1985)

Kitching, Christopher J., 'The quest for the concealed lands in the reign of Elizabeth I', *Transactions of the Royal Historical Society*, 5th series, xxiv (1974)

Knowles, D. and R.N. Hadcock, *Medieval Religious Houses of England and Wales* (1953, 1971)

Latham, R.E., *Revised Medieval Latin Word-list* (Oxford, 1983)

Levey, Santina M., *An Elizabethan Inheritance: the Hardwick Hall Textiles* (1998)

Livingstone, E.A., *Concise Oxford Dictionary of the Christian Church* (Oxford, 1997)

Lobel, M.D., 'A list of the Aldermen and Bailiffs of Bury St Edmunds from the twelfth to the sixteenth century', *PSIA*, xxii (1934)

Lobel, Mary D., *The Borough of Bury St Edmund's: a study in the government and development of a monastic town* (Oxford, 1935)

Lotteries in the City of London (Corporation of London Record Office, 1994)

MacCulloch, Diarmaid (ed.) 'Henry Chitting's Suffolk Collections', *PSIAH*, xxxxiv (1978)

MacCulloch, Diarmaid, *Suffolk and the Tudors: Politics and Religion in an English County, 1500–1600* (Oxford, 1986)

Martin, G., *The Story of Colchester* (Colchester, 1959)

Memorials of the Past relating to Bury St Edmunds and West Suffolk (reprinted from *Bury and Norwich Post*, 1890–1)

Metcalfe, Walter C. (ed.) *The Vistitations of Suffolk . . . 1561, 1577 and 1612* (Exeter, 1888)

Middle English Dictionary (1956–2001)

Milward, Rosemary, *A Glossary of Household, Farming and Trade Terms from Probate Inventories* (Chesterfield, 1982)

Morris, C. (ed.) *The Journeys of Celia Fiennes* (1949)

Mozley and Whiteley's Law Dictionary (1977)

Muskett, Joseph James, *Suffolk Manorial Families . . .*, 3 vols. (printed privately, 1900, 1908)

Northeast, Peter (ed.) *Wills of the Archdeaconry of Sudbury, 1439–1474*, vol. 1, SRS, xliv (2001)

O'Day, Rosemary, *The Professions in Early Modern England, 1450–1800: servants of the Commonweal* (Harlow, 2000)

Onions, C.T. (revised by Robert E. Eagleson) *A Shakespeare Glossary* (Oxford, 1986)

Oxford English Dictionary

Patterson, W.S.B., 'Educating the Greeks: Anglican scholarships for Greek Orthodox students in the early 17th century', in K. Robbins (ed.), *Religion and Humanism*, Studies in Church History, xvii (1981)

Pevsner, N., *The Buildings of England: Cambridgeshire* (Harmondsworth, 1954)

Platt, Colin, *The English Medieval Town* (1986)

Porter, Roy, *The Greatest Benefit to Mankind: a medical history of humanity from antiquity to the present* (1997)

Rackham, Oliver, *Trees and Woodland in the British Landscape* (1976)

Redstone, V.B., 'Chapels, chantries and gilds in Suffolk', *PSIA*, xii (1904)

Rowe, M. Joy, 'The Medieval Hospitals of Bury St Edmunds', *Medical History*, ii (1959)

Rupp, Gordon, *William Bedell, 1571–1642* (Cambridge, 1972)

Salzman, L.F., *Building in England down to 1540: a documentary history* (Oxford, 1992)

Simon, Jacob, *The Art of the Picture Frame: artists, patrons and the framing of portraits in Britain* (National Portrait Gallery, 1996)

Slack, Paul, *The Impact of Plague in Tudor and Stuart England* (Oxford, 1990)

Smith, A.H., *County and Court: government and politics in Norfolk 1558–1603* (Oxford, 1974)

Smith, A.H. and Baker, G.M. (eds.) *The Papers of Nathaniel Bacon of Stiffkey*, Norfolk Record Society, xlvi (1979)

Sperling, F.C.D., *Hodson's History of the Borough of Sudbury* (Sudbury, 1896)

Statham, Margaret, 'The Guildhall, Bury St Edmunds', *PSIA*, xxxi, part 2 (1968)

Statham, Margaret, *The Book of Bury St Edmunds* (revised edition, Whittlebury, 1996)

Statham, Margaret, 'The Medieval Town' in Antonia Gransden (ed.) *Bury St Edmunds, Medieval Art, Architecture and Economy*, BAA Conference Proceedings, xx (1998)

Statham, Margaret, 'John Baret of Bury' in Livia Visser-Fuchs (ed.) *The Ricardian*, xiii (2003, forthcoming)

Stephens, Sir Edgar, *The Clerks of the Counties, 1360–1960* (1961)

369

Strype, *Ecclesiastical Memorials of the Reign of Edward VI*, 3 vols. (Oxford 1822)

Tittler, Robert, *Nicholas Bacon: the making of a Tudor statesman* (1976)

Tittler, Robert, *Townspeople and Nation: English urban experiences, 1540–1640* (Stanford, California, 2001)

'Transcription of the Parish Registers of St Mary's church, Bury St Edmunds' (typescript, n.d., at SROB on open shelves)

Trenholme, N.M., 'The English Monastic Boroughs', *The University of Missouri Studies*, ii, no. 3 (1927)

Tymms, Samuel, *Wills and Inventories from the Registers of the Commissary of Bury St Edmunds and the Archdeacon of Sudbury*, Camden Society, xlix (1850)

Tymms, Samuel, *An Architectural and Historical Account of the Church of St Mary, Bury St Edmunds* (Bury St Edmunds, 1854)

Venn, J. and J.A. (eds.) *Alumni Cantabrigienses. Part I, from the earliest times to 1751*, 4 vols. (Cambridge, 1922–4)

Victoria County History: Suffolk

Walton, Issak, 'Life of Sir Henry Wotton' in *Lives by Isaak Walton* (Oxford, World's Classics, 1940)

Webb, John, *The Town Finances of Ipswich*, SRS, xxxviii (1996).

Whittingham, A.B., 'Bury St Edmunds Abbey: the plan, design and development of the church and monastic buildings', *Archaeological Journal*, cviii (1951)

Woodworth, Allegra, 'Purveyance for the Royal Household of Queen Elizabeth', *Transactions of the American Philosophical Society*, new series, xxxv, part I (1945)

Yates, Richard, *An Illustration of the Monastic History and Antiquities of the Town and Abbey of St Edmund's Bury* (illustrated edition, 1843)

Notes about the Indexes

No attempt has been made to indicate multiple references to entries found on the same page.

In the Index of Persons, where known, the Christian name of those about whom there is information in Notes on People is given in italics. Where entries are gathered under a Christian name, not all of them may relate to the same person. If it is certain that two or more people are involved, the Christian name has been repeated. The term 'receiver' has been used for all those who kept accounts, whatever term was used in the account book. However, in view of the different job performed by the distributors for the poor and orphans, they are described as 'distributors'. Where the term receiver is not qualified, the person concerned accounted for all the feoffees' properties. To avoid confusion, the person who acted as the caretaker of the Guildhall is always described in the index as the porter. Where appropriate a 'J' or an 'M' is used to indicate the parish to which the entry relates.

In the Index of Places, some buildings, notably the Angel, have been given their own headings rather than including them among entries for the street in which the building stands. Places are in Suffolk unless otherwise indicated. 'House' is always used, not 'tenement' or 'messuage'.

In the Index of Subjects, entries are brought together in groups, of which the more important are headed in bold. References to the Index of Places are to places in Bury St Edmunds unless otherwise stated.

Abbreviations

ac	acre	Midd	Middlesex
Berks	Berkshire	Norf	Norfolk
Cambs	Cambridgeshire	Northants	Northamptonshire
Cwt	hundredweight (56 lbs)	npl	new purchased lands
dau	daughter	nr	near
E	east	p and o	poor and orphans
Ess	Essex	s	son
Herts	Hertfordshire	S	south
Lincs	Lincolnshire	w	wife

Index of Persons

Index of Places

Index of Subjects

abbey, *see under* religious houses

accounts,
accounting terms, lvii, lviii
allowed and ratified, 103
copied into account book by clerk, xxxi, 308
of all properties, 27, 29, 31, 34, 103, 107, 113, 118, 122, 126, 130, 134, 139, 143, 147, 153, 160, 168, 178, 185, 191, 197, 209, 219, 228, 237, 245, 251, 257, 264, 270, 275
of all properties and the house of correction, 37, 40, 44, 47
of Revell and Gipps entered, 244
of the alderman, 5, 8, 11, 15, 19, 23, 26, 55, 59, 64
of distributors, p and o, 60, 65, 69, 76, 78, 81, 85, 91
of the keeper of Guildhall, lix, 4, 7, 11, 14, 19, 22, 25
of Hepworth, Smith's, Odeham's, Fish's, Newhawe's, Salter's and Tassell's, 17
of Hepworth, Smith's and others, Tassell's, and Jermyn's annuity, 21
of money to set the poor to work, 111
of npl, 4, 7, 10, 14, 22, 25, 74
to be made each year, 309, 310
npl and Jermyn' annuity, 18
npl and Tassell's, 63, 67, 84, 89, 95, 99
not allowed, 102
of Smith's, to be made each year, 285
of Smith's, Odeham's, Hepworth and Tassell's, 6, 9, 13
of Smith's, Odeham's, Fish's (Fissher's), Newhawe's, Salter's and almshouses, 51, 56, 61, 66, 71, 76, 81, 87, 92, 97
of Smith's, Odeham's, Hepworth and Tassell's, 3
of stock of £300 left by Thomas Bright I, 142, 147, 153, 160
supervision of, procedures for, 285
account books, *see also* books and stationery
arabic numerals introduced, lviii
description of, xiii
new, 1570, xxxii
alderman and burgesses of Bury St Edmunds, *see under* town administration; borough administration
almshouses, 76, 81, 87, 92, 97, 199, 321–3, 326
named, 294
penthouses for, 171
repaired, 98, 109, 115, 131, 149, 155, 163, 165, 170, 175, 189, 194, 226, 273, 279
amerciament, 119
animals, *see under* food

anniversaries, *see under* guilds and chantries

annuity,
given by Edmund Jermyn, *see* Index of Persons, Jermyn, Edmund
granted by governors to feoffees for St Peter's, 40
paid by order of Commissioners, 187
paid to John Bedwall, *see* Index of Persons, Bedwall John
paid to John Jermyn, *see* Index of Persons, Jermyn, John
apprenticing, *see under* poor
arms, coat of, royal, 268
arms, *see under* military matters
armour, *see under* military matters
armourer, *see under* occupations
bailiffs, *see under* office holders, local
badges, *see under* cognizaunces
bakers, *see under* occupations
banner (aunciante), 234
beadle, *see under* office holders
beef, *see under* food and drink
beer, *see under* food and drink
bellringing, liv
benefactors, *see* Appendix 8 for benefactors and their gifts
accounts of lands of named, xxix
discouraged by sale of Tassell's land, lv
with no direct heirs, 19 (n.36)
benevolences, churchgraces, *see* Index of Places *under* St James's church and St Mary's church
bin, meal, *see under* markets and fairs
bishop, of Norwich, present for, 267
blood hounds, xxxii
boards, *see under* building
books and stationery,
account book, paper, 8, 146, 249
book for orders (minutes), 73
books for receivers' receipts and expenditure, 282
books of Statutes, 201
Catechism, 253
ink, 179, 214, 249, 269
well (glasse to putt it in), 269
paper, 12, 20, 23, 26, 33, 43, 179, 188, 214, 238, 249
paper, a quire, 202, 203, 227, 269
pens, 269; pen knife, 179
Statutes at Large, 268
wax, 43, 238
borough administration
Almoner's Barns, purchase of, l
feoffees give financial assistance, 233

398

401

411

412